PRINCIPLES OF
MICROECONOMICS

THIRD EDITION

PRINCIPLES OF MICROECONOMICS

THIRD EDITION

Dirk Mateer
University of Arizona

Lee Coppock
University of Virginia

W. W. NORTON & COMPANY
Independent Publishers Since 1923

W. W. Norton & Company has been independent since its founding in 1923, when William Warder Norton and Mary D. Herter Norton first published lectures delivered at the People's Institute, the adult education division of New York City's Cooper Union. The firm soon expanded its program beyond the Institute, publishing books by celebrated academics from America and abroad. By midcentury, the two major pillars of Norton's publishing program—trade books and college texts—were firmly established. In the 1950s, the Norton family transferred control of the company to its employees, and today—with a staff of five hundred and hundreds of trade, college, and professional titles published each year—W. W. Norton & Company stands as the largest and oldest publishing house owned wholly by its employees.

Editor: Eric Svendsen

Developmental Editor: Kurt Norlin

Manuscript Editor: Carla Barnwell

Project Editor: Laura Dragonette

Media Editor: Miryam Chandler

Associate Media Editor: Victoria Reuter

Assistant Editor: Jeannine Hennawi

Media Editorial Assistant: Christina Fuery

Marketing Manager, Economics: Janise Turso

Production Manager: Eric Pier-Hocking

Photo Editor: Ted Szczepanski

Photo Researcher: Dena Digilio Betz

College Permissions Specialist: Elizabeth Trammell

Text Design: Jen Montgomery

Art Director: Rubina Yeh

Cover Design and "Snapshot" Infographics: Kiss Me I'm Polish

Composition: Graphic World

Manufacturing: Transcontinental Printing

Library of Congress Cataloging-in-Publication Data

Names: Mateer, G. Dirk, author. | Coppock, Lee, author.
Title: Principles of economics / Dirk Mateer, Lee Coppock.
Description: Third Edition. | New York : W. W. Norton & Company, 2020. |
  Revised edition of the authors' Principles of economics, [2018] |
  Includes bibliographical references and index.
Identifiers: LCCN 2019045451 | ISBN **9780393679175** (hardcover)
Subjects: LCSH: Economics.
Classification: LCC HB171.5 .M435 2020 | DDC 330—dc23
LC record available at https://lccn.loc.gov/2019045451

This edition: ISBN **978-0-393-67919-9** (pbk.)

W. W. Norton & Company, Inc., 500 Fifth Avenue, New York, NY 10110-0017
wwnorton.com

W. W. Norton & Company Ltd., 15 Carlisle Street, London W1D 3BS
1 2 3 4 5 6 7 8 9 0

In memory of our editor, Jack Repcheck, whose zest for life was contagious. Thanks for believing in us and challenging us to share our passion for economic education with others.

D.M. and L.C.

BRIEF CONTENTS

CONTENTS

PART I Introduction

1 Five Foundations of Economics 4

2 Model Building and Gains from Trade 26

PART II The Role of Markets

3 The Market at Work: Supply and Demand   72

4 Elasticity   114

7 Market Inefficiencies: Externalities and Public Goods 218

PART III The Theory of the Firm

PART IV Labor Markets and Earnings

14 The Demand and Supply of Resources 434

15 Income, Inequality, and Poverty   470

PART V Special Topics in Microeconomics

16 Consumer Choice   510

PREFACE

We are teachers of principles of economics. That is what we do. We each teach principles of microeconomics and macroeconomics to over a thousand students a semester, every single semester, at the University of Arizona and the University of Virginia. To date, we have taught over 50,000 students.

We decided to write our own text for one big reason. We simply were not satisfied with the available texts and felt strongly that we could write an innovative book to which dedicated instructors like us would respond. It's not that the already available texts were bad or inaccurate; it's that they lacked an understanding of what we, as teachers, have learned through fielding the thousands of questions that our students have asked us over the years. We do not advise policymakers, but we do advise students, and we know how their minds work.

For instance, there really was no text that showed an understanding for where students consistently trip up (for example, cost curves) and therefore provided an additional example or, better yet, a worked exercise. There really was no text that was careful to reinforce new terminology and difficult sticking points with explanations in everyday language. There really was no text that leveraged the fact that today's students are key participants in the twenty-first-century economy and that used examples and cases from markets in which they interact all the time (such as the markets for cell phones, social networking sites, computing devices, and online booksellers).

What our years in the classroom have brought home to us is the importance of meeting students where they are. This means knowing their cultural touchstones and trying to tell the story of economics with those touchstones in mind. In our text, we meet students where they are through resonance and reinforcement. In fact, these two words are our mantra—we strive to make each topic resonate and then make it stick through reinforcement.

Whenever possible, we use student-centered examples that resonate with students. For instance, many of our examples refer to jobs that students often hold and businesses that often employ them. If the examples resonate, students are much more likely to dig in to the material wholeheartedly and internalize key concepts. This revision process is not new to us; every time a new term begins, we update our course materials. What you see in the Third Edition of this book is a reflection of current economic theory, the contributions of students (past and present), and the changes in society around us. As professional instructors, we have an unfailing commitment to reach every student who crosses our paths and equip them for success. This book, like our classrooms, reflects this goal.

When we teach, we try to create a rhythm of reinforcement in our lectures that begins with the presentation of new material, is followed by a concrete example and then a reinforcing device, and then closes with a "make it stick" moment. We do this over and over again. We have tried to bring that rhythm to the book. We believe strongly that this commitment to reinforcement works. To give an example, in our chapter "Oligopoly and Strategic Behavior," while presenting the crucial yet difficult subject of game theory, we work through the concept of the prisoner's dilemma at least six different ways.

No educator is happy with the challenge we all face to motivate our students to read the assigned text. No matter how effective our lectures are, if our students are not reinforcing those lectures by reading the assigned text chapters, they are only partially absorbing the key takeaways that properly trained citizens need in order to thrive in today's world. A second key motivation for us to undertake this ambitious project was the desire to create a text that students would read, week in and week out, for the entire course. By following our commitment to resonance and reinforcement, we are confident that we have written a text that's a good read for today's students. So good, in fact, that we believe students will read entire chapters and actually enjoy them. Many users of the first two editions have indicated that this is the case.

What do we all want? We want our students to leave our courses having internalized fundamentals that they will remember for life. The fundamentals (such as understanding incentives, opportunity cost, and thinking at the margin) will help them to make better choices in the workplace, in their personal investments, in their long-term planning, in their voting, and in all their critical choices. The bottom line is that they will live more fulfilled and satisfying lives if we succeed. The purpose of this text is to help all of us succeed in this quest.

What does this classroom-inspired, student-centered text look like?

A Simple Narrative

First and foremost, we keep the narrative simple. We always bear in mind all those office-hour conversations with students where we searched for some way to make sense of this foreign language—for them—that is economics. It is incredibly satisfying when you find the right expression, explanation, or example that creates the "Oh, now I get it . . ." moment with your student. We have filled the narrative with those successful "now I get it" passages.

Real-World, Relatable Examples and Cases that Resonate

Nothing makes this material stick for students like good examples and cases that they relate to, and we have peppered our book with them. They are part of the narrative, set off with an Economics in the Real World heading. We further feature Economics in the Media boxed examples that use scenes from movies and TV shows that illustrate economic concepts. One of us has written the book (literally!) on economics in the movies, and we have used these clips year after year to make economics stick with students.

In addition, we have continued to work hard to create a text that represents the student population. Economics as a discipline is less diverse than many other fields of study, and that's something we've been trying to change, at the ground level, for decades. How do we do this? We listen to our students in our office hours, through email and informal conversations, and by observing the level of engagement in our classrooms. We also go out of our way to reach out and help those in need to learn and feel welcome. We hope you get this same feeling when you read this book! The style of writing is clear but intentionally conversational—the photos and captions are designed to draw you in, just as a lecture would. Take a quick read or flip through the pages, and you will see what we mean.

ECONOMICS IN THE REAL WORLD

EXPRESS LANES USE DYNAMIC PRICING TO EASE CONGESTION

Metro Washington, D.C., is notorious for traffic, especially on the Capital Beltway (Interstate 495). New express lanes keep traffic moving by using dynamic pricing, which adjusts t... manage the qu... I-495 express-... times to appro... higher rush-ho... congested. Mo... arrive faster, o... use the express... regularly drive... the express lan...

Because dy... motorists to w... the dynamic pr... in terms of the... evening rush, s... regular lanes. F... charged more t...

How much would you pay to avoid sitting in traffic?

Opportunity cost

ECONOMICS *in the* **MEDIA**

Costs in the Short Run

OCEAN'S 8

In *Ocean's 8* (2018), Sandra Bullock and Cate Blanchett recruit six partners in crime to help them steal a diamond necklace worth $150 million. Part of the joy in watching any of the *Ocean's* films is seeing a star-studded cast of A-list actors pull off the perfect heist. Each partner has a specific skill: one is a jewelry maker, another a computer hacker, a third a pickpocket, and so on.

Beyond a certain point, however, adding more specialists mostly just means an extra person to split the take with. The Bullock and Blanchett characters know exactly how big a core team they want. That's

Applying Economic Decision-Making Through Problem-Solving

Most instructors in this course want students to learn to think like economists and to apply economic principles to their decision-making. This text shares this goal. To get students thinking about economics, we open each chapter with a scenario to illustrate a popular concept or to point out a misconception. Students come to our classes with a number of strongly held beliefs about economics and the economy, so we begin each chapter recognizing that fact and then establishing what we will do to illuminate and clarify that subject area. Then, in each chapter, several Practice What You Know features allow students to self-check their comprehension while also laying the foundation for the step-by-step problem solving required for the end-of-chapter Study Problems. And throughout the text, key equations are used, and the five core foundations of economics (incentives, trade-offs, opportunity cost, marginal thinking, and trade creates value) are reinforced with a special icon to ensure that students are constantly connecting the dots.

Incentives
Trade-offs
Opportunity cost
Marginal thinking
Trade creates value

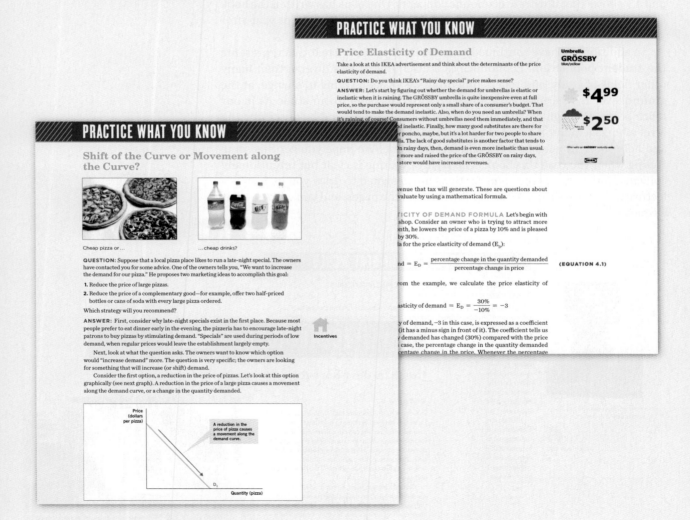

PRACTICE WHAT YOU KNOW

Price Elasticity of Demand

Take a look at this IKEA advertisement and think about the determinants of the price elasticity of demand.

QUESTION: Do you think IKEA's "Rainy day special" price makes sense?

ANSWER: Let's start by figuring out whether the demand for umbrellas is elastic or inelastic when it is raining. The GRÖSSBY umbrella is quite inexpensive even at full price, so the purchase would represent only a small share of a consumer's budget. That would tend to make the demand inelastic. Also, when do you need an umbrella? When it's raining, of course! Consumers without umbrellas need them immediately, and that [...] inelastic. Finally, how many good substitutes are there for [...] or poncho, maybe, but it's a lot harder for two people to share [...]la. The lack of good substitutes is another factor that tends to [...] n rainy days, then, demand is even more inelastic than usual. [...] e more and raised the price of the GRÖSSBY on rainy days, [...] store would have increased revenues.

Umbrella
GRÖSSBY
blue/yellow

$**4**⁹⁹

$**2**⁵⁰

[...]venue that tax will generate. These are questions about [...]valuate by using a mathematical formula.

[...]TICITY OF DEMAND FORMULA Let's begin with [...] shop. Consider an owner who is trying to attract more [...]nth, he lowers the price of a pizza by 10% and is pleased [...] by 30%.

[...]la for the price elasticity of demand (E_D):

$$\text{nd} = E_D = \frac{\text{percentage change in the quantity demanded}}{\text{percentage change in price}} \qquad \text{(EQUATION 4.1)}$$

[...]rom the example, we calculate the price elasticity of

$$\text{asticity of demand} = E_D = \frac{30\%}{-10\%} = -3$$

[...]y of demand, −3 in this case, is expressed as a coefficient [...] (it has a minus sign in front of it). The coefficient tells us [...] demanded has changed (30%) compared with the price [...] case, the percentage change in the quantity demanded [...]centage change in the price. Whenever the percentage

PRACTICE WHAT YOU KNOW

Shift of the Curve or Movement along the Curve?

Cheap pizza or...   ...cheap drinks?

QUESTION: Suppose that a local pizza place likes to run a late-night special. The owners have contacted you for some advice. One of the owners tells you, "We want to increase the demand for our pizza." He proposes two marketing ideas to accomplish this goal:

1. Reduce the price of large pizzas.

2. Reduce the price of a complementary good—for example, offer two half-priced bottles or cans of soda with every large pizza ordered.

Which strategy will you recommend?

ANSWER: First, consider why late-night specials exist in the first place. Because most people prefer to eat dinner early in the evening, the pizzeria has to encourage late-night patrons to buy pizzas by stimulating demand. "Specials" are used during periods of low demand, when regular prices would leave the establishment largely empty.

Next, look at what the question asks. The owners want to know which option would "increase demand" more. The question is very specific; the owners are looking for something that will increase (or shift) demand.

Consider the first option, a reduction in the price of pizzas. Let's look at this option graphically (see next graph). A reduction in the price of a large pizza causes a movement along the demand curve, or a change in the quantity demanded.

Incentives

Price
(dollars
per pizza)

A reduction in the
price of pizza causes
a movement along the
demand curve.

D_1

Quantity (pizza)

Big-Picture Pedagogy

For beginning students, economics can be a subject with many new concepts and seemingly many details to memorize. To help students stay focused on the big ideas of each chapter while continuing to emphasize critical thinking, we use several unique features. First we introduce students to the objectives in each chapter in the form of Big Questions that students will explore rather than memorize. Then we come back to the Big Questions in the conclusion to the chapter with Answering the Big Questions.

· BIG QUESTIONS ·

- What are the factors of production?
- Where does the demand for labor come from?
- Where does the supply of labor come from?
- What are the determinants of demand and supply in the labor market?
- What role do land and capital play in production?

Another notable reinforcement device is the Snapshot that appears in most chapters. We have used the innovation of modern infographics to create a memorable story that reinforces a particularly important topic. By combining pictures, text, and data in these unique features, we encourage students to think about and understand different components of a concept working together.

· ANSWERING the BIG QUESTIONS ·

What are the factors of production?
- Labor, land, and capital are the factors of production, or the inputs used in producing goods and services.

Where does the demand for labor come from?
- The demand for each factor of production is a derived demand that stems from a firm's desire to supply a good in another market. Labor demand is contingent on the value of the marginal product that is produced, and the value of the marginal product is equivalent to the firm's labor demand curve.

Where does the supply of labor come from?
- The supply of labor comes from the wage rate that is offered. Each worker faces the labor-leisure trade-off. At high wage levels, the income effect may become larger than the substitution effect and cause the labor supply curve to bend backward. Changes in the supply of labor can result from other employment opportunities, the changing composition of the workforce, immigration, and migration.

What are the determinants of demand and supply in the labor market?
- Labor markets bring the forces of demand and supply together in a wage signal that conveys information to both sides of the market. At wages above the equilibrium, the supply of workers exceeds the demand for labor. The result is a surplus of available workers that places downward pressure on wages until they reach the equilibrium wage, at which point the surplus is eliminated. At wages below the equilibrium, the demand for labor exceeds the available supply of workers, and a shortage develops. The shortage forces firms to offer higher wages to attract workers. Wages rise until they reach the equilibrium wage, at which point the shortage is eliminated.
- There is no definitive result for outsourcing of labor in the short run. In the long run, outsourcing moves jobs to workers who are more productive and enhances overall social welfare.

What role do land and capital play in production?
- Land and capital (as well as labor) are the factors of production across which firms compare the value of the marginal product per dollar spent. Firms seek to equalize the revenue per dollar spent on each input, thereby maximizing their efficiency.

Solved-Problems Pedagogy

Last but certainly not least, we conclude each chapter with a selection of fully solved problems. These problems show students how to approach material they will see in homework, quizzes, and tests.

Solved Problems

5a. The equilibrium price is $4, and the equilibrium quantity is 60 quarts. The next step is to graph the curves, as shown here.

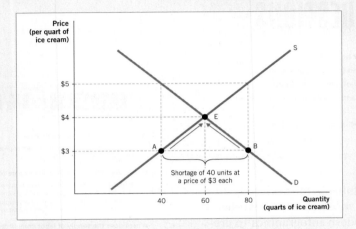

b. A shortage of 40 quarts of ice cream exists at $3 (quantity demanded is 80 and the quantity supplied is 40); therefore, there is excess demand. Ice cream sellers will raise their price as long as excess demand exists—that is, as long as the price is below $4. It is not until $4 that the equilibrium point is reached and the shortage is resolved.

8a. The first step is to set $Q_D = Q_S$. Doing so gives us $90 - 2P = P$. Solving for price, we find that $90 = 3P$, or $P = 30$. Once we know that $P = 30$, we can plug this value back into either of the original equations, $Q_D = 90 - 2P$ or $Q_S = P$. Beginning with Q_D, we get $90 - 2(30) = 90 - 60 = 30$, or we can plug it into $Q_S = P$, so $Q_S = 30$. Because we get a quantity of 30 for both Q_D and Q_S, we know that the price of $30 is correct.

b. In this part, we plug $20 into Q_D. Doing so yields $90 - 2(20) = 50$. Now we plug $20 into Q_S. Doing so yields 20.

c. Because $Q_D = 50$ and $Q_S = 20$, there is a shortage of 30 quarts.

d. Whenever there is a shortage of a good, the price will rise in order to find the equilibrium point.

9a. The reduction in consumer income led to a negative, or leftward, shift in the demand curve for gasoline. Because this is the only change, the equilibrium price of gasoline fell. In fact, by the end of 2008, the price of gasoline had fallen to under $2 per gallon in the United States.

b. The significant drop in the cost of production led to a large increase, or rightward, shift in the supply of gasoline. This increase in supply led to a decrease in price. In fact, by early 2015, the average price of a gallon of regular gasoline in the United States fell to under $2 per gallon.

Looking at parts (a) and (b) together, you can see that very different causes led to steep drops in the price of gasoline. In 2008 the cause was a decline in demand; in 2014 it was an increase in supply.

10. Because alcohol and Solo cups are complements, the key here is to recall that a change in the price of a complementary good shifts the demand curve for the related good. Lower alcohol prices will cause consumers to purchase more alcohol and therefore demand more Solo cups. In other words, the entire demand curve for Solo cups shifts to the right.

12a. The price of related goods is a demand shifter so, it is incorrect.

b. Income is a demand shifter so, it is incorrect.

c. The cost of inputs is a supply shifter so, it is correct.

d. The price causes a movement along the supply curve so, it is incorrect.

Principles of Microeconomics—Hallmarks and Updates to the Third Edition

When we wrote the First Edition of *Principles of Microeconomics*, we decided to follow the traditional structure found in most texts. Though every chapter is critical, we believe that those covering supply and demand, elasticity, and production costs are the *most* fundamental, since so many other insights and takeaways build on them. We tried triply hard to reinforce these chapters with extra examples and opportunities for self-assessment.

Enthusiastic feedback from the Second Edition told us that our readers were happy with the organization of the book, so in this edition we were able to drill down and focus our updates on elements that we believe add tremendous value. We did a big rethink on every example in the textbook, updating and changing examples so that they are relatable, inclusive, culturally relevant, and interesting, and so the reader is engaged. This involved updating text content, features boxes, images, and illustrations. We took a hard look at many chapters, considering where we might introduce the work of different economists, especially women, who are often not well represented in principles texts. In trying to be relatable to a varied student body, we always looked for places where we could make sure every reader finds themselves represented repeatedly throughout the book.

Several other important changes were made to the chapter pedagogy. Each chapter now starts with a large and engaging photo that works with the chapter opener and the caption. Images and stories engage students, and we wanted to improve on our treatment in previous editions. Each chapter now includes a challenge question in our practice boxes. These challenge questions give curious students the opportuntiy to analyze problems in-depth so that deeper learning occurs. Further, Economics for Life boxes have both revised content and bullets that summarize the key takeaways at a glance. Based on reviewer feedback, we have updated and simplified Snapshots, and we eliminated those that were found to be repetitive with the text material. We also have built a closer connection to the book and the media package, especially elements of Smartwork5 and Inquizitive. This is described in more detail below.

A sampling of specific updates to the text includes new material featuring the research of economists like Joan Robinson, Elinor Ostrom, and Ulrike Malmendier, among others. New media examples feature *Shark Tank, Ocean's 8, Breaking Bad, Superior Donuts, Mad Men, Superstore, Captain America: Civil War, Last Week Tonight with John Oliver, Worth It, Inside Out, The Onion*, and *Planet Money*. Updated examples include new data on the relationship between educational attainment and pay; a full explanation of the gender wage gap along with a study on why the gender gap exists at Uber; and a figure showing gender differences among the most common jobs. We dug deeper to give our students the best data so that they can become more informed.

One hallmark of this textbook that is not found anywhere else in the principles markets remains. This text includes a separate chapter on price discrimination. We have done this because the digital economy has made price discrimination much more common than it ever was before, so what was once a fun but somewhat marginal topic is no longer marginal. What's more, students really relate to it because they experience it in many of the markets in which they participate—for example, college sporting events.

We also place a stand-alone consumer theory chapter toward the end of the volume, but that does not mean that we consider it an optional chapter. We have learned that there is tremendous variation among instructors for when to present this material in the course, and we wanted to allow for maximum flexibility.

Supplements and Media

SMARTWORK5

Smartwork5 (SW5) for *Principles of Microeconomics* is an online learning environment that helps instructors meet the teaching goal of connecting concepts and showing applications. Richly varied questions and intuitive functionality give users the flexibility to create the type of learning that works best for their students. Try a demo of the following features at digital.wwnorton.com /prinecomi3.

Easy to launch, easy to use

Simple course setup and intuitive student registration minimize administrative headaches at the beginning of the semester. Instructors can use prebuilt activities or customize their own assignments and questions to suit their needs.

Integration with campus LMS platforms

Smartwork5 integrates with campus learning management systems. Student grades flow automatically to the instructor's LMS course. A single sign-on between the LMS and Norton digital products simplifies student access—and this means fewer password/log-in woes.

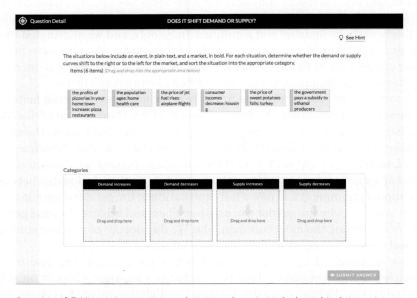

Smartwork5 Norton's easy-to-use homework system designed to integrate with your LMS.

Trusted economics tools and content

Smartwork5 teaches students not just how to solve problems but how to problem-solve, connecting concepts to learned skills through varied applications. Smartwork5 includes assignments based on real-world economic scenarios, "Office Hours" video tutorials presented in the learning moment, analytical and interactive graphing questions, and application problems. Rich answer-specific feedback builds students' confidence and economic skills. Questions are book specific, matching the terminology and conventions that students see in their textbook. They were developed in collaboration with instructors actively teaching with the Mateer and Coppock textbook.

NEW for this edition are several reviewer-tested improvements and content types. Smartwork5 now also includes questions keyed in to Practice What You Know examples in each chapter, building a strong support system between Smartwork5 and the text. Further, up-to-date news feature questions have been added to each chapter. In total, there are close to 500 new questions in the latest release of Smartwork5.

Rich performance reports

Intuitive performance reports for both individual students and entire classes help instructors gauge student comprehension and adjust their teaching accordingly.

An intuitive, easy-to-use graphing tool

The Smartwork5 graphing interface consistently uses the same colors and notation as the in-text art to enhance continuity and reduce confusion. The interface is easy to understand and was designed for both computers and tablet devices. Students are invited to manipulate existing graphs or to draw their own graphs from scratch.

Answer-specific feedback and hints

Smartwork5 teaches students to problem-solve, not just solve a single problem. Many online homework systems only offer solution explanations after the student has answered a question. Smartwork5, in contrast, provides explanations throughout the problem-solving process, giving answer-specific feedback and hints for common misconceptions.

INQUIZITIVE

Award-winning InQuizitive is Norton's gamelike, adaptive quizzing and practice system. Developed and revised for the new edition with even more book-specific questions and content, this system lets students compete with themselves as they prepare their material for class. Demo InQuisitive at digital .wwnorton.com/prinecomi3.

Play with a purpose

Gaming elements built into InQuizitive engage students and motivate them to keep working. Students wager points on every question based on their confidence level, gain additional points for high success rates and on bonus questions, and can improve their grade by continuing to work questions in InQuizitive.

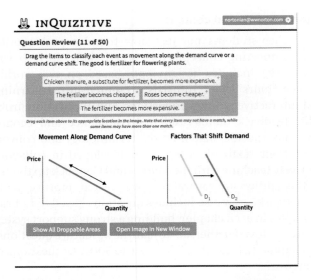

Inquizitive offers adaptive quizzing with gamelike features.

Active learning, helpful feedback

InQuizitive includes a variety of question types beyond basic multiple choice. Image-click, numeric entry, and various graph interpretation questions build economic skills and better prepare students for lecture, quizzes, and exams. Rich answer-specific feedback helps students understand their mistakes.

Easy to use, and integrates with your campus LMS

Instructors can set up InQuizitive for their students in less than 5 minutes. Students can access InQuizitive on tablet devices as well as on computers, making it easy to study on the go. InQuizitive integrates with campus learning management systems; when integration is enabled, grades flow automatically to campus LMS gradebooks. A single sign-on between the LMS and Norton digital products simplifies student access.

Formative assessment works

The efficacy of formative assessment is backed by education and psychology research (see inquizitive.wwnorton.com). Furthermore, performance-specific feedback, varied question types, and gaming elements built into InQuizitive have been shown to increase student engagement and retention of material.

NORTON COURSEPACK

Bring tutorial videos, assessment, and other online teaching resources directly into your new or existing online course with the Norton Coursepack. It's easily customizable and available for all major learning management systems, including Blackboard, Desire2Learn, Moodle, and Canvas.

The Norton Coursepack for *Principles of Economics* includes:

- Concept Check quizzes
- Homework quizzes

- Office Hours video tutorials
- Interactive Scratch Paper modules
- Flashcards
- Links to the digital landing page for the ebook, InQuizitive, and Smartwork5
- Test bank

THE ULTIMATE GUIDE TO TEACHING ECONOMICS—FULLY UPDATED WITH NEW TEACHING TYPES

The Ultimate Guide to Teaching Economics is much more than an instructor's manual; it is two handbooks for becoming a better teacher. *The Ultimate Guide*—the most innovative instructor's manual ever created for principles of economics—includes 1,000+ teaching tips from the classrooms of the authors and other innovative instructors. It can help instructors, both new and experienced, incorporate best-teaching practices and find inspiring ideas for enlivening their lectures.

The tips in *The Ultimate Guide to Teaching Microeconomics* and *The Ultimate Guide to Teaching Macroeconomics* include:

- Think-pair-share activities to promote small-group discussion and active learning
- "Recipes" for in-class activities and demonstrations that include descriptions of the activity, required materials, estimated length of time, estimated difficulty, recommended class size, and instructions. Improved and ready-to-use worksheets are also available for select activities, now with additional instructions to make them easier to use in class.
- Descriptions of movie clips, TV shows, commercials, and other videos that can be used in class to illustrate economic concepts
- Clicker questions and questions designed for other classroom signaling systems
- Ideas for music examples that can be used as lecture starters
- Suggestions for additional real-world examples to engage students
- A Taking It Online appendix in each chapter that shows how *The Ultimate Guide*'s class-tested teaching ideas can be adapted to online teaching environments
- Writing to Learn tips that give instructors short (one-page or less) paper prompts with ideas for potential student responses

Each chapter ends with solutions to the unsolved end-of-chapter problems in the textbook.

INTERACTIVE INSTRUCTOR'S GUIDE

The Interactive Instructor's Guide (IIG) brings all the great content from *The Ultimate Guide to Teaching Economics* into an online database that can be searched and filtered by a number of criteria, such as topic, chapter, key word, media format, and resource type. Instructors can even save their favorite assets to a list so they don't need to hunt for them each time they revisit the IIG.

To make it quick and easy for instructors to incorporate the tips from *The Ultimate Guide to Teaching Economics,* the IIG also includes:

- Downloadable versions of student worksheets for activities and demonstrations
- Downloadable PowerPoint slides for clicker questions
- Additional teaching resources not found in *The Ultimate Guide*

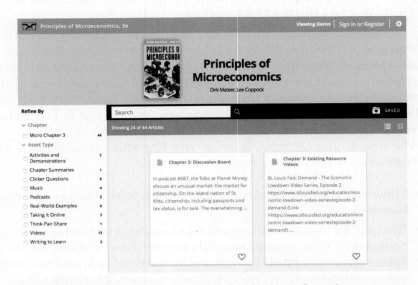

Interactive Instructor's Guide This searchable database of premium resources makes lecture development easy.

OFFICE HOURS VIDEO TUTORIALS

This collection of now more than 85 videos brings the office-hours experience online. Each video explains a fundamental concept. Videos were developed and filmed working with the authors, as well as a new team of presenters.

Perfect for online courses, each Office Hours video tutorial is succinct (90 seconds to 2 minutes in length) and mimics the office-hours experience. The videos focus on topics that are typically difficult to explain just in writing (or over email), such as shifting supply and demand curves.

The Office Hours videos have been incorporated throughout the Smartwork5 online homework system as video feedback for questions, integrated into the ebook, and included in the Norton Coursepack.

TEST BANK

NEW Two versions of the test bank are now available to better serve very large courses and offer you more question options for quizzes and tests each semester you teach. Each version has over 6,000 questions, with over 3,000 of those questions either new or substantively revised. Both test banks have been fully updated and expanded based on reviewer feedback. Each chapter includes between 100 and 150 questions and incorporates graphs and images where appropriate. The test bank has been developed using the Norton Assessment

Guidelines. Each question in the test bank is classified according to Bloom's taxonomy of knowledge types (remembering, understanding and applying, analyzing and evaluating, and creating). Questions are further classified by section and difficulty, making it easy to construct tests and quizzes that are meaningful and diagnostic.

PRESENTATION TOOLS

Norton offers a variety of presentation tools so that new instructors and veteran instructors alike can find the resources that are best suited for their teaching style.

Enhanced lecture PowerPoint slides

NEW Revised lecture PowerPoints now also use key images from the text to convey complex economic concepts. All slides are supported with complete lecture notes. These comprehensive, lecture-ready slides are perfect for new instructors and instructors who have limited time to prepare for lecture. The slides include elements such as images from the book, stepped-out versions of in-text graphs, additional examples not included in the chapter, and clicker questions.

Student note-taking slides

This resource is a trimmed-down version of the lecture slides with instructor notes removed for instructors who prefer slides that are more visual and with limited bullets. These are great for posting to the LMS for students to download for note-taking during lecture.

Art slides and art JPEGs

For instructors who simply want to incorporate in-text art into their existing slides, all art from the book (tables, graphs, photos, and Snapshot infographics) is available in both PowerPoint and .jpeg formats. Stepped-out versions of in-text graphs and Snapshot infographics are also provided and optimized for screen projection.

DIRKMATEER.COM

Visit dirkmateer.com to find a library of hundreds of recommended movie and TV clips and links to online video sources to use in class.

LEECOPPOCK.COM

This blog serves as a one-stop-shop for all the "econ news you can use." Here you will find timely economic data, graphics, and teaching materials you will need to keep your course fresh and topical.

ACKNOWLEDGMENTS

We would like to thank the literally hundreds of fellow instructors who have helped us refine both our vision and the actual words on the page for three editions of this text. Without your help, we would never have gotten to the finish line. We hope that the result is the economics teacher's text that we set out to write.

Our class testers:

Jennifer Bailly, California State University, Long Beach
Mihajlo Balic, Harrisburg Community College
Erol Balkan, Hamilton College
Susan Bell, Seminole State College
Scott Benson, Idaho State University
Joe DaBoll-Lavoie, Nazareth College
Michael Dowell, California State University, Sacramento
Abdelaziz Farah, State University of New York, Orange
Shelby Frost, Georgia State University
Karl Geisler, University of Nevada, Reno
Nancy Griffin, Tyler Junior College
Lauren Heller, Berry College
John Hilston, Brevard Community College
Kim Holder, University of West Georgia
Todd Knoop, Cornell College
Katharine W. Kontak, Bowling Green State University
Daniel Kuester, Kansas State University

Herman Li, University of Nevada, Las Vegas
Gary Lyn, University of Massachusetts, Lowell
Kyle Mangum, Georgia State University
Shah Mehrabi, Montgomery College
Sean Mulholland, Stonehill College
Vincent Odock, State University of New York, Orange
J. Brian O'Roark, Robert Morris University
Michael Price, Georgia State University
Matthew Rousu, Susquehanna University
Tom Scales, Southside Virginia Community College
Tom Scheiding, University of Wisconsin, Stout
Clair Smith, St. John Fisher College
Tesa Stegner, Idaho State University
James Tierney, State University of New York, Plattsburgh
Nora Underwood, University of Central Florida
Michael Urbancic, University of Oregon
Marlon Williams, Lock Haven University

Our reviewers and advisors from focus groups:

Mark Abajian, California State University, San Marcos
Teshome Abebe, Eastern Illinois University
Casey R. Abington, Northwest Missouri State University
Charity-Joy Acchiardo, University of Arizona
Rebecca Achee Thornton, University of Houston
Mehdi Afiat, College of Southern Nevada
Carlos Aguilar, El Paso Community College
Clelia Aguirre, Miami Dade College
Seemi Ahmad, State University of New York, Dutchess
Abdullah Al-Bahrani, Northern Kentucky University
Frank Albritton, Seminole State College
Rashid Al-Hmoud, Texas Tech University
Farhad Ameen, Westchester Community College
Giuliana Andreopoulos, William Paterson University
Tom Andrews, West Chester University
Becca Arnold, San Diego Mesa College
Giant Aryani, Collin College
Lisa Augustyniak, Lake Michigan College
Dennis Avola, Bentley University

Roberto Ayala, California State University, Fullerton
Nahata Babu, University of Louisville
Philip Baca, New Mexico Military Institute
Sahar Bahmani, University of Wisconsin, Parkside
Diana Bajrami, Diablo Valley College
Ron Baker, Millersville University
Saad Bakir, Alabama State University
Mihajlo Balic, Harrisburg Area Community College
Kuntal Banerjee, Florida Atlantic University
Gyanendra Baral, Oklahoma City Community College
Ryan Baranowski, Coe College
Ruth Barney, Edison Community College
David Barrus, Brigham Young University, Idaho
Clare Battista, California Polytechnic State University
Jude Bayham, Washington State University
Mary Beal-Hodges, University of North Florida
Michael Bech, University of Southern Denmark
Stacie Beck, University of Delaware
Q Beckman, Delta College
Christian Beer, University of North Carolina, Wilmington

Jodi Beggs, Northeastern University
Richard Beil, Auburn University
Ari Belasen, Southern Illinois University
Doris Bennett, Jacksonville State University
Karen Bernhardt-Walther, The Ohio State University
Joel Beutel, Delta College
Prasun Bhattacharjee, East Tennessee State University
Richard Bilas, College of Charleston
Kelly Blanchard, Purdue University
Wesley Blundell, California State University, East Bay
Inácio Bo, Boston College
Michael Bognanno, Temple University
Antonio Bojanic, California State University, Sacramento
David Boldt, University of West Georgia
Michael Bonnal, University of Tennessee, Chattanooga
Heather Bono, University of West Georgia
Andrea Borchard, Hillsborough Community College
Feler Bose, Alma College
Inoussa Boubacar, University of Wisconsin, Stout
Donald Boudreaux, George Mason University
Austin Boyle, Penn State
Jared Boyd, Henry Ford Community College
Elissa Braunstein, Colorado State University
Elizabeth Breitbach, University of Southern California
Kristie Briggs, Creighton University
Stacey Brook, University of Iowa
Bruce Brown, California State Polytechnic University, Pomona
John Brown, Clark University
Vera Brusentsev, Swarthmore College
Laura Maria Bucila, Texas Christian University
Bryan Buckley, Northeastern State University
Benjamin Burden, Temple College
Richard Burkhauser, Cornell University
Whitney Buser, Young Harris College
W. Jennings Byrd, Troy University
Joseph Calhoun, Florida State University
Charles Callahan, State University of New York, Brockport
Douglas Campbell, University of Memphis
Giorgio Canarella, University of Nevada, Las Vegas
Laura Carolevschi, Winona State University
Nancy Carter, Kilgore College
Mike Casey, University of Central Arkansas
Amber Casolari, Riverside Community College
Nevin Cavusoglu, James Madison University
Valbona Cela, TriCounty Technical College
Semih Cekin, Texas Tech University
Rebecca Chambers, University of Delaware
Jason Chang, California Polytechnic State University, Pomona
Myong-Hun Chang, Cleveland State University
June Charles, North Lake College
Sanjukta Chaudhuri, University of Wisconsin, Eau Claire
Parama Chaudhury, University College of London
Chuiping Chen, American River College
Shuo Chen, State University of New York, Geneseo
Monica Cherry, State University of New York, Buffalo
Larry Chisesi, University of San Diego

David L. Cleeton, Illinois State University
Marcelo Clerici-Arias, Stanford University
Steve Cobb, University of North Texas
John Colletti, North Central College
Kristen Collett-Schmitt, University of Notre Dame
Rhonda Collier, Portland Community College
Simon Condliffe, West Chester University
Christopher K. Coombs, Louisiana State University
Michael Coon, Hood College
Gary Cooper, University of Minnesota
William Cooper, University of Kentucky
Doug Copeland, Johnson County Community College
Joab Corey, University of California, Riverside
Carlos Cortinhas, University of Exeter
Allen Coson, East Los Angeles College
Chad D. Cotti, University of Wisconsin, Oshkosh
Richard Cox, Arizona State University
Erik Craft, University of Richmond
Antoinette Criss, University of South Florida
Zachary Cronin, Hillsborough Community College
Glynice Crow, Wallace State Community College
Patrick Crowley, Texas A&M University, Corpus Christi
Sarah E. Culver, University of Alabama at Birmingham
Damian Damianov, University of Texas, Pan American
Morassa Danai, California State University, Fullerton
Alexander Danel, University of Virginia
Ribhi Daoud, Sinclair Community College
Patrick Dolenc, University of Massachusetts, Amherst
John Donahue, Estrella Mountain Community College
Oswaldo Donoso, Lone Star College, North Harris
Kacey Douglas, Mississippi State University
Whitney Douglas-Buser, Young Harris College
Chelsea Dowell, Upper Iowa University
Alissa Dubnicki
William Dupor, The Ohio State University
Renee Edwards, Houston Community College
Harold W. Elder, University of Alabama
Diantha Ellis, Abraham Baldwin Agricultural College
Harry Ellis, University of North Texas
Amani Elobeid, Iowa State University
Tisha Emerson, Baylor University
Lucas Englehardt, Kent State University
Michael Enz, Framingham State University
Erwin Erhardt, University of Cincinnati
Jonathan Ernest, Clemson University
Mary Ervin, El Paso Community College
Molly Espey, Clemson University
Jose Esteban, Palomar Community College
Sarah Estelle, Hope College
Patricia Euzent, University of Central Florida
Brent Evans, Mississippi State University
Carolyn Fabian Stumph, Indiana University–Purdue
University, Fort Wayne
Leila Farivar, The Ohio State University
Ben Fitch-Fleischmann, University of Oregon
Va Nee Van Fleck, California State University, Fresno

Oscar Flores, Minnesota State University, Moorhead
Michael Forney, Austin Community College
Irene Foster, George Washington University
Roger Frantz, San Diego State University
Shelby Frost, Georgia State University
Gnel Gabrielyan, Washington State University
Craig Gallet, California State University, Sacramento
Susan Garrigan-Piela, Hudson Valley Community College
Wayne Geerling, Pennsylvania State University
Karl Geisler, Idaho State University
Elisabetta Gentile, University of Houston
Erin George, Hood College
Menelik Geremew, Texas Tech University
Linda Ghent, Eastern Illinois University
Dipak Ghosh, Emporia State University
Edgar Ghossoub, University of Texas at San Antonio
J. Robert Gillette, University of Kentucky
Gregory Gilpin, Montana State University
Joana Girante, Arizona State University
Lisa Gloege, Grand Rapids Community College
Robert Godby, University of Wyoming
John Goddeeris, Michigan State University
Rajeev Goel, Illinois State University
Bill Goffe, State University of New York, Oswego
Michael Gootzeit, University of Memphis
Aspen Gorry, Clemson University
Paul Graf, Indiana University, Bloomington
Alan Green, Stetson University
Barbara Grey, Brown Foundation
Natalia Grey, Southeastern Missouri State University
Daniel Grossman, West Virginia University
Jeremy Groves, Northern Illinois University
Sheryl Hadley, Johnson County Community College
Gail Hayne Hafer, St. Louis Community College
Dan Hamermesh, University of Texas at Austin
Gabriela Q. Hamilton, Hillsborough Community College-
Dale Mabry Campus
Mehdi Haririan, Bloomsburg University
Oskar Harmon, University of Connecticut
David Harrington, The Ohio State University
David Harris, Benedictine College
Darcy Hartman, The Ohio State University
Jenny Hawkins, Case Western Reserve University
John Hayfron, Western Washington University
Beth Haynes, East Tennessee State University
Jill Hayter, East Tennessee State University
Densie Hazlett, Whitman College
Phil Heap, James Madison University
Douglas Heiwig, Ivy Tech Community College
Marc Hellman, Oregon State University
Amy Henderson, St. Mary's College Maryland
Jessica Hennessey, Furman State
Wayne Hickenbottom, University of Texas at Austin
Mike Hilmer, San Diego State University
John Hilston, Eastern Florida State College
Ashley Hodgson, St. Olaf College
Adam Hoffer, University of Wisconsin, La Crosse

Jan Höffler, University of Göttingen
Lora Holcombe, Florida State University
Suneye Holmes, Spelman College
Charles Holt, University of Virginia
James Hornsten, Northwestern University
Nancy Howe, Hudson Valley Community College
Gail M. Hoyt, University of Kentucky
Yu-Mong Hsiao, Campbell University
Alice Hsiaw, College of the Holy Cross
Yu Hsing, Southeastern Louisiana University
Amanda Hughey, University of Delaware
Brad R. Humphreys, West Virginia University
Greg W. Hunter, California State Polytechnic University, Pomona
Rebecca Innerarity, Angelina College
Miren Ivankovic, Anderson University
Oleg Ivashchenko, University of Albany
Meredith Jackson, Snead State Community College
Sarah Jenyk, Youngstown State University
Michal M. Jerzmanowski, Clemson University
Kristen Johnson, Metropolitan State University of Denver
Paul Johnson, University of Alaska, Anchorage
David Kalist, Shippensburg University of Pennsylvania
Mustafa Karakaplan, Oregon State University
Nicholas Karatjas, Indian University of Pennsylvania
Reza Karim, Des Moines Area Community College
Hossein Kazemi, Stonehill College
Janis Kea, West Valley College
Michael Kelley, Oakwood University
Sukanya Kemp, University of Akron
Carrie B. Kerekes, Florida Gulf Coast University
Frank Kim, University of San Diego
Sandra Kinel, Monroe Community College
Linda Kinney, Shepherd University
Vivian Kirby, Kennesaw State University
Ara Khanjian, Ventura College
Colin Knapp, University of Florida
Mary Knudson, University of Iowa
Brian Koralewski, Suffolk County Community College,
Ammerman
Dmitri Krichevskiy, Elizabethtown College
Lone Grønbæk Kronbak, University of Southern Denmark
Daniel Kuester, Kentucky State University
Jean Kujawa, Lourdes University
Sylvia Kuo, Brown University
MAJ James Lacovara, United States Military Academy at
West Point
Becky Lafrancois, Colorado School of Mines
Ermelinda Laho, LaGuardia Community College
Bree Lang, University of California, Riverside
David Lang, California State University, Sacramento
Ghislaine Lang, San Jose State University
Nancy Lang, Northern Kentucky University
Carsten Lange, California State Polytechnic University,
Pomona
Tony Laramie, Merrimack College
Paul Larson, University of Delaware
Teresa Laughlin, Palomar College

Jason Lee, University of California, Merced
Logan Lee, University of Oregon
Jenny Lehman, Wharton County Junior College
Mike Leonard, Kwantlen Polytechnic
Tesa Leonce, Columbus State University
Amy Leung, Cosumnes River College
Eric Levy, Florida Atlantic University
Herman Li, University of Nevada, Las Vegas
Ishuan Li, Minnesota State University, Mankato
Daniel Lin, American University
Jaclyn Lindo, University of Hawaii, Manoa
Charles Link, University of Delaware
Delores Linton, Tarrant County College
Arthur Liu, East Carolina University
Bo Liu, Southern New Hampshire University
Weiwei Liu, Saginaw Valley State University
Xuepeng Liu, Kennesaw State University
Monika Lopez-Anuarbe, Connecticut College
Heriberto Lozano, Mississippi State University
Josephine Lugovskyy, University of Kansas
Ed Lukco, Ohio State University at Marion and Ohio
Dominican University
Brian Lynch, Lake Land College
Martin Ma, Brigham Young University-Idaho
Lynn MacDonald, St. Cloud State University
Zachary Machunda, Minnesota State University, Moorhead
Bruce Madariaga, Montgomery College
Brinda Mahalingam, University of California, Riverside
Chowdhury Mahmoud, Concordia University
David Mahon, University of Delaware
Mark Maier, Glendale Community College
Lucy Malakar, Lorain County Community College
Len Malczynski, University of New Mexico
Ninos Malek, San Jose State University
Margaret Malixi, California State University, Bakersfield
Khawaja Mamun, Sacred Heart University
Nimantha Manamperi, St. Cloud University
Amber Mann, Corretta Scott King High School
Sonia Mansoor, Westminster College
Fady Mansour, Columbus State University
Daniel Marburger, Arkansas State University
Emily Marshall, Dickinson College
Kerry Martin, Wright State University
Erika Martinez, University of South Florida
Jim McAndrew, Luzerne County Community College
Michael McAvoy, State University of New York, Oneonta
Kate McClain, University of Georgia
Myra McCrickard, Bellarmine University
Cara McDaniel, Arizona State University
Scott McGann, Grossmont College
Christopher McIntosh, University of Minnesota, Duluth
Craig McLaren, University of California, Riverside
Kris McWhite, University of Georgia
Shah Mehrabi, Montgomery College
Mark Melichar, Tennessee Technical University
Diego Mendez-Carbajo, Illinois Wesleyan University
Evelina Mengova, California State University, Fullerton

William G. Mertens, University of Colorado, Boulder
Charles Meyrick, Housatonic Community College
Frannie Miller, Texas A&M University
Laurie Miller, University of Nebraska, Lincoln
Edward L. Millner, Virginia Commonwealth University
Ida Mirzaie, The Ohio State University
Kaustav Misra, Saginaw Valley State University
Kara Mitchell, Belmont University
Michael A. Mogavero, University of Notre Dame
Mehdi Mohaghegh, Norwich University
Conor Molloy, Suffolk County Community College
Moon Moon Haque, University of Memphis
Francis Mummery, Fullerton College
Sheena Murray, University of Colorado, Boulder
Yolunda Nabors, Tennessee Technical University
Max Nagiel, Daytona State University
Mijid Naranchimeg, Central Connecticut State University
Mike Nelson, Oregon State University
Gibson Nene, University of Minnesota, Duluth
Boris Nikolaev, University of South Florida
Jasminka, Ninkovic, Emory University
Caroline Noblet, University of Maine
Daniel Norgard, Normandale Community College
Stephen Norman, University of Washington, Tacoma
Farrokh Nourzad, Marquette University
Grace O, Georgia State University
Ichiro Obara, University of California, Los Angeles
Fola Odebunmi, Cypress College
Vincent Odock, State University of New York, Orange
Constantin Ogloblin, Georgia Southern University
Lee Ohanian, University of California, Los Angeles
Paul Okello, Tarrant County College
Gregory Okoro, Georgia Perimeter College, Clarkston Campus
Ifeakandu Okoye, Florida A&M University
Neal Olitsky, University of Massachusetts, Dartmouth
Martha Olney, University of California, Berkeley
EeCheng Ong, National University of Singapore
Stephen Onyeiwu, Allegheny College
Sandra Orozco-Aleman, Mississippi State University
Lynda Marie Ortega, Saint Phillip's College
Christopher Otrok, University of Missouri
Stephanie Owings, Fort Lewis College
Caroline Padgett, Francis Marion University
Jennifer Pakula, Saddleback College
Kerry Pannell, DePauw University
Pete Parcells, Whitman College
Darshak Patel, University of Kentucky
R. Scott Pearson, Charleston Southern University
Jodi Pelkowski, Wichita State University
Faye Peng, University of Wisconsin, Richland
Erica Perdue, Virginia Polytechnic Institute and State University
Andrew Perumal, University of Massachusetts, Boston
Brian Peterson, Central College
Dorothy Peterson, Washington University
Michael Petrowsky, Austin Community College
Van T.H. Pham, Salem State University
Rinaldo Pietrantonio, West Virginia University

Inna Pomorina, Bath Spa University
Steve Price, Butte College
Irina Pritchett, North Carolina State University
Guangjun Qu, Birmingham—Southern College
Jason Query, Western Washington University
Gabriela Quevado, Hillsborough Community College
Sarah Quintanar, University of Arkansas at Little Rock
Aleksander Radisich, Glendale Community College
Tobi Ragan, San Jose State University
Robi Ragan, Mercer University
Nahreen Rahman, University of Cincinnati
Mona Ray, Morehouse College
Ranajoy Ray-Chaudhuri, The Ohio State University
Mitchell Redlo, Monroe Community College
Dawn Renninger, Penn State Altoona
Ann Rhoads, Delaware State University
Jennifer Rhoads, St. Catharine University
Samual Riewe, Sonoma State University
Matthew Rolnick, City College of New York
Leanne Roncolato, American University
Debasis Rooj, Northern Illinois University
Brian Rosario, American River College
Ildiko Roth, North Idaho College
Matthew Rousu, Susquehanna University
Jason Rudbeck, University of Georgia
Nicholas G. Rupp, East Carolina University
Anne-Marie Ryan-Guest, Normandale Community College
Martin Sabo, Community College of Denver
Hilary Sackett, Westfield State University
Shrawantee Saha, College of St. Benedict
Ravi Samitamana, Daytona State College
Rolando Sanchez, Northwest Vista College
Jeff Sarbaum, University of North Carolina, Greensboro
Naveen Sarna, Northern Virginia Community College
Supriya Sarnikar, Westfield State University
Noriaki Sasaki, McHenry County College
Thomas Scheiding, University of Hawaii-West Oahu
Douglas Schneiderheinze, Lewis & Clark Community College
Jessica Schuring, Central College
Robert Schwab, University of Maryland
James Self, Indiana University, Bloomington
Sean Severe, Drake University
Sheikh Shahnawaz, California State University, Chico
Gina Shamshak, Goucher College
Neil Sheflin, Rutgers University
Brandon Sheridan, North Central College
Dorothy R. Siden, Salem State College
Cheri Sides, Lane College
Joe Silverman, Mira Costa College
Scott Simkins, North Carolina A&T State University
Robert Simonson, Minnesota State University, Mankato
Michael C. Slagel, College of Southern Idaho
Brian Sloboda, University of Phoenix
Gordon Smith, Anderson University
Kara Smith, Belmont University
John Solow, University of Iowa
Robert Sonora, Fort Lewis Collge

Todd Sorensen, University of California, Riverside
Maria Sorokina, West Virginia University
Christian Spielman, University College London
Denise Stanley, California State University, Fullerton
Leticia Starkov, Elgin Community College
Kalina Staub, University of North Carolina, Chapel Hill
Tesa Stegner, Idaho State University
Rebecca Stein, University of Pennsylvania
Joe Stenard, Hudson Valley Community College
Heather Stephens, California State University, Long Beach
Liliana Stern, Auburn University
Joshua Stillwagon, University of New Hampshire
Burak Sungu, Miami University
Paul Suozzo, Centralia College
Dan Sutter, Troy University
David Switzer, St. Cloud Sate University
Vera Tabakova, East Carolina University
Ariuna Taivan, University of Minnesota, Duluth
Yuan Emily Tang, University of California, San Diego
Anna Terzyan, Loyola Marymount University
David Thomas, Ball State University
Henry Thompson, Auburn University
James Tierney, Pennsylvania State University
Aleksander Tomic, Macon State College
Suzanne Toney, Savannah State University
Mehmet Tosun, University of Nevada, Reno
Steve Trost, Virginia Polytechnic Institute and State University
Mark Trueman, Macomb College
Melissa Trussell, College of Coastal Georgia
Phillip Tussing, Houston Community College
Nora Underwood, University of Central Florida
Gergory B. Upton, Jr., Louisiana State University
Mike Urbancic, University of Oregon
Jesus Valencia, Slippery Rock University
Robert Van Horn, University of Rhode Island
Adel Varghese, Texas A&M University
Marieta Velikova, Belmont University
Tatsuma Wada, Wayne State University
Jaime Wagner, University of Nebraska, Lincoln
Annie Walker, Boise State University
Will Walsh, Samford University
Yongqing Wang, University of Wisconsin, Waukesha
Mark V. Wheeler, Western Michigan University
Thomas White, Assumption College
Katie Wick, Abilene Christian University
Johnathan Wight, University of Richmond
Eric Wilbrandt, Auburn University
Nick Williams, University of Cincinnati
Douglas Wills, University of Washington, Tacoma
Ann Wimmer, Iowa Lakes Community College
Kafu Wong, University of Hong Kong
Kelvin Wong, University of Minnesota
Ken Woodward, Saddleback College
Jadrian Wooten, Washington State University
Ranita Wyatt, Paso-Hernando State College
Kuzey Yilmaz, Cleveland State University
Young-Ro Yoon, Wayne State University

Anne York, Meredith College
Han Yu, Southern Connecticut State University
Kristen Zaborski, State College of Florida
Arindra Zainal, Oregon State University
Erik Zemljic, Kent State University

Tianwei Zhang, University of Georgia
Ying Zhen, Wesleyan College
Dmytro Zhosan, Glendale Community College
Alex Zhylyevskyy, Iowa State University
Kent Zirlott, University of Alabama

All of the individuals listed above helped us to improve the text and ancillaries for the first three editions, but a smaller group of them offered us extraordinary insight and support. They went above and beyond, and we would like them to know just how much we appreciate it. In particular, we want to recognize Alicia Baik (University of Virginia), Jodi Beggs (Northeastern University), Dave Brown (Penn State University), Jennings Byrd (Troy University), Douglas Campbell (University of Memphis), Shelby Frost (Georgia State University), Wayne Geerling (Penn State University), Karl Geisler (Idaho State University), Paul Graf (Indiana University), Oskar Harmon (University of Connecticut), Jill Hayter (East Tennessee State University), Phil Heap (James Madison University), John Hilston (Brevard Community College), Kim Holder (University of West Georgia), Todd Knoop (Cornell College), Katie Kontak (Bowling Green State University), Brendan LaCerda (University of Virginia), Paul Larson (University of Delaware), David Mahon (University of Delaware), Lucy Malakar (Lorain County Community College), Kerry Martin (Wright State University), Kris McWhite (University of Georgia), Ida Mirzaie (The Ohio State University), Yolunda Nabors (Tennessee Technical University), Charles Newton (Houston Community College), Boris Nikolaev (University of South Florida), J. Brian O'Roark (Robert Morris University), Andrew Perumal (University of Massachusetts, Boston), Irina Pritchett (North Carolina State University), Robi Ragan (Mercer University), Matt Rousu (Susquehanna College), Tom Scheiding (University of Hawaii-West Oahu), Brandon Sheridan (North Central College), Clair Smith (Saint John Fisher College), James Tierney (Penn State University), Phillip Tussing (Houston Community College), Nora Underwood (University of Central Florida), Joseph Whitman (University of Florida), Erin Yetter (University of Arizona), Erik Zemljic (Kent State University), and Zhou Zhang (University of Virginia).

We would also like to thank our partners at W. W. Norton & Company, on all three editions, who have been as committed to this text as we've been. They have been a pleasure to work with and we hope that we get to work together for many years. We like to call them Team Econ: Melissa Atkin, Hannah Bachman, Jack Borrebach, Miryam Chandler, Cassie del Pilar, Laura Dragonette, Christina Fuery, Sam Glass, Jeannine Hennawi, John Kresse, Pete Lesser, Sasha Levitt, Lindsey Osteen, Eric Pier-Hocking, Jack Repcheck, Victoria Reuter, Spencer Richardson-Jones, Carson Russell, Nicole Sawa, Megan Schindel, Eric Svendsen, Elizabeth Trammel, Janise Turso, and Stefani Wallace. Our development editors, Becky Kohn, Steve Riglosi, and Kurt Norlin were a big help, as were our copy editors, Alice Vigliani, Janet Greenblatt, and Carla Barnwell. The visual appeal of the book is the result of our photo researchers, Dena Digilio Betz, Nelson Colón, and Ted Szczepanski, and the design teams at W. W. Norton and Kiss Me I'm Polish: Jen Montgomery, Debra Morton-Hoyt, Tiani Kennedy, Rubina Yeh, Agnieszka Gasparska, Andrew Janik, and Annie Song.

Finally, we would like to thank Kaitlyn Amos for the help she provided generating photo ideas. Thanks to all.

ABOUT THE AUTHORS

Dirk Mateer is the Gerald J. Swanson Chair in Economic Education at the University of Arizona. His research has appeared in the *Journal of Economic Education* as well as other journals and focuses on media-enriched learning. He is the author of *Economics in the Movies* (2005) and is an award-winning instructor. He has been featured in the "Great Teachers in Economics" series and he was also the inaugural winner of the Economic Communicator Contest sponsored by the Association of Private Enterprise Education. While he was at Penn State, he received the George W. Atherton Award, the university's highest teaching award, and was voted the best overall teacher in the Smeal College of Business by the readers of *Critique Magazine*. Now at Arizona, he received the best large class lecture award in the Eller College of Management.

Lee Coppock is professor of economics and director of undergraduate studies in the Department of Economics at the University of Virginia, where he has taught more than 15,000 students in principles of macroeconomics. He has received several teaching awards, including the 2017 Kenneth G. Elzinga Distinguished Teaching Award from the Southern Economics Association and the 2018 UVA Alumni Distinguished Professor Award. Along with Krista, his wife of 30 years, he has four children: Bethany, Lee III, Kara, and Jackson.

PRINCIPLES OF MICROECONOMICS

THIRD EDITION

PART I

Introduction

Five Foundations of Economics

Economics Is About More Than Money.

Have you ever thought about what it would be like to have a money tree in your backyard? Imagine walking outside, picking cash off the branches, and using it to buy whatever you desired. If that sounds too good to be true, it is—and not just because money doesn't grow on trees. The problem is, if money did grow on trees, it wouldn't be scarce. Everyone would have their own money tree, and therefore they wouldn't have any reason to give you something in return for the greenbacks you waved in front of them. You'd have all the money you could possibly want, and yet in practical terms you'd be as poor as if you had none at all.

The money-tree story teaches a lesson about the value-destroying nature of inflation; we'll get to that in a later chapter. But there's another, even more basic moral, namely that money itself is not really what we care about. What we care about is what we use money to acquire: the actual goods and services that make our lives more enjoyable.

Economist Carol Graham, who studies "the economics of happiness," argues that human happiness provides an alternative measure of well-being, one that covers more than a snapshot of people's finances at a single point in time. For many people, income is variable, with periods of unemployment causing them to move in and out of poverty. Even when these folks are working, uncertainty about the future subtracts from their happiness. Other people's variations in

A personal money tree would be awesome, especially if no one else had one!

income follow a more predictable course: these folks are relatively poor when young, earn more and build up savings during middle age, and then draw down those savings once they retire. These people, for the most part, avoid the happiness-undermining effects of financial uncertainty.

Money also can't tell us about neighborhood effects, like the fact that New York City is a way more expensive place to live than Charlottesville, Virginia, or Tubac, Arizona (where your authors live). These are some reasons why economists are concerned about human happiness just as much, if not more, than simply how much money you make.

This textbook provides the tools you need to fill in more of the picture and make your own assessments about the economy. What other discipline helps you discover how the world works, how to be an informed citizen, and how to live your life to the fullest? Economics can improve your understanding of the stock market and help you make better decisions. If you are concerned about Social Security, this textbook explains how it

Even in New York's pricey Greenwich Village, money doesn't grow on trees. The people living here do make a lot more money than most people, though. So do the residents of Miami Beach and Beverly Hills. Does that make them happier? Not necessarily.

works. If you are interested in learning more about the economics of health care and some of the challenges it faces, the answers are here.

In this chapter, you will learn about five foundations of economics—incentives, trade-offs, opportunity cost, marginal thinking, and the principle that trade creates value. You will find that many of the more complex problems presented later in the text are based on these foundations, either singly or in combination. Think of this chapter as a road map that provides a broad overview of your first journey into economics. Let's get started!

· BIG QUESTIONS ·

* What is economics?
* What are five foundations of economics?

What Is Economics?

Economists study how decisions are made. Examples of economic decisions include whether you should buy or lease a car, sublet your apartment, or buy that Gibson guitar you've been eyeing. And just as individuals must choose what to buy within the limits of their income, society as a whole must determine what to produce from its limited set of resources.

Of course, life would be a lot easier if we could have whatever we wanted whenever we wanted it. Unfortunately, life does not work that way. Our wants and needs are practically unlimited, but the resources available to satisfy these wants and needs are always limited. The term used to describe the limited nature of society's resources is **scarcity**. Even the most abundant resources, like the water we drink and the air we breathe, are not always abundant enough everywhere to meet the wants and needs of every person. So how do individuals and societies make decisions about scarce resources? This is the basic question economists seek to answer. **Economics** is the study of how individuals and societies allocate their limited resources to satisfy their practically unlimited wants.

Scarcity
refers to the inherently limited nature of society's resources, given society's unlimited wants and needs.

Economics
is the study of how individuals and societies allocate their limited resources to satisfy their practically unlimited wants.

Water is scarce...

...and so are diamonds!

Microeconomics and Macroeconomics

Microeconomics
is the study of the individual units that make up the economy.

Macroeconomics
is the study of the overall aspects and workings of an economy.

The study of economics is divided into two subfields: microeconomics and macroeconomics. **Microeconomics** (micro) is the study of the individual units that make up the economy, such as households and businesses. **Macroeconomics** (macro) is the study of the overall aspects and workings of an economy, such as inflation (an overall increase in prices), growth, employment, interest rates, and the productivity of the economy as a whole. To understand the difference, consider a worker who gets laid off and becomes unemployed. Is this an issue that would be addressed in microeconomics or macroeconomics? The question seems to fit parts of both definitions. The worker is an individual, which is micro, but employment is one of the broad areas of concern for the economy as a whole, which is macro. However, because only one worker is laid off, this is a micro issue. If many workers were laid off and the result was a higher unemployment rate across the entire economy, the issue would be broad enough to be studied by macroeconomists. However, macroeconomics is more than just an aggregation of microeconomics. Macroeconomists examine, among other things, government policies regarding the federal budget and money supply, the reasons for inflation and unemployment, economic growth, international trade, and government borrowing—topics that are too complex to be understood using only microeconomic analysis.

What Are Five Foundations of Economics?

The study of economics can be complicated, but we can make it very accessible by breaking it down into a set of component parts. The five foundations presented here are key components of economics. They are a bit like the natural laws of physics or chemistry. Almost every economic subject can be analyzed through the prism of one of these foundations. By mastering the five

Scarcity

NATION JUST WANTS TO BE SAFE, HAPPY, RICH, COMFORTABLE, ENTERTAINED AT ALL TIMES

A short video from the satirical website *The Onion* describes a fictitious report from the Pew Research Center, about what Americans want and expect from life. After a graphic details how practically all Americans would like to be everything from "safe" to "romantically fulfilled," the video segues to interviews with individuals whose "all I want" lists range from the endearing (a big happy dog) to the quirky (a new Wes Anderson movie), the unrealistic (quick and easy weight loss), and the impossible ("I don't want to die").

We live in a world of scarcity. But that alone doesn't explain why we're unable to meet everyone's wants. Couldn't we just redistribute goods and services more evenly, to satisfy everyone? No chance, because our wants exceed our needs, and when all our wants are met, we come up with new ones. Many people spend their lives trying to "keep up with the Joneses." This isn't all bad, because competitive drive causes people to work longer and harder, which makes the economy more productive. At the same time, when we purchase

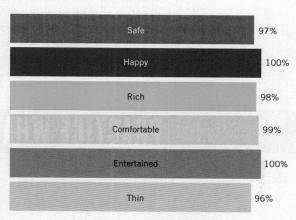

Safe	97%
Happy	100%
Rich	98%
Comfortable	99%
Entertained	100%
Thin	96%

the ONION

Based on a fictitious report on the satirical website *The Onion,* this graphic shows what Americans want. Of course, part of the joke is that this is not far from the truth for most of us, right?

one good, we have less to spend on other goods we also desire, and therefore we face trade-offs and opportunity costs.

foundations, you will be on your way to succeeding in this course and thinking like an economist. The five foundations of economics are:

- Incentives
- Trade-offs
- Opportunity cost
- Marginal thinking
- Trade creates value

Each of these five foundations reappears throughout the book and enables you to solve complex problems. Every time you encounter one of the five concepts, you will see an icon of a house in the margin. As you become more adept at economic analysis, you will often use two or more of these foundational ideas to understand the economic world around you.

Incentives
Trade-offs
Opportunity cost
Marginal thinking
Trade creates value

Incentives

When you are faced with making a decision, you usually make the choice that you think will most improve your situation. In making your decision, you respond to **incentives**—factors that motivate you to act or exert effort. For example, your choice to study for an exam you have tomorrow, instead of spending the evening with your friends, is based on your belief that doing well on the exam will provide a greater benefit. You have an incentive to study because you know that an A in the course will raise your grade-point average and make you a more attractive candidate on the job market when you are finished with school. We can further divide incentives into two paired categories: positive and negative; and direct and indirect.

PRACTICE WHAT YOU KNOW

Microeconomics and Macroeconomics: The Big Picture

Decide whether each of the following statements identifies a microeconomic issue or a macroeconomic issue.

STATEMENT: The national savings rate is less than 2% of income.

ANSWER: The national savings rate is a statistic based on the average amount each household saves as a percentage of income. As such, it is a broad measure of savings that describes a macroeconomic issue.

STATEMENT: Maya was laid off from her job and is currently unemployed.

ANSWER: Maya's personal financial circumstances constitute a microeconomic issue, because she is an individual worker.

STATEMENT: Apple decides to open 100 new stores.

ANSWER: Even though Apple is a very large corporation and 100 new stores will create many new jobs, Apple's decision is a microeconomic issue because it is best understood as part of an individual firm's competitive strategy.

STATEMENT: The government passes a jobs bill designed to stabilize the economy during a recession (an economic downturn).

ANSWER: You might be tempted to ask how many jobs are created, but that information is not relevant to answering this question. The key part of the statement refers to "stabilize the economy during a recession," which is an example of the government taking an active role in managing the overall workings of the economy. Therefore, it is a macroeconomic issue.

This mosaic of the flag illustrates the difference between micro and macro. The tiny pictures represent microeconomics and the roles that individual decisions play in the overall health of the economy, which is the composite we see when we look at the entire picture.

POSITIVE AND NEGATIVE INCENTIVES *Positive incentives* encourage action by offering rewards or payments. For example, end-of-year bonuses motivate employees to work hard throughout the year, higher oil prices cause suppliers to extract more oil, and tax rebates encourage citizens to spend more money. *Negative incentives* discourage action by providing undesirable consequences or punishments. For instance, the fear of receiving a speeding ticket keeps motorists from driving too fast, higher oil prices might spur some consumers to use less oil, and the dread of a trip to the dentist motivates people to brush their teeth regularly. In each case, we see that incentives spur individuals to action.

Conventional wisdom tells us that "learning is its own reward," but try telling that to most students. Teachers are aware that incentives, both positive and negative, create additional interest among their students to learn the course material. Positive incentives include bonus points, gold stars, public praise, and extra credit. Many students respond to these encouragements by studying more. However, positive incentives are not enough. Suppose your instructor never gave any grade lower than an A. Your incentive to participate actively in the course, do assignments, or earn bonus points would be small. For positive incentives to work, they generally need to be coupled with negative incentives. This is why instructors require students to complete assignments, take exams, and write papers. Students know that if they do not complete these requirements, they will get a lower grade, or perhaps even fail the class.

Incentives

DIRECT AND INDIRECT INCENTIVES Incentives can also be direct or indirect. For instance, if one gas station lowers its prices, it most likely will get business from customers who would not usually stop there. This is a *direct incentive*. Lower gasoline prices also work as an *indirect incentive*, because lower prices might encourage consumers to use more gas.

Direct incentives are easy to recognize. "Cut my grass and I'll pay you $30" is an example of a direct incentive. Indirect incentives are more difficult to recognize. But learning to recognize them is one of the keys to mastering economics. For instance, consider the indirect incentives at work in welfare programs. Almost everyone agrees that societies should provide a safety net for those without employment or whose income isn't enough to meet their basic needs. In other words, a society has a direct incentive to alleviate suffering caused by poverty. But how does a society provide this safety net without taking away the incentive to work? If the amount of welfare a person receives is higher than the amount that person can hope to make from a job, the welfare recipient might decide to stay on welfare rather than go to work. The indirect incentive to stay on welfare creates an *unintended consequence*: people who were supposed to use government assistance as a safety net until they can find a job use it instead as a permanent source of income.

Policymakers have the tough task of deciding how to balance such conflicting incentives. To decrease the likelihood that a person will stay on welfare, policymakers could cut benefits. But this decision might leave some people without enough to live on. For this reason, many

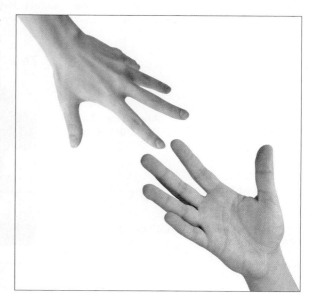
Public assistance: a hand in time of need or an incentive not to work?

government programs specify limits on the amount of time people can receive benefits. Ideally, this limit allows the welfare programs to continue meeting people's basic needs while creating incentives that encourage recipients to search for a job and acquire skills that will help them get a job. We'll learn more about welfare issues in Chapter 15.

ECONOMICS IN THE REAL WORLD

WHY ARE THERE SO MANY DASHBOARD CAMERAS IN RUSSIA?

Let's look at an example of how incentives operate in the real world and how they can produce surprising consequences. Compared to the United States, Russia is quite a dangerous place to drive (see Figure 1.1). On top of the collisions that occur due to chaotic traffic conditions, insurance scammers regularly stage accidents. To protect themselves against scammers, most Russian motorists have "dash cams," which provide video evidence of a driver's innocence in court. The fact that so many Russian drivers are willing to invest in dash cams strongly suggests that the benefits of having a cam exceed the cost.

In the United States, and in most other countries where there are fewer annual deaths (and accidents) per vehicle, staged accidents are much less common, and consequently dash cams are much less prevalent.

FIGURE 1.1

Global Status Report on Safety

Compared to the United States, Russia is quite a dangerous place to drive. Widespread insurance scamming in Russia has led most motorists to install dash cams. The fact that insurance scammers exist is an unintended consequence of mandated insurance, especially in Russia where the rules of the road and safe driving are often ignored.

Country	Annual deaths per 100,000 vehicles
Russia	53.4
Europe	19.0
United States	12.9
Australia	7.3

Source: See, WHO, ed., "Global Status Report on Road Safety 2015" (2015).

INCENTIVES AND INNOVATION Incentives also play a vital role in innovation, the engine of economic growth. An excellent example is Steve Jobs. He and the company he founded, Apple, held over 300 patents at the time of his death in 2011.

In the United States, the patent system and copyright laws guarantee inventors a specific period of time in which they have the exclusive right to sell their work. This system encourages innovation by creating a powerful financial reward for creativity. Without patents and copyright laws, inventors would bear all the costs, and almost none of the rewards, for their efforts. Why would firms invest in research and development or artists create new music if others could immediately copy and sell their work? To reward the perspiration and inspiration required for innovation, society allows patents and copyrights to create the right incentives for economic growth.

In recent years, new forms of technology have made the illegal sharing of copyrighted material quite easy. As a result, illegal downloads of books, music, and movies are widespread. When writers, musicians, actors, and studios cannot effectively protect what they have created, they earn less. So illegal downloads reduce the incentive to produce new content. Will the next John Lennon or Jay-Z work so hard? Will the next Suzanne Collins (author of *The Hunger Games*) or J. K. Rowling (author of the Harry Potter books) hone their writing craft so diligently if there is so much less financial reward for success? Is the "I want it for free" culture causing the truly gifted to be less committed to their craft, thus depriving society of excellence? Maintaining the right rewards, or incentives, for hard work and innovation is essential for making sure that inventors and other creative people are compensated for their creativity and vision. Some see services like Spotify, Tidal, and Soundcloud as the answer. While streaming services are now very successful, the amount artists receive is still far lower than is used to be.

Incentives

INCENTIVES ARE EVERYWHERE One very powerful incentive is saving time. You can test out your time-savings skills when you walk across campus to a class. An app will give you a detailed route and an estimated time of arrival, but your app won't know the local shortcuts. Sometimes the shortcuts everyone takes are through buildings or along dirt paths. Sometimes all you have to do is crowdsource the best route by following others. The paths worn into greens by students' feet will show you how to get across campus as quickly as possible.

Understanding incentives, from positive to negative and direct to indirect, is the key to understanding economics. If you remember only one concept from this course, it should be that incentives matter.

Trade-Offs

In a world of scarcity, each and every decision incurs a cost. Even time is a scarce resource; after all, there are only 24 hours in a day. So deciding to play Fortnite now means you won't be able to read one of the

Taking a shortcut saves time.

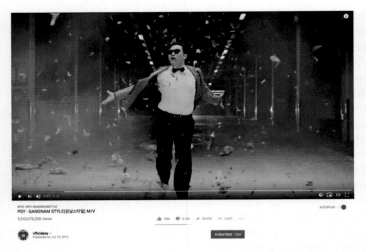

Trade-offs

What might have been achieved in the time it has taken to watch this video over 3 billion times?

Harry Potter books until later. More generally, doing one thing often means you will not have the time, resources, or energy to do something else. Similarly, paying for a college education can require spending tens of thousands of dollars that might be used elsewhere instead.

Understanding the trade-offs that exist in life can completely change how you view the world. Let's look at Psy's song "Gangnam Style." The video for this song has been viewed over 3 billion times on YouTube, making it one of the most watched videos of all time. Imagine what could have been accomplished if people had used that time differently. *The Economist* magazine considered this question and came up with a list of the trade-offs. "Gangnam Style" is 4 minutes and 12 seconds long, which means that more than 200 million hours have been spent watching the video. In the same amount of time, eight Burj Khalifas (one of the world's tallest buildings, located in Dubai, United Arab Emirates) or five Great Egyptian Pyramids could have been built or the entire contents of Wikipedia entered—twice!

People who don't understand economics sometimes ignore the trade-offs that are natural in a world of scarcity. They unconsciously assume that we can (as individuals or a group) have more of everything we want. But in fact, decision-making generally involves trade-offs. For example, if you decide to increase your time allotment for studying economics, you need to give up something else: you might study less for other courses, work fewer hours at your job, or socialize less. That is, there is a trade-off between higher economics grades and other things you desire. As a nation, we may wish to increase subsidies to college education, or to increase international aid, or to strengthen our national defense. Economists are the ones who then ask: What about the trade-offs? That is, what must we give up to increase spending on education or international aid, or on a stronger military?

Here's how President Dwight Eisenhower put the point in a 1953 speech:

> The cost of one modern heavy bomber is this: a modern brick school in more than 30 cities. It is two electric power plants, each serving a town of 60,000 population. It is two fine, fully equipped hospitals. It is some 50 miles of concrete highway. We pay for a single fighter plane with a half million bushels of wheat. We pay for a single destroyer with new homes that could have housed more than 8,000 people.

Ultimately, thinking about trade-offs means that we will make more informed decisions about how to utilize our scarce resources.

Opportunity Cost

Opportunity cost

The existence of trade-offs requires making hard decisions. Trade-offs are about having to give something up, and opportunity cost quantifies "what" or "how much" is being given up. Choosing one thing means giving up something else. Suppose you receive two invitations—the first to spend the day hiking and the second to go to a concert—and both events occur at the same time. No matter which event you choose, you have to sacrifice the other option. In this example, you can think of the cost of going to the concert as the lost opportunity to go on the hike. Likewise, the cost of going hiking is the lost opportunity to go to the concert. No matter what choice you make, there is an opportunity cost, or next-best alternative, that must be sacrificed. **Opportunity cost** is the highest-valued alternative that must be sacrificed to get something else.

Every time we make a choice, we experience an opportunity cost. The key to making the best possible decision is to minimize your opportunity cost by selecting the option that gives you the largest benefit. If you prefer going to a concert, you should go to the concert. What you give up (the hike) has less value to you than the concert, so it represents an opportunity cost.

The hiking/concert choice is a simple and clear example of opportunity cost. Usually, it takes deliberate effort to see the world through the opportunity cost prism. But it is a worthwhile practice because it will help you make better decisions. For example, imagine you are a small business owner. Your financial officer informs you that you have had a successful year and made a sizable profit. So everything is good, right? Not so fast. An economist will tell you to ask yourself, "Could I have made *more* profit doing something else?" Good economic thinkers ask this question all the time. "Could I be using my time, talents, or energy on another activity that would be even more profitable for me?"

Profits on an official income statement are only part of the story, because they only measure how well a business does relative to the bottom line. Accountants cannot measure what *might* have been better. For example, suppose you had decided not to open a new store. A few months later, a rival opened a very successful store in the same location you had considered. Your profits were good for the year, but if you had opened the new store, your profits could have been even better. So when economists talk about opportunity cost, they are assessing whether the alternatives are better than what you are currently doing, which considers a larger set of possible outcomes.

Before Ellen DeGeneres achieved stardom, she spent one semester studying communication at the University of New Orleans. Ellen defied the usual wisdom about staying in school and completing her degree, because she understood opportunity cost. Given her show's success and her entrepreneurial acumen starting a number of successful derivative companies, it is hard to fault her decision. If Ellen had finished her degree, she most likely never would have become the likeable star we know today.

Opportunity cost
is the highest-valued alternative that must be sacrificed to get something else.

Can you come up with a witty one-liner as fast as Ellen can?

Opportunity cost

The Opportunity Cost of Attending College

QUESTION: What is the opportunity cost of attending college?

ANSWER: When people think about the cost of attending college, they usually think of tuition, room and board, course materials, and travel-related expenses. While those

Spending thousands on college expenses? You could be working instead!

expenses are indeed a part of going to college, they are not its full cost. The opportunity cost is the next-best alternative that is sacrificed. This opportunity cost—or what you potentially could have done if you were not in college—includes the lost income you could have earned working a full-time job. If you consider the cost of attending college plus the forgone income lost while in college, you can see that college is a very expensive proposition. Setting aside the question of how much more you might have to pay for room and board at college rather than elsewhere, consider the cost of tuition, which can be $40,000 or more at many of the nation's most expensive colleges. Add that out-of-pocket expense to the forgone income from a full-time job that might pay $40,000 a year, and your four years in college can easily cost over a quarter of a million dollars.

CHALLENGE QUESTION: Ellen DeGeneres honed her trademark comedy routines in small venues until she became famous. But for every Ellen, there are thousands of other comedians who never made it big. What advice would you give to someone wrestling with the decision to leave college?

ANSWER: The question is tricky. We can't know the future, and staying in college and leaving college both have opportunity costs. By staying, you forgo the opportunity to try new things and, perhaps, discover in the process something else you excel at. However, leaving means a college degree will not be part of your resume. Making decisions when there is uncertainty about how the future will unfold is what makes choices difficult, because there are opportunity costs in both directions.

ECONOMICS IN THE REAL WORLD

HOW LONG WOULD YOU WAIT IN LINE ON BLACK FRIDAY TO SAVE $300?

How long would you wait in line to save $300?

A few years ago in Beaumont, California, Vicky Torres and Juanita Alva were first in line to secure a large-screen television at Best Buy during the Black Friday Sale. The TV they wanted was advertised at $199. Let's say that was a markdown from $499. How many hours would you wait in line to save $300? Two hours? Five? Ten? How about 500 hours? That's how long the two women waited, because they arrived *three weeks* early. By all accounts they enjoyed their time waiting, spending their days talking to strangers and taking turns saving each other's spots in line over night. However, there's an opportunity cost here that makes Vicky and Juanita's decision puzzling. Think of the many trade-offs they faced: missed sleep, time they could have spent with friends and family, and the time they could be working instead of waiting in line, to name just a few. It is hard to justify the women's choices using marginal analysis. Saving $300 by spending 500 hours makes their time worth 60 cents an hour. They could have spent 30 hours working an extra job at $10 an hour and each earned enough money to purchase the TV at full price—and still had 470 hours to do other things. In short, they don't seem to have been aware of the opportunity cost of waiting in line.

Marginal Thinking

The process of systematically evaluating a course of action is called economic thinking. **Economic thinking** involves a purposeful evaluation of the available opportunities to make the best decision possible. In this context, economic thinkers use a process called *marginal analysis* to break down decisions into smaller parts. Often, the choice is not between doing and not doing something, but between doing more or less of something. For instance, if you take on a part-time job while in school, you probably wrestle with the question of how many hours to work. If you work a little more, you can earn additional income. If you work a little less, you have more time to study. Working more has a tangible benefit (more money) and a tangible cost (lower grades). All of this should sound familiar from our earlier discussion about trade-offs. The work-study trade-off affects how much money you have and what kind of grades you earn.

An economist would say that your decision—weighing how much money you want against the grades you want—is a decision at the *margin*. What exactly does the word "margin" mean as used in economics? In economics, **marginal thinking** requires decision-makers to evaluate whether the benefit of one more unit of something is greater than its cost. Understanding how to analyze decisions at the margin is essential to thinking like a good economist.

For example, have you ever wondered why people vacuum, dust, scrub the bathrooms, clean out their garages, and wash their windows, but leave the dust bunnies under the refrigerator? The answer lies in thinking at the margin. Moving the refrigerator out from the wall to clean requires a significant effort for a small benefit. Guests who enter the kitchen can't see under the refrigerator. So most of us ignore the dust bunnies and just clean the visible areas of our homes. In other words, when economists say you should think at the margin, what they really mean is that you should weigh the costs and benefits of your actions and choose to do the things with the greatest payoff. For most of us, that means being willing to live with dust bunnies. The *marginal cost* of cleaning under the refrigerator (or on top of the cabinets or even behind the sofa cushions) is too high, and the added value of making the effort, or the *marginal benefit*, is too low to justify the additional cleaning.

Economic thinking requires a purposeful evaluation of the available opportunities to make the best decision possible.

Marginal thinking requires decision-makers to evaluate whether the benefit of one more unit of something is greater than its cost.

Marginal thinking

Trade

Imagine trying to find food in a world without grocery stores. The task of getting what you need to eat each day would require visiting many separate locations. Many centuries ago, this need to bring buyers and sellers together was met by weekly markets, or bazaars, in central locations like town squares. **Markets** bring buyers and sellers together to exchange goods and services. As commerce spread throughout the ancient world, trade routes developed. Markets grew from infrequent gatherings, where exchange involved trading goods and services for other goods and services, into more sophisticated systems that use cash, credit, and other financial instruments. Today, when we think of markets, we often think of eBay or Craigslist. For instance, if you want to find a rare Hot Wheels Black Panther Movie Die-Cast Vehicle, an excellent place to look is eBay, which allows users to search for just about any product, bid on it, and then have it sent directly to their home.

Markets bring buyers and sellers together to exchange goods and services.

Trade creates value

THE CIRCULAR FLOW When we consider all the trade that occurs in an economy, it is helpful to use a **circular flow diagram**. This shows how goods, services, and resources flow through the economy via commerce between households and firms. Households are made up of consumers, as we usually picture them. Firms are businesses. Households desire the goods and services produced by firms, but to produce those goods and services, firms require the resources owned by households. The circular flow diagram illustrates the movement of goods, services, and resources that results when firms and households do business with each other.

In the circular flow in Figure 1.2, households are on the left and firms on the right. Households buy goods and services from firms in product markets, at the top of the diagram. This is the kind of transaction you undertake all the time: when you buy groceries or school supplies, you purchase these in product markets, from firms. But households are also sellers, in that they provide the inputs or resources that firms use to produce their output. These transactions take place in resource markets, at the bottom of the diagram. When you put in time at your job and get a paycheck in return, that is a resource market transaction.

The green arrows that form the counterclockwise outer loop show goods and services flowing from firms to households across the top of the circle and resources flowing from households to firms across the bottom. Goods, services, and resources are paid for with *funds*. The red arrows forming the inner loop show how funds flow in the opposite direction of whatever they are paying for. Each loop is closed. On the outside, resources go into the production of goods and services, which in turn go into sustaining households so they can continue to provide firms with resources. On the inside, funds are transferred from households' bank accounts to firms' accounts as

FIGURE 1.2

The Circular Flow

Goods and services move counterclockwise from one part of the economy to another. Firms produce goods and services and trade them for funds from households in the product market. Households sell resources to produce goods and services in the resource market. The circular flow of goods and services appears as the green outer loop, and the circular flow of funds to purchase goods and services appears as the red inner loop.

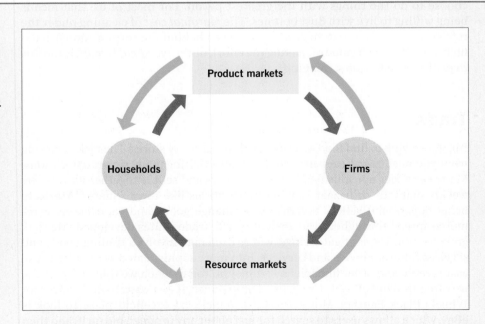

payment for goods and services, and then return to households as payment for resources.

Consider a simple example. Let's say you spend $1,000 on a new Dell computer. You trade for your computer in a product market, and Dell gets the $1,000: this takes place in the top half of the circular flow diagram. Then Dell uses the $1,000 to pay its workers' wages and other suppliers for the use of resources. This happens in the bottom half of the diagram. In the end, the funds make the complete circuit back to households.

This simple circular flow diagram leaves out some details. For one thing, government is an important player in any economy. Funds flow into and out of governments, which participate in both the product and resource markets. In addition, households and firms also interact with foreign firms and households. We consider the roles of government and foreign firms and households later in the text, but for now, this simple circular flow diagram serves as a schematic summary of how households and firms interact through trade in an economy.

TRADE CREATES VALUE **Trade** is the voluntary exchange of goods and services between two or more parties. Voluntary trade among rational individuals creates value for everyone involved. Imagine you are on your way home from class and you want to pick up a gallon of milk. You know that milk will be more expensive at a convenience store than at the grocery store 5 miles away, but you are in a hurry to study for your economics exam and are willing to pay up to $5 for the convenience of getting the milk quickly. At the store, you find that the price is $4 and you happily purchase the milk. This ability to buy for less than the price you are willing to pay provides a positive incentive to make the purchase. But what about the seller? If the store owner paid $3 to buy the milk from a supplier, and you are willing to pay the $4 price she has set in order to make a profit, the store owner has an incentive to sell. This simple voluntary transaction has made both of you better off.

By fostering the exchange of goods, trade helps to create additional growth through specialization. **Comparative advantage** refers to the situation in which an individual, business, or country can produce at a lower opportunity cost than a competitor can. Comparative advantage harnesses the power of specialization, a topic we discuss in more detail in Chapter 2. As a result, it is possible to be a physician, teacher, or plumber and not worry about how to do everything yourself. The physician becomes proficient at dispensing medical advice, the teacher at helping students, and the plumber at fixing leaks. The physician and the teacher call the plumber when they need work on their plumbing. The teacher and the plumber see the doctor when they are sick. The physician and the plumber send their children to school to learn from the teacher.

The same process is at work among businesses. For instance, Starbucks specializes in making coffee, Honda in making automobiles. You would not want to get your morning cup of joe at Honda any more than you would want to buy a car from Starbucks!

On a broader scale, specialization and trading of services exist at the international level as well. Some countries have highly developed workforces capable of managing and solving complex processes. Other countries have large pools of relatively unskilled labor. As a result, businesses that need skilled labor gravitate to countries where they can easily find the workers they need. Likewise,

Trade
is the voluntary exchange of goods and services between two or more parties.

Incentives
Trade creates value

Comparative advantage
refers to the situation where an individual, business, or country can produce at a lower opportunity cost than a competitor can.

Our economy depends on specialization.

firms with production processes that rely on unskilled labor look for employees in less developed countries, where workers are paid less. By harnessing the power of increased specialization, global companies and economies create value through increased production and growth.

However, globalized trade is not without controversy. When goods and jobs are free to move across borders, not everyone benefits equally, nor should we expect this outcome. Consider the case of a U.S. worker who loses her job when her position is outsourced to a call center in India. The jobless worker now has to find new employment—a process that requires significant time and energy. In contrast, the new position in the call center in India provides a job and an income that improve the life of another worker. Also, the U.S. firm enjoys the advantage of being able to hire lower-cost labor elsewhere. The firm's lower costs often translate into lower prices for domestic consumers. None of those advantages make the outsourcing of jobs any less painful for affected workers, but outsourcing is an important component of economic growth in the long run.

Conclusion

Economists ask, and answer, big questions about life. This is what makes the study of economics so fascinating. Understanding how an entire economy functions may seem like a daunting task, but it is not nearly as difficult as it sounds. Remember when you learned to drive? At first, everything was difficult and unfamiliar. But as you probably found, becoming a good driver is just a matter of mastering a few key principles, and then, with a little experience under your belt, you can drive any car on the road. In the same way, once you have learned the fundamentals of economics, you can use them to analyze almost any problem. In the next chapter, we use the ideas developed in this chapter to explore trade in greater depth. ✳

Five Foundations of Economics

In this book, we study five foundations of economics—incentives, trade-offs, opportunity cost, marginal thinking, and the principle that trade creates value. Once you have mastered these five concepts, even complex economic processes can be reduced to smaller, more easily understood parts. If you keep these foundations in mind, you'll find that understanding economics is rewarding and fun.

INCENTIVES

TRADE-OFFS

OPPORTUNITY COST

MARGINAL THINKING

TRADE CREATES VALUE

REVIEW QUESTIONS

- Which of the five foundations explains what you give up when you choose to buy a new pair of shoes instead of attending a concert?

- What are four types of incentives discussed in the chapter? Why do incentives sometimes create unintended consequences?

So You Wanna Be a Billionaire? Study Economics

- Economics majors are more likely to become billionaires than majors in any other subject.
- Economics majors, on average, make 3.4 million dollars in career earnings.
- Economics majors are also top performers on the Law School Admission Test.

Travie McCoy and Bruno Mars collaborated on the mega-hit "Billionaire" in 2010. Little did they know that majors in economics are most likely to make the Forbes 400, a list of the richest people in the United States. In this graphic, we report the six majors that produce the highest number of billionaires and cross-reference those findings with projected lifetime earnings to give you a sense of how much the average college graduate with one of these degrees is likely to earn. We've intentionally used lifetime earnings, since they are a better indicator of financial well-being than the typical starting salary ranges you might be more familiar with. It is how much money you make over your entire career that matters!

Majoring in economics gives you the best chance of becoming a billionaire.

The financial rewards are nice, but that's not the only reason to choose economics. Economics majors are also versatile in other ways: they are top performers on the LSAT (Law School Admission Test) and are in demand as policy experts, consultants, and forecasters.

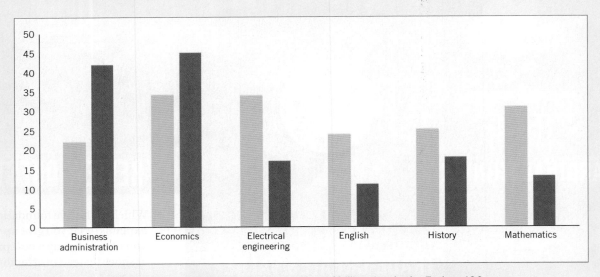

Green is lifetime income (in $100,000s) and red is the number of billionaires in the Forbes 400.

· ANSWERING *the* BIG QUESTIONS ·

What is economics?

- Economics is the study of how people allocate their limited resources to satisfy their practically unlimited wants. Because of the limited nature of society's resources, even the most abundant resources are not always plentiful enough everywhere to meet the wants and needs of every person. So how do individuals and societies make decisions about how to use the scarce resources at their disposal? This is the basic question economists seek to answer.

What are five foundations of economics?

Five foundations of economics are incentives, trade-offs, opportunity cost, marginal thinking, and the principle that trade creates value.

- Incentives are important because they help explain how rational decisions are made.
- Trade-offs exist when a decision-maker has to choose a course of action.
- Each time we make a choice, we experience an opportunity cost, or a lost chance to do something else.
- Marginal thinking requires a decision-maker to weigh the extra benefits against the extra costs.
- Trade creates value because participants in markets are able to specialize in the production of goods and services they have a comparative advantage in making.

· CHAPTER PROBLEMS ·

Concepts You Should Know

circular flow diagram (p. 18)
comparative advantage (p. 19)
economics (p. 7)
economic thinking (p. 17)

incentives (p. 10)
macroeconomics (p. 8)
marginal thinking (p. 17)
markets (p. 17)

microeconomics (p. 8)
opportunity cost (p. 15)
scarcity (p. 7)
trade (p. 19)

Questions for Review

1. How would you respond if your instructor gave daily quizzes on the course readings? Are these quizzes a positive incentive or a negative incentive?

2. Explain why many seniors often earn lower grades in their last semester before graduation. (**Hint:** This is an incentive problem.)

3. What is the opportunity cost of reading this textbook?

4. Evaluate the following statement: "Trade is like football: one team wins and the other loses."

Study Problems *(✷ solved at the end of the section)*

✷ 1. What role do incentives play in each of the following situations? Are there any unintended consequences?

   a. You learn you can resell a ticket to next week's homecoming game for twice what you paid.

   b. A state government announces a "sales tax holiday" for back-to-school shopping during one week each August.

2. Compare your standard of living with that of your parents when they were the age you are now. Ask them or somebody you know around their age to recall where they were living and what they owned. How has the well-being of the typical person changed over the last 25 years? Explain your answer.

3. By referencing events in the news or something from your personal experiences, describe one example of each of the five foundations of economics discussed in this chapter.

✷ 4. Suppose that Colombia is good at growing coffee but not very good at making computer software and that Canada is good at making computer software but not very good at growing coffee. If Colombia decided only to grow coffee and Canada only to make computer software, would both countries be better off or worse off? Explain. Can you think of a similar example from your life?

5. After some consideration, you decide to hire someone to help you move from one apartment to another. Wouldn't it be cheaper to move yourself? Do you think the choice to hire someone is a rational choice? Explain your response.

✷ 6. When a town gets snowed in for a couple of days—the urban legend goes—the local hospital is likely to see a boost in births nine months later. In other words: blizzards might be prime baby-making time. Explain, using *economic* reasoning, why snowstorms may indeed cause an uptick in births nine months down the road.

7. *Whiplash* (2014) is about an aspiring college-age drummer who wants to become the best drummer in the world. He is willing to sacrifice personal relationships, practices tens of thousands of hours, and suffers mental and physical abuse from his teacher in order to achieve his goal and earn the recognition he craves. Watch the full movie trailer on IMDB.com or go to www.youtube.com/watch?v=MsWlktW0kj4 and watch the break-up scene with his girlfriend. What trade-offs are you making in your life right now to achieve your goals?

* 8. We have talked about how trade creates value. Use the information in each example below to compute the total value created in each exchange:

  a. Patrick bought an orange pen from Jill for $2.00. Patrick would have been willing to pay $2.50 for the pen, and Jill would have been willing to sell the pen for $1.25.

  b. Hillary found a car on Craigslist for which she would have been willing to pay up to $10,000.

The car's owner, Jason, needed to sell the car right away and would have accepted $6,000. The price they agreed on was $7,500.

9. What concept best explains why you wouldn't want to make your own clothes completely from scratch and instead will normally prefer to buy them from a retailer?

Solved Problems

1.a. Because your tickets are worth more than you paid for them, you have a direct positive incentive to resell them.

  b. The "sales tax holiday" is a direct positive incentive to buy more clothes during the back-to-school period. An unintended consequence of this policy is that fewer purchases are likely to be made both before and after the tax holiday.

4. If Colombia decided to specialize in the production of coffee, it could trade coffee to Canada in exchange for computer software. This process illustrates gains from specialization and trade. Both countries have a comparative advantage in producing one particular good. Colombia has ideal coffee-growing conditions, and Canada has a workforce that is more adept at writing software. Since both countries specialize in what they do best, they are able to produce more value than they could produce by trying to make both products on their own.

6. The situation has changed the incentives people face. In other words, the perceived costs and benefits of their choices have changed. Inclement weather makes it more costly to go outside; thus, more people will choose to stay home and engage in at-home activities.

8.a. In this example, Patrick is better off by $0.50, because he was willing to pay $2.50 but paid just $2.00. And Jill is better off by $0.75, because she would have accepted $1.25 but received $2.00. So the total value created is the additional value to Patrick ($0.50) plus the additional value to Jill ($0.75), which sums to $1.25.

  b. The value added for Jason is $1,500, which is the difference between the minimum price he would have accepted ($6,000) and the price he received ($7,500). The value added for Hillary is $2,500, which is the difference between the maximum price she would have paid ($10,000) and the price she actually paid ($7,500). In total, $1,500 + $2,500 = $4,000 in new value was created through the exchange.

02 Model Building and Gains from Trade

When People Trade, Both Sides Normally Win.

It's only common sense that trade benefits both parties. After all, if it's voluntary, both sides must be getting something out of it. But there's more to the story: we can quantify the extent to which trade makes each side better off. We do this by establishing how much more productive a person can become through trade, given that trade allows people to specialize in what they're good at. That's what we're going to learn about in this chapter.

Consider the interaction between a contractor and an architect. They each have a vital role to play in the building process. The architect designs the plans to the buyer's specifications. The contractor is an expert at bringing the architect's design to fruition by organizing the equipment, supplies, and labor to complete the project on time. The architect is the creative genius and the contractor is a genius at managing the construction workflow. The architect understands how to design plans that pass engineering tests and meet building codes. The contractor understands the supply chain. By specializing, each becomes more productive and gets their part of the project done faster, trading their expertise and time for monetary payment.

In 2004, world-renowned architect Zaha Hadid became the first woman to win the Pritzker Architecture Prize. She was well aware that building her designs, like this Riverside Museum in Glasgow, Scotland, required the work of many specialized builders, all managed by a highly skilled contractor. She also looked to other specialists for creative inspiration. "Our designs become more ambitious," she says, "as we see the new possibilities created by the technology of other industries."

To help understand how trade works, we will develop our first economic model, the production possibilities frontier, so we can explore the more nuanced reasons why trade creates value.

· BIG QUESTIONS ·

- How do economists study the economy?
- What is a production possibilities frontier?
- What are the benefits of specialization and trade?
- What is the trade-off between having more now and having more later?

How Do Economists Study the Economy?

Economics is a social science that uses the scientific method to develop *economic models*. To create these models, economists make many assumptions to simplify reality. These models help economists understand the key relationships that drive economic decisions.

The Scientific Method in Economics

The television show *MythBusters* puts popular myths to the test by replicating the circumstances and then showing the results. The entire show is dedicated to scientific testing of the myths. At the end of each episode, the myth is confirmed, deemed plausible, or busted. For instance, in a memorable episode, the show explored the reasons behind the *Hindenburg* disaster. The *Hindenburg* was a German passenger airship, or zeppelin, that caught fire and became engulfed in flames as it attempted to dock in New Jersey on May 6, 1937. Thirty-six people died.

Some people have claimed that the fire was sparked by the painted fabric in which the zeppelin was wrapped. Others have suggested that the hydrogen used to give the airship lift was the primary cause of the disaster. To test the hypothesis (proposed explanation) that the paint used on the fabric was to blame, the MythBusters built two small-scale models. The first model was filled with hydrogen and had a nonflammable skin. The second model used a replica of the original fabric for the skin but did not contain any hydrogen. Hyneman and Savage then compared their models' burn times with original footage of the disaster.

After examining the results, they "busted" the myth that the paint was to blame. Why? The model containing the hydrogen burned twice as fast as the one with just the painted fabric skin. It seems reasonable to conclude that hydrogen caused the disaster, not paint.

Economists work in much the same way as the Myth-Busters: they use the scientific method to answer questions about observable phenomena and to explain how the world works. The scientific method consists of four steps:

- First, researchers observe a phenomenon that interests them.
- Next, based on these observations, researchers develop a *hypothesis*, which is a proposed explanation for the phenomenon.
- Then they construct a model to test the hypothesis.
- Finally, they look for opportunities to test how well the model (which is based on the hypothesis) works. After collecting data, they use statistical methods to verify, revise, or refute the hypothesis.

The scientific method was used to discover why the *Hindenburg* caught fire.

The economist's laboratory is the world around us, and it ranges from the economy as a whole to the decisions made by firms and individuals. As a result, economists cannot always design experiments to test their hypotheses. Often, they must gather historical data or wait for real-world events to take place—for example, the Great Recession (economic downturn) of 2007–2009—to better understand the economy. When real-world events meet the criteria of an experiment designed to test a hypothesis, we have what's called a *natural* experiment.

Positive and Normative Analysis

As scientists, economists strive to approach their subject with objectivity. This means they rigorously avoid letting personal beliefs and values influence the outcome of their analysis. To be as objective as possible, economists deploy positive analysis. A **positive statement** can be tested and validated. Each positive statement can be thought of as a description of "what is." For instance, the statement "The unemployment rate is declining" is a positive statement, because it can be tested by gathering data. If the unemployment rate is indeed going down, then the statement is true, whereas if instead unemployment is rising, the statement is false.

A **positive statement** can be tested and validated; it describes "what is."

In contrast, a **normative statement** cannot be tested or validated; it is about "what ought to be." For instance, the statement "An unemployed worker should receive financial assistance to help make ends meet" is a matter of opinion. One can reasonably argue that financial assistance to the unemployed is beneficial for society as a whole because it helps eliminate poverty. However, many argue that financial assistance to the unemployed provides the wrong incentives. If the financial assistance provides enough to meet basic needs, workers may end up spending more time unemployed than they otherwise would. Neither opinion is right or wrong; they are differing viewpoints based on values, beliefs, and opinions.

A **normative statement** is an opinion that cannot be tested or validated; it describes "what ought to be."

Incentives

The Wright brothers' wind tunnel.

Economists are concerned with positive analysis. In contrast, normative statements are the realm of policymakers, voters, and philosophers. For example, if the unemployment rate rises, economists try to understand the conditions that created the situation. Economics does not attempt to determine who should receive unemployment assistance, which involves normative analysis. Maintaining a positive framework is crucial for economic analysis because it allows decision-makers to observe the facts objectively.

Economic Models

Thinking like an economist means learning how to analyze complex issues and problems. Many economic topics, such as international trade, Social Security, job loss, and inflation, are complicated. To analyze these phenomena and to determine the effect of various government policy options related to them, economists use economic models, which are simplified versions of reality. Models help us analyze the components of the economy.

A good model should be simple, flexible, and useful for making accurate predictions. Let's consider one of the most famous models in history, designed by Wilbur and Orville Wright. Before the Wright brothers made their famous first flight in 1903, they built a small wind tunnel out of a 6-foot-long wooden box. Inside the box they placed a device to measure aerodynamics, and at one end they attached a small fan to supply the wind. The brothers then tested over 200 different wing configurations to determine the lifting properties of each design. Using the data they collected, the Wright brothers were able to determine the best type of wing to use on their aircraft.

Similarly, economic models provide frameworks that help us to predict the effects of changes in prices, production processes, and government policies on real-life behavior.

Ceteris paribus
[pronounced KETeris PAReebus] means "other things being equal" or "all else equal" and is used to build economic models. It allows economists to examine a change in one variable while holding everything else constant.

CETERIS PARIBUS Using a controlled setting that held many other variables constant enabled the Wright brothers to experiment with different wing designs. By altering only a single element—for example, the angle of the wing—they could test whether the change in design was advantageous. The process of examining a change in one variable while holding everything else constant involves a concept known as ***ceteris paribus***, from the Latin meaning "other things being equal" or "all else equal."

The *ceteris paribus* assumption is central to model building. If the Wright brothers had changed many design elements simultaneously and found that a new version of the wing worked better, they would have had no way of knowing which change was responsible for the improved performance. For this reason, engineers generally modify only one design element at a time and test only that one element before testing additional elements.

Like the Wright brothers, economists start with a simplified version of reality. Economists build models, change one variable at a time, and ask whether the change in the variable had a positive or negative impact on performance. Perhaps the best-known economic model is supply and demand, which we study in Chapter 3.

ENDOGENOUS VERSUS EXOGENOUS FACTORS Models must account for factors we can control (*endogenous*) and factors we can't (*exogenous*). Factors that are accounted for inside the model are **endogenous factors**. The Wright brothers' wind tunnel was critical to their success because it allowed them to control for as many endogenous factors as possible. For example, the wind tunnel enabled the Wright brothers to see how well each wing design—an important part of the model—performed under controlled conditions.

Endogenous factors are the variables that are inside a model.

Factors beyond our control—outside the model—are **exogenous factors**. Once the Wright brothers had determined the best wing design, they built the full-scale airplane that took flight at Kitty Hawk, North Carolina. At that point the plane, known as the "Flyer," was no longer in a controlled environment. It was subject to the gusting wind and other exogenous factors that made the first flight so challenging.

Exogenous factors are the variables that are outside a model.

Building an economic model is very similar to the process Wilbur and Orville used. We need to be mindful of three factors: (1) what we include in the model, (2) the assumptions we make when choosing what to include in the model, and (3) the outside conditions that can affect the model's performance. In the case of the first airplane, the design was an endogenous factor because it was within the Wright brothers' control. In contrast, the weather (wind, air pressure, and other atmospheric conditions) was an exogenous factor because the Wright brothers could not control it. Because the world is a complex place, an airplane model that flies perfectly in a wind tunnel may not fly reliably when it is exposed to the elements. Therefore, if we add more exogenous variables, or factors we cannot control—for example, wind and rain—to test our model's performance, the test becomes more realistic.

THE IMPORTANCE OF ASSUMPTIONS When we build a model, we need to make choices about which variables to include. Ideally, we would like to include all the important variables inside the model and exclude all the variables that can safely be ignored. Then we have made reasonable simplifying assumptions. Excluding the wrong variables, on the other hand, can lead to spectacular failures. So can making *false* assumptions. An excellent example is the financial crisis and Great Recession that began in December 2007.

In the years leading up to the crisis, banks sold and repackaged mortgage-backed investments under the faulty assumption that real estate prices will always rise. This assumption seemed perfectly reasonable in a world where real estate prices were rising annually. Unfortunately, the assumption turned out to be false. From 2007 to 2008, real estate prices fell dramatically. Because of one faulty assumption, the entire financial market teetered on the edge of collapse.

In the early 2000s, some investors believed that real estate prices could only rise.

Throughout this textbook we will assume that firms and households are rational benefit-maximizers who both respond to incentives predictably and thoughtfully consider the costs and benefits of their actions. Rationality is a cornerstone of most economic theory. It's a simplifying assumption, and in Chapter 17 we will see how it sometimes fails in real life, but for the most part we treat it as 'true enough.'

Positive versus Normative Statements

QUESTION: Which of the following statements are positive and which ones are normative?

1. Winters in Arkansas are too cold.
2. Everyone should work at a bank to learn the true value of money.
3. The current exchange rate is 0.7 British pound per U.S. dollar.
4. On average, people save 15% on insurance when they switch to Geico.
5. Everyone ought to have a life insurance policy.
6. University of Virginia graduates earn more than Duke University graduates.
7. Harvard University is the top educational institution in the country.
8. The average January temperature in Fargo, North Dakota, is 56°F.

ANSWERS

1. The phrase "too cold" is a matter of opinion. This is a normative statement.
2. While working at a bank might give someone an appreciation for the value of money, the word "should" indicates an opinion. This is a normative statement.
3. This is a positive statement. You can look up the current exchange rate and verify if this statement is true or false.
4. Geico made this claim in one of its commercials. It is a positive statement because it is a testable claim. If you had the data from Geico, you could determine if the statement were correct or not.
5. This sounds like a true statement, or at least a very sensible one. However, the word "ought" makes it an opinion. This is a normative statement.
6. You can look up the data and see which university's graduates earn more. This is a positive statement.
7. Some national rankings indicate that this statement is true, but others do not. Because different rankings are based on different assumptions, it is not possible to identify a definitive "top" school. This is a normative statement.
8. This is a positive statement, but the statement is wrong. North Dakota is much colder than that in January. The statement can be verified (in this case, proved wrong) by climate data.

CHALLENGE QUESTION: Some statements aren't simple declarative sentences but instead take the form of hypotheticals. Are the following hypotheticals positive or normative?

9. If Steph Curry makes 50% of his two-point shots and 40% of his three-point shots, his "effective field goal percentage" calculates higher than 50% since this statistic weighs three-point shots more than two-point shots.
10. If Steph Curry makes 40% of his three-point shots, he should shoot only three-pointers.
11. If you earn a college degree, you may earn less income than someone who only completes high school.
12. If you earn a college degree, you should share what you learned with the less fortunate.

NBA star Steph Curry has made three-pointers his trademark.

ANSWERS

9. This hypothetical statement is mathematically verifiable, so the statement is positive.

10. This is a hypothetical statement where the second part is an opinion, so the statement is normative.

11. This statement is factually verifiable, so the statement is positive.

12. The second part of this statement is an opinion, so the statement is normative.

What Is a Production Possibilities Frontier?

Now it's time to learn our first economic model. However, before you go on, you might want to review the appendix on graphing at the end of this chapter. Graphs are a key tool in economics because they display the relationship between two variables. Your ability to read a graph and understand the model it represents is crucial to learning economics.

In Chapter 1, we learned that economics is about the trade-offs individuals and societies face every day. For instance, you may frequently have to decide between spending more time studying or hanging out with your friends. The more time you study, the less time you have for your friends. Similarly, a society has to determine how to allocate its resources. The decision to build new roads will mean that there is less money available for new schools, and vice versa.

A **production possibilities frontier (PPF)** is a model that illustrates the combinations of outputs a society can produce if all of its resources are being used efficiently. An outcome is considered *efficient* when resources are fully utilized and potential output is maximized. To preserve *ceteris paribus*, we assume that the technology available for production and the quantity of resources remain fixed, or constant. These assumptions allow us to model trade-offs more clearly.

Let's begin by imagining a society that produces only two goods—pizza and chicken wings. This may not seem like a very realistic assumption, since a real economy produces millions of different goods and services, but this approach helps us understand trade-offs by keeping the analysis simple.

Figure 2.1 shows the production possibilities frontier for our simplified two-product society. Remember that the number of people and the total resources in this two-product society are fixed. If the economy uses all of its resources to produce pizza, it can produce 100 pizzas and 0 wings. If it uses all of its resources to produce wings, it can make 300 wings and 0 pizzas. These outcomes are represented by points A and B, respectively, on the production possibilities frontier. It is unlikely the society will choose either of these extreme outcomes, because it is human nature to enjoy variety.

If our theoretical society decides to spend some of its resources producing pizzas and some of its resources making wings, its economy will end up with a combination of pizza and wings somewhere along the PPF between points A and B. At point C, for example, the society would deploy its resources to produce

Trade-offs

A **production possibilities frontier (PPF)** is a model that illustrates the combinations of outputs a society can produce if all of its resources are being used efficiently.

FIGURE 2.1

The Production Possibilities Frontier for Pizza and Chicken Wings

The production possibilities frontier (PPF) shows the trade-off between producing pizza and producing wings. Any combination of pizza and wings is possible along, or inside, the line. Combinations of pizza and wings beyond the production possibilities frontier—for example, at point E—are not possible with the current set of resources. Point F and any other points located in the shaded region are inefficient.

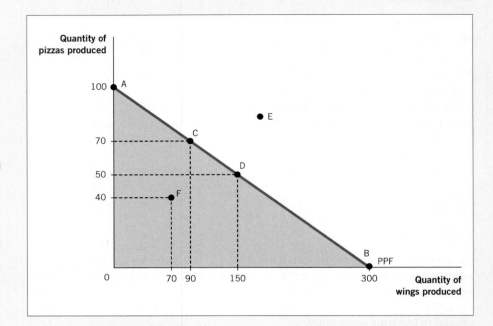

70 pizzas and 90 wings. At point D, the combination would be 50 pizzas and 150 wings. Each point along the production possibilities frontier represents a possible set of outcomes the society can choose if it uses all of its resources efficiently.

Notice that some combinations of pizza and wings cannot be produced because not enough resources are available. Our theoretical society would enjoy point E, but given the available resources, it cannot produce that output level. Points beyond the production possibilities frontier are desirable but not feasible with the available resources and technology.

At any combination of wings and pizzas along the production possibilities frontier, the society is using all of its resources in the most efficient way possible. But what about point F and any other points located in the shaded region? These points represent outcomes inside the production possibilities frontier, and they indicate an inefficient use of the society's resources. Consider, for example, the labor resource. If employees spend many hours at work surfing the Web instead of doing their jobs, the output of pizza and wings will drop and the outcome will no longer be efficient. As long as workers use all of their time efficiently, they will produce an efficient amount of pizza and wings, and output will lie somewhere on the PPF.

Whenever society is producing on the production possibilities frontier, the only way to get more of one good is to accept less of another. Because an economy operating at a point on the frontier will be efficient, every point on the frontier represents full-capacity output. But a society may favor one point over another because it prefers that combination of goods. For example, in our theoretical two-good society, if wings suddenly become more popular, the movement from point C to point D will represent a desirable trade-off. The society will produce 20 fewer pizzas (decreasing from 70 to 50) but 60 additional wings (increasing from 90 to 150).

Trade-offs

The Production Possibilities Frontier and Opportunity Cost

Because our two-good society produces only pizza and wings, the trade-offs that occur along the production possibilities frontier represent the opportunity cost of producing one good instead of the other. As we saw in Chapter 1, an opportunity cost is the highest-valued alternative given up to pursue another course of action. As Figure 2.1 shows, when society moves from point C to point D, it gives up 20 pizzas; this is the opportunity cost of producing more wings. The movement from point D to point C has an opportunity cost of 60 wings.

Until now, we have assumed a constant trade-off between the number of pizzas and the number of wings produced. However, not all resources in our theoretical society are perfectly adaptable for use in making pizza and wings. Some workers are good at making pizza, and others are not so good. When the society tries to make as many pizzas as possible, it will be using both types of workers. That is, to get more pizzas, the society will have to use workers who are increasingly less skilled at making them. For this reason, pizza production will not expand at a constant rate. You can see this effect in the new production possibilities frontier in Figure 2.2; it is bowed outward rather than a straight line.

Opportunity cost

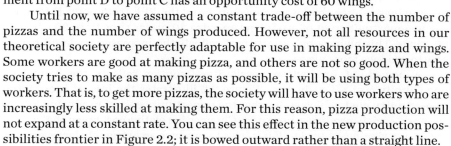

The Production Possibilities Frontier and Economic Growth

FIGURE 2.2

The Law of Increasing Opportunity Cost

To make more pizzas, the society will have to use workers who are increasingly less skilled at making them. As a result, as we move up along the PPF, the opportunity cost of producing an extra 20 pizzas rises from 30 wings between points D and C to 80 wings between points B and A.

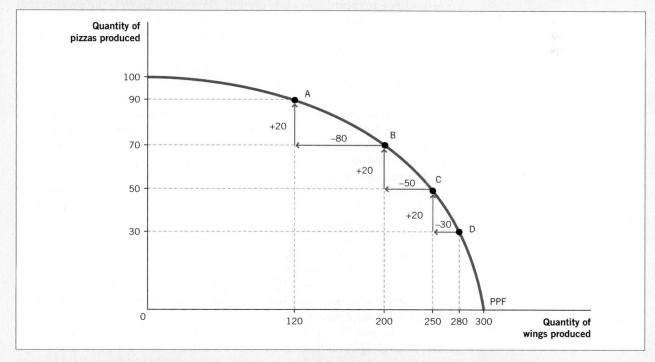

Opportunity cost

The **law of increasing opportunity cost** states that the opportunity cost of producing a good rises as a society produces more of it.

Because resources are not perfectly adaptable, production does not expand at a constant rate. For example, to produce 20 extra pizzas, the society can move from point D (30 pizzas) to point C (50 pizzas). But moving from point D (280 wings) to point C (250 wings) means giving up 30 wings. So moving from point D to point C has an opportunity cost of 30 wings.

Now suppose that the society decides it wants even more pizzas and moves from point C (50 pizzas) to point B (70 pizzas). Now the opportunity cost of 20 more pizzas is 50 wings, because wing production declines from 250 to 200. If the society decides that 70 pizzas are not enough, it can expand pizza production from point B (70 pizzas) to point A (90 pizzas). Now the society gives up 80 wings. Notice that as we move up along the PPF from point D to point A, the opportunity cost of producing an extra 20 pizzas rises from 30 wings to 80 wings. This higher opportunity cost reflects the increased trade-off necessary to produce more pizzas.

A bowed-out production possibilities frontier reflects the increasing opportunity cost of production. Figure 2.2 illustrates the **law of increasing opportunity cost**, which states that the opportunity cost of producing a good rises as a society produces more of it. Changes in relative cost mean that a society faces a significant trade-off if it tries to produce an extremely large amount of a single good.

The Production Possibilities Frontier and Economic Growth

So far, we have modeled the production possibilities frontier based on the resources available to society at a particular moment in time. However, most societies hope to create economic growth. *Economic growth* is the process that enables a society to produce more output in the future.

We can use the production possibilities frontier to explore economic growth. For example, we can ask what would happen to the PPF if our two-good society develops a new technology that increases productivity. Suppose that a new pizza assembly line improves the pizza production process and that the new assembly line does not require the use of more resources—it simply redeploys the resources that already exist. This development would allow the society to make more pizza with the same number of workers. Or it would allow the same amount of pizza to be made with fewer workers than previously. Either way, the society has expanded its resource base. Figure 2.3 shows this change as a shift in the PPF.

With the new technology, it becomes possible to produce 120 pizzas using the same number of workers and in the same amount of time it previously took to produce 100 pizzas. Although the ability to produce wings has not changed, the new pizza-making technology expands the production possibilities frontier outward from PPF_1 to PPF_2. It is now possible for the society to move from point A to point B, where it can produce more of both goods (80 pizzas and 220 wings). Why can the society produce more of both? Because the improvement in pizza-making technology—the assembly line—allows a redeployment of the labor force that also increases the production of wings. Improvements in technology make point B possible.

The production possibilities frontier will also expand if the population grows. A larger population means more workers to make pizza and wings. Figure 2.4 illustrates what happens when the society adds workers to help

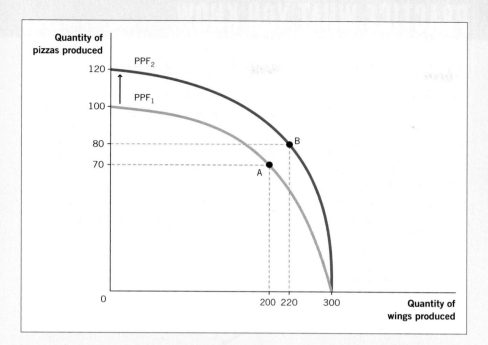

FIGURE 2.3

A Shift in the Production Possibilities Frontier

A new pizza assembly line that improves the productive capacity of pizza makers shifts the PPF upward from PPF_1 to PPF_2. More pizzas can be produced. Comparing points A and B, you can see that the enhanced pizza-making capacity also makes it possible to produce more wings at the same time.

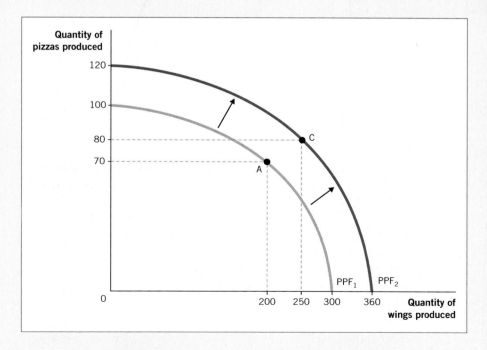

FIGURE 2.4

More Resources and the Production Possibilities Frontier

When more resources (such as additional workers) are available for the production of either pizza or wings, the entire PPF shifts upward and outward. This shift makes point C, along PPF_2, possible.

The Production Possibilities Frontier: Bicycles and Cars

There is a trade-off between making bicycles and making cars.

QUESTION: Are the following statements true or false? Base your answers on the PPF shown below.

1. Point A represents possible numbers of cars and bicycles that can be sold.
2. The movement along the curve from point A to point B shows the opportunity cost of producing more bicycles.
3. If society experiences a substantial increase in unemployment, the PPF shifts inward.
4. If an improved process for manufacturing cars is introduced, the entire PPF will shift outward.

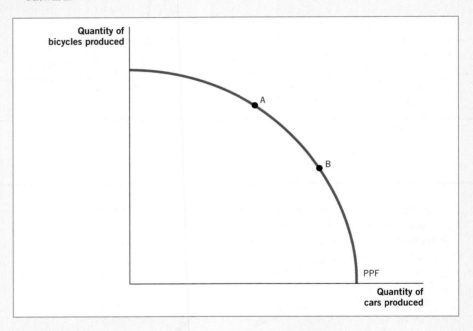

ANSWERS

1. False. Point A represents numbers of cars and bicycles that can be *produced*, not sold.
2. False. Moving from point A to point B shows the opportunity cost of producing more cars, not more bicycles.
3. False. Higher unemployment does not shift the curve inward, because the PPF is the maximum that can be produced when all resources are being used efficiently. More unemployment would locate society at a point inside the PPF, because some people who could help produce more cars or bicycles would not be working.
4. False. The PPF will shift outward along the car axis, but it will not shift upward along the bicycle axis.

produce pizza and wings. With more workers, the society can produce more pizzas and wings than before. The PPF curve shifts from PPF$_1$ to PPF$_2$, expanding up along the y axis and out along the x axis. Like improvements in technology, additional resources expand the frontier and allow the society to reach a point—in this case, point C—that was not possible before. The extra workers have pushed the entire frontier out—not just one end of it, as the pizza assembly line did.

What Are the Benefits of Specialization and Trade?

We have seen that improving technology and adding resources make an economy more productive. A third way to create gains for society is through specialization and trade. **Specialization** is the limiting of one's work to a particular area. Determining what to specialize in is an important part of the process. Every worker, business, or country is relatively good at producing certain products or services. Suppose you decide to learn about information technology. You earn a certificate or degree and find an employer who hires you for your specialized skills. Your information technology skills determine your salary. You can then use your salary to purchase other goods and services that you desire and that you are not so skilled at making yourself.

In the next section, we explore why specializing and exchanging your skilled expertise with others makes gains from trade possible.

Specialization is the limiting of one's work to a particular area.

Gains from Trade

Let's return to our two-good economy. Now we'll make the further assumption that this economy has only two people. One person is better at making pizzas, and the other is better at making wings. In this case, the potential gains from trade are clear. Each person will specialize in what he or she is better at producing and then will trade to acquire some of the good produced by the other person.

Figure 2.5 shows the production potential of the two people in our economy, Gwen and Blake. From the table at the top of the figure, we see that if Gwen devotes all of her work time to making pizzas, she can produce 60 pizzas. If she does not spend any time on pizzas, she can make 120 wings. In contrast, Blake can spend all his time on pizzas and produce 24 pizzas or all his time on wings and produce 72 wings.

The graphs illustrate the amount of pizza and wings each person produces daily. Wing production is plotted on the x axis, pizza production on the y axis. Each production possibilities frontier is drawn from the data in the table at the top of the figure.

Because the production possibilities frontiers here are straight, not bowed, Gwen and Blake each face a *constant* trade-off between producing pizza and producing wings. Gwen produces 60 pizzas for every 120 wings; this means her trade-off between producing pizza and producing wings is fixed at 60:120, or 1:2. Blake produces 24 pizzas for every 72 wings. His trade-off between producing pizza and producing wings is fixed at 24:72, or 1:3. Because Gwen and

Trade creates value

Trade-offs

FIGURE 2.5

The Production Possibilities Frontier with No Trade

(a) If Gwen cannot trade with Blake, she chooses to produce 40 pizzas and 40 wings, because she likes both foods equally.
(b) If Blake cannot trade with Gwen, he chooses to produce 18 pizzas and 18 wings, because he likes both foods equally.

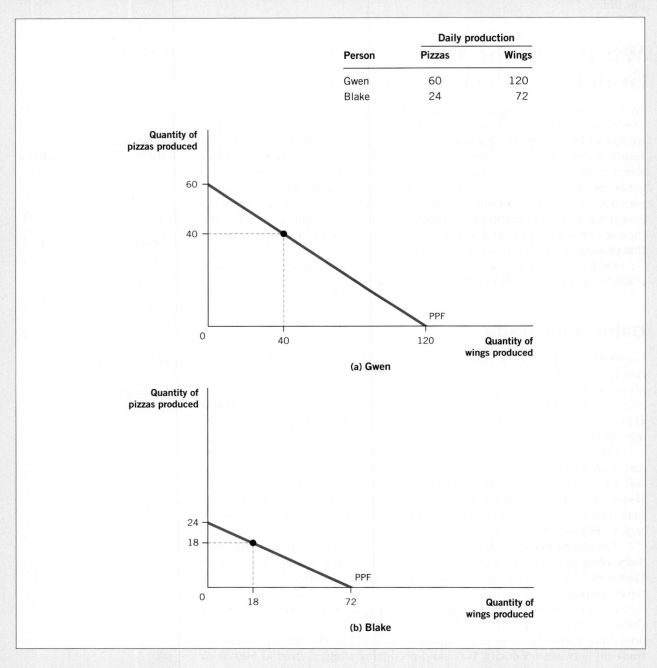

	Daily production	
Person	**Pizzas**	**Wings**
Gwen	60	120
Blake	24	72

(a) Gwen

(b) Blake

TABLE 2.1

The Gains from Trade

| Person | Good | Without trade | | With specialization and trade | | Gains from trade |
		Production	Consumption	Production	Consumption	
Gwen	Pizza	40	40	60	41 (keeps)	+1
	Wings	40	40	0	47 (from Blake)	+7
Blake	Pizza	18	18	0	19 (from Gwen)	+1
	Wings	18	18	72	25 (keeps)	+7

Blake can choose to produce at any point along their production possibilities frontiers, let's assume they each want to produce an equal number of pizzas and wings. In this case, Gwen produces 40 pizzas and 40 wings, while Blake produces 18 pizzas and 18 wings. Since Gwen is more productive in general, she produces more of each food. Gwen has an **absolute advantage**, meaning she can produce more than Blake can produce with the same quantity of resources.

At first glance, it would appear that Gwen should continue to work alone. But consider what happens if Gwen and Blake each specialize and then trade. Table 2.1 compares production with and without specialization and trade. Without trade, Gwen and Blake have a combined production of 58 units of pizza and 58 units of wings (Gwen's 40 + Blake's 18). But when Gwen specializes and produces only pizza, her production is 60 units. In this case, her individual pizza output is greater than the combined output of 58 pizzas (Gwen's 40 + Blake's 18). Similarly, if Blake specializes in wings, he is able to make 72 units. His individual wing output is greater than their combined output of 58 wings (Gwen's 40 + Blake's 18). Specialization has resulted in the production of 2 additional pizzas and 14 additional wings.

Specialization leads to greater output. But Gwen and Blake would like to eat both pizza and wings. So if they specialize and then trade with each other, they will benefit. If Gwen gives Blake 19 pizzas in exchange for 47 wings, they are each better off by 1 pizza and 7 wings. This result is evident in the final column of Table 2.1 and in Figure 2.6.

In Figure 2.6a, we see that at point A, Gwen produces 60 pizzas and 0 wings. If she does not specialize, she produces 40 pizzas and 40 wings, represented at point B. If she specializes and then trades with Blake, she can have 41 pizzas and 47 wings, shown at point C. Her value gained from trade is 1 pizza and 7 wings. In Figure 2.6b, we see a similar benefit for Blake. If he produces only wings, he will have 72 wings, shown at point A. If he does not specialize, he produces 18 pizzas and 18 wings (point B). If he specializes and trades with Gwen, he can have 19 pizzas and 25 wings, shown at point C. His value gained from trade is 1 pizza and 7 wings. In spite of Gwen's absolute advantage in making both pizza and wings, she is still better off trading with Blake. This amazing result occurs because of specialization. When Gwen and Blake spend their time on what they do best, they are able to produce more collectively and then divide the gain.

Absolute advantage
refers to one producer's ability to make more than another producer with the same quantity of resources.

Trade creates value

FIGURE 2.6

The Production Possibilities Frontier with Trade

(a) If Gwen produces only pizza, she will have 60 pizzas, shown at point A. If she does not specialize, she will produce 40 pizzas and 40 wings (point B). If she specializes and trades with Blake, she will have 41 pizzas and 47 wings (point C). (b) If Blake produces only wings, he will have 72 wings (point A). If he does not specialize, he will produce 18 pizzas and 18 wings (point B). If he specializes and trades with Gwen, he can have 19 pizzas and 25 wings (point C).

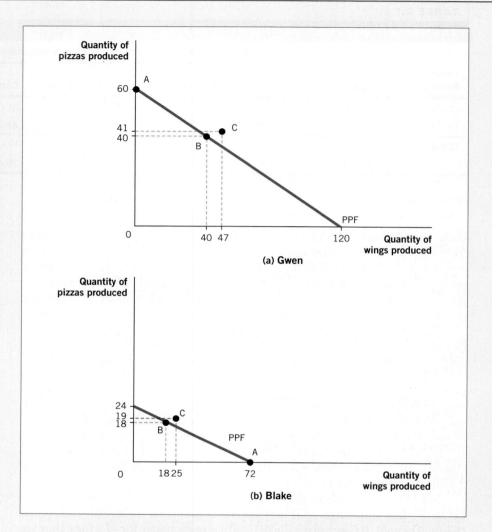

Comparative Advantage

Opportunity cost

We have seen that specialization enables workers to enjoy gains from trade. The concept of opportunity cost provides us with a second way of validating the principle that trade creates value. Recall that opportunity cost is the highest-valued alternative that is sacrificed to pursue something else. Looking at Table 2.2, you can see that in order to produce 1 more pizza, Gwen must give up producing 2 wings. We can say that the opportunity cost of 1 pizza is 2 wings. We can also reverse the observation and say that the opportunity cost of one wing is $\frac{1}{2}$ pizza. In Blake's case, each pizza he produces means giving up the production of 3 wings. In other words, the opportunity cost for him to produce 1 pizza is 3 wings. In reverse, we can say that when he produces 1 wing, he gives up $\frac{1}{3}$ pizza.

TABLE 2.2

The Opportunity Cost of Pizza and Wings

| Person | Opportunity cost | |
	1 Pizza	1 Wing
Gwen	2 wings	$\frac{1}{2}$ pizza
Blake	3 wings	$\frac{1}{3}$ pizza

Recall from Chapter 1 that comparative advantage is the ability to make a good at a lower opportunity cost than another producer. Looking at Table 2.2, you can see that Gwen has a lower opportunity cost of producing pizza than Blake does—she gives up 2 wings for each pizza she produces, while he gives up 3 wings for each pizza he produces. In other words, Gwen has a comparative advantage in producing pizzas. However, Gwen does not have a comparative advantage in producing wings. For Gwen to produce 1 wing, she would have to give up production of $\frac{1}{2}$ pizza. Blake, in contrast, gives up $\frac{1}{3}$ pizza each time he produces 1 wing. So Gwen's opportunity cost of producing wings is higher than Blake's. Because Blake is the low-opportunity-cost producer of wings, he has a comparative advantage in producing them. Recall that Gwen has an absolute advantage in the production of both pizzas and wings; she is better at making both. However, from this example we see that she cannot have a comparative advantage in making both goods.

Applying the concept of opportunity cost helps us see why specialization enables people to produce more. Gwen's opportunity cost of producing pizzas (she gives up 2 wings for every pizza) is less than Blake's opportunity cost of producing pizzas (he gives up 3 wings for every pizza). Therefore, Gwen should specialize in producing pizzas. If you want to double-check this result, consider who should produce wings. Gwen's opportunity cost of producing wings (she gives up $\frac{1}{2}$ pizza for every wing she makes) is more than Blake's opportunity cost of producing wings (he gives up $\frac{1}{3}$ pizza for every wing he makes). Therefore, Blake should specialize in producing wings. When Gwen produces only pizzas and Blake produces only wings, their combined output is 60 pizzas and 72 wings.

Finding the Right Price to Facilitate Trade

We have seen that Gwen and Blake will do better if they specialize and then trade. But how many wings should it cost to buy a pizza? How many pizzas for a wing? In other words, what trading price will benefit both parties? To answer this question, we need to return to opportunity cost. For context, think of the process you likely went through when trading lunch food with friends in grade school. Perhaps you wanted a friend's apple and he wanted a few of your Oreos. If you agreed to trade three Oreos for the apple, the exchange benefited both parties, because you valued your three cookies less than your friend's apple, and your friend valued your three cookies more than his apple.

In our example, Gwen and Blake will benefit from exchanging a good at a price that is lower than the opportunity cost of producing it. Recall that Gwen's opportunity cost is 1 pizza per 2 wings, or half a pizza per wing. This means that

Opportunity cost

Specialization

HOW TO MAKE A $1,500 SANDWICH IN ONLY SIX MONTHS

This video on the YouTube channel "How to Make Everything" features a YouTuber who takes building a sandwich from scratch to new lengths. We're not talking about going the store and getting the needed ingredients. We're talking 100% do-it-yourself: growing the vegetables, evaporating seawater for salt, milking a cow and using the milk to make cheese, slaughtering a chicken for the protein, and grinding wheat to make bread flour. It is all quite fascinating to watch. At the end he taste tests the sandwich. "Not bad" he says, "not bad for six months of my time"—and then he puts his head down on the table.

When you decide to forgo specialization and comparative advantage, you're effectively turning back the clock on economic progress and living like our ancestors did. Without any help, we end up doing everything ourselves. When that happens, we are not getting the benefits of comparative advantage. So the next time you think to yourself, "I can do this on my own," think again.

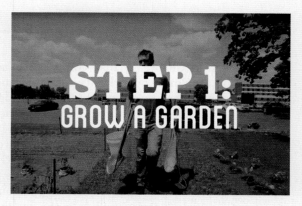

How long would it take you to make a sandwich from scratch?

Sandwiches only take a few minutes to make, precisely because in a modern economy we rely on others to make the component parts we want. You can even get your sandwich made to order for you at any number of shops, and that's a wonderful thing!

any exchange where she can get a wing for less than half a pizza will be beneficial to her, because she ends up with more pizza and wings than she had without trade. Blake's opportunity cost is 1 pizza per 3 wings, so any trade where he can get a pizza for less than three wings will be beneficial to him. For trade to be mutually beneficial, the exchange ratio must fall between Gwen's opportunity cost ratio of 1:2 (0.50) and Blake's opportunity cost ratio of 1:3 (0.33). Outside of that range, either Gwen or Blake will be better off without trade, because the trade will not be attractive to both parties. In the example shown in Table 2.3, Gwen trades 19 pizzas for 47 wings. The ratio of 19:47 (0.40) falls between Gwen's and Blake's opportunity cost ratios and is therefore advantageous to both of them.

As long as the terms of trade fall between the trading partners' opportunity costs, the trade benefits both sides. But if Blake insists on a trading ratio of 1 wing for 1 pizza, which would be a good deal for him, Gwen will refuse to trade because she will be better off producing both goods on her own. Likewise, if Gwen insists on receiving 4 wings for every pizza she gives to Blake, he will refuse to trade with her because he will be better off producing both goods on his own.

Trade creates value

TABLE 2.3

Gaining from Trade		
Person	**Opportunity cost**	**Ratio**
Gwen	1 pizza equals 2 wings	1:2 = 0.50
Terms of trade	19 pizzas for 47 wings	19:47 = 0.40
Blake	1 pizza equals 3 wings	1:3 = 0.33

PRACTICE WHAT YOU KNOW

Opportunity Cost

QUESTION: Imagine that you are planning to visit your family in Chicago. You can take a train or a plane. The plane ticket costs $300, and traveling by air takes 2 hours each way. The train ticket costs $200, and traveling by rail takes 12 hours each way. Which form of transportation should you choose?

ANSWER: The key to answering the question is learning to value time. The simplest way to do this is to calculate the cost savings of taking the train and compare that with the value of the time you would save if you took the plane.

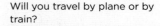

Opportunity cost

Cost savings with train	Round-trip time saved with plane
$300 − $200 = $100	24 hours − 4 hours = 20 hours
(plane) − (train)	(train) − (plane)

Will you travel by plane or by train?

A person who takes the train can save $100, but it will cost 20 hours to do so. At an hourly rate, the savings would be $100/20 hours = $5 per hour. If you value your time at exactly $5 an hour, you will be indifferent between plane and train travel (that is, you will be equally satisfied with both options). If your time is worth more than $5 an hour, you should take the plane. If your time is worth less than $5 an hour, you should take the train.

It is important to note that this approach to calculating opportunity cost gives us a more realistic answer than simply observing ticket prices. The train has a lower ticket price, but very few people ride the train instead of flying, because the opportunity cost of their time is worth more to them than the difference in the ticket prices. Opportunity cost explains why most business travelers fly—it saves valuable time. Good economists learn to examine the full opportunity cost of their decisions, which must include both the financials and the cost of time.

We have examined this question by holding everything else constant (that is, applying the principle of *ceteris paribus*). In other words, at no point did we discuss possible side issues such as the fear of flying, sleeping arrangements on the train, or anything else that might be relevant to someone making the decision.

WHY LEBRON JAMES HAS SOMEONE ELSE HELP HIM MOVE

LeBron James is a giant of a man—6′8″ and 260 pounds. He is a professional basketball player in the NBA, and he has moved from one team to another multiple times, requiring him to relocate to another city. Given his size and strength, you might think that LeBron would move his household himself. But despite the fact that he could likely do the work of two ordinary movers, he kept playing basketball and hired movers. Let's examine the situation to see if this was a wise decision.

Opportunity cost

LeBron has an absolute advantage in both playing basketball and moving furniture. But as we have seen, an absolute advantage doesn't mean that LeBron should do both tasks himself. When he signed with a new team, he could have asked for a few days to pack up and move, but each day spent moving would have been a day he was unable to work with his new team. When you are paid millions of dollars to play a game, the time spent moving is time lost practicing or playing basketball, which incurs a substantial opportunity cost. The movers, with a much lower opportunity cost of their time, have a comparative advantage in moving—so LeBron made a smart decision to hire them!

What Is the Trade-Off between Having More Now and Having More Later?

So far, we have examined short-run trade-offs. In looking at our wings–pizza trade-off, we were essentially living in the moment. But both individuals and society as a whole must weigh the benefits available today (the short run) with those available tomorrow (the long run). In the **short run**, we make decisions that reflect our immediate or short-term wants, needs, or limitations. In the short run, consumers can partially adjust their behavior. In the **long run**, we make decisions that reflect our wants, needs, and limitations over a much longer time horizon. In the long run, consumers have time to fully adjust to market conditions.

> The **short run** is the period in which we make decisions that reflect our immediate or short-term wants, needs, or limitations. In the short run, consumers can partially adjust their behavior.

> The **long run** is the period in which we make decisions that reflect our needs, wants, and limitations over a long time horizon. In the long run, consumers have time to fully adjust to market conditions.

Many of life's important decisions are about the long run. We must decide where to live, whether and whom to marry, whether and where to go to college, and what type of career to pursue. Getting these decisions right is far more important than simply deciding how many wings and pizzas to produce. For instance, the decision to save money requires giving up something you want to buy today for the benefit of having more money available in the future. Similarly, if you decide to go to a party tonight, you benefit today, while staying home to study creates a larger benefit at exam time. We are constantly making decisions that reflect this tension between today and tomorrow—eating a large piece of cake or a healthy snack, taking a nap or exercising at the gym, buying a jet ski or purchasing stocks in the stock market. Each of these decisions is a trade-off between the present and the future.

Trade-offs

Opportunity Cost

XBOX OR PLAYSTATION?

In *The Big Bang Theory*, Sheldon wants to buy either a new Xbox or a new PlayStation. He explains to his girlfriend, Amy, over dinner that because each system has many advantages, it is hard to choose. Eventually, he settles on an Xbox, but after picking one up at the store, he begins to have second thoughts. He starts by recalling decisions from his past that in hindsight were poor choices: he bought a Betamax instead of a VHS player, an HD-DVD player instead of a Blu-ray player, and a Zune instead of an iPod. Sheldon puts the Xbox back, because he doesn't want to experience regret.

Seeing that Sheldon is unable to choose, Amy intervenes and offers to buy him both systems! Problem solved, right? Not quite, because Sheldon only has one slot open on his entertainment system. Amy counters that she'll buy him a new entertainment center, only to have Sheldon respond, "Which one?" because he knows he won't be able to make that choice easily, either! Hours later, we see Sheldon and Amy lying on the floor while Sheldon is still deciding. Eventually the store closes and they are forced to come back another day.

We may not be as indecisive as Sheldon, but we face the same basic problem all the time. When you buy a new phone, rent a new apartment, buy a new outfit,

Which would you choose, an Xbox or a PlayStation?

go out to eat, or decide where to go to college, you give up your next-best option. The more important the decision and the better the alternatives, the harder the choice becomes. In those situations, the choice involves a high opportunity cost. If the choice is trivial or the second-best option isn't appealing, the choices we make involve low opportunity costs.

Consumer Goods, Capital Goods, and Investment

We have seen that the trade-off between the present and the future is evident in the tension between what we consume now and what we plan to consume later. Any good that is produced for present consumption is a **consumer good**. These goods help to satisfy our needs or wants now. Food, entertainment, and clothing are all examples of consumer goods. **Capital goods** help in the production of

Consumer goods
are produced for present consumption.

Capital goods
help produce other valuable goods and services in the future.

other valuable goods and services in the future. Capital goods are everywhere. Roads, factories, trucks, and computers are all capital goods.

Education is a form of capital. The time you spend earning a college degree makes you more attractive to future employers. When you decide to go to college instead of working, you are investing in your *human capital*. **Investment** is the process of using resources to create or buy new capital.

Because we live in a world with scarce resources, every investment in capital goods has an opportunity cost of forgone consumer goods. For example, if you decide to buy a new laptop, you cannot use the money to travel over spring break. Similarly, a firm that decides to invest in a new factory to expand future production is unable to use that money to hire more workers now.

The decision between whether to consume or to invest has a significant impact on economic growth in the future, or long run. What happens when society chooses to produce many more consumer goods than capital goods? Figure 2.7a shows the result. When relatively few resources are invested in producing capital goods in the short run, very little new capital is created. Because new capital is a necessary ingredient for economic growth in the future, the long-run production possibilities curve expands only a small amount.

What happens when society chooses to plan for the future by producing more capital goods than consumer goods in the short run? Figure 2.7b shows the result. With investment in new capital, the long-run production possibilities curve expands outward much more.

All societies face the trade-off between spending today and investing for tomorrow. Mexico and Turkey are good examples of emerging global economies investing in the future. Over the last 20 years, the citizens of these countries have invested significantly more in capital goods than have the citizens of wealthier nations in North America and Europe. Not surprisingly, economic growth rates in Mexico and Turkey are much higher than they are in more developed countries. Part of the difference in these investment rates can be explained by the fact that the United States and Europe already have large capital stocks per capita (per person) and therefore have less to gain from operating at point B in

Investment
is the process of using resources to create or buy new capital.

Trade-offs

Study Now...

...play later.

The Trade-Off between the Short Run and the Long Run

A KNIGHT'S TALE

In this movie, three peasants unexpectedly win a jousting tournament and earn 15 silver coins. Then they face a choice about what to do next. Two of the three want to return to England and live the high life for a while, but the third, played by Heath Ledger, suggests they take 13 of the coins and reinvest them in training for the next tournament. He offers to put in all 5 of his coins and asks the other two peasants for 4 coins each. His partners are skeptical about the plan because Ledger's character is good with the sword but not very good with the lance. For them to win additional tournaments, they will have to invest considerable resources in training and preparation.

The movie illustrates the trade-off between enjoying consumer goods in the short run and investing in capital goods in the long run. The peasants' choice to forgo spending their winnings to enjoy themselves now in order to prepare for the next tournament is not easy. None of the three has ever had any money. Five silver coins represent an opportunity, at least for a few days, to live the good life. However, the plan will elevate the three out of poverty in the long term if they

Learning to joust is a lifetime skill.

can learn to compete at the highest level. Therefore, investing the 13 coins is like choosing point B in Figure 2.7b. Investing now will allow their production possibilities frontier to grow over time, affording each of them a better life in the long run.

Figure 2.7b than developing countries do. Mexico clearly prefers point B at this stage of its economic development, but point B is not necessarily better than point A. Developing nations, such as Mexico, are sacrificing the present for a better future, while many developed countries, such as the United States, take a more balanced approach to weighing current needs against future growth. For Mexican workers, this trade-off typically means longer work hours and higher savings rates than their U.S. counterparts can claim, despite far lower average salaries for the Mexican workers. In contrast, U.S. workers have much more leisure time and more disposable (spendable) income, a combination that leads to much higher rates of consumption in the United States.

FIGURE 2.7

Investing in Capital Goods and Promoting Growth

(a) When a society chooses point A in the short run, very few capital goods are created. Because capital goods are needed to enhance future growth, the long-run PPF$_2$ expands, but only slightly.
(b) When a society chooses point B in the short run, many capital goods are created, and the long-run PPF$_2$ expands significantly.

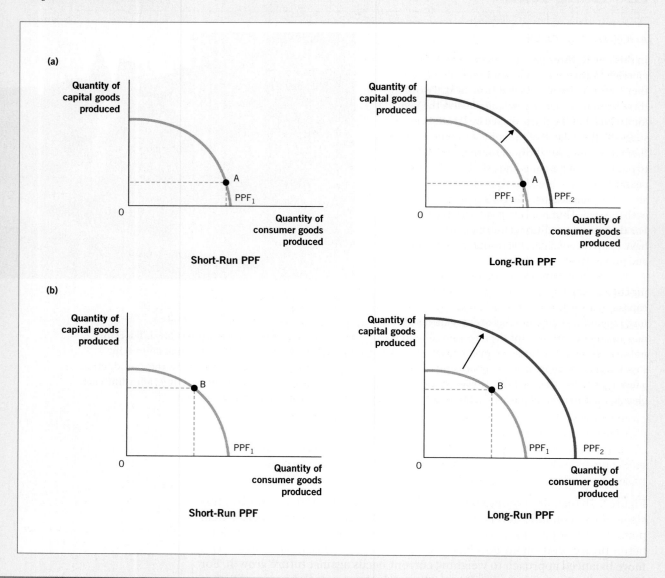

Trade-Offs

QUESTION: Your friend is fond of saying he will study later. He eventually does study, but he often doesn't get quite the grades he had hoped for because he doesn't study enough. Every time this happens, he says, "It's only one exam." What advice would you give him about trade-offs?

ANSWER: Your friend doesn't understand long-run trade-offs. You could start by reminding him that each decision has a consequence at the margin and also later in life. The marginal cost of not studying enough is a lower exam grade. To some extent, your friend's reasoning is correct. How well he does on one exam over four years of college is almost irrelevant. The problem is that many poor exam scores have a cumulative effect over the semesters. If your friend graduates with a 2.5 GPA instead of a 3.5 GPA because he did not study enough, his employment prospects will be significantly diminished.

No pain, no gain.

Marginal thinking

Incentives

ECONOMICS IN THE REAL WORLD

ZIFERBLAT CAFÉ UNDERSTANDS INCENTIVES

Ziferblat is a small but growing café chain with locations in the UK and Eastern Europe. Their slogan is "Everything is free inside; except the time you spend." Unlike most cafés, which charge for the items you order, Ziferblat charges 8 pence a minute (about $7.00/hour), and everything (Wi-Fi, dozens of brands of tea and coffee, biscuits, and cakes) is included.

In most cafés the scarcest resource is table space. The reason is that once a customer purchases something, they are allowed to sit as long as they want. Ziferblat has solved the "squatting" problem that plagues other cafés by giving each customer a clock that charges them based on how long they stay. This nontraditional pricing structure creates an incentive to take time into account, by raising the cost of staying after you have finished your refreshment.

Ziferblat is a good example of voluntary trade. Customers can use Ziferblat for a quick bite or beverage and also use it as a shared office or meeting space. Ziferblat sets a price per minute that allows it to make a profit, and customers are willing to pay for the comforts provided. That's a win-win exchange.

How long would you stay, if each minute costs you 12 cents?

Trade creates value

Conclusion

The simple, yet powerful idea that trade creates value has far-reaching consequences for how we should organize our society. Since we all win when voluntary trade takes place, creating opportunities for more trades to take place between consumers and producers and across countries enriches all of our lives.

We have developed our first model, the production possibilities frontier. This model illustrates the benefits of trade and also enables us to describe ways to grow the economy. Trade and growth rest on a more fundamental idea—specialization.

Why Men Should Do More Housework

- Men spend, on average, 50 minutes less than women on household chores.
- If labor in the household is allocated in a gender-neutral way, output-per-hour increases by 5.4%.
- Reducing the amount of time talented women spend doing household chores helps them earn pay equal to their male counterparts.

According to the U.S. Census Bureau's American Time Use Survey, the division of household chores falls disproportionately on females. It turns out that this imbalance is a contributor to the wage gap that exists between men and women (more on that in Chapter 15). Researchers at the National Bureau of Economic Research, a private nonprofit organization, found that women earn less than men do because they are less willing to work jobs that require long hours.

When men share chores equally, it's good for all of us.

The researchers determined that if labor in the household is allocated in a gender-neutral way, this increases output-per-hour by 5.4%, as people make better use of their time, given their respective skills. Freeing up talented women from household chores also helps them earn pay equal to that of their male counterparts.

The life lesson is clear here. When partners both work outside the home, they should each pull their weight by spending equal amounts of time completing chores at home. Each partner should specialize in the chores they are comparatively good at, enabling the other partner to do likewise.

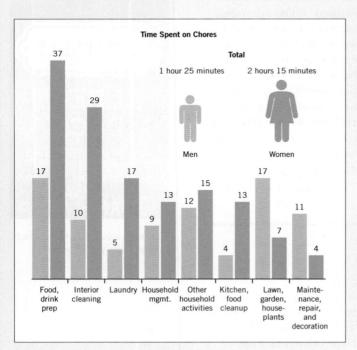

Time Spent on Chores

Total

Men: 1 hour 25 minutes
Women: 2 hours 15 minutes

Chore	Men	Women
Food, drink prep	17	37
Interior cleaning	10	29
Laundry	5	17
Household mgmt.	9	13
Other household activities	12	15
Kitchen, food cleanup	4	13
Lawn, garden, house-plants	17	7
Maintenance, repair, and decoration	11	4

Women on the average spend more of their time than men do on household activities. Households that break up tasks more based on skill increase household labor per hour by 5.4%. This earns the family more money. If women participated in the economy identically to men, one report estimates it would add $28 trillion or 26% to the annual global economy.

Sources: NBER Study, 2017; McKinsey & Company, www.mckinsey.com/featured-insights/employment-and-growth/how-advancing-womens-equality-can-add-12-trillion-to-global-growth.

When producers specialize, they focus their efforts on those goods and services for which they have the lowest opportunity cost and they trade with others who are good at making something else. To have something valuable to trade, each producer, in effect, must find its comparative advantage. As a result, trade creates value and contributes to an improved standard of living in society.

In the next chapter, we examine the supply and demand model to illustrate how markets work. While the model is different, the fundamental result we learned here—that trade creates value—still holds. ✳

Opportunity cost
Trade creates value

· ANSWERING *the* BIG QUESTIONS ·

How do economists study the economy?

* Economists design hypotheses (proposed explanations) and then test them by collecting real data. The economist's laboratory is the world around us.
* A good model should be simple, flexible, and useful for making accurate predictions. A model is both more realistic and harder to understand when it involves many variables. To keep models simple, economists often use the concept of *ceteris paribus*, or "all else equal." Maintaining a positive (as opposed to normative) framework is crucial for economic analysis because it allows decision-makers to observe the facts objectively.

What is a production possibilities frontier?

* A production possibilities frontier (PPF) is a model that illustrates the combinations of outputs a society can produce if all of its resources are being used efficiently. An outcome is considered efficient when resources are fully utilized and potential output is maximized. Economists use the PPF to illustrate trade-offs and to explain opportunity costs and the role of additional resources and technology in creating economic growth.

What are the benefits of specialization and trade?

* Society is better off if individuals and firms specialize and trade on the basis of the principle of comparative advantage.
* Parties that are better at producing goods and services than all their potential trading partners (and thus hold an absolute advantage) still benefit from trade. Trade allows them to specialize and trade what they produce for other goods and services they are relatively less skilled at making.
* As long as the terms of trade fall between the opportunity costs of both trading partners, the trade benefits both sides.

What is the trade-off between having more now and having more later?

* All societies face a crucial trade-off between consumption in the short run and economic growth in the long run. Investments in capital goods today help to spur economic growth in the future. However, because capital goods are not consumed in the short run, society must be willing to sacrifice how well it lives today in order to have more later.

· CHAPTER PROBLEMS·

Concepts You Should Know

absolute advantage (p. 41)
capital goods (p. 47)
ceteris paribus (p. 30)
consumer goods (p. 47)
endogenous factors (p. 31)
exogenous factors (p. 31)

investment (p. 48)
law of increasing opportunity
   cost (p. 36)
long run (p. 46)
normative statement (p. 29)
positive statement (p. 29)

production possibilities frontier
   (PPF) (p. 33)
short run (p. 46)
specialization (p. 39)

Questions for Review

1. What is a positive economic statement? What is a normative economic statement? Provide an example of each (other than those given in the chapter).

2. Is it important to build completely realistic economic models? Explain your response.

3. Draw a production possibilities frontier curve. Illustrate the set of points that is feasible, the set of points that is efficient, the set of points that is inefficient, and the set of points that is not feasible.

4. Why does the production possibilities frontier bow out?

5. Does having an absolute advantage mean that you should undertake to produce everything on your own? Why or why not?

6. What criteria would you use to determine which of two workers has a comparative advantage in performing a task?

7. Why does comparative advantage matter more than absolute advantage for trade?

8. What factors are most important for economic growth?

Study Problems (*solved at the end of the section)

* 1. Michael and Angelo live in a small town in Italy. They work as artists. Michael is the more productive artist. He can produce 10 small sculptures each day but only 5 paintings. Angelo can produce 6 sculptures each day but only 2 paintings.

	Output per day	
	Sculptures	**Paintings**
Michael	10	5
Angelo	6	2

a. What is the opportunity cost of a painting for each artist?
b. Based on your answer in part (a), who has a comparative advantage in producing paintings?
c. If the two men decide to specialize, who should produce the sculptures and who should produce the paintings?

* 2. The following table shows scores a student can earn on two upcoming exams according to the amount of time devoted to study:

Hours spent studying for economics	Economics score	Hours spent studying for history	History score
10	100	0	40
8	96	2	60
6	88	4	76
4	76	6	88
2	60	8	96
0	40	10	100

a. Plot the production possibilities frontier.
b. Does the production possibilities frontier exhibit the law of increasing relative cost?
c. If the student wishes to move from a grade of 60 to a grade of 88 in economics, what is the opportunity cost?

3. Think about comparative advantage when answering this question: Should your professor, who has highly specialized training in economics, take time out of his or her teaching schedule to mow the lawn? Defend your answer.

✳ **4.** Are the following statements positive or normative?

   a. My dog weighs 75 pounds.
   b. Dogs are required by law to have rabies shots.
   c. You should take your dog to the veterinarian once a year for a checkup.
   d. Chihuahuas are cuter than bulldogs.
   e. Leash laws for dogs are a good idea because they reduce injuries.

5. How does your decision to invest in a college degree add to your human capital? Use a projected production possibilities frontier for 10 years from now to compare your life with and without the college degree.

✳ **6.** Suppose that an amazing new fertilizer doubles the production of potatoes. How would this invention affect the production possibilities frontier for an economy that produces only potatoes and carrots? Would it now be possible to produce more potatoes *and* more carrots or only more potatoes?

7. Suppose that a politician tells you about a plan to create two expensive but necessary programs to build more production facilities for solar power and wind power. At the same time, the politician is unwilling to cut any other programs. Use the production possibilities frontier graph below to explain if the politician's proposal is possible.

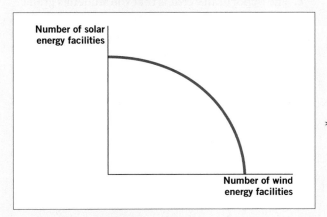

✳ **8.** Two friends, Rachel and Joey, enjoy baking bread and making apple pie. Rachel takes 2 hours to bake a loaf of bread and 1 hour to make a pie. Joey takes 4 hours to bake a loaf of bread and 4 hours to make a pie.

   a. What are Joey's and Rachel's opportunity costs of baking bread?
   b. Who has the absolute advantage in making bread?
   c. Who has a comparative advantage in making bread?
   d. If Joey and Rachel both decide to specialize to increase their joint production, what should Joey produce? What should Rachel produce?
   e. The price of a loaf of bread can be expressed in terms of an apple pie. If Joey and Rachel are specializing in production and decide to trade with each other, what range of ratios of bread and apple pie would allow both parties to benefit from trade?

9. Where would you plot unemployment on a production possibilities frontier? Where would you plot full employment on a production possibilities frontier? Now suppose that in a time of crisis everyone pitches in and works much harder than usual. What happens to the production possibilities frontier?

10. Read the poem "The Road Not Taken," by Robert Frost. What line(s) in the poem capture the opportunity cost of decision-making?

✳ **11.** Suppose that you must decide between attending a Taylor Swift concert or a Maroon 5 concert. The concerts are at the same time on the same evening, so you cannot see both. You love Taylor Swift and would pay as much as $200 to see her perform. Tickets to her concert are $135. You are not as big a Maroon 5 fan, but a friend has just offered you a free ticket to the concert. If you decide to take the free ticket to see Maroon 5, what is your opportunity cost?

✳ **12.** In this chapter we have seen that the PPF could be bowed-out or a straight line.

   a. Provide an example of two goods where the PPF would be bowed-out.
   b. Provide an example of two goods where the PPF would be a straight line.

c. It also turns out that the PPF can bow in. This occurs when the production process produces economies of scale, which means that it is possible to make *more* of each good as production expands. Can you think of two goods where the PPF would be bowed-in?

13. Barrville is a country that produces either all dumbbells, or all sandals, or a combination of the two.

   a. Draw a production possibilities frontier and label the *x* and *y* axes appropriately.

b. Place a point that shows where the country would be operating if a recession hits and companies are laying off workers. Label this point B.

c. Place a point that shows an unattainable point under the current situation. Label this point C.

d. If a point is unattainable now, will it always be unattainable? If you write that it can be attainable, what would cause it to become attainable?

Solved Problems

1.a. Michael's opportunity cost is 2 sculptures for each painting he produces. How do we know this? If he devotes all of his time to sculptures, he can produce 10. If he devotes all of his time to paintings, he can produce 5. The ratio 10:5 is the same as 2:1. Michael is therefore twice as fast at producing sculptures as he is at producing paintings. Angelo's opportunity cost is 3 sculptures for each painting he produces. If he devotes all of his time to sculptures, he can produce 6. If he devotes all of his time to paintings, he can produce 2. The ratio 6:2 is the same as 3:1.

b. For this question, we need to compare Michael's and Angelo's relative strengths. Michael produces 2 sculptures for every painting, and Angelo produces 3 sculptures for every painting. Because Michael is only twice as good at producing sculptures, his opportunity cost of producing each painting is 2 sculptures instead of 3. Therefore, Michael is the low-opportunity-cost producer of paintings.

c. If they specialize, Michael should paint and Angelo should sculpt. You might be tempted to argue that Michael should just work alone, but if Angelo does the sculptures, Michael can concentrate on the paintings. This is what comparative advantage is all about.

2.a.

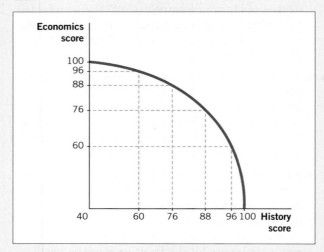

b. Yes, because it is not a straight line.

c. The opportunity cost is that the student's grade falls from 96 to 76 in history.

4.a. positive   **d.** normative

b. positive   **e.** normative

c. normative

6. A new fertilizer that doubles potato production will shift the entire PPF out along the potato axis but not along the carrot axis. Nevertheless, the added ability to produce more potatoes means that less acreage will have to be planted in potatoes and more land can be used to produce carrots. This makes it possible to produce more potatoes and carrots at many points along the production possibilities frontier. Figure 2.3 has a nice illustration if you are unsure how this process works.

8.a. Rachel gives up 2 pies for every loaf she makes. Joey gives up 1 pie for every loaf he makes.
   b. Rachel
   c. Joey
   d. Joey should make the bread and Rachel the pies.
   e. Rachel makes 2 pies per loaf and Joey makes 1 pie per loaf. So any trade between 2:1 and 1:1 would benefit them both.

11. Despite what you might think, the opportunity cost is *not* $200. You would be giving up $200 in enjoyment if you go to the Maroon 5 concert, but you would also have to pay $135 to see Taylor Swift, whereas the Maroon 5 ticket is free. The difference between the satisfaction you would have experienced at the Taylor Swift concert ($200) and the amount you must pay for the ticket ($135) is the marginal benefit you would receive from her concert. That amount is $200 − $135 = $65. You are not as big a Maroon 5 fan, but the ticket is free. As long as you think the Maroon 5 concert is worth more than $65, you will get a larger marginal benefit from seeing Maroon 5 perform than from seeing Taylor Swift perform. Therefore, the opportunity cost of using the free ticket is $65.

12.a. tattoos and (in-ground) swimming pools
   b. left shoes and right shoes
   c. The cost of producing some goods goes down as production increases. Computers, automobiles, and fast food are good examples. For such goods, the PPF would bow in.

Graphs in Economics

Many students try to understand economics without taking the time to learn how to read and interpret graphs. This approach is shortsighted. You can "think" your way to the correct answer in a few cases, but the models we build and illustrate with graphs are designed to help analyze the tough questions, where your intuition can lead you astray.

Economics is fundamentally a quantitative science. That is, economists often solve problems by finding a numerical answer. For instance, economists determine the unemployment rate, the inflation rate, the growth rate of the economy, prices, costs, and much more. Economists also like to compare present-day numbers with numbers from the immediate past and historical data. Throughout your study of economics, you will find that many data-driven topics—for example, financial trends, transactions, the stock market, and other business-related variables—naturally lend themselves to graphic display. You will also find that many theoretical concepts are easier to understand when depicted visually in graphs and charts.

Economists also find that graphing can be a powerful tool when attempting to find relationships between different sets of variables. For example, the production possibilities frontier model presented in this chapter involves the relationship between the production of pizza and the production of chicken wings. The graphical presentations make this relationship, the trade-off between pizza and wings, much more vivid.

In this appendix, we begin with simple graphs involving a single variable. We then move to graphs that consist of two variables.

Graphs That Consist of One Variable

A **variable** is a quantity that can take on more than one value.

There are two common ways to display data with one variable: bar graphs and pie charts. A **variable** is a quantity that can take on more than one value. Let's look at the market share of the largest carbonated-beverage companies. Figure 2A.1 shows the data in a bar graph. On the vertical (*y*) axis is the market share held by each firm. On the horizontal (*x*) axis are the three largest firms (Coca-Cola Co., PepsiCo Inc., and Keurig Dr Pepper) and a separate category for the remaining firms, called "Others." Coca-Cola Co. has the largest market

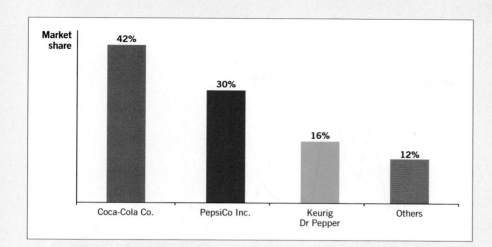

Bar Graphs

Each firm's market share in the beverage industry is represented by the height of the bar.

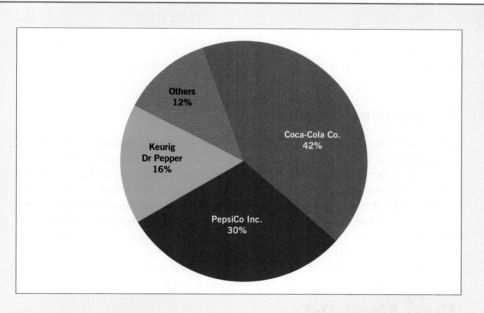

Pie Chart

Each firm's market share in the beverage industry is represented by the size of the pie slice.

share of the U.S. market at 42%, followed by PepsiCo Inc. at 30% and Keurig Dr Pepper at 16%. The height of each firm's bar represents its market-share percentage. The combined market share of the other firms in the market is 12%.

Figure 2A.2 illustrates the same data from the beverage industry on a pie chart. Now the market share is expressed as the size of the pie slice for each firm.

The information in a bar graph and a pie chart is the same, so does it matter which visualization you use? Bar graphs are particularly good for comparing sizes or quantities, while pie charts are generally better for illustrating proportions (parts of a whole).

Time-Series Graph

In a time-series graph, you immediately get a sense of when the inflation rate was highest and lowest, the trend through time, and the amount of volatility in the data.

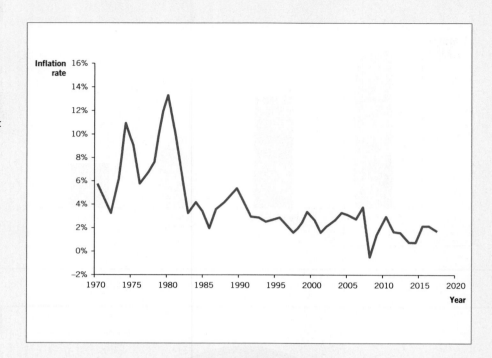

Time-Series Graphs

A time-series graph displays information about a single variable across time. For instance, if you want to show how the inflation rate has varied over a certain period of time, you could list the annual inflation rates in a lengthy table or you could illustrate each point as part of a time series in a graph. Graphing the points makes it possible to quickly determine when inflation was highest and lowest without having to scan through the entire table. Figure 2A.3 illustrates this point.

Graphs That Consist of Two Variables

Sometimes, understanding graphs requires you to visualize relationships between two economic variables. Each variable is plotted on a coordinate system, or two-dimensional grid. The coordinate system allows us to map a series of ordered pairs that show how the two variables relate to each other. For instance, suppose we examine the relationship between the amount of lemonade sold and the air temperature, as shown in Figure 2A.4.

The air temperature is graphed on the *x* axis (horizontal) and cups of lemonade sold on the *y* axis (vertical). Within each ordered pair (*x*, *y*), the first value, *x*, represents the value along the *x* axis and the second value, *y*, represents the value along the *y* axis. For example, at point A, the value of *x*, or the

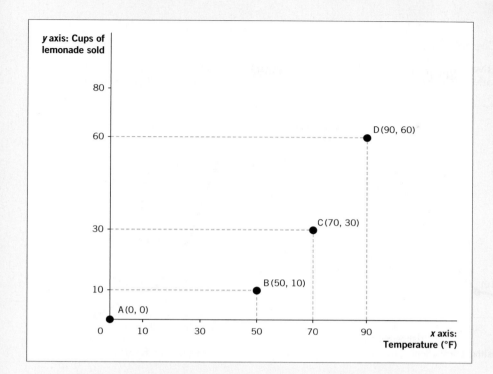

Plotting Points in a Coordinate System

Within each ordered pair (x, y), the first value, x, represents the value along the x axis, and the second value, y, represents the value along the y axis. The combination of all the (x, y) pairs is known as a scatterplot.

temperature, is 0 and the value of y, or the amount of lemonade sold, is also 0. No one would want to buy lemonade when the temperature is that low. At point B, the value of x, the air temperature, is 50°F, and the value of y, the number of cups of lemonade sold, is 10. By the time we reach point C, the temperature is 70°F and the amount of lemonade sold is 30 cups. Finally, at point D, the temperature has reached 90°F, and 60 cups of lemonade are sold.

The graph you see in Figure 2A.4 is known as a **scatterplot**; it shows the individual (x, y) points in a coordinate system. Note that in this example, the amount of lemonade sold rises as the temperature increases. When the two variables move together in the same direction, we say there is a **positive correlation** between them (see Figure 2A.5a). Conversely, if we graph the relationship between hot chocolate sales and temperature, we find they move in opposite directions; as the temperature rises, hot chocolate consumption goes down (see Figure 2A.5b). This data set reveals a **negative correlation**, which occurs when two variables, such as cups of hot chocolate sold and temperature, move in opposite directions. Economists are ultimately interested in using models and graphs to make predictions and test theories, and the coordinate system makes both positive and negative correlations easy to observe.

Figure 2A.5 illustrates the difference between a positive correlation and a negative correlation. Figure 2A.5a shows the same information as Figure 2A.4. When the temperature increases, the quantity of lemonade sold increases as well. However, in Figure 2A.5b we have a very different set of ordered pairs. As the temperature increases, the quantity of hot chocolate sold falls. We can see this relationship by starting with point E, where the temperature is 32°F and

A **scatterplot** is a graph that shows individual (x, y) points.

Positive correlation occurs when two variables move in the same direction.

Negative correlation occurs when two variables move in opposite directions.

Positive and Negative Correlations

(a) This graph displays the positive relationship, or correlation, between lemonade sales and higher temperatures.
(b) This graph displays the negative relationship, or correlation, between hot chocolate sales and higher temperatures.

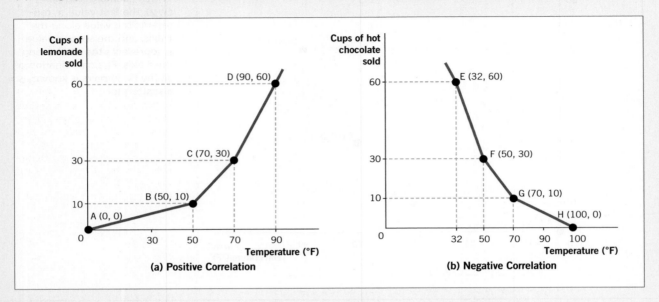

(a) Positive Correlation

(b) Negative Correlation

hot chocolate sales are 60 cups. At point F, the temperature rises to 50°F, but hot chocolate sales fall to 30 cups. At point G, the temperature is 70°F and hot chocolate sales are down to 10 cups. The purple line connecting points E–H illustrates the negative correlation between hot chocolate sales and temperature, because the line is downward sloping. This relationship contrasts with the positive correlation in Figure 2A.5a, where lemonade sales rise from point A to point D and the line is upward sloping. But what exactly is slope?

The Slope of a Curve

Slope
refers to the change in the rise along the *y* axis (vertical) divided by the change in the run along the *x* axis (horizontal).

A key element in any graph is the **slope**, or the rise along the *y* axis (vertical) divided by the run along the *x* axis (horizontal). The *rise* is the amount the vertical distance changes. The *run* is the amount the horizontal distance changes.

$$\text{Slope} = \frac{\text{change in } y}{\text{change in } x}$$

A slope can have a positive, negative, or zero value. A slope of zero—a straight horizontal line—indicates that there is no change in *y* for a given change in *x*. The slope can also be positive, as it is in Figure 2A.5a, or negative, as it is in Figure 2A.5b. Figure 2A.6 highlights the changes in *x* and *y* between the points

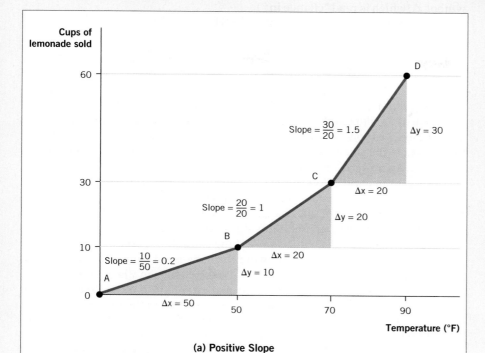

(a) Positive Slope

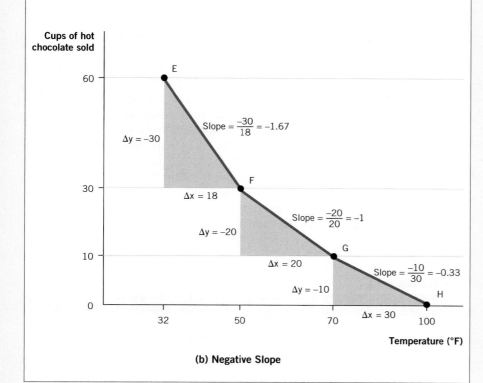

(b) Negative Slope

Positive and Negative Slopes

Notice that in both panels the slope changes value from point to point. Because of this changing slope value, we say that the relationships are nonlinear. In (a), the slopes are positive as you move along the curve from point A to point D. In (b), the slopes are negative as you move along the curve from point E to point H. An upward, or positive, slope indicates a positive correlation, while a negative, or downward, slope indicates a negative correlation.

on Figure 2A.5. (The change in a variable is often notated with a Greek delta symbol, Δ, which is read "change in.")

In Figure 2A.6a, the slope from point B to point C is

$$\text{Slope} = \frac{\text{change in } y}{\text{change in } x} = \frac{30 - 10 \text{ or } 20}{70 - 50 \text{ or } 20} = 1$$

All of the slopes in Figure 2A.6 are tabulated in Table 2A.1.

Each of the slopes in Figure 2A.6a is positive, and the values slowly increase from 0.2 to 1.5 as you move along the curve from point A to point D. However, in Figure 2A.6b, the slopes are negative as you move along the curve from point E to point H. An upward, or positive, slope indicates a positive correlation, while a downward, or negative, slope indicates a negative correlation.

Notice that in both panels of Figure 2A.6, the slope changes values from point to point. Because of this changing slope, we say that the relationships are *nonlinear*. (In contrast, the relationship is *linear* when slope does not change along the line.) The slope tells us something about how responsive consumers are to changes in temperature. Consider the movement from point A to point B in Figure 2A.6a. The change in y is 10, while the change in x is 50, and the slope (10/50) is 0.2. Because zero indicates no change and 0.2 is close to zero, we can say that lemonade customers are not very responsive as the temperature rises from 0°F to 50°F. However, they are much more responsive from point C to point D, when the temperature rises from 70°F to 90°F. At point D, lemonade consumption—the change in y—rises from 30 to 60 cups, and the slope is now 1.5. The strength of the positive relationship is much stronger, and as a result, the curve is much steeper, or more vertical. This part of the curve contrasts with the movement from point A to point B, where the curve is flatter, or more horizontal.

We can apply the same analysis to Figure 2A.6b. Consider the movement from point E to point F. The change in y is –30, the change in x is 18, and the slope is –1.7. This value represents a strong negative relationship, so we would say that hot chocolate customers were quite responsive; as the temperature rose from 32°F to 50°F, they cut their consumption of hot chocolate by 30 cups. However, hot chocolate customers are not very responsive from point G to point H, where the temperature rises from 70°F to 100°F. In this case, consumption falls from 10 cups to 0 cups and the slope is –0.3. The strength of the negative relationship is much weaker (closer to zero), and as a result, the line is much flatter, or more horizontal. This part of the curve contrasts with the movement from point E to point F, where the curve is steeper, or more vertical.

TABLE 2A.1

Positive and Negative Slopes

(a)		(b)	
Points	Slope	Points	Slope
A to B	0.2	E to F	−1.7
B to C	1.0	F to G	−1.0
C to D	1.5	G to H	−0.3

Formulas for the Area of a Rectangle and a Triangle

Sometimes, economists interpret graphs by examining the area of different sections below a curve. Consider the demand for Bruegger's Bagels shown in Figure 2A.7. The demand curve (labeled D) has a downward slope, which tells us that when the price of bagels falls, consumers will buy more bagels. (We will learn more about demand curves in Chapter 3.) But this curve also can tell us about the revenue the seller receives—one of the most important considerations for the firm. In this case, let's assume that the price of each bagel is $0.60 and Bruegger's sells 4,000 bagels each week. We can illustrate the total amount of Bruegger's revenue by shading the area bounded by the number of sales and the price—the green rectangle in the figure. In addition, we can identify the surplus benefit consumers receive from purchasing bagels; the blue triangle shows this amount. Because many buyers are willing to pay more than $0.60 per bagel, we can visualize the "surplus" consumers get from Bruegger's Bagels by highlighting the blue triangular area under the demand curve and above the price of $0.60.

To calculate the area of a rectangle, we use the formula

$$\text{Area of a rectangle} = \text{height} \times \text{base}$$

In Figure 2A.7, the green rectangle is the amount of revenue that Bruegger's Bagels receives when it charges $0.60 per bagel. The total revenue is $0.60 × 4,000, or $2,400.

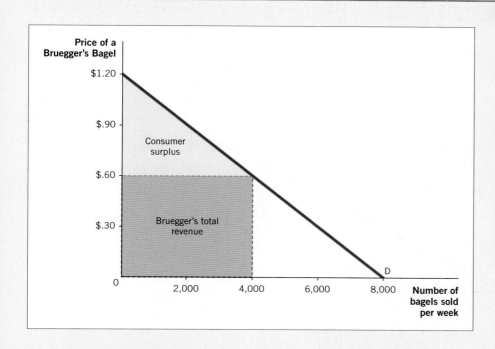

FIGURE 2A.7

Working with Rectangles and Triangles

We can determine the area of the green rectangle by multiplying the height by the base. This gives us $0.60 × 4,000, or $2,400 for the total revenue earned by Bruegger's Bagels. We can determine the area of a triangle by using the formula $\frac{1}{2} \times$ height × base. This gives us $\frac{1}{2} \times$ $0.60 × 4,000, or $1,200 for the area of consumer surplus.

To calculate the area of a triangle, we use the formula

$$\text{Area of a triangle} = \tfrac{1}{2} \times \text{height} \times \text{base}$$

In Figure 2A.7, the blue triangle represents the amount of surplus consumers get from buying bagels. The amount of consumer surplus is $\tfrac{1}{2} \times \$0.60 \times 4{,}000 = \$1{,}200$. Note that the value of the height, \$0.60, comes from reading the y axis: \$1.20 at the top of the triangle − \$0.60 at the bottom of the triangle = \$0.60.

Cautions in Interpreting Numerical Graphs

In Chapter 2, we utilized *ceteris paribus*, which entails holding everything else around us constant (unchanged) while analyzing a specific relationship. Suppose that you omitted an important part of the relationship. What effect would this omission have on your ability to use graphs as an illustrative tool? Consider the relationship between sales of lemonade and sales of bottles of suntan lotion. The graph of the two variables would look something like Figure 2A.8.

FIGURE 2A.8

Graph with an Omitted Variable

What looks like a strongly positive correlation is misleading. What underlying variable is causing lemonade and suntan lotion sales to rise? The demand for both lemonade and suntan lotion rises because the temperature rises.

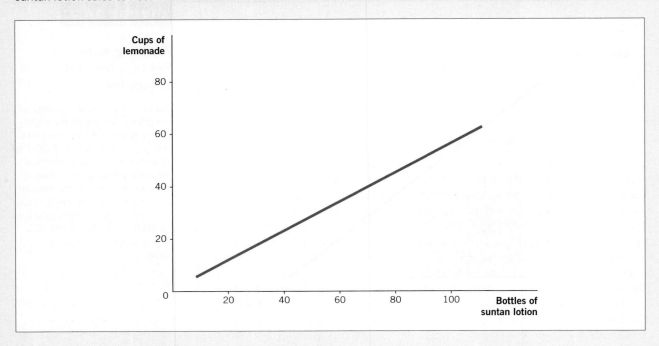

Reverse Causation

AIDS deaths are associated with having more doctors in the area. But the doctors are there to help and treat people, not harm them. Suggesting that more doctors in an area causes more deaths from AIDS would be a mistake—an example of reverse causation.

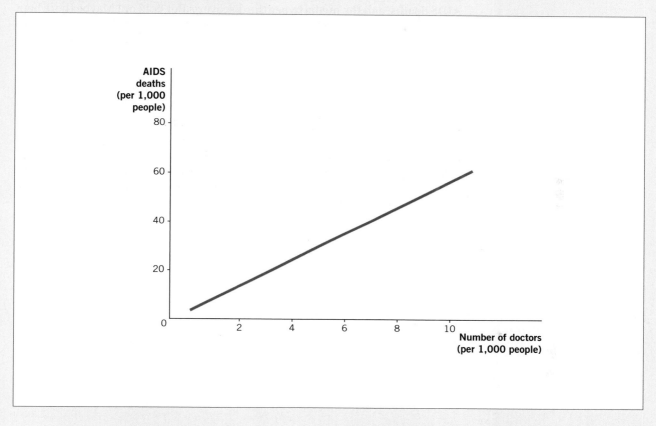

Looking at Figure 2A.8, you would not necessarily know that it is misleading. However, when you stop to think about the relationship, you quickly recognize that the graph is deceptive. Because the slope is positive, the graph indicates a positive correlation between the number of bottles of suntan lotion sold and the amount of lemonade sold. At first glance this relationship seems reasonable, because we associate suntan lotion and lemonade with summer activities. But the association does not imply **causality**, which occurs when one variable influences the other. Using more suntan lotion does not cause people to drink more lemonade. The **common cause** is that when it is hot outside, more suntan lotion is used and more lemonade is consumed. In this case, the causal factor is heat! The graph makes it look like the number of people using suntan lotion affects the amount of lemonade being consumed, when in fact the two variables are not directly related.

Causality
occurs when one variable influences another.

A **common cause** is a single cause responsible for two phenomena observed to correlate with each other.

Reverse causation occurs when causation is incorrectly assigned among associated events.

Another possible mistake is **reverse causation**, which occurs when causation is incorrectly assigned among associated events. Suppose that in an effort to fight the AIDS epidemic in Africa, a research organization notes the correlation shown in Figure 2A.9.

After looking at the data, it is clear that as the number of doctors per 1,000 people goes up, so do death rates from AIDS. The research organization puts out a press release claiming that doctors are responsible for increasing AIDS deaths, and the media hypes the discovery. But hold on! Maybe there happen to be more doctors in areas with high incidences of AIDS because that's where they are most needed. Coming to the correct conclusion about the data requires that we do more than simply look at the correlation.

·APPENDIX PROBLEMS·

Concepts You Should Know

causality (p. 67)
common cause (p. 67)
negative correlation (p. 61)

positive correlation (p. 61)
reverse causation (p. 68)
scatterplot (p. 61)

slope (p. 62)
variable (p. 58)

Study Problems *(＊solved at the end of the section)*

1. The following table shows the price and the quantity demanded of apples (per week).

Price per apple	Quantity demanded
$0.25	10
$0.50	7
$0.75	4
$1.00	2
$1.25	1
$1.50	0

a. Plot the data provided in the table into a graph.
b. Is the relationship between the price of apples and the quantity demanded negative or positive?

＊ **2.** In the following graph, calculate the value of the slope if the price rises from $20 to $40.

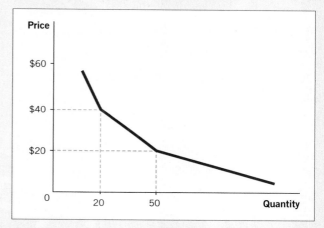

3. Explain the logical error in the following sentence: "As ice cream sales increase, the number of people who drown increases sharply. Therefore, ice cream causes drowning."

4. Of the following relationships, which are the result of a common cause or reverse causation?

a. Increased dash cam use causes more accidents to happen.
b. Increased sales of life jackets lead to more shark attacks.
c. When people wear sandals more often, it's because they're wearing shorts more often.

Solved Problem

2. The slope is calculated by using the formula:

$$\text{Slope} = \frac{\text{change in } y}{\text{change in } x} = \frac{\$40 - \$20}{20 - 50} = \frac{\$20}{-30} = -0.6667$$

PART

II

The Role of
MARKETS

The Market at Work: Supply and Demand

Buyers and Sellers Together Determine the Price of the Good.

What do Starbucks, Nordstrom, and Amazon have in common? If you guessed that they all have headquarters in Seattle, that's true. But even more interesting is that each company supplies a product much in demand by consumers. Starbucks supplies coffee from coast to coast and seems to be everywhere someone wants a cup of coffee. Nordstrom, a giant retailer with hundreds of department stores, supplies fashion apparel to meet a broad spectrum of individual demand, from the basics to designer collections. Amazon delivers online products to customers all over the world. Demand for Amazon's products has made Jeff Bezos the richest person in the world.

Notice the two recurring words in the previous paragraph: "supply" and "demand." Sometimes buyers set the price—through live auctions, on eBay, or at shopgoodwill.com. Other times, sellers set the price and then adjust it based on how well an item sells and how much inventory remains. Buyers and sellers each influence both prices and quantities traded, so that these end up being determined by how buyers' and sellers' price-versus-quantity calculations interact.

This chapter describes how markets work and discusses the nature of competition. To shed light on the process, we introduce the formal model of demand and supply. We begin

Black Friday rush at Macy's means more demand. Customers storm the door while taking selfies to share the moment with their friends. Macy's and other Black Friday retailers offer a limited supply of dramatically reduced merchandise to get customers into their stores.

by looking at demand and supply separately. Then we combine them to see how they interact to establish the market price and determine how much is produced and sold.

· BIG QUESTIONS ·

- What are the fundamentals of markets?
- What determines demand?
- What determines supply?
- How do supply and demand interact to create equilibrium?

What Are the Fundamentals of Markets?

In a **market economy**, resources are allocated among households and firms with little or no government interference.

The **invisible hand** is a phrase coined by Adam Smith to refer to the unobservable market forces that guide resources to their highest-valued use.

Peak season is expensive…

Markets bring trading partners together to create order out of chaos. Companies supply goods and services, and customers want to obtain the goods and services that companies supply. In a **market economy**, resources are allocated among households and firms with little or no government interference. Adam Smith, the founder of modern economics, described the dynamic best: "It is not from the benevolence of the butcher, the brewer, or the baker, that we expect our dinner, but from their regard to their own interest." In other words, producers earn a living by selling the products consumers want. Consumers are also motivated by self-interest; they must decide how to use their money to select the goods they need or want the most. This process, which Adam Smith called the **invisible hand**, guides resources to their highest-valued use.

The exchange of goods and services in a market economy happens through prices that are established in markets. Those prices change according to the level of demand for a product and how much is supplied. For instance, hotel rates near Disney World are reduced in the fall when demand is low, and they peak in March when spring break occurs. If spring break takes you to a ski resort instead, you will find lots of company and high prices. But if you are looking for an outdoor adventure during the summer, ski resorts have plenty of lodging available at great rates.

Similarly, many parents know how hard it is to find a reasonably priced hotel room in a college town on graduation weekend. Likewise, a pipeline break or unsettled political conditions in the Middle East can disrupt the supply of oil and cause the price of gasoline to spike overnight. When higher gas prices continue over a period of time, consumers respond by changing their driving habits or buying more fuel-efficient cars.

Why does all of this happen? Supply and demand tell the story. We begin our exploration of supply and demand by looking at where they interact—in markets. A firm's degree of control over the market price is the distinguishing feature between *competitive markets* and *imperfect markets*.

… but off-season is a bargain.

Competitive Markets

Buyers and sellers of a specific good or service come together to form a market. Formally, a *market* is a collection of buyers and sellers of a particular product or service. The buyers create the demand for the product, while the sellers produce the supply. The interaction of the buyers and sellers in a market establishes the price and the quantity produced of a particular good or the amount of a service offered.

Markets exist whenever goods and services are exchanged. Some markets are online, and others operate in traditional "brick and mortar" stores. Pike Place Market in Seattle is a collection of markets spread across 9 acres. For over a hundred years, it has brought together buyers and sellers of fresh, organic, and specialty foods. Because there is a large number of buyers and sellers for each type of product, we say that the markets at Pike Place are competitive. A **competitive market** is one in which there are so many buyers and sellers that each has only a small impact on the market price and output. In fact, the impact is so small that it is negligible.

At Pike Place Market, like other local markets, the goods sold by each vendor are similar. Because each buyer and seller is just one small part of the whole market, no single buyer or seller has any influence over the market price. These two characteristics—similar goods and many participants—create a highly competitive market in which the price and quantity sold of a good are determined by the market rather than by any one person or business.

To understand how competition works, let's look at sales of salmon at Pike Place Market. On any given day, dozens of vendors sell salmon at this market. If a single vendor is absent or runs out of salmon, the quantity supplied that day will not change significantly—the remaining sellers will have no trouble filling the void. The same is true for those buying salmon. Customers will have no trouble finding salmon at the remaining vendors. Whether a particular salmon buyer decides to show up on a given day makes little difference when hundreds of buyers visit the market each day. No single buyer or seller has any

Trade creates value

A **competitive market** exists when there are so many buyers and sellers that each has only a small (negligible) impact on the market price and output.

One of many vendors at Pike Place Market.

The Empire State Building has one of the best views in New York City.

An **imperfect market** is one in which either the buyer or the seller can influence the market price.

Market power is a firm's ability to influence the price of a good or service by exercising control over its demand, supply, or both.

A **monopoly** exists when a single company supplies the entire market for a particular good or service.

The **quantity demanded** is the amount of a good or service that buyers are willing and able to purchase at the current price.

appreciable influence on the price of salmon. As a result, the market for salmon at Pike Place Market is a competitive one.

Imperfect Markets

Markets are not always fully competitive. British economist Joan Robinson wrote that in imperfect competition, "a certain difficulty arises [because] the individual demand curve for the product of each of the firms . . . will depend to some extent upon the price policy of the others."* Accordingly, we define these **imperfect markets** as markets in which either the buyer or the seller can influence the market price. For example, the Empire State Building affords an iconic view of Manhattan. Not surprisingly, the cost of taking the elevator to the top of the building is not cheap. But many customers buy the tickets anyway because they have decided that the view is worth the price. The managers of the Empire State Building can set a high price for tickets because there is no other place in New York City with such a great view. From this example, we see that when sellers produce goods and services that are different from their competitors', they gain some control, or leverage, over the price they charge. The more unusual the product being sold, the more control the seller has over the price. When a seller has some control over the price, we say that the market is imperfect. Specialized products, such as popular video games, front-row concert tickets, or dinner reservations at a trendy restaurant, give the seller substantial pricing power. **Market power** is a firm's ability to influence the price of a good or service by exercising control over its demand, supply, or both.

In between the highly competitive environment at the Pike Place Market and markets characterized by a lack of competition, such as the Empire State Building with its iconic view, there are many other types of markets. Some, like the market for fast-food restaurants, are highly competitive but sell products that are not identical. Other businesses—for example, Comcast Cable—function like monopolies because they are the only provider of a service in a geographic area. A **monopoly** exists when a single company supplies the entire market for a particular good or service. We'll talk a lot more about different market structures, such as monopoly, in later chapters. But even in imperfect markets, the forces of supply and demand significantly influence producer and consumer behavior. For the time being, we'll keep our analysis focused on supply and demand in competitive markets.

What Determines Demand?

Demand exists when an individual or group wants something badly enough to pay or trade for it. How much an individual or group actually buys depends on the price of the good or service. In economics, the amount of a good or service that buyers are willing and able to purchase at the current price is known as the **quantity demanded**.

When the price of a good increases, consumers often respond by purchasing less of the good or buying something else. For instance, many consumers

---

*Source: Joan Robinson, *The Economics of Imperfect Competition* (London: Macmillan, 1933).

Markets and the Nature of Competition

QUESTION: Which of the following are competitive markets? How will each firm price its products, and how much market power does each firm have?

1. gas stations at a busy interstate exit

2. a furniture store in an isolated small town

3. a fresh produce stand at a farmers' market

ANSWERS

1. Because each gas station sells the same product and competes for the same customers, they often charge the same price. This is a competitive market. However, gas stations also differentiate themselves by offering conveniences such as fast food, clean restrooms, ATM machines, and so forth. The result is that individual stations have some market power.

2. Residents would have to travel a significant distance to find another furniture store. This situation allows the small-town store to charge more than other furniture stores. The furniture store has some monopoly power. This is not a competitive market.

3. Because consumers can buy fresh produce in season from many stands at a farmers' market, individual vendors have very little market pricing power. They must charge the same price as other vendors in order to attract customers. This is a competitive market.

Is this a competitive market?

who would buy salmon at $5 per pound would likely buy something else if the price of salmon rose to $20 per pound. Therefore, as price goes up, quantity demanded goes down. Similarly, as price goes down, quantity demanded goes up. This negative (opposite) relationship between the price and the quantity demanded is the law of demand. The **law of demand** states that, all other things being equal, the quantity demanded falls when the price rises, and the quantity demanded rises when the price falls. The law of demand holds true over a wide range of goods and settings.

Trade creates value

The **law of demand** states that, all other things being equal, quantity demanded falls when the price rises, and rises when the price falls.

The Demand Curve

A table that shows the relationship between the price of a good and the quantity demanded is known as a **demand schedule**. To discuss this idea (and to take a break from fish markets), let's introduce a new hypothetical involving action hero and former athlete Dwayne "The Rock" Johnson. The Rock gets a lot of bumps and bruises in his active career, and Table 3.1 shows The Rock's hypothetical demand schedule for healing crystals. When the price is $20.00 or more per crystal, The Rock will not purchase any crystals. However, below $20.00, the amount The Rock purchases is negatively related to the price. For instance, at a price of $10.00, The Rock demands 4 crystals. If the price rises to $12.50, he demands 3 crystals. Every time the price increases, The Rock buys fewer crystals. In contrast, every time the price falls, he buys more. If the price falls to zero, The Rock would demand 8 crystals. That is, even if the crystals are free, there is a limit to his demand because he would grow tired of using the crystals.

A **demand schedule** is a table that shows the relationship between the price of a good and the quantity demanded.

Incentives

TABLE 3.1

The Rock's Demand for Healing Crystals

Price of healing crystals	Number demanded
$20.00	0
17.50	1
15.00	2
12.50	3
10.00	4
7.50	5
5.00	6
2.50	7
0.00	8

A **demand curve** is a graph of the relationship between the prices in the demand schedule and the quantity demanded at those prices.

The numbers in The Rock's demand schedule from Table 3.1 are plotted on a graph in Figure 3.1, known as a demand curve. A **demand curve** is a graph of the relationship between the prices in the demand schedule and the quantity demanded at those prices. For simplicity, the demand "curve" is often drawn as a straight line. Economists always place the independent variable, which is the price, on the *y* (vertical) axis and the dependent

FIGURE 3.1

The Rock's Demand Curve for Healing Crystals

The Rock's demand curve for healing crystals plots the data from Table 3.1. When the price of a crystal is $10.00, he buys 4. If the price rises to $12.50, The Rock reduces the quantity he buys to 3. The figure illustrates the law of demand by showing a negative relationship between price and the quantity demanded.

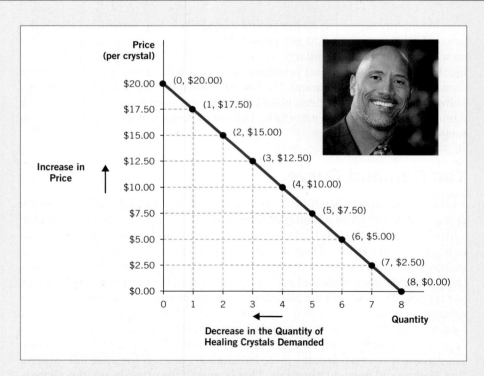

variable, which is the quantity demanded, on the *x* (horizontal) axis. The relationship between the price and the quantity demanded produces a downward-sloping curve. In Figure 3.1, we see that as the price rises from $0.00 to $20.00 along the *y* axis, the quantity demanded decreases from 8 to 0 along the *x* axis.

Market Demand

So far, we have studied individual demand, but a market is composed of many different buyers. In this section, we examine the collective demand of all of the buyers in a given market.

The **market demand** is the sum of all the individual quantities demanded by each buyer in a market at each price. During a typical day, thousands of individuals buy healing crystals. However, to make our analysis simpler, let's assume that our market consists of only two buyers, The Rock and Emma Stone, each of whom enjoys using healing crystals. Figure 3.2 shows individual demand schedules for the two people in this market, a combined market demand schedule, and the corresponding graphs. At a price of $10, Emma buys 2 crystals, while The Rock buys 4. To determine the market demand curve, we add Emma's 2 to The Rock's 4 for a total of 6 crystals. As you can see in the table within Figure 3.2, by adding Emma's demand and The Rock's demand, we arrive at the total (that is, combined) market demand. Any demand curve shows the law of demand with movements along (up or down) the curve that reflect the effect of a price change on the quantity demanded of the good or service. Only a change in price can cause a movement along a demand curve.

Shifts of the Demand Curve

We have examined the relationship between price and quantity demanded. This relationship, described by the law of demand, shows us that when price changes, consumers respond by altering the amount they purchase. But in addition to price, many other variables influence how much of a good or service is purchased. For instance, news about the possible risks or benefits associated with the consumption of a good or service can change overall demand.

Suppose the government issues a nationwide safety warning that cautions against eating cantaloupe because of a recent discovery of *Listeria* bacteria in some melons. The government warning would cause consumers to buy fewer cantaloupes at any given price, and overall demand would decline. Looking at Figure 3.3, we see that an overall decline in demand will cause the entire demand curve to shift to the left of the original curve, from D_1 to D_2. Note that though the price remains at $5 per cantaloupe, demand has moved from 6 melons to 3. Figure 3.3 also shows what does *not* cause a shift of the demand curve: the price. The orange arrow alongside D_1 indicates that the quantity demanded will rise or fall in response to a price change. *A price change causes a movement along a given demand curve, but it cannot cause a shift of the demand curve.*

FIGURE 3.2

Calculating Market Demand

To calculate the market demand for healing crystals, we add Emma Stone's quantity demanded and The Rock's quantity demanded.

Price of healing crystals	Emma's demand	The Rock's demand	Combined market demand
$20.00	0	0	0
17.50	0	1	1
15.00	1	2	3
12.50	1	3	4
10.00	2	4	6
7.50	2	5	7
5.00	3	6	9
2.50	3	7	10
0.00	4	8	12

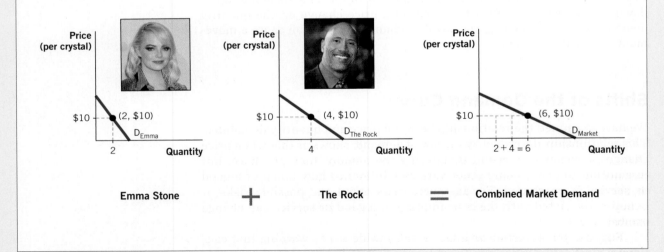

Emma Stone + The Rock = Combined Market Demand

A decrease in overall demand shifts the demand curve to the left. What happens when a variable causes overall demand to increase? Suppose that the news media have just announced the results of a medical study indicating that cantaloupe contains a natural substance that lowers cholesterol. Because of the newly discovered health benefits of cantaloupe, overall demand for it will increase. This increase in demand shifts the demand curve to the right, from D_1 to D_3, as Figure 3.3 shows.

Incentives

FIGURE 3.3

A Shift of the Demand Curve

When the price changes, the quantity demanded changes along the existing demand curve, as indicated by the orange arrow. A shift of the demand curve, indicated by the black arrows, occurs when something other than price changes.

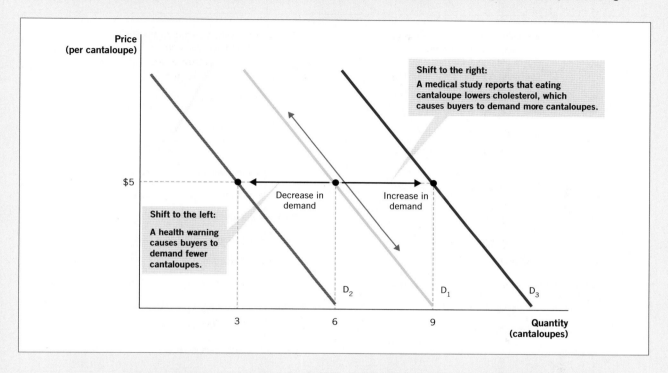

In our cantaloupe example, we saw that demand shifted because of changes in consumers' tastes and preferences. However, many different variables can shift demand. These include changes in buyers' income, the price of related goods, changes in buyers' tastes and preferences, price expectations, the number of buyers, and taxes.

Figure 3.4 provides an overview of the variables, or factors, that can shift demand. The easiest way to keep all of these elements straight is to ask yourself a simple question: Would this change cause me to buy more or less of the good? If the change reduces how much you would buy at any given price, you shift the demand curve to the left. If the change increases how much you would buy at any given price, you shift the curve to the right.

CHANGES IN BUYERS' INCOME When your income goes up, you have more to spend. Assuming that prices don't change, individuals with higher incomes are able to buy more of what they want. Similarly, when your income

If a new medical study indicates that eating more cantaloupe lowers cholesterol, would this finding cause a shift in demand, or a movement along the demand curve?

FIGURE 3.4

Factors That Shift the Demand Curve

The demand curve shifts to the left when a factor decreases demand. The demand curve shifts to the right when a factor increases demand. (*Note*: A change in price does not cause a shift. Price changes cause movements along the demand curve.)

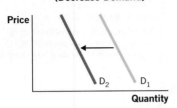

Factors That Shift Demand to the Left (Decrease Demand)

- Income falls (demand for a normal good).
- Income rises (demand for an inferior good).
- The price of a substitute good falls.
- The price of a complementary good rises.
- The good falls out of style.
- There is a belief that the future price of the good will decline.
- The number of buyers in the market falls.
- Excise or sales taxes increase.
- Subsidies to consumers decrease.

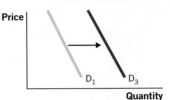

Factors That Shift Demand to the Right (Increase Demand)

- Income rises (demand for a normal good).
- Income falls (demand for an inferior good).
- The price of a substitute good rises.
- The price of a complementary good falls.
- The good is currently in style.
- There is a belief that the future price of the good will rise.
- The number of buyers in the market increases.
- Excise or sales taxes decrease.
- Subsidies to consumers increase.

Purchasing power is the value of your income expressed in terms of how much you can afford.

Consumers buy more of a **normal good** as income rises, holding all other factors constant.

An **inferior good** is one where demand declines as income rises.

declines, your **purchasing power**, or how much you can afford, falls. In either case, your income affects your overall demand.

When economists look at how consumers spend, they often differentiate between two types of goods: normal and inferior. Consumers will buy more of a **normal good** as their income goes up (assuming all other factors remain constant). An example of a normal good is a meal at a restaurant. When income goes up, the demand for restaurant meals increases and the demand curve shifts to the right. Similarly, if income falls, the demand for restaurant meals goes down and the demand curve shifts to the left.

While consumers with an increased income may purchase more of some things, the additional purchasing power will mean they purchase fewer inferior goods. An **inferior good** is one where demand declines as income rises. Examples include rooms in boarding houses, as opposed to one's own apartment or house, and hamburgers and ramen noodles, as opposed to filet mignon. As income goes up, consumers buy less of an inferior good because they can afford something better. Within a specific product market, you can often find examples of inferior and normal goods in the form of different brands.

THE PRICE OF RELATED GOODS Another factor that can shift the demand curve is the price of related goods. Certain goods directly influence the demand for other goods. **Complements** are two goods that are used together. **Substitutes** are two goods that are used in place of each other.

Consider this pair of complements: smartphones and phone cases. What happens when the price of one of the complements—say, the smartphone—rises? As you would expect, the quantity demanded of the smartphone goes down. The demand for its complement, the phone case, also goes down because people are not likely to use one without the other.

Substitute goods work the opposite way. When the price of a substitute good increases, the quantity demanded declines, and the demand for the alternative good increases. For example, if the price of the PlayStation 4 goes up and the price of Microsoft's Xbox remains unchanged, the demand for Xbox will increase while the quantity demanded of the PS4 will decline.

Complements
When the price of a complementary good rises, the quantity demanded of that good falls and the demand for the related good goes down.

Substitutes
are two goods that are used in place of each other. When the price of a substitute good rises, the quantity demanded of that good falls and the demand for the related good goes up.

CHANGES IN TASTES AND PREFERENCES Fashion goes in and out of style quickly. Walk into Nordstrom or another clothing retailer, and you will see that fashion changes from season to season and year to year. For instance, what do you think of heavily distressed jeans? They became popular a few years ago and are still a common sight today, but it is safe to assume that in a few years they will once again go out of style. While something is popular, demand increases. As soon as it falls out of favor, you can expect demand for it to decrease. Tastes and preferences can change quickly, and this fluctuation alters the demand for a particular good.

Though changes in fashion trends are usually purely subjective, other changes in preferences are the result of new information about the goods and services we buy. Recall our example of shifting demand for cantaloupe as the result of either the *Listeria* infection or new positive medical findings. This is one example of how information can influence consumers' preferences. Contamination would cause a decrease in demand because people would no longer want to eat cantaloupe. In contrast, if people learn that eating cantaloupe lowers cholesterol, their demand for the melon will go up.

Are these jeans stylish or fit for the dumpster? It depends on consumers' tastes in fashion at the time.

PRICE EXPECTATIONS Have you ever waited to purchase a sweater because warm weather was right around the corner and you expected the price to come down? Conversely, have you ever purchased an airline ticket well in advance because you figured that the price would rise as the flight filled up? In both cases, expectations about the future influenced your current demand. If we expect a price to be higher tomorrow, we are likely to buy more today to beat the price increase. The result is an increase in current demand. Likewise, if you expect a price to decline soon, you might delay your purchases to try to get a lower price in the future. An expectation of a lower price in the future will therefore decrease current demand.

Shifting the Demand Curve

THE HUDSUCKER PROXY

This 1994 film by the Coen brothers, who would go on to bring us *Fargo* (1996) and the TV series based on it, chronicles the introduction of the hula hoop, a toy that set off one of the greatest fads in U.S. history. According to Wham-O, the manufacturer of the hoop, when the toy was first introduced in the late 1950s over 25 million were sold in four months.

One scene from the movie clearly illustrates the difference between movements along the demand curve and a shift of the entire demand curve.

The Hudsucker Corporation has decided to sell the hula hoop for $1.79. We see a toy store owner leaning next to the front door waiting for customers to enter. But business is slow. The movie cuts to the president of the company, played by Tim Robbins, sitting behind a big desk waiting to hear about sales of the new toy. It is not doing well. So the store lowers the price, first to $1.59, then to $1.49, and so on, until finally the hula hoop is "free with any purchase." But even this generous offer is not enough to attract consumers, so the toy store owner throws the unwanted hula hoops into the alley behind the store.

One of the unwanted toys rolls across the street and around the block before landing at the foot of a boy who is skipping school. He picks up the hula hoop and tries it out. He is a natural. When school lets out, a throng of students round the corner and see him

How did the hula hoop craze start?

playing with the hula hoop. Suddenly, everyone wants a hula hoop and there is a run on the toy store. Now preferences have changed, and the overall demand has increased. The hula hoop craze is born. In economic terms, we say that the increased demand has shifted the entire demand curve to the right. The toy store responds by ordering new hula hoops and raising the price to $3.99—the new market price after the increase, or shift, in demand.

This example reminds us that changes in price cannot shift the demand curve. Shifts in demand can happen only when an outside event influences human behavior.

THE NUMBER OF BUYERS Recall that the market demand curve is the sum of all individual demand curves. Therefore, another way for market demand to increase is for more individual buyers to enter the market. The United States adds 3 million people each year to its population through immigration and births. All those new people have needs and wants, just as the existing population of 325 million does. Collectively, the new people add about 1% to the overall size of many existing markets on an annual basis.

The number of buyers also varies by age. Consider two markets—one for baby products (such as diapers, high chairs, and strollers) and the other for health care (including medicine, cancer treatments, hip replacement surgery,

Shift of the Curve or Movement along the Curve?

Cheap pizza or...

...cheap drinks?

QUESTION: Suppose that a local pizza place likes to run a late-night special. The owners have contacted you for some advice. One of the owners tells you, "We want to increase the demand for our pizza." He proposes two marketing ideas to accomplish this goal:

1. Reduce the price of large pizzas.

2. Reduce the price of a complementary good—for example, offer two half-priced bottles or cans of soda with every large pizza ordered.

Which strategy will you recommend?

ANSWER: First, consider why late-night specials exist in the first place. Because most people prefer to eat dinner early in the evening, the pizzeria has to encourage late-night patrons to buy pizzas by stimulating demand. "Specials" are used during periods of low demand, when regular prices would leave the establishment largely empty.

Incentives

Next, look at what the question asks. The owners want to know which option would "increase demand" more. The question is very specific; the owners are looking for something that will increase (or shift) demand.

Consider the first option, a reduction in the price of pizzas. Let's look at this option graphically (see next graph). A reduction in the price of a large pizza causes a movement along the demand curve, or a change in the quantity demanded.

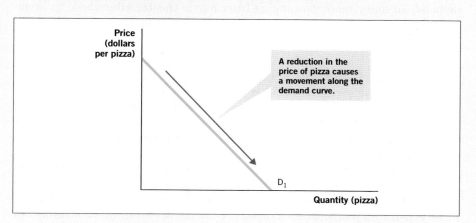

A reduction in the price of pizza causes a movement along the demand curve.

Now consider the second option, a reduction in the price of a complementary good. Let's look at this option graphically (next graph). A reduction in the price of a complementary good (for example, soda) causes the entire demand curve to shift. This is the correct answer, because the question asks which marketing idea would increase (or shift) demand more.

Recall that a reduction in the price of a complementary good shifts the demand curve to the right. The other answer, cutting the price of pizzas, causes a movement along the existing demand curve, which does not increase demand.

If you move along a curve instead of shifting it, you will analyze the problem incorrectly.

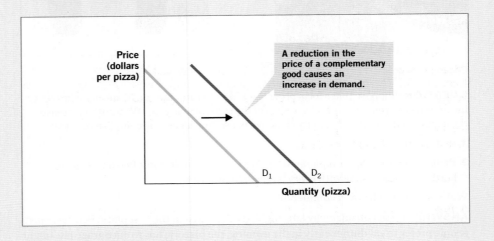

and nursing facilities). In countries with aging populations—for example, in Italy, where the birthrate has plummeted over several generations—the demand for baby products will decline and the demand for health care will expand. In other words, demographic changes in society are another source of shifts in demand. In many markets, ranging from movie theater attendance to home ownership, population trends play an important role in determining whether the market is expanding or contracting.

TAXES AND SUBSIDIES Changes in *excise taxes* (which are taxes on a single product or service) and *sales taxes* (which are general taxes on most goods and services) affect demand as well. Higher taxes lower demand because consumers must now pay the higher tax in addition to the price they pay for the good. Lower taxes reduce the overall cost to consumers and therefore increase demand.

The reverse is true for a **subsidy**, which is a payment made by the government to encourage the consumption or production of a good or service. A lot of times it's a tax break, like the mortgage interest tax deduction, or tax credits on eco-friendly cars. In both cases, the tax break encourages consumers to purchase more of the subsidized good.

Incentives

A **subsidy** is a payment made by the government to encourage the consumption or production of a good or service.

What Determines Supply?

Even though we have learned a great deal about demand, our understanding of markets is incomplete without also analyzing supply. Let's go back to Seattle's Pike Place Market and focus on the behavior of producers selling goods there.

We have seen that with demand, price and output are *negatively related*. That is, they move in opposite directions. With supply, however, the price level and quantity supplied are *positively related*. That is, they move in the same direction. For instance, few producers would sell salmon if the market price were $2.50 per pound, but many would sell it at a price of $20.00 per pound. (At $20.00, producers earn more profit than they do at a price of $2.50.) The **quantity supplied** is the amount of a good or service that producers are willing and able to sell at the current price. Higher prices cause the quantity supplied to increase. Conversely, lower prices cause the quantity supplied to decrease.

When price increases, producers often respond by offering more for sale. As price goes down, quantity supplied also goes down. This direct positive relationship between price and quantity supplied is the law of supply. The **law of supply** states that, all other things being equal, the quantity supplied increases when the price rises, and the quantity supplied falls when the price falls. This law holds true over a wide range of goods and settings.

The **quantity supplied** is the amount of a good or service producers are willing and able to sell at the current price.

The **law of supply** states that, all other things being equal, the quantity supplied of a good rises when the price of the good rises, and falls when the price of the good falls.

The Supply Curve

A **supply schedule** is a table that shows the relationship between the price of a good and the quantity supplied. The supply schedule for salmon in Table 3.2 shows how many pounds of salmon Sol Amon, owner of Pure Food Fish, would sell each month at different prices. (Pure Food Fish is a fish stand that sells all kinds of freshly caught seafood.) When the market price is $20.00 per pound, Sol is willing to sell 800 pounds. At $12.50, Sol's quantity offered is 500 pounds. If the price falls to $10.00, he offers 400 pounds. Every time the price falls, Sol offers less salmon. This means he is constantly adjusting the amount he offers.

A **supply schedule** is a table that shows the relationship between the price of a good and the quantity supplied.

TABLE 3.2

Pure Food Fish's Supply Schedule for Salmon

Price of salmon (per pound)	Pounds of salmon supplied (per month)
$20.00	800
17.50	700
15.00	600
12.50	500
10.00	400
7.50	300
5.00	200
2.50	100
0.00	0

FIGURE 3.5

Pure Food Fish's Supply Curve for Salmon

Pure Food Fish's supply curve for salmon plots the data from Table 3.2. When the price of salmon is $10.00 per pound, Pure Food Fish supplies 400 pounds. If the price rises to $12.50 per pound, Pure Food Fish increases its quantity supplied to 500 pounds. The figure illustrates the law of supply by showing a positive relationship between price and the quantity supplied.

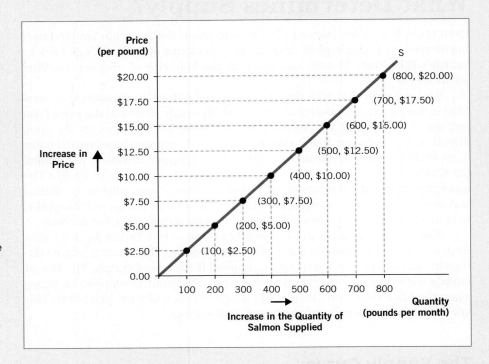

As the price of salmon falls, so does Sol's profit from selling it. Because Sol's livelihood depends on selling seafood, he has to find a way to compensate for the lost income. So he might offer more cod instead.

Sol and the other seafood vendors must respond to price changes by adjusting what they offer for sale in the market. This is why Sol offers more salmon when the price rises and less salmon when the price declines.

When we plot the supply schedule in Table 3.2, we get the supply curve shown in Figure 3.5. A **supply curve** is a graph of the relationship between the prices in the supply schedule and the quantity supplied at those prices. As you can see in Figure 3.5, this relationship produces an upward-sloping curve. Sellers are more willing to supply the market when prices are high, because this higher price generates more profits for the business. The upward-sloping curve means that the slope of the supply curve is positive, which illustrates a direct (positive) relationship between the price and the quantity offered for sale. For instance, when the price of salmon increases from $10.00 per pound to $12.50 per pound, Pure Food Fish will increase the quantity it supplies to the market from 400 pounds to 500 pounds.

A **supply curve** is a graph of the relationship between the prices in the supply schedule and the quantity supplied at those prices.

Incentives

Market Supply

Market supply is the sum of the quantities supplied by each seller in the market at each price.

Sol Amon is not the only vendor selling fish at the Pike Place Market. The **market supply** is the sum of the quantities supplied by each seller in the market at each price. However, to make our analysis simpler, let's assume that

FIGURE 3.6

Calculating Market Supply

Market supply is calculated by adding together the quantity supplied by individual vendors. The total quantity supplied, shown in the last column of the table, is illustrated in the market supply graph below.

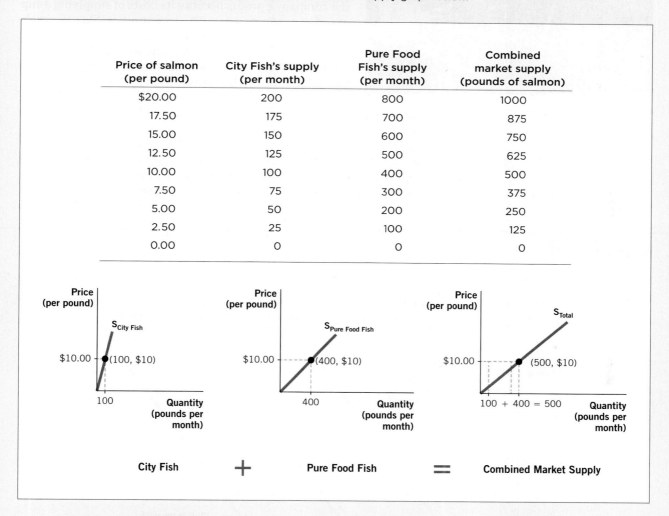

Price of salmon (per pound)	City Fish's supply (per month)	Pure Food Fish's supply (per month)	Combined market supply (pounds of salmon)
$20.00	200	800	1000
17.50	175	700	875
15.00	150	600	750
12.50	125	500	625
10.00	100	400	500
7.50	75	300	375
5.00	50	200	250
2.50	25	100	125
0.00	0	0	0

City Fish **+** Pure Food Fish **=** Combined Market Supply

our market consists of just two sellers, City Fish and Pure Food Fish, each of which sells salmon. Figure 3.6 shows supply schedules for those two fish sellers and the combined, total-market supply schedule and the corresponding graphs.

Looking at the supply schedule (the table within the figure), you can see that at a price of $10.00 per pound, City Fish supplies 100 pounds of salmon, while Pure Food Fish supplies 400 pounds. To determine the total market supply, we add City Fish's 100 pounds to Pure Food Fish's 400 pounds for a total market supply of 500 pounds.

The first Starbucks opened in 1971 in Pike Place Market.

Incentives

Shifts of the Supply Curve

When a variable other than the price changes, the entire supply curve shifts. For instance, suppose that beverage scientists at Starbucks discover a new way to brew a richer coffee at half the cost. The new process would increase the company's profits because its costs of supplying a cup of coffee would go down. The increased profits as a result of lower costs motivate Starbucks to sell more coffee and open new stores. Therefore, overall supply increases. Looking at Figure 3.7, we see that the supply curve shifts to the right of the original curve, from S_1 to S_2. Note that the retail price of coffee ($3 per cup) has not changed. When we shift the curve, we assume that price is constant and that something else has changed.

We have just seen that an increase in supply shifts the supply curve to the right. But what happens when a variable causes supply to decrease? Suppose that a hurricane devastates the coffee crop in Colombia and reduces the world coffee supply by 10% for that year. There is no way to make up for the destroyed

FIGURE 3.7

A Shift of the Supply Curve

When the price changes, the quantity supplied changes along the existing supply curve, illustrated here by the orange arrow. A shift in supply occurs when something other than price changes, illustrated by the black arrows.

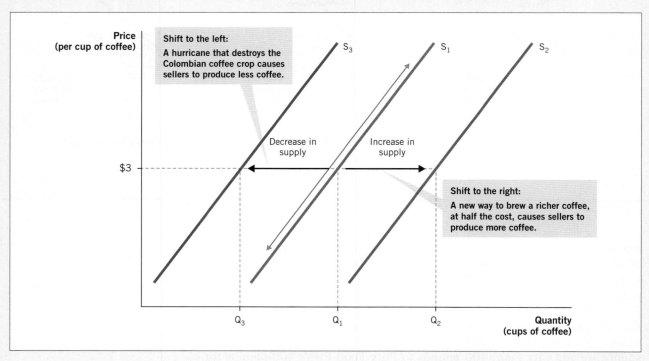

coffee crop, and for the rest of the year at least, the quantity of coffee supplied will be less than the previous year. This decrease in supply shifts the supply curve in Figure 3.7 to the left, from S_1 to S_3.

Many variables can shift supply, but Figure 3.7 also reminds us of what does *not* cause a shift in supply: the price. Recall that price is the variable that causes the supply curve to slope upward. The orange arrow alongside S_1 indicates that the quantity supplied will rise or fall in response to a price change. *A price change causes a movement along the supply curve, not a shift in the curve.*

Factors that shift the supply curve include the cost of inputs, changes in technology or the production process, taxes and subsidies, the number of firms in the industry, and price expectations. Figure 3.8 provides an overview of these variables that shift the supply curve. The easiest way to keep them straight is to ask yourself a simple question: Would the change cause a business to produce more of the good or less of the good? If the change would reduce the amount of a good or service a business is willing and able to supply at every given price, the supply curve shifts to the left. If the change would increase the amount of a good or service a business is willing and able to supply at every given price, the supply curve shifts to the right.

THE COST OF INPUTS **Inputs** are resources used in the production process. Inputs may include workers, equipment, raw materials, buildings, and capital goods. Each of these resources is critical to the production process.

Inputs
are resources used in the production process.

FIGURE 3.8

Factors That Shift the Supply Curve

The supply curve shifts to the left when a factor decreases supply. The supply curve shifts to the right when a factor increases supply. (*Note*: A change in price does not cause a shift. Price changes cause movements along the supply curve.)

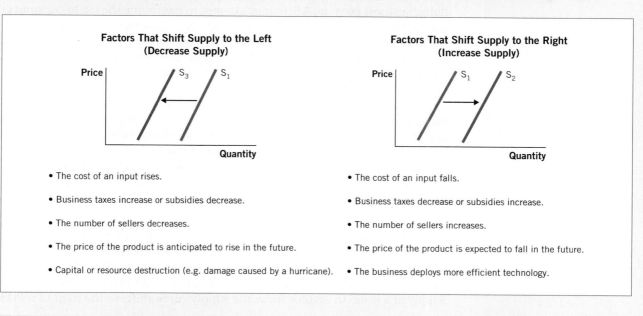

Factors That Shift Supply to the Left (Decrease Supply)

Price / Quantity — S_3, S_1

- The cost of an input rises.
- Business taxes increase or subsidies decrease.
- The number of sellers decreases.
- The price of the product is anticipated to rise in the future.
- Capital or resource destruction (e.g. damage caused by a hurricane).

Factors That Shift Supply to the Right (Increase Supply)

Price / Quantity — S_1, S_2

- The cost of an input falls.
- Business taxes decrease or subsidies increase.
- The number of sellers increases.
- The price of the product is expected to fall in the future.
- The business deploys more efficient technology.

Baristas' wages make up a large share of the cost of selling coffee.

When the cost of inputs change, so does the seller's profit. If the cost of inputs declines, profits improve. Improved profits make the firm more willing to supply the good. So, for example, if Starbucks is able to purchase coffee beans at a significantly reduced price, it will want to supply more coffee. Conversely, higher input costs reduce profits. For instance, at Starbucks, the salaries of Starbucks store employees (or baristas, as they are commonly called) are a large part of the production cost. An increase in the minimum wage would require Starbucks to pay its workers more. This higher minimum wage would raise the cost of making coffee and make Starbucks less willing to supply the same amount of coffee at the same price.

CHANGES IN TECHNOLOGY OR THE PRODUCTION PROCESS *Technology* encompasses knowledge that producers use to make their products. An improvement in technology enables a producer to increase output with the same resources or to produce a given level of output with fewer resources. For example, if a new espresso machine works twice as fast as the old machine, Starbucks could serve its customers more quickly, reduce long lines, and increase its sales. As a result, Starbucks would be willing to produce and sell more espressos at each price in its established menu. In other words, if the producers of a good discover a new and improved technology or a better production process, there will be an increase in supply. That is, the supply curve for the good will shift to the right.

TAXES AND SUBSIDIES Taxes placed on suppliers are an added cost of doing business. For example, if property taxes are increased, the cost of doing business goes up. A firm may attempt to pass along the tax to consumers through higher prices, but higher prices will discourage sales. So, in some cases, the firm will simply have to accept the taxes as an added cost of doing business. Either way, a tax makes the firm less profitable. Lower profits make the firm less willing to supply the product; thus, the supply curve shifts to the left and the overall supply declines.

The reverse is true for a subsidy. Consider a hypothetical example where the government wants to promote flu shots for high-risk groups like the young and the elderly. One approach would be to offer large subsidies to clinics and hospitals, thus offsetting those firms' costs of immunizing the targeted groups. The supply curve of immunizations greatly shifts to the right under the subsidy, so the price falls. As a result, vaccination rates increase over what they would be in a market without the subsidy.

THE NUMBER OF FIRMS IN THE INDUSTRY We saw that an increase in total buyers (population) shifts the demand curve to the right. A similar dynamic happens with an increase in the number of sellers in an industry. Each additional firm that enters the market increases the available supply of a good. In graphic form, the supply curve shifts to the right to reflect

WHY DO THE PRICES OF NEW ELECTRONICS ALWAYS DROP?

The first personal computers (PCs) released in the 1980s cost as much as $10,000. Today, you can purchase a laptop computer for less than $500. When a new technology emerges, prices are initially very high and then tend to fall rapidly. The first PCs profoundly changed the way people could work with information. Before the PC, complex programming could be done only on large mainframe computers that often took up an entire room. But at first only a few people could afford a PC. What makes emerging technology so expensive when it is first introduced and so inexpensive later in its life cycle? Supply tells the story. Advances in manufacturing methods lead to an increased willingness to supply, and therefore the supply curve shifts out. When the supply expands, there is both an increase in the quantity sold and a lower price.

Technological progress is also driving newer markets, like the market for custom shoes. 3D printing makes it possible for anyone go online, or enter information at a kiosk in a store, and order shoes that are 100% customized. You can design the uppers, insoles, and tread however you like, and in about an hour, your shoes will be printed for you. If your two feet are slightly different sizes, you will get two different-size insoles, to match your feet perfectly! Fully customized 3D printed shoes are still pretty pricey (about $300), but the price is dropping rapidly as the process becomes more efficient and designers build templates that make it easier for customers to get exactly what they want. As the technology continues to improve, the supply curve will continue to shift out. With time, customized shoes may eventually become so cheap that almost everyone will be able to afford them easily—just like computers today!

Why did consumers pay $5,000 for this?

the increased production. By the same reasoning, if the number of firms in the industry decreases, the supply curve shifts to the left.

Changes in the number of firms in a market are a regular part of business. For example, if a new pizza joint opens up nearby, more pizzas can be produced and supply expands. Conversely, if a pizzeria closes, the number of pizzas produced falls and supply contracts.

PRICE EXPECTATIONS A seller who expects a higher price for a product in the future may wish to delay sales until a time when the product will bring a higher price. For instance, florists know that the demand for roses spikes on Valentine's Day and Mother's Day. Because of higher demand, they can charge higher prices. To be able to sell more flowers during the times of peak demand, many florists work longer hours and hire temporary employees. These actions allow them to make more deliveries, so supply increases.

Likewise, the expectation of lower prices in the future will cause sellers to offer more while prices are still relatively high. This effect is particularly noticeable in the electronics sector, where newer—and much better—products are constantly being developed and released. Sellers know that their current offerings will soon be replaced by something better and that consumer demand for the existing technology will then plummet. This means that prices typically fall when a product has been on the market for a time. Because producers know that the price will fall, they supply as many of the current models as possible before the next wave of innovation cuts the price they can charge.

PRACTICE WHAT YOU KNOW

Ice Cream: Supply and Demand

I scream, you scream, we all scream for ice cream.

QUESTION: Which one of the following will increase the demand for ice cream?

a. a decrease in the price of the butterfat used to make ice cream

b. a decrease in the price of ice cream

c. an increase in the price of the milk used to make ice cream

d. an increase in the price of frozen yogurt, a substitute for ice cream

ANSWER: If you answered b, you made a common mistake. A change in the price of a good cannot change overall market demand; it can only cause a movement along an existing curve. So, as important as price changes are, they are not the right answer. Instead, you need to look for an event that shifts the entire curve.

Choices a and c refer to the prices of butterfat and milk. Because these are the inputs of production for ice cream, a change in their prices will shift the supply curve, not the demand curve. That leaves choice d as the only possibility. Choice d is correct because the increase in the price of frozen yogurt will cause consumers to substitute away from frozen yogurt and toward ice cream. This shift in consumer behavior will result in an increase in the demand for ice cream even though its price remains the same.

QUESTION: Which one of the following will decrease the supply of chocolate ice cream?

a. a medical report finding that consuming chocolate prevents cancer

b. a decrease in the price of chocolate ice cream

c. an increase in the price of chocolate, an ingredient used to make chocolate ice cream

d. an increase in the price of whipped cream, a complementary good

ANSWER: We know that b cannot be the correct answer because a change in the price of the good cannot change supply; it can only cause a movement along an existing curve. Choices a and d would both cause a change in demand without affecting the supply curve. That leaves choice c as the only possibility. Chocolate is a necessary ingredient in the production process. Whenever the price of an input rises, profits are squeezed. The result is a decrease in supply at the existing price.

How Do Supply and Demand Interact to Create Equilibrium?

We have examined supply and demand separately. Now it is time to see how the two interact. The real power of supply and demand analysis is in how well it predicts prices and output in the entire market.

Supply, Demand, and Equilibrium

Let's consider the market for salmon again. This example meets the conditions for a competitive market because the salmon sold by one vendor is essentially the same as the salmon sold by another, and there are many individual buyers.

In Figure 3.9, we see that when the price of salmon fillets is $10 per pound, consumers demand 500 pounds and producers supply 500 pounds. This situation is represented graphically at point E, known as the point of **equilibrium**, where the demand curve and the supply curve intersect. At this point, the two opposing forces of supply and demand are perfectly balanced.

Notice that at $10 per pound, the quantity demanded equals the quantity supplied. At this price, and only this price, the entire supply of salmon in the market is sold. Moreover, every buyer who wants salmon is able to find some and every producer is able to sell his or her entire stock. We say that $10 is the **equilibrium price** because the quantity supplied equals the quantity demanded. The equilibrium price is also called the *market-clearing price*, because this is the only price at which no surplus or shortage of the good exists. Similarly, there is also an **equilibrium quantity** at which the quantity supplied equals the quantity demanded (in this example, 500 pounds). When the market is in equilibrium, we sometimes say that *the market clears* or that *the price clears the market*.

The equilibrium point has a special place in economics because movements away from that point throw the market out of balance. The equilibrium process is so powerful that it is often referred to as the **law of supply and demand**, the idea that market prices adjust to bring the quantity supplied and the quantity demanded into balance.

Equilibrium occurs at the point where the demand curve and the supply curve intersect.

The **equilibrium price** is the price at which the quantity supplied is equal to the quantity demanded. It is also known as the *market-clearing price.*

The **equilibrium quantity** is the amount at which the quantity supplied is equal to the quantity demanded.

The **law of supply and demand** states that the market price of any good will adjust to bring the quantity supplied and the quantity demanded into balance.

FIGURE 3.9

The Salmon Market

At the equilibrium point, E, quantity supplied and quantity demanded are perfectly balanced. At prices above the equilibrium price, a surplus exists. At prices below the equilibrium price, a shortage exists.

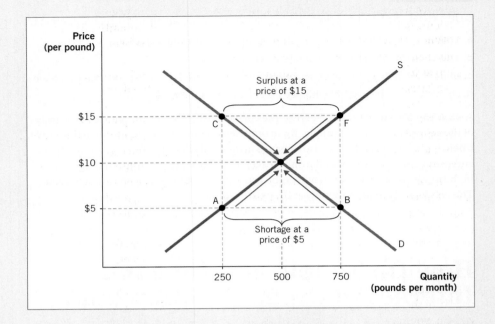

SHORTAGES AND SURPLUSES How does the market respond when it is not in equilibrium? Let's look at two other prices for salmon shown on the *y* axis in Figure 3.9: $5 per pound and $15 per pound.

At a price of $5 per pound, salmon is quite attractive to buyers but not very profitable to sellers. The quantity demanded is 750 pounds, represented by point B on the demand curve (D). However, the quantity supplied, which is represented by point A on the supply curve (S), is only 250 pounds. So at $5 per pound there is an excess quantity of 750 − 250 = 500 pounds demanded. This excess demand creates disequilibrium in the market.

When there is more demand for a product than sellers are willing or able to supply, we say there is a shortage. A **shortage**, or *excess demand*, occurs whenever the quantity supplied is less than the quantity demanded. In our case, at a price of $5 per pound of salmon, there are three buyers for each pound. New shipments of salmon fly out the door, providing a strong signal for sellers to raise the price. As the market price increases in response to the shortage, sellers continue to increase the quantity they offer. You can see the increase in quantity supplied on the graph in Figure 3.9 by following the upward-sloping arrow from point A to point E. At the same time, as the price rises, buyers demand an increasingly smaller quantity, represented by the arrow from point B to point E along the demand curve. Eventually, when the price reaches $10 per pound, the quantity supplied and the quantity demanded are equal. The market is in equilibrium.

What happens when the price is set above the equilibrium point—say, at $15 per pound? At this price, salmon is quite profitable for sellers but not very attractive to buyers. The quantity demanded, represented by point C on the demand curve, is 250 pounds. However, the quantity supplied, represented by point F on the supply curve, is 750 pounds. In other words, sellers provide 500 pounds more than buyers wish to purchase. This excess supply creates disequilibrium in the

A **shortage** occurs whenever the quantity supplied is less than the quantity demanded. A shortage is also called *excess demand*.

market. Any buyer who is willing to pay $15 for a pound of salmon can find some because there are 3 pounds available for every customer. A **surplus**, or *excess supply*, occurs whenever the quantity supplied is greater than the quantity demanded.

When there is a surplus, sellers realize that salmon has been oversupplied, giving them a strong signal to lower the price. As the market price decreases in response to the surplus, more buyers enter the market and purchase salmon. Figure 3.9 represents this situation on the demand side by the downward-sloping arrow moving from point C to point E along the demand curve. At the same time, sellers reduce output, represented by the arrow moving from point F to point E on the supply curve. As long as the surplus persists, the price will continue to fall. Eventually, the price reaches $10 per pound. At this point, the quantity supplied and the quantity demanded are equal and the market is in equilibrium again.

In competitive markets, surpluses and shortages are resolved through the process of price adjustment. Buyers who are unable to find enough salmon at $5 per pound compete to find the available stocks; this competition drives the price up. Likewise, businesses that cannot sell their product at $15 per pound must lower their prices to reduce inventories; this desire to sell all inventory drives the price down.

Every seller and buyer has a vital role to play in the market. Venues like the Pike Place Market bring buyers and sellers together. Amazingly, market equilibrium occurs without the need for government planning to ensure an adequate supply of the goods consumers want or need. You might think that a decentralized system would create chaos, but nothing could be further from the truth. Markets work because buyers and sellers can rapidly adjust to changes in prices. These adjustments bring balance. When markets were suppressed in communist countries during the twentieth century, shortages were commonplace, in part because there was no market price system to signal that additional production was needed.

In summary, Figure 3.10 provides four examples of what happens when either the supply curve or the demand curve shifts. As you study these examples, you should develop a sense for how price and quantity are affected by changes in supply and demand. When one curve shifts, we can make a definitive statement about how price and quantity will change.

In Appendix 3A, we consider what happens when supply and demand change at the same time. There you will discover the challenges in simultaneously determining price and quantity when more than one variable changes.

PRACTICE WHAT YOU KNOW

Bacon: Supply and Demand

QUESTION: Suppose that the government decides to subsidize bacon producers. What is the impact on the equilibrium market price and output?

ANSWER: In order to answer this question, you first need to determine whether the supply curve or the demand curve shifts in response to the subsidy. Since the subsidy is given to the bacon producers, the supply curve shifts out. The end result is that the market price falls to P_2 and the market output increases to Q_2.

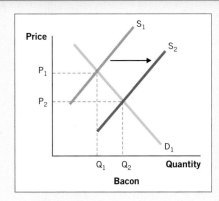

CHALLENGE QUESTION: Is the statement in the meme true or false?

ANSWER: By now you should know that a price decrease causes a change in the quantity demanded, not a change in demand. Therefore, you might be tempted to judge the meme false. But if you did, you would be wrong! Let's see why. The first step is recognizing that bacon and eggs are complements. Therefore, a reduction in the price of the one increases the demand for the other. Recall that a reduction in the price of a complementary good shifts the demand curve to the right. The second step is to look at this graphically (see the graphs below). Using the color-coded letters, we see that (B_1) the price drop on bacon causes an increase in the quantity demanded of bacon (a slide along the existing demand curve) and (E_2) since consumers buy more bacon than before, this increases the demand for eggs (demand shifts to the right) in the egg market. At the same time, (E_1) the price drop on eggs causes an increase in the quantity demanded of eggs (a slide along the existing demand curve) and (B_2) since consumers buy more eggs than before, this increases the demand for bacon (demand shifts to the right) in the bacon market. We model this by showing the two related markets, bacon and eggs, side by side so you can see how a price reduction of the related goods increases the "demand for each other." Since both curves shift out, the meme is true!

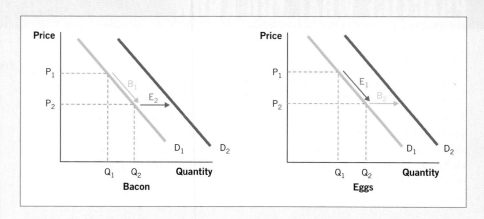

FIGURE 3.10

Price and Quantity When Either Supply or Demand Changes

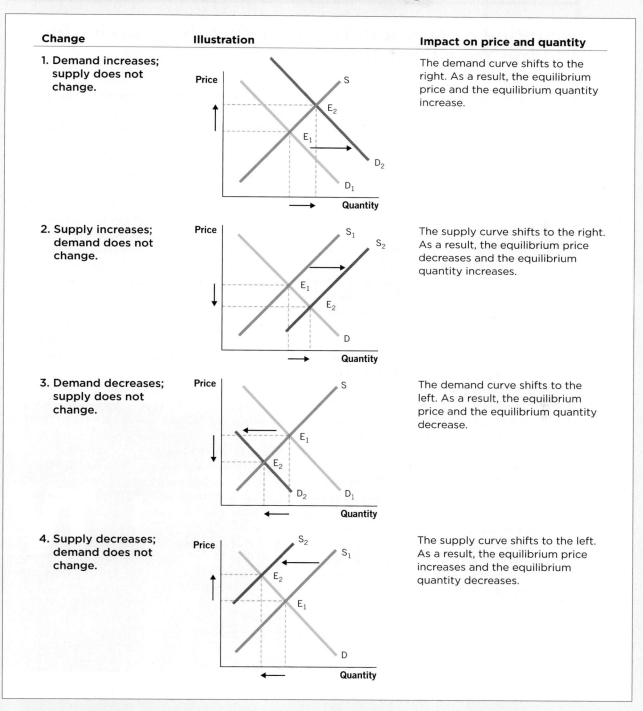

Change	Illustration	Impact on price and quantity
1. Demand increases; supply does not change.		The demand curve shifts to the right. As a result, the equilibrium price and the equilibrium quantity increase.
2. Supply increases; demand does not change.		The supply curve shifts to the right. As a result, the equilibrium price decreases and the equilibrium quantity increases.
3. Demand decreases; supply does not change.		The demand curve shifts to the left. As a result, the equilibrium price and the equilibrium quantity decrease.
4. Supply decreases; demand does not change.		The supply curve shifts to the left. As a result, the equilibrium price increases and the equilibrium quantity decreases.

Bringing Supply and Demand Together: Advice for Buying Your First Home

- The first rule of real estate is, "location, location, location."
- Consider the school district, even if you don't have children, because properties in better districts command higher prices.
- A home along a busy street may sell for half the price of a similar property a few blocks away that backs up to a quiet park.

There are a number of popular HGTV shows, such as *Flip or Flop*, *Property Brothers*, *Love It or List It*, and *House Hunters*, that help viewers become better informed about the process of buying a home. If you have seen any of these shows, or almost any show on HGTV involving buying or fixing up a property, you know that watching an episode is one of the best lessons in economics you will ever get.

One real estate adage you're eventually bound to pick up, if you watch one of these shows long enough, is "location, location, location." Why does location matter so much? Simple. Supply and demand. There are only so many places to live in any given location—that is the supply. The most desirable locations have many buyers who'd like to purchase in that area—that is the demand.

Consider for a moment all of the variables that can influence where you want to live. As you're shopping for your new home, you may want to consider proximity to where you work and your favorite restaurants, public transportation, and the quality of the schools. You'll also want to pay attention to the crime rate, differences in local tax rates, traffic concerns, noise issues, and zoning restrictions. In addition, many communities have *restrictive covenants* that limit how owners can use their property. Smart buyers determine how the covenants work and whether they would be happy to give up some freedom in order to maintain an attractive neighborhood. Finally, it is always a good idea to visit the neighborhood in the evening or on the weekend to meet your future neighbors before you buy. All of these variables determine the demand for any given property.

Once you've done your homework and settled on a neighborhood, you will find that property values can vary tremendously across very short distances. A home along a busy street may sell for half the price of a similar property a few blocks away that backs up to a quiet park. Properties near a subway line command a premium, as do properties with views or close access to major employers and amenities (such as parks, shopping centers, and places to eat). Here is the main point to remember, even if some of these things aren't important to you: when it comes time to sell, the location of the home will always matter. The number of potential buyers depends on the characteristics of your neighborhood and the size and condition of

your property. If you want to be able to sell your home easily, you'll have to consider not only where you want to live now but who might want to live there in the future.

All of this discussion brings us back to supply and demand. The best locations are in short supply and high demand. The combination of low supply and high demand causes property values in those areas to rise. Likewise, less desirable locations have lower property values because demand is relatively low and the supply is relatively high. Because first-time buyers often have wish lists that far exceed their budgets, considering the costs and benefits will help you find the best available property.

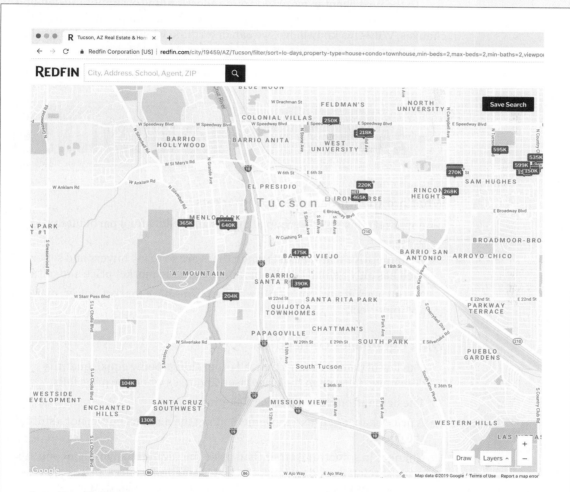

Location Matters
This graphic shows listings for prices of 2-bedroom, 2-bath houses on the market in Tucson, AZ. Prices range from $104–640K. What are some rules of thumb to remember?

Conclusion

Five years from now, if someone asks you what you remember about your first course in economics, you will probably respond with two words: "supply" and "demand." These two forces allow us to model market behavior through prices. Supply and demand help establish the market equilibrium, or the price at which quantity supplied and quantity demanded are in balance. At the equilibrium point, every good and service produced has a corresponding buyer who wants to purchase it. When the market is out of equilibrium, either a shortage or surplus exists. This condition persists until buyers and sellers have a chance to adjust the quantity they demand and the quantity they supply, respectively.

In the next chapter, we extend our understanding of supply and demand by examining how sensitive, or responsive, consumers and producers are to price changes. With this knowledge, we can determine whether price changes have a big effect on behavior or not. ✳

- ANSWERING *the* BIG QUESTIONS -

What are the fundamentals of markets?

- A market consists of a group of buyers and sellers for a particular product or service.
- A competitive market exists when there are so many buyers and sellers that each has only a small (negligible) impact on the market price and output.
- Not all markets are competitive. When firms have market power, markets are imperfect.

What determines demand?

- The law of demand states that, all other things being equal, quantity demanded falls when the price rises, and rises when the price falls.
- The demand curve is downward sloping.
- A price change causes a movement along the demand curve, not a shift of the curve.
- Changes in something other than price (including changes in income, the price of related goods, changes in tastes and preferences, price expectations, the number of buyers, and taxes) shift the demand curve.

What determines supply?

- The law of supply states that, all other things being equal, the quantity supplied of a good rises when the price of the good rises, and falls when the price of the good falls.

- The supply curve is upward sloping.
- A price change causes a movement along the supply curve, not a shift of the curve.
- Changes in something other than price (the cost of inputs, changes in technology or the production process, taxes and subsidies, the number of firms in the industry, and price expectations) shift the original supply curve.

How do supply and demand interact to create equilibrium?

- Supply and demand work together in a market-clearing process that leads to equilibrium, the balancing point between the two forces. The market-clearing price and output are determined at the equilibrium point.
- When the price is above the equilibrium point, a surplus exists and inventories build up. Suppliers lower their price in an effort to sell the unwanted goods. The process continues until the equilibrium price is reached.
- When the price is below the equilibrium point, a shortage exists and inventories are depleted. Suppliers raise the price until the equilibrium point is reached.

▪ CHAPTER PROBLEMS ▪

Concepts You Should Know

competitive market (p. 75)
complements (p. 83)
demand curve (p. 78)
demand schedule (p. 77)
equilibrium (p. 95)
equilibrium price (p. 95)
equilibrium quantity (p. 95)
imperfect market (p. 76)
inferior good (p. 82)
inputs (p. 91)

invisible hand (p. 74)
law of demand (p. 77)
law of supply (p. 87)
law of supply and
  demand (p. 95)
market demand (p. 79)
market economy (p. 74)
market power (p. 76)
market supply (p. 88)
monopoly (p. 76)

normal good (p. 82)
purchasing power (p. 82)
quantity demanded (p. 76)
quantity supplied (p. 87)
shortage (p. 96)
subsidy (p. 86)
substitutes (p. 83)
supply curve (p. 88)
supply schedule (p. 87)
surplus (p. 97)

Questions for Review

1. What is a competitive market, and why does it depend on the existence of many buyers and sellers?

2. Why does the demand curve slope downward?

3. Does a price change cause a movement along a demand curve or a shift of the entire curve? What factors cause the entire demand curve to shift?

4. Describe the difference between inferior goods and normal goods. Give an example of each type of good.

5. Why does the supply curve slope upward?

6. Does a price change cause a movement along a supply curve or a shift of the entire curve? What factors cause the entire supply curve to shift?

7. Describe the process that leads a market toward equilibrium.

8. What happens in a competitive market when the price is above the equilibrium price? Below the equilibrium price?

9. What roles do shortages and surpluses play in the market?

Study Problems (∗ solved at the end of the section)

1. In the song "Money, Money, Money" by ABBA, one of the lead singers, Anni-Frid Lyngstad, is tired of the hard work that life requires and plans to marry a wealthy man. If she is successful, how will this marriage change her demand for goods? How will it change her supply of labor? Illustrate both changes with supply and demand curves. Be sure to explain what is happening in the diagrams. (*Note*: The full lyrics for the song can be found by Googling the song title and ABBA. For inspiration, try listening to the song while you solve the problem.)

2. For each of the following scenarios, determine if there is an increase or a decrease in demand for the good in *italics*.

   a. The price of *oranges* increases.
   b. The cost of producing *tires* increases.

   c. Samantha Brown, who is crazy about *air travel*, gets fired from her job.
   d. A local community has an unusually wet spring and a subsequent problem with mosquitoes, which can be deterred with *citronella*.
   e. Many motorcycle enthusiasts enjoy riding without *helmets* (in states where this is not prohibited by law). The price of new motorcycles rises.

3. For each of the following scenarios, determine if there is an increase or a decrease in supply for the good in *italics*.

   a. The price of *silver* increases.
   b. Growers of *tomatoes* experience an unusually good growing season.

c. New medical evidence reports that consumption of *organic products* reduces the incidence of cancer.

d. The wages of low-skilled workers, a resource used to help produce *clothing*, increase.

e. The price of movie tickets, a substitute for *Netflix video rentals*, goes up.

4. Are laser pointers and cats complements or substitutes? (Not sure? Search for videos of cats and laser pointers online.) Discuss.

✳ **5.** The market for ice cream has the following demand and supply schedules:

Price (per quart)	Quantity demanded (quarts)	Quantity supplied (quarts)
$2	100	20
3	80	40
4	60	60
5	40	80
6	20	100

a. What are the equilibrium price and equilibrium quantity in the ice cream market? Confirm your answer by graphing the demand and supply curves.

b. If the actual price is $3 per quart, what would drive the market toward equilibrium?

6. Starbucks Entertainment announced in a 2007 news release that Dave Matthews Band's *Live Trax* CD was available only at the company's coffee shops in the United States and Canada. The compilation features recordings of the band's performances dating back to 1995. Why would Starbucks and Dave Matthews have agreed to partner in this way? To come up with an answer, think about the nature of complementary goods and how both sides can benefit from this arrangement.

7. The Seattle Mariners baseball team wishes to determine the equilibrium price for seats for each of the next two seasons. The supply of seats at the ballpark is fixed at 45,000.

Price (per seat)	Quantity demanded in year 1	Quantity demanded in year 2	Quantity supplied
$25	75,000	60,000	45,000
30	60,000	55,000	45,000
35	45,000	50,000	45,000
40	30,000	45,000	45,000
45	15,000	40,000	45,000

Draw the supply curve and each of the demand curves for years 1 and 2.

✳ **8.** Demand and supply curves can also be represented with equations. Suppose that the quantity demanded, Q_D, is represented by the following equation:

$$Q_D = 90 - 2P$$

The quantity supplied, Q_S, is represented by the equation

$$Q_S = P$$

a. Find the equilibrium price and quantity. (**Hint:** Set $Q_D = Q_S$ and solve for the price, P, and then plug your result back into either of the original equations to find Q.)

b. Suppose that the price is $20. Determine Q_D and Q_S.

c. At a price of $20, is there a surplus or a shortage in the market?

d. Given your answer in part (c), will the price rise or fall in order to find the equilibrium point?

✳ **9.** Let's take a look at two real-world episodes in the market for gasoline and try to figure out why the price fluctuates so much.

a. In the summer of 2008, the price of regular gasoline in the United States soared to over $4 per gallon. Then, in the fall of that year, the U.S. economy fell into a deep recession that significantly reduced consumers' income. Use the supply and demand model to determine which curve shifted and what happened to the equilibrium price of gasoline. For this part of the question, assume no other changes in the market for gasoline.

b. By the summer of 2014, the price of regular gasoline in the United States was hovering around $3.50 per gallon. But innovations in oil extraction technology, such as hydraulic fracking, reduced the price of crude oil significantly. Crude oil is the primary input for gasoline production. Use the supply and demand model to determine which curve shifted and then what happened to the equilibrium price of gasoline. For this part of the question, assume no other changes in the market for gasoline.

✱ **10.** If the price of alcohol decreases, what happens to the demand for red Solo (plastic) cups?

11. Consider the market for the Samsung Galaxy S9.

   a. Scenario 1: Using a supply and demand graph, show what will happen to the current equilibrium price and quantity of Galaxy S9s

if people expect the price of S9s to fall in the future.

   b. Scenario 2: Now, using a second supply and demand graph, show instead what will happen to the equilibrium price and quantity of S9s if the price of the iPhone X falls. In answering your question, assume that the S9 and iPhone X are substitutes in consumption.

   c. Scenario 3: You observe that the price of S9s increases. Can you definitively conclude that there has been an increase in demand? If not, what besides an increase in demand could explain the price increase?

✱ **12.** One of the responses completes this list of things that shift the supply curve: technology, expectations, the number of sellers, and _____. Identify the correct answer and also explain why the other three responses are incorrect.

   a. the price of related goods
   b. income
   c. the cost of inputs
   d. the price

Solved Problems

5a. The equilibrium price is $4, and the equilibrium quantity is 60 quarts. The next step is to graph the curves, as shown here.

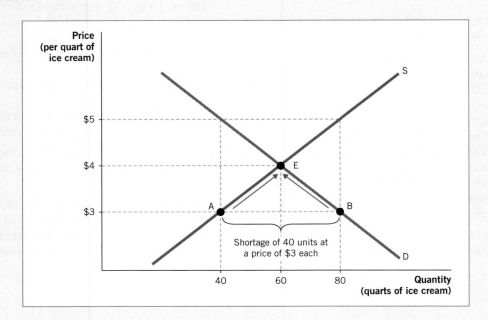

b. A shortage of 40 quarts of ice cream exists at $3 (quantity demanded is 80 and the quantity supplied is 40); therefore, there is excess demand. Ice cream sellers will raise their price as long as excess demand exists—that is, as long as the price is below $4. It is not until $4 that the equilibrium point is reached and the shortage is resolved.

8.a. The first step is to set $Q_D = Q_S$. Doing so gives us $90 - 2P = P$. Solving for price, we find that $90 = 3P$, or $P = 30$. Once we know that $P = 30$, we can plug this value back into either of the original equations, $Q_D = 90 - 2P$ or $Q_S = P$. Beginning with Q_D, we get $90 - 2(30) = 90 - 60 = 30$, or we can plug it into $Q_S = P$, so $Q_S = 30$. Because we get a quantity of 30 for both Q_D and Q_S, we know that the price of $30 is correct.

b. In this part, we plug $20 into Q_D. Doing so yields $90 - 2(20) = 50$. Now we plug $20 into Q_S. Doing so yields 20.

c. Because $Q_D = 50$ and $Q_S = 20$, there is a shortage of 30 quarts.

d. Whenever there is a shortage of a good, the price will rise in order to find the equilibrium point.

9a. The reduction in consumer income led to a negative, or leftward, shift in the demand curve for gasoline. Because this is the only change, the equilibrium price of gasoline fell. In fact, by the end of 2008, the price of gasoline had fallen to under $2 per gallon in the United States.

b. The significant drop in the cost of production led to a large increase, or rightward, shift in the supply of gasoline. This increase in supply led to a decrease in price. In fact, by early 2015, the average price of a gallon of regular gasoline in the United States fell to under $2 per gallon.

Looking at parts (a) and (b) together, you can see that very different causes led to steep drops in the price of gasoline. In 2008 the cause was a decline in demand; in 2014 it was an increase in supply.

10. Because alcohol and Solo cups are complements, the key here is to recall that a change in the price of a complementary good shifts the demand curve for the related good. Lower alcohol prices will cause consumers to purchase more alcohol and therefore demand more Solo cups. In other words, the entire demand curve for Solo cups shifts to the right.

12a. The price of related goods is a demand shifter so, it is incorrect.

b. Income is a demand shifter so, it is incorrect.

c. The cost of inputs is a supply shifter so, it is correct.

d. The price causes a movement along the supply curve so, it is incorrect.

03A

Changes in Both Demand and Supply

We have considered what would happen if supply *or* demand changes. But life is often more complex than that. To provide a more realistic analysis, we need to examine what happens when supply and demand both shift at the same time.

Suppose that a major drought hits the northwestern United States. The water shortage reduces both the amount of farmed salmon and the ability of wild salmon to spawn in streams and rivers. Figure 3A.1a shows the ensuing decline in the salmon supply, from S_1 progressively leftward, represented by the dotted supply curves. At the same time, a medical journal reports that people who consume at least 4 pounds of salmon a month live five years longer than those who consume an equal amount of cod. Figure 3A.1b shows the ensuing rise in the demand for salmon, from D_1 progressively rightward, represented by the dotted demand curves. This scenario leads to a twofold change. Because of the water shortage, the supply of salmon shrinks. At the same time, new information about the health benefits of eating salmon causes demand for salmon to increase.

It is impossible to predict exactly what happens to the equilibrium point when both supply and demand are shifting. We can, however, determine a region where the resulting equilibrium point must reside.

In this situation, we have a simultaneous decrease in supply and increase in demand. Since we do not know the magnitude of the supply reduction or demand increase, the overall effect on the equilibrium quantity cannot be determined. This result is evident in Figure 3A.1c, as illustrated by the purple region. The points where supply and demand cross within this area represent the set of possible new market equilibria. Because each of the possible points of intersection in the purple region occurs at a price greater than $10 per pound, we know that the price must rise. However, the left half of the purple region produces equilibrium quantities that are lower than 500 pounds of salmon, while the right half of the purple region results in equilibrium quantities that are greater than 500. Therefore, the equilibrium quantity may rise, fall, or stay the same if both shifts are of equal magnitudes.

The world we live in is complex, and often more than one variable will change simultaneously. In such cases, it is not possible to be as definitive as when only one variable—supply or demand—changes. You should think of the new equilibrium not as a single point but as a range of outcomes represented by the purple area in Figure 3A.1c. Therefore, we cannot be exactly sure at what point the new price *and* new quantity will settle. For a closer look at four possibilities, see Figure 3A.2, where E_1 equals the original equilibrium point and the new equilibrium (E_2) lies somewhere in the purple region.

A Shift in Supply and Demand

When supply and demand both shift, the resulting equilibrium can no longer be identified as an exact point. We can see this effect in (c), which combines the supply shift in (a) with the demand shift in (b). When supply decreases and demand increases, the result is that the price must rise, but the equilibrium quantity can either rise or fall, or stay the same if both shifts are of equal magnitudes.

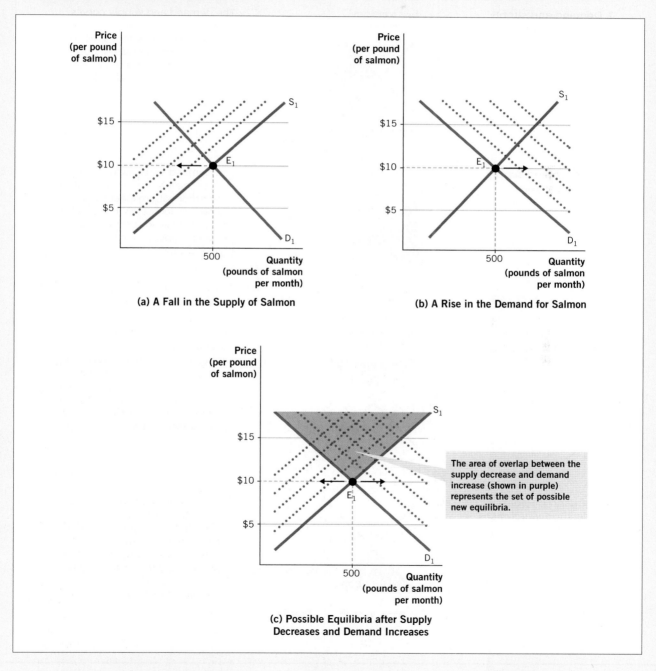

(a) A Fall in the Supply of Salmon

(b) A Rise in the Demand for Salmon

The area of overlap between the supply decrease and demand increase (shown in purple) represents the set of possible new equilibria.

(c) Possible Equilibria after Supply Decreases and Demand Increases

Price and Quantity When Demand and Supply Both Change

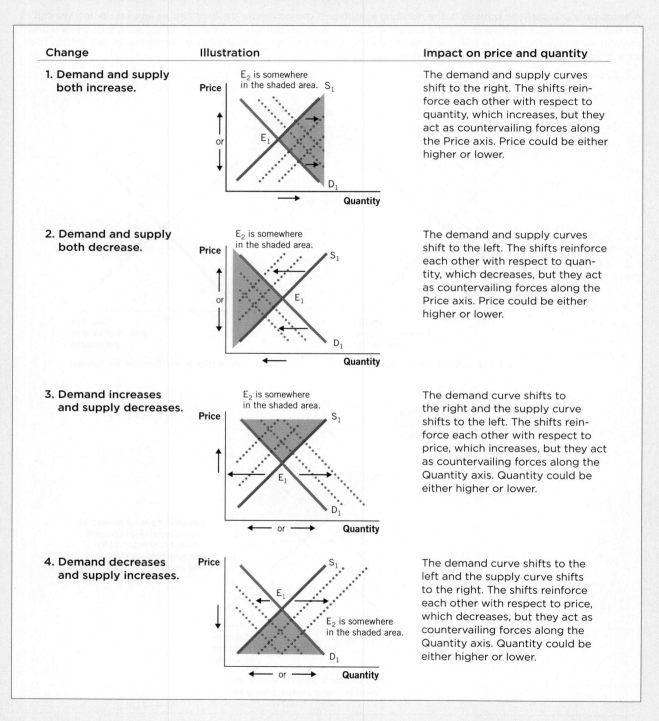

Change	Illustration	Impact on price and quantity
1. Demand and supply both increase.	E_2 is somewhere in the shaded area.	The demand and supply curves shift to the right. The shifts reinforce each other with respect to quantity, which increases, but they act as countervailing forces along the Price axis. Price could be either higher or lower.
2. Demand and supply both decrease.	E_2 is somewhere in the shaded area.	The demand and supply curves shift to the left. The shifts reinforce each other with respect to quantity, which decreases, but they act as countervailing forces along the Price axis. Price could be either higher or lower.
3. Demand increases and supply decreases.	E_2 is somewhere in the shaded area.	The demand curve shifts to the right and the supply curve shifts to the left. The shifts reinforce each other with respect to price, which increases, but they act as countervailing forces along the Quantity axis. Quantity could be either higher or lower.
4. Demand decreases and supply increases.	E_2 is somewhere in the shaded area.	The demand curve shifts to the left and the supply curve shifts to the right. The shifts reinforce each other with respect to price, which decreases, but they act as countervailing forces along the Quantity axis. Quantity could be either higher or lower.

When Supply and Demand Both Change: Hybrid Cars

QUESTION: At lunch, two friends are engaged in a heated argument. Their exchange goes like this:

The first friend begins, "The supply of hybrid cars and the demand for hybrid cars will both increase. I'm sure of it. I'm also sure the price of hybrids will go down."

The second friend replies, "I agree with the first part of your statement, but I'm not sure about the price. In fact, I'm pretty sure that hybrid prices will rise."

They go back and forth endlessly, each unable to convince the other, so they turn to you for advice. What do you say to them?

ANSWER: Either of your friends could be correct. In this case, supply and demand both shift out to the right, so we know that the quantity bought and sold will increase. However, an increase in supply would normally lower the price, and an increase in demand would typically raise the price. Without knowing which of these two effects on price is stronger, you can't predict how price will change. The overall price will rise if the increase in demand is larger than the increase in supply. However, if the increase in supply is larger than the increase in demand, prices will fall. But your two friends don't know which condition will be true—so they're locked in an argument that neither can win! As an aside, Tesla came out with their priciest model first, then their midrange model, and they're now trying to roll out the model for the masses, which suggests that they are betting on hybrid prices going down over time.

Hybrid cars are becoming increasingly common.

POLAR VORTEX ECONOMICS

Every few years, the jet stream buckles and the polar vortex drops into the eastern United States. When the vortex descends, temperatures plummet, the demand for propane skyrockets, and supplies of propane are tight. The economic effects of the polar vortex provide a textbook example of a positive demand shock and negative supply shock (a "shock" is an unexpected event) hitting at the same time. Let's consider the effects of the polar vortex that hit the United States in the winter of 2013–2014.

First, the positive demand shock. It is easy to understand. Bitter cold dramatically increases (that's why we say "positive") the demand for propane, because much more propane than usual is needed to heat homes.

Second, the negative supply shock. There are actually two negative shocks. It turns out that farmers used more propane than usual in the fall of 2013 to dry out their grain crops, thus lowering (that's why we say "negative") supplies of propane for heating homes. Then, during the first cold snap, pipelines across the Midwest froze, disrupting the delivery of propane to holding tanks and then to homes. The frozen pipes were the second negative supply shock.

Third, the complication. Because of the booming supply of natural gas (propane is made from natural gas) in the United States, the price had dropped so low (again, basic supply and demand at work) that very large quantities of propane were exported to markets where suppliers could get a higher price. The supplies that were exported out of the country could have been used in the United States in the winter of 2013–2014, but because they were not here, the shortage was exacerbated.

Incentives

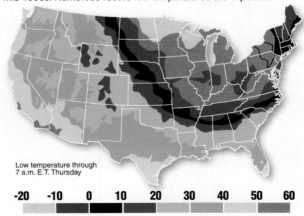

Bitter cold to continue all week

The unusually cold weather is forecast to continue through much of the week for the eastern U.S. Some places from the Carolinas to the Mid-Atlantic may see some of the coldest weather since the mid-1990s. Numerous record low temperatures are expected.

Low temperature through
7 a.m. E.T. Thursday

-20   -10   0   10   20   30   40   50   60

Source: NOAA
Graphic: Tribune News Service

The polar vortex is coming. Do you have enough propane?

▪ APPENDIX PROBLEMS ▪

Questions for Review

1. What happens to price and quantity when supply and demand change at the same time?

2. Is there more than one potential equilibrium point when supply and demand change at the same time? Explain.

Study Problems (✱ *solved at the end of the section*)

✱ **1.** Assume that, over time, consumer incomes generally increase but also that technological advancements in oil extraction lead to lower prices of crude oil (the primary input for gasoline).

   a. If consumer incomes increase by significantly more than input prices fall, what happens to both the price and quantity of gasoline?

   b. If, instead, consumer incomes increase relatively less than input prices fall, what happens to the price and quantity of gasoline?

2. Every Valentine's Day, the price of roses spikes. Using your understanding of the factors that shift both demand and supply, draw the equilibrium in the rose market on January 31 and then draw the new equilibrium that occurs on February 14.

Solved Problem

1a. The increase in consumer income increases demand and shifts the demand curve to the right. The decrease in input prices increases supply and shifts the supply curve to the right. Equilibrium quantity unequivocally increases. The demand shift is relatively larger, so price also increases.

   b. Again, we see that the increase in consumer income increases demand and shifts the demand

curve to the right; and the decrease in input prices increases supply and shifts the supply curve to the right. Equilibrium quantity increases. But in this question, the demand shift is relatively smaller, so price falls. This example provides a good description of events in the gasoline market at the end of 2014, when price was falling even though consumer incomes were rising.

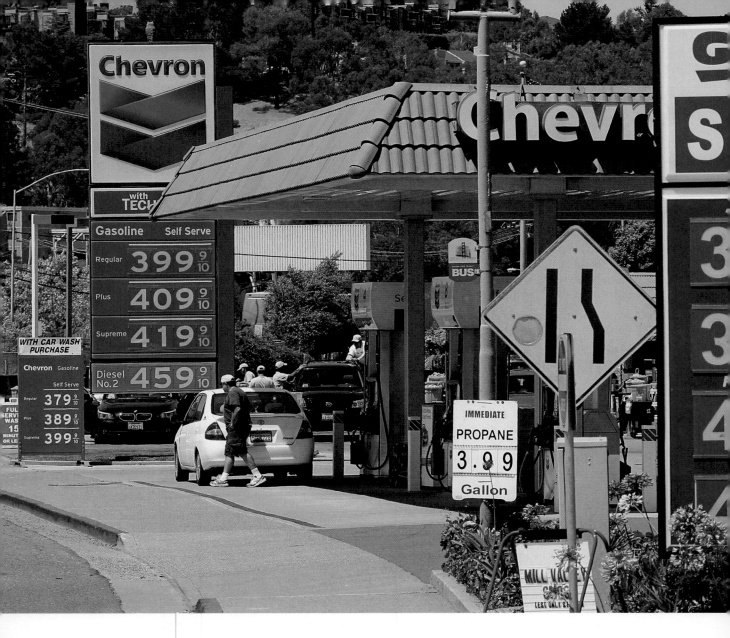

Elasticity

Should Sellers Charge the Highest Price Possible?

Many people believe that sellers charge the highest price possible for their product or service—that if sellers can get one more penny from a customer, they will, even if it makes the customer angry. It turns out that this belief is wrong. What *is* accurate is that producers charge the highest price they can while maintaining the goodwill of most of their customers.

Suppose that your gas tank is nearly empty. How much of a price difference would it take for you to switch from one station to another? Charging a high price might seem like a good strategy, because the station would make a sizable profit on each gallon sold, but this only works if most customers are not price sensitive. If customers are price sensitive, the station with the lower price might get two or three times more customers than the more expensive station does, and they could end up making more profits because they had more sales.

In the previous chapter, we learned that demand and supply regulate economic activity by balancing the interests of buyers and sellers. We also observed how that balance is achieved through prices. A higher price causes the quantity supplied to rise and the quantity demanded to fall. In contrast, a lower price causes the quantity supplied to fall

Where would you fill up? A ten-cent price difference may not seem like a lot but when you multiply that price difference by the number of gallons in your tank, you can easily save a couple of dollars by driving a few feet more.

and the quantity demanded to rise. In this chapter, we examine how decision-makers respond to differences in price and also to changes in income.

The concept of *elasticity*, or responsiveness to a change in market conditions, is a concept that we need to grasp if we are to fully understand supply and demand. Understanding elasticity helps us to determine the impact of government policy on the economy, to vote more intelligently, and even to make wiser day-to-day decisions.

· BIG QUESTIONS ·

- What is the price elasticity of demand, and what are its determinants?
- How do changes in income and the prices of other goods affect elasticity?
- What is the price elasticity of supply?
- How do the price elasticities of demand and supply relate to each other?

What Is the Price Elasticity of Demand, and What Are Its Determinants?

Trade-offs

Many things in life are replaceable, or have substitutes: boyfriends come and go, people stream videos instead of going out to a movie, and students ride their bikes to class instead of taking the bus. Pasta fans may prefer linguini to spaghetti or angel hair, but all three taste about the same and can be substituted for one another in a pinch. With goods like pasta, where consumers can easily purchase a substitute, we think of demand as being *responsive*. That is, a small change in price will likely cause many people to switch from one good to another.

In contrast, many things in life are irreplaceable or have few good substitutes. Examples include electricity and a hospital emergency room visit. A significant rise in price for either of these items would probably not cause you to consume a smaller quantity. If the price of electricity goes up, you might try to cut your usage somewhat, but you would probably not start generating your own power. Likewise, you could try to treat a serious medical crisis without a visit to the ER—but the consequences of making a mistake would be enormous. In these cases, we say that consumers are *unresponsive*, or unwilling to change their behavior, even when the price of the good or service changes.

Elasticity is a measure of the responsiveness of buyers and sellers to changes in price or income. Elasticity is a useful concept because it allows us to measure *how much* consumers and producers change their behavior when either price or income changes. In the next section, we look at the factors that determine the price elasticity of demand.

Elasticity
is a measure of the responsiveness of buyers and sellers to changes in price or income.

Determinants of the Price Elasticity of Demand

The law of demand tells us that as price goes up, quantity demanded goes down, and as price goes down, quantity demanded goes up. In other words, there is a negative relationship between the price of a good and the quantity demanded. Elasticity allows us to measure how much the quantity demanded changes in response to a change in price. If the quantity demanded changes significantly as a result of a price change, then demand is *elastic*. If the quantity demanded changes a small amount as a result of a price change, then demand is *inelastic*.

The **price elasticity of demand** measures the responsiveness of quantity demanded to a change in price. For instance, if the price of a sweatshirt with a college logo rises by $10 and the quantity demanded falls by a large amount (say, half), we'd say that the demand for those sweatshirts is elastic. But if the $10 rise in price results in very little or no change in the quantity demanded, the demand for the sweatshirts is inelastic.

The **price elasticity of demand** measures the responsiveness of quantity demanded to a change in price.

Five determinants play a crucial role in influencing whether demand will be elastic or inelastic: the existence of substitutes, the share of the budget spent on a good, whether the good is a necessity or a luxury good, how broadly defined the market is, and time.

THE EXISTENCE OF SUBSTITUTES The most important determinant of price elasticity is the number of substitutes available. When substitutes are plentiful, market forces tilt in favor of the consumer. For example, imagine that an unexpected freeze in Florida reduces the supply of oranges. As a result, the supply of orange juice shifts to the left (picture the supply curves we discussed in Chapter 3). Because demand remains unchanged, the price of orange juice rises. However, the consumer of orange juice can find many good substitutes. Because cranberries, grapes, and apple crops are unaffected by the Florida freeze, prices for juices made from those fruits remain constant. This situation leads to a choice: a consumer can continue to buy orange juice at a higher price or choose to pay a lower price for a fruit juice that may not be his first choice but is nonetheless acceptable. Faced with higher orange juice prices, some consumers will switch. How quickly this switch takes place, and to

Your "average"-looking boyfriend is replaceable.

Beyoncé is irreplaceable.

what extent consumers are willing to replace one product with another, determines whether demand is elastic or inelastic. Because many substitutes for orange juice exist, the demand for orange juice is elastic, or responsive to price changes.

What if there are no good substitutes? There is no amusement park quite like Disney. Where else can you see all your favorite Disney characters? Nowhere! Because the experience is unique, the number of close substitutes is small. Therefore, demand is more inelastic, or less responsive to price changes.

To some degree, the price elasticity of demand depends on consumer preferences. For instance, sports fans are often willing to shell out big bucks to follow their passions. Amateur golfers can play the same courses that professional golfers do. But the opportunity to golf where the professionals play does not come cheaply. A round of golf at the Tournament Players Club at Sawgrass, a famous course in Florida, costs close to $300. Why are some golfers willing to pay that much? For an avid golfer with the financial means, the experience of living out the same shots seen on television tournaments is worth $300. In this case, demand is inelastic—the avid golfer does not view other golf courses as good substitutes. However, a less enthusiastic golfer, or one without the financial resources, is happy to golf on a less expensive course even if the pros don't play it on TV. When less expensive golf courses serve as good substitutes, the price tag makes demand elastic. Ultimately, whether demand is inelastic or elastic depends on the buyer's preferences and resources.

Incentives

Saving 10% on this purchase amounts to a few pennies.

THE SHARE OF THE BUDGET SPENT ON THE GOOD Despite our example of an avid and affluent golfer willing to pay a premium fee to play at a famous golf course, in most cases price is a critical element in determining what we can afford and what we choose to buy. If you plan to purchase an 80-inch-screen TV, which can cost as much as $2,000, you will probably be willing to take the time to find the best deal. Because of the high price, even a small percentage discount can cause a relatively large change in consumer demand. A 10% off sale may not sound like much, but when purchasing a big-ticket item like a TV, it can mean hundreds of dollars in savings. In this case, the willingness to shop for the best deal indicates that the price matters, so demand is elastic.

Demand is much more inelastic for inexpensive items on sale. For example, if a candy bar is discounted 10%, the price falls by pennies. The savings from switching candy bars is not enough to make a difference in what you can afford elsewhere. Therefore, the incentive to switch is small. Most consumers still buy their favorite candy because the price difference is so insignificant. In this case, demand is inelastic because the savings gained by purchasing a less desirable candy bar are small in comparison to the consumer's budget.

NECESSITIES VERSUS LUXURY GOODS A big-screen TV and a candy bar are both luxury goods. You don't need to have either one. But some goods are necessities. For example, you have to pay your rent and water bill, purchase gasoline for your car, and eat. When consumers purchase a necessity, they are generally thinking about the need, not the price. When the need trumps the price, we expect demand to be relatively inelastic. Therefore, the demand for things like cars, textbooks, and heating oil all tend to have inelastic demand.

Saving 10% on this purchase adds up quickly.

WHETHER THE MARKET IS BROADLY OR NARROWLY DEFINED The more broadly we define a market for a good, the harder it is to live without. For instance, demand for housing in general is quite inelastic because without some form of housing you'd be living on the street. However, the demand for a particular apartment or house is much more price sensitive because you don't need to live in *that* exact place. Therefore, a good falling into a narrowly defined category, such as Crest toothpaste, will have more elastic demand than a broadly defined category, such as toothpaste, which has more inelastic demand.

TIME AND THE ADJUSTMENT PROCESS When the market price changes, consumers and sellers respond. But that response does not remain the same over time. As time passes, both consumers and sellers are able to find substitutes. To understand these different market responses, when considering elasticity economists consider time in three distinct periods: the *immediate run*, the *short run*, and the *long run*.

In the **immediate run**, there is no time for consumers to adjust their behavior. Consider the demand for gasoline. When the gas tank is empty, you have to stop at the nearest gas station and pay the posted price. Filling up as soon as possible is more important than driving around searching for the lowest price. Inelastic demand exists whenever price is secondary to the desire to attain a certain amount of the good. So in the case of an empty tank, the demand for gasoline is inelastic.

But what if your tank is not empty? The **short run** is a period of time when consumers can partially adjust their behavior (in this case, can search for a good deal on gas). In the short run, we make decisions that reflect our immediate or short-term wants, needs, or limitations. When consumers have some time to make a purchase, they gain flexibility. They can shop for lower prices at the pump, carpool to save gas, or even change how often they drive. In the short run, flexibility reduces the demand for expensive gasoline and makes consumer demand more elastic.

Finally, if we relax the time constraint completely, it is possible to use even less gasoline. The **long run** is a period of time when consumers have time to fully adjust to market conditions. In the long run, we make decisions that reflect our wants, needs, and limitations over a long time horizon. If gasoline prices are high in the long run, consumers can relocate closer to work and purchase fuel-efficient cars. These changes further reduce the demand for gasoline. As a result of the flexibility that additional time gives the consumer, the demand for gasoline becomes more elastic.

This is *not* the time to try and find cheap gas.

In the **immediate run**, there is no time for consumers to adjust their behavior.

The **short run** is a period of time when consumers can partially adjust their behavior. In the short run, we make decisions that reflect our immediate or short-term wants, needs, or limitations.

The **long run** is a period of time when consumers have time to fully adjust to market conditions. In the long run, we make decisions that reflect our wants, needs, and limitations over a long time horizon.

TABLE 4.1

Developing Intuition for the Price Elasticity of Demand

Example	Discussion	Overall elasticity
Football tickets for a true fan	Being able to watch a game in person and go to pregame and postgame tailgates is a unique experience. For many fans, the experience of going to the game has few close substitutes. In addition, this is a narrowly defined experience. Therefore, the demand is relatively inelastic.	Tends to be relatively inelastic
Assigned textbooks for a course in your major	The information inside a textbook is valuable. Substitutes such as older editions and free online resources are not exactly the same. As a result, most students buy the required course materials. Acquiring the textbook is more important than the price paid; therefore, the demand is inelastic. The fact that a textbook is needed in the short run (for a few months while taking a class) also tends to make the demand inelastic.	Tends to be inelastic
A slice of pizza from Domino's	In most locations, many pizza competitors exist, so there are many close substitutes. The presence of so much competition tends to make the demand for a narrowly defined brand of pizza elastic.	Tends to be elastic
A Yellow Kia Soul	There are many styles, makes, and colors of cars to choose from. With large purchases, consumers are sensitive to smaller percentages of savings. Moreover, people typically plan their car purchases many months or years in advance. The combination of all these factors makes the demand for any narrowly defined model relatively elastic.	Tends to be relatively elastic

We have looked at five determinants of elasticity—substitutes, the share of the budget spent on the good, necessities versus luxury goods, whether the market is broadly or narrowly defined, and time. Each is significant, but the number of substitutes tends to be the most influential factor and dominates the others. Table 4.1 will help you develop your intuition about how different market situations influence the overall elasticity of demand.

Computing the Price Elasticity of Demand

Until this point, our discussion of elasticity has been descriptive. However, to apply the concept of elasticity in decision-making, we need to view it more quantitatively. For example, if the owner of a business is trying to decide whether to put a good on sale, he or she needs to estimate how many new customers would purchase it at the sale price. If a government is considering a new tax, it needs

Price Elasticity of Demand

Take a look at this IKEA advertisement and think about the determinants of the price elasticity of demand.

QUESTION: Do you think IKEA's "Rainy day special" price makes sense?

ANSWER: Let's start by figuring out whether the demand for umbrellas is elastic or inelastic when it is raining. The GRÖSSBY umbrella is quite inexpensive even at full price, so the purchase would represent only a small share of a consumer's budget. That would tend to make the demand inelastic. Also, when do you need an umbrella? When it's raining, of course! Consumers without umbrellas need them immediately, and that also tends to make demand inelastic. Finally, how many good substitutes are there for an umbrella? A raincoat or poncho, maybe, but it's a lot harder for two people to share a raincoat than an umbrella. The lack of good substitutes is another factor that tends to make demand inelastic. On rainy days, then, demand is even more inelastic than usual. If IKEA decided to charge more and raised the price of the GRÖSSBY on rainy days, instead of lowering it, the store would have increased revenues.

Umbrella
GRÖSSBY
blue/yellow

$\$4^{99}$

$\$2^{50}$ Rainy day special

Offer valid on **GRÖSSBY** umbrella **only**.

IKEA

to know how much revenue that tax will generate. These are questions about elasticity that we can evaluate by using a mathematical formula.

THE PRICE ELASTICITY OF DEMAND FORMULA Let's begin with an example of a pizza shop. Consider an owner who is trying to attract more customers. For one month, he lowers the price of a pizza by 10% and is pleased to find that sales jump by 30%.

Here is the formula for the price elasticity of demand (E_D):

$$\text{price elasticity of demand} = E_D = \frac{\text{percentage change in the quantity demanded}}{\text{percentage change in price}}$$

(EQUATION 4.1)

Using the data from the example, we calculate the price elasticity of demand as follows:

$$\text{price elasticity of demand} = E_D = \frac{30\%}{-10\%} = -3$$

The price elasticity of demand, −3 in this case, is expressed as a coefficient (3) with a specific sign (it has a minus sign in front of it). The coefficient tells us how much the quantity demanded has changed (30%) compared with the price change (−10%). In this case, the percentage change in the quantity demanded is three times the percentage change in the price. Whenever the percentage change in the quantity demanded is larger than the percentage change in price, the demand is elastic. In other words, the price drop made a big difference in how much pizza consumers purchased from the pizza shop. If the opposite occurs and a price drop makes a small difference in the quantity that consumers purchase, demand is inelastic (see Table 4.2).

Price Elasticity of Demand

THE BIG BANG THEORY

The Mystic Warlords of Ka'a (an obvious spoof of Magic: The Gathering) is a fictional trading card game that Sheldon, Leonard, Raj, and Howard all enjoy playing. Howard complains about the release of a new expansion pack called Wild West Witches:

RAJ: Hey, look, the new Warlords of Ka'a expansion pack is out.

HOWARD: A new one? Unbelievable. They just keep making up more cheesy monsters, slapping them on cards, and selling them at 25 bucks a pop.

RAJ: Stuart, settle an argument for us. Who would win, Billy the Kid or the White Wizard?

STUART: If I tell you that, I'm robbing you of the hours of fun you could have for the magical, rootin' tootin' low price of $24.95.

RAJ: I'll take one.

HOWARD: Mmm, make it two.

LEONARD: I hate all of you and myself. Three.

STUART: I'll ring it up. Like shooting nerds in a barrel.

Analysis: Expansion packs allow players of Mystic (and other role-playing games) the opportunity to

Howard considers buying an expansion pack.

improve the deck of cards with which they play the game. Because all of the guys are smart and competitive, new expansion packs make Mystic more challenging to play and also increases the chance of winning when you play against others who do not have the latest cards. The demand for new expansion packs is quite inelastic because the purchase is made in the short run, the share of the budget that each guy spends on the item ($25) is relatively small, and the number of available substitutes for cards with new powers is effectively zero.

The negative (minus) sign in front of the coefficient is equally important. Recall that the law of demand describes a negative relationship between the price of a good and the quantity demanded; when price rises, the quantity demanded falls. The E_D coefficient reflects this negative relationship with a negative sign. In other words, the pizza shop drops its price and consumers buy more pizza. Because the price of pizza and consumer purchases of pizza generally move in opposite directions, the sign of the price elasticity of demand is almost always negative.

THE MIDPOINT METHOD Our earlier calculation was simple because we looked at the change in price and the change in the quantity demanded from only one direction—that is, from a high price to a lower price and from the corresponding lower quantity demanded to the higher quantity demanded. However, the complete—and proper—way to calculate elasticity is from both directions. Consider the following demand schedule for pizza:

Price	Quantity demanded
$12	20
6	30

Let's calculate the elasticity of demand. If the price drops from $12 to $6—a drop of 50%—the quantity demanded increases from 20 to 30—a rise of 50%. Plugging the percentage changes into the E_D formula yields

$$\text{price elasticity of demand} = E_D = \frac{50\%}{-50\%} = -1.0$$

But if the price rises from $6 to $12—an increase of 100%—the quantity demanded falls from 30 to 20, or decreases by 33%. Plugging the percentage changes into the E_D formula yields

$$\text{price elasticity of demand} = E_D = \frac{-33\%}{100\%} = -0.33$$

This result occurs because percentage changes are usually calculated by using the initial value as the base, or reference point. In this example, we worked the problem two ways: by using $12 as the starting point and dropping the price to $6, and then by using $6 as the starting point and increasing the price to $12. Even though we are measuring elasticity over the same range of values, the percentage changes are different.

To avoid this problem, economists use the *midpoint method*, which gives the same answer for the elasticity no matter what point you begin with. Equation 4.2 uses the midpoint method to express the price elasticity of demand. While this equation looks more complicated than Equation 4.1, it is not. The midpoint method merely specifies how to plug in the initial and ending values for price and quantity to determine the percentage changes. Q_1 and P_1 are the initial values, and Q_2 and P_2 are the ending values.

$$E_D = \frac{\text{change in Q} \div \text{average value of Q}}{\text{change in P} \div \text{average value of P}}$$

$$= \frac{(Q_2 - Q_1) \div [(Q_1 + Q_2) \div 2]}{(P_2 - P_1) \div [(P_1 + P_2) \div 2]}$$

(EQUATION 4.2)

The change in the quantity demanded, $(Q_2 - Q_1)$, and the change in price, $(P_2 - P_1)$, are each divided by the average of the initial and ending values, or $[(Q_1 + Q_2) \div 2]$ and $[(P_1 + P_2) \div 2]$.

The midpoint method is the preferred method for solving elasticity problems. To see why, let's return to our pizza demand example.

If the price rises from \$6 to \$12, the quantity demanded falls from 30 to 20. Here the initial values are $P_1 = \$6$ and $Q_1 = 30$. The ending values are $P_2 = \$12$ and $Q_2 = 20$. Using the midpoint method,

$$E_D = \frac{(20 - 30) \div [(30 + 20) \div 2]}{(\$12 - \$6) \div [(\$6 + \$12) \div 2]} = \frac{-10 \div 25}{\$6 \div \$9} = -0.60$$

If the price falls from \$12 to \$6, quantity demanded rises from 20 to 30. This time, the initial values are $P_1 = \$12$ and $Q_1 = 20$. The ending values are $P_2 = \$6$ and $Q_2 = 30$. Using the midpoint method,

$$E_D = \frac{(30 - 20) \div [(20 + 30) \div 2]}{(\$6 - \$12) \div [(\$12 + \$6) \div 2]} = \frac{10 \div 25}{-\$6 \div \$9} = -0.60$$

When we calculated the price elasticity of demand from \$6 to \$12 using \$6 as the initial point, $E_D = -0.33$. Moving in the opposite direction, from \$12 to \$6, made \$12 the initial reference point and $E_D = -1.0$. The midpoint method splits the difference and uses \$9 and 25 pizzas as the midpoints. This approach makes the calculation of the elasticity coefficient the same, -0.60, no matter what direction the price moves. Therefore, economists use the midpoint method to standardize the results.

So, using the midpoint method, we arrive at an elasticity coefficient of -0.60, which is between 0 and -1. What does that number mean? In this case, the percentage change in the quantity demanded is less than the percentage change in the price. Whenever the percentage change in the quantity demanded is smaller than the percentage change in price, we say that demand is inelastic. In other words, the price drop does not make a big difference in how much pizza consumers purchase from the pizza shop. When the elasticity coefficient is less than -1, the opposite is true, and demand is elastic.

Graphing the Price Elasticity of Demand

Visualizing elasticity graphically helps us understand the relationship between elastic and inelastic demand. Figure 4.1 shows elasticity graphically. As demand becomes increasingly elastic, or responsive to price changes, the demand curve flattens. The range of elasticity runs from perfectly inelastic through perfectly elastic.

For many pet owners, the demand for veterinary care is perfectly inelastic.

PERFECTLY INELASTIC DEMAND   Figure 4.1, panel (a), depicts the price elasticity for pet care. Many pet owners report that they would pay any amount of money to help their sick or injured pet get better. For these pet owners, the demand curve is a vertical line. If you look along the quantity axis in panel (a), you will see that the quantity of pet care demanded (Q_D) remains constant no matter what it costs. At the same time, the price increases from P_0 to P_1. We can calculate the price elasticity coefficient as follows:

$$E_{\text{pet care}} = \frac{\text{percentage change in } Q_D}{\text{percentage change in P}} = \frac{0}{\text{percentage change in P}} = 0$$

When zero is in the numerator, we know that the answer will be zero no matter what we find in the denominator. This conclusion makes sense. Many pet owners will try to help their pet feel better no matter what the cost, so we can say that their demand is *perfectly inelastic*. This means that the value of E_D will always be zero. (Of course, pet care is not perfectly inelastic, because there is certainly a price beyond which some pet owners would not or could not pay; but for illustrative purposes, let's say that pet care *is* perfectly elastic.) As you continue reading this section, refer to Table 4.2 on page 128 to help you keep track of the different types of elasticity.

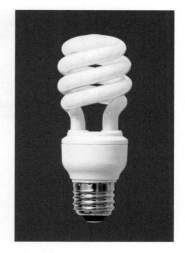

The demand for electricity is relatively inelastic.

RELATIVELY INELASTIC DEMAND Moving on to panel (b) of Figure 4.1, we consider the demand for electricity. Whereas many pet owners will not change their consumption of health care for their pet no matter what the cost, consumers of electricity will modify their use of electricity in response to price changes. When the price of electricity goes up, they will use less, and when the price goes down, they will use more. Because living without electricity is not practical, using less is a matter of making relatively small lifestyle adjustments—buying energy-efficient light bulbs or adjusting the thermostat a few degrees. As a result, the demand curve in panel (b) is relatively steep, but not completely vertical as in panel (a).

When the change on the quantity axis is small compared with the change on the price axis, the price elasticity is *relatively inelastic*. Plugging these changes into the elasticity formula, we get

$$E_{electricity} = \frac{\text{percentage change in } Q_D}{\text{percentage change in P}} = \frac{\text{\small small } \text{change}}{\text{\large large } \text{change}}$$

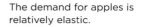

The demand for apples is relatively elastic.

Recall that the law of demand describes a negative relationship between price and quantity demanded. Therefore, the changes along the price and quantity axes will always be in opposite directions. A price elasticity of zero tells us there is no change in the quantity demanded when price changes. So when demand is relatively inelastic, the price elasticity of demand must be relatively close to zero. The easiest way to think about this scenario is to consider how a 10% increase in electric rates affects most households. How much less electricity would you use? The answer for most people would be a little less, but not 10% less. You can adjust your thermostat, but you still need electricity to run your appliances and lights. When the price changes more than quantity changes, there is a larger change in the denominator. Therefore, the price elasticity of demand is between 0 and –1 when demand is relatively inelastic.

RELATIVELY ELASTIC DEMAND In Figure 4.1, panel (c), we consider apples. Because there are many good substitutes for apples, the demand for apples is *relatively elastic*. The flexibility of consumer demand for apples is illustrated by the degree of responsiveness we see along the quantity axis relative to the change exhibited along the price axis. We can observe this responsiveness by noting that a relatively elastic demand curve

The demand for a $10 bill is perfectly elastic.

is flatter than an inelastic demand curve. So, whereas perfectly inelastic demand shows no change in demand with an increase in price, and relatively inelastic demand shows a small change in quantity demanded with an increase in price, relatively elastic demand shows a relatively large change in quantity demanded with an increase in price. Placing this information into the elasticity formula gives us

$$E_{apples} = \frac{\text{percentage change in } Q_D}{\text{percentage change in P}} = \frac{\text{large change}}{\text{small change}}$$

Now the numerator—the percentage change in Q_D—is large, and the denominator—the percentage change in P—is small. E_D is less than −1. Recall that the sign must be negative, because there is a negative relationship between price and the quantity demanded. As the price elasticity of demand moves farther away from zero, the consumer becomes more responsive to a price change. Because many other fruits are good substitutes for apples, a small change in the price of apples will have a large effect on the quantity demanded.

PERFECTLY ELASTIC DEMAND Figure 4.1, panel (d), provides an interesting example: the demand for a $10 bill. Would you pay $11.00 to get a $10 bill? No. Would you pay $10.01 for a $10 bill? Still no. However, when the price drops to $10.00, you will probably become indifferent (that is, you will be equally satisfied with paying $10.00 for the $10 bill or not making the trade). The real magic here occurs when the price drops to $9.99. How many $10 bills would you buy if you could buy them for $9.99 or less? The answer: as many as possible! This is exactly what happens in currency markets, where small differences among currency prices around the globe motivate traders to buy and sell large quantities of currency and clear a small profit on the difference in exchange rates. This extreme form of price sensitivity is illustrated by a perfectly horizontal demand curve, which means that demand is *perfectly elastic*. Solving for the elasticity yields

$$E_{\$10\,bill} = \frac{\text{percentage change in } Q_D}{\text{percentage change in P}} = \frac{\text{nearly infinite change}}{\text{very small (\$0.01) change}}$$

We can think of this very small price change, from $10.00 to $9.99, as having essentially an unlimited effect on the quantity of $10 bills demanded. Traders go from being uninterested in trading at $10.00 to seeking to buy as many $10 bills as possible when the price drops to $9.99. As a result, the price elasticity of demand approaches negative infinity ($-\infty$).

UNITARY ELASTICITY There is a fifth type of elasticity, not depicted in Figure 4.1. *Unitary elasticity* describes the situation in which elasticity is neither elastic nor inelastic. This situation occurs when E_D is exactly −1, and it happens when the percentage change in price is exactly equal to the percentage change in quantity demanded. This characteristic of unitary elasticity will be important when we discuss the connection between elasticity and total revenue later in this chapter. You're probably wondering what an example of a unitary good would be. Relax. It is impossible to find a good that has a price elasticity

FIGURE 4.1

Elasticity and the Demand Curve

For any given price change across two demand curves, demand will be more elastic on the flatter demand curve than on the steeper demand curve. In (a), the demand is perfectly inelastic, so the price does not matter. In (b), the demand is relatively inelastic, so the price is less important than the quantity purchased. In (c), the demand is relatively elastic, so the price matters more than quantity. In (d), the demand is perfectly elastic, so price is all that matters.

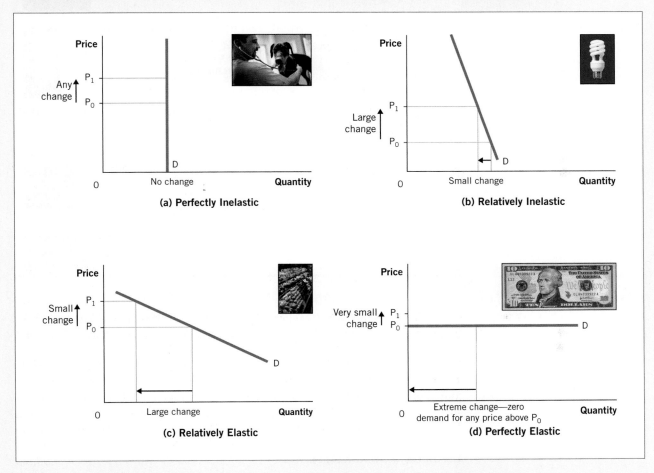

of exactly −1 at all price points. It is enough to know that unitary demand represents the crossover from elastic to inelastic demand.

PRICE ELASTICITY OF DEMAND: A SUMMARY Now that you have had a chance to look at all four panels in Figure 4.1, here is a handy trick you can use to keep the difference between inelastic and elastic demand straight.

$$\text{I} = \text{inelastic and} \quad \text{E} = \text{elastic}$$

TABLE 4.2

The Relationship between Price Elasticity of Demand and Price

Elasticity	E_D coefficient	Interpretation	Example in Figure 4.1
Perfectly inelastic	$E_D = 0$	Price does not matter.	Saving your pet
Relatively inelastic	$0 > E_D > -1$	Price is less important than the quantity purchased.	Electricity
Unitary	$E_D = -1$	Price and quantity are equally important.	
Relatively elastic	$-1 > E_D > -\infty$	Price is more important than the quantity purchased.	Apples
Perfectly elastic	$E_D \rightarrow -\infty$	Price is everything.	A $10 bill

The "I" in the word "inelastic" is vertical, just like the inelastic relationships we examined in Figure 4.1. Likewise, the letter "E" has three horizontal lines to remind us that elastic demand is flat.

Finally, it is possible to pair the elasticity coefficients with an interpretation of how much price matters. Table 4.2 provides a convenient summary. When price does not matter, demand is perfectly inelastic (denoted by the coefficient of zero). Conversely, when price is the only thing that matters, demand becomes perfectly elastic (denoted by $-\infty$). Between these two extremes, the extent to which price matters determines whether demand is relatively inelastic, unitary, or relatively elastic.

TIME, ELASTICITY, AND THE DEMAND CURVE We have already seen that increased time makes demand more elastic. Figure 4.2 shows this result graphically. When the price rises from P_1 to P_2, consumers cannot avoid the price increase in the immediate run, and demand is represented by the perfectly inelastic demand curve, D_1. For example, if your gas tank is almost empty, you must purchase gas at the new, higher price. Over a slightly longer time horizon—the short run—consumers are more flexible and drive less in order to buy less gasoline. Demand rotates to D_2, and in the short run consumption declines to Q_2. In the long run, when consumers have time to purchase a more fuel-efficient vehicle or move closer to work, demand rotates to D_3 and gas purchases fall even further. As the demand curve continues to flatten, the quantity demanded falls to Q_3.

FIGURE 4.2

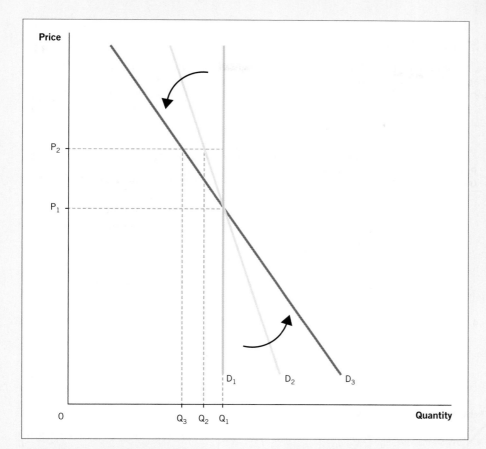

Demand becomes more elastic over time. When the price rises from P_1 to P_2, consumers are unable to avoid the price increase in the immediate run (D_1). In the short run (D_2), consumers become more flexible and consumption declines to Q_2. Eventually, in the long run (D_3), there is time to make lifestyle changes that further reduce consumption. As a result, the demand curve continues to flatten and the quantity demanded falls to Q_3 in response to the higher price.

SLOPE AND ELASTICITY In this section, we pause to make sure that you understand what you are observing in the figures. The demand curves shown in Figures 4.1 and 4.2 are straight lines, and therefore they have a constant slope, or steepness. (A refresher on slope is found in the appendix to Chapter 2.) So, looking at Figures 4.1 and 4.2, you might think that slope is the same as the price elasticity. But slope does not equal elasticity.

Consider, for example, a trip to Starbucks. Would you buy a tall skinny latte if it costs $10? How about $7? What about $5? Say you decide to buy the skinny latte because the price drops from $5 to $4. In this case, a small price change, a drop from $5 to $4, causes you to make the purchase. You can say that the demand for skinny lattes is relatively elastic. Now look at Figure 4.3, which shows a demand curve for skinny lattes. At $5 the consumer purchases zero lattes, at $4 she purchases one latte, at $3 she purchases two, and she continues to buy one additional latte with each $1 drop in price. As you progress downward along the demand curve, price becomes less of an inhibiting factor, and as a result, the price elasticity of demand slowly becomes more inelastic. Notice that the slope of a linear demand curve is constant. However, when we calculate the price elasticity of demand between the various points in Figure 4.3, it becomes clear that demand is increasingly inelastic as we move

FIGURE 4.3

The Difference between Slope and Elasticity

Along any straight demand curve, the price elasticity of demand (E_D) is not constant, as you can see by noting how the price elasticity of demand changes from highly elastic near the top of the demand curve to highly inelastic near the bottom of the curve. In the table, note that all the numbers in the third, fourth, and fifth columns are based on the midpoint formula.

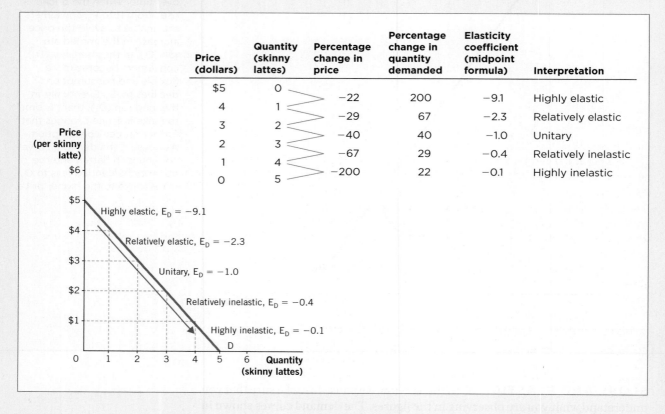

Price (dollars)	Quantity (skinny lattes)	Percentage change in price	Percentage change in quantity demanded	Elasticity coefficient (midpoint formula)	Interpretation
$5	0				
4	1	−22	200	−9.1	Highly elastic
3	2	−29	67	−2.3	Relatively elastic
2	3	−40	40	−1.0	Unitary
1	4	−67	29	−0.4	Relatively inelastic
0	5	−200	22	−0.1	Highly inelastic

down the demand curve. You can see this in the change in E_D; it steadily increases from −9.1 to −0.1.

Perfectly inelastic demand would exist if the elasticity coefficient reached zero. Recall that a value of zero means that there is no change in the quantity demanded as a result of a price change. Therefore, values close to zero reflect inelastic demand, while those farther away from zero reflect more elastic demand.

Price Elasticity of Demand and Total Revenue

Understanding the price elasticity of demand for the product you sell is important when running a business. Consumer responsiveness to price changes determines whether a firm would be better off raising or lowering its price for

TABLE 4.3

The Price Elasticity of Demand and Total Revenue

Price (P) (per skinny latte)	Quantity (Q) (skinny lattes)	Total revenue P × Q	Percentage change in price	Percentage change in quantity	Elasticity coefficient	Interpretation
$5	0	$0				
			−22	200	−9.1	Highly elastic
4	1	4				
			−29	67	−2.3	Relatively elastic
3	2	6				
			−40	40	−1.0	Unitary
2	3	6				
			−67	29	−0.4	Relatively inelastic
1	4	4				
			−200	22	−0.1	Highly inelastic
0	5	0				

a given product. In this section, we explore the relationship between the price elasticity of demand and a firm's total revenue.

But first we need to understand the concept of total revenue. **Total revenue** is the amount that a firm receives from the sale of goods and services. Total revenue for a particular good is calculated by multiplying the price of the good by the quantity of the good that is sold. Table 4.3 reproduces the table from Figure 4.3 (with numbers based on the midpoint formula) and adds a column for the total revenue. We find the total revenue by multiplying the price of a tall skinny latte by the quantity purchased.

After calculating total revenue at each price, we can look at the column of elasticity coefficients to determine the relationship. When we link revenues with the price elasticity of demand, a trade-off emerges. (This trade-off occurs because total revenue and elasticity relate to price differently. Total revenue involves multiplying the price by the quantity, while elasticity involves dividing the percentage change in quantity demanded by the percentage change in price.) Total revenue is zero when the price is too high ($5 or more) and when the price is too low ($0). Between these two extremes, prices from $1 to $4 generate positive total revenue.

Consider what happens when the price drops from $5 to $4. At $4, the first latte is purchased. Total revenue is $4 × 1 = $4. This is also the range at which the price elasticity of demand is highly elastic. As a result, lowering the price increases revenue. Revenue continues to increase when the price drops from $4 to $3. Now two lattes are sold, so the total revenue rises to $3 × 2 = $6. At the same time, demand remains elastic. We thus conclude that when demand is elastic, lowering the price will increase total revenue. This relationship is shown in panel (a) of Figure 4.4. By lowering the price from $4 to $3, the business has generated $2 more in revenue. But to generate this extra revenue, the business has lowered the price from $4 to $3 and therefore has given up $1 for each unit it sells. This lost revenue is represented by the red area under the demand curve in panel (a).

When the price drops from $3 to $2, the total revenue stays at $6. This result occurs because demand is unitary, as shown in panel (b). This special condition exists when the percentage price change is exactly offset by an equal percentage change in the quantity demanded. In this situation, revenue remains constant. At $2, three lattes are purchased, so the total revenue is $2 × 3, which is the same as it was when the price was $3. As a result, we can

Total revenue
is the amount that a firm receives from the sale of goods and services. Total revenue for a particular good is calculated by multiplying the price of the good by the quantity of the good that is sold.

Trade-offs

FIGURE 4.4

(a) The Total Revenue Trade-Off When Demand Is Elastic

In the elastic region of the demand curve, lowering the price will increase total revenue. The gains from increased purchases, shown in the light green area, are greater than the losses from a lower purchase price, shown in the red area. The dark green area is part of the total revenue that exists at both prices.

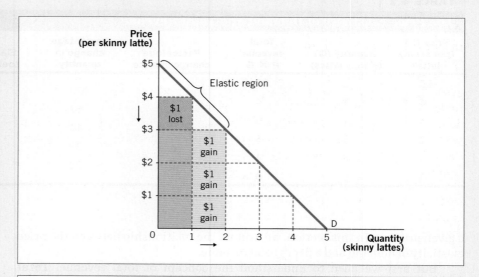

(b) ...When Demand Is Unitary

When demand is unitary, lowering the price will no longer increase total revenue. The gains from increased purchases, shown in the light green area, are equal to the losses from a lower purchase price, shown in the red area.

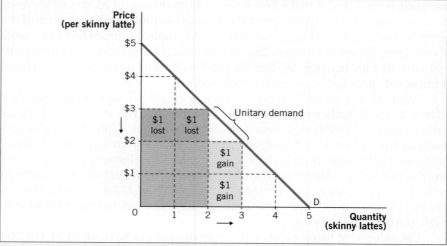

(c) ...When Demand Is Inelastic

In the inelastic region of the demand curve, lowering the price will decrease total revenue. The gains from increased purchases, shown in the light green area, are smaller than the losses from a lower purchase price, shown in the red area.

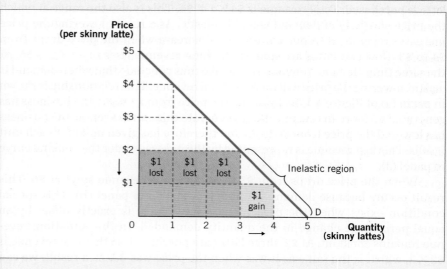

see that total revenue has reached a maximum. Between $3 and $2, the price elasticity of demand is unitary. This finding does not necessarily mean that the firm will operate at the unitary point. Maximizing profit, not revenue, is the ultimate goal of a business, and we have not yet accounted for costs in our calculation of profits.

Once we reach a price below unitary demand, we move into the realm of inelastic demand, shown in panel (c). When the price falls to $1, total revenue declines to $4. This result occurs because the price elasticity of demand is now relatively inelastic, or price insensitive. Even though the price is declining by $1, price is increasingly unimportant; as you can see by the light green square, lowering the price to $1 does not spur a large increase in consumption.

As we see in panel (c), at a price of $2, three units are sold and total revenue is $2 \times 3 = $6. When the price falls to $1, four units are sold, so the total revenue is now $4 \times 1 = $4. By lowering the price from $2 to $1, the business has lost $2 in extra revenue because it does not generate enough extra revenue from the lower price. Lowering the price from $2 to $1 causes a loss of $3 in existing sales revenue (the red boxes). At the same time, it generates only $1 in new sales (the light green box), so the net change is a loss of $2.

In this analysis, we see that once the demand curve enters the inelastic area, lowering the price decreases total revenue. This outcome is unambiguously bad for a business. The lower price brings in less revenue and requires the business to produce more goods. Because making goods is costly, it does not make sense to lower prices into the region where revenues decline. We can be sure that no business will intentionally operate in the inelastic region of the demand curve because it will earn less profit.

ECONOMICS IN THE REAL WORLD

PRICE ELASTICITY OF DEMAND: THE NUTELLA RIOTS OF 2018

Nutella is a chocolate hazelnut spread with a distinctive flavor and legions of loyal fans (32 million Facebook followers). There's even a medical condition known as "Nutella Addiction." When Intermarché supermarkets in France slashed their Nutella prices by 70% from €4.50 to €1.40 ($5.00 to $1.50), people went crazy. Want to see the reaction for yourself? Check out this link: www.youtube.com/watch?v=UyjM62yLGFQ.

What makes this story so interesting is the overwhelming reaction the price drop created. Nutella is a brisk seller in many European countries at its retail price. But when Intermarché lowered the price, sales exploded and Nutella sold out in every store. The overwhelming reaction is strong evidence that the demand for Nutella is quite elastic, since the price reduction caused a massive increase in the quantity demanded.

What would you do if the price of Nutella suddenly dropped 70%?

Incentives

Price Elasticity of Demand

The following two questions ask you to compute price elasticity of demand. Before we do the math, ask yourself whether the price elasticity of demand for sandwiches or the antibiotic amoxicillin is elastic.

Is the demand for a sandwich elastic or inelastic?

QUESTION: A deli manager decides to lower the price of a featured sandwich from $3 to $2, and she finds that sales during the week increase from 240 to 480 sandwiches. Is demand elastic?

ANSWER: Consumers were flexible and bought significantly more sandwiches in response to the price drop. Let's calculate the price elasticity of demand (E_D) using Equation 4.2. Recall that

$$E_D = \frac{(Q_2 - Q_1) \div [(Q_1 + Q_2) \div 2]}{(P_2 - P_1) \div [(P_1 + P_2) \div 2]}$$

Plugging in the values from the question yields

$$E_D = \frac{(480 - 240) \div [(240 + 480) \div 2]}{(\$2 - \$3) \div [(\$3 + \$2) \div 2]} = \frac{240 \div 360}{-\$1 \div \$2.50}$$

Therefore, $E_D = -1.67$.

Whenever the price elasticity of demand is less than −1, demand is elastic: the percentage change in the quantity demanded is greater than the percentage change in price. This outcome is exactly what the store manager expected. But sandwiches are just one option for a meal; there are many other choices, such as salads, burgers, and chicken—all of which cost more than the now-cheaper sandwich. Therefore, we should not be surprised that there is a relatively large percentage increase in sandwich purchases by price-conscious customers.

QUESTION: A local pharmacy manager decides to raise the price of a 50-pill prescription of amoxicillin (an antibiotic) from $8 to $10. The pharmacy tracks the sales of amoxicillin over the next month and finds that sales decline from 1,500 boxes to 1,480. Is demand elastic?

Is the demand for amoxicillin elastic or inelastic?

ANSWER: First, let's consider the potential substitutes for amoxicillin. To be sure, it's possible to substitute other drugs, but they might not be as effective. Therefore, most patients prefer to use the drug prescribed by their doctor. Also, in this case the cost of the drug is relatively small. Finally, patients' need for amoxicillin is a short-run consideration. They want the medicine now so they will get better! All three factors would lead us to believe that the demand for amoxicillin is relatively inelastic. Let's find out if the data confirm that intuition.

The price elasticity of demand using the midpoint method is

$$E_D = \frac{(Q_2 - Q_1) \div [(Q_1 + Q_2) \div 2]}{(P_2 - P_1) \div [(P_1 + P_2) \div 2]}$$

Plugging in the values from the question yields

$$E_D = \frac{(1480 - 1500) \div [(1500 + 1480) \div 2]}{(\$10 - \$8) \div [(\$8 + \$10) \div 2]}$$

Simplifying produces this equation:

$$E_D = \frac{-20 \div 1490}{\$2 \div \$9}$$

Therefore, $E_D = -0.06$.

Recall that an E_D near zero indicates that the price elasticity of demand is highly inelastic, which is what we suspected. The price increase does not cause consumption to fall very much. If the store manager was hoping to bring in a little extra revenue from the sales of amoxicillin, his plan is successful. Before the price increase, the business sold 1,500 units at $8, so total revenue was $12,000. After the price increase, sales decrease to 1,480 units, but the new price is $10, so total revenue is now $14,800. Raising the price of amoxicillin has helped the pharmacy make an additional $2,800 in total revenue.

CHALLENGE QUESTION: Now suppose that the local pharmacy manager decides to raise the price of a 50-pill prescription of amoxicillin from $8 to $40, instead of just to $10. Again the pharmacy tracks the sales, and this time it finds that sales decline from 1,500 boxes all the way down to 50 boxes. Is demand still elastic?

ANSWER:

Plugging in the values from the question using the midpoint method yields

$$E_D = \frac{(50 - 1500) \div [(1500 + 50) \div 2]}{(\$40 - \$8) \div [(\$8 + \$40) \div 2]}$$

Simplifying produces

$$E_D = \frac{-1450 \div 775}{\$32 \div \$24}$$

Therefore $E_D = -1.41$

An E_D value below -1 represents relatively elastic demand. At this point, the price increase has clearly backfired. Total revenue has gone from $12,000 (1,500 boxes at $8 each) down to 50 boxes $\times$ $40 per box = $2,000. Raising the price of amoxicillin to a point where demand is elastic has cost the pharmacy $10,000 in total revenue. This is a vivid reminder that the elasticity of demand steadily becomes more elastic as the price rises.

Price Elasticity of Demand

Determining the price elasticity of demand for a product or service involves calculating the responsiveness of quantity demanded to a change in the price. The chart below gives the actual price elasticity of demand for ten common products and services. Remember, the number is always negative because of the negative relationship between price and the quantity demanded. Why is price elasticity of demand important? It reveals consumer behavior and allows for better pricing strategies by businesses.

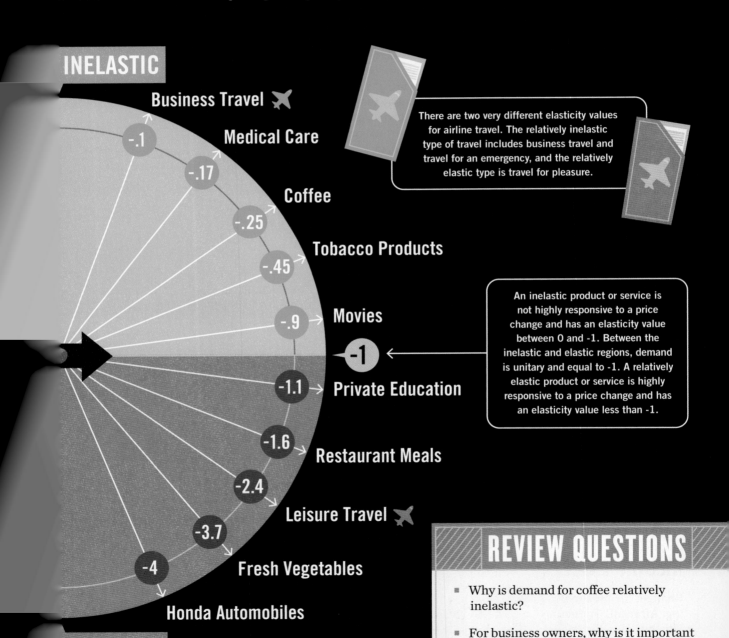

INELASTIC

Business Travel ✈ — -.1

Medical Care — -.17

Coffee — -.25

Tobacco Products — -.45

Movies — -.9

-1

Private Education — -1.1

Restaurant Meals — -1.6

-2.4

Leisure Travel ✈ — -3.7

Fresh Vegetables — -4

Honda Automobiles

ELASTIC

> There are two very different elasticity values for airline travel. The relatively inelastic type of travel includes business travel and travel for an emergency, and the relatively elastic type is travel for pleasure.

> An inelastic product or service is not highly responsive to a price change and has an elasticity value between 0 and -1. Between the inelastic and elastic regions, demand is unitary and equal to -1. A relatively elastic product or service is highly responsive to a price change and has an elasticity value less than -1.

REVIEW QUESTIONS

- Why is demand for coffee relatively inelastic?

- For business owners, why is it important to understand whether demand for their products is elastic or inelastic?

Price Elasticity of Demand and Total Revenues

SHARK TANK: VURTEGO POGO

Do you increase revenue by lowering or raising prices?

The answer, according to economist Charity-Joy Acchiardo, is that "it all depends on the price elasticity of demand for your product or service." Acchiardo is one of the creators of econshark.com, a website dedicated to dissecting the economic principles on display in the popular TV show *Shark Tank*. In one episode, Brian Spencer is looking for an investment from the Sharks so he can mass-market his amazingly cool, extreme-sport pogo stick, the "Vurtego Pogo." However, Shark Robert Herjavec questions whether high-end pogo sticks are a good fit for the mass market. Spencer's current price of $330, Robert feels, is too low for a specialty product like a high-performance pogo stick, but too high for the mass market. The other Sharks agree. They urge Spencer to raise his price and concentrate on dominating the niche he's carved out for himself. Spencer leaves the Shark Tank empty-handed but realizing that he's been given good advice. When something is cool and there is nothing else exactly like it on the

How much would you pay to be able to do flips on a pogo stick?

market, people are willing to pay more to buy one. Translation: when demand is inelastic, don't price your product too low.

How Do Changes in Income and the Prices of Other Goods Affect Elasticity?

We have seen how consumer demand responds to changes in the price of a single good. In this section, we examine how responsive demand is to changes in income and to price changes in other goods.

Income Elasticity

Changes in personal income can have a large effect on consumer spending. After all, the money in your pocket influences not only how much you buy, but also the types of purchases you make. A consumer who is low on money may opt to buy a cheap generic product, while someone with a little extra cash can afford to upgrade. The grocery store aisle reflects different shoppers' budgets. Store brands and name products compete for shelf space. Lower-income shoppers can choose the store brand to save money, while more affluent shoppers can choose their favorite brand-name product without worrying about the purchase price. The **income elasticity of demand** (E_I) measures how a change in income affects spending. It is calculated by dividing the percentage change in the quantity demanded by the percentage change in personal income:

(EQUATION 4.3)

$$E_I = \frac{\text{percentage change in the quantity demanded}}{\text{percentage change in income}}$$

The **income elasticity of demand** (E_I) measures how a change in income affects spending.

Unlike the price elasticity of demand, which is negative, the income elasticity of demand can be positive or negative. When a higher level of income enables the consumer to purchase more, the goods that are purchased are *normal goods*, a term we learned in Chapter 3. Because the demand for normal goods goes up with income, they have a positive income elasticity; a rise in income causes a rise in the quantity demanded. For instance, if you receive a 20% pay raise and you decide to pay an extra 10% on your cable TV bill to add HBO, the resulting income elasticity is positive, because 10% divided by 20% is 0.5. Whenever a good is normal, the result is a positive income elasticity of demand, and purchases of the good rise as income expands and purchases of the good fall as income falls.

Normal goods fall into two categories: *necessities* and *luxuries*. Goods that people consider necessities generally have income elasticities between 0 and 1. For example, expenditures on items such as clothing, electricity, and gasoline are unavoidable, and consumers at any income level must buy them no matter what. Although purchases of necessities will increase as income rises, they do not rise as fast as the increase in income does. Therefore, as income increases, spending on necessities will expand at a slower rate than the increase in income.

Rising income enables consumers to enjoy significantly more luxuries, producing an income elasticity of demand greater than 1 for luxuries. For instance, a family of modest means may travel almost exclusively by car. However, as the family's income rises, they can afford air travel. A relatively small jump in income can cause the family to fly instead of drive.

Clothing purchases expand with income.

In Chapter 3, we saw that *inferior goods* are those that people will choose not to purchase when their income goes up. Inferior goods have a negative income elasticity, because as income expands, the demand for these goods declines. We see this effect in Table 4.4 with the example of macaroni and cheese, an inexpensive meal. As a household's income rises, it is able to afford healthier food and more variety in its meals. Consequently, the number of times that mac and cheese is purchased declines. The decline in consumption indicates that mac and cheese is an inferior good, as reflected in the negative sign of the income elasticity.

Cross-Price Elasticity

Now we will look at how a price change in one good can affect the demand for a related good. For instance, if you enjoy pizza, the choice between ordering from Domino's or Pizza Hut is influenced by the price of both goods. The **cross-price elasticity of demand** (E_C) measures the percentage change in the quantity demanded of one good to the percentage change in the price of a related good:

Air travel is a luxury good.

$$E_C = \frac{\text{percentage change in the quantity demanded of one good}}{\text{percentage change in the price of a related good}}$$

(EQUATION 4.4)

The **cross-price elasticity of demand** (E_C) measures the percentage change in the quantity demanded of one good to the percentage change in the price of a related good.

Consider how two goods are related. If the goods are substitutes, a price rise in one good will cause the quantity demanded of that good to decline. At the same time, because consumers can purchase the substitute good for the same price as before, demand for the substitute good will increase. When the price of Domino's pizza rises, consumers will buy more pizza from Pizza Hut. This means that the cross-price elasticity of demand is positive.

The opposite is true if the goods are complements. In that case, a price increase in one good will make the joint consumption of both goods more expensive. Therefore, the consumption of both goods will decline. For example, a price increase for turkeys will cause the quantity demanded of both turkey and gravy to decline, and a price decrease for turkeys will cause the quantity demanded of both turkey and gravy to increase. This means that the cross-price elasticity of demand is negative.

What if there is no relationship between two goods? For example, if the price of basketballs goes up, that price increase probably will not affect the quantity demanded of bedroom slippers. In this case, the cross-price elasticity is neither positive nor negative; it is zero. Table 4.5 lists cross-price elasticity values according to type of good.

Trade-offs

TABLE 4.4

Income Elasticity

Type of good	Subcategory	E_I coefficient	Example	
Inferior		$E_I < 0$	Macaroni and cheese	
Normal	Necessity	$0 < E_I < 1$	Milk	
Normal	Luxury	$E_I > 1$	Diamond ring	

TABLE 4.5

Cross-Price Elasticity

Type of good	E_C coefficient	Example	
Substitutes	$E_C > 0$	Pizza Hut and Domino's	
No relationship	$E_C = 0$	A basketball and bedroom slippers	
Complements	$E_C < 0$	Turkey and gravy	

PRACTICE WHAT YOU KNOW

Cross-Price Elasticity of Demand

To learn how to calculate cross-price elasticity, let's consider enjoying the soft drink Mr. Pibb with Red Vines candy. If you have never tried this combination, you should!

QUESTION: Suppose that the price of a 2-liter bottle of Mr. Pibb falls from $1.49 to $1.29. In the week immediately preceding the price drop, a local store sells 60 boxes of Red Vines. After the price drop, sales of Red Vines increase to 80 boxes. What is the cross-price elasticity of demand for Red Vines when the price of Mr. Pibb falls from $1.49 to $1.29?

ANSWER: The cross-price elasticity of demand using the midpoint method is

$$E_C = \frac{(Q_{RV2} - Q_{RV1}) \div [(Q_{RV1} + Q_{RV2}) \div 2]}{(P_{MP2} - P_{MP1}) \div [(P_{MP1} + P_{MP2}) \div 2]}$$

Notice that there are now additional subscripts to denote that we are measuring the percentage change in the quantity demanded of good RV (Red Vines) in response to the percentage change in the price of good MP (Mr. Pibb).

Plugging in the values from the example yields

$$E_C = \frac{(80 - 60) \div [(60 + 80) \div 2]}{(\$1.29 - \$1.49) \div [(\$1.49 + \$1.29) \div 2]}$$

Simplifying produces

$$E_C = \frac{20 \div 70}{-\$0.20 \div \$1.39}$$

Solving for E_C gives us a value of −1.99. The result's negative value confirms our intuition that two goods that go well together are complements, since the decrease in the price of Mr. Pibb causes consumers to buy more Red Vines.

Have you tried Mr. Pibb and Red Vines together?

TENNIS, ANYONE?

Are you a casual tennis player or passionate about your game? The answer to that question helps us understand a real-life elasticity experiment.

In 2011, the New York City Parks Department doubled the prices paid by tennis players between the ages of 18 and 61. Single-pay passes for an hour of court time jumped from $7 to $15, while season passes rose from $100 to $200.

Far fewer tennis permits were sold under the new prices, according to data from the Parks Department. Sales of season passes for most players slipped by 40%, with 7,400 sold in 2011 as compared to 12,400 in 2010. Sales of one-day passes took a big hit as well, dropping by nearly a third from more than 40,000 for the 2010 season to 27,000.

How much would you be willing to pay for court time?

Type of pass	Price in 2010	Price in 2011	Passes sold in 2010	Passes sold in 2011	Total revenue in 2010 (in millions)	Total revenue in 2011 (in millions)	E$_D$
One-day	$7	$15	40,000	27,000	$0.28	$0.41	−0.53
Annual	100	200	12,400	7,400	1.24	1.48	−0.75
Total					**$1.52**	**$1.89**	

We calculated the price elasticity of demand, E$_D$, using the midpoint formula. Because the coefficients for the one-day and annual passes are between 0 and −1, we know that demand is relatively inelastic at these prices. We also know that when demand is inelastic and prices increase, total revenue should increase, and that is exactly what happened. Tennis court revenues increased from $1.52 million in 2010 to $1.89 million in 2011.

As you might guess, many tennis players in New York City were quite upset with the sudden price increase. However, the data show that many tennis players decided to keep playing rather than quit. This result shouldn't surprise you too much. Tennis is good exercise, a social experience, and a hobby that many people enjoy. While the price increases were dramatic on a percentage basis (they doubled!), the increase in price is a relatively small part of most New Yorkers' budgets. Because there are not many good substitutes for tennis available in New York City, we'd expect many to continue playing, as the data confirmed.

Sources: Author's calculations. Data from Matt McCue, "Tennis Fees Ace Out Many," *Wall Street Journal*, August 5, 2012. http://www.wsj.com/articles/SB10000872396390443687504577564933033308176.

Yummy, or all you can afford?

Income Elasticity

QUESTION: A college student eats ramen noodles twice a week and earns $300 a week working part-time. After graduating, the student earns $1,000 a week and eats ramen noodles once every other week , or 0.5 time a week. What is the student's income elasticity?

ANSWER: The income elasticity of demand using the midpoint method is

$$E_I = \frac{(Q_2 - Q_1) \div [(Q_1 + Q_2) \div 2]}{(I_2 - I_1) \div [(I_1 + I_2) \div 2]}$$

Plugging in the values from the question yields

$$E_I = \frac{(0.5 - 2.0) \div [(2.0 + 0.5) \div 2]}{(\$1000 - \$300) \div [(\$300 + \$1000) \div 2]}$$

Simplifying yields

$$E_I = \frac{-1.5 \div 1.25}{\$700 \div \$650}$$

Therefore, $E_I = -1.1$.

The income elasticity of demand is positive for normal goods and negative for inferior goods. Therefore, the negative coefficient indicates that ramen noodles are an inferior good over this person's range of income—in this example, between $300 and $1,000 per week. This result should confirm your intuition. The higher postgraduation income enables the student to substitute away from ramen noodles and toward other meals that provide more nourishment and enjoyment.

What Is the Price Elasticity of Supply?

The price elasticity of supply is a measure of the responsiveness of the quantity supplied to a change in price.

Like consumers, sellers are sensitive to price changes. However, the determinants of the price elasticity of supply are substantially different from the determinants of the price elasticity of demand. The **price elasticity of supply** is a measure of the responsiveness of the quantity supplied to a change in price.

In this section, we examine how much sellers respond to price changes. For instance, if the market price of gasoline increases, how will oil companies respond? The answer depends on the elasticity of supply. Oil must be refined into gasoline. If it is difficult for oil companies to increase their output of gasoline significantly, the quantity of gasoline supplied will not increase much even if the price increases a lot. In this case, we say that supply is inelastic, or unresponsive. However, if the price increase is small and suppliers respond by offering significantly more gasoline for sale, then supply is elastic. We would expect to observe this outcome if it is easy to refine oil into gasoline.

When supply is not able to respond to a change in price, we say it is inelastic. Think of an oceanfront property in Southern California. The amount of land next to the ocean is fixed. If the price of oceanfront property rises, the supply of land cannot adjust to the price increase. In this case, the supply is perfectly inelastic and the price elasticity of supply is zero. Recall that a price elasticity coefficient of zero means that quantity supplied does not change as price changes.

When the supplier's ability to make quick adjustments is limited, the elasticity of supply is less than 1. For instance, when a cellular network becomes congested, it takes suppliers a long time to provide additional capacity. They have to build new cell towers, which requires the purchase of land and additional construction costs. In contrast, a local hot dog vendor can easily add another cart in relatively short order. As a result, for the hot dog vendor, supply is elastic, with an elasticity coefficient that is greater than 1.

Table 4.6 examines the price elasticity of supply (E_s). Recall the law of supply, which states that there is a direct relationship between the price of a good and the quantity that a firm supplies. As a result, the percentage change in the quantity supplied and the percentage change in price move in the same direction. The E_s coefficient reflects this direct relationship with a positive sign.

What would it take to own a slice of paradise?

Determinants of the Price Elasticity of Supply

When we examined the determinants of the price elasticity of demand, we saw that consumers have to consider the number of substitutes, how expensive the item is compared to their overall budget, whether the good is a necessity or

TABLE 4.6

A Closer Look at the Price Elasticity of Supply

Elasticity	E_s coefficient	Example	
Perfectly inelastic	$E_s = 0$	Oceanfront land	
Relatively inelastic	$0 < E_s < 1$	Cell phone tower	
Relatively elastic	$E_s > 1$	Hot dog vendor	

a luxury, and the amount of time they have to make a decision. Time and the adjustment process are also key elements in determining the price elasticity of supply. However, there is a critical difference: the degree of flexibility that producers have in bringing their product to the market quickly.

The Flexibility of Producers

When a producer can quickly ramp up output, supply tends to be elastic. One way to maintain flexibility is to have spare production capacity. Extra capacity enables producers to quickly meet changing price conditions, so supply is more responsive, or elastic. The ability to store the good is another way to stay flexible. Producers who have stockpiles of their products can respond more quickly to changes in market conditions. For example, De Beers, the international diamond conglomerate, stores millions of uncut diamonds. As the price of diamonds fluctuates, De Beers can quickly change the quantity of diamonds it offers to the market. Likewise, hot dog vendors can relocate quickly from one street corner to another or add carts if demand is strong. However, many businesses cannot adapt to changing market conditions quickly. For instance, a golf course cannot easily add nine new holes to meet additional demand. This constraint limits the golf course owner's ability to adjust quickly, preventing the owner from quickly increasing the supply of golfing opportunities as soon as the fee changes.

Time and the Adjustment Process

In the immediate run, businesses are stuck with what they have on hand. For example, a pastry shop that runs out of chocolate glazed doughnuts cannot bake more instantly. As we move from the immediate run to the short run and a price change persists through time, supply—just like demand—becomes more elastic. For instance, a golf resort may be able to squeeze extra production out of its current facility by staying open longer hours or moving tee times closer together, but those short-run efforts will not match the production potential of adding another golf course in the long run.

Figure 4.5 shows how the two determinants of supply elasticity are mapped onto the supply curve. In the immediate run, the supply curve is vertical (S_1). A vertical curve tells us that there is no responsiveness when the price changes. As producers gain additional time to make adjustments, the supply curve rotates from S_1 (the immediate run) to S_2 (the short run) to S_3 (the long run). Like the demand curve, the supply curve becomes flatter through time. The only difference is that the supply curve rotates clockwise; in contrast, as we saw in Figure 4.2, the demand curve rotates counterclockwise. With both supply and demand, the most important thing to remember is that more time allows for greater adjustment, so the long run is always more elastic.

CALCULATING THE PRICE ELASTICITY OF SUPPLY We can use a simple formula to calculate the price elasticity of supply. Doing so is useful when a business owner must decide how much to produce at various prices. The elasticity of supply measures how quickly the producer is able to change production in response to changes in price. When supply is elastic, producers

FIGURE 4.5

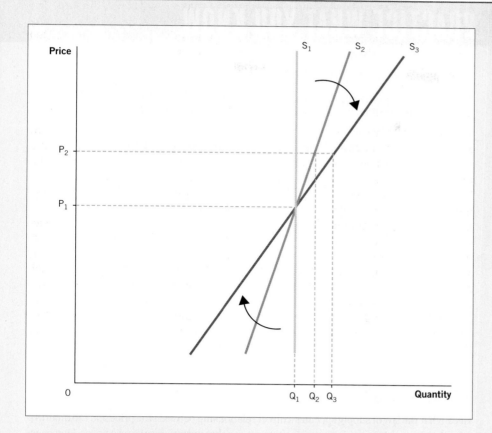

Elasticity and the Supply Curve

Increased flexibility and more time make supply more elastic. When price rises from P_1 to P_2, producers are unable to expand output immediately and the supply curve remains at Q_1 in the immediate run. In the short run (S_2), the firm becomes more flexible and output expands to Q_2. Eventually, in the long run (S_3), the firm is able to produce even more, and it moves to Q_3 in response to higher prices.

are able to quickly adjust production. If supply is inelastic, production tends to remain roughly constant, despite large swings in price.

Here is the formula for the price elasticity of supply (E_S):

$$E_S = \frac{\text{percentage change in the quantity supplied}}{\text{percentage change in the price}}$$

(EQUATION 4.5)

Consider how the manufacturer of Solo cups might respond to an increase in demand that causes the cups' market price to rise. The company's ability to change the amount it produces depends on the flexibility of the manufacturing process and the length of time needed to ramp up production. Suppose that the price of the cups rises by 10%. The company can increase its production by 5% immediately, but it will take many months to expand production by 20%. What can we say about the price elasticity of supply in this case? Using Equation 4.5, we can take the percentage change in the quantity supplied immediately (5%) and divide that by the percentage change in price (10%). This calculation gives us $E_S = 0.5$, which signals that supply is relatively inelastic. However, with time the firm is able to increase the quantity supplied by 20%. If we divide 20% by the percentage change in the price (10%), we get $E_S = 2.0$, which indicates that supply is relatively elastic in the long run.

How would the manufacturer of Solo cups respond to a price increase in the short run and in the long run?

The Price Elasticity of Supply

QUESTION: Suppose that the price of a barrel of oil increases from $50 to $100. The new output is 2 million barrels a day, and the old output is 1.8 million barrels a day. What is the price elasticity of supply?

ANSWER: The price elasticity of supply using the midpoint method is

$$E_s = \frac{(Q_2 - Q_1) \div [(Q_1 + Q_2) \div 2]}{(P_2 - P_1) \div [(P_1 + P_2) \div 2]}$$

Oil companies cannot quickly respond to rising prices.

Plugging in the values from the example yields

$$E_s = \frac{(2.0M - 1.8M) \div [(1.8M + 2.0M) \div 2]}{(\$100 - \$50) \div [(\$50 + \$100) \div 2]}$$

Simplifying yields

$$E_s = \frac{0.2M \div 1.9M}{\$50 \div \$75}$$

Therefore, $E_s = 0.16$.

Recall that the law of supply specifies a direct relationship between the price and the quantity supplied. Because E_s in this case is positive, we see that output rises as price rises. However, the magnitude of the output increase is quite small, as reflected in the coefficient 0.16. Because oil companies cannot easily change their production process, they have a limited ability to respond quickly to rising prices. That inability is reflected in a coefficient that is relatively close to zero. A zero coefficient would mean that suppliers could not change their output at all. Here suppliers are able to respond, but only in a limited capacity.

How Do the Price Elasticities of Demand and Supply Relate to Each Other?

The interplay between the price elasticity of supply and the price elasticity of demand allows us to explain more fully how the economy operates. With an understanding of elasticity at our disposal, we can conduct a much richer and deeper analysis of the world around us.

For instance, suppose that we are concerned about what will happen to the price of oil as economic development spurs additional demand in China and India. An examination of the determinants of the price elasticity of supply quickly confirms that oil producers have a limited ability to adjust production in response to rising prices. Oil wells can be uncapped to meet rising demand, but it takes years to bring the new capacity online. Moreover, storing oil reserves, while possible, is expensive. Therefore, the short-run supply of oil is quite inelastic. Figure 4.6 shows the combination of inelastic supply-side production constraints in the short run and the inelastic short-run demand for oil (D_1).

An increase in global demand from D_1 to D_2 will create significantly higher prices (from $50 to $90 per barrel) in the short run. This result occurs because increasing oil production is difficult in the short run. Therefore, the short-run supply curve (S_{SR}) is relatively inelastic. In the long run, though, oil producers are able to bring more oil to the market when prices are higher, so the supply curve rotates clockwise (to S_{LR}), becoming more elastic, and the market price falls to $80 per barrel (point E_3). (Note that we are using an arbitrary price for a barrel of oil. The price of oil has swung widely over the last decade, making it difficult to predict.)

What does this example tell us? It reminds us that the interplay between the price elasticity of demand and the price elasticity of supply determines the magnitude of the resulting price change. We cannot observe demand in isolation without also considering how supply responds. Similarly, we cannot simply think about the short-run consequences of demand and supply shifts; we also must consider how prices and quantity will vary in the long run. Armed with this knowledge, you can begin to see the power of the supply and demand model to explain the world around us.

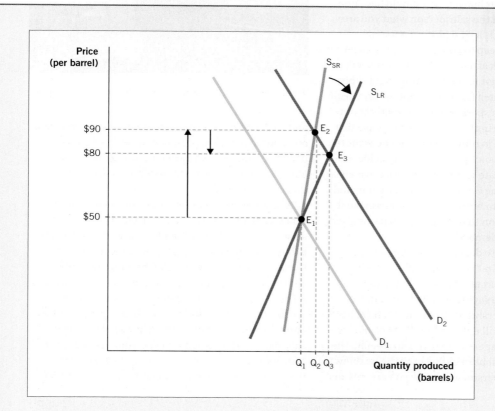

FIGURE 4.6

A Demand Shift and the Consequences for Short- and Long-Run Supply

When an increase in demand causes the price of oil to rise from $50 to $90 per barrel, initially producers are unable to expand output very much—production expands from Q_1 to Q_2. However, in the long run, as producers expand their production capacity, the price will fall to $80 per barrel.

Price Elasticity of Supply and Demand: Buying Your First Car

- Never buy a car on your first visit. Walking away shows that your demand is elastic and gives you a bargaining advantage.
- Don't give the salesperson information about your budget or allow them to run your credit.
- Shop when prices tend to be lower (end of the month, end of the model year, on a Sunday).

When you buy a car, your knowledge of price elasticity can help you negotiate the best possible deal.

Recall that three of the determinants of price elasticity of demand are (1) the share of the budget, (2) the number of available substitutes, and (3) the time you have to make a decision.

Let's start with your budget. You should have one in mind, but don't tell the salesperson what you are willing to spend; that is a vital piece of personal information you want to keep to yourself. If the salesperson suggests that you look at a model that is too expensive, just say that you are not interested. You might reply, "Buying a car is a stretch for me; I've got to stay within my budget." If the salesperson asks indirectly about your budget by inquiring whether you have a particular monthly payment in mind, reply that you want to negotiate over the invoice price once you decide on a vehicle. Never negotiate on the sticker price, which is the price you see in the car window, because it includes thousands of dollars in markup. You want to make it clear to the salesperson that the price you pay matters to you—that is, your demand is elastic.

Taking your time to decide is also important. Never buy a car the first time you walk onto a lot. If you convey the message that you want a car immediately, you are saying that your demand is inelastic. If the dealership thinks that you have no flexibility, the staff will not give you their best offer. Instead, tell the salesperson that you appreciate the help and that you will be deciding over the next few weeks. A good salesperson will know you are serious

Watch out for shady negotiation practices!

and will ask for your phone number or email address and contact you. The salesperson will sweeten the deal if you indicate you are narrowing down your choices and his or her dealership is in the running. You wait. You win.

Also know that salespeople and dealerships have times when they want to move inventory. The price elasticity of supply is at work here as well. A good time to buy is when the dealer is trying to move inventory to make room for new models (the autumn months), because prices fall for end-of-the-model-year closeouts. Likewise, many sales promotions and sales bonuses are tied to the end of the month, so salespeople will be more eager to sell at that time. The day of the week also matters. Here is some advice from TrueCar.com: "buyers on a Friday can pay as much as $2,000 more than those who shop on a Sunday for the same vehicle."

Elasticity: Trick or Treat Edition

QUESTION: An unusually bad growing season leads to a small pumpkin crop. What will happen to the price of pumpkins as Halloween approaches? Use elasticity to explain your answer.

ANSWER: The demand for pumpkins peaks in October and rapidly falls after Halloween. Purchasing a pumpkin is a short-run decision to buy a unique product that takes up a relatively small share of the consumer's budget. As a result, the price elasticity of demand for pumpkins leading up to Halloween tends to be quite inelastic. At the same time, a small crop causes the entire supply curve to shift left. As a result, the market price of pumpkins rises. Because the demand is relatively inelastic in the short run and the supply of pumpkins is fixed, we expect the price to rise significantly. After Halloween, the price of any remaining pumpkins falls, because demand declines dramatically.

How much would you spend on a Halloween pumpkin?

Conclusion

Do sellers charge the highest price possible? We can now address this misconception definitively: no. Sellers like higher prices in the same way consumers like lower prices, but that does not mean that sellers will charge the highest price possible. At very high prices, consumer demand is quite elastic. Therefore, a seller who charges too high a price will not sell much. As a result, firms learn that they must lower their price to attract more customers and maximize their total revenue.

Incentives

The ability to determine whether demand and supply are elastic or inelastic enables economists to calculate the effects of personal, business, and policy decisions. When you combine the concept of elasticity with the supply and demand model from Chapter 3, you get a very powerful tool. In subsequent chapters, we use elasticity to refine our models of economic behavior and make our results more realistic. ✳

· ANSWERING *the* BIG QUESTIONS ·

What is the price elasticity of demand, and what are its determinants?

- The price elasticity of demand is a measure of the responsiveness of quantity demanded to a change in price.
- Demand will generally be more elastic if there are many substitutes available, if the item accounts for a large share of the consumer's budget, if the item is a luxury good, if the market is more narrowly defined, or if the consumer has plenty of time to make a decision.

- Economists categorize time in three distinct periods: (1) the immediate run, when there is no time for consumers to adjust their behavior; (2) the short run, when consumers can adjust, but only partially; and (3) the long run, when consumers have time to fully adjust to market conditions.

- The price elasticity of demand is calculated by dividing the percentage change in the quantity demanded by the percentage change in price. A value of zero indicates that the quantity demanded does not respond to a price change; if the price elasticity is zero, demand is said to be perfectly inelastic. When the price elasticity of demand is between 0 and −1, demand is inelastic. If the price elasticity of demand is less than −1, demand is elastic. When price elasticity is exactly −1, the item has unitary elasticity.

How do changes in income and the prices of other goods affect elasticity?

- The income elasticity of demand measures how a change in income affects spending. Normal goods have a positive income elasticity. Inferior goods have a negative income elasticity.

- The cross-price elasticity of demand measures the responsiveness of the quantity demanded of one good to a change in the price of a related good. Positive values for the cross-price elasticity mean that the two goods are substitutes, while negative values indicate that the two goods are complements. If the cross-price elasticity is zero, then the two goods are not related to each other.

What is the price elasticity of supply?

- The price elasticity of supply is a measure of the responsiveness of the quantity supplied to a change in price. Supply will generally be more elastic if producers have flexibility in the production process and ample time to adjust production.

- The price elasticity of supply is calculated by dividing the percentage change in the quantity supplied by the percentage change in price. A value of zero indicates that the quantity supplied does not respond to a price change; if the price elasticity of supply is zero, supply is said to be perfectly inelastic. When the price elasticity of supply is between 0 and 1, demand is relatively inelastic. If the price elasticity of supply is greater than 1, supply is elastic.

How do the price elasticities of demand and supply relate to each other?

- The interplay between the price elasticity of demand and the price elasticity of supply determines the magnitude of the resulting price change.

· CHAPTER PROBLEMS ·

Concepts You Should Know

cross-price elasticity of
    demand (p. 139)
elasticity (p. 117)
immediate run (p. 119)

income elasticity of demand
    (p. 138)
long run (p. 119)
price elasticity of demand (p. 117)

price elasticity of supply (p. 142)
short run (p. 119)
total revenue (p. 131)

Questions for Review

1. Define the price elasticity of demand.

2. What are the four determinants of the price elasticity of demand?

3. Give an example of a good that has elastic demand. What is the value of the price elasticity if demand is elastic? Give an example of a good that has inelastic demand. What is the value of the price elasticity if demand is inelastic?

4. What is the connection between total revenue and the price elasticity of demand? Illustrate this relationship along a demand curve.

5. Explain why slope is different from elasticity.

6. Define the price elasticity of supply.

7. What are the two determinants of the price elasticity of supply?

8. Give an example of a good that has elastic supply. What is the value of the price elasticity if supply is elastic? Give an example of a good that has an inelastic supply. What is the value of the price elasticity if supply is inelastic?

9. Give an example of a normal good. What is the income elasticity of a normal good? Give an example of a luxury good. What is the income elasticity of a luxury good? Give an example of a necessity. What is the income elasticity of a necessity? Give an example of an inferior good. What is the income elasticity of an inferior good?

10. Define the cross-price elasticity of demand. Give an example of a good with negative cross-price elasticity, another with zero cross-price elasticity, and a third with positive cross-price elasticity.

Study Problems (✱ solved at the end of the section)

✱ 1. If the government decided to impose a 50% tax on gray T-shirts, would this policy generate a large increase in tax revenues or a small increase? Use elasticity to explain your answer.

✱ 2. College logo T-shirts priced at $15 sell at a rate of 25 per week, but when the bookstore marks them down to $10, it finds that it can sell 50 T-shirts per week. What is the price elasticity of demand for the logo T-shirts?

3. Black Friday, the day after Thanksgiving, is the largest shopping day of the year. Do the early shoppers, who often wait in line for hours in the cold to get doorbuster sale items, have elastic or inelastic demand? Explain your response.

4. If a 20% increase in price causes a 10% drop in the quantity demanded, is the price elasticity of demand for this good elastic, unitary, or inelastic?

5. Characterize the demand for each of the following goods or services as perfectly elastic, relatively elastic, relatively inelastic, or perfectly inelastic.

    a. a lifesaving medication
    b. photocopies at a copy shop, when all competing shops charge 10 cents per copy
    c. a fast-food restaurant located in the food court of a shopping mall
    d. the water you buy from your local utility company

6. A local paintball business receives a total revenue of $8,000 a month when it charges $10 per person and $9,600 in total revenue when it charges $6 per person. Over that range of prices, does the business face elastic, unitary, or inelastic demand?

7. At a price of $200, a cell phone company manufactures 300,000 phones. At a price of $150, the

company produces 200,000 phones. What is the price elasticity of supply?

8. Do customers who visit convenience stores at 3 a.m. have a price elasticity of demand that is more elastic or less elastic than those who visit at 3 p.m.?

✳ 9. A worker eats at a restaurant once a week. He then gets a 25% raise. As a result, he decides to eat out twice as much as before and cut back on the number of frozen lasagna dinners from one frozen dinner a week to one every other week. Determine the income elasticity of demand for eating at a restaurant and for having frozen lasagna dinners.

10. The cross-price elasticity of demand between American Eagle and Hollister is 2.0. What does that coefficient tell us about the relationship between these two stores?

11. A local golf course is considering lowering its fees in order to increase its total revenue. Under what conditions will the fee reduction achieve its goal?

12. A private university notices that in-state and out-of-state students seem to respond differently to tuition changes.

Tuition	Quantity demanded (in-state applicants)	Quantity demanded (out-of-state applicants)
$10,000	6,000	12,000
15,000	5,000	9,000
20,000	4,000	6,000
30,000	3,000	3,000

As the price of tuition rises from $15,000 to $20,000, what is the price elasticity of demand for in-state applicants and also for out-of-state applicants?

✳ 13. The TV show *Extreme Couponing* features coupon users who go to extraordinary measures to save money on their weekly purchases. The show follows these coupon users throughout the week as they assemble coupons and scout out stores to see which have the best deals, and then follows them to the store for the big buy. Do extreme "couponers" have extremely elastic demand or extremely inelastic demand? Explain. (*Note:* If you are unfamiliar with the show, you can Google it and watch a segment.)

14. Suppose a hotel raises the price of the bottled water in the minibar in each room from $3 to $5. The hotel tracks the number of customers who buy the bottled water and finds that consumption drops from 1,000 bottles a week to 900 bottles. Is demand elastic or inelastic? Explain.

15. Americans bought 143 billion gallons of gas in 2016 when the price was $2.25. Back in 2012, when the price was $3.64, they bought 133 billion gallons. Is the demand for gasoline elastic, unitary, or inelastic?

16. In 2018, the NFC football team the Atlanta Falcons moved to a new stadium. As part of this move, they dropped their stadium's food and beverage prices 50% versus prices at the old stadium. In order for this pricing strategy to work, the Falcons must believe that consumer demand is _____. Explain your answer.

Solved Problems

1. To answer this question, we need to consider the price elasticity of demand. The tax is only on gray T-shirts. This means that T-shirt customers who buy other colors can avoid the tax entirely—which means that the demand for gray T-shirts is relatively elastic. Not many gray T-shirts will be sold, so the government will generate only a small increase in revenues from the tax.

2. Plugging into the formula for E_D gives us

$$E_D = \frac{(50 - 25) \div [(25 + 50) \div 2]}{(10 - 15) \div [(15 + 10) \div 2]} = -1.67$$

9. In this question a worker gets a 25% (or 0.25) raise, so we can use this information in the denominator when determining the income elasticity of demand. We are not given the percentage change for the meals out, so we need to plug in how often the worker ate out before (once a week) and the amount he eats out after the raise (twice a week) into the numerator.

Plugging into E_I gives us

$$E_I = \frac{(2 - 1) \div [(1 + 2) \div 2]}{0.25}$$

Simplifying yields

$$E_I = \frac{1 \div 1.5}{0.25}$$

Therefore, $E_I = 2.67$.

The income elasticity of demand for eating at a restaurant is positive for normal goods. Therefore, eating at a restaurant is a normal good. This result should confirm your intuition.

Let's see what happens with frozen lasagna once the worker gets the 25% raise. Now he cuts back on the number of lasagna dinners from once a week to once every other week. This information is plugged into the numerator, while the 25% change in income, or 0.25, is plugged into the denominator.

Plugging into E_I gives us

$$E_I = \frac{(0.5 - 1) \div [(1 + 0.5) \div 2]}{0.25}$$

Simplifying yields

$$E_I = \frac{-0.5 \div 0.75}{0.25}$$

Therefore, $E_I = -2.67$.

The income elasticity of demand for having frozen lasagna is negative. Therefore, frozen lasagna is an inferior good. This result should confirm your intuition.

13. The show is called *Extreme Couponing* for a reason. Ordinary people don't spend more than 20 hours a week trying to find the best deals on grocery items, scouting stores, comparing prices, and make purchases based solely on what's on sale. The persons featured in the show are obsessive about saving money. When the price you pay is the most important determinant of what you buy, demand is extremely elastic.

Market Outcomes and Tax Incidence

Taxes on Firms Affect Consumers.

Many people believe that when the government taxes businesses, consumers catch a break because firms pay the tax. If only life worked that way! As this chapter explains, who actually pays the tax often is quite different from the party that is legally responsible for making the tax payment.

Gasoline prices are a common and visible sign of the market at work. It is hard not to notice when gasoline prices rise or fall, because every gas station posts its prices prominently. But there are a few things you might not know. First, gasoline taxes vary significantly from state to state, and they vary wildly from country to country. Residents of Saudi Arabia pay some of the lowest gasoline prices in the world, while Israelis have to put up with the world's third-highest gas prices. This occurs because the governments of certain oil-rich countries, such as Saudi Arabia, subsidize gasoline so that their citizens pay less than the market price. In countries where gasoline is subsidized, consumers drive their cars everywhere, mass transportation is largely unavailable, and there is less concern for fuel efficiency. As you might imagine, the opposite is true in countries with high gasoline taxes, like Israel, where consumers drive less, use public transportation more often, and tend to purchase fuel-efficient vehicles.

In countries with high gasoline taxes, close to $50 for every fill-up can be for taxes. However, in Saudi Arabia, gasoline taxes are almost nonexistent and gasoline is less expensive than bottled water.

What do gasoline taxes and subsidies around the world have in common? They are all folded into the price you see at the pump, which might lead you to believe that the seller is paying all of the tax or receiving the entire subsidy. Nothing could be further from the truth. The firm will try to pass along the tax to consumers in the form of higher prices. Likewise, in countries with subsidies, the firm must pass along lower prices to consumers. After reading this chapter, you will understand how this process works.

We begin this chapter by discussing consumer and producer surplus, two concepts that illustrate gains from trade. These concepts help us measure the efficiency of markets and the effects of taxation. Then we examine how taxation creates distortions in economic behavior by altering the incentives people and firms face when consuming and producing goods that are taxed.

· BIG QUESTIONS ·

- What are consumer surplus and producer surplus?
- When is a market efficient?
- Why do taxes create deadweight loss in otherwise efficient markets?

What Are Consumer Surplus and Producer Surplus?

Trade creates value

Welfare economics
is the branch of economics that studies how the allocation of resources affects economic well-being.

Markets create value by bringing together buyers and sellers so that consumers and producers can mutually benefit from trade. **Welfare economics** is the branch of economics that studies how the allocation of resources affects economic well-being. In this section, we develop two concepts that help us measure the value markets create: *consumer surplus* and *producer surplus*.

In competitive markets, the equilibrium price is simultaneously low enough to attract consumers and high enough to encourage producers. This balance between demand and supply enhances the *welfare* (well-being) of society. That is not to say that society's welfare depends solely on markets. People also find satisfaction in many nonmarket settings, including spending time with families and friends, doing hobbies, and helping with charity work. We incorporate aspects of personal satisfaction into our economic model in Chapter 16. For now, let's focus on how markets enhance human welfare.

Consumer Surplus

Consider three students: Ron, Leslie, and Donna, all city government employees in the small Midwestern town of Pawnee (you may recognize them from the TV series *Parks and Recreation*). They need to take a class in basic economics, to better understand Pawnee's business environment. Like students everywhere, each of them has a maximum price he or she is willing to pay for a new economics textbook. Ron has a keen interest in financial matters, and he is prepared to invest quite a bit of money in a new book. Leslie is extremely conscientious but on a tighter budget than Ron and also not quite so committed to that particular class. Donna is a departmental colleague who is a confident negotiator and is also successful in her outside life. Table 5.1 shows the value each student places on the textbook. This value, called the **willingness to pay**, is the maximum price a consumer will pay for a good or service. The willingness to pay is also known as the *reservation price*. In an auction or a negotiation, the willingness to pay, or reservation price, is the price beyond which the consumer decides to walk away from the transaction.

Consider what happens when the price of the book is $151. If Ron purchases the book at $151, he pays $49 less than the $200 maximum he was willing to pay. He values the textbook at $49 more than the purchase price, so buying the book makes him better off.

Consumer surplus is the difference between the willingness to pay for a good (or service) and the price paid to get it. While Ron gains $49 in consumer surplus, a price of $151 is more than either Leslie or Donna is willing to pay. Because Leslie is willing to pay only $150, if she purchases the book she will experience a consumer loss of $1. Donna's willingness to pay is $100, so if she buys the book for $151 she will experience a consumer loss of $51. Whenever

These Pawnee city employees want to earn a consumer surplus.

Willingness to pay
also known as the *reservation price,* is the maximum price a consumer will pay for a good or service.

Consumer surplus
is the difference between the willingness to pay for a good (or service) and the price paid to get it.

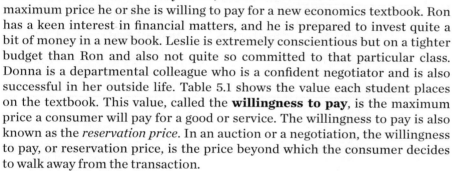

TABLE 5.1

Willingness to Pay for a New Economics Textbook

Buyer	Willingness to pay
Ron	$200
Leslie	150
Donna	100

FIGURE 5.1

Demand Curve for an Economics Textbook

The demand curve has a step for each additional textbook purchase. As the price goes down, more students buy the textbook.

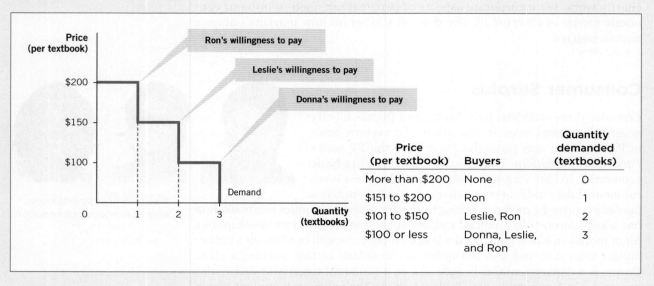

Price (per textbook)	Buyers	Quantity demanded (textbooks)
More than $200	None	0
$151 to $200	Ron	1
$101 to $150	Leslie, Ron	2
$100 or less	Donna, Leslie, and Ron	3

the price is greater than the willingness to pay, a rational consumer will decide not to buy.

Using Demand Curves to Illustrate Consumer Surplus

In the previous section, we discussed consumer surplus as a dollar amount. We can illustrate it graphically with a demand curve. Figure 5.1 shows the demand curve drawn from the data in Table 5.1. Notice that the curve looks like a staircase with three steps—one for each additional textbook purchase. Each point on a market demand curve corresponds to a specific number of units sold.

At any price above $200, none of the students wants to purchase a textbook. This relationship is evident on the *x* axis where the quantity demanded is 0 at a price of $200. At any price between $151 and $200, Ron is the only buyer, so the quantity demanded is 1. At prices between $101 and $150, Ron and Leslie are both willing to buy the textbook, so the quantity demanded is 2. Finally, if the price is $100 or less, all three students are willing to buy the textbook, so the quantity demanded is 3. As the price falls, the quantity demanded increases.

We can measure the total extent of consumer surplus by examining the area under the demand curve for each of our three consumers, as shown in Figure 5.2. In panel (a), the price is $175, and only Ron decides to buy. Because his willingness to pay is $200, he is better off by $25, which is his consumer

FIGURE 5.2

Determining Consumer Surplus from a Demand Curve

(a) At a price of $175, Ron is the only buyer, so the quantity demanded is 1. (b) At a price of $125, Ron and Leslie are both willing to buy the textbook, so the quantity demanded is 2.

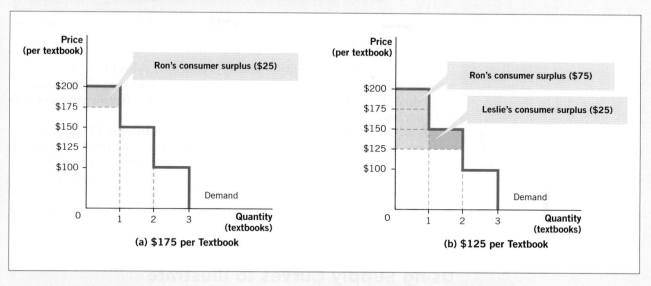

(a) $175 per Textbook

(b) $125 per Textbook

surplus. The light blue area under the demand curve and above the price represents the benefit Ron receives from purchasing a textbook at a price of $175. When the price drops to $125, as shown in panel (b), Leslie also decides to buy a textbook. Now the total quantity demanded is 2. Leslie's willingness to pay is $150, so her consumer surplus, represented by the darker blue area, is $25. However, since Ron's willingness to pay is $200, his consumer surplus rises from $25 to $75. So a textbook price of $125 raises the total consumer surplus from $25 at a price of $200 to $75 + $25 = $100. In other words, lower prices create more consumer surplus in this market—and in any other.

Producer Surplus

Sellers also benefit from market transactions. In this section, three other Pawnee city employees, Ann, April, and Andy, discover that they are good at economics and decide to go into the tutoring business. They do not want to provide this service for free, but each has a different minimum price. The **willingness to sell** is the minimum price a seller will accept to sell a good or service. Table 5.2 shows each tutor's willingness to sell their services.

Consider what happens at a tutoring price of $25 per hour. Because Ann is willing to tutor for $10 per hour, every hour she tutors at $25 per hour earns her $15 more than her willingness to sell. This extra $15 per hour is her producer surplus. **Producer surplus** is the difference between the willingness to sell a good or service and the price the seller receives. April is willing

Willingness to sell
is the minimum price a seller will accept to sell a good or service.

Producer surplus
is the difference between the willingness to sell a good (or service) and the price the seller receives.

TABLE 5.2	
Willingness to Sell Tutoring Services	
Seller	**Willingness to sell**
Andy	$30/hr
April	20/hr
Ann	10/hr

to tutor for $20 per hour and earns a $5 producer surplus for every hour she tutors at $25 per hour. Finally, Andy's willingness to tutor, at $30 per hour, is more than the market price of $25. If he tutors, he will have a producer loss of $5 per hour.

Opportunity cost

How do producers determine their willingness to sell? They must consider two factors: the direct costs of producing the good and the indirect costs, or opportunity costs. Students who are new to economics often mistakenly assume that the cost of producing an item is the only cost to consider in making the decision to produce. But producers also have opportunity costs. Ann, April and Andy each has a unique willingness to sell because each has a different opportunity cost.

Using Supply Curves to Illustrate Producer Surplus

Continuing our example, the supply curve in Figure 5.3 shows the relationship between the price for an hour of tutoring and the number of tutors who are willing to sell their services. As you can see on the supply schedule (the table within the figure), at any price less than $10 per hour, no one wants to tutor. At prices between $10 and $19 per hour, Ann is the only tutor, so the quantity supplied is 1. Between $20 and $29 per hour, Ann and April are willing to tutor, so the quantity supplied rises to 2. Finally, if the price is $30 or more, all three coworkers are willing to tutor, so the quantity supplied is 3. As the price they receive for tutoring rises, the number of tutors increases from 0 to 3.

What do these relationships between price and quantity supplied tell us about producer surplus? Let's turn to Figure 5.4. By examining the area above the supply curve, we can measure the extent of producer surplus. In panel (a), the price of an hour of tutoring is $15. At that price, only Ann decides to tutor. Since she would be willing to tutor even if the price were as low as $10 per hour, she is $5 per hour better off tutoring. Ann's producer surplus is represented by the light red area between the supply curve and the price of $15. Because April and Andy do not tutor when the price is $15 per hour, they do not receive any producer surplus. In panel (b), the price for tutoring is $25 per hour. At this price, April also decides to tutor. Her willingness to tutor is $20, so when the price is $25 per hour, her producer surplus is $5 per hour, represented by the darker red area. Since Ann's willingness to tutor is $10, at $25 per hour her producer surplus rises to $15 per hour. By looking at the shaded boxes in panel (b), we see that an increase in the rates for tutoring raises the combined producer surplus of Ann and April to $15 + $5 = $20 per hour.

FIGURE 5.3

Supply Curve for Economics Tutoring

The supply curve has three steps, one for each additional coworker who is willing to tutor. Progressively higher prices will induce more coworkers to become tutors.

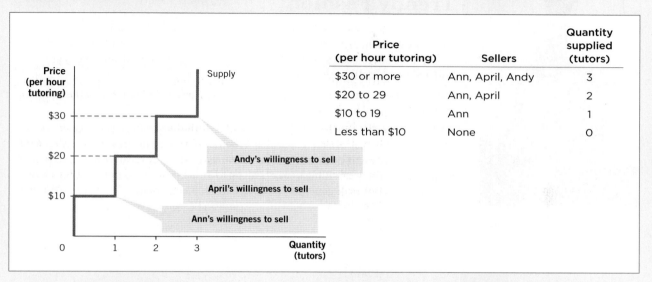

Price (per hour tutoring)	Sellers	Quantity supplied (tutors)
$30 or more	Ann, April, Andy	3
$20 to 29	Ann, April	2
$10 to 19	Ann	1
Less than $10	None	0

FIGURE 5.4

Determining Producer Surplus from a Supply Curve

(a) The price of an hour of tutoring is $15. At this price, only Ann decides to tutor. (b) The price for tutoring is $25 per hour. At this price, April also decides to tutor.

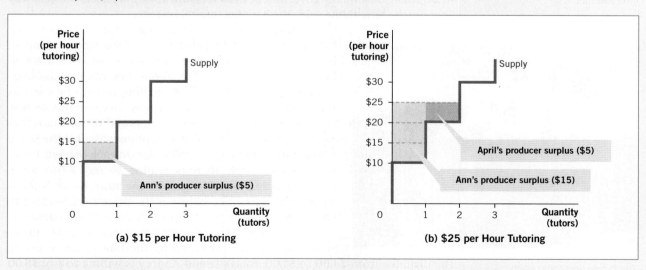

(a) $15 per Hour Tutoring

(b) $25 per Hour Tutoring

Cardi B looking regal in a D&G dress.

Consumer and Producer Surplus: Trendy Fashion

Leah decides to buy a used Dolce & Gabbana dress for $80. She was willing to pay $100. When her friend Becky sees the dress, she loves it and thinks it is worth $150. So she offers Leah $125 for the dress, and Leah accepts. Leah and Becky are both thrilled with the exchange.

QUESTION: Determine the total surplus from the original purchase and the additional surplus generated by the resale of the dress.

ANSWER: Leah was willing to pay $100 and the dress cost $80, so she keeps the difference, or $20, as consumer surplus. When Leah resells the dress to Becky for $125, Leah earns $25 in producer surplus. At the same time, Becky receives $25 in consumer surplus, since she was willing to pay Leah up to $150 for the dress but Leah sells it to her for $125. The resale generates an additional $50 in surplus.

When Is a Market Efficient?

Total surplus, also known as **social welfare**, is the sum of consumer surplus and producer surplus. It measures the well-being of all participants in a market, absent any government intervention.

We have seen how consumers benefit from lower prices and how producers benefit from higher prices. When we combine the concepts of consumer and producer surplus, we can build a complete picture of the welfare of buyers and sellers. Adding consumer and producer surplus gives us **total surplus**, also known as **social welfare**, because it measures the well-being of all participants in a market, absent any government intervention. Total surplus is the best way economists have to measure the benefits markets create.

Figure 5.5 illustrates the relationship between consumer surplus and producer surplus for a slice of pumpkin pie. The demand curve shows that some customers are willing to pay more for a slice of pie than others. Likewise, some sellers (producers) are willing to sell pie for less than others. The demand and supply curves in this section are drawn as straight lines (as opposed to the stairsteps we have seen so far), since we will now assume there are a large number of buyers and sellers in each market.

Let's say that Russ is willing to pay $7.00 for a slice of pie, but when he gets to the store he finds it for $4.00. The difference between the price he is willing to pay, represented by point A, and the price he actually pays, represented by E (the equilibrium price), is $3.00 in consumer surplus, as indicated by the blue arrow showing the distance from $4.00 to $7.00. Russ's friend Audrey is willing to pay $5.00 for a slice of pie, but, like Russ, she finds it for $4.00. Therefore, she receives

The buyer and seller each benefit from this exchange.

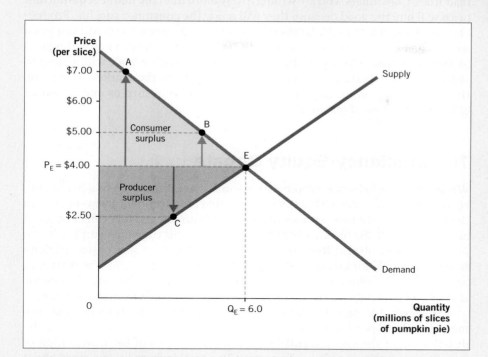

FIGURE 5.5

Consumer and Producer Surplus for Pumpkin Pie

Consumer surplus is the difference between the willingness to pay along the demand curve and the equilibrium price, P_E. It is illustrated by the blue triangle. Producer surplus is the difference between the willingness to produce along the supply curve and the equilibrium price. It is illustrated by the red triangle.

$1.00 in consumer surplus, as indicated by the green arrow at point B showing the distance from $4.00 to $5.00. In fact, all consumers who are willing to pay more than $4.00 are better off when they purchase the slice of pie at $4.00. We can show this total area of consumer surplus on the graph as the blue triangle bordered by the demand curve, the y axis, and the equilibrium price (P_E). At every point in this area, consumers who are willing to pay more than the equilibrium price for pie are better off.

Continuing with Figure 5.5, to identify producer surplus we follow a similar process. Suppose that Ellen's Bakery is willing to sell pumpkin pie for $2.50 per slice, represented by point C. Because the equilibrium price is $4.00, the business makes $1.50 per slice in producer surplus, as indicated by the red arrow at point C showing the distance from $4.00 to $2.50. If we think of the supply curve as representing the costs of many different sellers, we can calculate the total producer surplus as the red triangle bordered by the supply curve, the y axis, and the equilibrium price. The blue triangle (consumer surplus) and the red triangle (producer surplus) describe the increase in total surplus, or social welfare, created by the production and exchange of the good at the equilibrium price. At the equilibrium quantity of 6 million slices of pie, output and consumption reach the largest possible combination of producer and consumer surplus. In the region of the graph beyond 6 million units, buyers and sellers will experience a loss of surplus.

When an allocation of resources maximizes total surplus, the result is said to be **efficient**. In Figure 5.5, efficiency occurs at point E, where the market is in equilibrium. To think about why the market creates the largest possible total surplus, or social welfare, it is important to recall how the market allocates

Trade creates value

An outcome is **efficient** when an allocation of resources maximizes total surplus.

resources. Consumers who are willing to pay more than the market equilibrium price will buy the good because they will enjoy the consumer surplus. Producers who are willing to sell the good for less than the market equilibrium price will enjoy the producer surplus. In addition, consumers with a low willingness to buy (less than $4.00 per slice) and producers with a high willingness to sell (more than $4.00 per slice) do not participate in the market. Therefore, the equilibrium output at point E maximizes the total surplus and is also an efficient allocation of resources.

The Efficiency-Equity Debate

When modeling behavior, economists assume that participants in a market are rational decision-makers. That is, we assume that producers will always operate in the region of the triangle representing producer surplus, and that consumers will always operate in the region of the triangle representing consumer surplus. We do not, for example, expect Russ to pay more than $7.00 for a slice of pie or Ellen's Bakery to sell pie for less than $2.50 per slice. In other words, for the market to work efficiently, voluntary instances of consumer loss must be rare. We assume that self-interest helps to ensure that all participants benefit from an exchange.

However, the fact that both parties benefit from an exchange does not mean that both parties benefit equally. Economists are also interested in the distribution of the gains. **Equity** refers to the fairness of the distribution of benefits among the members of a society. In a world where no one cared about equity, only efficiency would matter and no particular division would be preferred. Another way of thinking about fairness versus efficiency is to consider a pie. If our only concern is efficiency, we will simply want to make sure that none of the pie goes to waste. But if we care about equity, we will also care about how the pie is divvied up, perhaps making sure that everyone gets a bite of the pie or at least has access to the pie.

In our first look at consumer and producer surplus, we have assumed that markets produce efficient outcomes. But in the real world, efficient outcomes are not guaranteed. Markets also fail; their efficiency can be compromised in a number of ways. We discuss market failure in much greater detail in subsequent chapters. For now, all you need to know is that failure can occur.

Trade creates value

Equity
refers to the fairness of the distribution of benefits among the members of a society.

Efficiency only requires that the pie get eaten. Equity is a question of how the pie gets divided.

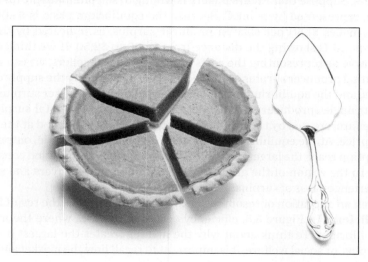

Efficiency

ADAM RUINS EVERYTHING: WHY GIFT GIVING MAKES NO ECONOMIC SENSE

In this 2016 episode of the truTV series *Adam Ruins Everything*, Adam Conover pops into Emily and Murph's living room on the morning of their first Christmas together, just as they are opening gifts. Adam begins his lecture by defining economic value. He states that the value of an object is "how much it's worth to you," and immediately dollar amounts appear next to items throughout the room. Adam observes that a giant cardboard cutout of The Rock (a.k.a. Dwayne Johnson) standing in one corner is worth $100 to Emily. "But I only paid $50 for it," she happily replies. Adam then explains that in that case, "when you bought it, you literally created $50 in value. You're $50 richer." Emily is pleased. "Let's go to Vegas!" she exclaims.

While this lesson in basic economics is going on, a voice from the chimney signals the arrival of another visitor—not Santa, to Murph's disappointment, but economist Joel Waldfogel. He explains that while we are all really good at knowing what we like, we are not so good at knowing what others want. As Waldfogel talks, Emily unwraps a gift from Murph, a "Rock the Vote" T-shirt. Emily is less than impressed. She says she will probably wear it to bed but wouldn't have paid more than $15 for it. Murph, annoyed, declares that he paid $50 for it, to which Waldfogel responds, "Well, Murph, you just destroyed $35 worth of value." Adam piles on: "You might as well have set it on fire."

The cameo by Joel Waldfogel is a result of his research on "The Deadweight Loss of Christmas." He found that poor gift buying results in a loss of economic value of anywhere from 10 to 33% of the money spent during the holidays. That has led some economists to conclude that cash is the most efficient gift, since the recipient can simply spend the money as they see fit. Angus Deaton, however, pointed out that Waldfogel did not ask respondents to include any sentimental value they received from the gifts.

When we spend more on a gift than the recipient values it at, we destroy economic value.

Deaton states, "Money would be better than a gift if you define the problem narrowly enough. And that insight, like a lot of insights in economics, is valuable to have. But stopping there is the problem." Judy Chevalier thinks that Waldfogel and Deaton both make good points. She agreed with Waldfogel that giving gifts is often inefficient, but she also agrees with Deaton: "You can't stop there. If you ask people after Christmas how much they value this sweater, it's almost always less than what the giver spent on it. Does that mean I don't give Christmas gifts? No, I give Christmas gifts!" Most of us merrily exchange gifts each year, and we don't feel worse off for it. We value the sense of family that gift giving creates, and many gifts we receive convey a message that has immense intangible value: we know that someone loves us. It's hard to put a price on that.

Does less consumer income affect total surplus?

Total Surplus: How Would Lower Consumer Income Affect Urban Outfitters?

QUESTION: If a drop in consumer income occurs, what will happen to the consumer surplus that customers enjoy at Urban Outfitters? What will happen to the amount of producer surplus Urban Outfitters receives? Illustrate your answer by shifting the demand curve appropriately and labeling the new and old areas of consumer and producer surplus.

ANSWER: Because the items sold at Urban Outfitters are normal goods, a drop in income shifts the demand curve (D) to the left. The black arrow shows the leftward shift in the second graph below. When you compare the area of consumer surplus (in blue) before and after the drop in income—that is, graphs (a) and (b)—you can see that consumer surplus shrinks. Producer surplus (in red) also shrinks.

Your intuition might already confirm what the graphs tell us. Because consumers have less income, they buy fewer clothes at Urban Outfitters—so consumer surplus falls. Likewise, because fewer customers buy the store's clothes, Urban Outfitters sells less—so producer surplus falls. This result is also evident in graph (b), because $Q_2 < Q_1$.

CHALLENGE QUESTION: Now let's add an additional consideration. Suppose that Urban Outfitters also faces high manufacturing costs at the same time that consumer income drops. Will consumer and producer surplus continue to shrink in size or rebound?

ANSWER: Higher manufacturing costs will cause the supply curve to shift left. If you look at the second panel, you can visualize how a leftward shift in the supply curve will cause the new equilibrium to occur at a price above P_2 and the new equilibrium quantity to be less than Q_2. Since the overall quantity supplied shrinks, the areas of consumer and producer surplus will shrink as well.

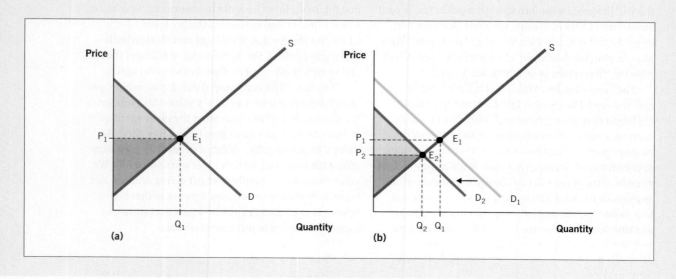

Why Do Taxes Create Deadweight Loss in Otherwise Efficient Markets?

Taxes provide many benefits. Taxes help to pay for many of society's needs—public transportation, schools, police, the court system, and the military, to name just a few. Most of us take these services for granted, but without taxes it would be impossible to pay for them. How much do all of these services cost? When you add all the federal, state, and local government budgets in the United States, you get over $6 trillion a year in taxes!

Spending tax dollars incurs opportunity costs, because the money could have been used in other ways. In this section, we use the concepts of consumer and producer surplus to explain the effect of taxation on social welfare and market efficiency. Taxes come in many sizes and shapes. There are taxes on personal income, payroll, property, corporate profits, sales, and inheritance, for example. Fortunately, we do not have to examine the entire tax code all at once. In the pages that follow, we explore the impact of taxes on social welfare by looking at one of the simplest taxes, the *excise tax*.

Opportunity cost

Tax Incidence

Economists want to know how taxes affect the choices that consumers and producers make. When a tax is imposed on an item, do buyers switch to alternative goods that are not taxed? How do producers respond when the products they sell are taxed? Because taxes cause prices to rise, they can affect how much of a good or service is bought and sold. This outcome is especially evident with **excise taxes**, which are taxes levied on a particular good or service. For example, all 50 states levy excise taxes on cigarettes, but the amount assessed varies tremendously. In New York, cigarette taxes are over $4.00 per pack, while in a handful of tobacco-producing states (including Virginia and North Carolina), the excise tax is less than $0.50 per pack. Overall, excise taxes, such as those on cigarettes, alcohol, and gasoline, account for less than 4% of all tax revenues. But because we can isolate changes in consumer behavior that result from taxes on one item, excise taxes help us understand the overall effect of a tax.

In looking at the effect of a tax, economists are also interested in the **incidence** of taxation, which refers to the burden of taxation on the party who pays the tax. To understand this idea, consider a $1.00 tax on milk purchases. We consider two cases: a tax placed directly on buyers and a tax placed directly on sellers.

Excise taxes
are taxes levied on a particular good or service.

Incidence
refers to the burden of taxation on the party who pays the tax through higher prices, regardless of whom the tax is actually levied on.

EXAMPLE 1: TAX ON BUYERS Each time a consumer buys a gallon of milk, the cash register adds $1.00 in tax. This means that to purchase the milk, the consumer must be willing to pay the price of the milk plus the $1.00 tax.

The result of the $1.00 tax on milk is shown in Figure 5.6. Because of the tax, consumers' willingness to pay for milk goes down, and the demand curve shifts down from D_1 to D_2. Why does the demand curve shift? The extra cost makes consumers less likely to buy milk at every price,

Why do we place excise taxes on cigarettes . . .

. . . and gasoline?

FIGURE 5.6

A Tax on Buyers

After the tax, the new equilibrium price (E$_2$) is $3.50, but the buyer must also pay $1.00 in tax. Therefore, despite the drop in equilibrium price, the buyer still pays more for a gallon of milk: $4.50 instead of the original equilibrium price of $4.00. A similar logic applies to the producer. Because the new equilibrium price after the tax is $0.50 lower, the producer shares the tax incidence equally with the buyer in this example. The consumer pays $0.50 more, and the seller nets $0.50 less.

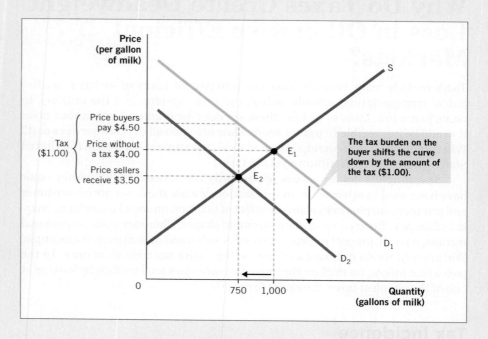

Price buyers pay $4.50

Tax ($1.00) Price without a tax $4.00

Price sellers receive $3.50

The tax burden on the buyer shifts the curve down by the amount of the tax ($1.00).

which causes the entire demand curve to shift down. The intersection of the new demand curve (D$_2$) with the existing supply curve (S) creates a new equilibrium price of $3.50 (E$_2$), which is $0.50 lower than the original price of $4.00 per gallon. But even though the base price is lower, consumers are still worse off. Because they must also pay part of the $1.00 tax, the total price to them rises to $4.50 per gallon. Many students mistakenly believe that the new equilibrium price will be $5.00, but that would only be the case if demand were perfectly inelastic. We will take a look at that scenario shortly.

At the same time, because the new equilibrium price after the tax is $0.50 lower than it was before the tax, the producer splits the tax incidence with the buyer. The producer receives $0.50 less, and the buyer pays $0.50 more.

The tax on milk purchases also affects the amount sold in the market, which we also see in Figure 5.6. Because the after-tax equilibrium price (E$_2$) is lower, producers of milk reduce the quantity they sell to 750 gallons. Therefore, the market for milk becomes smaller than it was before the good was taxed.

Excise taxes are rarely levied on consumers because these taxes are highly visible. If you were reminded that you have to pay a $1.00 tax every time you buy a gallon of milk, it would be hard for you to ignore the tax. As a result, politicians often prefer to place the tax on the seller.

EXAMPLE 2: TAX ON SELLERS Now let's look at what happens when the $1.00 tax on milk is placed on sellers. Figure 5.7 shows the result. First, look at the shift in the supply curve. Why does it shift? The $1.00-per-gallon tax on milk lowers willingness to sell, which causes producers to offer less milk at every price level. As a result, the entire supply curve shifts up in response to the tax that milk producers owe the government. The intersection of the new supply curve (S$_2$)

FIGURE 5.7

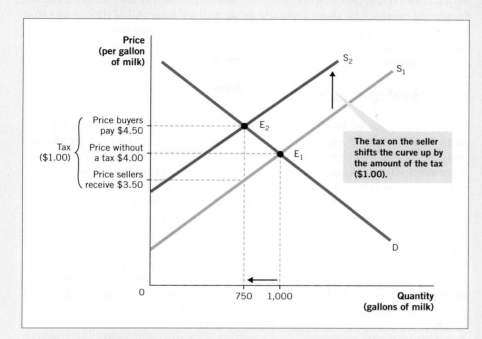

Price
(per gallon of milk)

S_2
S_1

Price buyers
pay $4.50

E_2

Tax
($1.00)

Price without
a tax $4.00

E_1

The tax on the seller
shifts the curve up by
the amount of the tax
($1.00).

Price sellers
receive $3.50

D

0   750   1,000   Quantity
(gallons of milk)

A Tax on Sellers

After the tax, the new equilibrium price (E_2) is $4.50, but $1.00 must be paid in tax to the government. Therefore, despite the rise in price, the seller nets only $3.50. Similar logic applies to the consumer. Because the new equilibrium price after the tax is $0.50 higher, the consumer shares the $1.00-per-gallon tax incidence equally with the seller. The consumer pays $0.50 more, and the seller nets $0.50 less.

with the existing demand curve creates a new equilibrium price (E_2) of $4.50 per gallon—which is $0.50 higher than the original equilibrium price of $4.00 ($E_1$). Many students mistakenly believe that the new equilibrium price will be $5.00, but again, that would only be the case if supply were perfectly inelastic. This higher equilibrium price occurs because the seller passes part of the tax increase along to the buyer in the form of a higher price. However, the seller is still worse off. After the tax, the new equilibrium price is $4.50 per gallon, but $1.00 goes as tax to the government. Therefore, despite the rise in price, the seller nets only $3.50 per gallon, which is $0.50 less than the original equilibrium price.

The tax also affects the amount of milk sold in the market. Because the new equilibrium price after the tax is higher, consumers reduce the quantity demanded from 1,000 gallons to 750 gallons.

SO WHO BEARS THE INCIDENCE OF THE TAX? It's important to notice that the result in Figure 5.7 looks much like that in Figure 5.6 because it does not matter whether a tax is levied on the buyer or the seller. The tax places a wedge of $1.00 between the price buyers ultimately pay ($4.50) and the net price sellers ultimately receive ($3.50), regardless of who is actually responsible for paying the tax.

Continuing with our milk example, when the tax was levied on sellers, they were responsible for collecting the entire tax ($1.00 per gallon), but they transferred $0.50 of the tax to the consumer by raising the market price to $4.50. Similarly, when the tax was levied on consumers, they were responsible for paying the entire tax, but they essentially transferred $0.50 of it to producers, because the market price fell to $3.50. Therefore, we can say that the incidence of a tax is independent of whether it is levied on the buyer or the seller. However, depending on the price elasticity of supply and demand, the tax incidence need not be shared equally, as we will see later. All of this means that the government doesn't get to determine whether consumers or producers bear the tax incidence—the market does!

Deadweight Loss

Deadweight loss
is the decrease in economic activity caused by market distortions.

Recall that economists measure economic efficiency by looking at total consumer and producer surplus. We have seen that a tax raises the total price consumers pay and lowers the net price producers receive. For this reason, taxes reduce the amount of economic activity. **Deadweight loss** is the decrease in economic activity caused by market distortions, such as taxes.

In the previous section, we observed that the tax on milk caused the amount purchased to decline from 1,000 to 750 gallons—a reduction of 250 gallons sold in the market. In Figure 5.8, the yellow triangle represents the deadweight loss caused by the tax. When the price rises to $4.50 per gallon, consumers who would have paid between $4.01 and $4.50 will no longer purchase milk. Likewise, the reduction in the price the seller can charge means that producers who were willing to sell a gallon of milk for between $3.50 and $3.99 will no longer do so. The combined reductions in consumer and producer surplus equal the deadweight loss produced by a $1.00 tax on milk.

In the next three sections, we examine how differences in the price elasticity of demand lead to varying amounts of deadweight loss. The tax is placed on the seller, and we evaluate what happens when the demand curve is perfectly inelastic, somewhat elastic, and perfectly elastic.

FIGURE 5.8

The Deadweight Loss from a Tax

The yellow triangle represents the deadweight loss caused by the tax. When the price rises, all consumers who would have paid between $4.01 and $4.50 no longer purchase milk. Likewise, the reduction in revenue the seller receives means that producers who were willing to sell a gallon of milk for between $3.50 and $3.99 will no longer do so.

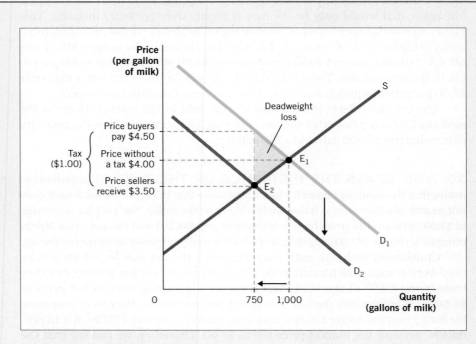

Is Soda Demand Elastic or Inelastic?

PARKS AND RECREATION: SODA TAX

Leslie Knope, now serving on the Pawnee city council, has to decide whether to vote for a citywide tax on sugary soda drinks. Leslie wants to understand both sides of the issue, so she meets with Pawnee Restaurant Association spokeswoman Kathryn Pinewood, to discuss the city's growing drink sizes. Leslie is concerned about the obesity problem in Pawnee, so she is horrified to learn that the sodas come in 64-, 128- and 512-ounce containers. She can't imagine why anyone would want so much soda. Kathryn won't allow Leslie to drag her into that discussion and instead touts the incredible value for consumers. Kathryn also argues that the tax would mean lost jobs in the local restaurant industry. Leslie and Kathryn, though on opposite sides, agree on this much: if passed, the tax will have a negative effect on the quantity demanded.

Since this episode first aired in 2012, soda taxes have been implemented throughout Mexico (2014) and in a number of major U.S. cities (San Francisco, Chicago, and Philadelphia). Researchers studied the impact of the sugary drink tax in Mexico and found that a 10% increase in the price of sweetened sugar beverages was associated with an 11.6% decrease

Mexico's sugary drink tax cut consumption by about 12%.

in quantity consumed.* That translates into a price elasticity of demand of −1.16 (slightly elastic). For proponents of soda taxes, this indicates that even a relatively small increase in price will meaningfully reduce consumption and lessen obesity.

---

*Source: M. A. Colchero, J. C. Salgado, M. Unar-Munguía, M. Hernández-Ávila, and J. A. Rivera-Dommarco. "Price elasticity of the demand for sugar sweetened beverages and soft drinks in Mexico," *Economics & Human Biology*, vol. 19 (December 2015): 129–137.

TAX REVENUE AND DEADWEIGHT LOSS WHEN DEMAND IS INELASTIC In Chapter 4, we saw that necessary goods and services—for example, water, electricity, and phone service—have highly inelastic demand. These goods and services are often taxed. For example, consider all the taxes associated with your cell phone bill: sales tax, city tax, county tax, federal excise tax, and annual regulatory fees. In addition, many companies add surcharges, including activation fees, local-number portability fees, telephone number pooling charges, emergency 911 service, directory assistance, telecommunications relay service surcharges, and cancellation fees. Of course, there is a way to avoid all these fees: don't use a cell phone! However, many people today feel that cell phones are a necessity. Cell phone providers and government agencies take advantage of consumers' strongly inelastic demand by tacking on these extra charges.

How do phone companies get away with all the added fees per month? Answer: inelastic demand.

FIGURE 5.9

A Tax on Products with Almost Perfectly Inelastic Demand

(a) Before the tax, the consumer enjoys the consumer surplus (C.S.) shaded in blue, and the producer enjoys the producer surplus (P.S.) shaded in red. (b) After the tax, the incidence, or the burden of taxation, is borne entirely by the consumer. A tax on a good with perfectly inelastic demand, such as phone service, represents a transfer of welfare from consumers to the government, as reflected by the reduced size of the blue rectangle in (b) and the creation of the green tax revenue rectangle between P_1 and P_2.

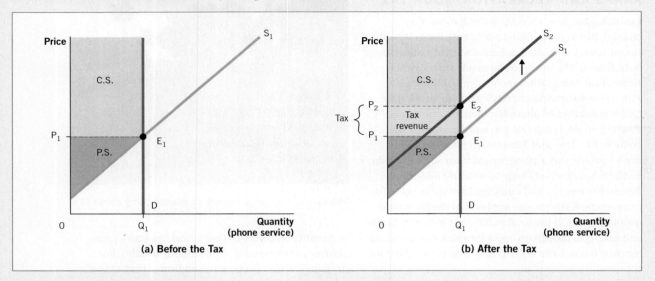

(a) Before the Tax

(b) After the Tax

Figure 5.9 shows the result of a tax on products with perfectly inelastic demand, such as phone service—something people feel they need to have no matter what the price. For our purposes, the demand for access to a phone (either a landline or a cell phone) can be considered perfectly inelastic. Recall that whenever demand is perfectly inelastic, the demand curve is vertical. Panel (a) shows the market for phone service before the tax. The blue rectangle represents consumer surplus (C.S.), and the red triangle represents producer surplus (P.S.). Now imagine that a tax is levied on the seller, as shown in panel (b). The supply curve shifts from S_1 to S_2. The shift in supply causes the equilibrium point to move from E_1 to E_2 and the price to rise from P_1 to P_2, but the quantity supplied, Q_1, remains the same. We know that when demand is perfectly inelastic, a price increase does not alter how much consumers purchase. So the quantity demanded remains constant at Q_1 even after the government collects tax revenue equal to the green rectangle.

There are two reasons why the government may favor excise taxes on goods with almost perfectly (or highly) inelastic demand. First, because these goods do not have substitutes, the tax will not cause consumers to buy less. Thus, the revenue from the tax will remain steady. Second, because the number of transactions, or quantity demanded (Q_1), remains constant, there will be no deadweight loss. As a result, the yellow triangle we observed in Figure 5.8 disappears in Figure 5.9 because the tax does not alter the efficiency of the market. Looking at Figure 5.9, you can see that the same number of transactions exist in panels

(a) and (b); the total surplus, or social welfare, is equal in both panels. You can also see this equality by comparing the full shaded areas in both panels. The sum of the blue area of consumer surplus and the red area of producer surplus in panel (a) is equal to the sum of the consumer surplus, producer surplus, and tax revenue in panel (b). The green area in panel (b) is subtracted entirely from the blue rectangle in panel (a), which indicates that the surplus is redistributed from consumers to the government. But society overall enjoys the same total surplus (even though some of this surplus is now in the form of a tax). Thus, we see that when demand is perfectly inelastic, the incidence, or the burden of taxation, is borne entirely by the consumer. A tax on a good with almost perfectly inelastic demand represents a transfer of welfare from consumers of the good to the government, reflected by the reduced size of the blue rectangle in panel (b).

TAX REVENUE AND DEADWEIGHT LOSS WHEN DEMAND IS MORE ELASTIC Now consider a tax on a product with more elastic demand, such as milk, the subject of our earlier discussion. The demand for milk is price sensitive, but not overly so. This elasticity is reflected in a demand curve with a typical slope as shown in Figure 5.10. Let's compare the after-tax price, P_2, in panel (b) of Figures 5.9 and 5.10. When demand is perfectly inelastic, as it is in panel (b) of Figure 5.9, the price increase from P_1 to P_2 is absorbed entirely by consumers. But in panel (b) of Figure 5.10, because demand is flatter and

FIGURE 5.10

A Tax on Products with More Elastic Demand

(a) Before the tax, the consumer enjoys the consumer surplus (C.S.) shaded in blue, and the producer enjoys the producer surplus (P.S.) shaded in red. (b) A tax on a good for which demand and supply are both somewhat elastic will cause a transfer of welfare from consumers and producers to the government, the revenue shown as the green rectangle. It will also create deadweight loss (D.W.L.), shaded in yellow, because the quantity bought and sold in the market declines (from Q_1 to Q_2).

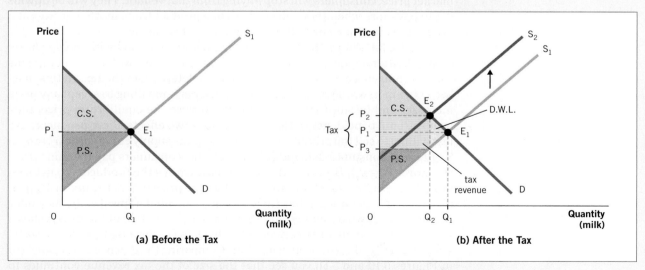

therefore more sensitive to price, suppliers must absorb part of the tax themselves (from P_1 to P_3). Thus, the net price they charge, P_3, is less than what they received when the good was not taxed. In addition, the total tax revenue generated (the green area) is not as large in panel (b) of Figure 5.10 as in panel (b) of Figure 5.9 because as the price of the good rises to P_2, some consumers no longer buy it and the quantity demanded falls from Q_1 to Q_2.

Notice that both consumer surplus (C.S., the blue triangle) and producer surplus (P.S., the red triangle) in Figure 5.10, panel (b), are smaller after the tax. Because the price rises after the tax increase (from P_1 to P_2), those consumers with a relatively low willingness to pay for the good are priced out of the market. Likewise, sellers with relatively high costs of production will stop producing the good, because the price they net after paying the tax drops to P_3. The total reduction in economic activity, the change from Q_1 to Q_2, is the deadweight loss (D.W.L.) indicated by the yellow triangle.

A tax on a good for which demand and supply are both somewhat elastic will cause a transfer of welfare from consumers and producers of the good to the government. At the same time, because the quantity bought and sold in the market declines, deadweight loss is created. Another way of seeing this result is to compare the red and blue areas in Figure 5.10, panel (a), with the red and blue areas in panel (b) of Figure 5.10. The sum of the consumer surplus and producer surplus in panel (a) is greater than the sum of the consumer surplus, tax revenue, and producer surplus in panel (b) because the deadweight loss in panel (b) is no longer a part of the surplus. Therefore, the total surplus is lower, which means that the efficiency of the market is smaller. The tax is no longer a pure transfer from consumers to the government, as was the case in Figure 5.9 with perfectly inelastic demand.

TAX REVENUE AND DEADWEIGHT LOSS WHEN DEMAND IS HIGHLY ELASTIC We have seen the effect of taxation when demand is inelastic and somewhat elastic. What happens when demand is highly elastic? For example, a customer who wants to buy fresh lettuce at a produce market will find many local growers charging the same price and many varieties to choose from. If one of the vendors decides to charge $1 per pound above the market price, consumers will stop buying from that vendor. They will be unwilling to pay more when they can get the same product from another grower at a lower price. In other words, their demand is highly elastic.

Figure 5.11 shows the result of a tax on lettuce, a good with highly elastic demand. After all, when lettuce is taxed, consumers can switch to other greens such as spinach, cabbage, or endive and completely avoid the tax. In this market, consumers are so price sensitive that they are unwilling to accept any price increase. And because sellers are unable to raise the equilibrium price, they bear the entire incidence of the tax. There are two effects. First, producers are less willing to sell the product at all prices, and the supply curve shifts from S_1 to S_2. Because consumer demand is highly elastic, consumers pay the same price as before ($P_1 = P_2$). However, the tax increase causes the producers to net less, or P_3. Because P_3 is substantially lower than the price before the tax, or P_2, producers offer less for sale after the tax is implemented. (Specifically, they offer the amount shown on supply curve S_2 at price P_2.) Panel (b) of Figure 5.11 shows the movement of quantity demanded from Q_1 to Q_2. Because Q_2 is significantly smaller than Q_1, there is deadweight loss. Comparing the green areas of panel (b) in Figures 5.10 and 5.11, you see that the size of the tax revenue continues to shrink. There is an important lesson here for policymakers. They should tax

FIGURE 5.11

A Tax on Products with Highly Elastic Demand

(a) Before the tax, the producer enjoys the producer surplus (P.S.) shaded in red. (b) When consumer demand is highly elastic, consumers pay the same price after the tax as before. But they are worse off because less is produced and sold; the quantity produced moves from Q_1 to Q_2. The result is deadweight loss (D.W.L.), as shown by the yellow triangle. The total surplus, or efficiency of the market, is much smaller than before. The size of the tax revenue (shaded in green) is also noticeably smaller in the market with highly elastic demand compared to the market with highly inelastic demand.

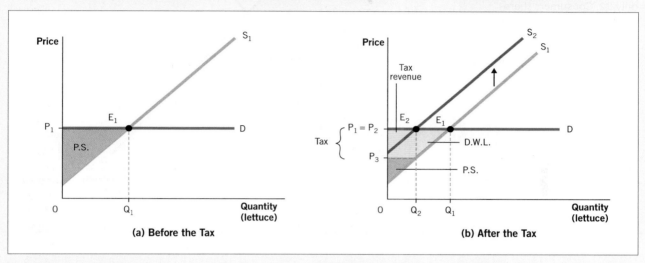

(a) Before the Tax

(b) After the Tax

goods with relatively inelastic demand (if the goal is to generate tax revenue or minimize efficiency losses). Doing so will not only lessen the deadweight loss of taxation, but also generate larger tax revenues for the government.

INTERACTION OF DEMAND ELASTICITY AND SUPPLY ELASTICITY

The incidence of a tax is determined by the relative steepness of the demand curve compared with the supply curve. When the demand curve is steeper (more inelastic) than the supply curve, consumers bear more of the incidence of the tax. When the supply curve is steeper (more inelastic) than the demand curve, suppliers bear more of the incidence of the tax. Also, whenever the supply and/or demand curves are relatively steep, deadweight loss is minimized.

How much would you pay per pound for these mushrooms?

Let's explore an example in which we consider how the elasticity of demand and elasticity of supply interact. Suppose that a $5-per-pound tax is placed on shiitake mushrooms. Given the information in Figure 5.12, we will compute the incidence, deadweight loss, and tax revenue from the tax.

Let's start with the incidence of the tax. After the tax is implemented, the market price rises from $18 per pound (at E_1) to $20 per pound (at E_2). But since sellers must pay $5 per pound to the government, they keep only $15.

FIGURE 5.12

A Realistic Example

A $5-per-pound tax is placed on mushroom suppliers, driving the equilibrium price up from E₁ ($18) to E₂ ($20). Notice that the price rises by only $2. Consumers therefore pick up $2 of the $5 tax and the seller must pay the remaining $3. Therefore, most of the incidence is borne by the seller.

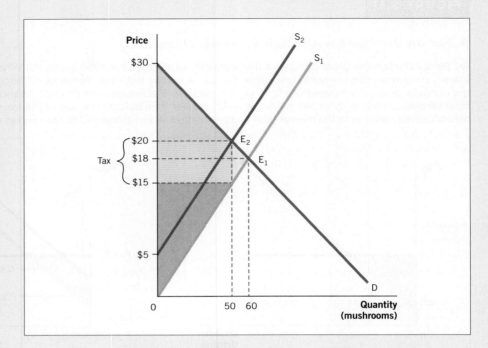

Tax incidence measures the share of the tax paid by buyers and sellers, so we need to compare the incidence of the tax paid by each party. Because the market price rises by $2 (from $18 to $20), buyers are paying $2 of the $5 tax, or $\frac{2}{5}$. Because the amount the seller keeps falls by $3 (from $18 to $15), sellers are paying $3 of the $5 tax, or $\frac{3}{5}$. Notice that the demand curve is slightly more elastic (flatter) than the supply curve; therefore, sellers have a limited ability to raise their price.

Now let's determine the deadweight loss caused by the tax—that is, the decrease in economic activity. Deadweight loss is represented by the decrease in the total surplus found in the yellow triangle in Figure 5.12. To compute the amount of the deadweight loss, we need to determine the area of the triangle:

(EQUATION 5.1)

$$\text{area of a triangle} = \frac{1}{2} \times \text{base} \times \text{height}$$

The triangle in Figure 5.12 is sitting on its side, so its height is $60 - 50 = 10$, and its base is $\$20 - \$15 = \$5$.

$$\text{deadweight loss} = \frac{1}{2} \times 10 \times \$5 = \$25$$

This means that $25 worth of mushroom sales will not take place because of the tax.

THE SHORT-LIVED LUXURY TAX

The Budget Reconciliation Act of 1990 established a special luxury tax on the sale of new aircraft, yachts, automobiles, furs, and jewelry. The act established a 10% surcharge on new purchases as follows: aircraft over $500,000; yachts over $100,000; automobiles over $25,000; and furs and jewelry over $10,000. The taxes were expected to generate approximately $2 billion a year. However, revenue fell far below expectations, and thousands of jobs were lost in each of the affected industries. Within three years, the tax was repealed. Why was the luxury tax such a failure?

If you were rich, would this be your luxury toy?

When passing the Budget Reconciliation Act, lawmakers failed to consider basic demand elasticity. Because the purchase of a new aircraft, yacht, car, fur, or jewelry is highly discretionary, many wealthy consumers decided that they would buy substitute products that fell below the tax threshold or buy a used product and refurbish it. Therefore, the demand for these luxury goods turned out to be highly elastic. We have seen that when goods with elastic demand are taxed, the resulting tax revenues are small. Moreover, in this example, the resulting decrease in purchases was significant. As a result, jobs were lost in the middle of an economic downturn. The combination of low revenues and crippling job losses was enough to convince Congress to repeal the tax in 1993.

The failed luxury tax is a reminder that the populist idea of taxing the rich is far more difficult to implement than it appears. In simple terms, it is nearly impossible to tax the toys that the rich enjoy because wealthy people can spend their money in so many different ways. They have options about whether to buy or lease, as well as many good substitutes to choose from. In other words, in many cases, they can avoid paying luxury taxes.

Finally, what is the tax revenue generated by the tax? In Figure 5.12, the tax revenue is represented by the green-shaded area, which is a rectangle. We can calculate the tax revenue by determining the area of the rectangle:

$$\text{area of a rectangle} = \text{base} \times \text{height}$$

(EQUATION 5.2)

The height of the tax revenue rectangle is the amount of the tax ($5), and the number of units sold after the tax is 50 (the base).

$$\text{tax revenue} = \$5 \times 50 = \$250$$

Balancing Deadweight Loss and Tax Revenues

Up to this point, we have kept the size of the tax increase constant. Doing so enabled us to examine the impact of the elasticity of demand and supply on deadweight loss and tax revenues. But what happens when a tax is high enough to significantly alter consumer or producer behavior? For instance, in 2002, the Republic of Ireland instituted a tax of 15 euro cents on each plastic bag in order to curb litter and encourage recycling. Since the cost of production of each plastic bag is just a few pennies, a 15-euro-cent tax is enormous by comparison. As a result, consumer use of plastic bags quickly fell by over 90%. Thus, the tax was a major success because the government achieved its goal of curbing litter. In this section, we consider how consumers respond to taxes of different sizes, and we determine the relationship between the size of a tax, the deadweight loss, and tax revenues.

Figure 5.13 shows the market response to a variety of tax increases. The five panels in the figure begin with a reference point, panel (a), where no tax is levied, and progress toward panel (e), where the tax rate becomes so extreme that it curtails all economic activity.

As taxes rise, so do prices. You can trace this price rise from panel (a), where there is no tax and the price is P_1, all the way to panel (e), where the extreme tax causes the price to rise to P_5. At the same time, deadweight loss (D.W.L.) also rises. You can see this increase by comparing the sizes of the yellow triangles. The trade-off is striking. Without any taxes, deadweight loss does not occur. But as soon as taxes are in place, the market equilibrium quantity demanded begins to decline, moving from Q_1 to Q_5. As the number of transactions (quantity demanded) declines, the area of deadweight loss rapidly expands.

When taxes are small, as in panel (b), the tax revenue (green rectangle) is large relative to the deadweight loss (yellow triangle). However, as we progress through the panels, this relationship slowly reverses. In panel (c), the size of the tax revenue remains larger than the deadweight loss. In panel (d), however, the

Incentives

Trade-offs

PRACTICE WHAT YOU KNOW

What is the optimal tax rate?

Deadweight Loss of Taxation: The Politics of Tax Rates

Imagine that you and two friends are discussing the politics of taxation. One friend, who is fiscally conservative, argues that tax rates are too high. The other friend, who is more progressive, argues that tax rates are too low.

QUESTION: Is it possible that both friends are right?

ANSWER: Surprisingly, the answer is yes. When tax rates become extraordinarily high, the amount of deadweight loss dwarfs the amount of tax revenue collected. We observed this result in our discussion of the short-lived luxury tax. Fiscal conservatives often note that taxes inhibit economic activity. They advocate lower tax rates and limited government involvement in the market, preferring to minimize the deadweight loss on economic activity—see panel (b) in Figure 5.13. However, progressives prefer somewhat higher tax rates than fiscal conservatives, because a moderate tax rate—see panel (c)—generates more tax revenue than a small tax does. The additional revenues that moderate tax rates generate can fund more government services.

Therefore, a clear trade-off exists between the size of the public (government) sector and market activity. Depending on how you view the value created by markets versus the value added through government provision, there is ample room for disagreement about the best tax policy.

Trade-offs

FIGURE 5.13

Examining Deadweight Loss and Tax Revenues

The panels show that increased taxes result in higher prices. Progressively higher taxes lead to more deadweight loss (D.W.L.), but higher taxes do not always generate more tax revenue, as evidenced by the reduction in tax revenue that occurs when tax rates become too large in panels (d) and (e).

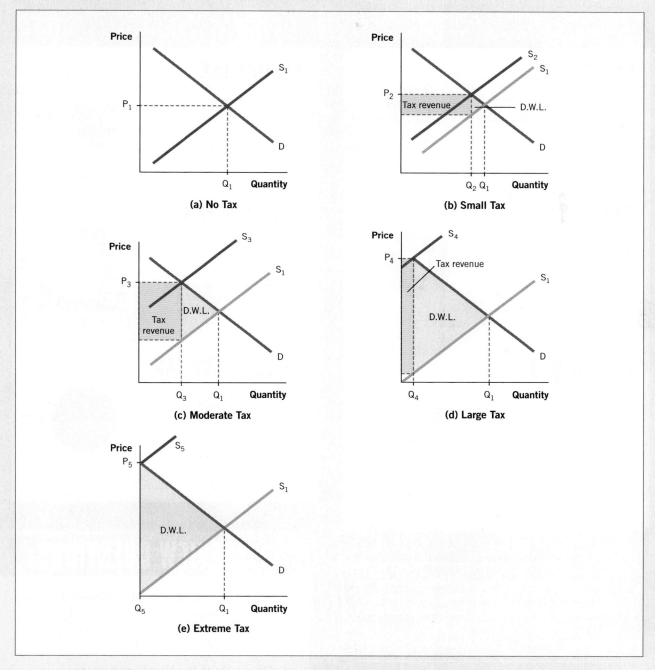

(a) No Tax

(b) Small Tax

(c) Moderate Tax

(d) Large Tax

(e) Extreme Tax

Unusual Taxes

Governments tax their citizens for a variety of reasons. Often it's to raise revenue. Sometimes, taxes are levied to influence citizens' behavior. Occasionally, both of these reasons are in play. These two motivations have led to some creative tax initiatives, as seen below.

FLUSH TAX

Maryland's "flush tax," a fee added to sewer bills, went up from $2.50 to $5.00 a month in 2012. The tax is paid only by residents who live in the Chesapeake Bay Watershed, and it generates revenue for reducing pollution in Chesapeake Bay.

BAGEL TAX

New Yorkers love their bagels and cream cheese from delis. In the state, any bagel that has been sliced or has any form of spread on it (like cream cheese) is subject to an 8-cent tax. Any bagel that is purchased "unaltered" is classified as unprepared and is not taxed.

GOSSIP TAX

In 2018, Uganda passed a "social media tax" of 200 shillings (about $0.05) per day on anyone using online services like Facebook, WhatsApp, and Twitter. President Yoweri Museveni declared that Internet messaging platforms encourage gossip, and that the revenue from the tax would help the country "cope with the consequences."

TATTOO TAX

Arkansas imposes a 6% tax on tattoos and body piercings, meaning that the people of Arkansas pay extra when getting inked or pierced.

WINDOW TAX

England passed a tax in 1696 targeting wealthy citizens—the more windows in one's house, the higher the tax. Many homeowners simply bricked over their windows. But they could not seal all of them, and the government did indeed collect revenue.

BLUEBERRY TAX

Maine levies a penny-and-a-half tax per pound on anyone growing, handling, processing, selling, or purchasing the state's delicious wild blueberries. The tax is an effort to make sure that the blueberries are not overharvested.

Maine produces 99% of the wild blueberries consumed in the USA, meaning that blueberry lovers have few substitutes available to avoid paying the tax and that demand is therefore inelastic.

Marylanders are being taxed on a negative externality, which we cover in Chapter 7.

REVIEW QUESTIONS

- Uganda's social media tax reportedly caused a drop in the amount of commercial activity conducted online. What is this kind of loss of economic activity called?

- Do you think the New York bagel tax is an effective tool to raise government revenue? Think about how the tax may or may not affect the purchasing behavior of New Yorkers.

magnitude of the deadweight loss is far greater than the tax revenue. The size of the tax in panel (d) is creating a significant cost in terms of economic efficiency. Finally, panel (e) shows an extreme case in which all market activity ceases as a result of the tax. Because nothing is produced and sold, there is no tax revenue.

Conclusion

The government largely taxes goods that have inelastic demand, which means that firms are able to transfer most of the tax incidence to consumers through higher prices.

In the first part of this chapter, we learned that society benefits from unregulated markets because they generate the largest possible total surplus. However, society also needs the government to provide an infrastructure for the economy. The taxation of specific goods and services gives rise to a form of market failure called deadweight loss, which reflects reduced economic activity. Thus, any intervention in the market requires a deep understanding of how society will respond to the incentives created by the legislation. In addition, unintended consequences can affect the most well-intentioned tax legislation and, if the process is not well thought through, can cause inefficiencies with far-reaching consequences. None of this means that taxes are undesirable. Rather, society must balance (1) the need for tax revenues and the programs those revenues help fund with (2) trade-offs in the market. ✳

Incentives

Trade-offs

Excise Taxes Are Almost Impossible to Avoid

- Excise taxes are placed on specific products.
- Excise taxes are typically levied on goods with inelastic demand.
- A typical household of four pays over $1,000 in excise taxes annually.

The federal government collected $83 billion in excise taxes in 2017. Excise taxes are placed on many different products, making them almost impossible to avoid. They also have the added advantages of being easy to collect, hard for consumers to detect since the producer is responsible for paying the tax, and easier to enact politically than other types of taxes. You'll find federal excise taxes on many everyday household expenses—what you drink, the gasoline you purchase, plane tickets, and much more. Let's add them up over the course of a typical year.

Excise taxes are everywhere.

1. **Gasoline (and Diesel).** 18.4 cents per gallon (and 24.4 cents per gallon), generating $41 billion to help finance the interstate highway system.
2. **Cigarettes.** $1.01 per pack, generating $10 billion for the general federal budget.
3. **Air travel.** 7.5% of the base price of the ticket plus $4 per flight segment, generating $14 billion for the Transportation Security Administration and the Federal Aviation Administration.
4. **Alcohol.** 5 cents per can of beer, 21 cents per bottle of wine, and $2.14 per bottle of spirits, generating $10 billion for the general federal budget.

These four categories account for $75 billion in excise taxes. You could still avoid the taxman with this simple prescription: don't drink, don't travel, and don't smoke. Where does that leave you? Way out in the country somewhere far from civilization. Since you won't be able to travel to a grocery store, you'll need to live off the land, grow your own crops, and hunt or fish.

But there is still one last federal excise tax to go.

5. **Hunting and fishing.** Taxes range from 3 cents for fishing tackle boxes to 11% for archery equipment, generating over $1 billion for fish and wildlife services.

Living off the land and avoiding taxes just got much harder, and that's the whole point. The government taxes products with relatively inelastic demand because most people will still purchase them after the tax is in place. As a result, avoiding excise taxes isn't practical.

What are consumer surplus and producer surplus?

- Consumer surplus is the difference between the willingness to pay for a good or service and the price is paid to get it. Producer surplus is the difference between the price the seller receives and the price at which the seller is willing to sell the good or service.

- Total surplus (social welfare) is the sum of consumer and producer surplus that exists in a market.

When is a market efficient?

- Markets maximize consumer and producer surplus, provide goods and services to buyers who value them most, and reward sellers who can produce goods and services at the lowest cost. As a result, markets create the largest amount of total surplus possible.

- Whenever an allocation of resources maximizes total surplus, the result is said to be efficient. However, economists are also interested in the distribution of the surplus. Equity refers to the fairness of the distribution of the benefits within the society.

Why do taxes create deadweight loss in otherwise efficient markets?

- Deadweight loss occurs because taxes increase the purchase price, which causes consumers to buy less and producers to supply less. Deadweight loss can be lessened by taxing goods or services that have inelastic demand or supply.

- Economists are also concerned about the incidence of taxation. Incidence refers to the burden of taxation on the party who pays the tax through higher prices, regardless of whom the tax is actually levied on. The incidence is determined by the balance between the elasticity of supply and the elasticity of demand.

Concepts You Should Know

consumer surplus (p. 157)
deadweight loss (p. 170)
efficient (p. 163)
equity (p. 164)

excise taxes (p. 167)
incidence (p. 167)
producer surplus (p. 159)
social welfare (p. 162)

total surplus (p. 162)
welfare economics (p. 156)
willingness to pay (p. 157)
willingness to sell (p. 159)

Questions for Review

1. Explain how consumer surplus is derived from the difference between the willingness to pay and the market equilibrium price.

2. Explain how producer surplus is derived from the difference between the willingness to sell and the market equilibrium price.

3. Why do economists focus on consumer and producer surplus and not on the possibility of consumer and producer loss? Illustrate your answer on a supply and demand graph.

4. How do economists define efficiency?

5. What type of goods should be taxed in order to minimize deadweight loss?

6. Suppose that the government taxes a good that has very elastic demand. Illustrate what will happen to consumer surplus, producer surplus, tax revenue, and deadweight loss on a supply and demand graph.

7. What happens to tax revenues as tax rates increase?

Study Problems (✳ solved at the end of the section)

1. A college student enjoys eating pizza. Her willingness to pay for each slice is shown in the following table:

Number of pizza slices	Willingness to pay (per slice)
1	$6
2	5
3	4
4	3
5	2
6	1
7	0

a. If pizza slices cost $3 each, how many slices will she buy? How much consumer surplus will she enjoy?

b. If the price of slices falls to $2, how much consumer surplus will she enjoy?

2. A cash-starved town decides to impose a $6 excise tax on T-shirts sold. The following table shows the quantity demanded and the quantity supplied at various prices.

Price per T-shirt	Quantity demanded	Quantity supplied
$19	0	60
16	10	50
13	20	40
10	30	30
7	40	20
4	50	10

a. What are the equilibrium quantity demanded and the quantity supplied before the tax is implemented? Determine the consumer and producer surplus before the tax.

b. What are the equilibrium quantity demanded and quantity supplied after the tax is implemented? Determine the consumer and producer surplus after the tax.

c. How much tax revenue does the town generate from the tax?

3. Andrew pays $30 to buy a potato cannon, a cylinder that shoots potatoes hundreds of feet. He was willing to pay $45. When Andrew's friend Nick learns that Andrew bought a potato cannon, he asks Andrew if he will sell it for $60, and Andrew agrees. Nick is thrilled, since he would have paid Andrew up to $80 for the cannon. Andrew is also delighted. Determine the consumer surplus from the original purchase and the additional surplus generated by the resale of the cannon.

4. If the government wants to raise tax revenue, which of the following items are good candidates for an excise tax? Why?

a. granola bars
b. cigarettes
c. toilet paper
d. automobile tires
e. bird feeders

✳ **5.** If the government wants to minimize the deadweight loss of taxation, which of the following items are good candidates for an excise tax? Why?

a. bottled water
b. prescription drugs
c. oranges
d. batteries
e. luxury cars

6. A new medical study indicates that eating blueberries helps prevent cancer. If the demand for blueberries increases, what will happen to the size of the consumer surplus and producer surplus? Illustrate your answer by shifting the demand curve appropriately and labeling the new and old areas of consumer and producer surplus.

7. Use the following graph to answer questions a–f.

a. What area represents consumer surplus before the tax?

b. What area represents producer surplus before the tax?

c. What area represents consumer surplus after the tax?

d. What area represents producer surplus after the tax?

e. What area represents the tax revenue after the tax?

f. What area represents the deadweight loss after the tax?

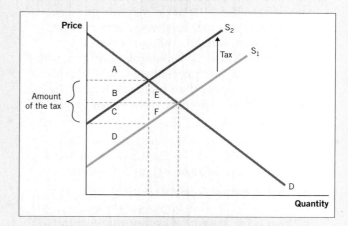

8. The cost of many electronic devices has fallen appreciably since they were first introduced. For instance, computers, cell phones, microwave ovens, and calculators not only provide more functions but also do so at a lower cost. Illustrate the impact of lower production costs on the supply curve. What happens to the size of the consumer surplus and producer surplus? If consumer demand for cell phones is relatively elastic, who is likely to benefit the most from the lower production costs?

9. Suppose that the demand for a concert, Q_D, is represented by the following equation, where P is the price of concert tickets and Q is the number of tickets sold:

$$Q_D = 2500 - 20P$$

The supply of tickets, Q_S, is represented by the equation

$$Q_S = -500 + 80P$$

a. Find the equilibrium price and quantity of tickets sold. (*Hint:* Set $Q_D = Q_S$ and solve for the price, P, and then plug the result back into either of the original equations to find Q_E.)

b. Carefully graph your result from part a.

c. Calculate the consumer surplus at the equilibrium price and quantity. (***Hint:*** Because the area of consumer surplus is a triangle, you will need to use the formula for the area of a triangle, $\frac{1}{2} \times$ base $\times$ height, to solve the problem.)

10. In this chapter, we focused on the effect of taxes on social welfare. However, governments also subsidize goods, making them cheaper to buy or sell. How would a $2,000 subsidy on the purchase of a new hybrid car impact the consumer surplus and producer surplus in the hybrid-car market? Use a supply and demand diagram to illustrate your answer. Does the subsidy create deadweight loss?

✳ **11.** Suppose that a new $50 tax is placed on each new cell phone sold. Use the information in the following graph to answer these questions.

    a. What is the incidence of the tax?
    b. What is the deadweight loss of the tax?
    c. What is the amount of tax revenue generated?

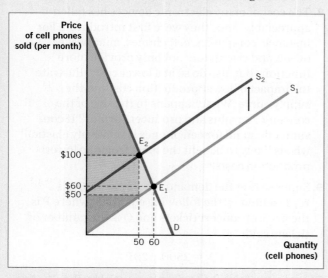

✳ **12.** A well-known saying goes, "Honesty is not only morally right, it is also highly efficient." Explain why firms that practice honesty generate more social welfare than firms that practice dishonesty.

13. We defined deadweight loss as the decrease in economic activity caused by market distortions. One place where we see deadweight loss is during Halloween's trick-or-treat. Children of all ages return home with bags of candy, some of which they love and some of which they don't care for. A lot of candy ends up uneaten. In this context, we can think of uneaten candy as not being distributed effectively by the market; therefore, deadweight loss occurs. What ways can you think of to improve how candy is given away during trick-or-treat so that children would receive more candies they enjoy? Provide three possible solutions.

✳ **14.** Assume that a $0.25/gallon tax on milk causes a loss of $300 million in consumer and producer surplus and creates a deadweight loss of $75 million. From this information, we know that the tax revenue from the tax is _____.

✳ **15.** For each of three potential buyers of avocados, the table displays the willingness to pay for the first three avocados of the day. Assume Carri, Carina, and Carlos are the only three buyers of avocados.

	First avocado	Second avocado	Third avocado
Carri	$2.00	$1.50	$0.75
Carina	1.50	1.00	0.80
Carlos	0.75	0.25	0.00

If the market price of avocados increases from $0.70 to $1.40, what is the change in total consumer surplus?

16. Suppose that the government imposes a $2 tax on consumers of donuts. What will happen to the market price?

Solved Problems

5.a. Many good substitutes are available: consumers can drink tap water, filtered water, or other healthy beverages instead of bottled water. Therefore, bottled water is not a good candidate for an excise tax.

b. Taxing prescription drugs will generate significant revenues without reducing sales much, if at all. There is almost no deadweight loss because consumers have few, if any, alternatives. Thus, prescription drugs are a good candidate for an excise tax.

c. Consumers can select many other fruits to replace oranges. The deadweight loss will be quite large. Therefore, oranges are not a good candidate for an excise tax.

d. Without batteries, many devices won't work. The lack of substitutes makes demand quite inelastic, so the deadweight loss will be small. Thus, batteries are an excellent candidate for an excise tax.

e. Wealthy consumers can spend their income in many ways. They do not have to buy luxury cars. As a result, the tax will create a large amount of deadweight loss. Therefore, luxury cars are a poor candidate for an excise tax.

11.a. After the tax is implemented, the market price rises from \$60 to \$100; but because sellers must pay \$50 to the government, they net only \$50. Tax incidence measures the share of the tax paid by buyers and sellers. Because the market price rises by \$40 (from \$60 to \$100), buyers are paying \$40 of the \$50 tax, or $\frac{4}{5}$. Because the net price falls by \$10 (from \$60 to \$50), sellers are paying \$10 of the \$50 tax, or $\frac{1}{5}$.

b. The deadweight loss is represented by the decrease in the total surplus found in the yellow triangle. To compute the amount of the deadweight loss, we need to determine the area inside the triangle. The area of a triangle is found by taking $\frac{1}{2} \times$ base $\times$ height. The triangle is sitting on its side, so the height of the triangle is 10 (60 – 50) and the base is \$50 (\$100 – \$50). Hence the deadweight loss is $\frac{1}{2} \times 10 \times \$50 = \$250$.

c. The tax revenue is represented by the green area. You can calculate the tax revenue by multiplying the amount of the tax (\$50) by the number of units sold after the tax (50), which equals \$2,500.

12. For markets to benefit both the buyer and the seller, both parties must have accurate information about the good. We learned that an efficient allocation maximizes total surplus. Think about how dishonesty disrupts trade. Suppose a seller misrepresents the qualities of the good she is selling. A consumer buys the good and finds it to be defective or undesirable. As a result, the consumer does not get any consumer surplus from the transaction. In this case, total surplus is less than it otherwise would be. In addition, the consumer will no longer purchase from the dishonest seller, which means that potential gains from trade in the future will be lost as well.

14. The tax revenue is the lost consumer surplus plus the lost producer surplus minus the deadweight loss. Therefore the answer is \$300M – \$75M = \$225M.

15. When avocados are \$0.70, Carri buys three and receives (\$2.00 + \$1.50 + \$0.75 – \$0.70×3 =) \$2.15 in consumer surplus, and Carina buys three and receives (\$1.50 + \$1.00 + \$0.80 – \$0.70×3 =) \$1.20 in consumer surplus. Carlos buys one and receives (\$0.75 – \$0.70 =) \$0.05 in consumer surplus. Totaling the combined consumer surplus gives us \$2.15 + \$1.20 + \$0.05 = \$3.40.

After the price rises to \$1.40, Carri buys two and receives (\$2.00 + \$1.50 – \$1.40×2 =) \$0.70 in consumer surplus, and Carina buys one and receives (\$1.50 – \$1.40 =) \$0.10 in consumer surplus. Carlos no longer buys avocados. Totaling the combined consumer surplus gives us \$0.70 + \$0.10 = \$0.80.

Therefore the change in consumer surplus is \$0.80 – \$3.40 = –\$2.60.

06

Price Controls

Price Controls Do More Harm Than Good.

Nineteen-year-old Monica Savaleta is just like a lot of us, but she lives in Caracas, Venezuela, where the prices charged for basic necessities are strictly regulated. On the surface this sounds like an intriguing idea. Lower prices for essential items, like rice and sugar, means that those items are more affordable for everyone, right? Unfortunately, nothing in life is free. Sure, Venezuelan supermarkets sell food staples at prices that are kept low not just by law but though government subsidies. But the reality is that to buy those products you have to wait in line for many hours, with no assurance that there will be any left when it's your turn to roam the aisles.

Meanwhile, black market profiteers called *bachaqueros* do sell commodities like rice and sugar—for more than $5 a pound, a tremendous expense for a typical Venezuelan earning the minimum wage, equivalent to about $50 month. Monica is faced with two bad choices: wait in line at the supermarkets, or pay the bachaqueros. "I've been waiting in line since 3 a.m. and have only managed to get two tubes of toothpaste," she says. "If I buy from the bachaqueros, my whole salary is blown on three kilos of rice."[*]

Price controls are not a new idea. The first recorded attempt to regulate prices was 4,000 years ago in ancient

[*]Source: Charner, Flora, Clarke, Rachel, Venezuale, "Where flour, pasta, and milk can cost a month's pay," CNN.com, August 2, 2016. http://edition.cnn.com/2016/08/02/americas/venezuela-food-prices/index.html.

Price controls in Venezuela have made it harder for stores to keep basic necessities in stock. Here, shoppers in the nation's capital, Caracas, wait their turn to enter a supermarket and hope to find at least a few of the items they came for.

Babylon, when King Hammurabi decreed how much corn a farmer could pay for a cow. Similar attempts to control prices occurred in ancient Egypt, Greece, and Rome. Each attempt ended badly. History has shown us that price controls generally do not work. Why? Because they disrupt the normal functioning of the market. By the end of this chapter, you will understand why price controls are rarely the win-win propositions that legislators often claim. To help you understand why price controls lead to disequilibrium in markets, this chapter focuses on the two most common types of price controls: *price ceilings* and *price floors*.

· BIG QUESTIONS ·

- When do price ceilings matter?
- What effects do price ceilings have on economic activity?
- When do price floors matter?
- What effects do price floors have on economic activity?

When Do Price Ceilings Matter?

Price controls
attempt to set prices through government regulations in the market.

A **price ceiling** is a legally established maximum price for a good or service.

Price controls attempt to set prices through government regulations in the market. In most cases, and certainly in the United States, price controls are enacted to ease perceived burdens on society. A **price ceiling** creates a legally established maximum price for a good or service. In the next section, we consider what happens when a price ceiling is in place. Price ceilings create many unintended effects that policymakers rarely acknowledge.

Understanding Price Ceilings

To understand how price ceilings work, let's try a simple thought experiment. Suppose that most prices are rising as a result of *inflation*, an overall increase in prices. The government is concerned that people with low incomes will not be able to afford to eat. To help the disadvantaged, legislators pass a law stating that no one can charge more than $0.50 for a loaf of bread. (Note that this price ceiling is about one-third the typical price of a loaf of generic white bread.) Does the new law accomplish its goal? What happens?

The law of demand tells us that if the price drops, the quantity that consumers demand will increase. At the same time, the law of supply tells us that the quantity supplied will fall because producers will be receiving lower profits for their efforts. This combination of increased quantity demanded and reduced quantity supplied will cause a shortage of bread.

On the demand side, consumers will want more bread than is available at the legal price. There will be long lines for bread, and many people will not be able to get the bread they want. On the supply side, producers will look for ways to maintain their profits. They can reduce the size of each loaf they produce. They can also use cheaper ingredients, thereby lowering the quality of their product, and they can stop making fancier varieties.

In addition, *black markets* will develop. For instance, in 2014 Venezuela instituted price controls on flour, which has led to severe shortages of bread. In this real-life example, many people who do not want to wait in line for bread or who do not obtain it despite waiting in line will resort to illegal means to obtain it. In other words, sellers will go "underground" and charge higher prices to customers who want bread. **Black markets** are illegal markets that arise when price controls are in place.

Table 6.1 summarizes the likely outcomes of price controls on bread.

Long lines for bread in Venezuela.

Incentives

Black markets
are illegal markets that arise
when price controls are in place.

TABLE 6.1

A Price Ceiling on Bread

Question	Answer / Explanation	Result
Will there be more bread or less bread for sale?	Consumers will want to buy more because the price is lower (the law of demand), but producers will manufacture less (the law of supply). The net result will be a shortage of bread.	Empty shelves
Will the size of a typical loaf change?	Because the price is capped at $0.50 per loaf, manufacturers will try to maintain profits by reducing the size of each loaf.	No more giant loaves
Will the quality change?	Because the price is capped, producers will use cheaper ingredients, and many expensive brands and varieties will no longer be profitable to produce. Thus the quality of available bread will decline.	Focaccia bread will disappear
Will the opportunity cost of finding bread change?	The opportunity cost of finding bread will rise. Consumers will spend significant resources going from store to store to see if a bread shipment has arrived and waiting in line for a chance to get some.	Bread lines will become the norm
Will people have to break the law to buy bread?	Because bread will be hard to find and people will still need it, a black market will develop. Those selling and buying on the black market will be breaking the law.	Black-market bread dealers will help reduce the shortage

If you can touch the ceiling, you can't go any higher. A binding price ceiling stops prices from rising.

Incentives

The Effect of Price Ceilings

Now that we have some understanding of how a price ceiling works, we can transfer that knowledge into the supply and demand model for a deeper analysis of how price ceilings affect the market. To explain when price ceilings matter in the short run, we examine two types of price ceilings: nonbinding and binding. Both are set by law, but only one actually makes a difference to prices.

NONBINDING PRICE CEILINGS The effect of a price ceiling depends on the level at which it is set relative to the equilibrium price. When a price ceiling is above the equilibrium price, we say it is *nonbinding*. Figure 6.1 shows a price ceiling of $2.00 per loaf in a market where $2.00 is above the equilibrium price (P_E) of $1.00. All prices at or below $2.00 (the green area) are legal. Prices above the price ceiling (the red area) are illegal. But because the market equilibrium (E) occurs in the green area, the price ceiling does not influence the market; it is nonbinding. As long as the equilibrium price remains below the price ceiling, price will continue to be regulated by supply and demand.

BINDING PRICE CEILINGS When a price ceiling is below the market price, it creates a binding constraint that prevents supply and demand from clearing the market. In Figure 6.2, the price ceiling for bread is set at $0.50 per loaf. Because $0.50 is well below the equilibrium price of $1.00, the price ceiling is *binding*. Notice that at a price of $0.50, the quantity demanded (Q_D) is greater than the quantity supplied (Q_S); in other words, a shortage exists. Shortages typically cause prices to rise, but the imposed price ceiling prevents that from happening. A price ceiling of $0.50 allows only the prices in the green area. The market cannot reach the equilibrium point E at $1.00 per loaf because it is located above the price ceiling, in the red area.

The black-market price is also set by supply and demand. Because prices above $0.50 are illegal, sellers are unwilling to produce more than Q_S. Because a shortage exists, an illegal market will form in response to the shortage. In the black market, purchasers can illegally resell what they have just bought at $0.50 for far more than what they just paid. Because the supply of legally produced bread is Q_S, the intersection of the vertical dashed line that reflects Q_S with the demand curve D_{SR} at point $E_{black\ market}$ establishes a black-market price ($P_{black\ market}$) at $2.00 per loaf for illegally sold bread. The black-market price is substantially more than the market equilibrium price (P_E) of $1.00. As a result, the black-market price eliminates the shortage caused by the price ceiling. However, the price ceiling has created two unintended consequences: a smaller quantity of bread supplied (Q_S is less than Q_E), and a higher price for those who purchase it on the black market.

Price Ceilings in the Long Run

In the long run, supply and demand become more elastic, or flatter. Recall from Chapter 4 that when consumers have additional time to make choices, they find more ways to avoid high-priced goods and more ways to take advantage of low prices. Additional time also gives producers the opportunity to

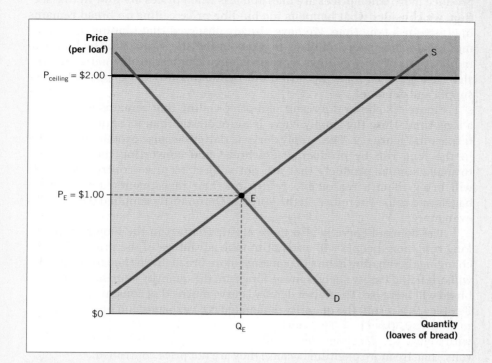

FIGURE 6.1

A Nonbinding Price Ceiling

The price ceiling ($2.00) is set above the equilibrium price ($1.00). Because market prices are set by the intersection of supply (S) and demand (D), as long as the equilibrium price is below the price ceiling, the price ceiling is nonbinding and has no effect.

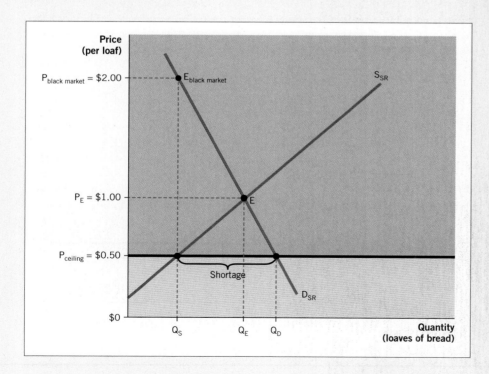

FIGURE 6.2

The Effect of a Binding Price Ceiling in the Short Run

A binding price ceiling prevents sellers from increasing the price and causes them to reduce the quantity they offer for sale. As a consequence, prices no longer signal relative scarcity. Consumers desire to purchase the product at the price ceiling level, which creates a shortage in the short run (SR); many will be unable to obtain the good. As a result, those who are shut out of the market will turn to other means to acquire the good, establishing an illegal market for the good at the black-market price.

produce more when prices are high and less when prices are low. In this section, we consider what happens if a binding price ceiling on bread remains in effect for a long time. We have already observed that binding price ceilings create shortages and black markets in the short run. Are the long-run implications of price ceilings more problematic or less problematic than the short-run implications? Let's find out by looking at what happens to both supply and demand.

Figure 6.3 shows the result of a price ceiling that remains in place for a long time. Here the supply curve is more elastic than its short-run counterpart in Figure 6.2. The supply curve is flatter because producers respond in the long run by producing less bread and converting their facilities to make similar products that are not subject to price controls and that will bring them a reasonable return on their investments—for example, bagels and rolls. Therefore, in the long run the quantity supplied (Q_S) shrinks even more.

The demand curve is also more elastic (flatter) in the long run. In the long run, more people will attempt to take advantage of the price ceiling by changing their eating habits to consume more bread. Even though consumers will often find empty shelves in the long run, the quantity demanded of cheap bread will increase. The flatter demand curve means that consumers are more flexible. As a result, the quantity demanded (Q_D) expands and bread is harder to find at $0.50 per loaf. The shortage will become so acute (compare Figure 6.3 with Figure 6.2) that consumers will turn to bread substitutes, like bagels and rolls, that are more plentiful because they are not price controlled.

FIGURE 6.3

The Effect of a Binding Price Ceiling in the Long Run

In the long run (LR), increased elasticity on the part of both producers and consumers makes the shortage larger than it was in the short run. Consumers adjust their demand to the lower price and want more bread. Producers adjust their supply and make less of the unprofitable product. As a result, the product becomes progressively harder to find.

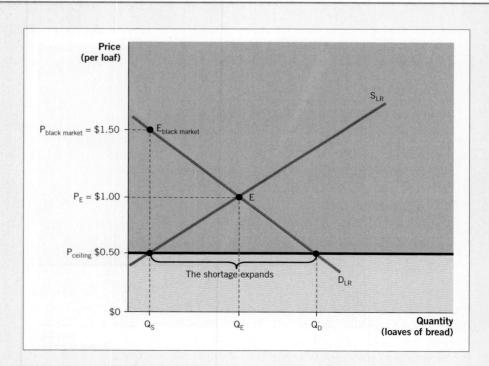

Price Ceilings

SLUMDOG MILLIONAIRE

The setting for the Academy Awards Best Picture of 2008 is Mumbai, India. Eighteen-year-old Jamal Malik is an Indian Muslim who is a contestant on the Indian version of *Who Wants to Be a Millionaire?* Dharavi, where the film is set, is a Mumbai slum about half the size of New York's Central Park. Over 1 million people call Dharavi home. Malik is one question away from the grand prize. However, he is detained by the authorities, who suspect him of cheating because they cannot comprehend how a "slumdog" could know all the answers. The movie beautifully chronicles the events in Jamal's life that provided him with the answers. Jamal, contrary to the stereotype of the people that live in the Dharavi slum, is intelligent, entrepreneurial, and fully capable of navigating life in the 21st century.

Rent controls have existed in Mumbai since 1947. Under the Rents, Hotel and Lodging House Rates Control Act, the government placed a cap on the amount of rent a tenant pays to a landlord. This limit has remained virtually frozen despite the consistent rise in market prices over time. As economists, we know that this policy will create excess demand. Renters are lined up for housing, and therefore, landlords can offer substandard accommodations and still have many takers. When this process continues for generations, as it has in Mumbai, the cumulative effect is that many buildings are unsafe to live in.

Price ceilings set the regulated price below the market equilibrium price determined by supply and demand. As a result, there is an increase in the quantity

The Dharavi slum in Mumbai is the setting for *Slumdog Millionaire.*

demanded. At the same time, since the price that landlords can charge is below the market equilibrium price, many landlords have left the apartment market to sell and invest elsewhere. As a consequence, the supply of rental units is reduced over time, which leads to long wait lists for apartments. Since demand exceeds supply, some landlords also impose additional requirements on potential tenants, leading to discrimination against certain groups of people.

Increased elasticity on the part of producers and consumers magnifies the unintended consequences we observed in the short run. Therefore, products subject to a price ceiling become progressively harder to find in the long run and the black market continues to operate. However, in the long run our bread consumers will choose substitutes for expensive black-market bread, leading to somewhat lower black-market prices in the long run.

Price Ceilings: Ridesharing

QUESTION: Surge pricing is the practice of raising prices during periods of increased demand, sometimes for just a few hours at a stretch. Suppose that users of rideshare services, such as Lyft and Uber, persuade Congress to ban surge pricing when emergencies are declared. How will this policy affect the number of people who can use ridesharing in times of crisis?

ANSWER: The price that makes quantity supplied equal to quantity demanded is now illegal, because of the binding price ceiling. As a result, there will be a shortage of drivers willing to supply their service. Because rideshare drivers control when and where they choose to work, many will choose to stay home or work other areas not affected by the emergency. Consumers seeking a ride in the affected areas will turn to taxi cabs, buses and other forms of mass transit, but those services are also likely to be disrupted. In sum, the supply of available transportation options will dwindle. So the answer to the question is that fewer people will be able to get a rideshare, and this problem will be most acute in the worst-hit areas.

Need a Lyft in an emergency? Better hope there's one available!

What Effects Do Price Ceilings Have on Economic Activity?

We have seen the logical repercussions of a hypothetical price ceiling on bread and the incentives it creates. Now let's use supply and demand analysis to examine two real-world price ceilings: *rent control* and *price gouging laws*.

Rent Control

Rent control is a price ceiling that applies to the market for apartment rentals.

Under **rent control**, a local government caps the price of apartment rentals to keep housing affordable. While this goal may be laudable, rent control doesn't work. In fact, it doesn't help the poor residents of a city find affordable housing or gain access to housing at all. In addition, these policies contribute to dangerous living conditions.

Mumbai, India, provides a chilling example of what can happen when rent controls are applied over an extended period. In Mumbai, many rent-controlled buildings have become dilapidated. Every monsoon season, several of these buildings fall—often with tragic consequences. Because the rent that property owners are permitted to charge is so low, they have less income to use for maintenance on the buildings. They cannot make a reasonable profit and afford to maintain the buildings properly. As a result, rent control policies have led to the decay of many apartment buildings. Similar controls have caused the same problem in cities worldwide.

To understand how a policy can backfire so greatly, let's look at the history of rent control in New York City. In 1943, in the midst of World War II, the federal government established the Emergency Price Control Act. The act was designed to keep inflation in check during the war, when many essential commodities were scarce. After the war, the federal government ended price controls, but New York City continued rent control. Today, there are approximately 1 million rent-controlled units in New York City. Rent controls limit the price a landlord can charge a tenant for rent. They also require that the landlord provide certain basic services; but not surprisingly, landlords keep maintenance to a minimum.

Does the presence of so many rent-controlled apartments mean that less affluent households can easily find a cheap place to rent? Hardly. When a rent-controlled unit is vacated, the property is generally no longer subject to rent control. Laws allow the tenants of rent-controlled apartments to pass those apartments from generation to generation, which keeps the apartments in the rent control program. Because so many rent-controlled apartments are inherited, rent control no longer even remotely serves its original purpose of helping low-income households. Clearly, the law was never intended to subsidize fancy vacation homes, but that's what it does! This outcome has happened, in part, because some tenants who can afford to live elsewhere choose not to. Their subsidized rent enables them to afford a second or third home in places such as upstate New York, Florida, or Europe.

The attempt to make housing more affordable in New York City has, ironically, made housing harder to obtain. It has encouraged the building of upscale properties rather than low-income units, and it has created a set of behaviors among landlords that is inconsistent with the affordability that rent control was designed to address. Figure 6.4 shows why rent control fails.

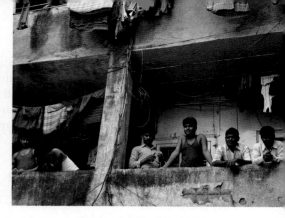

Many apartment buildings in Mumbai, India, are dilapidated as a result of rent control laws.

Incentives

FIGURE 6.4

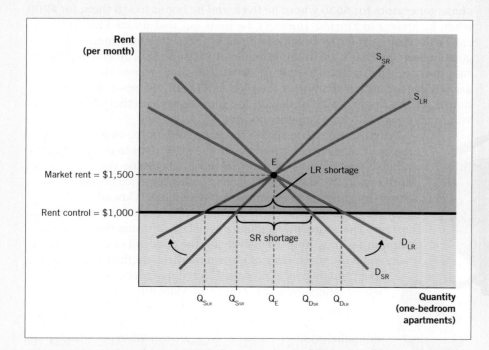

Rent Control in the Short Run and the Long Run

Because rent-controlled apartments are vacated slowly, the quantity supplied decreases in the short run and the supply curve becomes more elastic in the long run, causing the quantity supplied to fall. Demand also becomes more elastic in the long run, causing the quantity demanded to rise. The combination of fewer units available to rent and more consumers looking to find rent-controlled units leads to a larger shortage in the long run.

As with any binding price ceiling, rent control causes a shortage because the quantity demanded in the short run ($Q_{D_{SR}}$) is greater than the quantity supplied in the short run ($Q_{S_{SR}}$). The combination of fewer available units and more consumers looking for rent-controlled units leads to a larger shortage in the long run.

Price Gouging

Price gouging laws
place a temporary ceiling on the prices that sellers can charge during times of emergency.

Another kind of price control, **price gouging laws**, places a temporary ceiling on the prices that sellers can charge during times of emergency until markets function normally again. Over 30 U.S. states have laws against price gouging. Like all price controls, price gouging laws have unintended consequences. These consequences became very apparent after Hurricane Irma in 2017.

When Hurricane Irma hit Florida in September, a state of emergency activated the state's price gouging laws. The statute makes it illegal to charge an "excessive" price immediately following a natural disaster. The law is designed to prevent the victims of natural disasters from being exploited in a time of need. As Irma approached Florida, there were hundreds of complaints about suspected price gouging, including one retailer wanting $99.99 for cases of bottled water that normally retailed for $10.00—clear gouging under the statute. Airline prices, however, are not covered by gouging laws because they fluctuate quite a bit even in normal times. Prices on flights out of the affected areas skyrocketed to as much as $2,000 for last-minute bookings, as people tried to escape the storm.

Incentives

So what's better? Try to keep a lid on prices, or let them shoot up? Suppose that an entrepreneur from North Carolina is interested in delivering generators to parts of Florida about to be hit by Hurricane Irma. He can purchase generators for $530 where he lives, and he hopes to sell them for $900 when he arrives in Florida. However, he finds out that under Florida law he can be fined up to $1,000 for each sale he makes above the maximum under the gouging law (which is $700 in this example) during a state of emergency. Facing this prospect, he decides to stay in North Carolina, where the generators are not needed, rather than incur the risk. As a result, the residents of Florida never get the opportunity to decide for themselves whether they wish to voluntarily pay $900 for a generator or not.

Large generator: demand increased after Hurricane Irma hit.

Prices act to ration scarce resources. When the demand for generators or other necessities is high, the price rises to ensure that the available units are distributed to those who value them the most. More important, the ability to charge a higher price provides sellers with an incentive to make more units available. If laws limit the ability for the price to change when demand increases, the result will be a shortage. Therefore, price gouging legislation means that devastated communities must rely exclusively on the goodwill of others and the slow-moving machinery of government relief efforts. In addition, price gouging laws close off entrepreneurial activity, which would otherwise be a means to alleviate dire conditions.

Figure 6.5 shows how price gouging laws work and the shortage they create. If the demand for gas generators increases immediately after a disaster (D_{after}), the market price rises from $530 to $900. But because $900 is considered excessive, sales

FIGURE 6.5

Price Gouging

Price gouging laws serve as a nonbinding price ceiling during normal times. However, when a natural disaster strikes, price gouging laws go into effect. In our example, the demand curve for generators shifts to the right as a result of the natural disaster, causing the new equilibrium price (E_{after}) to rise above the legal limit. The result is a shortage. When the emergency is lifted, the market demand returns to normal, and the temporary shortage created by price gouging legislation is eliminated.

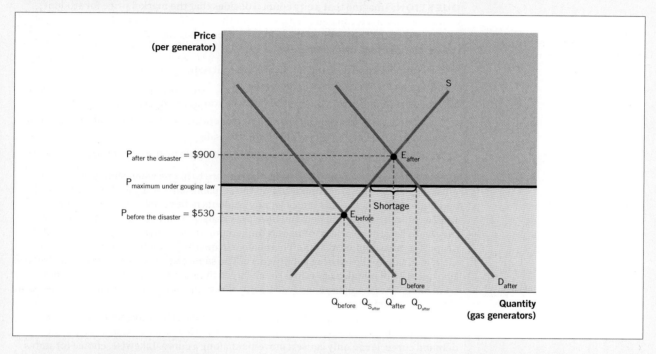

at that price are illegal. The result is a binding price ceiling for as long as a state of emergency is in effect. A binding price ceiling creates a shortage. You can see the shortage in Figure 6.5 in the difference between quantity demanded and quantity supplied at the price ceiling mandated by the law. In this case, the normal ability of supply and demand to ration the available generators is short-circuited. Because more people demand generators after the disaster than before it, those who do not get to the store soon enough are out of luck. When the emergency is lifted and the market returns to normal, the temporary shortage created by price gouging laws is eliminated.

When Do Price Floors Matter?

A **price floor** creates a legally established minimum price for a good or service. The minimum wage law is an example of a price floor in the market for labor. Like price ceilings, price floors create many unintended effects that policymakers rarely acknowledge. However, unlike price ceilings, price floors result

A **price floor** is a legally established minimum price for a good or service.

Price Ceilings: Student Rental Apartments

Here is a question that often confuses students.

QUESTION: Imagine that a city council decides that the market price for student rental apartments is too high. It passes a law that establishes a rental price ceiling of $600 per month. The result of the price ceiling is a shortage. Which of the following has caused the shortage of apartments?

a. Both suppliers and demanders. Landlords will reduce the supply of apartments, and the demand from renters will increase.

b. A spike in demand from many students who want to rent cheap apartments

c. The drop in supply caused by apartment owners pulling their units off the rental market and converting them into condos for sale

d. The change in price as a result of the price ceiling set by the city council

ANSWER: Many students think that markets are to blame when shortages (or surpluses) exist. The first reaction is to find the culpable party—either the supplier or the demander, or both. For this reason, many students believe that choice (a) is correct. But be careful. Supply and demand have not changed—they are exactly the same as they were before the price ceiling was implemented. What has changed is the quantity of apartments supplied at $600. This change in quantity supplied is represented by a movement along the existing supply curve. The same type of analysis applies to renters. The quantity demanded at $600 is much larger than it was when the price was not controlled. Therefore, the change in quantity demanded is represented by a movement along the demand curve.

The same logic applies to choices (b) and (c). Choice (b) states that there is a spike in student demand caused by the lower price. But price cannot cause a shift in the demand curve; it can only cause a movement along a curve. Likewise, choice (c) states that apartment owners supply fewer units for rent. The fact that fewer apartments are available at $600 per month would be represented by a movement along the apartment supply curve.

So we are left with choice (d), which is the correct answer. There is only one change in market conditions: the city council has passed a new price ceiling law. A binding price ceiling disrupts the market's ability to reach equilibrium. Therefore, we can say that the change in the price as a result of the price ceiling has caused the shortage.

from the political pressure of suppliers to keep prices high. Most consumers prefer lower prices when they shop, so the idea of a law that keeps prices high may sound like a bad one to you. However, if you are selling a product or service, you might think that legislation to keep prices high is a very good idea. For instance, many states establish minimum prices for milk. As a result, milk prices are higher than they would be if supply and demand set the price.

In this section, we follow the same progression that we did with price ceilings. We begin with a simple thought experiment. Once we understand how price floors work, we use supply and demand analysis to examine the short- and long-run implications for economic activity.

Understanding Price Floors

To understand how price floors affect the market, let's try a thought experiment. Suppose that a politician suggests we should encourage dairy farmers to produce more milk so that supplies will be plentiful and everyone will get enough calcium. To accomplish these goals, the government sets a price floor of $6 per gallon—about twice the price of a typical gallon of fat-free milk—to make production more attractive to milk producers. What repercussions should we expect?

First, more milk will be available for sale because the higher price will cause dairies to increase the quantity that they supply. At the same time, because consumers must pay more, the quantity demanded will fall. The result will be a surplus of milk. Because every gallon of milk that is produced but not sold hurts the dairies' bottom line, sellers will want to lower their prices enough to get as many sales as possible before the milk goes bad. But the price floor will not allow the market to respond, and sellers will be stuck with milk that goes to waste. They will be tempted to offer illegal discounts in order to recoup some of their costs.

What happens next? Because the surplus cannot be resolved through lower prices, the government will try to help equalize the quantity supplied and the quantity demanded through other means. It can do so in one of two ways: by restricting the supply of the good or by stimulating additional demand. Both solutions are problematic. If production is restricted, dairy farmers will not be able to generate a profitable amount of milk. Likewise, stimulating additional demand is not as simple as it sounds. Let's consider how these government programs work with other crops.

In many cases, the government purchases surplus agricultural production, most notably with corn, soybeans, cotton, and rice. Once the government buys the surplus production, it often sells the surplus below cost to developing countries to avoid wasting the crop. This strategy has the unintended consequence of making it cheaper for consumers in these developing nations to buy excess agricultural output from developed nations like the United States than to have local farmers grow the crop. International treaties ban the practice of dumping surplus production, but it continues under the guise of humanitarian aid. This practice makes little economic sense. Table 6.2 summarizes the result of our price floor thought experiment using milk.

If you're doing a handstand, you need the floor for support. A binding price floor keeps prices from falling.

The Effect of Price Floors

We have seen that price floors create unintended consequences. Now we will use the supply and demand model to analyze how price floors affect the market. We look at the short run first.

Got milk? Maybe not, if there's a price floor.

NONBINDING PRICE FLOORS Like price ceilings, price floors can be binding or nonbinding. Figure 6.6 illustrates a nonbinding price floor of $2 per gallon on milk. As you can see, at $2 the price floor is below the equilibrium price (P_E), so the price floor is nonbinding. Because the actual market price is above the legally established minimum price (P_{floor}), the price floor does not prevent the market from reaching equilibrium at point E. Consequently, the

TABLE 6.2

A Price Floor on Milk

Question	Answer / Explanation		Result
Will the quantity of milk for sale change?	Consumers will purchase less because the price is higher (the law of demand), but producers will manufacture more (the law of supply). The net result will be a surplus of milk.	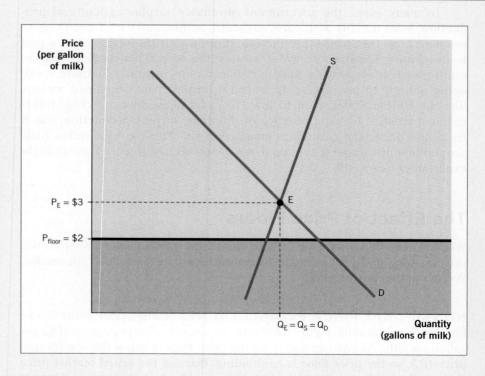	There will be a surplus of milk
Would producers sell below the price floor?	Yes. A surplus of milk would give sellers a strong incentive to undercut the price floor to avoid having to discard leftover milk.	REDUCED MILK AHEAD	Illegal discounts will help reduce the milk surplus
Will dairy farmers be better off?	Not if they have trouble selling what they produce.	not for Sale no good.	There might be a lot of spoiled milk

FIGURE 6.6

A Nonbinding Price Floor

Under a nonbinding price floor, price is regulated by supply and demand. Because the price floor ($2) is below the equilibrium price ($3), the market will voluntarily charge more than the legal minimum. Therefore, this nonbinding price floor will have no effect on sales and purchases of milk.

Price (per gallon of milk)

S

$P_E = \$3$ — E

$P_{floor} = \$2$

D

$Q_E = Q_S = Q_D$

Quantity (gallons of milk)

price floor has no impact on the market. As long as the equilibrium price remains above the price floor, price is determined by supply and demand.

BINDING PRICE FLOORS For a price floor to have an impact on the market, it must be set above the market equilibrium price. In that case, it is a binding price floor. With a binding price floor, the quantity supplied will exceed the quantity demanded. Figure 6.7 illustrates a binding price floor in the short run. Continuing our example of milk prices, at $6 per gallon the price floor is above the equilibrium price of $3. Market forces always attempt to restore the equilibrium between supply and demand at point E. So we know that there is downward pressure on the price. At a price floor of $6, we see that $Q_{S_{SR}} > Q_{D_{SR}}$. The difference between the quantity supplied and the quantity demanded is the surplus. Because the market's price adjustment mechanism is not permitted to work, sellers find themselves holding unwanted inventories of milk. To eliminate the surplus, which will spoil unless it is sold, a black market may develop with prices substantially below the legislated price. At a price ($P_{black\ market}$) of $2, the black market eliminates the surplus that the price floor caused. However, the price floor has created two unintended consequences: a smaller demand for milk ($Q_{D_{SR}} < Q_{E_{SR}}$) and a black market to eliminate the glut.

Full shelves signal a market at equilibrium.

Incentives

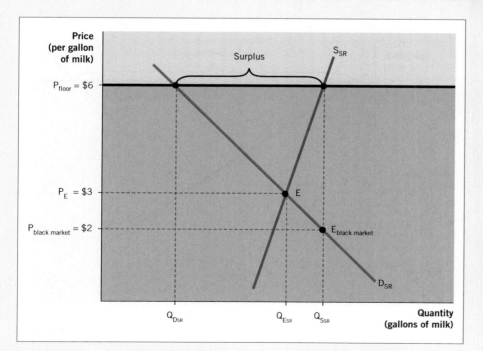

FIGURE 6.7

A Binding Price Floor in the Short Run

A binding price floor creates a surplus, which has two unintended consequences: (1) a smaller quantity demanded than the equilibrium quantity ($Q_{D_{SR}} < Q_{E_{SR}}$) and (2) a lower black-market price to eliminate the glut of the product.

Price Floors in the Long Run

Once price floor legislation is passed, it can be politically difficult to repeal. What happens if a binding price floor on milk stays in effect for a long time? To answer that question, we need to consider elasticity. We have already observed that in the short run, binding price ceilings cause shortages and that black markets follow.

Figure 6.8 shows a price floor for milk that remains in place well past the short run. The long run gives consumers a chance to find milk substitutes—for example, products made from soy, rice, or almond that are not subject to the price floor—at lower prices. This added consumer flexibility makes the long-run demand for milk more elastic. As a result, the demand curve depicted in Figure 6.8 is more elastic than its short-run counterpart in Figure 6.7. The supply curve also becomes flatter (more elastic) because firms (dairy farms) are able to produce more milk by acquiring additional land and production facilities. Therefore, a price floor ($6) that remains in place over time causes the supply and demand curves to become more elastic, magnifying the surplus.

What happens to supply? In the long run, producers are more flexible and therefore supply is more elastic. The pool of potential milk producers rises as other closely related businesses retool their operations to supply more milk. The flatter supply curve in Figure 6.8 reflects this flexibility. As a result, $Q_{S_{LR}}$ expands and becomes much larger than it was in Figure 6.7. The increased elasticity on the part of both producers and consumers makes the surplus larger in the long run and magnifies the unintended consequences we observed in the short run.

FIGURE 6.8

The Effect of a Binding Price Floor in the Long Run

When a price floor is left in place over time, supply and demand both become more elastic. The result is a larger surplus ($Q_{S_{LR}} < Q_{D_{LR}}$) in the long run. Because sellers are unable to sell all that they produce at $6 per gallon, a black market develops to eliminate the glut of milk.

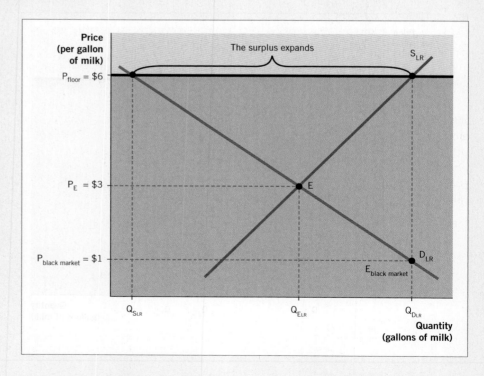

Price Floors: Fair-Trade Coffee

Fair-trade coffee is sold through organizations that purchase directly from growers. The coffee is usually sold for a higher price than standard coffee. The goal is to promote more humane working conditions for the coffee pickers and growers. Fair-trade coffee has become more popular but still accounts for a small portion of all coffee sales, in large part because it is substantially more expensive to produce.

QUESTION: Suppose that the price of a 1-pound bag of standard coffee is $8 and the price of a 1-pound bag of fair-trade coffee is $12. Congress decides to impose a price floor of $10 per pound on all 1-pound bags of coffee. What will most likely happen?

ANSWER: Fair-trade producers typically sell their product at a higher price than mass-produced coffee brands. Therefore, a $10 price floor is binding for inexpensive brands like Folgers but nonbinding for premium coffees, which include fair-trade sellers. The price floor will reduce the price disparity between fair-trade coffee and mass-produced coffee.

To see how the market will respond, consider a fair-trade coffee producer who charges $12 per pound and a mass-produced brand that sells for $8 per pound. A price floor of $10 reduces the difference between the price of fair-trade coffee and the inexpensive coffee brands, which now must sell for $10 instead of $8. The consumer's opportunity cost of choosing fair-trade coffee is now lower. Therefore, some consumers of the inexpensive brands will opt for fair-trade coffee instead. As a result, fair-trade producers will benefit indirectly from the price floor. Thus, the answer to the question is that more people will buy fair-trade coffee as a result of this price floor policy.

CHALLENGE QUESTION: Suppose the price floor is imposed and consumption of fair-trade coffee actually goes down. How might you explain this?

ANSWER: This could happen in a setting where the consumers are low-income, socially conscious coffee addicts. These consumers buy regular coffee when money is tight but fair-trade coffee when they feel they can afford it. When regular coffee gets more expensive, these consumers buy more of it and less of the fair-trade stuff. Since few locales have a large population of socially conscious coffee guzzlers on tight budgets, this scenario would require exceptionally strong consumer preferences.

Would fair-trade coffee producers benefit from a price floor?

Opportunity cost

· ECONOMICS *in the* MEDIA ·

Unintended Consequences

College Humor created a short YouTube video, "Buy Food Ethically, Unless It is Too Hard," that illustrates the trade-offs people face when they make purchases at a local farmer's market. The people interviewed in the video have the best of intentions: they want to save the environment, eat healthier, and support local growers. But their responses indicate that they don't always buy at the farmer's market despite their stated intentions. One of the primary reasons they don't go there as often as they would like to is the price. Each of the persons interviewed is young and socially conscious, but prices matter to them as well, and that, combined with the inconvenience of going to the farmer's market, means that they rarely go. The video illustrates a very important point: prices matter, whether those prices are naturally set in the market or artificially set through price controls.

Do you buy your produce at the farmer's market?

Trade-offs
Incentives

What Effects Do Price Floors Have on Economic Activity?

We have seen the logical repercussions of a hypothetical price floor on milk and the incentives it creates. Now let's use supply and demand analysis to examine two real-world price floors: *minimum wage laws* and *sugar subsidies*.

The Minimum Wage

The minimum wage is the lowest hourly wage rate that firms may legally pay their workers.

The **minimum wage** is the lowest hourly wage rate that firms may legally pay their workers. Minimum wage workers can be skilled or unskilled and experienced or inexperienced. The common thread is that these workers, for a variety of reasons, lack better prospects.

A minimum wage functions as a price floor. Figure 6.9 shows the effect of a binding minimum wage. Note that the wage, or the cost of labor, on the *y* axis ($10 per hour) is the price that must be paid. However, the market equilibrium wage ($7), or W_E, is below the minimum wage. The minimum wage prevents the market from reaching W_E at E (the equilibrium point) because only the wages

FIGURE 6.9

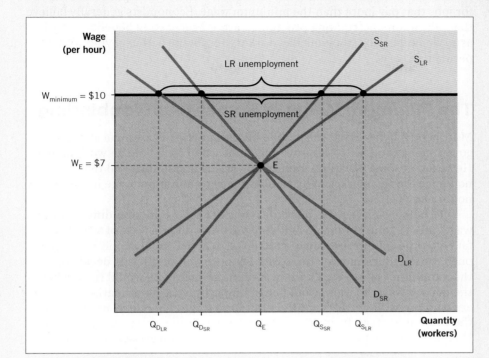

Price Floors and a Binding Minimum Wage Market in the Short Run and Long Run

A binding minimum wage is a price floor above the current equilibrium wage, W_E. At $10 per hour, the number of workers willing to supply their labor ($Q_{S_{SR}}$) is greater than the quantity demanded of workers ($Q_{D_{SR}}$). The result is a surplus of workers (which we recognize as unemployment). Because the supply of workers and demand for workers both become more elastic in the long run, unemployment expands $(Q_{S_{LR}} - Q_{D_{LR}}) > (Q_{S_{SR}} - Q_{D_{SR}})$.

in the green area are legal. The minimum wage raises the cost of hiring workers. Therefore, a higher minimum wage will lower the quantity of labor demanded. At the same time, firms will look for ways to substitute capital for workers. As a result, a binding minimum wage results in unemployment in the short run because $Q_{S_{SR}} > Q_{D_{SR}}$.

Businesses generally want to keep costs down, so in the long run they will try to reduce the amount they spend on labor. They might replace workers with machinery, shorten work hours, offer reduced customer service, or even relocate to countries that do not have minimum wage laws. As we move past the short run, more people will attempt to take advantage of higher minimum wages. Like firms, workers will adjust to the higher minimum wage over time. Some workers who might have decided to go to school full-time or remain retired or who simply want some extra income will enter the labor market because the minimum wage is now higher. As a result, minimum wage jobs will become progressively harder to find and unemployment will increase. The irony is that in the long run, the minimum wage, just like any other price floor, has created two unintended consequences: a smaller demand for workers by employers ($Q_{D_{LR}}$ is significantly less than Q_E) and a larger supply of workers ($Q_{S_{LR}}$) looking for jobs.

Proponents of minimum wage legislation are aware that it often creates unemployment. To address this problem, they support investment in training, education, and the creation of government jobs programs to provide more work opportunities. While jobs programs increase the number of minimum wage

Incentives

jobs, training and additional education enable workers to acquire skills needed for jobs that pay more than the minimum wage. Economists generally believe that education and training programs have longer-lasting benefits to society as a whole because they enable workers to obtain better-paying jobs on a permanent basis.

The Minimum Wage Is Sometimes Nonbinding

Most people believe that raising the minimum wage is a simple step that the government can take to improve the standard of living of the working poor. However, in some places the minimum wage is nonbinding and therefore has no impact on the market. Why would we have a minimum wage if it is largely nonbinding?

   To help us answer this question, consider the two nonbinding minimum wage rates ($7 and $9) shown in Figure 6.10. A minimum wage of $7 per hour is far below the equilibrium wage of $10 ($W_E$), so at that point supply and demand push the equilibrium wage up to $10. Suppose that politicians decide to raise the minimum wage to $9. This new minimum wage of $9 would remain below the market wage, so there would be no impact on the labor market for workers who are willing to accept the minimum wage. Therefore, an increase in the minimum wage from $7 to $9 an hour will not create unemployment. Unemployment will occur only when the minimum wage rises above $10.

FIGURE 6.10

A Nonbinding Minimum Wage

An increase in the minimum wage from $7 to $9 remains nonbinding. Therefore, it will not change the quantity demanded for labor or the unemployment rate. If the minimum wage rises above the market wage, unemployment will occur.

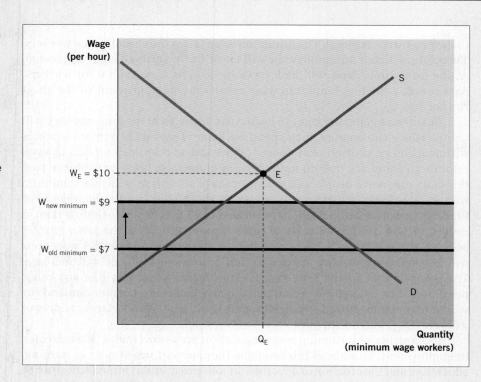

Minimum Wage: Always the Same?

A minimum wage is a price floor, a price control that doesn't allow prices—in this case the cost of labor—to fall below an assigned value. Although the media and politicians often discuss the minimum wage in the United States as if there is only one minimum wage, there are numerous minimum wages in the USA. In states where the state minimum wage is not the same as the federal minimum wage, the higher of the two wage rates takes effect.

- Minimum Wage Higher than Federal
- Minimum Wage Equal to Federal
- Minimum Wage Lower than Federal (Federal Rate Applies)
- No Minimum Wage (Federal Rate Applies)

WASHINGTON

Washington's minimum wage of $13.50/hour is significantly higher than the federal rate and takes precedence over the federal rate in that state.

FEDERAL MINIMUM WAGE $7.25

$13.50

Washington, DC

Georgia has a minimum wage of $5.15/hour on the books, but employers must pay their workers the higher federal rate.

GEORGIA $5.15

Puerto Rico

REVIEW QUESTIONS

- Suppose you live in Oklahoma and are looking for a job. The state minimum wage rate is $7.25/hour, the federal minimum wage rate is $7.25/hour, and the market equilibrium wage for the job is $8.00/hour. What wage will you be paid? Are the state and national minimum wages binding or non-binding price floors?

- Suppose Wisconsin increases its minimum wage from $7.25/hour, which is below the market wage for low-skill labor, to $11.00/hour, which is above the market wage. Using supply and demand curves, show how this might increase the number of unemployed workers.

HIGHEST MINIMUM WAGES, 2020

District of Columbia	$14.00
Washington	$13.50
California	$13.00
Massachusetts	$12.75

Source: U.S. Department of Labor.

In many locations there is a push to raise the minimum wage to $15 an hour. To consider the effectiveness of such a move, let's look at Seattle, Washington. Researchers who examined the Seattle Minimum Wage Ordinance have found conflicting results. What would explain the differences in their findings? For an answer we turn to a group of economists, including Ekaterina Jardim, who evaluated the wage, employment, and work hours of the first and second phase-in of the ordinance, which raised the minimum wage from $9.47 to $11 per hour in 2015 and to $13 per hour in 2016. For the first increase, from $9.47 to $11 an hour, the team found that the overall effect on low-wage workers' earnings was minimal. However, Jardim and the other researchers found that the second wage increase, to $13, reduced hours worked in low-wage jobs by around 9%, while hourly wages in such jobs increased by around 3%. Consequently, total payroll fell for such jobs, implying that the Minimum Wage Ordinance lowered low-wage employees' earnings by an average of $125 per month in 2016. Somewhere between $11 and $13 per hour, then, the minimum wage became binding.

That's not to say that efforts to raise the minimum wage in other places will have the same impact as Seattle. San Francisco became the first city with a $15 minimum wage in 2018. It is too early to tell whether that wage is binding or nonbinding. Moreover, just because a minimum wage is binding does not mean that low-wage workers can't benefit as a whole. If enough low-wage workers retain their jobs when the minimum wage is increased, the total payroll that workers receive can still increase even though some workers will have lost their jobs.

ECONOMICS IN THE REAL WORLD

WHY IS SUGAR CHEAPER IN CANADA, WHEN CANADA DOESN'T GROW SUGARCANE?

Sugar is one of life's small pleasures. It can be extracted and refined from sugarcane and sugar beets, two crops that can be grown in a variety of climates around the world. Sugar is both plentiful and cheap. As a result, Americans enjoy a lot of it—an average of over 100 pounds of refined sugar per person each year!

We would consume a lot more sugar if it were not subject to price controls. After the War of 1812, struggling sugarcane producers asked the government to pass a tariff (tax) that would protect domestic production. Over the years, price supports of all kinds have served to keep domestic sugar production high. The result is an industry that depends on a high price to survive. Under the current price-support system, the price of U.S.-produced sugar is roughly two to three times the world price. This situation has led to a bizarre set of incentives whereby U.S. farmers grow more sugar than they should and use land that is not well suited to the crop. For instance, sugarcane requires a subtropical climate, but most of the U.S. crop is grown in Louisiana, a region that is prone to hurricanes in the summer. As a result, many sugarcane crops there are completely lost. Have farmers turned to other, more locally suited crops? Not so much! What's happened is that frost-resistant strains have been developed that will grow farther inland, at colder locations.

Why do farmers persist in growing sugarcane in Louisiana? The answer lies in the political process: sugar growers have effectively lobbied to keep prices high

Incentives

through tariffs on foreign imports. Because lower prices would put many U.S. growers out of business and cause the loss of many jobs, politicians have given in to their demands.

Meanwhile, the typical sugar consumer is largely oblivious to the political process that sets the price floor. It has been estimated that the sugar subsidy program costs consumers over $1 billion a year. To make matters worse, thanks to corn subsidies, high-fructose corn syrup has become a cheap alternative to sugar and is often added to processed foods and soft drinks. In 1980, Coca-Cola replaced sugar with high-fructose corn syrup in its U.S. factories to reduce production costs. However, Coca-Cola continues to use sugarcane in many Latin American countries because it is cheaper there. Research shows that high-fructose corn syrup causes a metabolic reaction that makes people who ingest it more inclined to obesity. This is an example of an unintended consequence that few policymakers could have imagined. There is no reason why the United States must produce its own sugarcane. Ironically, sugar is cheaper in Canada than in the United States, primarily because Canada has no sugar growers—and thus no trade restrictions or government support programs. So here's another unintended consequence: Life Savers moved production of their quintessentially American candy treat to Canada, as a result of high U.S. production costs.

Which of these is the *real* thing? The Coke on the right, with high-fructose corn syrup, was made in the United States; the others, with sugar, were made in Mexico.

PRACTICE WHAT YOU KNOW

Price Ceilings and Price Floors: Would a Price Control on Internet Access Be Binding?

A recent study found the following demand and supply schedule for high-speed Internet access:

In today's Internet age, four degrees of separation are all that stand between you and the rest of the world.

Price of Internet	Connections demanded (millions of units)	Connections supplied (millions of units)
$60	10.0	62.5
50	20.0	55.0
40	30.0	47.5
30	40.0	40.0
20	50.0	32.5
10	60.0	25.0

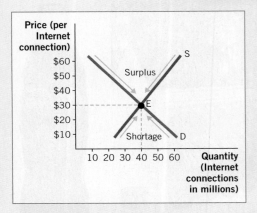

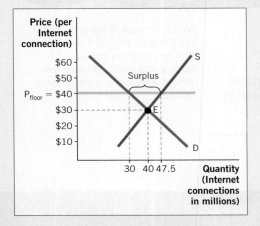

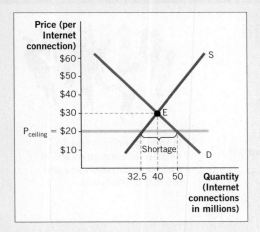

QUESTION: What are the equilibrium price and equilibrium quantity of Internet service?

ANSWER: First, look at the table on the previous page to see where quantity supplied and quantity demanded are equal. At a price of $30, consumers purchase 40 million units and producers supply 40 million units. Therefore, the equilibrium price is $30 and the equilibrium quantity is 40 million. At any price above $30, the quantity supplied exceeds the quantity demanded, so there is a surplus. The surplus gives sellers an incentive to cut the price until it reaches the equilibrium point, E. At any price below $30, the quantity demanded exceeds the quantity supplied, so there is a shortage. The shortage gives sellers an incentive to raise the price until it reaches the equilibrium point, E.

QUESTION: Suppose that providers convince the government that maintaining high-speed access to the Internet is an important element of technology infrastructure. As a result, Congress approves a price floor at $10 above the equilibrium price to help companies provide Internet service. How many people are able to connect to the Internet?

ANSWER: Adding $10 to the market price of $30 gives us a price floor of $40. At $40, consumers demand 30 million connections. Producers provide 47.5 million connections. The result is a surplus of 17.5 million units (shown in the graph). A price floor means that producers cannot cut the price below that point to increase the quantity that consumers demand. As a result, only 30 million units are sold. So only 30 million people connect to the Internet.

QUESTION: When consumers realize that fewer people are purchasing Internet access, they demand that the price floor be repealed and a price ceiling be put in its place. Congress acts immediately to remedy the problem, and a new price ceiling is set at $10 below the market price. Now how many people are able to connect to the Internet?

ANSWER: Subtracting $10 from the market price of $30 gives us a price ceiling of $20. At $20 per connection, consumers demand 50 million connections. However, producers provide only 32.5 million connections. The result is a shortage of 17.5 million units (shown in the graph). A price ceiling means that producers cannot raise the price, which will cause an increase in the quantity supplied. As a result, only 32.5 million units are sold, so only 32.5 million people connect to the Internet.

QUESTION: Which provides the greatest access to the Internet: free markets, price floors, or price ceilings?

ANSWER: With no government intervention, 40 million connections are sold. Once the price floor is established, 30 million people have an Internet connection. Under the price ceiling, 32.5 million people have an Internet connection. Despite legislative efforts to satisfy both producers and consumers of Internet service, the best solution is to allow free markets to allocate the good.

Price Gouging: Disaster Preparedness

- Set aside money in a long-term emergency fund.
- Keep a simple disaster supply kit.
- Safeguard your financial and legal records.

During a disaster, shortages of essential goods and services become widespread. In the more than 30 states where price gouging laws are on the books, merchants are prevented from charging unusually high prices. If you live in one of these states, cash alone can't save you. You will have to survive on your own for a time before help arrives and communication channels are restored.

"(It was) a little bit of a pandemonium," Orlando-area resident Diane Williams said, describing shoppers' efforts to stock up on supplies just before Hurricane Irma struck Florida in 2017. "It's just that everybody is panicked, so they are preparing, which is wise, but it's just, like, crazy."[*]

Taking measures to prepare for a disaster reduces the likelihood of injury, loss of life, and property damage far more than anything you can do after a disaster strikes. An essential part of disaster planning should include financial planning. Let's begin with the basics. Get adequate insurance to protect your family's health and property; plan for the possibility of job loss or disability by building a cash reserve; and safeguard your financial and legal records. It is also important to set aside extra money in a long-term emergency

Will you be ready if disaster strikes?

fund. Nearly all financial experts advise saving enough money to cover your expenses for six months. Most households never come close to reaching this goal, but don't let that stop you from trying.

Preparing a simple disaster supply kit is also a must. Price gouging laws make it important to stock a bunch of stuff, because you can't rely on just having cash on hand to buy what you need on short notice. Keep enough water, nonperishable food, sanitation supplies, batteries, medications, and cash on hand for three days. Often, the power is out after a disaster, so you cannot count on ATMs or banks to be open. These measures will help you to weather the immediate impact of a disaster.

---

*Source: "Irma Eyes the U.S.: 'Everybody Is Panicked'; Shelves Empty; Gas Pumps Run Dry," Offthegridnews.com, September 7, 2017. https://www.offthegridnews.com/current-events/irma-eyes-the-u-s-everybody-is-panicked-shelves-empty-gas-pumps-run-dry/.

Conclusion

The policies presented in this chapter—rent control, price gouging laws, the minimum wage, and agricultural price controls—create unintended consequences. Attempts to control prices should be viewed cautiously. When the price signal is suppressed through a binding price floor or a binding price ceiling, the market's ability to allocate goods and services is diminished, surpluses and shortages develop and expand through time, and obtaining goods and services becomes difficult.

The role of markets in society has many layers, and we've only just begun our analysis. In the next chapter, we consider two cases—externalities and public goods—in which the unregulated market produces an output that is not socially desirable. ✳

- ANSWERING *the* BIG QUESTIONS -

When do price ceilings matter?

* A price ceiling is a legally imposed maximum price. When the price is set below the equilibrium price, the quantity demanded will exceed the quantity supplied. The result is a shortage. Price ceilings matter when they are binding (below the equilibrium price).

What effects do price ceilings have on economic activity?

* Price ceilings create two unintended consequences: a smaller quantity supplied of the good (Q_S) and a higher price for consumers who turn to the black market.

When do price floors matter?

* A price floor is a legally imposed minimum price. The minimum wage is an example of a price floor. If the minimum wage is set above the equilibrium wage, a surplus of labor will develop. However, if the minimum wage is nonbinding, it will have no effect on the market wage. Thus, price floors matter when they are set above the equilibrium price.

What effects do price floors have on economic activity?

* Price floors lead to many unintended consequences, including surpluses, the creation of black markets, and artificial attempts to bring the market back into balance. For example, proponents of a higher minimum wage are concerned about finding ways to alleviate the resulting surplus of labor, or unemployment.

· CHAPTER PROBLEMS ·

Concepts You Should Know

black markets (p. 191)
minimum wage (p. 206)
price ceiling (p. 190)

price controls (p. 190)
price floor (p. 199)

price gouging laws (p. 198)
rent control (p. 196)

Questions for Review

1. Does a binding price ceiling cause a shortage or a surplus? Provide an example to support your answer.

2. Does a nonbinding price floor cause a shortage or a surplus? Provide an example to support your answer.

3. Will a surplus or a shortage caused by a price control become smaller or larger over time? Explain.

4. Are price gouging laws an example of a price floor or a price ceiling?

5. What will happen to the market price when a price control is nonbinding?

6. Why do most economists oppose attempts to control prices? Why does the government attempt to control prices anyway in a number of markets?

Study Problems (✱ solved at the end of this section)

1. In the song "Minimum Wage," the punk band Fenix TX comments on the inadequacy of the minimum wage for making ends meet. Using the poverty thresholds provided by the Census Bureau,* determine whether the federal minimum wage of $7.25 an hour provides enough income for a single full-time worker to escape poverty.

✱ **2.** Imagine that the community you live in decides to enact a rent control of $700 per month on every one-bedroom apartment. Using the following table, determine the market price and equilibrium quantity without rent control. How many one-bedroom apartments will be rented after the rent control law is passed?

Monthly rent	Quantity demanded	Quantity supplied
$600	700	240
700	550	320
800	400	400
900	250	480
1,000	100	560

*Source: https://www.census.gov/data/tables/2017/demo/supplemental-poverty-measure/poverty-thresholds.html.

3. Suppose that the federal government places a binding price floor on chocolate. To help support the price floor, the government purchases all of the leftover chocolate that consumers do not buy. If the price floor remains in place for a number of years, what do you expect to happen to each of the following?

a. quantity of chocolate demanded by consumers
b. quantity of chocolate supplied by producers
c. quantity of chocolate purchased by the government

4. Suppose that a group of die-hard sports fans are upset about the high price of tickets to many games. As a result of their lobbying efforts, a new law caps the maximum ticket price to any sporting event at $50. Will more people be able to attend the games? Explain your answer. Will certain teams and events be affected more than others? Provide examples.

5. Many local governments use parking meters on crowded downtown streets. However, the parking spaces along the street are typically hard to find because the metered price is often set below the market price. Explain what happens when local governments set the meter price too low. Why do you think the price is set below the market-clearing price?

6. Imagine that local suburban leaders decide to enact a minimum wage. Will the community lose more jobs if the nearby city votes to increase the minimum wage to the same rate? Discuss your answer.

✳ **7.** Examine the following graph, showing the market for low-skilled laborers.

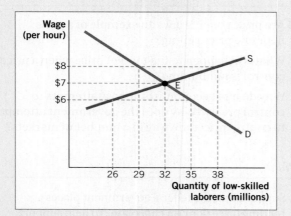

How many low-skilled laborers will be unemployed when the minimum wage is $8 an hour? How many low-skilled workers will be unemployed when the minimum wage is $6 an hour?

8. Demand and supply curves can be represented with equations. Suppose that the demand for low-skilled labor, Q_D, is represented by the following equation, where W is the wage rate:

$$Q_D = 53,000,000 - 3,000,000W$$

The supply of low-skilled labor, Q_S, is represented by the equation

$$Q_S = -10,000,000 + 6,000,000W$$

a. Find the equilibrium wage. (**Hint:** Set $Q_D = Q_S$ and solve for the wage, W.)

b. Find the equilibrium quantity of labor. (**Hint:** Now plug the value you got in part (a) back into Q_D or Q_S. You can double-check your answer by plugging the answer from part (a) into both Q_D and Q_S to see that you get the same result.)

c. What happens if the minimum wage is $8? (**Hint:** Plug W = 8 into both Q_D and Q_S.) Does this minimum wage cause a surplus or a shortage?

d. What happens if the minimum wage is $6? (**Hint:** Plug W = 6 into both Q_D and Q_S.) Does this minimum wage cause a surplus or a shortage?

9. Most of us would agree that movie theater popcorn is outrageously priced. Why don't price gouging laws result in arrests and prosecutions of theater operators and other firms that charge prices far beyond the actual cost of production?

✳ **10.** More than 5,000 people in the United States die each year because they cannot find a suitable kidney donor. Under U.S. law, citizens cannot sell their spare kidney, which effectively means that there is a price ceiling on the sale of kidneys equal to $0. What do you think would happen to the number of deaths caused by kidney failure each year if the law prohibiting the sale of kidneys were repealed?

✳ **11.** Scotland has introduced price floors on alcohol as a public health measure. Higher alcohol prices will lower sales, which would seem to hurt producers. If you were a producer in Scotland, would you necessarily be against this proposal?

12. Suppose the equilibrium rent for one-bedroom apartments in your neighborhood is $1,000 per month. If the government imposes a rent ceiling of $750 per month, what will happen to the number of one-bedroom apartments rented out each month?

a. It will increase, since more people will want to rent apartments when they are cheaper.

b. It will decrease, since fewer landlords will want to rent out their apartments when they can't charge as much.

c. It will not change, since the rent control is set below the equilibrium rent.

d. None of the above

✳ **13.** Suppose the government imposes a minimum wage that is above the equilibrium wage. Will workers be better off or worse off?

Solved Problems

2. The equilibrium price occurs where the quantity demanded is equal to the quantity supplied. This equilibrium occurs when $Q_D = Q_S = 400$. When the quantity is 400, the monthly rent is $800. Next, the question asks how many one-bedroom apartments will be rented after a rent control law limits the rent to $700 a month. When the rent is $700, the quantity supplied is 320 apartments. It is also worth noting that the quantity demanded when the rent is $700 is 550 units, so there is a shortage of $550 - 320 = 230$ apartments once the rent control law goes into effect.

7. The first question asks how many low-skilled laborers will be unemployed when the minimum wage is $8 an hour. The quantity demanded is 29 million, and the quantity supplied is 38 million. The result is 38 million $-$ 29 million $=$ 9 million unemployed low-skilled workers.

   The next question asks how many low-skilled workers will be unemployed when the minimum wage is $6 an hour. Because $6 an hour is below the market equilibrium wage of $7, it has no effect. In other words, a $6 minimum wage is nonbinding, and therefore no unemployment is caused.

10. Despite the repugnant nature of organ sales, there is no doubt that a price exists that would alleviate the kidney shortage and save lives. Under the current system, market prices are unable to identify people who would sell their spare kidney and match those sellers with the people who would be willing to buy a kidney. In the absence of a legal market, black markets have arisen to bring buyers and sellers together. The black-market price for a kidney ($250,000) is far higher than the market equilibrium price ($20,000) that economists estimate would exist if organ sales were legal.

11. If demand for alcohol is relatively inelastic, a price floor could increase revenues for most suppliers.

13. This is an empirical question. Low-wage workers may be better off, if enough of them keep their jobs and subsequently earn a higher wage, compared to the number of workers who lose their jobs and become unemployed.

CHAPTER

07 Market Inefficiencies: Externalities and Public Goods

Should We Eliminate All Pollution?

We would all agree that it's important to protect the environment. So when we face pollution and other environmental degradation, should we eliminate it? If your first thought is "yes, always," you're not alone. After all, there's only one Earth, and we'd better get tough on environmental destruction wherever we find it, whatever it takes. Right?

It's tempting to think this way, but the prescription comes up short as a useful social policy. No one wants to go back to the way it was when businesses were free to dump their waste anywhere they chose, but it is also impractical to eliminate all pollution. Some amount of environmental damage is inevitable whenever we extract resources, manufacture goods, fertilize croplands, or power our electrical grid—all activities that are integral to modern society. But how do we figure out what the "right" level of pollution is, and how do we get there? The answer is to examine the tension between social costs and benefits and to ensure that participants in markets are fully accounting for both.

In the preceding chapters, we saw that markets provide many benefits and that they work because participants pursue their own self-interests. But sometimes markets need a

This outflow looks like lava flow from Mount Kilauea in Hawaii, but it's from a nickel refinery in Canada—what a catastrophe! No doubt we'd like to make it go away. But are we willing to do without the jobs the factory provides? What if we could keep the factory open and have just a *little* outflow? The scary red color is mostly iron oxides, a.k.a. rust. Are we willing to shut down any factory that puts even a little bit of rust into the groundwater? For an economist, deciding what to do about pollution isn't as easy as it may at first seem.

helping hand. For example, some market exchanges harm innocent bystanders, and some trades are not efficient because the ownership of property is not clearly defined or actively enforced. To help explain why markets do not always operate efficiently, this chapter explores two important concepts: externalities and the differences between private and public goods.

· BIG QUESTIONS ·

- What are externalities, and how do they affect markets?
- What are private goods and public goods?
- What are the challenges of providing nonexcludable goods?

What Are Externalities, and How Do They Affect Markets?

We have seen that buyers and sellers benefit from trade. But what about the effects trade might have on bystanders? **Externalities**, or the costs and benefits of a market activity that affect a third party, often lead to undesirable consequences. **Market failure** occurs when there is an inefficient allocation of resources in a market. Externalities are a type of market failure. For example, in 2010, an offshore oil rig in the Gulf of Mexico operated by British Petroleum (BP) exploded, causing millions of barrels of oil to spill into the water and resulting in over $40 billion in damage. Even though both BP and its customers benefit from the production of oil, others along the Gulf Coast had their lives severely disrupted. Industries dependent on high environmental quality, like tourism and fishing, were hit particularly hard by the costs of the spill.

For a market to work as efficiently as possible, two things must happen. First, each participant must be able to evaluate the **internal costs** of participation—the costs that only the individual participant pays. For example, when we choose to drive somewhere, we typically consider our internal (also known as personal) costs—the time it takes to reach our destination, the amount we pay for gasoline, and what we pay for routine vehicle maintenance. Second, for a market to work efficiently, the external costs must also be paid. **External costs** are the costs of a market activity imposed on people who are not participants in that market. In the case of driving, the congestion and pollution our cars create are external costs. Economists define **social costs** as the sum of the internal costs and external costs of a market activity.

Externalities
are the costs or benefits of a market activity that affect a third party.

Market failure
occurs when there is an inefficient allocation of resources in a market.

Internal costs
are the costs of a market activity paid only by an individual participant.

External costs
are the costs of a market activity imposed on people who are not participants in that market.

Social costs
are the sum of the internal costs and external costs of a market activity.

In this section, we consider some of the mechanisms that encourage consumers and producers to account for the social costs of their actions.

The Third-Party Problem

An externality exists whenever an internal cost (or benefit) diverges from a social cost (or benefit). For example, manufacturers who make vehicles and consumers who purchase them benefit from the transaction, but making and using those vehicles lead to externalities—including air pollution and traffic congestion—that adversely affect others. A **third-party problem** occurs when those not directly involved in a market activity experience negative or positive externalities.

A **third-party problem** occurs when those not directly involved in a market activity experience negative or positive externalities.

If a third party is adversely affected, the externality is negative. For example, a negative externality occurs when the number of vehicles on the roads causes air pollution. Negative externalities present a challenge to society because it is difficult to make consumers and producers take responsibility for the full costs of their actions. For example, drivers typically consider only the internal costs (their own costs) of reaching their destination. Likewise, manufacturers generally prefer to ignore the pollution they create, because addressing the problem would raise their costs without providing them with significant direct benefits.

In general, society would benefit if all consumers and producers considered both the internal and external costs of their actions. Because this expectation is not reasonable, governments design policies that create incentives for firms and people to limit the amount of pollution they emit.

Incentives

An effort by the city government of Washington, D.C., shows the potential power of this approach. Like many communities throughout the United States, the city instituted a 5-cent tax on every plastic bag a consumer picks up at a store. While 5 cents may not sound like much of a disincentive, shoppers have responded by switching to cloth bags or reusing plastic ones. In Washington, D.C., the number of plastic bags used every month fell from 22.5 million in 2009 to 3 million in 2018, significantly reducing the amount of plastic waste entering landfills in the process.

Many of the most successful businesses associated with Stanford have made large donations to the university.

Not all externalities are negative, however. Positive externalities also exist. For instance, education creates a large positive externality for society beyond the benefits to individual students, teachers, and support staff. A more knowledgeable workforce benefits employers looking for qualified employees and is more efficient and productive than an uneducated workforce. And because local businesses experience a positive externality from a well-educated local community, they have a stake in the educational process.

A good example of the synergy between local business and higher education is California's Silicon Valley, which is home to many high-tech companies and Stanford University. As early as the late nineteenth century, Stanford's leaders felt that the university's mission should include fostering the development of self-sufficient local

When oil refineries are permitted to pollute the environment without any limitations, they are likely to overproduce.

The **social optimum** is the price and quantity combination that would exist if there were no externalities.

industry. After World War II, Stanford encouraged faculty and graduates to start their own companies, which led to the creation of Hewlett-Packard, Bell Labs, and Xerox. A generation later, this nexus of high-tech firms gave birth to leading software and Internet firms like 3Com, Adobe, Facebook, and Snapchat, and—more indirectly—Cisco, Apple, and Alphabet.

Recognizing the benefits they received, many of the most successful businesses associated with Stanford have donated large sums to the university. For instance, the Hewlett Foundation gave $400 million to Stanford's endowment for the humanities and sciences and for undergraduate education—an act of generosity that highlights the positive externality Stanford University had on Hewlett-Packard.

CORRECTING FOR NEGATIVE EXTERNALITIES In this section, we explore ways to correct for negative externalities. To do so, we use supply and demand analysis to understand how the externalities affect the market. Let's begin with supply and compare the difference between what market forces produce and what is best for society in the case of an oil refinery. A refinery converts crude oil to gasoline. This complex process generates many negative externalities, including the release of pollutants into the air and the dumping of waste by-products.

Figure 7.1 illustrates the contrast between the market equilibrium and the social optimum in the case of an oil refinery. The **social optimum** is the price

FIGURE 7.1

Negative Externalities and Social Optimum

When a firm is required to internalize the external costs of production, the supply curve shifts to the left, pollution is reduced, and output falls to the socially optimal level, Q_s. The deadweight loss that occurs from overproduction is eliminated.

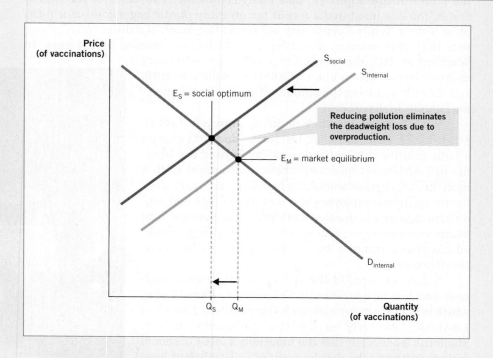

and quantity combination that would exist if there were no externalities. The supply curve $S_{internal}$ represents how much the oil refinery will produce if it does not have to pay for the negative consequences of its activity. In this situation, the market equilibrium, E_M, accounts only for the internal costs of production.

When a negative externality occurs, the government may be able to restore the social optimum by requiring externality-causing market participants to pay for the cost of their actions. In this case, there are three potential solutions. First, the refinery can be required to install pollution abatement equipment or change production techniques to reduce emissions and waste by-products. Second, the government can levy a tax on the refinery as a disincentive to produce. Finally, the government can require the firm to pay for any environmental damage it causes. Each solution forces the firm to **internalize** the externality, meaning that the firm must take into account the external costs (or benefits) to society that occur as a result of its actions.

Having to pay the costs of imposing pollution on others reduces the amount of the pollution-causing activity. This result is evident in the shift of the supply curve to S_{social}. The new supply curve reflects a combination of the internal and external costs of producing the good. Because each corrective measure requires the refinery to spend money to correct the externality and therefore increases overall costs, the willingness to sell the good declines, or shifts to the left. The result is a social optimum at a lower quantity, Q_S, than at the market equilibrium quantity demanded, Q_M. The trade-off is clear. We can reduce negative externalities by requiring producers to internalize the externality. However, doing so does not come without cost. Because the supply curve shifts to the left, the quantity produced is lower and the price rises. In the real world, there is always a cost.

In addition, when an externality occurs, the market equilibrium creates deadweight loss, as shown by the yellow triangle in Figure 7.1. In Chapter 5, we considered deadweight loss in the context of government regulation or taxation. These measures, when imposed on efficient markets, create deadweight loss, or an undesirable amount of economic activity. In the case of a negative externality, the market is not efficient because it is not fully capturing the cost of production. Once the government intervenes and requires the firm to internalize the external costs of its production, output falls to the socially optimal level, Q_S, and the deadweight loss from overproduction is eliminated.

Table 7.1 outlines the basic decision-making process that guides private and social decisions. Private decision-makers consider only their internal costs, but society as a whole experiences both internal and external costs. To align the incentives of private decision-makers with the interests of society, we must find mechanisms that encourage the internalization of externalities.

Incentives

Firms **internalize** an externality when they take into account the external costs (or benefits) to society that occur as a result of their actions.

Trade-offs

TABLE 7.1

Private and Social Decision-Making

Personal decision	Social optimum	The problem	The solution
Based on internal costs	Social costs = internal costs plus external costs	To get consumers and producers to take responsibility for the externalities they create	Encourage consumers and producers to *internalize* externalities

EXPRESS LANES USE DYNAMIC PRICING TO EASE CONGESTION

Metro Washington, D.C., is notorious for traffic, especially on the Capital Beltway (Interstate 495). New express lanes keep traffic moving by using dynamic pricing, which adjusts tolls based on real-time traffic conditions. Dynamic pricing helps manage the quantity demanded and keeps motorists moving at highway speeds. I-495 express-lane tolls can range from as low as $0.20 per mile during less busy times to approximately $1.25 per mile in some sections during rush hour. The higher rush-hour rates are designed to ensure that the express lanes do not become congested. Motorists thus have a choice: pay more to use the express lanes and arrive faster, or use the regular lanes and arrive later. The decision about whether to use the express lanes is all about opportunity cost. High-opportunity-cost motorists regularly drive the express lanes, while others with lower opportunity costs avoid the express lanes.

Because dynamic prices become part of a motorist's internal costs, they cause motorists to weigh the costs and benefits of driving into congested areas. In addition, the dynamic pricing of express lanes causes motorists to make marginal adjustments in terms of the time when they drive. High-demand times, such as the morning and evening rush, see higher tolls for using the express lanes and also longer waits in the regular lanes. Faced with either sitting in traffic (if they don't pay the toll) or being charged more to enter the express lanes at peak-demand times, many motorists attempt to use the Beltway at off-peak times. Since drivers internalize the external costs as a result of the dynamic toll prices even more precisely, the traffic flow spreads out over the course of the day so the existing road capacity is used more efficiently.

How much would you pay to avoid sitting in traffic?

Opportunity cost

Marginal thinking

CORRECTING FOR POSITIVE EXTERNALITIES Positive externalities, such as vaccines, are the result of economic activities that have benefits for third parties. As with negative externalities, economists use supply and demand analysis to compare the efficiency of the market with the social optimum. This time, we focus on the demand curve. Consider a person who gets a flu shot. When the vaccine is administered, the recipient is immunized, which creates an internal benefit. But there is also an external benefit. Because the recipient likely will not come down with the flu, fewer other people will catch the flu and become contagious, which helps to protect even those who do not get flu shots. Therefore, we can say that vaccines provide a positive externality to the rest of society.

Why do positive externalities exist in the market? Using our example of flu shots, there is an incentive for people in high-risk groups to get vaccinated for the sake of their own health. In Figure 7.2, we capture this internal benefit in the demand curve labeled $D_{internal}$. However, the market equilibrium, E_M, only accounts for the internal benefits of individuals deciding whether to get vaccinated. To maximize the health benefits for everyone, public health officials need to find a way to encourage people to consider the external benefit of their vaccination, too. For instance, making flu shots mandatory for hospital staff and other healthcare workers produces positive benefits for all members of society, by internalizing the externality, and helps nudge the market toward the socially optimal number of vaccinations.

Despite the benefits, however, vaccination rates in the United States have been steadily falling for years. The lower vaccination rate led to an outbreak of measles at Disneyland in California in late 2014, where it was believed a foreign visitor introduced the disease and unvaccinated children were exposed to it. The outbreak eventually spread to six U.S. states, Mexico, and Canada—demonstrating just how quickly measles can spread when the vaccination rate is not 100%. This disease continues to be a problem, worldwide, with major outbreaks in 2018 in places like Algeria, Greece, and Indonesia.

Vaccines offer both internal and external benefits.

Government can also promote the social optimum by encouraging economic activity that helps third parties. For example, it can offer a subsidy, or price break, to encourage more people to get vaccinated. The subsidy lowers the price to individuals but increases the demand for vaccines, which raises the overall market price.

Governments routinely provide free or reduced-cost vaccines to those most at risk from flu and to their caregivers. Because the subsidy enables

FIGURE 7.2

Positive Externalities and Social Optimum

The subsidy encourages consumers to internalize the externality. As a result, consumption moves from the market equilibrium (Q_M) to a social optimum at a higher quantity (Q_S), vaccinations increase, and the deadweight loss from insufficient market demand is eliminated.

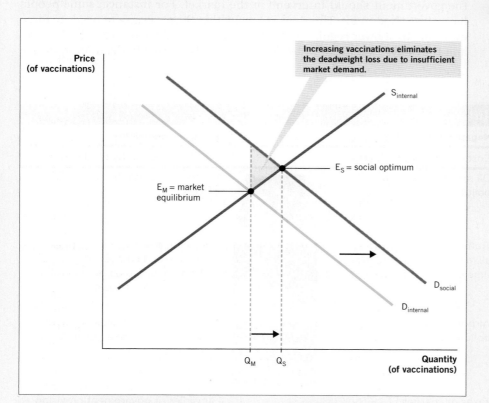

Increasing vaccinations eliminates the deadweight loss due to insufficient market demand.

$S_{internal}$

E_S = social optimum

E_M = market equilibrium

D_{social}

$D_{internal}$

Price (of vaccinations)

Quantity (of vaccinations)

Q_M Q_S

Incentives

consumers to spend less money, their willingness to get the vaccine increases, shifting the demand curve in Figure 7.2 from $D_{internal}$ to D_{social}. The social demand curve reflects the sum of the internal and external benefits of getting the vaccination. In other words, the subsidy encourages consumers to internalize the externality. As a result, the output moves from the market equilibrium quantity demanded, Q_M, to a social optimum at a higher quantity, Q_S.

Markets do not handle externalities well. With a negative externality, the market produces too much of a good. But in the case of a positive externality, the market produces too little. In both cases, the market equilibrium creates deadweight loss. When positive externalities are present, the private market is not efficient because it is not fully capturing the social benefits. In other words, the market equilibrium does not maximize the gains for society as a whole. When positive externalities are internalized, the demand curve shifts outward and output rises to the socially optimal level, Q_S. The deadweight loss that results from insufficient market demand, and therefore underproduction, is eliminated.

Table 7.2 summarizes the key characteristics of positive and negative externalities and presents additional examples of each type.

Before moving on, it is worth noting that not all externalities warrant corrective measures. There are times when the size of the externality is negligible and does not justify the cost of increased regulations, charges, taxes, or subsidies that might achieve the social optimum. Because corrective measures have costs, the presence of negligible externalities does not by itself imply that the government should intervene in the market. For instance, some people have strong body odor. This does not mean that the government needs to force everyone to shower regularly. Persons with bad body odor are the exception and they have every reason to shower, use extra-strength deodorant, or use

TABLE 7.2

A Summary of Externalities

	Negative externalities		Positive externalities
Definition	Costs borne by third parties		Benefits received by third parties
Examples	Oil refining creates air pollution.		Flu shots prevent the spread of disease.
	Traffic congestion causes all motorists to spend more time on the road waiting.		Education creates a more productive workforce and enables citizens to make more informed decisions for the betterment of society.
	Airports create noise pollution.		Restored historic buildings enable people to enjoy beautiful architectural details.
Corrective measures	Taxes or charges		Subsidies or government provision

Externalities: Fracking

In 2003, energy companies began using a process known as hydraulic fracturing, or fracking, to extract underground reserves of natural gas in certain states, including Pennsylvania, Texas, West Virginia, and Wyoming. Fracking involves injecting water, chemicals, and sand into rock formations more than a mile deep. The process releases the natural gas that is trapped in those rocks, allowing it to escape up the well. The gas comes to the surface along with much of the water and chemical mixture, which now must be disposed of. Unfortunately, the chemicals in the mix make the water toxic. Consequently, as fracking has expanded to more areas, controversy has grown about the potential environmental effects of the process.

What the frack?

QUESTION: What negative externalities might fracking generate?

ANSWER: People who live near wells worry about the pollutants in the water mixture and their potential to leach into drinking-water supplies. Additionally, the drilling of a well is a noisy process. Drilling occurs 24 hours a day for a period of a few weeks. This noise pollution affects anyone who lives close by. Another issue is that the natural gas has to be trucked away from the well. Additional truck traffic can potentially damage local roads and cause even more pollution.

QUESTION: What positive externalities might fracking generate?

ANSWER: Fracking has brought tremendous economic growth to the areas where it is occurring. The resulting jobs have employed many people, providing them with a good income. Local hotels and restaurants have seen an increase in business as temporary employees move from one area to another. As permanent employees take over the operation of a well, housing prices climb as a result of increasing demand, which benefits local homeowners.

cologne to mask the smell on their own. If they choose not to avail themselves of these options, they'll be ostracized in many social situations. Because the magnitude of the negative externality is small and government regulations to completely eliminate the externality would be quite onerous, it is best to leave well enough alone.

What Are Private Goods and Public Goods?

The presence of externalities reflects a divide between the way markets operate and the social optimum. What creates this divide? The answer is often related to property rights. **Property rights** give the owner the ability to exercise control over a resource. When property rights are not clearly defined, resources

Property rights
give the owner the ability to exercise control over a resource.

can be mistreated. For instance, because no one owns the air, manufacturing firms often emit pollutants into it.

Incentives

To understand why firms sometimes overlook their actions' effects on others, we need to examine the role of property rights in market efficiency. When property rights are poorly established or not enforced effectively, the wrong incentives come into play. The difference is apparent when we compare situations in which people do have property rights. Private owners have an incentive to keep their property in good repair because they bear the costs of fixing what they own when it breaks or no longer works properly. For instance, if you own a personal computer, you will probably protect your investment by treating it with care and dealing with any problems immediately. However, if you access a public computer terminal in a campus lab or library and find that it is not working properly, you will most likely ignore the problem and simply look for another computer that is working. The difference between solving the problem and ignoring it is crucial to understanding why property rights matter.

Private Property

Private property
provides an exclusive right of ownership that allows for the use, and especially the exchange, of property.

One way to minimize externalities is to establish well-defined private property rights. **Private property** provides an exclusive right of ownership that allows for the use, and especially the exchange, of property. This right creates incentives to maintain, protect, and conserve property and to trade with others. Let's consider these four incentives in the context of automobile ownership.

1. *The incentive to maintain property.* Car owners have an incentive to maintain their vehicles. Routine maintenance, replacement of worn parts, and repairs keep the vehicle safe and reliable. In addition, a well-maintained car can be sold for more than one in poor condition.

Incentives

2. *The incentive to protect property.* Owners have an incentive to protect their vehicles from theft or damage. They protect their property by using alarm systems, locking the doors, and parking in well-lit areas.

3. *The incentive to conserve property.* Car owners also have an incentive to extend the usable life of their automobiles by limiting the number of miles they put on their cars each year.

Opportunity cost

4. *The incentive to trade with others.* Car owners have an incentive to trade with others because they may profit from the transaction. Suppose someone offers to buy your car for $5,000 and you think it is worth only $3,000. Because you own the car, you can do whatever you want with it. If you decline to sell, you will incur an opportunity cost: you will be giving up $5,000 to keep something you value at $3,000. There is no law requiring you to sell your vehicle, so you *could* keep the car—but you probably won't. Why? Because private property gives you as the owner an incentive to trade for something better in the market.

The incentives to maintain, protect, and conserve property help to ensure that owners keep their private property in good shape. The fourth incentive, to trade with others, helps to ensure that private property is held by the person with the greatest willingness to pay for it.

THE COASE THEOREM In 1960, Nobel-prize winning economist Ronald Coase argued that establishing private property rights can close the gap between internal costs and social costs.

Consider an example involving two adjacent landowners, one who raises cattle and another who grows wheat. Because neither landowner has built a fence, the cattle wander onto the neighboring land to eat the wheat. Coase concluded that in this situation, both parties are responsible for the dilemma. He arrived at that conclusion by considering two possible scenarios.

The first scenario supposes that the wheat farmer has the legal right to expect cattle-free fields. In this scenario, the cattle rancher is liable for the damage caused to the wheat farmer. If the damage is costly and the rancher is liable, the rancher will build a fence to keep the cattle in rather than pay for the damage they cause. The fence internalizes the negative externality and forces the rancher to bear the full cost of the damage. If the cost of the damage to the crop is much smaller than the cost of building a fence, then the rancher is more likely to compensate the wheat farmer for his losses rather than build the fence.

What if the wheat farmer does not have the legal right to expect cattle-free fields? In this scenario, the cattle rancher is not liable for any damages his cattle cause to the wheat farmer. If the damage to the nearby wheat field is large and the rancher is *not* liable, the wheat farmer will build a fence to keep the cattle out. The fence internalizes the negative externality and forces the wheat farmer to bear the full cost of the damage. If the amount of damage is smaller than the cost of a fence, the farmer may accept occasional damage as the lower-cost option.

From comparing these two scenarios, Coase determined that whenever the externality is large enough to justify the expense, the externality gets internalized. As long as the property rights are fully specified (and there are no barriers to negotiations), either the cattle rancher or the wheat farmer will build a fence. The fence will keep the cattle away from the wheat, remove the externality, and prevent the destruction of property.

Selling a car, an exchange of private property, benefits both the owner and the buyer.

The cattle are near the wheat to the same extent . . .

. . . that the wheat is near the cattle.

With these scenarios in mind, we can now appreciate the **Coase theorem**, which states that if there are no barriers to negotiations, and if property rights are fully specified, interested parties will bargain privately to correct externalities. As a result, the assignment of property rights under the law gives each party an incentive to internalize any externalities. If it is difficult to bargain (because the costs of reaching an agreement are too high), private parties will be unable to internalize the externality between themselves. Therefore, the Coase theorem also suggests that private solutions to externality problems are not always possible, implying a role for government in solving complex externality issues.

A fence internalizes the externality.

To think about the case for a government role, consider the difference between the example of a rancher and a farmer with adjacent land and the example of a community-wide problem such as pollution. With two landowners, a private solution should be possible because the parties can bargain with each other at a low cost. With pollution, though, so many individuals are affected that the polluting company cannot afford to bargain with each one. Because bargaining costs are high in the case of pollution, an intermediary, like the government, may be necessary to ensure that externalities are internalized.

Private and Public Goods

When we think of private goods, most of us imagine something that we enjoy, like a slice of pizza or a favorite jacket. When we think of public goods, we think of goods provided by the government, like roads, the post office, and the military. The terms "private" and "public" typically imply ownership or production, but that is not the criterion economists use to categorize private and public goods. To understand the difference between private and public goods, you need to know whether a good is excludable, rival in consumption, or both. An **excludable good** is one for which access can be limited to paying customers. A **rival good** is one that cannot be enjoyed by more than one person at a time.

PRIVATE GOODS A **private good** is both excludable and rival in consumption. For instance, a slice of pizza is excludable because you must purchase it before you can eat it. Also, a slice of pizza is rival; only one person can eat it. These two characteristics, excludability and rivalry, allow the market to work efficiently in the absence of externalities. Consider a pizza business. The pizzeria bakes pizza pies because it knows it can sell them to consumers. Likewise, consumers are willing to buy pizza because it is a food they enjoy. Because the producer gets to charge a price and the consumer gets to acquire a rival good, the stage is set for mutual gains from trade.

Trade creates value

PUBLIC GOODS Markets have no difficulty producing purely private goods, like pizza, because in order to enjoy them you must first purchase them. But when was the last time you paid to see a fireworks display? Hundreds of thousands of people view many of the nation's best fireworks displays, but only a small percentage of them pay admission to get a preferred seat. Fireworks displays are a **public good** because (1) they are consumed by more than one person and (2) it is difficult to exclude nonpayers. Because consumers cannot be easily forced to pay to observe fireworks, they may desire more of the good than is typically supplied. As a result, a market economy underproduces fireworks displays and many other public goods.

Public goods are often underproduced because people can get them without paying for them. This means that public goods, like externalities, also result in market failure. Consider Joshua Bell, one of the most famous violinists in the world. The day after giving a concert in Boston for which patrons paid $100 a ticket, he decided to reprise the performance in a Washington, D.C., subway station and just ask for donations.* Any passerby could listen to the music—it did not need to be purchased to be enjoyed. In other words, it was nonexcludable and nonrival in consumption. But because it is impossible for a street musician to force bystanders to pay, it is difficult for the musician—even one as good as Joshua

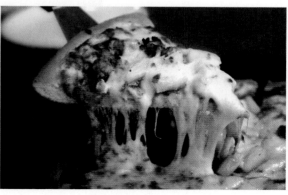

Bell—to make a living. Suppose he draws a large crowd and the music creates $500 worth of enjoyment among the audience. At the end of the performance, he receives a loud round of applause and then motions to the donation basket. A number of people come up and donate, but when he counts up the contributions, he finds only $30—the actual amount he earned while playing in the Metro.

Pizza is a private good.

Why did Joshua Bell receive $30 when he created many times that amount in value? This phenomenon, known as a **free-rider problem**, occurs whenever people receive a benefit they do not pay for. A street musician provides a public good and must rely on the generosity of the audience to contribute. If very few people contribute, many potential musicians will not find it worthwhile to perform. We tend to see very few street performances because free-riding lowers the returns to performing, and the private equilibrium amount of street performances is undersupplied in comparison to the social optimum. When payment cannot be linked to production or consumption, the efficient quantity is not produced.

Street performances are just one example of a public good. National defense, lighthouses, streetlights, clean air, and open-source software such as Mozilla Firefox are other examples. Let's examine national defense because it is a particularly clear example of a public good that is subject to a free-rider problem. All citizens value security, but consider the difficulty of trying to organize and provide adequate national defense through private contributions alone. How could you get enough people to voluntarily coordinate a missile defense system or pay for an aircraft carrier and the personnel to operate it? Society would be underprotected because many people would not

---

*This really happened! The *Washington Post* and Bell conducted an experiment to test the public's reaction to performances of "genius" in unexpected settings. Our discussion here places the event in a hypothetical context. For the real-life result, see Gene Weingarten, "Pearls before Breakfast," *Washington Post,* April 8, 2007.

Concerned about security? Only the government is capable of providing adequate national defense.

voluntarily contribute their fair share of the expense. For this reason, defense expenditures are normally provided by the government and funded by tax revenues. Because most people pay taxes, the free-rider problem is almost eliminated in the context of national defense.

Most people agree that government should provide certain public goods for society, including national defense, the interstate highway system, and medical and science-related research to fight pandemics. In each case, public-sector provision helps to eliminate the free-rider problem and create the socially optimal level of activity.

ECONOMICS IN THE REAL WORLD

GROUP WORK

Perhaps you've taken a class where group work is required. These assignments are valuable opportunities to develop a skill businesses are looking for in potential employees: the ability to work as a team to accomplish a task. However, group work in class or in the workplace creates an environment for the free-rider problem. In many groups, one of the members doesn't put in the time or effort to complete the project. This person realizes he or she will get the benefit of the group grade without incurring the full cost. You may think that this behavior is lazy or inconsiderate, and it is, but it is nonetheless quite rational. The question for the free-rider is whether his or her actions will marginally affect the group's grade. Does the cost of completing part of the project justify what is likely to be only a small change in the grade earned by every member in the group? If the work raises the group's grade from a B– to a B, the free-rider may find that it is too costly to participate. To avoid the free-rider problem, teachers often ask the group to grade each group member's contribution to the group's overall output, and this determines the part of the project grade attributed to individual effort. The hope is that this system will give free-riders the incentive to pull their own weight.

Incentives

CLUB GOODS AND COMMON-RESOURCE GOODS

There are two additional types of goods we have not yet introduced. Because club goods and common-resource goods have characteristics of both private and public goods, the line between private provision and public provision is often blurred.

A **club good** is nonrival in consumption and excludable. Satellite television is an example. It is excludable because you must pay to receive the signal, but it is nonrival in consumption because more than one customer can receive the signal at the same time. Because customers who wish to enjoy club goods can be excluded, markets typically provide these goods. However, once a satellite television network is in place, the cost of adding customers is low. Firms are motivated to maximize profits, not the number of people they serve, so the market price is higher and the output is lower than what society desires.

A **common-resource good** is rival in consumption but nonexcludable. King crab in the Bering Sea off Alaska is an example. Because any particular crab can be caught by only one boat crew, the crabs are a rival resource. At the same time, exclusion is not possible because any boat crew that wants to brave the elements can catch crab.

We have seen that the market generally works well for private goods. In the case of public goods, the market generally needs a hand. In between, club and common-resource goods illustrate the tension between the private and public provision of many goods and services. Table 7.3 summarizes the four types of goods we have discussed.

4-20
© 2006 Bil Keane, Inc.
Dist. by King Features Synd.
www.familycircus.com

"How much would it cost to see a sunset if God decided to charge for it?"

A **club good** has two characteristics: it is nonrival in consumption and excludable.

A **common-resource good** has two characteristics: it is rival in consumption and nonexcludable.

Satellite television is a club good.

Alaskan king crab is a common-resource good.

TABLE 7.3

The Four Types of Goods

	Consumption	
	Rival	**Nonrival**
Excludable? **Yes**	*Private goods* are rival and excludable: pizza, watches, automobiles.	*Club goods* are nonrival and excludable: satellite television, education, country clubs.
No	*Common-resource goods* are rival and nonexcludable: Alaskan king crab, a large shared popcorn at the movies, congested roads.	*Public goods* are nonrival and nonex-cludable: street performers, national defense, tsunami warning systems.

PRACTICE WHAT YOU KNOW

Are Parks Public Goods?

Many goods have the characteristics of a public good, but few goods meet the exact definition.

QUESTION: Are parks public goods?

ANSWER: We tend to think of public parks as meeting the necessary requirements to be a public good. But not so fast. Have you been to any of America's top national parks on a peak summer weekend? Parks are subject to congestion, which makes them rival. In addition, most national and state parks require an admission fee—translation: they are excludable. Therefore, public parks do not meet the exact definition of a public good.

Not surprisingly, there are many good examples of private parks that maintain, protect, and conserve the environment alongside their public counterparts. For instance, Meteor Crater is a privately owned and operated park in Arizona that showcases an extremely well-preserved meteor strike. The United States is dotted with private parks that predate the establishment of the national park system. Like their public counterparts, private parks are also not public goods.

CHALLENGE QUESTION: Suppose you have pitched your tent at a campsite with a lovely view, when another party comes along and prepares to pitch their tent where it will block your view. They explain that the ground is conveniently level and soft in the spot they chose. What could be done about this, assuming that people have a right to pitch their tent wherever they want? What would the solution be if instead whoever arrived first had a right, by park rules, to an unobstructed view?

ANSWER: To answer this question we recall the Coase Theorem. In the first case you could offer them money to shift to an acceptable if less comfortable part of their campsite. In the second case they could offer you money as compensation for your loss of view so they can pitch their tent where they want.

Meteor Crater in Arizona.

What Are the Challenges of Providing Nonexcludable Goods?

Understanding the four types of goods provides a solid foundation for understanding the role of markets and the government in society. Next, we consider some of the special challenges that arise in providing nonexcludable goods.

Cost-Benefit Analysis

To help make decisions about providing public goods, economists turn to **cost-benefit analysis**, a process used to determine whether the benefits of providing a public good outweigh the costs. Costs are easier to quantify than benefits. For instance, if a community puts on a Fourth of July celebration, it will have to pay for the fireworks and labor involved in setting up the event. The costs are a known quantity. But benefits are difficult to quantify. Because people do not need to pay to see the fireworks, it is hard to determine how much benefit the community receives. If asked, people might misrepresent the social benefit in two ways. First, some residents who value the celebration highly might claim that the fireworks bring more benefit than they actually do, because they want the community fireworks to continue. Second, those residents who dislike the crowds and noise might understate the benefit of the fireworks, because they want the fireworks to cease. Since there is no way to know how truthful people are when responding to a questionnaire, the actual social benefit of a fireworks show is hard to measure.

Because people do not pay to enjoy public goods, and because the government provides them without charging a direct fee, determining the socially optimal amount typically takes place through the political system. Generally speaking, elected officials do not get reelected if the populace believes they have not done a good job with their cost-benefit analyses.

Cost-benefit analysis is a process that economists use to determine whether the benefits of providing a public good outweigh the costs.

Figuring out the social benefit of a fireworks display is quite difficult.

INTERNET PIRACY

The digitization of media, along with the speed with which it can be transferred across the Internet, has made the protection of *intellectual property rights* (that is, the protection of patents, copyrights, and trademarks) very difficult to enforce. Many countries either do not have strict copyright standards or fail to enforce them. The result is a black market filled with bootlegged copies of movies, music, and other media.

Because digital "file sharing" is so common these days, you might not fully understand the harm that occurs. Piracy is an illegal form of free-riding. Every song and every movie that is transferred takes away royalties that would have gone to the original artist or the studio. After all, producing content is expensive, and violations of copyright law prevent businesses from making a fair return on their investments. However, consumers of content don't often see it this way. Some believe that breaking the copyright encryption is fair game because they "own" the object in question or bought it legally or got it from a friend. The reality is different. One reason copyright law exists is to limit free-riding. When copyrights are fully specified and enforced across international boundaries, content creators receive compensation for their efforts. But if copyrights are routinely violated, revenues to private businesses will decline and the amount of music and movies produced will decrease. In the long run, artists will produce less and society will suffer. (For other benefits of copyright law, see Chapter 10.)

Incentives

Think about the relationship between artists and the public as reciprocal: each side needs the other. In that sense, the music you buy or the movie you watch is not a true public good, but more of a club good. Copyright laws make the good excludable but nonrival. For this reason, some people will always have an incentive to violate copyright law, artists and studios will insist on ever more complicated encryption methods to protect their interests, and for the betterment of society as a whole, the government will have to enforce copyright law to prevent widespread free-riding.

Common Resources and the Tragedy of the Commons

The **tragedy of the commons** occurs when a common-resource good becomes depleted.

Incentives

Common resources often give rise to the **tragedy of the commons**, a situation that occurs when a common-resource good becomes depleted. The term "tragedy of the commons" refers to a phenomenon ecologist Garrett Hardin wrote about in the magazine *Science* in 1968. Hardin described the hypothetical use of a common pasture shared by local herders in a pastoral community. Herders know that intensively grazed land will be depleted and that this depletion is very likely to happen to common land. Knowing that the pasture will be depleted creates a strong incentive for individual herders to bring their animals to the pasture as much as possible while it is still green, because every other herder will be doing the same thing. Each herder has the same incentive to overgraze, which quickly makes the pasture unusable. The overgrazing is a negative externality brought about by poorly designed incentives and the absence of clearly defined private property rights.

Even though the concept of common ownership sounds ideal, it can be a recipe for resource depletion and economic disaster. Common ownership, unlike private ownership, leads to overuse. With a system of private property rights, an owner can seek damages in the court system if his property is damaged or destroyed. But the same cannot be said for common property, because joint ownership allows any party to use the resource as he or she sees fit. This situation creates incentives to use the resource now rather than later and to neglect it. In short, common property leads to abuse and depletion of the resource.

Consider global warming. Scientific evidence clearly links increasing amounts of CO_2 (carbon dioxide) in the atmosphere and global warming. This negative externality is caused by some but borne jointly by everyone. Because large CO_2 emitters consider only the internal costs of their actions and ignore the social costs, the amount of CO_2 released, and the corresponding increase in global warming, is larger than optimal. The air, a common resource, is being "overused" and degraded.

Private property rights give owners an incentive to maintain, protect, and conserve their property and to transfer it if someone else values it more than they do. How are those incentives different under a system of common ownership? Let's examine a real-world example of the tragedy of the commons: the collapse of cod populations off Newfoundland, Canada, in the 1990s. Over the course of three years, cod hauls fell from over 200,000 tons annually to close to zero. Why did the fishing community allow this to happen? The answer: incentives. Let's consider the incentives associated with common property in the context of the cod industry.

Incentives

1. *The incentive to neglect.* No one owns the ocean. As a result, fishing grounds in international waters cannot be protected. Even fishing grounds within territorial waters are problematic because fish do not adhere to political borders. Moreover, the fishing grounds in the North Atlantic cannot be maintained in the same way one can, say, check the oil in an automobile. The grounds are too large, and the cod population depends on variations in seawater temperature, salinity, and availability of algae and smaller fish to eat. The idea that individuals or communities could "maintain" a population of cod in this wild environment is highly impractical.

2. *The incentive to overuse.* Each fishing boat crew would like to maintain a sustainable population of cod to ensure future harvests. However, conservation on the part of one boat is irrelevant because other boats would catch whatever the first boat leaves behind. Because cod are a rival and finite resource, boats have an incentive to harvest as much as they can before another vessel does. With common resources, no one has the authority to define how much of a resource can be used. Maintaining economic activity at a socially optimal level would require the coordination of thousands of vested interests, each of which could gain by free-riding. For instance, if a socially responsible boat crew (or country) limits its catch in order to protect the species from depletion, this action does not guarantee that rivals will follow suit. Instead, rivals who disregard the socially optimal behavior stand to benefit by overfishing what remains.

Because cod are a common resource, the incentives we discussed under a system of private ownership do not apply. With common property, resources are neglected and overused.

Common resources, such as cod, encourage overuse (in this case, overfishing).

Possible Solutions to the Tragedy of the Commons

Preventing the tragedy of the commons requires planning and coordination. Unfortunately, in our cod example, officials were slow to recognize that there was a problem with Atlantic cod until it was too late to prevent the collapse. Ironically, just as they placed a moratorium on catching northern cod, the collapse of the fish population became an unprecedented disaster for all of Atlantic Canada's fisheries. Cod populations dropped to 1% of their former sizes. The collapse of cod and many other species led to the loss of 40,000 jobs and over $300 million in income annually. Because communities in the affected region relied almost exclusively on fishing, this outcome crippled their economies.

The lesson of the northern cod is a powerful reminder that efforts to avoid the tragedy of the commons must begin before a problem develops. For example, king crab populations off the coast of Alaska have fared much better than cod, thanks to proactive management. To prevent the collapse of the king crab population, the state and federal governments enforce several regulations. First, the length of the fishing season is limited so that populations have time to recover. Second, there are limitations on how much fishing boats can catch. Third, to promote sustainable populations, only adult males are harvested. It is illegal to harvest females and young crabs, because these are necessary for repopulation. Government regulations like these help avoid a tragedy of the commons.

Trade-offs

Nobel-winning economist Elinor Ostrom examined how some commons are sustainably managed without government, despite the tragedy of the commons and free-rider problems. She understood many of the problems we face today. "[N]o one communicates, everyone acts independently, no attention is paid to the effects of one's actions, and the costs of trying to change the structure of the situation are high."* Her advice was for individuals to communicate often with one another, in order to develop shared norms from which intuitional arrangements would naturally arise to address common-resource dilemmas.

Can the misuse of a common resource be foreseen and prevented? If predictions of rapid global warming are correct, our analysis points to a number of solutions to minimize the tragedy of the commons. Businesses and individuals can be discouraged from producing emissions through carbon pricing, which charges firms by the ton for the CO_2 they put into the atmosphere. This policy encourages parties to internalize the negative externality, because carbon pricing acts as an internal cost that must be considered before creating carbon pollution.

Cap and trade
is an approach used to curb pollution by creating a system of emissions permits that are traded in an open market.

Another solution, known as **cap and trade**, is an approach to emissions reduction that has received much attention lately. The idea behind cap and trade policy is to encourage carbon producers to internalize the externality by establishing markets for tradable emissions permits. As a result, a profit motive is created for some firms to purchase, and others to sell, emissions permits. Under cap and trade, the government sets a *cap*, or limit, on the amount

---

*Source: Elinor Ostrom. *Governing the Commons: The Evolution of Institutions for Collective Action* (New York: Cambridge University Press, 1990).

of CO_2 that can be emitted. Businesses and individuals are then issued permits to emit a certain amount of carbon each year. Also, permit owners may *trade* permits. In other words, companies that produce fewer carbon emissions can sell the permits they do not use. By establishing property rights that control emissions permits, cap and trade causes firms to internalize externalities and to seek out methods that lower emissions. Global warming is an incredibly complex process, but cap and trade policy is one tangible step that minimizes free-riding, creates incentives for action, and promotes a socially efficient outcome.

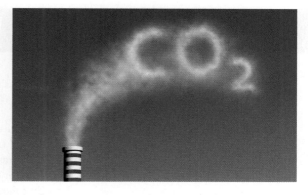

What is the best way to curb global warming?

Trade creates value

Cap and trade is a good idea, but there are issues that must be overcome to make it work effectively. For example, cap and trade presumes that nations can agree on and enforce emissions limits, but international agreements have proved difficult to negotiate. Without binding international agreements, nations that adopt cap and trade policies will experience higher production costs, while nations that ignore them—and free-ride in the process—will benefit.

ECONOMICS IN THE REAL WORLD

THE GREAT PACIFIC GARBAGE PATCH

The Great Pacific Garbage Patch is an immense swirl of floating debris in the central North Pacific Ocean. It was first discovered in 1988 and is roughly twice the size of Texas! One would think that an environmental calamity of that scale would prompt significant intervention. That has not happened, because no one person or country "owns" the open Pacific. When trash makes its way out to sea from the shorelines of the Philippines, Vietnam, China, Japan, South and North Korea, Russia, Canada, the United States, and Mexico, it all eventually ends up in the Garbage Patch.

Can anything be done to clean up the Great Pacific Garbage Patch?

The Great Pacific Garbage Patch is an extreme example of the tragedy of the commons. Its tragedy is especially striking because many people care deeply about marine quality. The tragedy occurs because no one individual, group, or country has the means to solve the problem on its own. Even if you and I, and all our friends, consciously make sure we never let any trash enter the ocean, this won't stop debris from elsewhere. Likewise, if Japan unilaterally decided to filter the outflow from all its rivers before entering the ocean, debris from other countries would still litter the garbage patch. Complicating matters, once in the ocean the debris is hard to detect from satellites and even harder to collect and dispose of properly. The only real solution would be a cooperative agreement among all North Pacific Rim nations to filter ocean-bound debris. That's a very expensive proposition to a problem in a location so remote that it is out of sight, and therefore, out of mind.

Common Resources: Why Do Tailgaters Trash Parking Lots?

Tailgating can be one of the best parts of attending a big game or concert. You enjoy a great time with your friends and take in the action, leaving quickly afterward with little concern about the trash left behind. Consider this example: In 2014, country artist Luke Bryan played at Heinz Field in Pittsburgh. No doubt his fans care about the environment, but they absolutely trashed the parking lot. It was so bad, it made the local news. On the plus side, some city officials said the trash wasn't as bad as the Kenny Chesney concert the year before!

Why don't these tailgaters make a "concerted" effort to clean up?

QUESTION: What economic concept explains why so many people left so much trash behind?

ANSWER: Tailgaters brought snacks, drinks, cups, napkins, and all kinds of things to party before the concert, so a lot of trash was generated. Would you throw your trash on your driveway? Of course not. But otherwise conscientious individuals often don't demonstrate the same concern for public property. As a public space, the Heinz Field parking lot is subject to the tragedy of the commons. No one person can keep the lot clean, so overuse and littering occur. The effects of littering can be especially apparent when 50,000 people fill a stadium at one time.

Conclusion

Trade-offs

Although it's tempting to believe that the appropriate response to pollution is always to eliminate it, this belief is a misconception. As with all things, there are trade-offs. When pollution is taxed or regulated, business activity declines. It's possible to eliminate too much pollution, forcing businesses to shut down, creating undesirably high prices for anything from groceries to gasoline to electronics, and all in all creating an enormous deadweight loss to society. When you think about pollution like an environmental economist, you realize that eliminating pollution would create benefits and also costs. A truly "green" environment without any pollution would leave most people without enough "green" in their wallets. Therefore, the goal for pollution isn't zero, because the cost of attaining zero pollution outweighs the benefit.

In this chapter, we have considered two types of market failure: externalities and public goods. When externalities and public goods exist, the market does not provide the socially optimal amount of the good or service. One solution is to encourage businesses to internalize externalities. The government can aid the process through taxes and regulations that force producers to account for the negative externalities they create. Similarly, subsidies can spur the production of activities that generate positive externalities.

· ECONOMICS *in the* MEDIA ·

Tragedy of the Commons

SOUTH PARK AND WATER PARKS

If you have ever been to a water park or community pool, you know that the staff checks the pH of the water regularly to make sure it is clean. However, in an episode of *South Park*, everyone is peeing in Pi Pi's water park. The resulting pee concentration ends up being so high that it triggers a disaster-movie-style cataclysm, unleashing a flood of pee that destroys the place.

Why did this happen? Because each person looked at all the water and thought it wouldn't matter if *he* or *she* peed in it. But when *everyone* thought the same way, the water quality was affected. This led to the tragedy of the commons, in which the overall water quality became degraded. Pee-ew.

Thankfully, the real world is cleaner than South Park!

Likewise, public goods present a challenge for the market. Free-riding leads to the underproduction of goods that are nonrival and nonexcludable. Because not enough is produced privately, one solution is to eliminate free-riding by making involvement compulsory through taxation or regulation. A second problem occurs whenever goods are nonexcludable, as is the case with common-resource goods. This condition gives rise to the tragedy of the commons and can lead to the overuse of valuable resources. ✳

Buying Used Can Be Good for Your Wallet and for the Environment

- When you buy used you don't pay the "new" price markup.
- When you buy used you extend the usable life of a product, which is good for the environment.
- Some items are available for significant discounts soon after they are first sold.

Many people often spend their hard-earned money buying new, when choices to buying *almost* new instead are available. While some customers are willing to pay a premium for that "new" feeling, if you avoid that price markup for untouched goods, you'll usually save money *and* extend the usable life of a product. Here are a few ideas.

Listen to Macklemore's "Thrift Shop" advice: "It was 99 cents!"

1. **Thrift-shop clothing**. Why would you buy something that immediately drops in value by 70%? When you buy new clothes at a retail store, you'll rarely get even a third of it back if you need to sell it at a consignment store or garage sale. Pick up bargains on lightly used clothing at your local thrift store instead.

2. **Sports equipment**. Let the enthusiasts buy the latest equipment. When they tire of it and switch to the newest golf clubs or buy a new kayak, you can swoop in and save big bucks. Play It Again Sports is a retailer that sells new and used equipment side-by-side so you can decide for yourself if new is worth the price difference.

3. **Video game consoles and games**. You can buy used and pay half price or less. The catch is you'll have to wait. But the good news is that you'll never find out that your expensive new system isn't as exciting as advertised. Waiting means better information *and* lower prices. That's how you find a good deal.

4. **Automobiles**. The average new car can lose as much as 20% of its value during the first year after purchase. For a $30,000 car, that means $6,000 in lost value. Let someone else take that hit and buy a used vehicle instead.

5. **Tools and yard equipment**. Think twice before heading to the hardware store. Many tools like hammers and shovels are designed to last. Used tools might not look shiny-new, but they work just as well.

Every time you buy used, you extend the usable life of a product, which helps maximize the value society gets from its resources. These examples also illustrate the benefit of private property: recall that owners have incentives to (1) maintain, (2) protect, and (3) conserve the products they own so that they can (4) maximize the value when they sell them.

· ANSWERING *the* BIG QUESTIONS ·

What are externalities, and how do they affect markets?

- An externality exists whenever an internal cost (or benefit) diverges from a social cost (or benefit). Third parties can experience negative or positive externalities from market activity. Externalities are a type of market failure, which occurs when there is an inefficient allocation of resources in a market.

- Social costs are the sum of an activity's internal costs and external costs.

- When a negative externality exists, government can restore the social optimum by discouraging economic activity that harms third parties. When a positive externality exists, government can restore the social optimum by encouraging economic activity that benefits third parties.

- An externality is internalized when decision-makers must pay for the externality created by their participation in the market.

What are private goods and public goods?

- Private goods (or private property) ensures that owners have an incentive to maintain, protect, and conserve their property and also to trade it with others.

- A public good has two characteristics: it is nonexcludable and nonrival in consumption. Public goods give rise to the free-rider problem and result in the underproduction of the good in the market. Public goods give rise to market failure.

What are the challenges of providing nonexcludable goods?

- Economists use cost-benefit analysis to determine whether the benefits of providing a particular good outweigh the costs, but benefits can be hard to determine.

- Under a system of common property, the incentive structure encourages neglect and overuse.

Concepts You Should Know

cap and trade (p. 238)
club good (p. 233)
Coase theorem (p. 230)
common-resource good (p. 233)
cost-benefit analysis (p. 235)
excludable good (p. 230)
external costs (p. 220)

externalities (p. 220)
free-rider problem (p. 231)
internal costs (p. 220)
internalize (p. 223)
market failure (p. 220)
private good (p. 230)
private property (p. 228)

property rights (p. 227)
public good (p. 231)
rival good (p. 230)
social costs (p. 220)
social optimum (p. 222)
third-party problem (p. 221)
tragedy of the commons (p. 236)

Questions for Review

1. Does the market overproduce or underproduce when third parties enjoy positive externalities? Show your answer on a supply and demand graph.

2. Is it possible to use bargaining to solve externality problems involving many parties? Explain your reasoning.

3. Describe all of the ways in which externalities can be internalized.

4. Does cost-benefit analysis apply to public goods only? If yes, why? If not, name situations in which economists would use cost-benefit analysis.

5. What is the tragedy of the commons? Give an example that is not in the chapter.

6. What are the four incentives of private property? How do they differ from the incentives found in common property?

7. Give an example of a good that is nonrival in consumption and nonexcludable. What do economists call goods that share these characteristics?

Study Problems (* solved at the end of the section)

1. Many cities have noise ordinances that impose especially harsh fines and penalties for early-morning and late-evening disturbances. Explain why these ordinances exist.

2. Indicate whether the following activities create a positive or negative externality:

   a. Late-night road construction begins on a new bridge. As a consequence, traffic is rerouted past your house while the construction takes place.
   b. An excavating company pollutes a local stream with acid rock.
   c. A homeowner whose property backs up on a city park enjoys the sound of kids playing soccer.
   d. A student uses her cell phone discreetly during class.
   e. You and your friends volunteer to plant wildflowers along the local highway.

3. Indicate whether the following are private goods, club goods, common-resource goods, or public goods:

   a. a bacon double cheeseburger
   b. an NHL hockey game between the Detroit Red Wings and Boston Bruins
   c. a Fourth of July fireworks show
   d. a swimming pool
   e. a vaccination for the flu
   f. streetlights

4. Can you think of a reason why making cars safer would create negative externalities? Explain.

5. Which of the following activities give rise to the free-rider problem?

   a. recycling programs
   b. biking
   c. studying for an exam
   d. riding a bus

✳ **6.** The students at a crowded university have trouble waking up before 10 a.m., and most work jobs after 3 p.m. As a result, there is a great deal of demand for classes between 10 a.m. and 3 p.m., and classes before and after those hours are rarely full. To make matters worse, the university has a limited amount of classroom space and faculty. As a result, not every student can take classes during the most desirable times. Building new classrooms and hiring more faculty are not options. The administration asks for your advice about the best way to solve the problem of demand during the peak class hours. What advice would you give?

7. Two roommates are opposites. One enjoys playing Modern Warfare with his friends all night. The other likes to get to bed early for a full 8 hours of sleep. If Coase is right, the roommates have an incentive to solve the noise externality issue themselves. Name at least two solutions that will internalize, or eliminate, the externality.

✳ **8.** Two companies, Toxic Waste Management and Sludge Industries, both pollute a nearby lake. Each firm dumps 1,000 gallons of goo into the lake every day. As a consequence, the lake has lost its clarity and the fish are dying. Local residents want to see the lake restored. But Toxic Waste's production process depends heavily on being able to dump the goo into the lake. It would cost Toxic Waste $10 per gallon to clean up the goo it generates. Sludge can clean up its goo at a cost of $2 per gallon.

   a. If the local government cuts the legal goo emissions in half for each firm, what are the costs to each firm to comply with the law? What is the total cost to both firms in meeting the goo-emissions standard?

   b. Another way of cutting goo emissions in half is to assign each firm tradable pollution permits that allow 500 gallons of goo to be dumped into the lake every day. Under this approach, will each firm still dump 500 gallons of goo? Would the firms be willing to trade permits with one another?

9. A study finds that leaf blowers make too much noise, so the government imposes a $10 tax on the sale of every unit to correct for the social cost of the noise pollution. The tax completely internalizes the externality. Before the corrective tax, Blown Away Manufacturing regularly sold blowers for $100. After the tax is in place, the consumer price for leaf blowers rises to $105.

   a. Describe the impact of the tax on the number of leaf blowers sold.

   b. What is the socially optimal price to the consumer?

   c. What is the private market price?

   d. What net price is Blown Away receiving after it pays the tax?

10. In most areas, developers are required to submit an environmental impact study before work can begin on a new construction project. Suppose that a commercial developer wants to build a new shopping center on an environmentally protected piece of property that is home to a rare three-eyed toad. The shopping complex, if approved by the local planning commission, will cover 10 acres. The planning commission wants the construction to go forward because the shopping complex means additional jobs for the local community, but it also wants to be environmentally responsible. One member of the commission suggests that the developer relocate the toads. She describes the relocation process as follows: "The developer builds the shopping mall and agrees to create 10 acres of artificial toad habitat elsewhere." Will this proposed solution make the builder internalize the externality? Explain.

✳ **11.** Describe the difference between the way an environmental economist thinks about policy and the way an environmentalist thinks about policy. (**Hint:** Recall the difference between positive economics and normative economics from Chapter 2.)

12. If a company pollutes the water and transactions costs are high, which of the following makes the most economic sense?

   a. All parties connected with the pollution should negotiate.

   b. The company should be allowed to pollute.

   c. The company should be liable for the damages it causes.

   d. The company should go out of business.

13. A homeowner is piling debris near his lot line. It would be $300 worth of trouble to put it elsewhere. The next-door neighbor is worried that the unsightly debris drops $5,000 from the market value of the home she's trying to sell.

  a. How might the two parties voluntarily resolve this conflict?

  b. If the local homeowners association prohibits debris piles, how is the dispute likely to get resolved? Is this a socially beneficial solution?

✷ **14.** Does antibiotic use entail an external cost or an external benefit?

✷ **15.** Suppose Heesun lives alone. She has two pet hamsters; she likes the hamsters because they are cute. But cleaning their cage every day is a hassle. In this case, Heesun's hamsters entail

  a. an external cost.

  b. an external benefit.

  c. neither an external cost nor an external benefit.

16. A cattle rancher and a wheat farmer own adjacent properties. The accompanying table identifies the annual profit received by each party in the event there is, or there is not, a fence. If there is no fence, one can be installed and maintained at an annual cost of $15,000.

	Fence	No fence
Cattle rancher	$40,000	$50,000
Wheat farmer	50,000	20,000

If legal rights are assigned to the wheat farmer so that the cattle rancher is liable for any damage caused by her cattle to the wheat crop, will the cattle rancher build a fence?

Solved Problems

6. A flat-fee congestion charge is a good start, because this charge would reduce the quantity demanded between 10 a.m. and 3 p.m., but such a fee is a blunt instrument. Making the congestion charge dynamic (or varying the price by the hour) will encourage students to move outside the window with the most popular class times in order to pay less. For instance, classes between 11 a.m. and 2 p.m. would have the highest fee. Classes between 10 and 11 a.m. and between 2 and 3 p.m. would be slightly discounted. Classes between 9 and 10 a.m. and between 3 and 4 p.m. would be cheaper still, and those earlier than 9 a.m. and after 4 p.m. would be the cheapest. By altering the price of different class times, the university would be able to offer classes at less popular times and fill them up regularly, thus efficiently using its existing resources.

8.a. If the local government cuts the legal goo emissions in half for each firm, Toxic Waste will cut its goo by 500 gallons at a cost of $10 per gallon, for a total cost of $5,000. Sludge Industries will also cut its goo by 500 gallons; at $2 per gallon, the cost is $1,000. The total cost to both firms in meeting the goo-emissions standard is $5,000 + $1,000 = $6,000.

  b. It costs Toxic Waste $10 per gallon to clean up its goo. It is therefore more efficient for Toxic to buy all 500 permits from Sludge—which enables Toxic to dump an additional 500 gallons in the lake and saves the company $5,000 minus the price it pays to Sludge for its permits. At the same time, Sludge could decide not to dump any goo in the lake. Because it costs Sludge $2 per gallon to clean up its goo, it will have to pay $1,000 unless it sells its permits to Toxic, in which case it might actually make a profit. Because Toxic is saving more than it costs Sludge to clean up the goo, the two sides have an incentive to trade the permits.

11. Thinking like an economist requires one to consider the marginal benefits and the marginal costs of every policy. This perspective allows environmental economists to assess whether a particular policy will create enough benefits to outweigh the costs. It is this positive (dispassionate) perspective that causes an environmental economist to argue that the optimal rate of pollution is above zero. In contrast, an environmentalist sees policy solutions through a normative lens. Environmentalists weigh the benefits of protecting the environment much more heavily than the costs and therefore advocate for policies that protect the environment even when the costs are quite high.

14. Antibiotics create both an external cost and an external benefit. There is external cost because overuse makes bacteria more resistant to future treatment, and an external benefit because the use of antibiotics helps to slow the spread of bacteria.

15. The correct answer is c. There is no third party, so there is no negative or positive externality.

PART III

The Theory of THE FIRM

Business Costs and Production

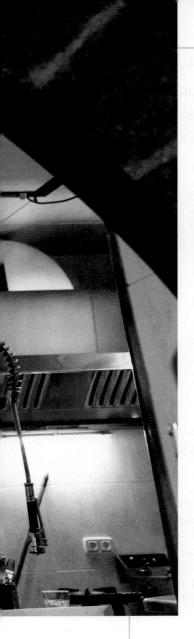

Do Larger Firms Always Have a Cost Advantage Over Their Smaller Rivals?

Walmart, the nation's largest retailer, leverages its size to get price breaks on bulk purchases from its suppliers. People commonly believe that this kind of leverage enables larger firms to operate at lower costs than smaller firms do. It is true that large firms have broader distribution networks, and they benefit from more specialization and automation compared with their smaller competitors. However, not all industries enjoy lower costs with additional sales the way retailers do. Even Walmart, known for its very low prices, can be undercut by online outlets that have lower costs and therefore lower prices. In other words, larger firms do not always have the lowest costs.

More generally, in any industry where transportation and advertising costs are high, smaller localized firms are not always at a disadvantage in terms of pricing. In fact, they often have the edge. For instance, in most college towns you will find many pizza shops—the national brands (Pizza Hut, Domino's, Little Caesars) and the local shops. Often, the local shop is the one with the cheapest pizza special, while the name brands charge more. By the end of this chapter, you will appreciate the importance of cost and understand why smaller and more nimble firms are sometimes able to undercut the prices of larger companies.

The guy flipping pizza dough at this pizzeria is happy, because he knows there's nothing the big national chains can do that he can't. Making pizza is a craft, not a factory process, and what he's doing here took years of practice.

We begin the chapter with an examination of costs and how they relate to production. After we understand the basics, we consider how firms can keep their costs low in the long run by choosing a scale of operation that best suits their needs.

· BIG QUESTIONS ·

- How are profits and losses calculated?
- How much should a firm produce?
- What costs do firms consider in the short run and the long run?

How Are Profits and Losses Calculated?

To determine the potential profits of a business, the first step is to look at how much it will cost to run it. Consider a McDonald's restaurant. While you are probably familiar with the products McDonald's sells, you may not know how an individual franchise operates. For one thing, the manager at a McDonald's must decide how many workers to hire and how many to assign to each shift. Other managerial decisions involve the equipment needed and what supplies to have on hand each day—everything from hamburger patties to paper napkins. In fact, behind each purchase a consumer makes at McDonald's, there is a complicated symphony of delivery trucks, workers, and managers.

For a company to be profitable, it is not enough to provide products consumers want. It must simultaneously manage its costs. In this section, we discuss how profits and costs are calculated.

The first McDonald's—much like the one pictured here—opened in San Bernardino, California, in 1940.

Total revenue is the amount a firm receives from the sale of goods and services.

Total cost is the amount a firm spends to produce and/or sell goods and services.

A **profit** results when total revenue is higher than total cost.

Calculating Profit and Loss

The simplest way to determine profit or loss is to calculate the difference between revenue and expenses (costs). The **total revenue** of a business is the amount the firm receives from the sale of goods and services. In the case of McDonald's, the total revenue is determined by the number of items sold and their prices. **Total cost** is the amount a firm spends to produce and/or sell goods and services. To determine total cost, the firm adds the individual costs of the resources used in producing and/or selling the goods. A **profit** occurs whenever total revenue is higher than total cost. A **loss** occurs whenever total revenue is less than total cost. We can express this relationship as an equation:

$$\text{profit (or loss)} = \text{total revenue} - \text{total cost}$$

(EQUATION 8.1)

To calculate total revenue, we look at the dollar amount the business takes in over a specific period. For instance, suppose that in a given day McDonald's sells 1,000 hamburgers for $1.00 each, 500 orders of large fries for $2.00 each, and 100 shakes for $2.50 each. The total revenue is the sum of all of these values, or $2,250. The profit is therefore $2,250 (total revenue) minus the total cost.

Calculating costs, however, is a little more complicated than calculating revenue; we don't simply tally the cost of making each hamburger, order of large fries, and shake. Total cost has two parts—one that is visible and one that is largely invisible. In the next section, we will see that determining total costs is part art and part science.

Explicit Costs and Implicit Costs

Economists break costs into two components: explicit costs and implicit costs. **Explicit costs** are tangible out-of-pocket expenses. To calculate explicit costs, we add every expense incurred to run the business. For example, in the case of a McDonald's franchise, the weekly supply of hamburger patties is one explicit cost; the owner receives a bill from the meat supplier and has to pay it. **Implicit costs** are the costs of resources already owned, for which no out-of-pocket payment is made. Implicit costs are also opportunity costs, because the use of owned resources means that the next-best alternative use is forgone.

Explicit costs are tangible out-of-pocket expenses.

Implicit costs are the costs of resources already owned, for which no out-of-pocket payment is made.

Let's consider an example. Purchasing a McDonald's franchise costs about $1 million; this is an explicit cost. However, there is also a high opportunity cost—the next-best possibility for investing $1 million. That money could have earned interest in a bank, been used to start a different business, or been invested in the stock market. Each alternative is an implicit cost.

Implicit costs are hard to calculate and easy to miss. For example, it is difficult to determine how much an investor could have earned from an

TABLE 8.1

Examples of a Firm's Explicit and Implicit Costs

Explicit costs	Implicit costs
The electricity bill	The labor of an owner who works for the company but does not draw a salary
Advertising in the local newspaper	The opportunity cost of the capital invested in the business
Employee wages	The use of the owner's car, computer, or other personal equipment to conduct company business

Opportunity cost

alternative activity. Is the opportunity cost the 3% interest he might have earned by placing the money in a bank, the 10% he might have hoped to earn in the stock market, or the 15% he might have gained by investing in a different business? We can be sure there is an opportunity cost for owner-provided capital, but we can never know exactly how much that might be.

In addition to the opportunity cost of capital, implicit costs include the opportunity cost of the owner's labor. Often, business owners do not pay themselves a direct salary. However, because they could have been working somewhere else, it is reasonable to consider the fair value of the owner's time—income the owner could have earned by working elsewhere—as part of the business's costs.

To fully account for all the costs of doing business, we must calculate the explicit costs, determine the implicit costs, and add them together:

(EQUATION 8.2)

$$\textbf{total cost} = \text{explicit costs} + \text{implicit costs}$$

A simple way of thinking about the distinction between explicit costs and implicit costs is to consider someone who wants to build a bookcase. Suppose that John purchases $30 in materials and takes half a day off from work, where he normally earns $12 an hour. After 4 hours, he completes the bookcase. His explicit cost is $30, but his total cost is much higher because he also gave up 4 hours of work at $12 an hour. His implicit cost is therefore $48. When we add the explicit cost ($30) and the implicit cost ($48), we get John's total cost ($78).

Table 8.1 shows examples of a firm's explicit and implicit costs.

Accounting Profit versus Economic Profit

Now that you know about explicit and implicit costs, we can refine our definition of profit. In fact, there are two types of profit—accounting profit and economic profit.

A firm's **accounting profit** is calculated by subtracting only the explicit costs from total revenue. Accounting figures permeate company reports, quarterly and annual statements, and the media.

Accounting profit is calculated by subtracting the explicit costs from total revenue.

(EQUATION 8.3)

$$\textbf{accounting profit} = \text{total revenues} - \text{explicit costs}$$

As you can see, accounting profit does not take into account the implicit costs of doing business. To calculate the full cost of doing business, we need to consider both implicit and explicit costs. Doing so yields a firm's economic profit. **Economic profit** is calculated by subtracting both the explicit and the implicit costs from total revenue. Economic profit gives a more complete assessment of how a firm is doing.

$$\text{economic profit} = \text{total revenues} - (\text{explicit costs} + \text{implicit costs})$$

(EQUATION 8.4)

Simplifying Equation 8.4 gives us

$$\text{economic profit} = \text{accounting profit} - \text{implicit costs}$$

(EQUATION 8.5)

Therefore, economic profit is always less than accounting profit.

The difference in accounting profits among various types of firms can be misleading. For instance, if a company with $1 billion in assets reports an annual profit of $10 million, we might think it is doing well. After all, wouldn't you be happy to make $10 million in a year? However, that $10 million is only 1% of the $1 billion the company holds in assets. As Table 8.2 shows, a 1% return is far less than the typical return available in a number of other places, including the stock market, bonds, or a savings account at a financial institution.

If the return on $1 billion in assets is low compared with what an investor can expect to make elsewhere, the firm with the $10 million accounting profit actually has a negative economic profit. For instance, if the firm had invested the $1 billion in a savings account, according to Table 8.2 it would have earned 2% on $1 billion—that is, $20 million. In that case,

$$\begin{aligned}\text{economic profit} &= \text{accounting profit} - \text{implicit costs} \\ &= \$10 \text{ million} - \$20 \text{ million} \\ &= -\$10 \text{ million}\end{aligned}$$

As you can see, economic profit can be negative, since the minus dollar amount is a loss. If a business has an economic profit, its revenues are larger than the combination of its explicit costs and implicit costs. Likewise, a business has an economic loss when its revenues are smaller than the combination of its explicit and implicit costs. The difficulty in determining economic profit lies in calculating the tangible value of implicit costs.

TABLE 8.2	
Historical Rates of Return in Stocks, Bonds, and Savings Accounts, 1928–2018	
Financial instrument	**Historical average rate of return since 1928 (adjusted for inflation)**
Stocks	8%
Bonds	3
Savings account at a financial institution	2

Source: Federal Reserve database in St. Louis (FRED) and author's adjustments. Data from 1928–2018.

Accounting Profit versus Economic Profit: Calculating Summer Job Profits

How much economic profit do you make from painting?

Kyle is a college student who works during the summer to pay for tuition. Last summer he worked at a fast-food restaurant and earned $2,500. This summer he is working as a painter and will earn $4,000. To do the painting job, Kyle had to spend $200 on supplies.

QUESTION: What is Kyle's accounting profit?

ANSWER: accounting profit = total revenues − explicit cost
$$= \$4,000 - \$200 = \$3,800$$

QUESTION: If working at the fast-food restaurant was Kyle's next-best alternative, how much economic profit will Kyle earn from painting?

ANSWER: To calculate economic profit, we need to subtract the explicit and implicit costs from the total revenue. Kyle's total revenue from painting will be $4,000. His explicit costs are $200 for supplies, and his implicit cost is $2,500—the salary he would have earned in the fast-food restaurant. So Kyle's

economic profit = total revenue − explicit cost + implicit cost
$$= \quad \$4,000 \quad - \quad (\$200 \quad + \quad \$2,500) \quad = \quad \$1,300$$

QUESTION: Suppose that Kyle can get an internship at an investment bank. The internship provides a stipend of $3,000 and tangible work experience that will help him get a job after graduation. Should Kyle take the painting job or the internship?

ANSWER: The implicit costs have changed because Kyle now has to consider the $3,000 stipend and the increased chance of securing a job after graduation versus what he can make painting houses. Calculation of economic profit from painting is now

$$\text{economic profit} = \$4,000 - (\$200 + \$3,000) = \$800$$

So at this point, Kyle's economic profit from painting would be only $800. But this number is incomplete. There is also the value of the internship experience. If Kyle wants to work in investment banking after graduation, then this decision is a no-brainer. He should take the internship—that is, unless some investment banks value painting houses more than work experience!

How Much Should a Firm Produce?

Every business must decide how much to produce. In this section, we describe the factors that determine output, and we explain how firms use inputs to maximize their production. Because it is possible for a firm to produce too little or too much, we must also consider when a firm should stop production.

Keeping Costs Down

INCREDIBLES 2

The 2018 sequel to *The Incredibles* opens where the original left off, with the Incredible family fighting to stop The Underminer. By now, all superheroes have been forced into hiding by public outrage over the collateral damage that the crime-fighting Supers habitually leave in their wake. Enter Winston Deavor, the head of a major telecommunications company. Not long after the Supers were banned, robbers broke into the Deavor mansion and shot his father. Winston always believed that if the Supers had been allowed to continue helping people, his father would still be alive. So when he and his sister inherited the company, they decided to create a campaign to bring back the superheroes.

To do this, Winston wants to change the public's perception by filming a superhero saving the day. He wants Elastigirl to lead the campaign, because a cost-benefit analysis by his sister determined that Elastigirl is able to solve crimes with far less damage than her husband, Mr. Incredible. That leaves the

Winston Deavor explains why he wants Elastigirl to fight the villains, while Mr. Incredible stays home with the kids.

big guy in the role of stay-at-home dad. Elastigirl changes public opinion about the Supers as she defeats the villains, because she is adept at minimizing property damage and loss of life. Good economists do likewise, by keeping costs as low as possible while getting the job done.

The Production Function

For a firm to earn an economic profit, it must produce a product that consumers want. This product is the firm's **output**. A firm should produce an output that is consistent with the largest possible economic profit.

Output
is the product the firm creates.

The firm must also control its costs. To do so, the firm must use resources efficiently. There are three primary **factors of production**: labor, land, and capital. Each factor of production is an *input*, or a resource used in the production process to generate the firm's output. *Labor* consists of workers, *land* consists of the geographical location used in production, and *capital* consists of all the resources the workers use to create the final product. Consider McDonald's as an example. The labor input includes managers, cashiers, cooks, and janitorial staff. The land input includes the land on which the McDonald's building sits. The capital input includes the building itself, the equipment used, the parking lot, the signs, and all the hamburger patties, buns, fries, ketchup, and other foodstuffs.

Factors of production
are the inputs (labor, land, and capital) used in producing goods and services.

To keep costs down in the production process, a firm needs to find the right mix of these inputs. The **production function** describes the relationship between the inputs a firm uses and the output it creates. As we saw at the beginning of the chapter, the manager of a McDonald's must make many decisions about inputs. If she hires too little labor, some of the land and capital will be underutilized. Likewise, with too many workers and not enough land or capital, some workers will not have enough to do to stay busy. For example, suppose that only a single worker shows up at McDonald's one day. This employee will have to do all the cooking; bag up the meals; handle the register, the drive-through, and the drinks; and clean the tables. This single worker, no matter how productive, will not be able to keep up with demand. Hungry customers will grow tired of waiting and take their business elsewhere—maybe for good!

When a second worker shows up, the two employees can begin to specialize in what they do well. Recall that specialization and comparative advantage lead to higher levels of output (see Chapter 2). Therefore, individual workers will be assigned to tasks that match their skills. For example, one worker can take the orders, fill the bags, and get the drinks. The other can work the grill area and drive-through. When a third worker comes on, the specialization process can extend even further. Specialization and division of labor are key to the way McDonald's operates. Production per worker expands as long as additional workers become more specialized and there are enough capital resources to keep each worker occupied.

McDonald's needs the correct amount of labor to maximize its output.

When only a few workers share capital resources, the resources each worker needs are readily available. But what happens when the restaurant is very busy? The manager can hire more staff for the busiest shifts, but the amount of space for cooking and the number of cash registers, drink dispensers, and tables in the seating area are fixed. Because the added employees have less capital to work with, beyond a certain point the additional labor will not continue to increase the restaurant's output at the same rate as it did at first. You might recognize this situation if you have ever gone into a fast-food restaurant at lunchtime. Even though the space behind the counter bustles with busy employees, they can't keep up with the orders. Only so many meals can be produced in a short time and in a fixed space; some customers have to wait.

The restaurant must also maintain an adequate supply of materials. If a shipment is late and the restaurant runs out of hamburger patties, sales (and total revenue) will decrease. The manager must therefore (1) decide how many workers to hire for each shift and (2) manage the inventory of supplies.

Let's look more closely at the manager's decision about how many workers to hire. On the left side of Figure 8.1, we see what happens when workers are added, one by one. When the manager adds one worker, output goes from 0 meals to 5 meals. Going from one worker to two workers increases total output to 15 meals. The second worker has increased the number of meals produced from 5 to 15, an increase of 10 meals. This increase in output is the **marginal product**, which is the change in output associated with one additional unit of an input. In this case, the change in output (10 additional

The Production Function and Marginal Product

(a) Total output rises rapidly in the green zone from zero to three workers, rises less rapidly in the yellow zone between three and eight workers, and falls in the red zone after eight workers. (b) The marginal product of labor rises in the green zone from zero to three workers, falls in the yellow zone from three to eight workers but remains positive, and becomes negative after eight workers. Notice that the marginal product becomes negative after total output reaches its maximum at eight workers. As long as marginal product is positive, total output rises. Once marginal product becomes negative, total output falls.

Marginal thinking

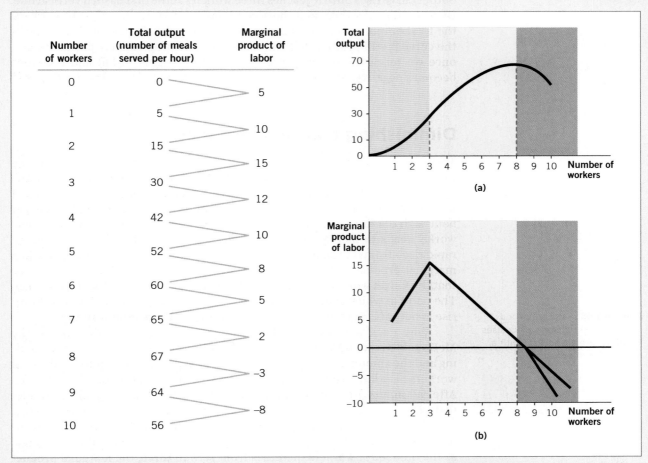

meals) divided by the increase in input (1 worker) gives us a marginal product of 10 ÷ 1, or 10. Because the table in Figure 8.1 adds one worker at a time, the marginal product is just the increase in output shown in the third column. Conversely, for any given number of workers, the total output is the sum of the individual workers' marginal products.

Looking down the three columns, we see that the total output continues to expand, and it keeps growing through eight workers. But after the first three workers, the rate of increase in the marginal product slows down. Why? The gains from specialization are slowly declining. With the ninth worker (going from 8 to 9), we see a negative marginal product. Once the cash registers, drive-through, grill area, and other service stations are fully staffed, there is not much for an extra worker to do. Eventually, extra workers will get in the way or distract other workers from completing their tasks.

The graphs on the right side of Figure 8.1 show (a) total output and (b) marginal product of labor. The graph of total output in (a) uses data from the second column of the table. As the number of workers goes from 0 to 3 on the *x* axis, total output rises at an increasing rate from 0 to 30. The slope of the total output curve rises until it reaches three workers at the first dashed vertical line. Between three workers and the second dashed vertical line at eight workers, the total output curve continues to rise, though at a slower rate; the slope of the curve is still positive, but the curve becomes progressively flatter. Finally, once we reach the ninth worker, total output begins to fall and the slope becomes negative. At this point, it is not productive to have so many workers.

Diminishing Marginal Product

The marginal product curve in panel (b) of Figure 8.1 explains the shape of the total output curve in panel (a). Consider that each worker's marginal productivity either adds to or subtracts from the firm's overall output. Marginal product increases from 5 meals served per hour with the first worker to 15 meals per hour with the third worker. From the first worker to the third, each additional worker leads to increased specialization and teamwork, which explains the rapid rise—from 0 to 30 meals—in the total output curve. By the fourth worker, marginal product begins to decline. Looking back to the table, you can see that the fourth worker produces 12 extra meals—3 fewer than the third worker. The point at which successive increases in inputs are associated with a slower rise in output is known as the point of **diminishing marginal product**.

Diminishing marginal product occurs when successive increases in inputs are associated with a slower rise in output.

Marginal thinking

Why does the rate of output slow? In our example, the size of the McDonald's restaurant is fixed in the short run. Because the size of the building and the amount of equipment do not increase, at a certain point additional workers have less to do or can even interfere with the output of other workers. After all inputs are fully utilized, additional workers cause marginal product to decline, which we see in the marginal product curve in Figure 8.1, panel (b).

What does diminishing marginal product tell us about the firm's labor input decision? Turning again to the two graphs, we see that in the green area, as the number of workers increases from zero to three, the marginal product and total output also rise. But when we enter the yellow zone with the fourth worker, we reach the point of diminishing marginal product where the curve starts to decline. Total output continues to rise, though at a slower rate. Finally, in the red zone, which we enter with the ninth worker, marginal product becomes negative and total output declines. No rational manager would hire more than eight workers in this scenario, because doing so would cause total output to drop.

A common mistake when considering diminishing marginal product is to assume that a firm should stop production as soon as marginal product starts to fall. This is not necessarily true. "Diminishing" does not mean "negative." There are many times when marginal product is declining but still relatively high. In our example, diminishing marginal product begins with the fourth worker. However, that fourth worker still produces 12 extra meals. If McDonald's can sell those 12 additional meals for more than it pays the fourth worker, the company's profits will rise.

What Costs Do Firms Consider in the Short Run and the Long Run?

Production is one part of a firm's decision-making process. If you have run even a simple business—for example, mowing lawns—you know that it requires decision-making. How many lawns do you want to be responsible for? Should you work on different lawns at the same time or specialize by task, with one person doing all the mowing and another taking care of the trimming? These are the kinds of production-related questions every firm must address. The other major component of production is cost. Should you invest in a big industrial-size mower? How much gasoline will you need to run your mowers? What does it cost to hire someone to help get the work done? These are some of the cost-related concerns firms face. Each one may seem like a small decision, but the discovery process that leads to the answers is crucial.

PRACTICE WHAT YOU KNOW

Diminishing Returns: Snow Cone Production

It's a hot day, and customers are lined up for snow cones at your small stand. The following table shows your firm's short-run production function for snow cones.

Number of workers	Total output of snow cones per hour
0	0
1	20
2	50
3	75
4	90
5	100
6	105
7	100
8	90

(CONTINUED)

QUESTION: When does diminishing marginal product begin?

ANSWER: You have to be careful when calculating this answer. Total output is maximized when you have six workers, but diminishing marginal return begins before you hire that many workers. Look at the following table, which includes a third column showing marginal product.

Number of workers	Total output of snow cones per hour	Marginal product
0	0	
		20
1	20	
		30
2	50	
		25
3	75	
		15
4	90	
		10
5	100	
		5
6	105	
		−5
7	100	
		−10
8	90	

How many workers are too many? Use marginal product to decide.

Marginal thinking

The marginal product is highest when you hire the second worker. After that, each subsequent worker you hire has a lower marginal product. Therefore, the answer to the question is that diminishing marginal product begins after the second worker.

Every firm, whether just starting out or already well established and profitable, can benefit by assessing how much to produce and how to produce it more efficiently. In addition, production and cost considerations are different in the short run and in the long run. We begin with the short run because the majority of firms are most concerned with making the best short-run decisions, and then we extend our analysis to the long run, where planning ahead plays a central role.

Costs in the Short Run

All firms experience some costs that are unavoidable in the short run. These unavoidable costs—for example, a lease on space or a contract with a supplier—are a large part of short-run costs. In the short run, costs can be variable or fixed.

Variable costs
change with the rate of output.

Variable costs change with the rate of output. Let's see what this means for a McDonald's and further simplify our example by assuming that the McDonald's produces only Big Macs. In this case, the variable costs include the number of workers the firm hires; the electricity the firm uses; the all-beef patties, special sauce, lettuce, cheese, pickles, onions, and sesame seed buns needed to create the Big Macs; and the packaging. These items are variable costs because the restaurant doesn't need them unless it has customers. The amount of these resources varies with the amount of output the restaurant produces. You might be thinking that a firm should decide to produce at an output where its average variable costs are lowest; but be careful—you don't have all the facts yet. In Chapter 9, we add demand to our analysis to determine how much the firm should produce. For now, we stay focused on the cost side.

Fixed costs are unavoidable; they do not vary with output in the short run. For instance, no matter how many Big Macs the McDonald's sells, most of the costs associated with the building remain the same and the business must pay for them. These fixed costs—also known as *overhead*—include rent, insurance, and property taxes.

Fixed costs
are unavoidable; they do not vary with output in the short run. Fixed costs are also known as overhead.

INTERPRETING TABULAR DATA Every business must be able to determine how much it costs to provide the products and services it sells. Table 8.3 lists many different ways to measure the costs associated with business decisions.

Let's begin with total variable cost (TVC) in column 2 and total fixed cost (TFC) in column 3. Notice that when output—the quantity (Q) of Big Macs produced per hour—is 0, total variable cost starts at $0 and rises with production at an uneven rate, depending on output and the cost of the ingredients that go into each Big Mac. We attribute this increase in TVC to the simple fact that additional workers and other inputs are needed to generate additional output. In contrast, total fixed cost starts at $100, even when output is 0, and remains constant as output rises. As already noted, fixed costs include overhead expenses such as rent, insurance, and property taxes.

TABLE 8.3

Measuring Costs

(1)	(2)	(3)	(4)	(5)	(6)	(7)	(8)
Quantity (Q = Big Macs produced per hour)	Total variable cost	Total fixed cost	Total cost	Average variable cost	Average fixed cost	Average total cost	Marginal cost
Abbreviation:	TVC	TFC	TC	AVC	AFC	ATC	MC
Formula:			TVC + TFC	TVC ÷ Q	TFC ÷ Q	TC ÷ Q or AVC + AFC	ΔTVC ÷ ΔQ or ΔTC ÷ ΔQ
0	$0.00	$100.00	$100.00				
10	30.00	100.00	130.00	$3.00	$10.00	$13.00	$3.00
20	50.00	100.00	150.00	2.50	5.00	7.50	2.00
30	65.00	100.00	165.00	2.17	3.33	5.50	1.50
40	77.00	100.00	177.00	1.93	2.50	4.43	1.20
50	87.00	100.00	187.00	1.74	2.00	3.74	1.00
60	100.00	100.00	200.00	1.67	1.67	3.34	1.30
70	120.00	100.00	220.00	1.71	1.43	3.14	2.00
80	160.00	100.00	260.00	2.00	1.25	3.25	4.00
90	220.00	100.00	320.00	2.44	1.11	3.55	6.00
100	300.00	100.00	400.00	3.00	1.00	4.00	8.00

For simplicity, we assume that this amount is $100 a day. When we add fixed cost and variable cost together, we get total cost (TC), listed in column 4: TC = TVC + TFC.

Columns 5 and 6 enable us to determine the cost of producing a Big Mac by examining the average cost of production. **Average variable cost (AVC)**, in column 5, is the total variable cost divided by the output produced: AVC = TVC ÷ Q. Notice that the average variable cost declines until 60 Big Macs are produced at an average variable cost of $1.67, which is the lowest average variable cost. Why should we care about AVC? Because it can be a useful signal. In this case, total variable costs in column 2 always rise, but the average variable cost falls until 60 Big Macs are produced.

Average fixed cost (AFC), listed in column 6, is calculated by dividing total fixed cost by the output: AFC = TFC ÷ Q. Because total fixed cost is constant, dividing these costs by the output means that as the output rises, the average fixed cost declines. In other words, higher output levels spread out the total fixed cost across more units. As Table 8.3 shows, average fixed cost is lowest at an output of 100 Big Macs, where

$$AFC = TFC ÷ Q$$
$$AFC = \$100 ÷ 100$$
$$AFC = \$1$$

What does this example tell a business that wants to lower its costs? Because overhead costs such as rent cannot be changed, the best way to lower average fixed costs is to raise output.

Average total cost (ATC), shown in column 7, is calculated by adding the AVC and AFC. It can also be calculated by dividing total cost by quantity (TC ÷ Q). Let's look at the numbers to get a better understanding of what average total cost tells us. Even though the average variable cost rises from $1.67 to $1.71 after 60 Big Macs are produced, the average fixed cost is still falling, from $1.67 to $1.43. The decline in average fixed cost is enough to pull the average total cost down to $3.14. Eventually, increases in variable cost overwhelm the cost savings achieved by spreading fixed cost across more production. We can see this result if we compare the average total costs of making 70 Big Macs and 80 Big Macs.

For 70 Big Macs:

$$ATC = AVC + AFC$$
$$ATC = \$1.71 + \$1.43 = \$3.14$$

For 80 Big Macs:

$$ATC = AVC + AFC$$
$$ATC = \$2.00 + \$1.25 = \$3.25$$

At 80 Big Macs, the average variable cost rises from $1.71 to $2.00. And the average fixed cost falls from $1.43 to $1.25. Therefore, the rise in average variable cost—$0.29—is higher than the fall in average fixed cost—$0.18. ATC therefore rises, removing the benefit of higher output.

Average variable cost (AVC) is determined by dividing total variable cost by the output.

Average fixed cost (AFC) is determined by dividing total fixed cost by the output.

Average total cost (ATC) is the sum of average variable cost and average fixed cost.

INTERPRETING DATA GRAPHICALLY Now that we have walked through the numerical results in Table 8.3, it is time to visualize the cost relationships with graphs. Figure 8.2 shows a graph of total cost curves (a) and the relationship between the marginal cost curve and the average cost curves (b).

In panel (a) of Figure 8.2, we see that although the total cost curve continues to rise, the rate of increase in total cost is not constant. For the first 50 Big Macs, the total cost rises at a decreasing rate, reflecting the gains of specialization and comparative advantage that come from adding workers who concentrate on specific tasks. After 50 Big Macs, diminishing marginal product causes the total cost curve to rise at an increasing rate. Because a McDonald's restaurant has a fixed capacity, producing more than 50 Big Macs requires a significantly higher investment in labor, and those workers do not have any additional space to work in—a situation that makes the total cost curve rise more rapidly at high production levels. The total cost (TC) curve is equal to the sum of the total fixed cost and total variable cost curves, as shown in panel (a). Total fixed cost (TFC) is constant, so it is the total variable cost (TVC) that gives the TC curve its shape.

But that is not the most important part of the story. Any manager at McDonald's can examine total costs. Likewise, she can look at the average cost

Marginal thinking

FIGURE 8.2

The Cost Curves

(a) The total variable cost (TVC) dictates the shape of the total cost (TC) curve. After 50 Big Macs, diminishing marginal product causes the total cost curve to rise at an increasing rate. Notice that the total fixed cost curve (TFC) stays constant, or flat. (b) The marginal cost curve (MC) reaches its minimum before average variable cost (AVC) and average total cost (ATC). Marginals always lead the average variable and average total costs either up or down. Average fixed cost (AFC), which has no variable component, continues to fall with increased quantity, because total fixed costs are spread across more units.

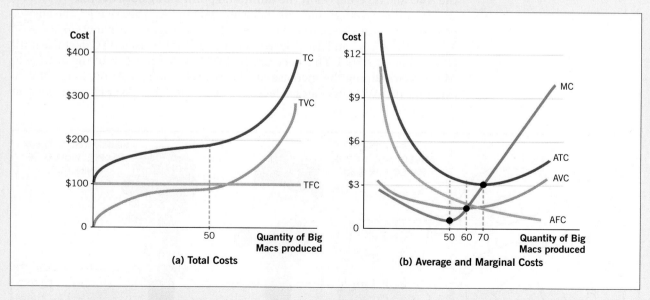

(a) Total Costs

(b) Average and Marginal Costs

and compare that information with the average cost at other local businesses. But neither the total cost of labor nor the average cost will tell her anything about the cost of making additional units—that is, Big Macs.

A manager can make even better decisions by looking at marginal cost. The **marginal cost** (**MC**) is the increase in cost that occurs from producing one additional unit of output. (In column 8 of Table 8.3, this relationship is shown as the change in TVC divided by the change in quantity produced, where "change" is indicated by Δ [the Greek letter delta]). For example, in planning the weekly work schedule, the manager has to consider how many workers to hire for each shift. She wants to hire additional workers when the cost of doing so is less than the expected boost in profits. In this situation, it is essential to know the marginal cost, or extra cost, of hiring one more worker.

In Table 8.3, marginal cost (MC) falls to a minimum of $1.00 when between 40 and 50 Big Macs are produced. Notice that the minimum MC occurs at a lower output level than average variable cost (AVC) and average total cost (ATC) in panel (b) of Figure 8.2. When output is less than 50 Big Macs, marginal cost is falling because over this range of production the marginal product of labor is increasing due to better teamwork and more specialization. After the fiftieth Big Mac, MC rises, acting as an early warning that average variable and total costs will soon follow suit. Why would a manager care about the marginal cost of the last few units being produced more than the average total cost of producing all the units? Because marginal cost helps the manager decide if making one more unit of output will increase profits or not!

The MC curve reaches its lowest point before the lowest point of the AVC and ATC curves. For this reason, a manager who is concerned about rising costs would look to the MC curve as a signal that average total cost will eventually increase as well. Once marginal cost begins to increase, it continues to pull down average variable cost until sales reach 60 Big Macs. After that point, MC is above AVC, and AVC begins to rise as well. However, ATC continues to fall until 70 Big Macs are sold. Note that the MC curve intersects the AVC and ATC curves at the minimum point along both curves.

Why does average total cost fall while MC and AVC are rising? The answer lies in the average fixed cost (AFC) curve shown in Figure 8.2, panel (b). Because ATC = AVC + AFC, and AFC always declines as output rises, ATC declines until 70 Big Macs are sold. This decrease in ATC is a direct result of the decline in AFC overwhelming the increase in AVC between 60 and 70 Big Macs. Notice also that the AVC curve stops declining at 60 Big Macs. Average variable cost

Marginal cost (MC)
is the increase in cost that occurs from producing one additional unit of output.

Marginal thinking

ECONOMICS *in the* MEDIA

Costs in the Short Run

OCEAN'S 8

In *Ocean's 8* (2018), Sandra Bullock and Cate Blanchett recruit six partners in crime to help them steal a diamond necklace worth $150 million. Part of the joy in watching any of the *Ocean's* films is seeing a star-studded cast of A-list actors pull off the perfect heist. Each partner has a specific skill: one is a jewelry maker, another a computer hacker, a third a pickpocket, and so on.

Beyond a certain point, however, adding more specialists mostly just means an extra person to split the take with. The Bullock and Blanchett characters know exactly how big a core team they want. That's why two people who play key but secondary roles—namely Yen, the acrobat from *Ocean's 11*, and Veronica, the younger sister of Nine Ball (Rihanna)—in effect function as contractors. They get a payoff, but they don't get a proportional share of the loot—because the marginal product of labor they contribute doesn't warrant a share.

How many accomplices does it take to pull off the perfect heist?

Marginal thinking

should initially decline as a result of increased specialization and teamwork. However, at some point the advantages of continued specialization are overtaken by diminishing marginal product, and average variable cost begins to rise. The transition from falling costs to rising costs is of particular interest because as long as average total cost is declining, the firm can lower its costs by increasing its output.

Once the marginal cost in Table 8.3 rises above the average total cost, the average total cost begins to rise as well. This result is evident if we compare the average total cost of making 70 Big Macs ($3.14) and 80 Big Macs ($3.25) with the marginal cost ($4.00) of making those extra 10 Big Macs. Since the marginal cost ($4.00) of making Big Macs 71 through 80 is higher than the average total cost at 70 ($3.14), the average total cost of making 80 Big Macs goes up (to $3.25).

Marginal cost always leads (or pulls) average variable cost and average total cost along. The MC eventually rises above the average total cost because of diminishing marginal product. Because the firm has to pay a fixed wage in our McDonald's example, the cost to produce each hamburger increases as each worker's output decreases.

Note that there is one "average" curve that the marginal cost does not affect: average fixed cost. Notice that the AFC curve in panel (b) of Figure 8.2 continues to fall even though marginal cost eventually rises. The AFC curve declines with increased output. Because McDonald's has $100.00 in fixed costs each day, we can determine the average fixed cost by dividing the total fixed cost ($100.00) by the number of Big Macs sold. When 10 Big Macs are sold, the average fixed cost is $10.00 per Big Mac, but this value falls to $1.00 per Big Mac if 100 burgers are sold. Because McDonald's is a high-volume business that relies on low costs to compete, being able to produce enough Big Macs to spread out the firm's fixed costs is essential.

Costs in the Long Run

We have seen that in the short run, businesses have fixed costs and fixed capacities. In the long run, all costs are variable and can be renegotiated. Thus, firms have more control over their costs in the long run, which enables them to reach their desired level of production. One way firms can adjust in the long run is by changing the **scale**, or size, of the production process. If the business is expected to grow, the firm can ramp up production. If the business is faltering, it can scale back its operations. This flexibility enables firms to avoid a situation of negative marginal product. Economists refer to the quantity of output that minimizes the average total cost in the long run as the **efficient scale**.

A long-run time horizon allows a business to choose a scale of operation that best suits its needs. For instance, if a local McDonald's is extremely popular, in the short run the manager can only hire more workers or expand the restaurant's hours to accommodate more customers. However, in the long run all costs are variable; the manager can add drive-through lanes, increase the number of registers, expand the grill area, and so on.

The absence of fixed factors in the long-run production process means that we cannot explain total costs in the long run in the same way we explained short-run costs. Short-run costs are a reflection of diminishing marginal product, whereas long-run costs are a reflection of scale and the cost of providing additional output. Because diminishing marginal product is no longer relevant in the long run, one might assume that costs would fall as output expands. However, this is not necessarily the case. Depending on the industry and the prevailing economic conditions, long-run costs can rise, fall, or stay approximately the same.

THREE TYPES OF SCALE In this section, we describe three different scenarios for a firm in the long run. A firm may experience *economies of scale*, *diseconomies of scale*, or *constant returns to scale*. Let's consider each of these in turn.

If output expands and long-run average total costs decline in the long run, a business experiences **economies of scale**. National homebuilders, such as Toll Brothers, provide a good example of economies of scale. All

Scale refers to the size of the production process.

The **efficient scale** is the output level that minimizes average total cost in the long run.

Building more than one house at a time would represent economies of scale.

Economies of scale occur when long-run average total costs decline as output expands.

builders, whether they are local or national, do the same thing—they build houses. Each builder needs lumber, concrete, excavators, electricians, plumbers, roofers, and many more specialized workers or subcontractors. A big company, such as Toll, is able to hire many specialists and also buy the equipment it needs in bulk. As a result, Toll can manufacture the same home as a local builder but at a much lower cost.

But bigger isn't always better! Sometimes a company grows so large that coordination problems make costs rise. For example, as an enterprise expands its scale, it might require more managers, highly specialized workers, and a coordination process to pull everything together. As the layers of management expand, the coordination process can break down. For this reason, a larger firm can become less effective at holding down long-run average total costs and experience **diseconomies of scale**, or higher costs as output expands in the long run.

The problem of diseconomies of scale is especially relevant in the service sector of the economy. For example, large regional hospitals have many layers of bureaucracy. These added management costs and infrastructure expenses can make medical care more expensive beyond a certain point. If you are not convinced, ask yourself why large cities have many smaller competing hospitals rather than one centralized hospital. The answer becomes obvious: bigger doesn't always mean less expensive (or better)!

When long-run average total costs remain constant even as output expands in the long run, we say that the firm has **constant returns to scale**. For example, large national restaurant chains like Panda Express, which specializes in Chinese cuisine, compete with local Chinese restaurants. In each case, the local costs to hire workers and build the restaurant are the same. Panda Express does have a few advantages; for example, it can afford to advertise on national television and buy food in bulk. But Panda Express also has more overhead costs for its many layers of management. Constant returns to scale in the bigger chain mean that a small local Chinese restaurant will have approximately the same menu prices as its bigger rivals.

LONG-RUN COST CURVES Now it is time to illustrate the long-run nature of cost curves. We have seen that increased output may not always lead to economies of scale. Average total costs can decline, be constant, or rise with output. Figure 8.3 illustrates each of the three scale possibilities graphically. The long-run average total cost curve (LRATC) is actually a composite of many short-run average total cost curves (SRATC), which appear as the faint U-shaped dashed curves drawn in gray. By visualizing the short-run cost curves at any given output level, we can develop a composite of them to create the LRATC curve, which comprises all the short-run cost curves the firm may choose to deploy in the long run. In the long run, the firm is free to choose

Would you rather see the ER's doctor du jour or your own physician?

Diseconomies of scale occur when long-run average total costs rise as output expands.

Constant returns to scale occur when long-run average total costs remain constant as output expands.

Will you find lower prices at Panda Express or your local Chinese restaurant?

any of its short-run curves, so it always picks the output/cost combination that minimizes costs.

In the long run, there are three distinct possibilities: economies of scale, constant returns to scale, and diseconomies of scale. At first, each LRATC curve exhibits economies of scale as a result of increased specialization, the utilization of mass production, bulk purchasing power, and increased automation. The main question in the long run is whether the cost curve will continue to decline, level off, or rise. In an industry with economies of scale at high output levels—for example, homebuilding—the cost curve continues to decline, and the most efficient output level is always the largest output: the purple curve in Figure 8.3. In this situation, we would expect only one large firm to dominate the industry because large firms have significant cost advantages. However, in an industry with constant returns to scale— for example, restaurants—the cost curve flattens out: the red line. Once the curve becomes constant, firms of varying sizes can compete equally with one another because they have the same costs. Finally, in the case of diseconomies of scale—for example, big-city hospitals—bigger firms have higher costs: the orange curve.

FIGURE 8.3

Costs in the Long Run

In the long run, there are three distinct possibilities: the long-run average total cost curve (LRATC) can exhibit economies of scale (the purple curve), constant returns to scale (the red curve), or diseconomies of scale (the orange curve).

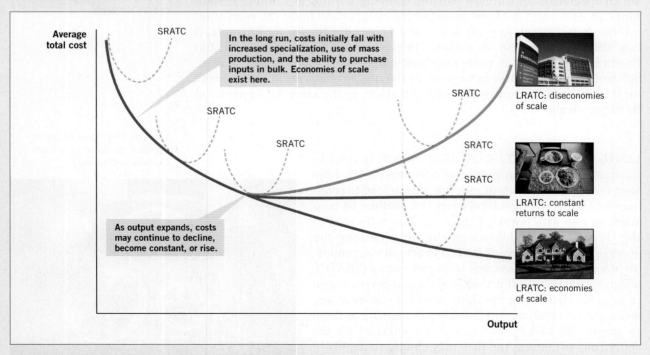

Economies of Scale

THE BIG BANG THEORY: THE WORK SONG NANOCLUSTER

In an episode of the long-running TV series *The Big Bang Theory*, Penny decides to make flower barrettes in her spare time to supplement her pay as a waitress. Because Penny is not very good at math, when Sheldon stops by she seeks his advice about how she can earn more money. What transpires can only be described as the best explanation of business costs you'll ever see.

As Sheldon explains to Penny: "If you took advantage of modern marketing techniques and optimized your manufacturing process, you might make this a viable business." They get to work and Sheldon starts timing how long it takes Penny to make a flower barrette. It takes her 12 minutes and 17 seconds, and Penny seems quite happy until Sheldon says, "That's 4.9 Penny Blossoms per hour. Based on your cost of materials and your wholesale selling price, you'll effectively be paying yourself $5.19 a day. There are children in a sneaker factory in Indonesia who outearn you." To increase Penny's productivity, he suggests they create an assembly line to lower the cost of manufacturing the barrettes, and they begin working together to make the Penny Blossoms, even singing a rhythmic work song to increase their productivity.

Creating flower barrettes by hand in your apartment misses out on economies of scale.

Together they can now make each Penny Blossom in under 3 minutes!

At this point, Leonard, Howard, and Raj enter Penny's apartment and start to ask questions about what is going on. Everyone quickly realizes they will have to expand the scale of the operation to fully optimize the production process to lower costs even further. The result is that you see the production process evolve from a small-scale operation in Penny's apartment in the short run to a sophisticated large-scale enterprise in the long run. All of this is done in one very funny 22-minute episode.

Costs are defined in a number of ways, but marginal cost plays the most crucial role in a firm's cost structure. By observing what happens to marginal cost, you can understand changes in average cost and total cost. This simple fact explains why economists place so much emphasis on marginal cost. Going forward, a solid grasp of marginal analysis will help you understand many of the most important concepts in microeconomics.

Marginal thinking

You now understand the cost, or supply side, of business decisions. However, to provide a complete picture of how firms operate, we still need to examine how markets work. Costs are only part of the story, and in the next chapter we take a closer look at profits.

ECONOMIES OF SCALE

Bike sharing is big business throughout China, with millions of bikes in use. It costs just pennies per hour to rent a bike, which means profit margins are thin, so firms have to be careful how quickly they expand into new markets. China's third-largest bike share company, Bluegogo, went out of business in 2017, when it expanded too rapidly and ran out of the cash needed to keep going. Bluegogo's chief executive said he had been "filled with arrogance" and believed that all they had to do was flood the market with bikes and people would use them.

Many firms mistakenly believe that expanding will make them more profitable. Bluegogo's two main rivals, Ofo and Mobike, followed the same strategy but survived because they generated more revenues. What does it look like when firms expand too rapidly? Check out this bicycle scrap pile, littered with broken shared bicycles that the companies would rather discard than fix.

Bike share graveyard in Xiamen, China, a testament to the perils of expanding too quickly.

PRACTICE WHAT YOU KNOW

Marginal Cost: The True Cost of Admission to Universal Studios

You and your family visit Orlando for a week. While there, you decide to go to Universal Studios. When you arrive, you notice that each family member can buy a day pass for $115 or a two-day pass for $150. Your parents are concerned about spending too much, so they decide to calculate the average cost of a two-day pass to see if it is a good value. The average cost is $150 \div 2$, or $75 per day. Their math is correct, but something you learned in economics tells you they are not thinking about this situation in the correct way.

QUESTION: What concept can you apply to make the decision clearer?

ANSWER: Tell your parents about *marginal cost*. The first day costs $115, but the marginal cost of going back to the park on the second day is only the extra cost per person, or $150 − $115, which equals $35. Your parents still might not want to spend the extra money, but spending only an extra $35 for a second day makes it an attractive value. Someone who does not appreciate economics might think the second day costs an extra $75 because that is the average cost, but the average cost is misleading. Looking at marginal cost is the best way to weigh these two options. By the way, if you want a three-day pass the price is $170, making the marginal cost of the third day just $170 − $150, which equals $20. That sounds ridiculously low, but the incremental increase in the price is low because no matter how much you like Harry Potter, a third straight day in the same theme park becomes repetitive quickly.

CHALLENGE QUESTION: Suppose you are considering a single-day three-park pass to Universal Studios, Islands of Adventure, and Volcano Bay. The price for the three-park pass is $170. If you value Universal Studios at $140, Islands of Adventure at $30, and Volcano Bay at $20, should you buy the three-park pass instead of the single-day pass to just Universal Studios?

ANSWER: The total value of the three-park pass to you is $140 + $30 + $20 = $190, which is more than enough to justify the expense of the park hopper ticket ($170), since you'd earn $20 in consumer surplus. However, you'd earn more consumer surplus if you purchased the day pass to just Universal Studios, since $140 − $115 = $25 in consumer surplus. That means you are better off sticking just with Universal Studios, since the price of the three-park pass doesn't save you enough money to justify the added expense.

Is one day enough to see Hogwarts?

Marginal thinking

Conclusion

Do larger firms have lower costs? Not always. When diseconomies of scale occur, average total costs will rise with output. This result contradicts the common misconception that bigger firms have lower costs than their smaller competitors. Simply put, sometimes a leaner firm with less overhead can beat its larger rivals on cost. ✳

How Much Does It Cost to Raise a Child?

- Raising a child costs approximately $250,000.
- Families that have three or more children spend an average of 22% less on each child.
- The cost of raising children also forces families to make trade-offs. In many households, both parents must work or work longer hours.

Raising a child is one of life's most rewarding experiences, but it can be very expensive. According to the U.S. Department of Agriculture, the cost for a middle-income, two-parent family to raise a child from birth to age 18 is about $250,000 (not including college). To determine this number, the government considers all the costs related to raising a child, such as food, clothing, medical care, and entertainment. In addition, the government apportions a share of the costs of the family home and vehicles to each child in the household. To put the cost of raising a child in perspective, the median home value in 2018 was $239,000. Talk about opportunity cost!

Opportunity cost

What if a family has more than one child? You wouldn't necessarily multiply the cost by 2 or 3, because there are economies of scale in raising more children. For example, some things can be shared: the children might share a bedroom and wear hand-me-downs. Also, the family can purchase food in bulk. As a result, families that have three or more children can manage to spend an average of 22% less on each child.

Trade-offs

The cost of raising children also forces families to make trade-offs. In many households, both parents must work or work longer hours. When one parent steps out of the workforce, the household loses a paycheck. While leaving the workforce may save in expenses associated with working, including certain clothes, transportation, and childcare, there are also hidden costs. For example, the lack of workplace continuity lowers the stay-at-home parent's future earning power.

Raising a child is an expensive proposition in both the short run and the long run. But don't let this discourage you; it is also one of the most rewarding personal investments you will ever make. More importantly, there are large benefits to society as well, as Nancy Folbre, author of *Valuing Children: Rethinking the Economics of the Family* notes. "When you raise children, they grow up to become workers and taxpayers and participants in an economic system that reproduces itself over time."[*] This has large implications for how the costs of raising children should be distributed among parents and society.

---

[*]Nancy Folbre, *Valuing Children: Rethinking the Economics of the Family* (Cambridge, M.A.: Harvard University Press, 2010).

Raising Hope, a TV show that ran from 2010 to 2014, is about Jimmy, a single father who wants to give his daughter a better childhood than the one he had.

- ANSWERING *the* BIG QUESTIONS -

How are profits and losses calculated?

- Profits and losses are determined by calculating the difference between expenses (total cost) and total revenue.

- There are two types of profit: economic profit and accounting profit. If a business has an economic profit, its revenue is larger than the combination of its explicit and implicit costs.

- Economists break costs into two components: explicit costs, which are easy to calculate, and implicit costs, which are hard to calculate. Because economic profit accounts for implicit costs, the economic profit is always less than the accounting profit.

How much should a firm produce?

- A firm should produce an output that is consistent with the largest possible economic profit.

- To maximize profit, firms must effectively combine land, labor, and capital in the right quantities.

- In any short-run production process, a point of diminishing marginal product will occur at which additional units of a variable input no longer generate as much output as before. Diminishing marginal product is a result of fixed inputs (such as capital and land) in the short run.

- Marginal cost (MC) is the key variable in determining a firm's cost structure. The MC curve always leads the average total cost (ATC) and average variable cost (AVC) curves up or down.

What costs do firms consider in the short run and the long run?

- In the short run, firms consider variable and fixed costs, as well as marginal cost. Firms also consider average variable cost (AVC), average fixed cost (AFC), and average total cost (ATC).

- With the exception of the average fixed cost (AFC) curve, which always declines, short-run cost curves are U-shaped. All variable costs initially decline due to increased specialization. At a certain point, the advantages of continued specialization give way to diminishing marginal product, and the MC, AVC, and ATC curves begin to rise.

- Long-run costs are a reflection of scale. Firms can experience diseconomies of scale, economies of scale, or constant returns to scale, depending on the industry.

·CHAPTER PROBLEMS·

Concepts You Should Know

accounting profit (p. 254)
average fixed cost (AFC) (p. 264)
average total cost (ATC) (p. 264)
average variable cost (AVC) (p. 264)
constant returns to scale (p. 269)
diminishing marginal
   product (p. 260)
diseconomies of scale (p. 269)
economic profit (p. 255)

economies of scale (p. 268)
efficient scale (p. 268)
explicit costs (p. 253)
factors of production (p. 257)
fixed costs (p. 263)
implicit costs (p. 253)
loss (p. 253)
marginal cost (MC) (p. 266)

marginal product (p. 258)
output (p. 257)
production function (p. 258)
profit (p. 252)
scale (p. 268)
total cost (p. 252)
total revenue (p. 252)
variable costs (p. 262)

Questions for Review

1. What is the equation for the profit (or loss) of a firm?

2. Why is economic profit a better measure of profit-ability than accounting profit? Give an example.

3. What role does diminishing marginal product play in determining the ideal mix of labor and capital a firm should use?

4. Describe what happens to the total product of a firm when marginal product is increasing, decreasing, and negative.

5. Explain why marginal cost is the glue that connects average variable cost and average total cost.

6. Compare the short-run and long-run cost curves. In a few sentences, explain their differences.

7. Name examples of industries that illustrate each of the following: economies of scale, constant returns to scale, and diseconomies of scale. Think creatively; do not use the textbook examples.

Study Problems (*solved at the end of this section)

1. Go to www.lemonadegame.com. This free online game places you in the role of a lemonade seller. Nothing could be simpler, right? Not so fast! You still need to control costs and ensure that you have the right ingredients on hand to be able to sell lemonade. You will need to manage your supply of lemons, sugar, ice, and cups. You will also have to set a price and decide how many lemons and how much sugar and ice to put in each glass of lemonade you produce. This is not a trivial process, so play the game. Your challenge is to make $20 in profit over the first five days. (Your business starts with $20, so you need to have $40 in your account by the end of day 5 to meet the challenge. Are you up to it?)

2. The following table shows a short-run production function for laptop computers. Use the data to determine where diminishing product begins.

Number of workers	Total output of laptop computers
0	0
1	40
2	100
3	150
4	180
5	200
6	205
7	200
8	190

3. A pizza business has the cost structure described below. The firm's fixed costs are $25 per day. Calculate the firm's average fixed costs, average variable costs, average total costs, and marginal costs.

Output (pizzas per day)	Total cost of output
0	$25
10	75
20	115
30	150
40	175
50	190
60	205
70	225
80	250

✳ **4.** A firm is considering changing its plant size, so it calculates the average cost of production for various plant sizes, shown below. If the firm is currently using plant size C, is the firm experiencing economies of scale, diseconomies of scale, or constant returns to scale?

Plant size	Average total cost
A (smallest)	$10,000
B	9,500
C	9,000
D	8,800
E	8,800
F (largest)	8,900

5. True or false?

a. The AFC curve can never rise.

b. Diminishing marginal product is a long-run constraint that prevents lower costs.

c. The MC curve intersects the AVC and ATC curves at the minimum point along both curves.

d. Accounting profit is smaller than economic profit.

e. Total cost divided by output is equal to marginal cost.

6. Digital media distributed over the Internet often have marginal costs of zero. For instance, people can download music and movies instantly through many providers. Do these products exhibit economies, diseconomies, or constant returns to scale?

7. An airline has a marginal cost per passenger of $30 on a route from Boston to Detroit. At the same time, the typical fare charged is $300. The planes that fly the route are usually full, yet the airline claims that it loses money on the route. How is this possible?

8. Many amusement parks offer two-day passes at dramatically discounted prices. If a one-day pass costs $40 but the two-day pass costs $50, what is the average cost for the two-day pass? What is the marginal cost of the second day pass?

✳ **9.** Suppose that you own a yard care business. You have your own mower, flatbed truck, and other equipment. You are also the primary employee. Why might you have trouble calculating your profits? (**Hint:** Think about the difference between accounting profits and economic profits.)

10. Use the information provided in the following table to fill in the blanks.

Output	Total fixed cost	Total variable cost	Total cost	Average fixed cost	Average variable cost	Average total cost	Marginal cost
0	$500	$0	$500	____	____	____	
1	500	200	____	____	____	____	____
2	____	____	800	____	____	____	____
3	____	____	875	____	____	____	____
4	____	____	925	____	____	____	$25
5	____	____		$100	____	____	____
6	____	450	____	____	____	____	____

11. If you are a fan of cold dessert treats, you'll recognize that the production process at Cold Stone Creamery differs a great deal from frozen yogurt places. At Cold Stone you give the server your order and the mix-ins you want, and the server creates your treat for you. This process is labor intensive. At a frozen yogurt place, you pick up a cup, choose your flavor from the self-serve machine, serve it yourself, and add in your own mix-ins. You put your creation on a scale and the worker then rings you up. This process is capital intensive. Given this information, which type of frozen dessert business will have the lower marginal cost of production?

✳ **12.** Watch the Reebok commercial on "Terry Tate, Office Linebacker" (www.youtube.com/watch?v=tbSpAsJSZPc). Is the firm that hires Terry Tate experiencing economies, constant returns, or diseconomies of scale? Explain your answer.

13. Take a look at the table in Problem 10. What is happening to the marginal cost as more and more units are produced? Can you think of an industry where this might be expected?

✳ **14.** All else equal, when the marginal product of labor is falling, the marginal cost of producing output
 a. is falling.
 b. is rising.
 c. could be rising or falling.

Solved Problems

4. The key to solving this problem is recognizing the direction of change in the average total cost. If the firm were to switch to a smaller plant, like B, its average total cost would rise to $9,500. Because the smaller plant would cost more, plant C is currently enjoying economies of scale. When we compare the average total cost of C ($9,000) to D ($8,800), it continues to fall. Because the average total cost is falling from B to D, we again know that the firm is experiencing economies of scale.

9. When calculating your costs for the mower, truck, and other expenses, you are computing your explicit costs. Subtracting the explicit costs from your total revenue will yield the accounting profit you have earned. However, you still do not know your economic profit because you haven't determined your implicit costs. Because you are the primary employee, you also have to add in the opportunity cost of the time you invest in the business. You may not know exactly what you might have earned doing something else, but you can be sure it exists—this is your implicit cost. Implicit costs are the reason you may have trouble computing your profits. You might show an accounting profit only to discover that what you thought you made was less than you could have made by doing something else. If that is the case, your true economic profit is actually negative.

12. Terry Tate enforces company policies and helps to reduce the amount of slacking, making the workforce more productive. However, at the same time, the company needs to hire Terry Tate to reduce slacking, and this is costly, which means that the company is experiencing diseconomies of scale.

14. When the marginal product of labor is falling, the marginal cost of production is rising, since each worker is becoming less productive and therefore each unit requires more labor to produce.

09

Firms in a Competitive Market

Why Do Firms Charge the Price They Do?

You want to send your mom flowers for Mother's Day, but when you check out the price of an arrangement from your favorite local florist, Diane's Flower Cottage, you have an attack of sticker shock. Why in the world are flowers so expensive?

Let's consider things from Diane's point of view, though. Growing flowers is labor intensive, since they must be carefully tended and then harvested by hand. Being highly perishable, they then have to be shipped rapidly, under refrigeration, to the point of sale. Diane has to charge enough to cover all the costs associated with getting the flowers to her shop. She then has to cover the expense of storing the flowers, again under refrigeration, and the spoilage loss of those that go unsold. Diane also has to pay the staff she relies on to market, design, and sell arrangements and deliver them on time. So while flower delivery might seem expensive to the consumer, Diane is just charging the market rate and can't go lower, due to her many behind-the-scenes costs. She might wish she could charge more, but since there are many florists, all of whom sell essentially the same services, competition drives prices down, which limits any one firm's ability to charge as much as it would like.

Such a lovely sight! But a lot of money probably went into this gorgeous display. These flowers may well have been grown in Colombia or Ecuador, the main foreign suppliers to the U.S. flower market. Getting them to the shop was not cheap.

In this chapter and the next four, we look in more detail at how markets work, the profits firms earn, and how market forces determine the price a firm can charge for its product or service. We begin our examination of *market structure*, or how individual firms are interconnected, by looking at the conditions necessary to create a competitive market. Although few real markets achieve the ideal market structure described in this chapter, this model provides a good starting point for understanding other market structures.

Our analysis of competitive markets shows that when competition is widespread, firms have little or no control over the price they can charge, and they make little or no economic profit. Thus, in competitive markets, firms are completely at the mercy of market forces that set the price. Let's find out why.

· BIG QUESTIONS ·

- How do competitive markets work?
- How do firms maximize profits?
- What does the supply curve look like in perfectly competitive markets?

How Do Competitive Markets Work?

Competitive markets exist when there are so many buyers and sellers that each one has only a small impact on the market price and output. Recall that in Chapter 3 we used the example of the Pike Place Market, where each fish vendor sells similar products. Because each fish vendor is small relative to the whole market, no single firm can influence the market price. It doesn't matter where you buy salmon because the price is the same or very similar at every fish stall. When buyers are willing to purchase a product anywhere, sellers have no control over the price they charge. These two characteristics—similar goods and many participants—create a highly competitive market where the price and quantity sold are determined by the market conditions rather than by any one firm.

In competitive markets, buyers can expect to find consistently low prices and a wide availability of the good they want. Firms that produce goods in competitive markets are known as price takers. A **price taker** has no control over the price set by the market. It "takes"—that is, accepts—the price determined by the overall supply and demand conditions that regulate the market. One of the reasons why firms are price takers is that each seller is small compared to the overall market. This means that any individual seller's decision (to either increase or decrease production) has no impact on the market price.

A **price taker** has no control over the price set by the market. It "takes" (accepts) the price determined from the overall supply and demand conditions that regulate the market.

Competitive markets have another important feature: new competitors can easily enter the market. If you want to open a copy shop, all you have to do is rent store space and several copy machines. There are no licensing or regulatory obstacles in your way. Likewise, there is very little to stop competitors from leaving the market. If you decide to shut down your business, you can lock the doors, return the equipment you rented, and move on to do something else. When barriers to entry into a marketplace are low, new firms are free to compete with existing businesses, which ensures the existence of competitive markets and low prices. Table 9.1 summarizes the characteristics of competitive markets.

Real-life examples of competitive markets usually fall short of perfection. Markets that are almost perfectly competitive, shown in Table 9.2, include the stock market, farmers' markets, online ticket auctions, and currency trading. Of all the market structures, perfect competition is the most beneficial to society because it creates the maximum combined consumer surplus and producer surplus (as we saw in Chapter 5). The more imperfectly competitive a market is, the lower is the total of the two types of surplus and the less beneficial it is to society overall.

In the next section, we examine the profits competitive firms make. After all, profits motivate firms to produce a product, so knowing how a business can make the most profit is central to understanding how competitive markets work.

TABLE 9.1
Characteristics of Competitive Markets

- Many sellers
- Similar products
- Free entry and exit
- Price taking
- Every firm is small

TABLE 9.2

Almost Perfect Markets

Example	How it works	Reality check
Stock market 	Millions of shares of stocks are traded every day on various stock exchanges, and generally the buyers and sellers have access to real-time information about prices. Because most of the traders represent only a small share of the market, they have little ability to influence the market price.	Because of the volume of shares that they control, large institutional investors, like Pacific Investment Management Company (PIMCO), manage billions of dollars in funds. As a result, they are big enough to influence the market price.
Farmers' markets 	In farmers' markets, sellers are able to set up at little or no cost. Many buyers are also present. The gathering of numerous buyers and sellers of similar products causes the market price for similar products to converge toward a single price.	Many produce markets do not have enough sellers to achieve a perfectly competitive result. With fewer vendors, individual sellers can often set their prices higher.
Online ticket auctions 	The resale market for tickets to major sporting events and concerts involves many buyers and sellers. The prices for seats in identical sections end up converging quickly toward a narrow range.	Some ticket companies and fans get special privileges that enable them to buy and sell blocks of tickets before others can enter the market.
Currency trading 	Hundreds of thousands of traders around the globe engage in currency buying and selling on any given day. Because all traders have very good real-time information, currency trades in different parts of the world converge toward the same price.	Currency markets are subject to intervention on the part of governments that want to strategically alter the prevailing price of their currency.

ECONOMICS IN THE REAL WORLD

AALSMEER FLOWER AUCTION

The world's largest flower auction takes place in Aalsmeer, a small town in the Netherlands. Each week, producers sell over 100 million flowers there. In fact, over one-third of all the flowers sold in the world pass through Aalsmeer. Because the Aalsmeer market serves thousands of buyers and sellers, it is one of the best examples of a competitive market you will ever find. The supply comes from approximately 6,000 growers worldwide. More than 2,000 buyers attend the auction to purchase flowers.

Aalsmeer uses a method known as a Dutch auction to determine the price for each crate of flowers sold. Most people think of an auction as a situation in which two or more individuals try to outbid each other. However, in Aalsmeer that process is reversed. As each crate of flowers goes on sale, the price on a huge board starts at 100 euros and then goes down until the lot is sold. This special kind of auction was invented here, and it is a very efficient way of getting the highest price out of the buyer who wants the lot the most.

At Aalsmeer, individual buyers and sellers are small compared with the overall size of the market. In addition, the flowers offered by one seller are almost indistinguishable from those offered by the other sellers. As a result, individual buyers and sellers have no control over the price set by the market.

The Aalsmeer flower market is almost perfectly competitive.

How Do Firms Maximize Profits?

All firms, whether they are active in a competitive market or not, attempt to maximize profits. Making a profit requires that a firm have a thorough grasp of its costs and revenues. In the previous chapter, we learned about the firm's cost structure. In this section, we examine its revenues. Combining the firm's revenues with its costs enables us to determine how much profit the firm makes.

Profits are a key goal of almost every firm, but they don't always materialize. Sometimes, firms experience losses instead of profits, so we also explore whether a firm should shut down or continue to operate in order to minimize its losses. Once we fully understand the firm's decision-making process, we

PRACTICE WHAT YOU KNOW

Price Takers: Mall Food Courts

Your instructor asks you to find an example of a competitive market nearby. Your friend suggests that you visit the food court at a nearby mall.

QUESTION: Does each restaurant in a food court meet the definition of a price taker, thereby signaling a competitive market?

ANSWER: Most food courts contain many sellers. Customers can choose among burgers, sandwiches, salads, pizza, and much more. Everywhere you turn, there is another place to eat and the prices at each place are comparable. Is this enough to make each restaurant a price taker? Not quite. Each restaurant has some market power because it serves different food, enabling the more popular places to charge somewhat more.

While the restaurants in the court are not price takers, the drinks (both fountain drinks and bottled water) that they sell are essentially the same. Any customer who is only interested in getting something to drink has a highly competitive market to choose from.

Are the restaurants in a food court price takers?

Competitive Markets

THE SIMPSONS: MR. PLOW

In this episode, Homer buys a snowplow and goes into the snow removal business. After a few false starts, his business, Mr. Plow, becomes a huge success. Every snowy morning, he looks out the window and comments about "white gold."

The episode illustrates each of the factors that go into making a competitive market. Businesses providing snow removal all offer the same service. Because there are many buyers (homeowners) and many businesses (the "plow people"), the market is competitive.

However, Homer's joy, profits, and notoriety are short-lived. Soon his friend Barney buys a bigger plow and joins the ranks of the "plow people." Barney's entry into the business shows how easy it is for competitors to enter the market. Then Homer, who has begun to get lazy and rest on his success, wakes up late one snowy morning to find all the driveways in

Homer's great idea is about to melt away.

the neighborhood already plowed. A nasty battle over customers ensues.

When firms can easily enter the market, any positive economic profit a firm enjoys in the short run will dissipate in the long run, due to increased competition. As a result, we can say that this *Simpsons* episode shows a market that is not just competitive; it is perfectly competitive.

will better comprehend how the entire market functions. To make this process easier, throughout this section we refer to Mr. Plow (from the *Simpsons* episode mentioned in the Economics in the Media box above) to examine the choices every business must make. We look at the price Mr. Plow (Homer Simpson) charges and how many driveways he clears, and then we compare his revenues to his costs to determine whether he is maximizing his profit.

The Profit-Maximizing Rule

Let's imagine how much revenue Mr. Plow will make if the competitive price is $10 for each driveway he clears. Table 9.3 shows how much profit he might make if he clears up to 10 driveways. As we learned in Chapter 8, total profit (column 4) is determined by taking the total revenue (column 2) and subtracting the total cost (column 3). Mr. Plow's profits start out at −$25 because even if he does not clear any driveways, he incurs a fixed cost of $25 to rent a snow plow each day. To recover the fixed cost, he needs to generate revenue by clearing driveways. As Mr. Plow clears more driveways, the losses (the negative numbers) shown in column 4 gradually contract; he begins to earn a profit by the time he plows 6 driveways.

What does Table 9.3 tell us about Mr. Plow's business? Column 4 shows the company's profits (π) at various output (Q) levels. Profit reaches a maximum of $10 at 8 driveways. From looking at this table, you might suppose that the firm can make a production decision based on the data in the profit column. However, firms don't work this way. The total profit (or loss) is typically determined after the fact. For example, Homer may have to fill up with gas at the end of the day, buy new tires for his plow, or purchase liability insurance. His accountant will take his receipts and deduct each expense to determine his accounting profit. This process takes time. An accurate understanding of Homer's profits may have to wait until the end of the quarter, or even the year, in order to fully account for all the irregular expenses associated with running a business. This means that the information found in the profit column is not available until long after the business decisions have been made. So, in day-to-day operations, the firm needs another way to make production decisions.

The key to determining Mr. Plow's profits comes from understanding the relationship between marginal revenue (column 5) and marginal cost (column 6). The **marginal revenue** is the change (Δ) in total revenue when the firm produces one additional unit of output. So, looking down column 5, we see that for every driveway Mr. Plow clears, he makes $10 in extra revenue. The marginal cost (column 6) is the change (Δ) in total cost when the firm produces one additional unit. Column 7 calculates the difference between the marginal revenue (column 5) and marginal cost (column 6).

Marginal thinking

Marginal revenue is the change in total revenue a firm receives when it produces one additional unit of output.

TABLE 9.3

Calculating Profits for Mr. Plow

(1) Quantity (Q = driveways cleared)	(2) Total revenue	(3) Total cost	(4) Total profit	(5) Marginal revenue	(6) Marginal cost	(7) Change (Δ) in profit
Abbreviation:	TR	TC	π	MR	MC	$\Delta\pi$
Formula:	P × Q		TR − TC	ΔTR	ΔTC	MR − MC
0	$0	$25	−$25			
				$10	$9	$1
1	10	34	−24			
				10	7	3
2	20	41	−21			
				10	5	5
3	30	46	−16			
				10	3	7
4	40	49	−9			
				10	2	8
5	50	51	−1			
				10	3	7
6	60	54	6			
				10	7	3
7	70	61	9			
				10	9	1
8	80	70	**10**			
				10	25	−15
9	90	95	−5			
				10	50	−40
10	100	145	−45			

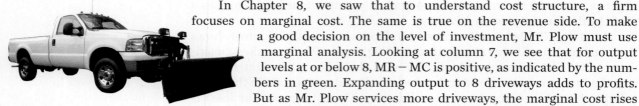

If you already own a truck and a plow, starting your own snow-plow business is inexpensive.

Marginal thinking

The **profit-maximizing rule** states that profit maximization occurs when a firm chooses the quantity of output that equates marginal revenue and marginal cost, or MR = MC.

In Chapter 8, we saw that to understand cost structure, a firm focuses on marginal cost. The same is true on the revenue side. To make a good decision on the level of investment, Mr. Plow must use marginal analysis. Looking at column 7, we see that for output levels at or below 8, MR − MC is positive, as indicated by the numbers in green. Expanding output to 8 driveways adds to profits. But as Mr. Plow services more driveways, the marginal cost rises dramatically. For instance, Mr. Plow may have to seek driveways farther away and thus incur higher transportation costs for those additional customers. Whatever the cause, increased marginal cost (column 6) eventually overtakes the constant marginal revenue (column 5), causing MR − MC to go negative (shown in red in column 7).

Recall that we began our discussion by saying that a firm can't wait for the yearly, or even quarterly, profit statements to make production decisions. By examining the marginal impact, shown in column 7, a firm can make good day-to-day operational decisions. Each time it snows, Mr. Plow has to decide whether or not to clear more driveways. For instance, if he is plowing 4 driveways, he may decide to work a little harder the next time it snows and plow one more. At 5 driveways, his profits increase by $8. Since he enjoys making this extra money, he could expand again from 5 to 6 driveways. This time, he makes an extra $7 in profit. From 6 to 7 driveways, he earns $3 more in profit, and from 7 to 8 driveways he earns $1 in profit. However, when Mr. Plow expands beyond 8 driveways, he discovers that at 9 driveways he loses $15. This loss would cause him to scale back his efforts to a more profitable level of output.

Marginal thinking helps Mr. Plow discover the production level at which his profits are maximized. The **profit-maximizing rule** states that profit maximization occurs when a firm expands output as long as marginal revenue is greater than marginal cost, stopping as close to MR = MC as practical. According to the MR = MC rule, production should stop at the point at which profit opportunities no longer exist. In the case of Mr. Plow, he should stop adding new driveways once he reaches 8.

Deciding How Much to Produce in a Competitive Market

We have observed that a firm in a highly competitive market is a price taker; it has no control over the price set by the market. Because all snow removal companies provide the same service, they must charge the price determined by the overall supply and demand conditions that regulate that particular market.

To better understand these relationships, we can look at them visually. In Figure 9.1, we use the MR and MC data from Table 9.3 to illustrate the profit calculation. For reference, we also include the average total cost curve. Recall from Chapter 8 that the marginal cost curve (MC, shown in orange) always crosses the average total cost curve (ATC) at the lowest point. Figure 9.1 illustrates the relationship between the marginal cost curve (MC) and the marginal revenue curve (MR). Because the price (P) Mr. Plow charges is constant at $10, marginal revenue is horizontal. Unlike MR, MC at first decreases and then rises due to diminishing marginal product. Therefore, the firm wants to expand production as long as MR is greater than MC, and it will stop production at the quantity where MR = MC = $10. When

FIGURE 9.1

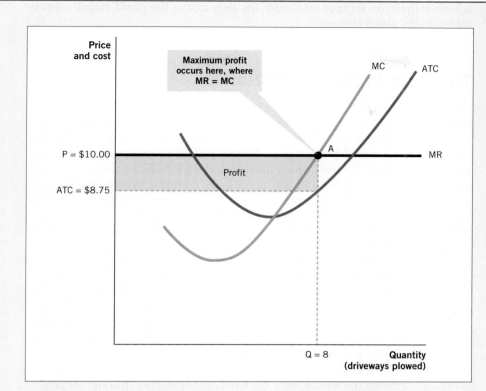

Price and cost

Maximum profit occurs here, where MR = MC

MC

ATC

P = $10.00

A

MR

Profit

ATC = $8.75

Q = 8

Quantity
(driveways plowed)

Mr. Plow uses the profit-maximizing rule to locate the point at which marginal revenue equals marginal cost, or MR = MC. This point determines the ideal output level, Q. The firm takes the price from the market; price is shown as the horizontal MR curve at P = $10.00. Because the price charged is higher than the average total cost curve along the dashed line at quantity Q, the firm makes the economic profit shown in the green rectangle.

$Q = 8$, MR = MC and profits are maximized. At quantities beyond 8, the MC curve is above the MR curve. Marginal cost is higher than marginal revenue, and the firm's profits fall.

Note that we can use the profit-maximizing rule, MR = MC, to identify the most profitable output in a two-step process:

1. Locate the point at which the firm will maximize its profits: MR = MC. This is the point labeled A in Figure 9.1.

2. Look for the profit-maximizing output: move down the vertical dashed line to the *x* axis at point Q. Any quantity greater than or less than Q would result in lower profits.

Once we know the profit-maximizing quantity, we can determine the average cost of producing Q units. From Q, we move up along the dashed line until it intersects with the ATC curve. From that point, we move horizontally until we come to the *y* axis. Doing so tells us the average cost of making 8 units. Because the total cost in Table 9.3 is $70 when 8 driveways are plowed, dividing 70 by 8 gives us $8.75 for the average total cost. We can calculate Mr. Plow's profit rectangle from Figure 9.1 as follows:

$$\text{profit} = (\text{price} - \text{ATC [along the dashed line at quantity Q]}) \times Q$$

This equation gives us $(10 - 8.75) \times 8 = \$10$, which is the profit we see in Table 9.3, column 4, in red. Because the MR is the price, and because the price is higher than the average total cost, the firm makes the profit visually represented in the green rectangle.

The Firm in the Short Run

Deciding how much to produce in order to maximize profits is the goal of every business in a competitive market. However, there are times when it is not possible to make a profit. When revenue is insufficient to cover cost, the firm suffers a loss—at which point it must decide whether to operate or temporarily shut down. Successful businesses make this decision all the time. For example, retail stores often close by 9 p.m. because operating overnight would not generate enough revenue to cover the costs of remaining open. Or consider the Ice Cream Float, which crisscrosses Smith Mountain Lake in Virginia during the summer months. You can hear the music announcing its arrival at the public beach from over a mile away. By the time the float arrives, there is usually a long line of eager customers waiting for the float to dock. This is a very profitable business on hot and sunny summer days. However, during the late spring and early fall, the float operates on weekends only. Eventually, colder weather forces the business to shut down until the crowds return the following season. This shutdown decision is a short-run calculation. If the float were to operate during the winter, it would need to pay for employees and fuel. Incurring these variable costs when there are so few customers would result in greater total costs than simply dry-docking the boat. When the float is dry-docked over the winter, only the fixed cost of storing the boat remains.

Fortunately, a firm can use a simple, intuitive rule to decide whether to operate or shut down in the short run: if the firm would lose less by shutting down than by staying open, it should shut down. Recall that costs are broken into two parts—fixed and variable. Fixed costs must be paid whether the business is open or not. Because variable costs are incurred only when the business is open, if it can make enough to cover its variable costs—for example, employee wages and the cost of the electricity needed to run the lighting—it will choose to remain open. Once the variable costs are covered, any extra money goes toward paying the fixed costs.

A business should operate if it can cover its variable costs, and it should shut down if it cannot. Figure 9.2 illustrates the decision using cost curves. As long as the firm's marginal revenue curve (MR) is greater than the minimum point on the average variable cost curve (AVC)—the green and yellow areas—the firm will choose to operate. (Note that the MR curve is not shown in Figure 9.2. The shaded areas in the figure denote the range of potential MR curves that are profitable and those that cause a loss.) Recalling our example of the Ice Cream Float, you can think of the green area as the months during the summer when the business makes a profit and the yellow area as the times during spring and fall when the float operates even though it is incurring a loss (because the loss is less than if the float were to shut down entirely). Finally, if the MR curve falls below the AVC curve—the red area—the firm should shut down. Table 9.4 summarizes these decisions.

The Ice Cream Float, a cool idea on a hot day at the lake.

FIGURE 9.2

When to Operate and When to Shut Down

If the MR (marginal revenue) curve is above the minimum point on the ATC (average total cost) curve, the Ice Cream Float will make a profit (shown in green). If the MR curve is below the minimum point on the ATC curve ($2.50) but above the minimum point on the AVC (average variable cost) curve ($2.00), the float will operate at a loss (shown in yellow). If the MR curve is below the minimum point on the AVC curve ($2.00), the float will temporarily shut down (shown in red).

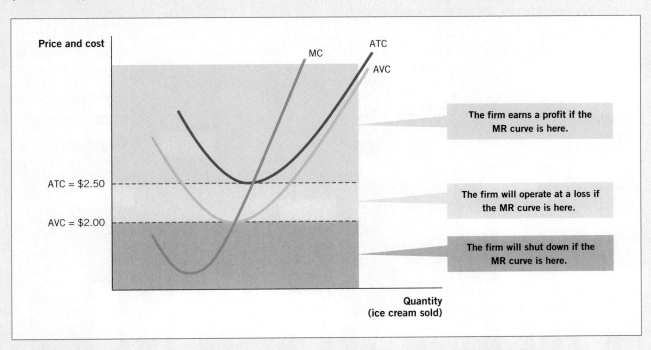

The firm earns a profit if the MR curve is here.

The firm will operate at a loss if the MR curve is here.

The firm will shut down if the MR curve is here.

TABLE 9.4

Profit and Loss in the Short Run

Condition	In words	Outcome
P > ATC	The price is greater than the average total cost of production.	The firm makes a profit.
ATC > P > AVC	The average total cost of production is greater than the price the firm charges, but the price is greater than the average variable cost of production.	The firm will operate to minimize loss.
AVC > P	The price is less than the average variable cost of production.	The firm will temporarily shut down.

Sunk Costs: If You Build It, They Will Come

Replacing an old stadium with a new one is sometimes controversial. People often misunderstand sunk costs and argue for continuing with a stadium until it's completely worn down. But economics tells us not to focus on the sunk costs of the old stadium's construction. Instead, we should compare the marginal benefit of a new stadium to the marginal cost of demolition and new construction.

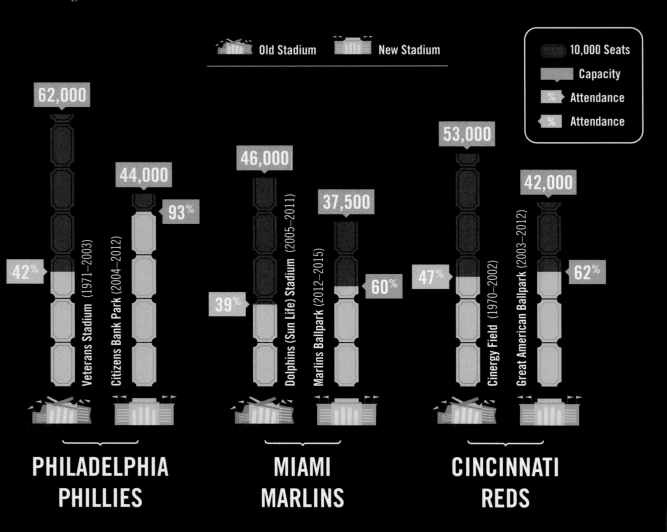

Old Stadium **New Stadium**

10,000 Seats
Capacity
% Attendance
% Attendance

62,000
42%
Veterans Stadium (1971–2003)

44,000
93%
Citizens Bank Park (2004–2012)

PHILADELPHIA PHILLIES

46,000
39%
Dolphins (Sun Life) Stadium (2005–2011)

37,500
60%
Marlins Ballpark (2012–2015)

MIAMI MARLINS

53,000
47%
Cinergy Field (1970–2002)

42,000
62%
Great American Ballpark (2003–2012)

CINCINNATI REDS

The three new stadiums shown are considered successes. Higher attendance (especially in Philadelphia) and higher revenue per ticket—thanks to luxury boxes and better concessions—make the franchises happy.

An economist's analysis of the stadiums would go beyond attendance, however. The additional revenue generated by the new stadiums must be weighed against the costs of imploding the old stadiums and building new venues.

REVIEW QUESTIONS

- What effect do you think the reduced seating capacities of the new stadiums has on ticket prices, and why?

- Use the idea of sunk costs to analyze switching majors in college.

To make the shutdown decision more concrete, imagine that the Ice Cream Float's minimum ATC (average total cost) is $2.50 and its minimum AVC is $2.00. During the summer, when many customers line up on the dock waiting for it to arrive, it can charge more than $2.50 and earn a substantial profit. However, as the weather cools, fewer people want ice cream. The Ice Cream Float still has to crisscross the lake to make sales, burning expensive gasoline and paying employees to operate the vessel. If the Ice Cream Float is to keep its revenues high, it needs customers; but cooler weather suppresses demand. If the Ice Cream Float charges $2.25 in the fall, it can make enough to cover its average variable cost of $2.00, but not enough to cover its average total cost of $2.50. Nevertheless, it will continue to operate because it makes enough in the yellow region to pay part of its fixed cost. Finally, it reaches a point at which the price drops below $2.00. Now the business is no longer able to cover its average variable cost. At this point, it shuts down for the winter. It does this because operating when MR is very low causes the business to incur a larger loss.

The Firm's Short-Run Supply Curve

Cost curves provide a detailed picture of a firm's willingness to supply a good or service. We have seen that when the MR curve is below the minimum point on the AVC curve, the firm shuts down and production, or output, falls to zero. In other words, when revenues are too low, no supply is produced. For example, during the winter, the Ice Cream Float is dry-docked, so the supply curve does not exist. However, when the firm is operating, it bases its output decisions on the marginal cost. Recall that the firm uses the profit-maximizing rule, or MR = MC, to determine how much to produce. The marginal cost curve is therefore the firm's short-run supply curve as long as the firm is operating.

Marginal thinking

Figure 9.3 shows the Ice Cream Float's short-run supply curve. In the short run, diminishing marginal product causes the firm's costs to rise as the quantity produced increases. This is reflected in the shape of the firm's short-run supply curve, shown in orange. The supply curve is upward sloping above the minimum point on the AVC curve. Below the minimum point on the AVC curve, the short-run supply curve is vertical at a quantity of zero, indicating that a willingness to supply the good does not exist below a price of $2.00. At prices above $2.00, the firm will offer more for sale as the price increases.

Sunk Costs

Unrecoverable costs that have been incurred as a result of past decisions are known as **sunk costs**. For example, the decision to build a new sports stadium is a good application of the principle of sunk costs. Many professional stadiums have been built in the past few years, even though the arenas they replaced were built to last much longer. For example, Three Rivers Stadium in Pittsburgh and Veterans Stadium in Philadelphia were built in the early 1970s as multiuse facilities for both football and baseball, each with an expected life span of 60 or more years. However, in the 2000s, both were replaced. Each city built two new stadiums with features such as luxury boxes and better seats that generate more revenue than Veterans and Three Rivers did. The additional revenue makes the

Sunk costs
are unrecoverable costs that have been incurred as a result of past decisions.

FIGURE 9.3

The Firm's Short-Run Supply Curve

The short-run supply curve (S_{SR}) and marginal cost curve (MC) are equivalent when the price is above the minimum point on the average variable cost curve (AVC). Below that point, the firm shuts down and no supply exists.

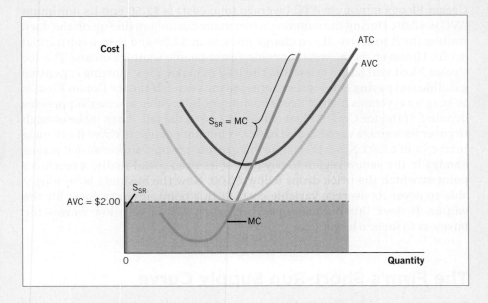

Opportunity costs can lead to stadium implosions.

Opportunity cost

new stadiums financially attractive even though the old stadiums were still structurally sound.

Demolishing a structure that is still in good working order may sound like a waste, but it can be good economics. When the extra benefit of a new stadium is large enough to pay for the cost of imploding the old stadium and constructing a new one, a city will do just that. In fact, because Pittsburgh and Philadelphia draw significantly more paying spectators with the new stadiums, the decision to replace the older stadiums has made the citizens in both cities better off. The new stadiums have created increased ticket sales, higher tax revenues, and a more enjoyable experience for fans.

Continuing to use an out-of-date facility has an opportunity cost. Those who do not understand sunk costs might point to the benefits of getting maximum use out of what already exists. But good economists learn to ignore sunk costs and focus on marginal value. They compare marginal benefits and marginal costs. If a new stadium and the revenue it brings in will create more value than the old stadium, the decision should be to tear the old one down.

The Firm's Long-Run Supply Curve

In the long run, a competitive firm's output decision is directly tied to profits. Because the firm is flexible in the long run, all costs are variable. As a result, the firm's long-run supply curve exists only when the firm expects to cover its total

The Profit-Maximizing Rule: Show Me the Money!

Here is a question that often confuses students.

QUESTION: At what point does a firm maximize profits: where the profit per additional unit is greatest, or where marginal revenue equals marginal cost?

ANSWER: Each answer sounds plausible, so the key is to think about each one in a concrete way. To help do that, we will refer back to the Mr. Plow data in Table 9.3. Making a large profit per unit sounds great. However, if the firm stops production when the profit per unit peaks—at $8 in column 7—it will fail to realize the additional profits, namely $7, then $3, and then $1 in column 7, that come from continuing to produce until MR = MC. The correct answer is where marginal revenue equals marginal cost. A firm maximizes profits where MR = MC, because at this point all profitable opportunities are exhausted. If Mr. Plow clears 8 driveways, his profit on the additional driveway is $1. If he clears 9 driveways, his profit on the additional driveway is −$15, because the marginal cost of clearing that ninth driveway, $25, is greater than the $10 he earns in marginal revenue.

What is the rule for making the most profit?

costs of production (because otherwise the firm would go out of business— that is, exit the market).

Returning to the Ice Cream Float example, recall that the boat shuts down over the winter instead of going out of business because demand is low but is expected to return. If for some reason the crowds do not come back, the float would go out of business. Turning to Figure 9.4, we see that at any point below the minimum point, $2.50, on the ATC curve, the float will experience a loss. Because firms are free to enter or exit the market in the long run, no firm will willingly produce in the market if the price is less than average total cost (P < ATC). As a result, no supply exists below $2.50. However, if price is greater than average total cost (P > ATC), the float expects to make a profit and thus will continue to produce.

The firm's long-run supply curve, shown in Figure 9.4 in orange, is upward sloping above the minimum point on the ATC curve, which is denoted by ATC on the y axis. The supply curve is vertical at a quantity of zero, indicating that a willingness to supply the good does not exist below a price of $2.50. In the long run, a firm that expects price to exceed ATC will continue to operate, because the conditions for making a profit seem favorable. In contrast, a firm that does not expect price to exceed ATC should cut its losses and exit the market. Table 9.5 outlines the long-run decision criteria.

So far, we have examined the firm's decision-making process in the short run in the context of revenue versus cost, which has enabled us to determine the profit each firm makes. However, a single firm represents only a small part of the overall supply in a competitive market. In the next section, we develop the short-run and long-run market supply curves.

FIGURE 9.4

The Firm's Long-Run Supply Curve

The long-run supply curve (S_{LR}) and marginal cost curve (MC) are equivalent when the price is above the minimum point on the average total cost curve (ATC). Below that point, the firm shuts down and no supply exists.

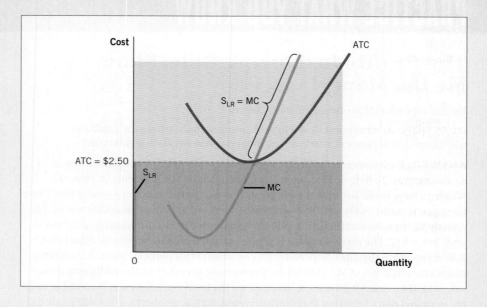

TABLE 9.5

The Long-Run Shutdown Criteria

Condition	In words	Outcome
P > ATC	The price is greater than the average total cost of production.	The firm makes a profit.
P < ATC	The price is less than the average total cost of production.	The firm should shut down.

ECONOMICS IN THE REAL WORLD

TOYS "R" US, CHANGES IN TECHNOLOGY, AND THE DYNAMIC NATURE OF CHANGE

What happens if your customers do not return? What if you simply had a bad idea to begin with, and the customers never arrived in the first place?

When the long-run profit outlook is bleak, the firm is better off shutting down. This is a normal part of the ebb and flow of business in a market economy. For example, once there were thousands of buggy whip companies. Today, as technology has improved and we no longer rely on horse-drawn carriages, few buggy whip makers remain. However, many companies now manufacture automobile parts.

Similarly, a succession of technological advances has transformed the music industry. Records were replaced by 8-track tapes, and then by cassettes and CDs. After that came iPods, MP3 players, and smartphones to help make music more portable. Websites and apps such as Pandora, Spotify, and the Apple music service allow streaming of almost any selection a listener wants to hear. However, there was a time when innovation meant playing music on the original Sony Walkman. What was cool in the early 1980s is antiquated today. Any business engaged in distributing music has had to adapt or shut down.

Similar changes are taking place in the toy industry. Toys "R" Us was founded in 1948 and experienced explosive growth. It was the nation's largest toy store seller until Walmart claimed that spot in 1998. By the early 2010s, Toys "R" Us faced stiff competition not only from large traditional retailers like Walmart but also from online vendors like Amazon. The last year Toys "R" Us made a profit was 2013. Eventually the firm filed for bankruptcy, and it closed its remaining stores in 2018.

In addition to changes in technology, other factors such as downturns in the economy, changes in tastes, demographic factors, and migration can all force businesses to close. These examples remind us that the long-run decision to go out of business has nothing to do with the short-term profit outlook.

Toys "R" Us once had over 1,600 stores worldwide.

What Does the Supply Curve Look Like in Perfectly Competitive Markets?

We have seen that a firm's willingness to supply a good or service depends on whether the firm is making a short-run or long-run decision. In the short run, a firm may choose to operate at a loss to recover a portion of its fixed costs. In the long run, there are no fixed costs, so a firm is willing to operate only if it expects the price it charges to cover total costs.

However, the supply curve for a single firm represents only a small part of the overall supply in a competitive market. We now turn to market supply and develop the short-run and long-run market supply curves.

The Short-Run Market Supply Curve

A competitive market consists of a large number of identical sellers. Because an individual firm's supply curve is equal to its marginal cost curve, if we add together all the individual supply curves in a market, we arrive at the short-run market supply curve. Figure 9.5 shows the short-run market supply curve in a two-firm model consisting of Mr. Plow and the Plow King. At a price of $10, Mr. Plow is willing to clear 8 driveways (Q_A) and the Plow King is willing to clear 20 driveways (Q_B). When we sum the output of the two firms, we get a total market supply of 28 driveways (Q_{market}), seen in the third graph.

The Long-Run Market Supply Curve

Recall that a competitive market is one in which a large number of buyers seek a product many sellers offer. Competitive markets are also characterized by easy entry and exit. Existing firms and entrepreneurs decide whether to enter and exit a market based on incentives. When existing firms are enjoying profits,

FIGURE 9.5

Short-Run Market Supply

The market supply is determined by summing the individual supplies of all the firms in the market. Although we have only shown this process for two firms, Mr. Plow and Plow King, the process extends to any number of firms in a market.

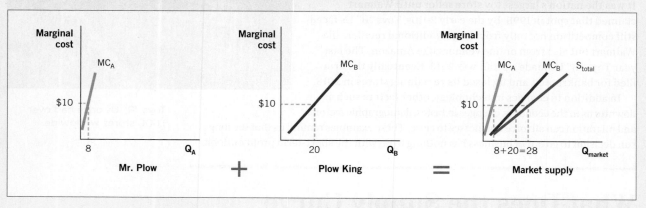

Incentives

The **signals** of profits and losses convey information about the profitability of various markets.

there is an incentive for them to produce more and also for entrepreneurs to enter the market. The result is an increase in the quantity of the good supplied. Likewise, when existing firms are experiencing losses, there is an incentive for them to exit the market; then the quantity supplied decreases.

Entry and exit have the combined effect of regulating the amount of profit a firm can hope to make in the long run. As long as profits exist, the quantity supplied will increase because existing firms expand production or other firms enter the market. When losses exist, the quantity supplied will decrease because existing firms reduce production or other firms exit the market. So both profits and losses signal a need for an adjustment in market supply. In other words, profits and losses act as signals for resources to enter or leave a market. **Signals** convey information about the profitability of various markets.

The only time an adjustment does not take place is when participants in the market make zero economic profit. In that case, the market is in long-run equilibrium. Existing firms and entrepreneurs are not inclined to enter or exit the market; the adjustment process that occurs through price changes ends.

The benefit of a competitive market is that profits guide existing firms and entrepreneurs to produce more goods and services that society values. Losses encourage firms to exit and move elsewhere. Without profits and losses acting as signals for firms to enter or exit the market, resources will be misallocated and surpluses and shortages will occur.

Figure 9.6 captures how entry and exit determine the market supply. The profit-maximizing point of the individual firm in panel (a), MR = MC, is located at the minimum point on the ATC curve. The price (P = min. ATC) that existing firms receive is just enough to cover costs, so profits are zero. As a result, new firms have no incentive to enter the market and existing firms have no reason to leave. At all prices above P = min. ATC, firms will earn a profit (the green

FIGURE 9.6

The Long-Run Market Supply Curve and Entry and Exit

Entry into the market and exit from it force the long-run price to be equal to the minimum point on the average total cost curve (ATC). At all prices above P = min. ATC, firms will earn a profit (the green area), and at all prices below P = min. ATC, firms will experience a loss (the red area). For this reason, the long-run supply curve (S_{LR}) must be horizontal at price P = min. ATC. If the price was any higher or lower, firms would enter or exit the market, and the market could not be in a long-run equilibrium.

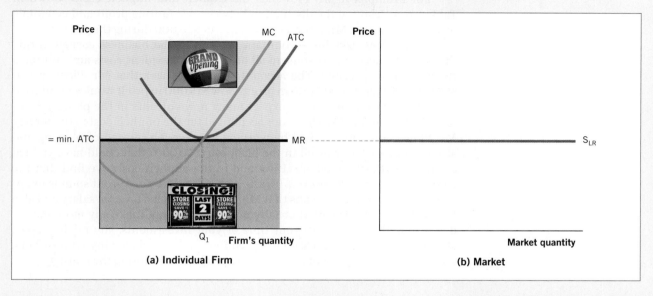

(a) Individual Firm

(b) Market

area), and at all prices below P = min. ATC, firms will experience a loss (the red area). This picture is consistent for all markets with free entry and exit; zero economic profit occurs at only one price, and that price is the lowest point of the ATC curve.

At this price, the supply curve in panel (b) must be a horizontal line at P = min. ATC. If the price were any higher, firms would enter, supply would increase, and price would be forced back down to P = min. ATC. If the price were any lower, firms would exit, supply would decrease, and price would be forced up to P = min. ATC. Because we know that these adjustments will have time to take place in the long run, the long-run supply curve must also be equal to P = min. ATC to satisfy the demand that exists at this price.

A REMINDER ABOUT ECONOMIC PROFIT Now that you have learned how perfect competition affects business profits in the long run, you may not think that a competitive market is a desirable environment for businesses seeking to earn profits. After all, if a firm cannot expect to make an economic profit in the long run, why bother? It's easy to forget the distinction between accounting profit and economic profit. Firms enter a market when they expect to be reasonably compensated for their investment. And they leave a market

Opportunity cost

when the investment does not yield a satisfactory result. Economic profit is determined by deducting the explicit and implicit costs from total revenue. The remaining examples (graphs) in this chapter focus on our benchmark, economic profit. Therefore, firms are willing to stay in perfectly competitive markets in the long run when they are breaking even because they are being reasonably compensated for the explicit expenses they have incurred and also for the implicit expenses—like the opportunity costs of other business ventures—they would expect to incur elsewhere.

For example, if Mr. Plow has the explicit and implicit costs shown in Table 9.6, we can see the distinction between accounting profit and economic profit more clearly. Mr. Plow has a revenue of $25,000 during the year.

If Mr. Plow asks his accountant how much the business earned during the year, the accountant adds up all of Mr. Plow's explicit costs and subtracts them from his revenue. The accountant reports back that Mr. Plow earned $25,000 − $10,000, or $15,000 in profit. Now $15,000 in profit would sound good to a lot of firms, so we would expect many new entrants in the plowing business. But not so fast! We have not accounted for the implicit costs—the money Mr. Plow could have earned by working another job instead of plowing and also the money he invested in the business ($50,000) that could have yielded a return ($5,000) elsewhere. If we add in the implicit costs, we find that the economic profit is $25,000 − $10,000 − $15,000 = $0. Zero profit sounds unappealing, but it is not. It means that Mr. Plow covered his forgone salary and also his next-best investment alternative. If you could not make any more money doing something else with your time or your investments, you might as well stay in the same place. So Mr. Plow is content to keep on plowing, while others, outside the market, do not see any likely profit from entering the market.

How the Market Adjusts in the Long Run: An Example

We have seen that profits and losses may exist in the short run; in the long run, the best the competitive firm can do is earn zero economic profit. This section looks in more detail at the adjustment process that leads to long-run equilibrium.

TABLE 9.6

Mr. Plow's Economic Profit and the Entry or Exit Decision

Explicit costs per year	
Payment on the loan on his snowplow	$7,000
Gasoline	2,000
Miscellaneous equipment (shovels, salt)	1,000
Implicit costs	
Forgone salary	$10,000
The forgone income that the $50,000 invested in the business could have earned if invested elsewhere	5,000
Total cost	$25,000

FIGURE 9.7

A Competitive Market in Long-Run Equilibrium

When a market is in long-run equilibrium, the short-run supply curve (S_{SR}) and short-run demand curve (D_{SR}) intersect along the long-run supply curve (S_{LR}). At this point, the price the firm charges is equal to the minimum point along the average total cost curve (ATC). The existing firms in the market earn zero economic profit, and there is no incentive for firms to enter or exit the market.

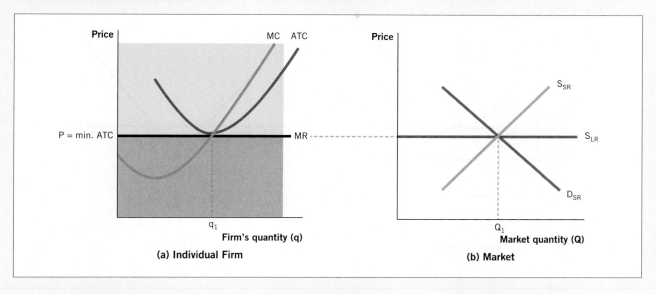

(a) Individual Firm

(b) Market

We begin with the market in long-run equilibrium, shown in Figure 9.7. Panel (a) represents an individual firm operating at the minimum point on its ATC curve. In long-run equilibrium, all firms are operating as efficiently as possible. Because the price is equal to the average cost of production, economic profit for the firm is zero. In panel (b), the short-run supply curve (S_{SR}) and the short-run demand curve (D_{SR}) intersect along the long-run supply curve (S_{LR}), so the market is also in equilibrium. But if the short-run supply curve and demand curve happened to intersect above the long-run supply curve, then the price would be higher than the minimum point on the ATC curve. The result would be short-run profits, indicating that the market is not in long-run equilibrium. And if the short-run supply curve and demand curve intersected below the long-run supply curve, then the price would be lower than the minimum point on the ATC curve. In that case, the result would be short-run losses.

Now suppose that demand declines, as shown in Figure 9.8. In panel (b), we see that the market demand curve shifts from D_1 to D_2. When demand falls, the equilibrium point moves from point A to point B. The price drops to P_2 and the market output drops to Q_2. The firms in this market take their price from the market, so the new marginal revenue curve shifts down from MR_1 to MR_2 at P_2 in panel (a). Because the firm maximizes profits where $MR = MC$, the firm will produce an output of q_2. When the output is q_2 the firm's costs, C_2, are higher than the price it charges, P_2, so it experiences a loss equal to the red area

FIGURE 9.8

The Short-Run Adjustment to a Decrease in Demand

A decrease in demand causes the price to fall in the market, as shown by the movement from D_1 to D_2 in panel (b). Because the firm is a price taker, the price it can charge falls to P_2. As we see in panel (a), the intersection of MR_2 and MC occurs at q_2. At this output level, the firm incurs the short-run loss shown by the red area in (a).

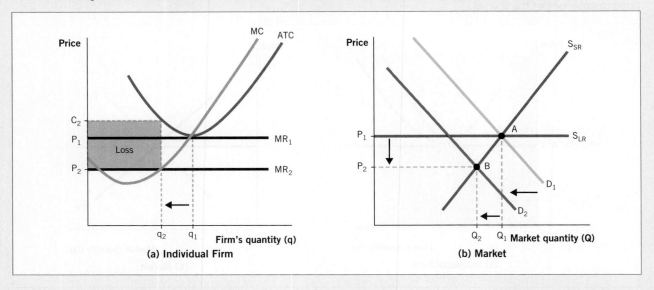

(a) Individual Firm

(b) Market

What does it take to produce more mangoes?

in panel (a). In addition, because the firm's output is lower, it is no longer producing at the minimum point on its ATC curve, so the firm is not as efficient as before.

Firms in a competitive market can exit the market easily. Some will do so to avoid further losses. Figure 9.9 continues the example from Figure 9.8. It shows that as firms exit, the market supply contracts from S_{SR1} to S_{SR2} and the market equilibrium moves from point B to point C. At point C, the price rises back to P_1 and the market output drops to Q_3. The firms that remain in the market no longer experience a short-run loss, because MR_2 returns to MR_1 and costs fall from C_2 to C_1. The end result is that the firm is once again efficient, and economic profit returns to zero.

For example, suppose there is a decline in demand for mangoes due to a false rumor that links the fruit to a salmonella outbreak. The decline in demand causes the price of mangoes to drop. As a consequence, mango producers experience negative economic profit—generating curves like the ones shown in Figure 9.8. In response to the negative profit, some mango growers will exit the market, the mango trees will be sold for firewood, and the land will be converted to other uses. With fewer mangoes being produced, the supply will contract. Eventually, the smaller supply will cause the price of mangoes to rise until a new long-run equilibrium is reached at a much lower level of output, as shown in Figure 9.9.

FIGURE 9.9

The Long-Run Adjustment to a Decrease in Demand

Short-run losses cause some firms to exit the market. Their exit shifts the market supply curve to the left in panel (b) until the price returns to long-run equilibrium at point C. Price is restored to P_1 and the MR_2 curve in panel (a) shifts up to MR_1. At P_1 the firm is once again earning zero economic profit.

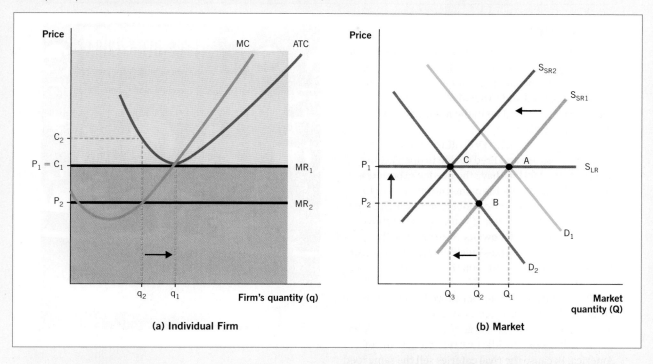

(a) Individual Firm

(b) Market

MORE ON THE LONG-RUN SUPPLY CURVE To keep the previous example as simple as possible, we assumed that the long-run supply curve was horizontal. However, this is not always the case. There are two reasons why the long-run supply curve may slope upward. First, some resources needed to produce the product may only be available in limited supplies. As firms try to expand production, they must bid to acquire those resources—a move that causes the average total cost curve to rise. For instance, a mango grower who wants to plant more trees must acquire more land. Because mangoes grow in tropical areas with warm, wet summers, not all land is perfectly suited to growing them. The limited supply of land will cause the price of producing more mangoes to rise, which will cause the supply curve to be positively sloped.

A second reason the long-run supply curve may be upward sloping is the opportunity cost of the labor used in producing the good. If you want to produce more mangoes, you will need more workers to pick the fruit. Hiring extra workers will mean finding people who are both willing and capable. Some workers are better than others at picking mangoes, and some workers have higher opportunity costs. As your firm attempts to expand production, it must increase

Opportunity cost

Entry and Exit

I LOVE LUCY

In the 1950s, the most-watched comedy on TV was *I Love Lucy*. The show features Lucy Ricardo and her singer-bandleader husband, Ricky, and their best friends, Fred and Ethel Mertz. The two couples regularly end up in the most unlikely situations together.

One episode finds Ricky disillusioned with show business. He and Fred decide to open a diner together. The Mertzes have the needed experience, and Ricky plans to use his name and star power to attract customers to the establishment, which they name A Little Bit of Cuba. If you've seen the show, you know that disaster awaits. Sure enough, the Ricardos and the Mertzes quickly start bickering over the division of labor, and soon the two couples decide to part ways.

The trouble is, neither can afford to buy out the other. So they decide to split the diner down the middle! On one side, guests go to A Little Bit of Cuba. On the other side, the Mertzes set up Big Hunk of America. Because the rival eateries sell the same food at the same facility, the only way they can differentiate themselves is through price. The result is a price war to attract customers.

When a new customer comes into the diner and starts to place an order for a 15-cent hamburger from Big Hunk of America, Lucy lowers the price at A Little Bit of Cuba to 10 cents. Ethel responds by lowering the price at Big Hunk of America to 5 cents. The two continue lowering the price until Ethel drops her price all the way down to 1 cent! (Even in the 1950s, a penny didn't cover the marginal cost of making a hamburger.) At this point, Lucy whispers in the customer's ear and gives him a dollar.

He then proceeds to Big Hunk of America and orders 100 hamburgers.

The scene illustrates how perfectly competitive markets work. Neither the Ricardos nor the Mertzes can stay in business selling one-cent burgers, so one of the couples will end up exiting the market. At that point, the remaining couple should be able to charge more. But if they end up making a profit, that profit will encourage entrepreneurs to enter the market. As the supply of hamburgers expands, the market price will be driven back down. Because we live in an economically dynamic world, prices are always moving toward long-run equilibrium.

Long-Run Profits: How Much Can a Firm Expect to Make?

QUESTION: True or false? "If firms in an industry are making economic profits, other firms will enter."

ANSWER: In the long run, a firm in a perfectly competitive market earns zero economic profit, so the opportunity in the short run to enjoy positive economic profits will cause existing firms to increase output and new firms to enter the market. The statement is true.

Calculating profits.

CHALLENGE QUESTION: The company you work for reported in its annual stockholder meeting that it made $1 million in profits last year. Should you invest?

ANSWER: The profit in the example is accounting profit. We don't know how large the firm is. If the firm had $5 million in assets, $1 million would represent a 20% return—which would be excellent. However, if the firm had $100 million in assets, the rate of return would only be 1%—which is poor. Economists are concerned with the rate of return adjusting for the implicit cost of the resources used. Recall that the stock market rises, on average, 8% a year. To account for this, when economists speak of profits they adjust the accounting profits downward for the implicit costs of doing business. For instance, let's take 8% off of the two hypothetical returns; 20% becomes a 12% return over the firm's next best alternative, that's why this outcome is "excellent." But when you subtract 8% from 1%, you get a return of −7%, which will drive firms out of the market. The firm could have used its assets more successfully by deploying them elsewhere.

So the answer to the question, "Should you invest?" is that it depends on the amount of economic profit—not the accounting profit—the firm expects to make going forward. Even then, you must be mindful about competition from other firms entering the market, since that will drive economic profits down to zero in the long run. Perhaps more pertinently, investing in a market characterized by no long-run economic profits should give you pause. In the next few chapters we will focus on imperfect competition. Firms with market power, barriers to entry, and differentiated products are able to consistently earn economic profits. That's where the smart investors look.

the wage it pays to attract additional help or accept new workers who are not quite as capable. Either way you slice it, the result is higher costs, which would be reflected in an upward-sloping long-run supply curve.

This discussion simply means that higher prices are necessary to induce suppliers to offer more for sale. None of it changes the basic ideas we have discussed throughout this section. The entry and exit of firms ensure that the market supply curve is much more elastic in the long run than in the short run.

Conclusion

In competitive markets, where firms are at the mercy of market forces that set the price, individual firms have no control over the price because they sell the same products as their competitors. In addition, profits and losses help regulate

Tips from the Sharks for Becoming a Millionaire

Before you go into business for yourself, you need to devise a plan. Over 80% of all small businesses fail within five years, because the businesses were ill-conceived or relied on unrealistic sales projections. Here is some advice from the stars of *Shark Tank*:

- **Barbara Corcoran:** "Every business is born out of an individual's intense passion and a real need to succeed, so you'll need enough passion to get started, but also enough to get through the intense 12-hour days when the chips are down and everything and everyone seems against you."
- **Mark Cuban:** "You've got to be good at something and not only be good at it, but you've got to love it, and then you're willing to work and do whatever it takes. Then, if you're fortunate, that turns into something that creates wealth for you."
- **Lori Greiner:** "Make sure you are hands-on and the one driving things because no one will care about your business like you do. Be involved in all details and be aggressive at attaining your goals, and know how to pivot when necessary."
- **Kevin O'Leary:** "If you can afford to take a risk and you're young enough, either start your own company or be involved with one where you're racking up equity."
- **Robert Herjavec:** "You've got to go back to the basics. Find a need, solve a problem and, most importantly, make sure you have a customer. If those things are in place, and you have the ability to scale, now we're talking. It's going to be incredibly hard work. Harder than you've ever

The Sharks may have a scary-sounding name, but they're rooting for you to succeed.

imagined, but it's the best time in America to start a business. The time is now!"
- **Daymond John:** "Go out there and do something that you really, really love, even if it's not something you went to school for. Find out what your passion is. I can't guarantee that you're ever going to make a dollar doing anything, but do something that you absolutely love and you're going to look back over the years and say that you enjoyed life."[*]

*Source: https://www.entrepreneur.com/slideshow/.

economic activity in competitive markets and promote economic efficiency. Profits reward producers for producing a good that is valued more highly than the resources used to produce it. Profits encourage entry into a market. Likewise, losses penalize producers who operate inefficiently or produce goods consumers do not want. Losses encourage exit from the market. The process of entry and exit ensures that resources flow into markets that are undersupplied and away from markets where too many firms exist.

In this chapter, we studied competitive markets to establish a benchmark that will help us understand how other market structures compare with this ideal. In the next few chapters, we explore imperfect markets, which provide a significant contrast with the results we have just seen. The closer a market is to meeting the criteria of perfect competition, the better the result for consumers and society in general. ✳

· ANSWERING *the* BIG QUESTIONS ·

How do competitive markets work?

* The firms in competitive markets sell similar products. Firms are also free to enter and exit the market whenever they wish.
* A price taker has no control over the price it receives in the market.
* In competitive markets, the price and quantity produced are determined by market forces instead of by the firm.

How do firms maximize profits?

* A firm maximizes profits by expanding output until marginal revenue is equal to marginal cost (MR = MC, or the profit-maximizing rule). The profit-maximizing rule is a condition for stopping production at the point where profit opportunities no longer exist.
* The firm should shut down in the short run if the price it receives does not cover its average variable costs. Because variable costs are incurred only when operating, if a firm can make enough to cover its variable costs in the short run, it will choose to continue to operate.
* In the long run, the firm should go out of business if it cannot cover its average total costs.

What does the supply curve look like in perfectly competitive markets?

* Profits and losses act as signals for firms to enter or leave a market. As a result, perfectly competitive markets drive economic profit to zero in the long run.
* The entry and exit of firms ensure that the market supply curve in a competitive market is much more elastic in the long run than in the short run.

· CHAPTER PROBLEMS ·

Concepts You Should Know

marginal revenue (p. 287)
price taker (p. 283)

profit-maximizing rule (p. 288)
signals (p. 298)

sunk costs (p. 293)

Questions for Review

1. What are the necessary conditions for a perfectly competitive market to exist?

2. Describe the two-step process used to identify the profit-maximizing level of output.

3. Under what circumstances will a firm have to decide whether to operate or to shut down?

4. What is the difference between the decision to go out of business and the decision to shut down?

5. How do profits and losses act as signals that guide producers to use resources to make what society wants most?

6. What are sunk costs? Give an example from your own experience.

7. Why do competitive firms earn zero economic profit in the long run?

Study Problems (✱ solved at the end of this section)

1. Using the definition of a price taker as your guide, explain why each of the following industries does not meet the definition.

   a. the pizza delivery business
   b. the home improvement business
   c. cell phone companies
   d. cereal producers

2. A local snow cone business sells snow cones in one size for $3 each. It has the following cost and output structure per hour:

Output (cones per hour)	Total cost (per hour)
0	$60
10	90
20	110
30	120
40	125
50	135
60	150
70	175
80	225

   a. Calculate the total revenue for the business at each rate of output.

   b. Calculate the total profit for the business at each rate of output.

   c. Is the business operating in the short run or the long run?

   d. Calculate the profit-maximizing rate of output using the MR = MC rule. (**Hint:** First compute the marginal revenue and marginal cost from the table.)

3. Determine whether the following statements are true or false. Explain your answers.

   a. A firm will make a profit when the price it charges exceeds the average variable cost of the chosen output level.

   b. To maximize profits in the short run, a firm must minimize its costs.

   c. If economic profit is positive, firms will exit the market in the short run.

   d. A firm that receives a price greater than its average variable cost but less than its average total cost should shut down.

4. In the following table, fill in the blanks. After you have completed the entire table, determine the profit-maximizing output.

Output	Price	Total revenue	Marginal revenue	Total cost	Marginal cost	Total profit
1	$20	___	___	$40	___	−$20
2	___	___	___	50	___	___
3	___	___	___	60	___	___
4	___	___	___	65	$5	___
5	___	___	___	85	___	___
6	___	$120	___	120	___	___

5. Use the graph to answer the questions that follow.

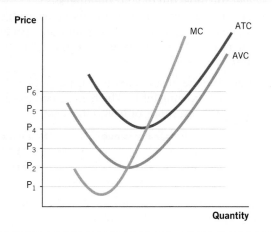

a. At what prices is the firm making an economic profit, breaking even, and experiencing an economic loss?

b. At what prices would the firm shut down?

c. At what prices does the firm's short-run supply curve exist? At what prices does the firm's long-run supply curve exist?

✱ 6. Identify as many errors as you can in the following graph.

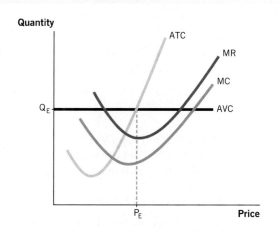

7. A firm is experiencing a loss of $5,000 per year. The firm has fixed costs of $8,000 per year.

a. Should the firm operate in the short run or shut down?

b. If the situation persists into the long run, should the firm stay in the market or go out of business?

c. Now suppose that the firm's fixed costs are $2,000. How would this level of fixed costs change the firm's short-run and long-run decisions?

8. Three students at the same school hear about the success of cookie delivery businesses on college campuses. Each student decides to open a local service. The individual supply schedules are shown below.

QUANTITY SUPPLIED

Delivery charge	Esra	Remzi	Camilo
$1	2	3	6
2	4	6	7
3	6	9	8
4	8	12	9
5	10	15	10
6	12	18	11

a. Draw the individual supply curves.
b. Sum the individual supply schedules to compute the short-run market supply schedule.
c. Draw the market supply curve.

9. Do you agree or disagree with the following statement? "A profit-maximizing, perfectly competitive firm should select the output level at which the difference between the marginal revenue and marginal cost is the greatest." Explain your answer.

10. Barney's snow removal service is a profit-maximizing, competitive firm. Barney clears driveways for $10 each. His total cost each day is $250, and half of his total costs are fixed. If Barney clears 20 driveways a day, should he continue to operate or shut down? If this situation persists, will Barney stay in the market or exit?

✳ 11. Suppose you are the owner of a firm producing jelly beans. Your production costs are shown in the following table. Initially, you produce 100 boxes of jelly beans per time period. Then a new customer calls and places an order for an additional box of jelly beans, requiring you to increase your output to 101 boxes. She offers you $1.50 for the additional box. Should you produce it? Why or why not?

JELLY BEAN PRODUCTION

Number of boxes	Average cost per box
100	$1.00
101	1.01
102	1.02
103	1.03

12. In which of the following examples does the decision-maker avoid the sunk cost fallacy?

a. You pay $10 to see *Furious 10* but realize 15 minutes into the film that the plot and acting are truly terrible, so you leave immediately.
b. You sign up for a year-long membership at a local fitness center. You tire of the club visits quickly, but still go regularly to make sure you get the most out of your membership.
c. A construction company builds a new bridge, but soon afterwards the traffic flow unexpectedly increases. The new bridge must be replaced before it needs repairs.

✳ 13. Determine the profit-maximizing output level from the following table. The firm has no fixed costs in this example, only variable costs.

Output	Marginal revenue	Marginal cost
1	$10	$13
2	10	10
3	10	8
4	10	7
5	10	9
6	10	11
7	10	14

14. Which of the following statements are true? Explain your reasoning.

a. The marginal cost curve passes through the lowest points of the ATC, AVC, and AFC curves.
b. The quantity for which MR = MC is the quantity for which the profit rectangle's area is maximized.
c. The AVC curve can be derived from the MC curve.
d. The AFC curve always slopes downward.

Solved Problems

6. Here is the corrected graph with the errors struck out and some explanation below.

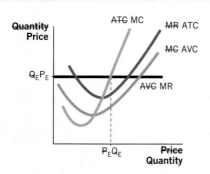

Also, the ATC and AVC curves did not intersect the MC curve at their minimum points. That is corrected here.

11. This problem requires marginal thinking. We know the profit-maximizing rule, MR = MC. Here all we need to do is compare the additional cost, or MC, against the additional revenue, or MR, to see if the deal is a good idea. We know that MR = $1.50, because that is what the customer is offering to pay for another box of jelly beans. Now we need to calculate the marginal cost of producing the additional box.

JELLY BEAN PRODUCTION

Number of boxes	Average cost per box	Total cost	Marginal cost
100	$1.00	$100.00	—
101	1.01	102.01	$2.01
102	1.02	104.04	2.03
103	1.03	106.09	2.05

First we compute the total cost. To do this, we multiply the number of boxes, listed in the first column, by the average cost, shown in the second column. The results are shown in the third column.

Next we find the marginal cost. Recall that the marginal cost is the amount it costs to produce one more unit. So we subtract the total cost of producing 101 boxes from the total cost of producing 100 boxes. For 101 boxes, MC = $102.01 − $100.00, or $2.01. Because MR − MC is $1.50 − $2.01, producing the 101st box would create a loss of $0.51. Therefore, at a price of $1.50, your firm should not produce the 101st box.

13. This problem confounds many students because if you've memorized only one thing from this chapter, it is the profit-maximizing rule, MR = MC, and it is clear that this condition is satisfied when the output is 2 (where MR and MC are both $10). But the answer 2 would be incorrect. A second part of the profit-maximizing rule is often overlooked: MR = MC, but MC must also be increasing. To see why 2 is not the profit-maximizing output, you should calculate the profit in a fourth column, as in the following table:

Output	Marginal revenue	Marginal cost	Profit (MR − MC)
1	$10	$13	− $3
2	10	10	0
3	10	8	2
4	10	7	3
5	10	9	1
6	10	11	−1
7	10	14	− 4

Profit is maximized at an output of 5, but why is this the case? Marginal cost is declining until output reaches 4, at which point the MR = $10 and MC = $7. So when the fourth unit is sold, it generates $3, and the firm is profitable for the first time. By the fifth unit, MC is rising but remains less than MR, so the profit rises. However, MC is higher than MR for the sixth unit, which causes profits to decline. The reason 2 is *not* the profit-maximizing output is that MC is falling, which means that the firm is at the point where additional output is just becoming profitable.

10

Understanding Monopoly

Monopolists Don't Always Make a Profit.

In this chapter, we explore another market structure: monopoly. Many people mistakenly believe that monopolists always make a profit. This is not true. Monopolists enjoy market power for their specific product, but they cannot force consumers to purchase what they are selling. The law of demand regulates how much a monopolist can charge. When a monopolist charges more, people buy less. If demand is low enough, a monopolist may even experience a loss instead of a profit.

While pure monopolies are unusual, it is important to study this market structure because many markets exhibit some form of monopolistic behavior. Google, the National Football League, the United States Postal Service (for first-class mail), and some small-town businesses are all examples of monopoly. The typical result of monopoly is higher prices and less output than we find in a competitive market.

Governments sometimes try to address the problems monopolies present. For example, governments split up the monopoly on phone service in the early eighties, which is generally seen as spurring the innovation that led to our modern systems. But governments can also be the cause of monopolies, sometimes in unexpected places. For example, in Winston-Salem, North Carolina, state law

Doctor Gajendra Singh wanted to make MRIs more affordable, but North Carolina wouldn't let him—so he took the state to court. Singh's lawyers are arguing that the certification requirement for MRI service providers interferes with his right, under the North Carolina constitution, to equal protection of the right to earn a living.

prevents doctors from becoming authorized providers of MRIs unless they first obtain a certificate of need, which can cost close to a half-million dollars. While this was originally done to regulate the quality of this service, the current result is that hospitals effectively have a monopoly on MRIs, keeping doctors or MRI centers from opening up and offering services at lower prices. So instead of Winston-Salem-area patients choosing the MRI provider they prefer, they are stuck going to a provider who charges $1,000 per MRI. Essentially, the state has made MRI services a monopoly market. In this chapter, we explore the conditions that give rise to monopolies and also the ways in which monopoly power can erode.

· BIG QUESTIONS ·

- How are monopolies created?
- How much do monopolies charge, and how much do they produce?
- What are the problems with, and solutions for, monopoly?

How Are Monopolies Created?

As we explained in Chapter 3, a monopoly exists when a single seller supplies the entire market for a particular good or service. Two conditions enable a single seller to become a monopolist. First, the firm must have something unique to sell—that is, something without close substitutes. Second, it must have a way to prevent potential competitors from entering the market.

Monopolies occur in many places and for several different reasons. For example, companies that provide natural gas, water, and electricity are all examples of monopolies that occur naturally because of economies of scale. But monopolies can also occur when the government regulates the amount of competition. For example, trash pickup, street vending, taxicab rides, and ferry service are often licensed by local governments. These licenses have the effect of limiting competition and creating **monopoly power**, which is a measure of a monopolist's ability to set the price of a good or service.

Monopoly power
is a measure of a monopolist's ability to set the price of a good or service.

A monopolist operates in a market with high **barriers to entry**, which are restrictions that make it difficult for new firms to enter a market. As a result, monopolists have no competition nor any immediate threat of competition. High barriers to entry insulate the monopolist from competition, which means that many monopolists enjoy long-run economic profits. There are two types of barriers to entry: natural barriers and government-created barriers. Let's look at each.

Barriers to entry are restrictions that make it difficult for new firms to enter a market.

Natural Barriers

Some barriers exist naturally within the market. These include control of resources, problems in raising capital, and economies of scale.

CONTROL OF RESOURCES The best way to limit competition is to control a resource that is essential in the production process. This extremely effective barrier to entry is hard to accomplish. But if you control a scarce resource, other competitors will not be able to find enough of it to compete. For example, in the early twentieth century, the Aluminum Company of America (ALCOA) made a concerted effort to buy bauxite mines around the globe. Within a decade, the company owned 90% of the world's bauxite, an essential element in making aluminum. This strategy enabled ALCOA to eliminate potential competitors and achieve dominance in the aluminum market.

PROBLEMS IN RAISING CAPITAL Monopolists are usually very big companies that have grown over an extended period. Even if you had a wonderful business plan, it is unlikely that a bank or a venture-capital company would lend you enough money to start a business that could compete effectively with a well-established company. For example, if you wanted to design a new operating system to compete with Microsoft and Apple, you would need tens of millions of dollars to fund your start-up. Lenders provide capital for business projects when the chance of success is high, but the chance of a new company successfully competing against an entrenched monopolist is not high. Consequently, raising capital to compete effectively is difficult.

ECONOMIES OF SCALE In Chapter 8, we saw that economies of scale occur when long-run average costs fall as production expands. Low unit costs and the low prices that follow give some larger firms the ability to drive rivals out of business. For example, imagine a market for electric power where companies compete to generate electricity and deliver it through their own grids. In such a market, it would be technically possible to run competing sets of wire to every home and business in the community, but the cost of installation and the maintenance of separate lines to deliver electricity would be both prohibitive and impractical. Even if a handful of smaller electric companies could produce electricity at the same cost, each would have to pay to deliver power through its own grid. This system would be highly inefficient.

In an industry that enjoys large economies of scale, production costs per unit continue to fall as a firm expands. Smaller rivals then have much higher average costs that prevent them from competing with a larger company. As a result, firms in the industry tend to combine over time. These mergers lead to

A **natural monopoly** occurs when a single large firm has lower costs than any potential smaller competitor.

the creation of a **natural monopoly**, which occurs when a single large firm has lower costs than any potential smaller competitor.

Government-Created Barriers

The creation of a monopoly can be either intentional or an unintended consequence of a government policy. Government-enforced statutes and regulations, such as laws and regulations covering licenses and patents, limit the scope of competition by creating barriers to entry.

LICENSING In many instances, it makes sense to give a single firm the exclusive right to sell a good or service. To minimize negative externalities, governments occasionally establish monopolies, or near monopolies, through licensing requirements. For example, in some communities trash collection is licensed to a single company. The rationale usually involves economies of scale, but there are additional factors to consider. Because firms cannot collect trash without a government-issued operating license, opportunities to enter the business are limited, which leaves consumers with a one-size-fits-all level of service. This outcome is the opposite of what we'd expect to see in a competitive market, where there would be many varieties of service at different price points.

Licensing also creates an opportunity for corruption. In fact, in many parts of the world, bribery is so common that it often determines which companies receive licenses in the first place.

PATENTS AND COPYRIGHT LAW Another area in which the government fosters monopoly is that of patents and copyrights. For example, when musicians create a new song and copyright their work, they earn royalties over the life of the copyright. The copyright is the government's assurance that no one else can play or sell the work without the artist's permission. Similarly, when a pharmaceutical company develops a new drug, the company receives a patent under which it has the exclusive right to market and sell the drug for as long as the patent is in force.

By granting patents and copyrights to developers and inventors, the government creates monopolies. Patents and copyrights create stronger incentives to develop new drugs and produce new music than would exist if market competitors could immediately copy inventions. As a result, pharmaceutical companies invest heavily in developing new drugs and musicians devote their time to writing new music. At least in theory, these activities make our society a healthier and culturally richer place. After the patent or copyright expires, rivals can mimic the invention. This new competition opens up the market and provides dual benefits: wider access to the innovation and more sellers—both of which are good for consumers in the long run.

Nonetheless, many economists wonder if patents and copyrights are necessary or have unintended consequences. Sometimes copyright holders benefit more from exposure than from exercising their right to charge consumers. For example, when a music video goes viral on YouTube, the exposure causes many people to buy the original artist's work. Consider Justin Bieber. He managed to leverage his YouTube fame into a successful album launch, concert tours,

Incentives

TABLE 10.1

The Characteristics of Monopolies

- One seller
- A unique product without close substitutes
- High barriers to entry
- Price making

and appearance fees that might never have occurred if a music studio had tightly controlled his sound while he was an emerging artist. Conversely, Taylor Swift refused to allow her music on Spotify from 2014 to 2017, because she felt the service did not properly compensate her and all the other people involved in creating the music. The point to remember is that copyright protection gives artists the right to decide how to distribute their work and what price to charge. It also gives them the ability to litigate when their work is stolen, illegally downloaded, or improperly used.

Though market-created and government-created barriers occur for different reasons, they have the same effect—they create monopolies. Table 10.1 summarizes the key characteristics of monopolies. In the next section, we examine how the monopolist determines the price it charges and how much to produce, explaining the term "price making" listed in Table 10.1.

Taylor's fans wanted her to *stay, stay, stay* but there was a *blank space* on Spotify for three years.

ECONOMICS IN THE REAL WORLD

PFIZER'S LIPITOR

Lipitor is the best-selling drug of all time. Pfizer corporation spent millions of dollars developing the drug and bringing it to the market. Lipitor is highly effective in lowering blood cholesterol. It was also highly profitable for Pfizer, generating over $11 billion in annual revenues before the patent ran out in 2011. Lipitor is now available in an inexpensive generic formulation at a price that is 80% lower than the original patent-protected price. Even after the patent expired, many customers continued to ask for Lipitor—not the generic—so brand recognition and customer loyalty represent another entry barrier.

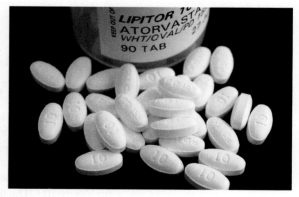

Would Lipitor have been developed without patent protection? Probably not. Pfizer would have had little incentive to incur the cost of developing a cholesterol treatment if other companies could immediately copy the drug. In this case, society benefits because of the twofold nature of patents: they give firms the incentive to innovate, but they also limit the amount of time the patent is in place (20 years from the time of filing), thereby guaranteeing that competitive forces will govern long-run access to the product.

Do you want fries with that cholesterol medication?

Incentives

Characteristics of Monopoly

THE OFFICE: PRINCESS UNICORN

Dwight Schrute buys up all of the Princess Unicorn dolls in local stores. As the Christmas holidays approach and parents become more desperate to find the dolls for their children, Dwight plans to sell his dolls marked way, way up—to $200! Toby wants to buy a doll for his daughter, Sasha, and is delighted to learn that Dwight has a stash he is selling, because now Toby has a chance to be a hero to his daughter. But he waits too long and learns that Dwight sold his last doll to Darryl. Distraught, Toby approaches Darryl, explains that he promised a doll to Sasha, and starts crying. Darryl decides to let Toby have the prized doll for $400, double what Darryl paid.

Dwight has a good understanding of the elements that create monopoly power. He is the sole seller in his area and he has a uniquely desirable product without close substitutes. That gives him monopoly power and the ability to raise the price he charges. Darryl also understands economics. He sees that Toby is desperate (has very inelastic demand) for the last doll and doubles Dwight's already high price.

FA-LA-LA-LA-LA, LA-LA, KA-CHING!

How Much Do Monopolies Charge, and How Much Do They Produce?

A **price maker** has some control over the price it charges.

Both monopolists and firms in a competitive market seek to earn a profit. However, a monopolist is the sole provider of its product and holds market power. Thus, monopolists are price makers. A **price maker** has some control over the price it charges. As you learned in Chapter 9, a firm in a competitive market is a price taker.

We can see the difference between price takers and price makers graphically in Figure 10.1. The demand curve for the product of a firm in a competitive market, shown in panel (a), is horizontal. When individual firms are price takers, they have no control over what they charge. In other words, demand is perfectly elastic—or horizontal—because every firm sells the same product. Demand for an individual firm's product exists only at the price determined by the market, and each firm is such a small part of the market that it can sell its entire output without lowering the price.

In contrast, because a monopolist is the only firm—the sole provider—in the industry, the demand curve for its product, shown in panel (b), constitutes the market demand curve. But the demand curve is downward sloping, which limits the monopolist's ability to make a profit. The monopolist would like to exploit its market power by charging a high price to many customers. However, the law of demand, which identifies a negative relationship between price and quantity demanded, dictates otherwise. Unlike the horizontal demand curve of a firm in a competitive market, the downward-sloping demand curve of the monopolist has many price-output combinations. If market demand is inelastic, a monopolist will choose a higher price. When market demand is more elastic, a monopolist will choose a lower price. As a result, monopolists must search for the profit-maximizing price and output.

PRACTICE WHAT YOU KNOW

Monopoly: Can You Spot the Monopolist?

Here are three questions to test your understanding of the conditions necessary for monopoly power to arise.

QUESTION: Is Amazon a monopolist?

ANSWER: Amazon is the nation's largest bookseller, with sales that dwarf those of its nearest retail rival, Barnes & Noble. Amazon is also by far the nation's leader in e-commerce with online sales that exceed the combined total of Walmart, Apple, Macy's, Home Depot, Best Buy, Costco, Nordstrom, Gap, and Target! Amazon's outsize market share, however, does not make it a monopolist. It still faces intense competition.

QUESTION: Is the only hairdresser in a small town a monopolist?

ANSWER: For all practical purposes, yes. He or she sells a unique service with inelastic demand. Because the nearest competitor is in the next town, the local hairdresser enjoys significant monopoly power. At the same time, the town's size limits potential competitors from entering the market, because the small community may not be able to support two hairdressers. Once one hairdresser is in place, a potential rival looks at the size of the market in the small town, calculates how many people he or she could expect to serve, and deduces that the potential revenue is too small to justify entrance into this market.

Monopoly profits!

CHALLENGE QUESTION: Which of these four firms do you think the government might, with good reason, allow to operate as a monopolist?

a. Tesla

b. Pacific Gas and Electric

c. Twitter

d. Walmart

ANSWER: The correct answer is B. Gas and electric companies are natural monopolies that have lower costs of production when they scale up. Dividing a natural monopolist into two or more smaller firms would drive costs significantly higher. Governments allow firms with significant economies of scale to remain monopolists and, as we shall learn, regulate the prices the firms can charge, to ensure that consumers are not gouged. Tesla, Walmart, and Twitter would, of course, like to be monopolists, too, but there is no compelling reason why society would be better off with just one large manufacturer of electric vehicles, or just one department store, or one social media outlet.

Barriers to Entry

FORREST GUMP

In this 1994 movie, Tom Hanks's character, Forrest Gump, keeps his promise to his deceased friend, Bubba, to go into the shrimping business after leaving the army. Forrest invests $25,000 in an old shrimp boat, but the going is tough—he catches only a handful of shrimp because of the competition for space in the shrimping waters. So Forrest tries naming his boat for good luck and brings on a first mate, Lieutenant Dan, who unfortunately is less knowledgeable and resourceful than Forrest. The fledgling enterprise continues to struggle, and eventually Forrest decides to pray for shrimp. Soon after, Forrest's boat, the *Jenny*, is caught out in the Gulf of Mexico during a hurricane. Miraculously, the *Jenny* makes it through the storm while the other shrimp boats, all anchored in the harbor, are destroyed. Boom! Forrest has a short-run monopoly.

The film suggests that Forrest's good luck—being in the right place at the right time—explains how he became a millionaire. But is Forrest's case realistic? Let's consider the situation in real-world economic terms.

Remember, Forrest was able to enter the business simply by purchasing a boat. To be sure, he will catch more shrimp in the short run, while the other boats are docked for repairs. However, once the competitors' boats return, they will resume catching shrimp, and Forrest's short-run profits will disappear. The reason we can be so confident of this result is that shrimping, with low barriers to entry and an undifferentiated product, is an industry that closely mirrors a perfectly competitive market. So when profits exist, new entrants will expand the supply produced and profits will return to the break-even level. Having Forrest become a "millionaire" makes for a good

If shrimping were easy, everyone would do it.

movie, but none of the elements are in place to suggest that he could attain a permanent monopoly. Forrest does not control an essential resource; the other shrimp captains will have little difficulty raising capital to repair their boats; and the economies of scale in this situation are small.

FIGURE 10.1

Comparing the Demand Curves of Perfectly Competitive Firms and Monopolists

(a) Firms in a competitive market face a horizontal demand curve. (b) Because the monopolist is the sole provider of the good or service, the demand for its product constitutes the industry—or market—demand curve, which is downward sloping. So while the perfectly competitive firm has no control over the price it charges, the monopolist gets to search for the profit-maximizing price and output.

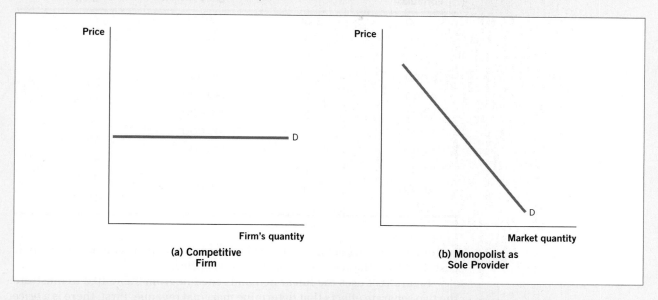

The Profit-Maximizing Rule for the Monopolist

A competitive firm can sell all it produces at the existing market price. But a monopolist, because of the downward-sloping demand curve, must search for the most profitable price. To maximize profits, a monopolist can use the profit-maximizing rule we introduced in Chapter 9: MR = MC. For the price-taking firm, MR is just the market price, full stop. For the monopolist, however, there's a calculation involved.

Marginal thinking

Table 10.2 shows the marginal revenue for a cable company that serves a small community. Notice the negative relationship between output (quantity of customers) and price in columns 1 and 2: as the price goes down, the quantity of customers goes up. Total revenue is calculated by multiplying output by price (TR = Q × P). At first, total revenue rises as the price falls. Once the price becomes too low ($40), total revenue begins to fall. As a result, the total revenue in column 3 initially rises to $250,000 before it begins to fall off. The final column, marginal revenue, shows the change (Δ) in total revenue. Here we see positive (though falling) marginal revenue associated with prices between $100 and $50 (see the green dollar amounts in column 4). Below $50, marginal revenue becomes negative (see the red dollar amounts in column 4).

The change in total revenue reflects the trade-off a monopolist encounters in trying to attract additional customers. To gain additional sales, the firm must lower its price. But the lower price is available to both new and existing

Trade-offs

TABLE 10.2

Calculating the Monopolist's Marginal Revenue

(1) Quantity of customers (Q)	(2) Price of service (P)	(3) Total revenue (TR)	(4) Marginal revenue per 1,000 customers (MR)
Formula:		$Q \times P$	Δ TR
0	$100	$0.00	
			$90,000
1,000	90	90,000	
			70,000
2,000	80	160,000	
			50,000
3,000	70	210,000	
			30,000
4,000	60	240,000	
			10,000
5,000	50	250,000	
			−10,000
6,000	40	240,000	
			−30,000
7,000	30	210,000	
			−50,000
8,000	20	160,000	
			−70,000
9,000	10	90,000	
			−90,000
10,000	0	0.00	

customers. The impact on total revenue therefore depends on how many new customers buy the good because of the lower price.

Figure 10.2 uses the linear demand schedule from Table 10.2 to illustrate the two separate effects that determine marginal revenue. First, there is a *price effect*, which reflects how the lower price affects revenue. If the price of service drops from $70 to $60, each of the 3,000 existing customers saves $10, and the firm loses $10 × 3,000, or $30,000 in revenue, represented by the red area on the graph. But dropping the price also has an *output effect*, which reflects how the lower price affects the number of customers. Because 1,000 new customers buy the product (that is, cable service) when the price drops to $60, revenue increases by $60 × 1,000, or $60,000, represented by the green area. The output effect ($60,000) is greater than the price effect ($30,000). When we subtract the $30,000 in lost revenue (the red rectangle) from the $60,000 in revenue gained (the green rectangle), the result is $30,000 in marginal revenue at an output level between 3,000 and 4,000 customers.

Lost revenues associated with the price effect are always subtracted from the revenue gains created by the output effect. Now let's think of this data at the individual level. Because the firm adds 1,000 new customers, the marginal revenue per customer—$30,000 ÷ 1,000 new customers—is $30. Notice that this marginal revenue is less than the price, $60, that the firm charges. Because there is a price effect whenever the price drops, the marginal revenue curve lies below the demand curve. Therefore, in Figure 10.2, the *y* intercept is the same for the demand and marginal revenue curves and the *x* intercept of the MR curve is half of the demand curve's.

At high price levels—where demand is elastic—the price effect is small relative to the output effect. As the price drops, demand slowly becomes more inelastic. The output effect diminishes and the price effect increases. In other words, as the price falls, it becomes harder for the firm to acquire enough new

FIGURE 10.2

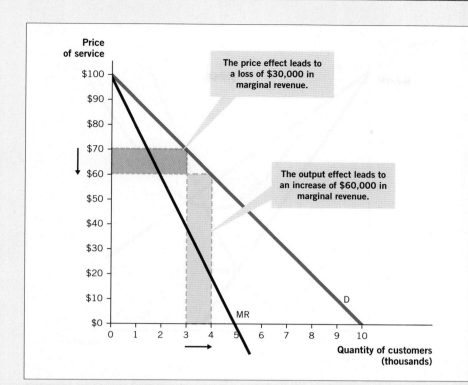

A price drop has two effects. (1) Existing customers now pay less—this is the price effect. (2) New customers decide to purchase the good for the first time—this is the output effect. The relative size of the two effects, as shown by the red and green rectangles, determines whether the firm is able to increase its revenue by lowering its price. In this case, marginal revenue increases by $30,000.

customers to make up for the difference in lost revenue. Eventually, the price effect becomes larger than the output effect. This means that the marginal revenue curve will have the same y intercept as the demand curve and be twice as steep. As a result, marginal revenue becomes negative and dips below the x axis, as shown by the MR curve in Figure 10.2. When the marginal revenue is negative, the firm cannot maximize profit. This outcome puts an upper limit on the amount the firm will produce. This outcome is evident in Table 10.2: once the price becomes too low, the firm's marginal revenue is negative.

Marginal thinking

DECIDING HOW MUCH TO PRODUCE In Chapter 9, we explored the profit-maximizing rule for a firm in a competitive market. This rule also applies to a monopolist: marginal revenue should be equal to marginal cost. However, there is one big difference: a monopolist does not charge a price equal to marginal revenue.

Figure 10.3 illustrates the profit-maximizing decision-making process for a monopolist. We use a two-step process to determine the monopolist's profit:

1. Locate the point at which the firm will maximize its profits: MR = MC.
2. Set the price: from the point at which MR = MC, determine the profit-maximizing output, Q. From Q, move up along the dashed line until it intersects with the demand curve (D). From that point, move horizontally until you come to the y axis. This point on the y axis tells us the price (P)

FIGURE 10.3

The Monopolist's Profit Maximization

The firm uses the profit-maximizing rule to locate the point at which MR = MC. This condition determines the ideal output level, Q. Because the price (which is determined by the demand curve) is higher than the average total cost curve (ATC) along the dashed line at quantity Q, the firm makes the profit shown in the green area.

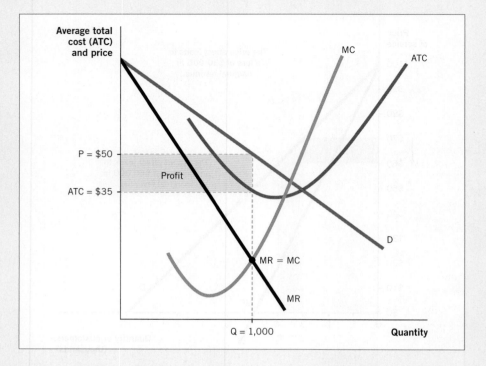

the monopolist should charge. Notice that the monopolist's price (P) is greater than MC (P > MC). This result differs from the competitive outcome, where P = MC.

Using this two-step process, we can determine the monopolist's profit. Locate the average total cost, ATC, of making Q units along the vertical dashed line. From that point, move horizontally until you come to the *y* axis. This point tells us the average total cost of making Q units. The difference between the price and the average total cost multiplied by Q tells us the profit (or loss) the firm makes. Any time the U-shaped ATC curve dips below the downward-sloping demand curve, D, there is a way to earn positive economic profits.

Because the price (P = $50) is higher than the average total cost (ATC = $35), the firm makes the profit shown in the green rectangle. For example, a profit-maximizing veterinarian will choose the point where MR = MC, and that means that the vet will serve 1,000 customers. Because the price at Q is $50 and the average total cost is $35, total profits are 1,000 × ($50 − $35) = $15,000.

Table 10.3 summarizes the differences between a competitive market and a monopoly. The competitive firm must take the price established in the market. If it does not operate efficiently, it cannot survive. Nor can it make an economic profit in the long run. The monopolist operates very differently. Because high barriers to entry limit competition, the monopolist may be able to earn long-run profits by restricting output. It operates inefficiently from society's perspective, and it has significant market power.

TABLE 10.3

The Major Differences between a Monopoly and a Competitive Market	
Competitive market	**Monopoly**
Many firms	One firm
Cannot earn long-run economic profits	May earn long-run economic profits
Has no market power (is a price taker)	Has significant market power (is a price maker)
Produces an efficient level of output (because P = MC)	Produces less than the efficient level of output (because P > MC)

ECONOMICS IN THE REAL WORLD

THE BROADBAND MONOPOLY

Many markets in the United States have only a single high-speed Internet provider. The technology race strongly favors cable transmission over competing telephone lines. Internet access is provided by telephone companies using aging copper wiring, whereas cable companies use the latest fiber-optic technology. When it comes to truly high-speed Internet access, cable companies benefit from considerable barriers to entry. In many places, Comcast and Charter, the two largest cable companies in the United States by far, effectively own access to the Internet and can price their services accordingly.

Is there only one provider in your area?

The cable monopoly on high-speed Internet access affects both consumers and businesses. First, consumers increasingly need more bandwidth to stream movies, view YouTube, and load media-rich web sites. A slow connection can make surfing the Internet a chore. In other words, consumer demand is high and very inelastic. Second, businesses rely on bandwidth to maintain web sites and provide services to customers. Companies such as Netflix, Amazon Prime, and Hulu Plus, which deliver streaming content over the Internet, rely on access to a relatively affordable broadband Internet connection. Therefore, businesses also have high demand that is quite inelastic. For this reason, many people argue that relatively inexpensive access to the Internet is crucial if it is to continue as an engine of economic growth. Without competition, access will remain expensive.

Our dependence on the Internet invites a larger question. Where only one provider controls the bandwidth, should the government have a role in providing the infrastructure, or cables, in order to allow greater (or less-expensive) access? This is a concern in metropolitan areas served by only one Internet provider. Meanwhile, small rural communities may have no Internet access at all. For example, it is estimated that more than 25 million people in rural areas remain off the grid. Cable companies wouldn't make enough profit to connect these low-density areas, making it more difficult for their residents to participate in today's economy. The unfeasibility of having separate infrastructure for every would-be Internet provider makes this an example of a natural monopoly, a topic we'll take up toward the end of the chapter.

Is there a key profit takeaway?

Monopoly Profits: How Much Do Monopolists Make?

QUESTION: A monopolist always earns ＿＿ economic profit.

a. a positive

b. zero

c. a negative

d. We cannot be sure about the profit a monopolist makes.

ANSWERS:

a. Incorrect. A monopolist is a price maker with considerable market power. This situation usually leads to a positive economic profit.

b. Incorrect. Zero economic profit exists in competitive markets in the long run. Because a monopolist, by definition, does not operate in competitive markets, it is protected from additional competition that would drive its profit to zero.

c. Incorrect. Whoa there! Negative profit? There is absolutely no reason to think that would happen. Monopolists sell a unique product without close substitutes in a market that is insulated from competitive pressures.

d. Correct. Because a monopolist benefits from barriers that limit the entry of competitors into the market, we would expect an economic profit. However, this outcome is not guaranteed. Monopolies do not control the demand for the product they sell. Consequently, in the short run the monopolist may experience a loss (if demand is low).

What Are the Problems with, and Solutions for, Monopoly?

Monopolies can adversely affect society by restricting output and charging higher prices than sellers in competitive markets do. This activity causes monopolies to operate inefficiently, provide less choice, promote an unhealthy form of competition known as *rent seeking* (addressed in a later section), and make economic profits that fail to guide resources to their highest-valued use. Recall that market failure occurs when there is an inefficient allocation of resources in a market. Once we have examined the problems with monopoly, we will turn to the potential solutions to the problems of monopoly.

The Problems with Monopoly

Monopolies result in an inefficient level of output, provide fewer choices to consumers, and encourage monopoly firms to lobby for government protection. Let's look at each of these concerns.

INEFFICIENT OUTPUT AND PRICE From an efficiency standpoint, the monopolist charges too much and produces too little. This result is evident in Figure 10.4, which shows what happens when a competitive market (denoted by the subscript C) ends up being controlled by a monopolist (denoted by the subscript M).

First, imagine a competitive fishing industry in which each boat catches a small portion of the fish, as shown in panel (a). Each firm is a price taker that must charge the market price. In contrast, panel (b) depicts pricing and output decisions for a monopoly fishing industry when it confronts the same cost structure as presented in panel (a). When a single firm controls the entire fishing ground, it is the sole supplier, so the supply curve becomes the monopolist's marginal cost curve. To set its price, it considers the downward-sloping demand and marginal revenue curves that serve the entire market. Therefore, it sets marginal revenue equal to marginal cost. The result is a smaller output than the competitive industry ($Q_M < Q_C$) and a higher price ($P_M > P_C$). The smaller output level is not efficient. In addition, the price the monopolist charges, P_M, is significantly above the marginal cost at the profit-maximizing level of output.

Figure 10.5 captures the deadweight loss (see Chapter 5) of the monopoly. The monopolist charges too high a price and produces too little of the product, so some consumers who would benefit from a competitive market lose out. Because the demand curve (the willingness to pay) is greater than the marginal

FIGURE 10.4

When a Competitive Industry Becomes a Monopoly

(a) In a competitive industry, the intersection of supply and demand determines the price (P_C) and quantity (Q_C).
(b) When a monopolist controls an entire industry, the supply curve becomes the monopolist's marginal cost curve. The monopolist uses MR = MC to determine its price (P_M) and quantity (Q_M). As a result, the monopolist charges a higher price and produces a smaller output than when an entire industry is populated with competitive firms.

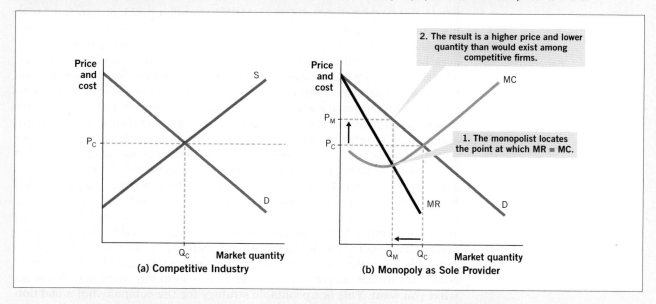

FIGURE 10.5

The Deadweight Loss of Monopoly

Because the profit-maximizing monopolist produces an output of Q_M, an amount that is less than Q_C, the result is the deadweight loss shown in the yellow triangle. The blue rectangle is the consumer surplus transferred to the monopolist.

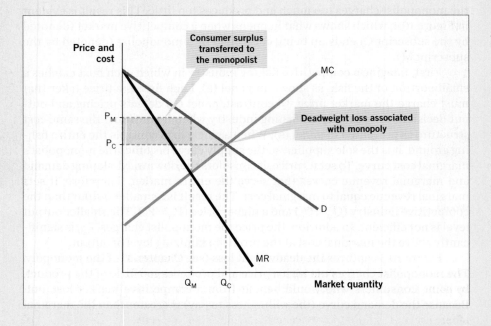

cost between output levels Q_M and Q_C, society would be better off if output expanded to Q_C. But a profit-maximizing monopolist will limit output to Q_M. The result, a deadweight loss equal to the area of the yellow triangle, is inefficient for society. Consumer surplus is also transferred to the monopolist, as shown in the blue rectangle.

Marginal thinking

FEW CHOICES FOR CONSUMERS Another problem associated with monopoly is the lack of choice. Have you ever wondered why cable companies offer their services in bundles? You can buy basic, digital, and premium packages, but the one thing you cannot do is buy just the cable channels you want. This situation prevails because cable companies function like monopolies, and monopolies limit consumer choice. Because the monopolist sells a good with few close substitutes, it can leverage its market power to offer product features that benefit the monopolist at the expense of consumer choice. With a monopolist, there is only one outlet: if you do not like the design, features, price, or any other aspect of the good provided, you have few (or no) other options. For example, in many communities there is only one cable television provider. In a hypothetical competitive market, we would expect each company to provide more options to satisfy consumer preferences. For instance, in a competitive market you should be able to find a firm willing to sell only ESPN and the Weather Channel. In a monopoly situation, though, the cable company forces you to choose between buying more cable than you really want or going without cable altogether. Because the cable company has a good deal of market power, it can restrict your options and force you to buy more in order to get what you want. This is a profitable strategy for the company but a bad outcome for consumers.

Would you rather watch the Weather Channel . . .   . . . or SportsCenter?

RENT SEEKING The term **rent seeking** was first coined by Anne Krueger in 1974. It refers to the attempt to gain monopoly power through the political process, by using lobbying and other means to secure legal monopoly rights. Throughout this text, we have seen the desirable effects of competition: lower prices, increased efficiency, and enhanced service and quality. However, rent seeking is a form of competition that produces an undesirable result. When firms compete to become monopolists, there is one winner without any of the benefits usually associated with competition. Consider the U.S. steel industry, which has been in decline for many years and has lost market share to steel firms in China, Japan, and Europe. If a U.S. steel company is losing money because of foreign competition, it can address the situation in one of two ways. It can modernize by building new facilities and using the latest equipment and techniques. (In other words, it can become competitive with the overseas competition.) Or it can lobby the government to limit imports. The domestic steel industry chose to lobby, and in 2002 the George W. Bush administration imposed tariffs of up to 30% on imported steel. Here is the danger: when lobbying is less expensive than building a new factory, the company will choose to lobby! If politicians give in and the lobbying succeeds, society is adversely affected because the gains from trade are smaller.

Supply and demand tell us that steel prices will rise in the absence of competition. This outcome is inefficient. Also, instead of pushing for legislation that grants market power, the lobbying resources could have gone into the production of useful products. As a result, the process of rent seeking potentially benefits the rent seeker but yields little direct benefit for society.

Rent seeking occurs when resources are used to secure monopoly rights through the political process.

Trade creates value

A former steel plant in Bethlehem, Pennsylvania.

Solutions to the Problems of Monopoly

We have learned that monopolies do not produce as much social welfare as competitive markets do. As a result, public policy approaches attempt to address this problem. The policy solutions include breaking up the monopoly, reducing trade barriers, and regulating markets.

Problems with Monopoly: Coffee Consolidation

A community has many competing coffee shops.

QUESTION: How can we use the market demand curve to illustrate the consumer surplus and producer surplus created by a competitive market?

When companies compete, consumers win.

ANSWER:

In a competitive market, supply and demand determine the price and quantity. In the figure, consumer surplus is represented by the blue area. Producer surplus is represented by the red area.

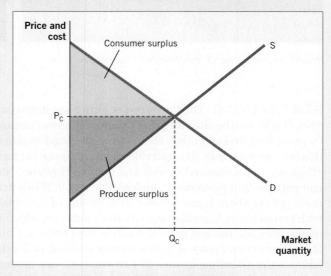

QUESTION: Now imagine that all the independent coffee shops combine under one fictional franchise, known as Harbucks. How can we create a new graph that illustrates the consumer surplus, producer surplus, and deadweight loss that occur when a monopolist takes over the market?

ANSWER:

In this figure, we see that the consumer surplus has shrunk, the producer surplus has increased, and the higher price charged by Harbucks creates deadweight loss. Allowing a monopolist to capture a market does not benefit consumers and is inefficient for society.

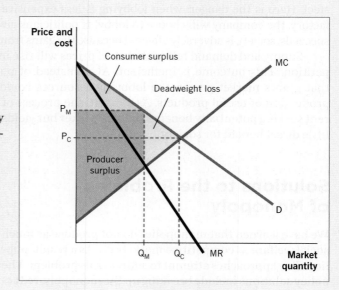

Monopoly Power

BREAKING BAD

Breaking Bad is widely regarded as one of the greatest television series of all time. It tells the story of Walter White, a depressed high school chemistry teacher diagnosed with lung cancer who turns to crime to secure his family's financial future before he dies. Together with a former student, Jesse Pinkman, the two produce and sell methamphetamine. Walt is the chemist who makes the best crystal meth in town. Jesse has the contacts Walt needs to sell it. Together, the two begin a long journey to take over the meth market in Albuquerque, NM.

In one scene Jesse is enthused about how well they are doing and says, "Gonna be some mad cheddar, yo. Cheddar, Mr. White. Fat stacks, dead presidents, cash money. Gonna own this city."

Walt immediately responds, "We're not charging enough."

JESSE: "What?

WALT: "You corner the market, then raise the price. Simple economics."

Walt understands that you have to corner the market before you can raise your price.

BREAKING UP THE MONOPOLY Eliminating deadweight loss and restoring efficiency can be as simple as promoting competition. From 1913 until 1982, AT&T had a monopoly on the delivery of telephone services in the United States. As the years passed, however, it became progressively harder for AT&T to defend its position that having a single provider of phone services was good for consumers. By the early 1980s, AT&T was spending over $300 million to fend off antitrust lawsuits from the states, the federal government, and many private firms. The AT&T monopoly ended in 1982, when enormous pressure from the government led the company to split into eight smaller companies. Suddenly, AT&T had to compete to survive. The newly competitive phone market forced each of the phone companies to expand the services it offered—and sometimes even lower its prices—to avoid losing customers. For example, rates on long-distance calls, which were quite high before the break-up, plummeted.

Incentives

From this example, we see that the government can help to limit monopoly outcomes and restore a competitive balance. The government can accomplish this goal through antitrust legislation. Antitrust laws are designed to prevent monopoly practices and promote competition. The government has exercised control over monopoly practices since the passage of the Sherman Act in 1890, and the task currently falls to the Department of Justice. We discuss these regulations at greater length in Chapter 13.

REDUCING TRADE BARRIERS Countries use *tariffs*, which are taxes on imported goods, as a trade barrier to prevent competition and protect domestic business. However, any barrier—whether a tariff, a quota, or a prohibition—limits the possible gains from trade. For monopolists, trade barriers prevent rivals from entering their territory. For example, imagine that Florida could place a tariff on California oranges. For every California orange sold in Florida, the seller would have to pay a fee. Florida orange producers might like this tariff because it would limit competition from California. But California growers would cry foul and reciprocate with a tariff on Florida oranges. Growers in both states would be happy, but consumers would be harmed. For example, if a damaging freeze in Florida depleted the crop, Florida consumers would have to pay more than the demand-driven price for imported oranges from California. If, in contrast, Florida had a bumper crop, the tariff would keep prices artificially high, and much of the extra harvest would go to waste.

The United States has achieved tremendous growth by limiting the ability of individual states to place import and export restrictions on goods and services. The Constitution reads, "No State shall, without the consent of Congress, lay any imposts or duties on imports or exports." Rarely have so few words been more profound. With this simple law in place, states must compete on equal terms.

Reducing trade barriers creates more competition, lessens the influence of monopoly, and promotes the efficient use of resources. For example, prior to 1994, private air carriers accounted for less than 0.5% of the air traffic in India. In 1994, Indian airspace was opened to allow private airlines to operate scheduled service. This move forced the state-owned Air India to become more competitive. These changes in Indian aviation policies had the effect of raising the share of private airline operators in domestic passenger carriage to over 85% by 2018. Air India—which once controlled the market—has fallen to third place.

Since 1994, reduced barriers to competition have transformed India's airline industry.

REGULATING MARKETS In the case of a natural monopoly, it is not practical to harness the benefits of competition. Consider the economies of scale that utility companies experience. Breaking up a company that provides natural gas, water, or electricity would result in higher production costs. For instance, a second water company would have to build infrastructure to each residence or business in a community. Having redundant water lines with only a fraction of the customers would make the delivery of water extremely expensive, such that the final price to the consumer, even with competition, would be higher. Therefore, keeping the monopoly intact is the best option. In this situation, policymakers might attempt to create a more efficient outcome and maximize society's welfare by regulating the monopolist's prices. Theoretically, this process would be straightforward. However, the reality is that few regulators are experts in the fields of electricity, natural gas, water, and other regulated industries, so they often lack sufficient knowledge to make the regulations work as designed.

When a natural monopoly exists, the government may choose to use the marginal cost pricing rule, $P = MC$, to generate the greatest welfare for society. Because the price is determined along the demand curve, setting $P = MC$ guarantees that the good or service will be produced as long as the willingness to pay exceeds the additional cost of production. Figure 10.6 shows the difference in pricing and profits for a regulated monopoly and an unregulated natural monopoly. Recall that a natural monopoly is characterized by economies of scale, which we can idealize as a constant marginal cost that leads to a steadily dropping ATC curve, as in Figure 10.6.

To maximize profits, an unregulated monopolist sets $MR = MC$ and produces quantity Q_M at a price of P_M. Because P_M is greater than the average total cost of producing Q_M units, or C_M, the monopolist earns the profit shown in the

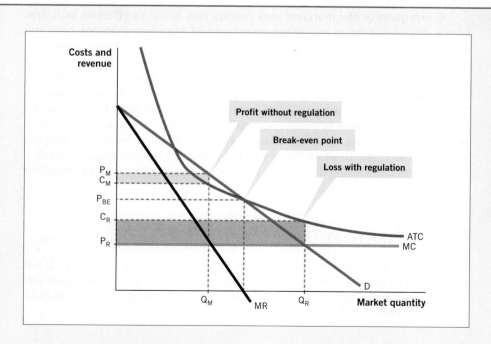

FIGURE 10.6

The Regulatory Solution for Natural Monopoly

An unregulated monopolist uses the profit-maximizing rule $MR = MC$ and earns a small profit, shown in the green rectangle. If the monopolist is regulated using the marginal cost pricing rule, $P = MC$, it will experience the loss shown in the red rectangle.

Marginal thinking

green rectangle. If the firm is regulated and the price is set at marginal cost, regulators can set P = MC, and the output expands to Q_R. (The subscript R denotes the regulated monopolist.) In this example, because the cost of production is subject to economies of scale, the cost falls from C_M to C_R and generates a large improvement in efficiency. The regulated price, P_R, is lower than the unregulated monopolist's price, P_M, and production increases. As a result, consumers are better off.

But what happens to the monopolist? It loses money in the amount of the red rectangle because the average total costs under the marginal cost pricing solution, C_R, are higher than the price allowed by regulators, P_R. This outcome is problematic because a firm that suffers losses will go out of business. That outcome is not desirable from society's standpoint, because the consumers of the product will be left without it. There are three possible solutions. First, to make up for the losses incurred at the higher output level, C_R, the government could subsidize the monopolist in order to achieve the socially efficient level of production. Second, the regulated price could be set at P_{BE}, where the ATC crosses the D curve, so that the firm breaks even; we can think of this as the second-best solution. Third, the government could own and operate the business in lieu of the private firm. This solution, however, has its own challenges, as we explore in the next section.

A CAVEAT ABOUT GOVERNMENT OVERSIGHT Firms with a profit motive have an incentive to minimize the costs of production, because lower costs translate directly into higher profits. If a firm's managers do a poor job reining in costs, they will be fired. The same cannot be said about government managers, or bureaucrats. Government employees are rarely let go, regardless of their performance. As a result, the government oversight and management of monopolies is problematic because there are fewer incentives to keep costs in check.

Incentives

Consequently, the marginal cost pricing rule is not as effective as it first seems. Regulated firms and government-owned businesses do not have the same incentives to keep costs down. Without the correct incentives in place, we would expect cost inefficiencies to develop.

Public policy can mitigate the power of monopolies. But this outcome is not guaranteed. While monopolies are not as efficient as firms in competitive markets, this comparison is not always relevant. We need to ask how the inefficiency of monopoly compares with the inefficiencies associated with government involvement in the market. Good economists assess the benefits as well as the costs, so when the costs of government involvement are greater than the efficiency gains that can be realized, the best solution to the problem of monopoly might be to do nothing.

Conclusion

It is tempting to believe that monopolies always earn a profit, but profit is not a guaranteed outcome. The monopolist controls the supply, not the demand, so monopolies occasionally suffer losses despite the advantages they enjoy. Still, many monopolists do make economic profits.

Playing Monopoly Like an Economist

- Buy and trade properties with others. Recall that trade is one of our Five Foundations!
- Some properties are landed on far more frequently than others. Buy or trade for them.
- If you obtain a monopoly, develop it as quickly as possible.

In the game Monopoly, you profit only by taking from other players. The assets of its world are fixed in number. The best player drives others into bankruptcy and is declared the winner only after gaining control of the entire board.

Here is some advice on how to play the game like an economist.

Apply some basic economic principles, and you can win big.

- Remember that a monopoly is built on trade. You are unlikely to acquire a monopoly by landing on the color groups you need. Instead, you have to trade properties in order to acquire the ones you need. Because every player knows this, acquiring the last property to complete a color group is nearly impossible. Your competitors will never willingly hand you a monopoly unless they get something of great value in return.

- Don't wait to trade until it is obvious what you need. Instead, try to acquire as many properties as you can in order to gain trading leverage as the game unfolds. Always pick up available properties if no other player owns one of the same color group; purchase properties that will give you two or three of the same group; or purchase a property if it blocks someone else from completing a set.

- Think about probability. Mathematicians have determined that Illinois Avenue is the property most likely to be landed on and that B&O is the best railroad to own. Know the odds, and you can weigh the risks and rewards of trade better than your opponents. This is just like doing market research before you buy. Being informed matters in Monopoly and in business.

- When you get a monopoly, develop it quickly. Build three houses as quickly as you can, but don't build a fourth house or put a hotel on your property—the returns to those additional investments are not worth the price.

- Finally, if you gain the upper hand and have a chance to bankrupt a player from the game, do it. Luck plays a key role in Monopoly, as it does in life. Although it may sound harsh, eliminating a competitor moves you one step closer to winning the game.

Trade creates value

The decisions you make while playing Monopoly are all about cost-benefit analysis. You have limited resources and only so many opportunities to use them to your advantage. The skilled player understands how to weigh the values of tradable properties, considers the risk-return proposition of every decision, manages money effectively, and eliminates competitors when given a chance.

In this chapter, we examined the monopoly model and, along the way, compared the results under monopoly with the results of the competitive model that we developed in the previous chapter. While competitive markets generally yield welfare-enhancing outcomes for society, monopolies often do the opposite. Because monopolists do not produce an efficient outcome, government often seeks to limit monopoly outcomes and promote competitive markets.

Competitive markets and monopoly are market structures at opposite extremes. Indeed, we rarely encounter the conditions necessary for either a pure monopoly or a perfectly competitive market. Most economic activity takes place between these two alternatives. In the upcoming chapters, we examine monopolistic competition and oligopoly—two markets that constitute the bulk of the economy. Fortunately, if you understand the market structures at the extremes, understanding the middle ground is straightforward. As we move forward, we will deploy the same tools we used to examine monopoly in order to understand monopolistic competition (Chapter 12) and oligopoly (Chapter 13) ✳.

· ANSWERING *the* BIG QUESTIONS ·

How are monopolies created?

* Monopoly is a market structure characterized by a single seller that produces a well-defined product with no good substitutes.
* Monopolies operate in a market with high barriers to entry, the chief source of market power.
* Monopolies are created when a single seller supplies the entire market for a particular good or service.

How much do monopolies charge, and how much do they produce?

* Monopolists are price makers who may earn long-run economic profits.
* Like perfectly competitive firms, a monopolist tries to maximize its profits. To do so, it uses the profit-maximizing rule, MR = MC, to select the optimal price and quantity combination of a good or service.

What are the problems with, and solutions for, monopoly?

* From an efficiency standpoint, the monopolist charges too much and produces too little. Because the monopolist's output is smaller than the output that would exist in a competitive market, monopolies lead to deadweight loss.

- Government grants of monopoly power encourage rent seeking, or the use of resources to secure monopoly rights through the political process.

- There are three potential solutions to the problem of monopoly. First, the government may break up firms that gain too much market power in order to restore a competitive market. Second, the government can promote open markets by reducing trade barriers. Third, the government can regulate a monopolist's ability to charge excessive prices.

- When the costs of government involvement in regulating a monopoly are greater than the efficiency gains that can be realized, it is better to leave the monopolist alone.

· CHAPTER PROBLEMS ·

Concepts You Should Know

barriers to entry (p. 315)
monopoly power (p. 314)

natural monopoly (p. 316)
price maker (p. 318)

rent seeking (p. 329)

Questions for Review

1. Describe the difference between a monopoly and a natural monopoly.

2. What are barriers to entry, and why are they crucial to the creation of potential long-run monopoly profits? Give an example of a barrier that can lead to monopoly.

3. Explain why a monopolist is a price maker but a perfectly competitive firm is a price taker.

4. Why is a monopolist's marginal revenue curve less than the price of the good it sells?

5. What is the monopolist's rule for determining the profit-maximizing output? What two steps does the monopolist follow to maximize profits?

6. Why does a monopolist operate inefficiently? Draw a demand curve, a marginal revenue curve, and a marginal cost curve to illustrate the deadweight loss from monopoly.

7. Why is it difficult to regulate a natural monopoly?

Study Problems (*solved at the end of the section)

1. In the figure below, identify the price the monopolist will charge and the output the monopolist will produce. How do these two decisions on the part of the monopolist compare with the efficient price and output?

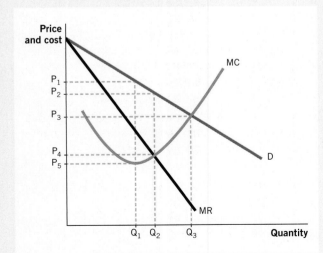

2. Which of the following could be considered a monopolist?

  a. your local water company
  b. Boeing, a manufacturer of airplanes
  c. Brad Pitt
  d. Walmart
  e. the only gas station along a 100-mile stretch of road

3. A monopolist has the following fixed and variable costs:

Price	Quantity	Fixed cost	Variable cost
$10	0	$8	$0
9	1	8	5
8	2	8	8
7	3	8	10
6	4	8	11
5	5	8	13
4	6	8	16
3	7	8	20
2	8	8	25

At what level of output will the monopolist maximize profits?

4. The year is 2278, and the starship *Enterprise* is running low on dilithium crystals, which are used to regulate the matter-antimatter reactions that propel the ship across the universe. Without the crystals, space-time travel is not possible. If there is only one known source of dilithium crystals, are the necessary conditions met to establish a monopoly? If the crystals are government owned or regulated, what price should the government set for them?

✴ 5. If demand falls, what is likely to happen to a monopolist's price, output, and economic profit?

✴ 6. A new musical group called The Incentives cuts a debut single. The record company determines a number of price points for the group's first single, "The Big Idea."

Price per download	Quantity of downloads
$2.99	25,000
1.99	50,000
1.49	75,000
0.99	100,000
0.49	150,000

The record company can produce the song with fixed costs of $10,000 and no variable cost.

a. Determine the total revenue at each price. What is the marginal revenue as the price drops from one level to the next?

b. What price would maximize the record company's profits? How much would the company make?

c. If you were the agent for The Incentives, what signing fee would you request from the record company? Explain your answer.

7. Recalling what you have learned about elasticity, what can you say about the connection between the price a monopolist chooses to charge and whether or not demand is elastic, unitary, or inelastic at that price? (**Hint:** Examine the marginal revenue curve of a monopolist. The fact that marginal revenue becomes negative at low prices implies that a portion of the demand curve cannot possibly be chosen.)

8. A small community is served by five independent gas stations. Gasoline is a highly competitive market. Use the market demand curve to illustrate the consumer surplus and producer surplus created by the market. Now imagine that the five independent gas stations are all combined under one franchise. Create a new graph that illustrates the consumer surplus, producer surplus, and deadweight loss after the monopolist enters the market.

9. A local community bus service charges $2.00 for a one-way fare. The city council is thinking of raising the fare to $2.50 to generate 25% more revenue. The council has asked for your advice as a student of economics. In your analysis, be sure to break down the impact of the price increase into the price effect and the output effect. Explain why the city council's estimate of the revenue increase is likely to be overstated. Use a graph to illustrate your answer.

10. Suppose that a monopolist's marginal cost curve shifts upward. What is likely to happen to the price the monopolist charges, the quantity it produces, and the profit it makes? Use a graph to illustrate your answer.

11. Suppose a firm collects $60 in revenues when it sells four units, $70 in revenues when it sells five units and $75 when it sells six units. You can infer that the firm is

a. perfectly competitive.

b. either a perfectly competitive firm or a monopolist.

c. a monopolist.

⁕ 12. Suppose Ambika, a graduate student in economics, tutors undergraduates to supplement her income as a teaching assistant. Ambika might tutor nine students each week. Their reservation prices for tutoring are given in the following table.

Student	Reservation price
A	$50
B	46
C	42
D	38
E	34
F	30
G	26
H	22
I	18

Each tutoring session lasts an hour. If the opportunity cost of Ambika's time is $20 per hour, and if she must charge each student the same price, how many students should she tutor each week? What price should she charge? What will be her economic profit?

Solved Problems

5. The following graph shows a monopolist making a profit:

Now we show what happens if demand falls:

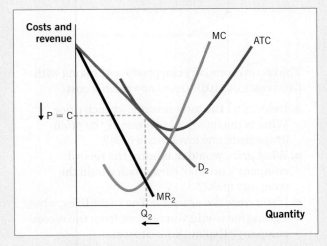

Lower demand causes the price to fall, the output to decline, and the profit to disappear.

6.a.

Price per download	Downloads	Total revenue	Marginal revenue
$2.99	25,000	$74,750	$74,750
1.99	50,000	99,500	24,750
1.49	75,000	111,750	12,250
0.99	100,000	99,000	−12,750
0.49	150,000	73,500	−25,500

b. Because marginal costs are $0, the firm would maximize its profits at $1.49. The company would make $111,750 − $10,000, or $101,750.

c. The company makes $101,750 from production, so as the agent you could request any signing fee up to that amount. Because determining a fee is a negotiation and both sides have to gain from trade, as the agent you should argue for a number close to $100,000, and you should expect the firm to argue for a much smaller fee.

12. She should tutor four students (students A–D). The marginal revenue of tutoring student D is $26, which is greater than Ambika's opportunity cost, but the marginal revenue of tutoring student E is only $18, which is less than Ambika's opportunity cost. So Ambika should stop at student D. She should charge $38, which is student D's reservation price. At this price, her economic profit will be 4($38) − 4($20) = $72.

Student	Reservation price	Total revenue	Marginal revenue
A	$50	$50	$50
B	46	92	42
C	42	126	34
D	38	152	26
E	34	170	18
F	30	180	10
G	26	182	2
H	22	176	−6
I	18	162	−14

■ CHAPTER ■

11

Price Discrimination

Is Charging Different Prices to Different People Unfair and Harmful? Actually, No.

Have you ever wondered why private colleges have high sticker prices and then offer tuition discounts to some students but not others? And why theaters charge more for adults than for children, when everyone sees the same movie? In these examples, some customers pay more and others pay less. Is this practice unfair? Not really: everyone's paying what they're willing to pay. Anyway, two-tiered pricing usually works to the advantage of people who need a financial break, and in the big picture there are net social benefits, in the form of greater market efficiency.

Discounts for college students are a prime example. Here's a rundown of companies that will give you a price break if you can prove you're a student:

- clothing retailers like J. Crew, Eastern Mountain Sports, and TopShop
- tech companies such as Apple, Microsoft, Adobe, and MathWorks (makers of MATLAB)
- entertainment companies like Cinemark, Major League Baseball, museums, and most ski resorts and amusement parks
- travel and transportation companies such as Greyhound, Amtrak, many hotel brands, and some air carriers
- your favorite news publications, like *The New York Times* or *The Economist* (!)

College students win big with price discrimination—your student I.D. gets you hundreds of discounts!

- auto insurance (if you have good grades)
- all the major cell phone carriers
- last, but certainly not least: many national restaurant chains and almost all local restaurants

Price discrimination makes big winners out of college students! In this chapter, we examine many real-life pricing situations and how businesses can make additional profits if they charge different prices to different groups of customers. The study of *price discrimination* adds a layer of complexity to the simple models of perfect competition and monopoly. A thorough understanding of how price discrimination works is especially useful as we complete our study of market structure with monopolistic competition and oligopoly in the next two chapters.

· BIG QUESTIONS ·

- What is price discrimination?
- How is price discrimination practiced?

What Is Price Discrimination?

Price discrimination
occurs when a firm sells the same good or service at different prices to different groups of customers.

Price discrimination occurs when a firm sells the same good or service at different prices to different groups of customers. The difference in price is not related to differences in cost. Although "price discrimination" sounds like something illegal, in fact it is beneficial to both sellers and buyers. When a firm can charge more than one price, markets work more efficiently. Because price-discriminating firms typically charge a "high" and a "low" price, some consumers are able to buy the product at a low price. Of course, firms are not in business to provide goods at low prices; they want to make a profit. Price discrimination enables them to make more money by dividing their customers into at least two groups: those who get a discount and others who pay more.

We have seen that in competitive markets, firms are *price takers*. If a competitive firm attempts to charge a higher price, its customers will likely buy elsewhere. To practice price discrimination, a firm must be a *price maker*; it must have some market power before it can charge more than one price. Both monopolies and nonmonopolistic companies use price discrimination to earn higher profits. Common examples of price discrimination are movie theater tickets, restaurant menus, college tuition, airline reservations, discounts on academic software, and coupons.

Conditions for Price Discrimination

For price discrimination to take place, two conditions must be met. First, there must be at least two different types of buyers. Second, the firm must be able to prevent resale of the product or service. Let's look at each in turn.

DISTINGUISHING GROUPS OF BUYERS To price-discriminate, a firm must be able to distinguish groups of buyers with different price elasticities of demand. Firms can generate additional revenues by charging more to customers with inelastic demand and less to customers with elastic demand. For instance, many restaurants offer lower prices, known as "early-bird specials," to people who eat dinner early. Who are these customers? Many, such as retirees and families with children, are on a limited budget. These early diners not only have lower demand but also represent demand that is more elastic; they eat out only if the price is low enough.

Trade-offs

Early-bird specials work for restaurants by separating customers into two groups: one that is price sensitive and another that is willing to pay full price. This strategy enables the restaurants to serve more customers and generate additional revenue.

PREVENTING RESALE For price discrimination to be a viable strategy, a firm must also be able to prevent resale of the product or service. In some cases, preventing resale is easy. For example, airlines require that electronic tickets match the passenger's government-issued photo ID. This system prevents a passenger who received a discounted fare from reselling it to another passenger who would be willing to pay more. The process works well for airlines and enables them to charge more to groups of flyers with more inelastic demand, such as business travelers. It also works well for restaurants offering early-bird specials, because the restaurants can easily distinguish between customers who arrive in time for the specials and those who arrive later.

One Price versus Price Discrimination

A business that practices price discrimination would prefer to differentiate every customer by selling the same good or service at a price unique to that customer—a situation known as **perfect price discrimination**. To achieve this result, a business would have to know exactly what any particular customer would be willing to pay and charge him or her exactly that price. Many jewelry stores and automobile dealerships attempt to practice perfect price discrimination by posting high sticker prices and then bargaining with each customer to reach a deal. When you enter a jewelry store or a vehicle showroom, the

Perfect price discrimination occurs when a firm sells the same good or service at a unique price to every customer.

salesperson tries to determine the highest price you are willing to pay. Then he or she bargains with you until that price is reached.

In practice, perfect price discrimination is hard to implement, so most firms instead settle for charging two or three prices based on sorting customers into a few easily identified groups. To see how this works, let's look at a hypothetical example. Consider two small airlines, Flat Earth Air and Discriminating Fliers. Each airline has a monopoly on the route it flies, and each faces the same market demand curves and marginal costs. What happens if one of the airlines price-discriminates but the other does not?

In Figure 11.1, Flat Earth Air charges the same price to every passenger, while Discriminating Fliers uses two different price structures. To keep our example easy to work with, the marginal cost (MC) is set at $100, shown as a horizontal line.

Flat Earth Air sets its price by using the profit-maximizing rule, MR = MC. It charges $300 for every seat and serves 100 customers (that is, passengers).

FIGURE 11.1

One Price versus Price Discrimination

(a) A firm that charges a single price uses MR = MC to earn a profit. (b) When a firm price-discriminates, it takes in more profit than a firm that charges a single price. The discriminating firm increases its revenue by charging some customers more and other customers less, as shown in the dark green areas. The increase in profit is partly offset by the loss of revenue from existing customers who receive a lower price, as shown in the red area.

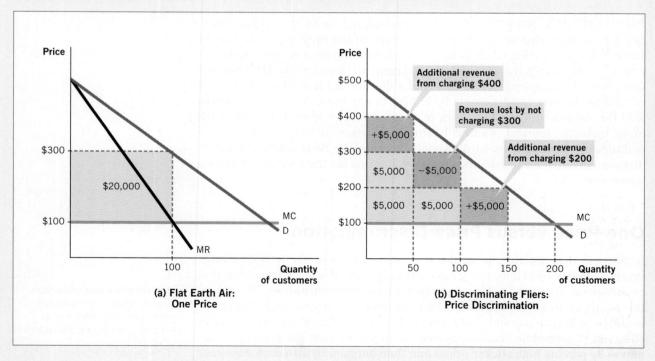

Because the marginal cost is $100, every passenger who gets on the plane generates $200 in producer surplus. The profit, represented by the green rectangle in panel (a), is $200 × 100, or $20,000. At 100 passengers, this airline has done everything it can to maximize profits at a single price. At the same time, there are plenty of unsold seats in the plane, which holds 200 passengers. Those unfilled seats represent a lost opportunity to earn additional revenue. As a result, airlines typically try to fill the plane by discounting the price of some seats. And this is precisely what Discriminating Fliers does.

Discriminating Fliers experiments with two prices, as shown in panel (b). Let's look at the reasoning behind these two prices. Because the firm faces a downward-sloping demand curve, the airline cannot sell every seat on the plane at the higher price. So it saves a number of seats, in this case 50, for last-minute bookings to capture customers with less flexibility who are willing to pay $400. These are travellers with inelastic demand, such as those who travel for business. The airline offers the rest of the seats at a low price, in this case $200, to capture customers with more elastic demand. The challenge for the airline is to make sure that the people who are willing to pay $400 do not purchase the $200 seats. So it makes the low fare available to customers who book far in advance, because these customers are typically more flexible and shop for the best deal. It is common for a business-person who needs to visit a client to make flight arrangements just days before the meeting, which precludes purchasing a $200 ticket weeks in advance. The customers who book early fill the seats that would otherwise be empty if the airline had charged only one price, as Flat Earth Air does. We can see this outcome by comparing the total number of passengers under the two strategies. Discriminating Fliers, with its two-price strategy, serves 50 passengers who pay $400 and 100 additional passengers who pay $200. Flat Earth Air's single price of $300 brings in only 100 passengers.

The net effect of price discrimination is apparent in the shaded areas of panel (b). By charging two prices, Discriminating Fliers generates more profit. The high price, $400, generates additional revenue equal to the upper dark green rectangle—$5,000—from passengers who must pay more than the $300 charged by Flat Earth Air. Discriminating Fliers also gains additional revenue with its low price of $200. The less-expensive tickets attract passengers with more elastic

Airlines offer lower fares if you are willing to take the red-eye.

Marginal thinking

· ECONOMICS *in the* MEDIA ·

Perfect Price Discrimination

LEGALLY BLONDE

In this 2001 film, Reese Witherspoon stars as Elle Woods, who defies others' expectations by attending Harvard Law School. Believing that her boyfriend is about to propose to her, Elle and two friends go shopping to find the perfect dress for the occasion. They enter an exclusive boutique and start trying on dresses.

The saleswoman comments to another associate, "There's nothing I love more than a dumb blonde with daddy's plastic." She grabs a dress off the clearance sale rack and removes the "half price" tag. Approaching Elle, she says, "Did you see this one? We just got it in yesterday." Elle fingers the dress, then the price tag, and looks at the saleswoman with excitement.

ELLE: "Is this a low-viscosity rayon?"

SALESWOMAN: "Uh, yes—of course."

ELLE: "With half-loop topstitching on the hem?"

SALESWOMAN (smiling a lie): "Absolutely. It's one of a kind."

(Elle hands the dress back to her, no longer pretending to be excited.)

ELLE: "It's impossible to use a half-loop topstitch on low-viscosity rayon. It would snag the fabric. And you didn't just get this in, because I remember it from the June *Vogue* a year ago, so if you're trying to sell it to me at full price, you picked the wrong girl."

Do you know how to get the best price? Elle does!

The scene is a wonderful example of an attempt at price discrimination gone wrong. Unbeknownst to the saleswoman, Elle is majoring in fashion merchandising in college and knows more about fashion than the saleswoman does. Her effort to cheat Elle fails miserably.

What makes the scene powerful is the use of stereotypes. When merchants attempt to price-discriminate, they look for clues to help them decide whether the buyer is willing to pay full price or needs an incentive, or discount, to make a purchase. In this case, the saleswoman misjudges Elle, assuming she is an uninformed buyer with highly inelastic demand. Consequently, her strategy backfires.

demand, such as college students, vacationers, and retirees. The low-price tickets generate $5,000 in revenue, as shown by the lower dark green rectangle.

Some customers would have paid Discriminating Fliers more if the airline had charged a single price. Customers willing to pay $300 can acquire tickets on Discriminating Fliers for $200. The red rectangle represents the lost profit, equal to $5,000. The $10,000 in revenue represented by the dark green rectangles more than offsets the $5,000 in lost profit represented by the red rectangle. The airline that price-discriminates, depicted in panel (b), generates a profit of $25,000. The airline that charges a single price, depicted in panel (a), generates a profit of $20,000.

In reality, airlines often charge many prices. For example, you will find higher prices for travel on Friday and for midday flights. If your stay includes a Saturday night or if you choose a red-eye flight, prices are lower. Airlines charge more for last-minute bookings and less to customers who book in advance. Airlines also change prices from day to day and even from hour to hour. All of these price changes reflect efforts to price-discriminate.

Because passengers cannot resell their tickets or easily change their plans, airlines can effectively price-discriminate. In fact, if an airline could charge unique prices for every passenger booking a flight, it would transform the entire area under the demand curve and above the marginal cost curve into more profit.

The Welfare Effects of Price Discrimination

Price discrimination is profitable for the companies that practice it. But it also increases the welfare of society. How, you might ask, can companies make more profit and also benefit consumers? The answer: because a price discriminator charges a high price to some and a low price to others, more consumers are able to buy the good.

To illustrate this point, let's imagine an airline, Perfect Flights, that is able to perfectly price-discriminate. Perfect Flights charges each passenger a price exactly equal to what that passenger is willing to pay. As a result, some customers pay more and others pay less than they would under a single-price system. This outcome is evident in Figure 11.2, where a profit-maximizing firm charges $300. At this price, the firm captures the profit in the light green rectangle, B.

FIGURE 11.2

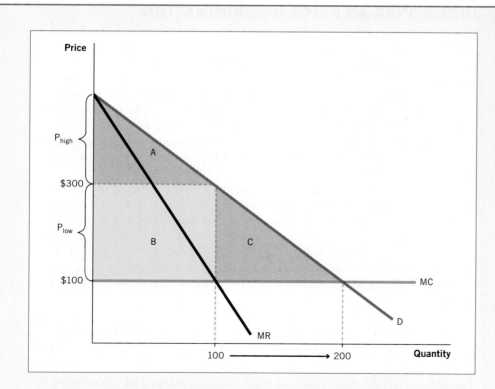

Perfect Price Discrimination

If the firm charges one price, the most it can earn is the profit in the light green rectangle. However, if a firm is able to perfectly price-discriminate, it can pick up the additional profit represented by the dark green triangles.

However, Perfect Flights charges each passenger a price based on his or her willingness to pay. Therefore, it earns significantly more profit. By charging higher prices (P_{high}) to those willing to pay more than $300, the firm is able to capture the additional profit in the upper dark green triangle, A. Likewise, by charging lower prices (P_{low}) to those not willing to pay $300, the firm is able to capture the additional profit in the lower dark green triangle, C. As a result, Perfect Flights is making more money and serving more customers.

By charging a different fare to every customer, Perfect Flights can also increase the quantity of tickets sold to 200. This strategy yields two results worth noting. First, in the long run, a perfectly competitive firm would charge a price just equal to marginal cost. In the case of Perfect Flights, the last customer who gets on the plane will pay an extraordinarily low price of $100—the price you might find in a competitive market. Second, this outcome mirrors the result of a government-regulated monopolist that uses the marginal cost pricing rule, $P = MC$, to enhance social welfare. Perfect Flights is therefore achieving the efficiency of a competitive market while also producing the output a regulated monopolist would choose. This strategy provides the firm with the opportunity to convert the area consisting of the two green triangles into more profit. In other words, the process maximizes the quantity sold. The efficiency of the market improves, and the firm generates more profit.

Marginal thinking

ECONOMICS IN THE REAL WORLD

Incentives

SANTA FE, NEW MEXICO: USING NEGATIVE INCENTIVES AS PRICE DISCRIMINATION

If you live in an arid climate, water rationing is the norm. Tiered pricing is one way to encourage water conservation. In most markets, bulk purchases get a volume discount. But as a way of encouraging water rationing, those who use more water pay much more for it.

Santa Fe, New Mexico, decided to use economics to address the issue of water conservation. Fifteen years ago, facing an acute water shortage (the city literally almost ran out of water), Santa Fe's city government introduced a tiered pricing system. The tiered system makes the heaviest users of water pay a premium for water used beyond a minimum. The heaviest users pay three times as much per gallon as modest users.

An article in the *New York Times* summarized the program's effects: "The tiered approach has worked as intended. Since 2001, Santa Fe's total water consumption has dropped by a fifth, even as the high desert city's population has increased more than 10%. When water costs more as its consumption increases, people respond exactly as an economics textbook would dictate: They use less."* This policy is truly economics in action, with a 20% reduction in water use even as the population increases!

The tiered pricing system involves several important economic concepts we have already learned about:

1. *Incentives matter* (Chapter 1). The people of Santa Fe have responded to the negative incentive of being penalized for using too much water.

Tiered pricing encourages water conservation.

---

*Nelson D. Schwartz, "Water Pricing in Two Thirsty Cities: In One, Guzzlers Pay More, and Use Less," *New York Times*, May 6, 2015.

2. *Internalizing the externality* (Chapter 7). Before 2001, heavy water users were affecting everyone in Santa Fe by creating periodic water shortages, but they did not have to pay extra for their actions. By paying much more for their water now, the heavy users are internalizing (paying for) the externality.

3. *Tragedy of the commons* (Chapter 7). Santa Fe has avoided a tragedy-of-the-commons scenario where all the water runs dry.

4. *The welfare effects of price discrimination* (this chapter). Dividing groups by their willingness to pay is beneficial to society, and that is what the Santa Fe water pricing system has achieved.

COMPARING PERFECT PRICE DISCRIMINATION WITH PERFECT COMPETITION AND MONOPOLY To understand the welfare effects of perfect price discrimination, we can compare the consumer and producer surplus in three scenarios: a competitive market, a market in which a monopolist charges a single price, and a market characterized by perfect price discrimination. The results, shown in Table 11.1, are derived by examining Figure 11.2.

In a perfectly competitive market, there are no barriers to entry and no firm has market power. In the long run, the price will be equal to the marginal cost. In our example of airline ticket prices, the price is driven down to $100. At this price, 200 tickets are sold. The entire area above the marginal cost curve (A + B + C) is consumer surplus, because the willingness to pay—as determined along the demand curve—is at least as great as the price. Because the ticket price is the same as the marginal cost, the producer surplus is zero. Because every customer who is willing to pay $100 or more can find a ticket, there is no deadweight loss. Under perfect competition, the market structure clearly favors consumers.

A monopoly holds substantial market power, so the firm in this scenario sets a price using the profit-maximizing rule, MR = MC, without having to worry about competition driving the price down to marginal cost. The monopolist's profit-maximizing price, or $300 in Figure 11.2, is higher than the $100 price under perfect competition. This higher price reduces the amount of consumer surplus to triangle A and creates a producer surplus equal to rectangle B. In addition, because the number of tickets sold falls to 100, there is now deadweight loss equal to triangle C. Economic activity associated with triangle C no longer exists, and the total welfare of society is now limited to A + B. From this analysis, we see that monopoly causes a partial transfer of consumer surplus to producers and a reduction in total welfare for society.

Marginal thinking

TABLE 11.1

The Welfare Effects of Perfect Price Discrimination

	Perfect competition	A monopolist that charges a single price	Perfect price discrimination
Consumer surplus	A + B + C	A	0
Producer surplus	0	B	A + B + C
Deadweight loss	0	C	0
Total welfare	A + B + C	A + B	A + B + C

In our third scenario, a firm that can practice perfect price discrimination is able to charge each customer a price exactly equal to the price that customer is willing to pay. This strategy enables the firm to convert the entire area of consumer surplus that existed under perfect competition into producer surplus (A + B + C). For the firm to capture the entire area of available consumer surplus, it must lower some prices all the way down to marginal cost. At that point, the number of tickets sold returns to 200, the market is once again efficient, and the deadweight loss disappears. Perfect price discrimination transfers the gains from trade from consumers to producers, but it also yields maximum efficiency.

Marginal thinking

Note that these examples give us a better understanding of what economists mean when they use the word "perfect" in connection with a market. It can mean that consumer surplus is maximized, as it is under perfect competition, or that producer surplus is maximized, as it is under perfect price discrimination. It does not specify an outcome from a particular perspective; instead, *perfect* describes any market process that produces no deadweight loss. If society's total welfare is maximized, economists do not distinguish whether the benefits accrue to consumers or producers. It is also important to note that while we compare the perfectly competitive result with the monopoly result and the result under perfect price discrimination as if those were the only three possible outcomes, those results are the extremes. Actual firms fall on a spectrum somewhere between these outcomes.

ECONOMICS IN THE REAL WORLD

OUTLET MALLS—IF YOU BUILD IT, THEY WILL COME

Incentives

Have you ever noticed that outlet malls along major roadways are often located a considerable distance from large population centers? Moreover, every item at an outlet mall can be found closer to home. The same clothes, shoes, and kitchenware are available nearby.

Logic tells us it would be more convenient to shop locally and forgo the time and hassle of getting to an outlet center. But that is not how many shoppers feel.

Discount shopping is a big deal. How big? Potomac Mills, 30 miles south of Washington, D.C., is Virginia's most popular attraction, with nearly 23 million visitors a year. (That figure rivals the number of annual visitors to Disney World's Magic Kingdom!)

How far would you drive to visit an outlet mall?

Outlet shopping is an example of price discrimination at work. Traditional malls are usually situated in urban settings and offer a wide variety of choices, but not necessarily low prices. If you want convenience, the local shopping mall is right around the corner. But if you want a bargain, shopping at a traditional local mall is not the best way to go.

What makes outlets so attractive are the discounts. Bargain hunters have much more elastic demand than their traditional mall-shopping counterparts who desire convenience. Moreover, the difference in the price elasticity of demand between these two groups means that traditional malls can more easily charge full price, while outlets must discount their merchandise to attract customers. The difference between these two groups of customers gives merchants a chance to price-discriminate on the basis of location—which is another way of separating customers into two groups and preventing resale at the same time. Retailers can therefore earn additional profits through price discrimination, while price-sensitive consumers can find lower prices at the outlets.

It is noteworthy that the convenience of finding discounts online threatens not only the traditional malls but also the outlets. When savvy shoppers can simply click to find the best deal, will they continue to drive to the outlets? Online retailers that have built user-friendly web sites with fast shipping and a seemingly endless list of products—think Amazon—are building platforms that many shoppers prefer to in-person shopping. Internet shopping also facilitates price discrimination. Cookies that record your search history can be used to influence the price you are offered, in effect enabling firms to discover a price closer to your willingness to pay. Online retailers also track whether you arrive at their address on a Mac or PC and what operating system you use. Did you know that many web sites routinely place more expensive products higher up in the search results if you are a Mac user? That's another example of price discrimination, but this time groups are differentiated based on the gadgets they use.

Opportunity cost

Price Discrimination: Taking Economics to New Heights

Consider the table below, which shows seven potential customers who are interested in taking a 30-minute helicopter ride. The helicopter has room for eight people, including the pilot. The cost to the helicopter company of taking on each additional passenger is $5.

How much would you pay to fly in a helicopter?

Customer	Maximum willingness to pay	Age
Amelia	$80	66
Orville	70	34
Wilbur	40	17
Neil	50	16
Charles	60	9
Chuck	100	49
Buzz	20	9

QUESTION: If the company can charge only one price, what should it be?

ANSWER: First, create an ordered array of the customers, from those willing to pay the most to those willing to pay the least.

If the firm charges $100, only Chuck will take the flight. When the firm drops the price to $80, Chuck and Amelia both buy tickets, so the total revenue (TR) is 80 × 2, or $160. Successively lower prices result in higher total revenue from the first five

Customer	Maximum willingness to pay	Price	TR	MR
Chuck	$100	$100	$100	$100
Amelia	80	80	160	60
Orville	70	70	210	50
Charles	60	60	240	30
Neil	50	50	250	10
Wilbur	40	40	240	−10
Buzz	20	20	140	−100

customers. The firm will benefit from lowering its price as long as the marginal revenue is greater than the marginal cost, $5. When the price is $50, five customers get on the helicopter, for a total of $250 in revenue. Adding the fifth passenger brings in $10 in marginal revenue. The marginal revenue for the sixth passenger is negative, so $50 is the best possible price to charge. Because each of the five passengers has a marginal cost of $5, the company makes $250 − (5 × $5) or $225 in profit.

QUESTION: If the company could charge two prices, what should they be, and who would pay them?

ANSWER: First, arrange the customers in two distinct groups: adults and children.

Adult customers	Willingness to pay	Age	Price	TR	MR
Chuck	$100	49	$100	$100	$100
Amelia	80	66	80	160	60
Orville	70	34	70	210	50

Young customers	Willingness to pay	Age	Price	TR	MR
Charles	$60	9	$60	$60	$60
Neil	50	16	50	100	40
Wilbur	40	17	40	120	20
Buzz	20	9	20	80	−40

As you can see, two separate prices emerge. For adults, profits are maximized at a price of $70. For children, total profits are maximized at $40. The company should charge $70 to the adult customers, which brings in $70 × 3, or $210 in total revenue. The company should charge $40 for each child under the age of 18, which brings in $40 × 3, or $120.

Price discrimination earns the company $210 + $120 − (6 × $5), or $300 in profit. This is a $75 improvement over charging a single price. In addition, six passengers are now able to get on the helicopter, instead of only five under the single-price model. Of course, leaving nine-year-old Buzz on the ground by himself isn't a great idea! Let's hope there's an adult friend or relative who was planning to sit the ride out.

How Is Price Discrimination Practiced?

Price discrimination is one of the most interesting topics in economics because each example is slightly different from the others. In this section, we take a closer look at real-world examples of price discrimination at movie theaters and on college campuses. Movie theaters and college campuses would like to achieve perfect price discrimination, but it simply isn't possible to know each customer's exact willingness to pay. As you will see, price discrimination takes many forms—some that are easy to describe and others that are more nuanced.

Price Discrimination at the Movies

Have you ever gone to the movies early so you can pay less for tickets? Movie theaters price-discriminate based on the time of day, age, student status, and whether or not you buy snacks. Let's examine these pricing techniques to see if they are effective.

PRICING BASED ON THE TIME OF THE SHOW Why are matinees priced less than evening shows? To encourage customers to attend movies during the afternoon, theaters discount ticket prices for matinees. This strategy makes sense because customers who can attend matinees (retirees, people on vacation, and those who do not work during the day) either have less demand or are more flexible, or price elastic. Work and school limit the options for many other potential customers. As a result, theaters discount matinee prices to encourage moviegoers who have elastic demand and are willing to watch at a less-crowded time. Movie theaters also discount the price of matinee shows because they pay to rent films on a weekly basis, so it is in their interest to show a film as many times as possible during a given week. Because the variable cost of being open during the day is essentially limited to paying a few employees relatively low wages, the theater can make additional profits even with a relatively small audience. On weekends, matinees also offer a discount to families that want to see a movie together—adding yet another layer of price discrimination.

Theaters charge two different prices based on showtime because they can easily distinguish between inelastic-demand customers and price-sensitive customers who have the flexibility to watch a matinee. Those with inelastic demand have less-flexible schedules and must pay higher ticket prices to attend in the evening.

PRICING BASED ON AGE OR STUDENT STATUS
Why are there different movie prices for children, seniors, students, and everyone else? This is a complex question. Income does not fully explain the discounts that the young, the old, and students receive. Movie attendance is highest among 13- to 24-year-olds and declines thereafter with age. Given the strong demand among teenagers, it is not surprising that "child" discounts are phased out at most theaters by age 12. But did you know that most "senior"

Even if you're at the matinee because your demand is highly elastic, be considerate of people who really want to watch the movie.

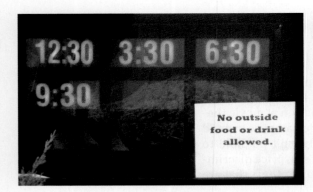
If you've ever smuggled food into a movie theater, it is because your demand for movie theater concessions is elastic.

discounts begin before age 65? In some places, senior discounts start at age 50. Now you might think that because people in their 50s tend to be at the peak of their earning power, discounting ticket prices for them would be a bad move. However, because interest in going to the movies declines with age, the "senior" discount actually provides an incentive for a population that might not otherwise go to a movie theater. However, as we have seen, age-based price discrimination does not always work perfectly. Theaters do not usually ask for proof of age, and it may be hard to tell the difference between a child who is just under 12 and one who is over 12. Nonetheless, price discrimination works well enough to make age or student status a useful revenue-generating tool. Empty seats represent lost revenue, so it makes sense to price-discriminate through a combination of high and low prices.

CONCESSION PRICING Have you ever wondered why it is so expensive to purchase snacks at the movie theater? The concession area is another arena in which movie theaters practice price discrimination. To understand why, we need to think of two groups of customers: those who want to eat while they watch movies and those who do not. By limiting outside food and drink, movie theaters push people with inelastic demand for snacks to buy from the concession area. Of course, that does not stop some customers with elastic demand from sneaking food into the theater. But as long as some moviegoers are willing to buy concession fare at exorbitant prices, the theater will generate more revenue. Movie theaters cannot prevent smuggling in of snacks, and they don't have to. All they really want to do is separate their customers into two groups: a price-inelastic group of concession-area snackers and a price-elastic group of nonsnackers and smugglers who fill up the remaining empty seats. This situation is very similar to the problem we examined with airlines.

Price Discrimination on Campus

Colleges and universities are experts at price discrimination. Think about tuition. Some students pay the full sticker price, while others enjoy a free ride. Some students receive the in-state rate, while out-of-state students pay substantially more. And once you get to campus, discounts for students are everywhere. In this section, we consider the many ways in which colleges and universities differentiate among their students.

TUITION Price discrimination begins before you ever set foot on campus, with the Free Application for Federal Student Aid (known as the FAFSA) that most families complete. The form determines eligibility for federal aid. Families that qualify are eligible for grants and low-interest loans, which effectively lower the tuition cost for low- and medium-income families. Therefore, the FAFSA enables colleges to separate applicants into two groups based on income. Because many colleges also use the FAFSA to determine eligibility for their own institutional grants of aid, the FAFSA makes it possible for colleges to precisely target grants and loans to the students who need the most financial help.

Many state institutions of higher education have a two-tiered pricing structure. In-state students get a discount on the tuition, while out-of-state students pay a much higher rate. Part of the difference is attributable to state subsidies that are intended to make in-state institutions more affordable for residents. In-state students pay less because their parents have been paying taxes to the state, often for many years, and the state then uses some of those tax dollars to support its system of higher education. However, in-state subsidies only partially explain the difference in pricing. Out-of-state tuition is higher than it would be if all students paid the same price because out-of-state students are generally less sensitive to price than in-state students.

This two-tiered pricing structure creates two separate groups of customers with distinctly different elasticities of demand. Students choose an out-of-state college or university because they like what that institution has to offer more than the institutions in their home state. It might be that a particular major or program is more highly rated or simply that they prefer the location of the out-of-state school. Whatever the reason, they are willing to pay more for the out-of-state school. Therefore, out-of-state students have a much more inelastic demand. Colleges know this and price their tuition accordingly. Conversely, in-state students often view the opportunity to attend a nearby college as the most economical decision. Because price is a big factor in choosing an in-state institution, it is not surprising that in-state demand is more elastic.

Selective private colleges also play the price discrimination game by advertising annual tuition and room and board fees that exceed $60,000. With price discrimination, the "sticker" price is often discounted. Depending on how much the college wants to encourage a particular student to attend, it can discount the tuition all the way to zero. This strategy enables selective private colleges to price-discriminate by offering scholarships based on financial need, while also guaranteeing placements for the children of wealthy alumni and others willing to pay the full sticker price.

Colleges and universities also use "early decision" and campus visits to determine how eager you are to attend. That information is a measure of your price elasticity of demand. At the margin, students who commit to an early decision or visit campus have more inelastic demand than those who only apply for regular admission. This is yet another way colleges fine-tune student aid packages based on observed behavior.

Resort or college? Sky-high tuition and room and board are one way to help pay for a beautiful campus.

STUDENT DISCOUNTS The edge of campus is a great place to look for price discrimination. Local bars, eateries, and shops all want college students to step off campus, so student discounts are the norm. Why do establishments offer student discounts? Think about the average college student. Price matters to that student. Knowing this, local merchants in search of college customers can provide student discounts without lowering their prices across the board. This means they can charge more to their regular clients while providing the necessary discounts to get college students to make the trek off campus.

Now Playing: Economics!

Have you ever gone to the movies early so you can pay less for tickets? Movie theaters price- discriminate based on the time of the movie and the age of the customer. In order to practice price discrimination, theaters must be able to identify different groups of moviegoers, where each group has a different price elasticity of demand.

MATINEE $9

Demand for matinees is typically low. These showings attract groups with relatively elastic demand, like families and those on a budget, who decide to attend matinees because of lower prices.

EVENING $13

Evening movie showings attract larger crowds that consist mainly of adults and couples on dates. This group has relatively inelastic demand, so price is not the determining factor of when and where they see a movie.

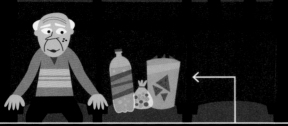

...e concession counter also generates profit for the movie theater. ...e high prices mean that patrons who are price– conscious (having ...atively elastic demand) skip the counter or smuggle in their own ...cks, while those who are more concerned about convenience than ...ce (having relatively inelastic demand) buy snacks at the counter.

REVIEW QUESTIONS

- Does price discrimination hurt all consumers? Think about the example of movie theaters as you craft your response.

- Your local movie theater is thinking about increasing ticket prices for just the opening day of a blockbuster movie. How would you explain the economics behind this price increase?

Price discrimination also occurs at entertainment venues near a college campus. For example, students typically receive discounts for campus activities like concerts and sporting events. Because students generally have elastic demand, price discrimination provides greater student access to events than charging a single price does.

PRACTICE WHAT YOU KNOW

Price Discrimination in Practice: Everyday Examples

QUESTION: Test your understanding by thinking about the examples below. Are they examples of price discrimination?

a. **Retail coupons.** Programs such as discount coupons, rebates, and frequent-buyer plans appeal to customers willing to spend time pursuing a deal.

b. **Using Priceline to make hotel reservations.** "Naming your price" on Priceline .com is a form of haggling that enables users to get hotel rooms at a discount. Hotels negotiate with Priceline to fill unused rooms while still advertising the full price on their web sites.

c. **The 1-2-3 Menu at McDonald's.** Customers who order off the 1-2-3 Menu get a variety of smaller menu items for $1, $2, or $3 each.

Are Black Friday deals price discrimination or not?

ANSWERS:

a. **Retail coupons.** Affluent customers generally do not bother with the hassle of clipping, sending in, and keeping track of coupons because they value their time more than the small savings. However, customers with lower incomes usually take the time to get the discount. This means that coupons, rebates, and frequent-buyer programs do a good job of price-discriminating.

b. **Using Priceline to make hotel reservations.** Priceline enables hotels to divide their customers into two groups: those who don't want to be bothered with haggling and those who value the savings enough to justify the time spent negotiating. This is a good example of price discrimination.

c. **The 1-2-3 Menu at McDonald's.** Anyone can buy off the 1-2-3 Menu at any time. Because McDonald's does not force customers to do anything special in order to get the deal, this is not price discrimination.

CHALLENGE QUESTION: Customers who line up in the early-morning hours after Thanksgiving get first dibs on a limited quantity of reduced-price items at many retailers. Are discounts for early shoppers on Black Friday a form of price discrimination?

ANSWER: The discounts are time sensitive. Shoppers who arrive before the deadline get a lower price; shoppers who arrive after the deadline do not. Any retailer can deploy this method and easily divide customers into two groups: those with elastic demand (willing to wait in line early in the morning to get a deal) and those with inelastic demand (they'd rather sleep and not hassle with waiting). Don't let the fact that anyone could wait in line distract you. Most people won't wait, and it is this fact that makes price discrimination possible.

Price Discrimination

JURASSIC PARK

Early on in the original *Jurassic Park* film, there's a discussion about the price of admission to the live-dinosaur theme park. "We can charge anything we want," muses the investors' lawyer, "two thousand a day, ten thousand a day, and people will pay it." Hammond, the park's visionary founder, objects, "This park was not meant to cater only for the super-rich. Everyone in the world has the right to enjoy these animals." The lawyer doesn't see a problem, "Sure. They will. We'll have a coupon day or something."

The ingenious thing about offering coupons, and about price discrimination in general, is that it would generate more total revenue for the firm while simultaneously increasing the number of visitors who are able to take in the park. The lawyer understands that some people's demand for dino-safaris is highly inelastic, but if that is the only market segment the park attracts, there may be times (off-season) when they can generate additional revenue by lowering the price to a separate group of tourists whose demand is more price-sensitive.

How much would you be willing to pay to see a real-life dinosaur in the wild?

Opportunity cost

Conclusion

The word "discrimination" has negative connotations, but not when combined with the word "price." Charging different prices to different groups of customers results in more economic activity and is more efficient than charging a single price across the board. Under price discrimination, many consumers pay less than they would if a firm had charged a single price, while other consumers will pay more because their demand is more inelastic. But overall, total social welfare increases, and the amount of deadweight loss in society is reduced.

Price discrimination also helps us understand how many markets actually function, because instances of perfectly competitive markets and monopoly are rare. ✳

Gender-Based Price Discrimination

On average, across the five industries surveyed, one report found that women paid:

- 7% more for toys and accessories.
- 4% more for children's clothing.
- 8% more for adult clothing.
- 13% more for personal care products.
- 8% more for senior/home health care products.

Why do the same jeans cost $50 more for women?

Throughout this chapter, we considered the shopping experience in the context of price discrimination. Here we focus on how firms separate men and women into different groups by making cosmetic changes to the products they sell.

In a report prepared for the New York City Department of Consumer Affairs, author Anna Bessendorf and her team compared nearly 800 products with clear male and female versions from more than 90 brands sold at two dozen New York City retailers, both online and in stores.

The report found that women frequently paid more than men for the same products. Specifically, the report found that women's products cost 7% more than similar products for men. To minimize differences between men's and women's items, Bessendorf's team selected products with male and female versions that were very similar in branding, appearance, materials, construction, and/or marketing. In all but five of the 35 product categories analyzed, products for female consumers were priced higher than those for male consumers. Across the entire sample, the report found that women's products cost more 42% of the time, while men's products cost more only 18% of the time.

Why would firms charge more for the female version of a product? The answer is price discrimination. When different groups (males and females) have different price elasticities of demand, price discrimination allows a firm to earn more revenue. In most of the products surveyed, females had more inelastic demand, which translates into higher prices for them in the marketplace compared to males.[*] If you are not happy about gender-based pricing there is a potential workaround: buy the comparable male product. Is a pink razor really something you have to have when a similar blue razor sells for less?

---

*Source: https://www1.nyc.gov/assets/dca/downloads/pdf/partners/Study-of-Gender-Pricing-in-NYC.pdf.

·ANSWERING *the* BIG QUESTIONS·

What is price discrimination?

- Price discrimination occurs when firms can identify different groups of customers with varying price elasticities of demand and can prevent resale among their customers.
- A firm must have some market power before it can charge more than one price.

How is price discrimination practiced?

- Under price discrimination, some consumers pay a higher price and others receive a discount. Price discrimination is profitable for the firm, reduces deadweight loss, and leads to a higher output level.

·CHAPTER PROBLEMS·

Concepts You Should Know

perfect price discrimination (p. 345)

price discrimination (p. 344)

Questions for Review

1. What two challenges must a price maker overcome to effectively price-discriminate?

2. Why does price discrimination improve the efficiency of the market?

3. Why is preventing resale a key to successful price discrimination?

4. If perfect price discrimination reduces consumer surplus to zero, how can this situation lead to the most socially desirable level of output?

Study Problems (✳ solved at the end of the section)

1. Seven potential customers are interested in seeing a movie. Because the marginal cost of admitting additional customers is zero, the movie theater maximizes its profits by maximizing its revenue.

Customer	Maximum willingness to pay	Age
Allison	$8	66
Becky	11	34
Charlie	6	45
David	7	16
Erin	6	9
Franco	10	28
Grace	9	14

a. What price would the theater charge if it could charge only one price?

b. If the theater could charge two prices, what prices would it choose? Which customers would pay the higher price, and which would pay the lower price?

c. How much profit does the theater make when it charges only one price? How much profit does the theater make if it price-discriminates?

2. Which of the following are examples of price discrimination? Explain your answers.

a. A cell phone carrier offers unlimited calling on the weekends for all of its customers.

b. Tickets to the student section for all basketball games are $5.

c. A restaurant offers a 20% discount for customers who order dinner between 4 and 6 p.m.

d. A music store has a half-price sale on last year's guitars.

e. A well-respected golf instructor charges each customer a fee just under the customer's maximum willingness to pay for lessons.

3. At many amusement parks, customers who enter after 4 p.m. receive a steep discount on the price of admission. Explain how this practice is a form of price discrimination.

4. Name three products for which impatience on the part of the consumer enables a firm to price-discriminate.

✳ 5. Prescription drug prices in the United States are often substantially higher than in Canada, the United Kingdom, and India. Today, pharmacies in these countries fill millions of low-cost prescriptions through the mail to U.S. citizens. Given that the pharmaceutical industry cannot prevent the resale of these drugs, are the industry's efforts to price-discriminate useless? Explain your answer.

✳ 6. Metropolitan Opera tickets are the most expensive on Saturday night. There are often a very limited number of "student rush tickets," with which a lucky student can wind up paying $20 for a $250 seat. The student rush tickets are available first-come, first-served. Why does the opera company offer these low-cost tickets? How does it benefit from this practice? Why are students, and not other groups of customers, offered the discounted tickets?

✳ 7. Have you ever tipped a restaurant host in order to bypass a long wait and get a table more quickly? Would this be an example of price discrimination? Why or why not? Discuss.

8. Orbitz, the travel web site, routinely offers PC and Apple users different search results. Apple users typically have higher-priced hotels show up on the top page of the results, while PC users are presented with somewhat lower prices. Is Orbitz practicing price discrimination? Discuss.

9. When Subway customers pay less per inch for footlong subs than they pay per inch for a six-inch sub, is this price discrimination or not?

10. When ride-sharing companies impose "surge pricing" during times of peak demand for rides and/or a low supply of drivers, is this price discrimination?

✳ 11. If an app uses geolocation to understand where you are and offers different prices based on your location, is this price discrimination or not?

Solved Problems

5. Buying prescription drugs outside the United States is increasingly common. Because the pharmaceutical companies charge three to four times more for drugs sold domestically than they do in most other countries, it would seem that the drug industry's efforts to price-discriminate aren't working, but that is not true. Not everyone fills their prescriptions from foreign sources; only a small fraction of U.S. customers go to that much effort. Because most U.S. citizens still purchase the more expensive drugs here, the pharmaceutical companies are benefiting from price discrimination, even though some consumers manage to navigate around their efforts.

6. The Met hopes to sell all of its $250 tickets, but not every show sells out and some tickets become available at the last minute. The student rush tickets benefit both the opera company and the students: the company can fill last-minute seats, and the students, who have elastic demand and low income, get a steep discount. The Met is able to price discriminate, because the rush tickets require a student ID. Other groups of operagoers are therefore unable to buy the rush tickets. This practice effectively separates the customer base into two groups: students and nonstudents. Students make ideal rush customers because they are more willing to change their plans in hopes of obtaining last-minute tickets than other groups. Some opera companies also open up the rush tickets to seniors, another group that is easy to identify and generally has significant flexibility.

7. As a college student you probably don't have a lot of money to tip the restaurant host. But if you do have the money, it would make sense to tip the host. Here is why: First, your tip gets you seated sooner and avoids the wait time. Time is money, so you save right there. Second, the host has an incentive to let tippers in sooner, and that's not just good for the host. It is also good for the business because tippers have much more inelastic demand, which translates into customers who spend more while dining. So the host is actually separating customers into two groups: tippers with inelastic demand and nontippers with much more elastic demand. Third, the restaurant wins because when tippers with inelastic demand get tables faster, the restaurant makes more revenue.

9. Anyone could conceivably get the better deal, but only those with big appetites or a willingness to eat leftovers will choose a footlong. Those with smaller appetites are stuck paying more per inch for a six-inch sub. Since Subway can differentiate between those with big and smaller appetites by the size of sandwich they order, this is a form of price discrimination based on making a "bulk" purchase.

11. This is a form of price discrimination, and like all price discrimination efforts it will generate more revenue. Companies can use your location to raise or lower the price shown on the app. For instance, in 2018 Burger King offered its app users a free Whopper if they happened to be near a McDonald's!

Monopolistic Competition and Advertising

Advertising and Product Differentiation are Notable Features of Monopolistic Competition.

If you drive down a busy street, you will find many competing businesses, often right next to one another. These competing firms advertise heavily. The temptation is to see advertising as driving up the price of a product without any benefit to the consumer. However, in markets where competitors sell slightly differentiated products, advertising enables firms to inform their customers about new products and services. Yes, costs rise, but consumers also gain information to help make purchasing decisions.

Consumers also benefit from added variety, and we all get a product that's pretty close to our vision of a perfect good—no other market structure delivers that outcome. Consider California Pizza Kitchen (CPK). Since its inception in 1985, CPK has grown to over 200 restaurants throughout the United States and expanded to over a dozen countries. How did CPK break into an already crowded pizza market? By doing pizza differently. Instead of making traditional Italian-style pies, CPK is widely known for serving nontraditional pies with innovative ingredients. They popularized gourmet pizza, a style of pizza that combines an Italian thin crust with toppings from the California cuisine cooking style. In other words, CPK made pizza even better!

What do you like on your pizza? CPK probably has you covered. Do you want just sliced tomatoes and basil? If not, what about carrots and bean sprouts? Or eggplant? Or baby broccoli? Poblano chilies, anyone? Take your pick and make sure to share with a tablemate.

In this chapter, we look at *monopolistic competition*, a widespread market structure that has features of both competitive markets and monopoly. We also explore the benefits and disadvantages of advertising, which is prevalent in markets with monopolistic competition.

· BIG QUESTIONS ·

- What is monopolistic competition?
- What are the differences among monopolistic competition, competitive markets, and monopoly?
- Why is advertising prevalent in monopolistic competition?

What Is Monopolistic Competition?

Monopolistic competition is a type of market structure characterized by low barriers to entry, many different firms, and product differentiation.

Product differentiation is the process firms use to make a product more attractive to potential customers.

Some consumers prefer the fries at McDonald's, while others may crave a salad at Panera Bread or the chicken at KFC. Each fast-food establishment has a unique set of menu items. The different products in fast-food restaurants give each seller a small degree of market power. This combination of market power and competition is typical of the market structure known as monopolistic competition. Indeed, **monopolistic competition** is characterized by low barriers to entry, many different firms, and product differentiation. **Product differentiation** is the process firms use to make a product more attractive to potential customers. Firms use product differentiation to contrast their product's unique qualities with competing products. The differences, which we will examine in detail, can be minor and can involve subtle changes in packaging, quality, availability, and promotion. Or the differences can be very significant. For example, some soup companies specialize in organic soups, which the consumers they are targeting would find an extremely important characteristic.

How does monopolistic competition compare with other market structures we have studied? As Table 12.1 shows, monopolistic competition falls between competitive markets and monopoly in terms of the number of sellers, the types of products sold, and competing firms' ability to enter and exit the market.

We have seen that firms in competitive markets do not have any market power. As a result, buyers can expect to find consistently low prices and wide availability. And we have seen that monopolies charge more and restrict the availability of a good or service. In markets that are monopolistically competitive, firms sell differentiated products. This differentiation gives the

TABLE 12.1

Competitive Markets, Monopolistic Competition, and Monopoly

Competitive markets	Monopolistic competition	Monopoly
Many sellers	Many sellers	One seller
Similar products	Differentiated products	A unique product without close substitutes
Free entry and exit	Low barriers to entry and exit	Significant barriers to entry and exit

monopolistic competitor some market power, though not as much as a monopolist, which controls the entire market. Monopolistically competitive firms have a small amount of market power that enables them to search for the most profitable price.

To understand how monopolistic competition works, we begin with a closer look at product differentiation.

Product Differentiation

Monopolistically competitive firms create some market power through product differentiation. Differentiation can occur in a variety of ways, including style or type, location, and quality.

STYLE OR TYPE A trip to a mall is a great way to see product differentiation firsthand. For example, you will find many clothing stores, each offering a unique array of styles and types of clothing. Some stores, such as Abercrombie & Fitch, carry styles that attract younger customers. Others, such as Ann Taylor, appeal to older shoppers. Clothing stores can also vary by the type of clothing they sell, specializing in apparel such as business clothing, plus sizes, or sportswear. Each store hopes to attract a specific type of customer.

When you're ready for lunch at the mall, you can go to the food court, where many different places to eat offer a wide variety of choices. Where you decide to eat is a matter of your personal preferences and the price you are willing to pay. Like most consumers, you will select the place that gives you what you want while providing the best value for your money. Consumers' differing tastes make it possible for a wide range of food vendors to compete side by side with rivals who provide many good substitutes.

LOCATION Many businesses attract customers because of their convenient location. Gasoline stations, dry cleaners, barber shops, and car washes provide products and services that customers tend to choose on the basis of convenience of location rather than price. When consumers prefer to save time and to avoid the inconvenience of shopping for a better deal, a firm with a more convenient location will have some pricing power. As a result, producers who sell very similar products can generate some market power by locating their businesses along routes to and from work or in other areas where customers frequently travel.

Would you like your Mexican food cheaper . . .   . . . or fresher?

QUALITY Firms also compete on the basis of quality. For instance, if you want Mexican food, you can go to Taco Bell, which is inexpensive and offers food cooked in advance. In contrast, at Moe's Southwest Grill the food is freshly prepared and, as a result, more expensive. This form of product differentiation serves consumers quite well. Budget-conscious consumers can feast at Taco Bell, while those with a larger budget and a taste for higher-quality Mexican food can consider Moe's as another option.

PRACTICE WHAT YOU KNOW

Is Hollister a monopolistic competitor?

Product Differentiation: Would You Recognize a Monopolistic Competitor?

QUESTION: Which of the following is a monopolistic competitor?

a. a local apple farm that grows Red Delicious apples

b. Hollister, an apparel store

c. your local water company

ANSWERS:

a. Because Red Delicious apples are widely available at grocery stores, this local apple farm does not have a differentiated product to sell. In addition, it has many competitors that grow exactly the same variety of apples. This apple farm is part of a competitive market; it is not a monopolistic competitor.

b. Hollister has a slightly different mix of clothes than competitors Abercrombie & Fitch and American Eagle Outfitters. This differentiation gives the brand some pricing power. Hollister is a good example of a monopolistically competitive firm.

c. Because water is essential and people cannot easily do without it, the local water company has significant monopoly power. Moreover, purifying and distributing water are subject to economies of scale. Your local water company is definitely a monopolist, not a monopolistic competitor.

What Are the Differences among Monopolistic Competition, Competitive Markets, and Monopoly?

Monopolistic competition occupies a place between competitive markets, which produce an efficient output at low prices, and monopoly, which produces an inefficient output at high prices. To help explain whether monopolistic competition is desirable or not, we consider the outcomes that individual firms can achieve when facing monopolistic competition in the short run and in the long run. Once you understand how monopolistic competition works, we will be able to compare the long-run equilibrium result with that of competitive markets and then determine if monopolistic competition is efficient.

Monopolistic Competition in the Short Run and the Long Run

A monopolistically competitive firm sells a differentiated product and for this reason has some market power. Recall that in perfect competition, each firm sells the same product, so competitors' products are perfect substitutes, which means that demand is perfectly elastic (flat). In monopolistic competition, each competitor provides a differentiated product, so competitors' products are imperfect substitutes for one another, which means that demand is relatively elastic (less flat), but still flatter (more elastic) than monopoly. Like a monopolist, the monopolistic competitor uses the profit-maximizing rule, MR = MC, and locates the corresponding point on its demand curve to determine the best price to charge and the best quantity to produce. Whether the firm earns a profit, experiences a loss, or breaks even is a function of other firms entering and exiting the market. Recall that entry and exit do not take place in the short run. In the long run, however, firms are free to enter an industry when they see a potential for profits or leave if they are making losses. Therefore, entry and exit regulate how much profit a firm can make in the long run.

Marginal thinking

Suppose you own a Hardee's fast-food restaurant in Asheville, North Carolina. Your business is doing well and making a profit. Then one day a Five Guys opens up across the street. Some of your customers will try Five Guys and switch, while others will still prefer your fare. But your profit will take a hit. Whether or not you stay in business will depend on how much business you lose. To understand how a business owner makes the decision to keep operating or to shut down, we now turn to the short-run and long-run implications of monopolistic competition.

MONOPOLISTIC COMPETITION IN THE SHORT RUN Figure 12.1 depicts a firm, like Hardee's, in a monopolistically competitive environment. In panel (a), the firm makes a profit. Panel (b) shows the same firm incurring a loss after a new competitor, like Five Guys, opens nearby. In each case, the firm uses the profit-maximizing rule to determine the best price to charge by locating the point at which marginal revenue equals marginal cost. This calculation

FIGURE 12.1

The Monopolistically Competitive Firm in the Short Run

In this figure, we see how a single monopolistically competitive firm may make a profit or incur a loss depending on the demand conditions it faces. Notice that the marginal cost curve (MC) and average total cost curve (ATC) are identical in both panels because we are considering the same firm. The only functional difference is the location of the demand curve (D) and marginal revenue curve (MR). The demand in (a) is high enough for the firm to make a profit. In (b), however, there is not enough demand, so the firm experiences a loss.

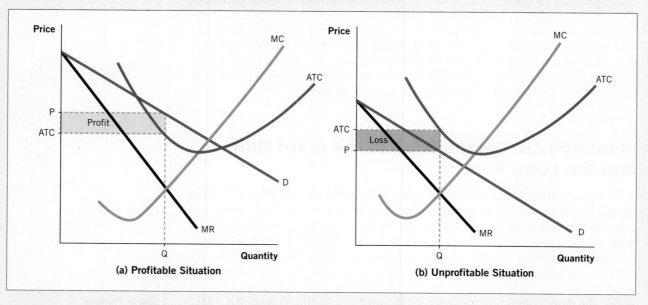

(a) Profitable Situation

(b) Unprofitable Situation

establishes the profit-maximizing output (Q) along the vertical dashed line. The firm determines the best price to charge (P) by following the dashed horizontal line from the demand curve to the vertical axis.

In panel (a), we see that because price is greater than average total cost (P > ATC), the firm makes a short-run economic profit. The situation in panel (b) is different. Because P < ATC, the firm experiences a short-run economic loss. What accounts for the difference? Because we are considering the same firm, the marginal cost (MC) and average total cost (ATC) curves are identical in both panels. The only functional difference is the location of the demand (D) and marginal revenue (MR) curves. The demand in panel (a) is high enough for the firm to make a profit. In panel (b), however, there is not enough demand; perhaps too many customers have switched to the new Five Guys. So even though the monopolistic competitor has some market power, if demand is too low, the firm may not be able to price its product high enough to make a profit.

MONOPOLISTIC COMPETITION IN THE LONG RUN In the long run, when firms can easily enter and exit a market, competition will drive economic profit to zero. This dynamic should be familiar to you from our previous discussions of competitive markets. If a firm is making an economic profit, that profit attracts new entrants to the business. Then the larger supply of competing firms will cause the demand for an individual firm's product to contract. Eventually, as more firms enter the market, it is no longer possible for existing firms to make an economic profit. A reverse process unfolds in the case of a market experiencing a loss. In this case, some firms exit the industry. Then consumers have fewer options to choose from, and the remaining firms experience an increase in demand. Eventually, demand increases to the point at which firms no longer experience a loss.

Figure 12.2 shows the market after the long-run adjustment process takes place. Price (P) is just equal to the average total cost of production (ATC) at the profit-maximizing rate of output (Q). At this point, firms are earning zero economic profit, as noted by P = ATC along the vertical axis; the market reaches a long-run equilibrium at the point where there is no reason for firms to enter or exit the industry. Note that the demand curve is drawn *tangent* to the average total cost curve (touching at one place). If demand were any larger, the result would look like panel (a) in Figure 12.1 and firms would experience an economic profit. Conversely, if demand were any lower, the result would look like panel (b) in Figure 12.1 and firms would experience an economic loss. Where entry and exit exist, profits and losses are not possible in the long run. In this way, monopolistic competition resembles a competitive market.

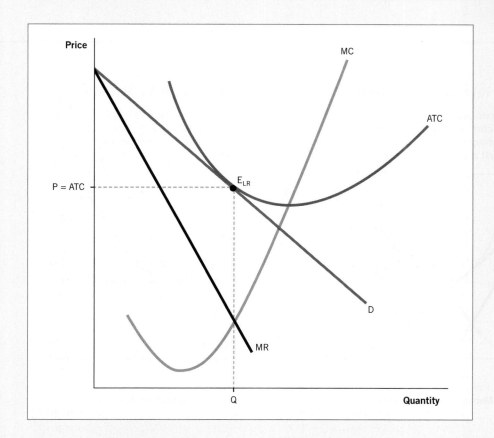

FIGURE 12.2

The Monopolistically Competitive Firm in the Long Run

Entry and exit cause short-run profits and losses to disappear in the long run, which means that the price charged (P) must be equal to the average total cost (ATC) of production. At this point, firms are earning zero economic profit, as noted by P = ATC along the vertical axis. The market reaches a long-run equilibrium (E_{LR}) at the point where there is no reason for firms to enter or exit the industry.

Incentives

Returning to our example of Hardee's, the firm's success will attract attention and encourage rivals, like Five Guys, to enter the market. As a result, the short-run profits that Hardee's enjoys will erode. As long as profits occur in the short run, other competitors will be encouraged to enter, while short-run losses will prompt some existing firms to close. The dynamic nature of competition guarantees that long-run profits and losses are not possible.

Monopolistic Competition and Competitive Markets

We have seen that monopolistic competition and competitive markets are similar; both market structures drive economic profit to zero in the long run. But monopolistic competitors enjoy some market power, which is a crucial difference. In this section, we compare pricing and output decisions in these two market structures. Then we look at issues of scale and output.

THE RELATIONSHIP BETWEEN PRICE, MARGINAL COST, AND LONG-RUN AVERAGE COST Monopolistically competitive firms have some market power, which enables them to charge slightly more than firms in competitive markets. Figure 12.3 compares the long-run equilibrium between monopolistic competition and a competitive market. Turning first to

FIGURE 12.3

The Long-Run Equilibrium in Monopolistic Competition and Competitive Markets

There are two primary differences between the long-run equilibrium in monopolistic competition (a) and a competitive market (b). First, monopolistic competition produces markup, because P is greater than MC. In a competitive market, P = MC. Second, the output in monopolistic competition is smaller than the efficient scale. In a competitive market, the firm's output is equal to the most efficient scale.

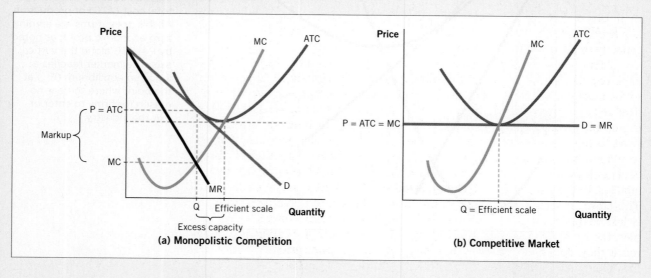

(a) Monopolistic Competition

(b) Competitive Market

the firm in a market characterized by monopolistic competition, shown in panel (a), notice that the price (P) is greater than the marginal cost (MC) of making one more unit. The difference between P and MC is known as the markup. **Markup** is the difference between the price the firm charges and the marginal cost of production.

A markup is possible when a firm enjoys some market power. Products such as bottled water, cosmetics, prescription medicines, eyeglass frames, brand-name clothing, restaurant drinks, and greeting cards all have hefty markups. Let's focus on bottled water. In most cases, it costs just pennies to produce a bottle of water, but you're unlikely to find it for less than $1; there is a lot of markup on every bottle! Some firms differentiate their product by marketing their water as the "purest" or the "cleanest." Other companies use special packaging. While the marketing of bottled water is unquestionably a successful business strategy, the markup means that consumers pay more. You can observe this result in panel (a) of Figure 12.3, where the price under monopolistic competition is higher than the price in a competitive market, shown in panel (b).

Next, look at the ATC curves in both panels. Because a monopolistic competitor has a downward-sloping demand curve, the point of tangency between the demand curve and the ATC curve is different from the point of tangency in a competitive market. The point where P = ATC is higher under monopolistic competition. Panel (b) shows the demand curve just tangent to the ATC curve at ATC's lowest point in a competitive market. Consequently, we can say that monopolistic competition produces higher prices than a competitive market does. If this result seems odd to you, recall that entry and exit do not ensure the lowest possible price, only that the price is equal to the average total cost of production. In a competitive market, where the demand curve is horizontal, the price is always the lowest possible average total cost of production. This is not the case under monopolistic competition. However, the price in monopolistic competition often reflects quality; cheap food is cheap for a reason. Firms may charge more for higher-quality food, but there will still be zero economic profit.

SCALE AND OUTPUT When a firm produces at an output level smaller than the output level needed to minimize average total costs, we say it has **excess capacity**. Turning back to panel (a) of Figure 12.3, we see excess capacity in the difference between Q and the efficient scale.

This result differs from what we see in panel (b) of Figure 12.3 for a competitive market. In a competitive market, the profit-maximizing output is equal to the most efficient scale of operation. This result is guaranteed because each firm sells an identical product and must therefore set its price equal to the minimum point on the average total cost curve. If, for instance, a corn farmer tried to sell a harvest for more than the prevailing market price, the farmer would not find any customers. In contrast, a monopolistic competitor in a food court enjoys market power because some customers prefer its product, which enables food court vendors to charge more than the lowest average total cost. Therefore, under monopolistic competition, the profit-maximizing output is less than the minimum efficient scale. Monopolistically competitive firms have the capacity to produce more output at a lower cost. But if they produced more, they would have to lower their price. Because a lower price decreases the firm's marginal revenue, it is more profitable for the monopolistic competitor to operate with excess capacity.

Markup
is the difference between the price the firm charges and the marginal cost of production.

Excess capacity
occurs when a firm produces at an output level smaller than the output level needed to minimize average total costs.

Monopolistic Competition, Inefficiency, and Social Welfare

Monopolistic competition produces a higher price and a lower level of output than a competitive market does. Recall that we looked at efficiency as a way to determine whether a firm's decisions are consistent with an output level beneficial to society. Does monopolistic competition display efficiency?

In Figure 12.3, panel (a), we observed that a monopolistic competitor has costs slightly above the lowest possible cost. So the average total costs of a monopolistically competitive firm are higher than those of a firm in a competitive market. This result is not efficient. To achieve efficiency, the monopolistically competitive firm could lower its price to what we would find in competitive markets. However, because a monopolistic competitor's goal is to make a profit, there is no incentive for the firm to lower its price. Every monopolistic competitor has a downward-sloping demand curve, so the demand curve cannot be tangent to the minimum point along the average total cost curve, as seen in panel (a).

Markup is a second source of inefficiency. We have seen that, for a monopolistically competitive firm at the profit-maximizing output level, $P > MC$ by an amount equal to the markup. The price reflects the consumer's willingness to pay, and this amount exceeds the marginal cost of production. A reduced markup would benefit consumers by lowering the price and decreasing the spread between the price and the marginal cost. If the firm did away with the markup entirely and set $P = MC$, the output level would benefit the greatest number of consumers. However, this result would not be practical. At the point where the greatest efficiency occurs, the demand curve would be below the average total cost curve and the firm would lose money. It is unreasonable to expect a profit-seeking firm to pursue a pricing strategy that would benefit its customers at the expense of its own profit.

What if the government intervened on behalf of the consumer? Increased efficiency could be achieved through government regulation. After all, the government regulates monopolists to reduce market power and restore social welfare. Couldn't the government do the same in monopolistically competitive markets? Yes and no! It is certainly possible, but not desirable. Monopolistically competitive firms have a limited amount of market power, so they cannot make a long-run economic profit like monopolists do. In addition, regulating the prices that firms in a monopolistically competitive market can charge would put many of them out of business. Bear in mind we are talking about firms in markets like the fast-food industry. Doing away with a significant percentage of these firms would mean fewer places for consumers to grab a quick bite. The remaining restaurants would be more efficient, but with fewer restaurants the trade-off for consumers would be less convenience and fewer choices.

Regulating monopolistic competition through marginal cost pricing, or setting $P = MC$, would also create a host of problems like those we discussed for monopoly. A good proportion of the economy consists of monopolistically competitive firms, so the scale of the regulatory effort would be enormous. And because implementing marginal cost pricing would result in widespread losses, the government would need to find a way to subsidize the regulated firms to keep them in business. Because the only way to fund these subsidies would be higher taxes, the inefficiencies present in monopolistic competition do not warrant government action.

Perrier has a distinctive look—but how different is it from other mineral water?

Trade-offs

VARYING DEGREES OF PRODUCT DIFFERENTIATION We have seen that products sold under monopolistic competition are more differentiated than those sold in a competitive market and less differentiated than those sold under monopoly. At one end of these two extremes we have competitive markets where firms sell identical products, have no market power, and face a perfectly elastic demand curve. At the other end we have a monopolist that sells a unique product without good substitutes and faces a steep downward-sloping demand curve indicative of highly inelastic demand. What about the firm that operates under monopolistic competition?

Figure 12.4 illustrates two monopolistic competitors with varying degrees of product differentiation. Firm A enjoys significant differentiation. High levels of differentiation occur when the firm has an especially attractive location, style, type, or quality of product that is in high demand among consumers and that competitors cannot easily replicate. H&M, Urban Outfitters, and Abercrombie & Fitch are good examples. Consumers have strong brand loyalty for the clothes these firms sell, so the demand curve is quite inelastic. The relatively steep slope of the demand curve means that the point of tangency between the demand curve (D) and the average total cost curve (ATC) occurs at a high price, which produces a large amount of excess capacity. In contrast,

---

FIGURE 12.4

Product Differentiation, Excess Capacity, and Efficiency

The difference in product differentiation is represented by the steepness (elasticity) of the demand curve, since the demand curve for firm A enjoys more product differentiation. As a result, it has more excess capacity and is less efficient. Firm B sells a product that is only slightly different from its competitors'. In this case, consumers have only weak preferences about which firm to buy from, and consumer demand is elastic. The results are a small amount of excess capacity and a more efficient result.

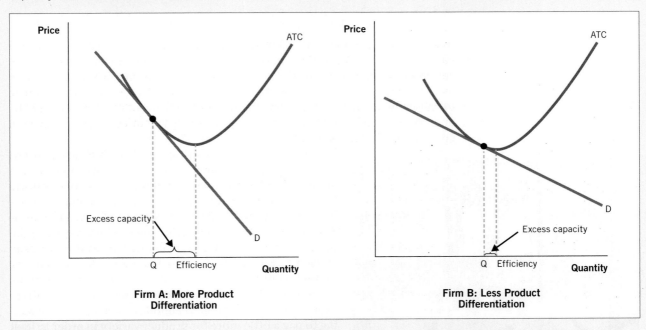

Firm A: More Product Differentiation

Firm B: Less Product Differentiation

Product Differentiation

SUPERIOR DONUTS

On the CBS sitcom *Superior Donuts,* Arthur is an old-school doughnut shop owner who runs the place with the help of a young employee, Franco. One day a new customer, Sofia, comes in and starts asking general questions about the neighborhood and how the shop operates. It turns out Sofia was doing recon, trying to gauge whether or not she should park her food truck out front! When she shows up a few minutes later, Arthur is incensed but Sofia doesn't care. She pops a few coins in a parking meter and opens her truck for business.

Sofia sells organic breakfast dishes at a much higher price point than Superior Donuts, so customers now have a second choice of where to eat. More importantly, since barriers to entering the market are low and the products served are differentiated, this is

Which do you prefer—an organic breakfast bowl or a donut?

a great example of how monopolistically competitive markets work to provide consumers with variety and reasonable prices.

Would you want to dress like this every day? Product variety is something consumers are willing to pay for.

firm B sells a product only slightly different from its competitors'. Here we can think of T.J. Maxx, Ross, and Marshalls—three companies that primarily sell discounted clothes. In this case, consumers have only weak preferences for a particular firm and consumer demand is elastic. The relatively flat nature of the demand curve means that the point of tangency between demand (D) and average total cost (ATC) occurs at a relatively low price, which produces a small amount of excess capacity.

Monopolistic competition leads to substantial product variety and greater selection and choice, all of which are beneficial to consumers. Therefore, any policy efforts to reduce inefficiency by lowering the prices that monopolistically competitive firms can charge will have the unintended consequence of limiting the product variety in the market. That sounds like a small price to pay for increased efficiency. But not so fast! Imagine a world without any product differentiation in clothes. One reason fashions go in and out of style is the desire among consumers to express their individuality. Therefore, consumers are willing to pay a little more for product variety in order to look different from everyone else.

Markup: Punch Pizza versus Pizza Hut

QUESTION: Punch Pizza is a small upscale chain in Minnesota that uses wood-fired ovens. In contrast, Pizza Hut is a large national chain. Which pizza chain would have a greater markup on each pizza?

ANSWER: If you ask people in the Twin Cities about their favorite pizza, you will find a cultlike following for Punch Pizza. That loyalty translates into inelastic demand. Punch Pizza claims to make the best Neapolitan pie. Fans of this style of pizza gravitate to Punch Pizza for the unique texture and flavor. In contrast, Pizza Hut competes in the middle of the pizza market and has crafted a taste that appeals to a broader set of customers. Pizza Hut's customers can find many other places that serve a similar product, so these customers are much more price sensitive.

Punch Pizza uses wood-fired ovens.

The marginal cost of making pizza at both places consists of the dough, the toppings, and wages for labor. At Pizza Hut, pizza assembly is streamlined for efficiency. Punch Pizza is more labor intensive, but its marginal cost is still relatively low. The prices at Punch Pizza are much higher than at Pizza Hut. As a result, the markup—or the difference between the price charged and the marginal cost of production—is greater at Punch Pizza than at Pizza Hut.

Marginal thinking

CHALLENGE QUESTION: If there's a higher markup for Punch Pizza, and therefore a higher economic profit, won't this attract new entrants?

ANSWER: Since barriers to entry into a monopolistically competitive market are relatively low, new firms will enter. As the supply expands, the market price drops and the demand for any particular pizza place becomes more elastic. This means that Punch Pizza's markup shrinks. So even though Punch Pizza is in an enviable position for now, competition will eventually reduce the price to a point where Punch Pizza earns zero economic profits—as is the case in every market where firms are free to enter.

Why Is Advertising Prevalent in Monopolistic Competition?

Advertising is a fact of daily life. It is also a means by which companies compete and therefore a cost of doing business in many industries. In the United States, advertising expenditures account for approximately 2% of all economic output annually. Worldwide, advertising expenses are a little less—about 1% of global economic activity. While the percentages are small in relative terms, in absolute terms worldwide advertising costs are over half a trillion dollars each year. Is this money well spent? Or is it a counterproductive contest that increases cost without adding value for the consumer? In this section, we will find that the answer is a little of both. Let's start by seeing who advertises.

Why Firms Advertise

No matter the company or slogan, the goal of advertising is to drive additional demand for the product being sold. Advertising campaigns use a variety of techniques to stimulate demand. In each instance, advertising is designed to highlight an important piece of information about the product (and remember the name of the company!). Table 12.2 shows how this process works. For instance, the FedEx slogan, "When it absolutely, positively has to be there overnight," conveys reliability and punctual service. Some customers who use FedEx are willing to pay a premium for overnight delivery because the company has differentiated itself from its competitors—UPS, DHL, and (especially) the United States Postal Service.

A successful advertising campaign will change the demand curve in two dimensions: it will shift the demand curve to the right and alter its shape. Turning to Figure 12.5, we see this change. First, the demand curve shifts to the right in response to the additional demand created by the advertising. Second, the demand curve becomes more inelastic, or slightly more vertical. This change in shape happens because advertising has highlighted features that make the product attractive to specific customers who are now more likely to want it. Because demand is more inelastic after advertising, the firm increases its market power and can raise its price.

In addition to increasing demand, advertising conveys information that consumers may find helpful in matching their preferences. Advertising tells us about the price of the goods offered, the location of products, and the introduction of new products. Firms also use advertising as a competitive mechanism to underprice one another. Finally, an advertising campaign signals quality. Firms that run expensive advertising campaigns are making a significant investment in their product. It is highly unlikely that a firm would spend a great deal on advertising if it did not think the process would yield a positive return. So a rational consumer can infer that firms spending a great deal on advertising are likely to have a higher-quality product than a competitor who does not advertise.

A wonderful example of this is Columbia Sportswear, a high-end maker and distributor of outerwear, sportswear, footwear, headgear, camping equipment, and ski apparel. Columbia ads feature the company CEO, Gert Boyle. She's better known as "Ma Boyle, One Tough Mother," thanks to a decades-long ad campaign for the company's outdoor apparel products. Columbia differentiated itself from its competitors, whose ads usually featured attractive young hikers and skiers, by chronicling the adventures of Boyle and her son, Tim, who gamely endured a variety of extreme conditions while bundled up in Columbia outerwear. The commercials reinforced the idea that Columbia products are worth a premium.

Advertising in Different Markets

Many firms engage in advertising, but advertising is not equally productive in all market structures. In our continuum from competitive markets to monopoly, markets that function under monopolistic competition invest the most in advertising.

ADVERTISING IN COMPETITIVE MARKETS As you know by now, competitive firms sell nearly identical products at an identical price. For this

TABLE 12.2

Advertising and Demand

Company / Product	Advertising slogan	How it increases demand
Convention and Visitors Authority / Las Vegas 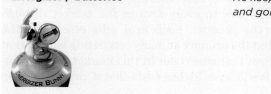	*What happens here stays here.*	The slogan attempts to convince travelers that they will have a better vacation than anywhere else.
John Deere / tractors 	*Nothing runs like a Deere.*	The emphasis on quality and performance appeals to buyers who desire a high-quality tractor.
Frito-Lay / potato chips 	*Betcha can't eat just one.*	The message that one potato chip is not enough to satisfy your craving appeals to chip buyers who choose better taste over lower-priced generics.
Energizer / batteries	*He keeps going and going and going.*	The campaign focuses attention on longevity in order to justify the higher prices of top-quality batteries.
FedEx / delivery service	*When it absolutely, positively has to be there overnight.*	Reliability and timeliness are crucial attributes of overnight delivery.
Visa / credit card	*It's everywhere you want to be.*	Widespread acceptance and usability are two of the major reasons for carrying a credit card.
Skittles / candy 	*Taste the rainbow.*	The emphasis is on taste and a variety of flavors.

FIGURE 12.5

Advertising and the Demand Curve

A successful advertising campaign increases demand. Advertising also makes the demand curve more inelastic, or vertical, by informing consumers about differences they care about. After advertising, consumers desire the good more intensely, which makes the demand curve for the firm's product somewhat more vertical.

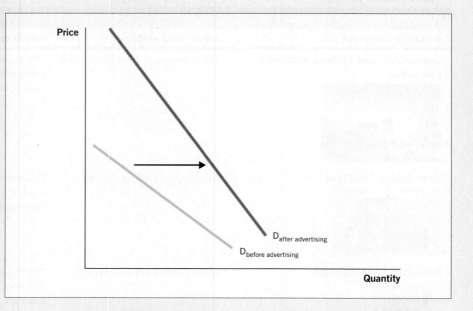

reason, advertising raises a firm's costs without directly influencing its sales. Advertising for an undifferentiated good functions like a public good for the industry as a whole: the benefits flow to every firm in the market through increased market demand for the product. Each firm sells essentially the same good, so consumers can find the product at many competing locations at the same price. An individual firm that advertises in this market is at a competitive disadvantage because it will have higher costs that it cannot pass on to the consumer.

This does not mean that we never see advertising in competitive markets. Although individual firms do not benefit from advertising, competitive industries as a whole can. For example, you have probably heard the slogan "Beef—it's what's for dinner." The campaign, which began in 1992, is recognized by over 80% of Americans and has been widely credited with increasing the demand for beef products. The campaign was funded by the National Cattlemen's Beef Association, an organization that puts millions of dollars a year into advertising. In fact, industrywide marketing campaigns such as "It's not just for breakfast anymore" by the Florida Orange Juice Growers Association or "Got milk?" by the National Milk Processor Board generally indicate that competitive firms have joined forces to advertise in an effort to increase demand. Other examples include "the incredible, edible egg" and "pork—the other white meat."

ADVERTISING UNDER MONOPOLISTIC COMPETITION Advertising is widespread under monopolistic competition because firms have differentiated products. Let's look at the advertising behavior of pizza companies.

Advertising

MAD MEN

Mad Men, which ran for seven seasons on AMC, is a show about the golden age of the advertising industry. The main character, Don Draper, is a marketing wiz. In season 6, he makes a pitch for a series of ads to sell ketchup. Gesturing at huge color photos of food that is just a condiment away from perfection, Draper explains the campaign's concept. "What's missing? One thing. Pass the Heinz." Draper understands that the goal of an ad campaign is to increase demand for a good or service and also to make the demand for whatever is being sold more inelastic. This gives the seller more pricing power and allows them charge a higher markup.

Draper's "Pass the Heinz" pitch is rejected, because the client can't wrap his head around the idea of ads that don't show the product. Fast forward fifty years, though, and in 2017, Heinz began running the ads, faithfully copied from Draper's presentation (with full credit given). The idea was brilliant—just ahead of its time.

This scene is missing just one thing.

Television commercials by national chains such as Domino's, Pizza Hut, Papa John's, and Little Caesars are widespread, as are flyers and advertisements for local pizza places. Because each pizza is slightly different, each firm's advertising increases the demand for its product and changes the slope of the demand curve. In short, the gains from advertising go directly to the firm spending the money. These benefits generate a strong incentive to advertise to gain new customers or to keep customers from switching to other products. Because each firm feels the same way, advertising becomes the norm among monopolistically competitive firms.

Incentives

Advertising and the Super Bowl

Super Bowl commercials are watched at least as closely as the football game itself. Fans love these usually creative and comedic ads. But economists pay close attention for different reasons. Who's advertising and what does it say about those industries? Are the ads money well spent, or do they increase business costs without making a noticeable difference in profits? Here we examine advertising from 1967 to 2019.

 **Inflation-adjusted Amount Spent**  **# of Super Bowls Advertised in** 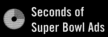 **Seconds of Super Bowl Ads**

ANHEUSER-BUSCH

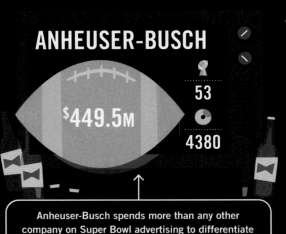

$449.5M

53

4380

> Anheuser-Busch spends more than any other company on Super Bowl advertising to differentiate its product and create brand awareness.

PEPSI CO

$289.5M

34

3780

> Coca-Cola has spent significantly less than PepsiCo on Super Bowl ads, yet it remains the market-leading soft drink brand. Coke has ramped up its Super Bowl efforts in the past few years to maintain this lead, however.

FORD

$109.8M

23

1800

COCA-COLA

$202M

29

2242

Some of these companies, especially Coca-Cola and Pepsi, are considered oligopolists rather than monopolistic competitors. We'll discuss oligopoly in the next chapter.

REVIEW QUESTIONS

- Draw what happens to a brand's demand curve when it successfully achieves product differentiation through advertising.

- Describe the risks and rewards of advertising from the perspective of both the brand and the consumer.

WHAT HAPPENED TO SEARS?

Sears, JCPenney, Kohl's, and The Gap are all famous brick-and-mortar retailers. Depending on how old you are, at some point in your life you probably spent a lot of time in one of these stores. Kohl's and The Gap struggled for a time but appear to be back on course for growth and viability. JCPenney and Sears, on the other hand, are all but done for. The last year Sears made a profit was 2010.

A few generations ago, a Sears credit card was as important as one from American Express. Sears is also historically important because it was the Sears catalog, first mailed in 1893, that allowed non-city dwellers access to products previously available only in cities.

So what has happened to Sears? Online giant Amazon and bad management have had major impacts since the mid-2000s. But Sears started losing business in the early 1990s. What happened then was the rapid rise of Walmart, which gave consumers significantly lower prices because of its sophisticated inventory control. By then, Sears had diversified into many areas, which caused it to lose focus on its main retail business. The rise of Walmart meant that Sears had to become more efficient (lower its markup) to survive, but because of the way Sears had expanded, its cost structure was higher than Walmart's.

What economics lesson can we extract from the Sears saga? A business must never take its success for granted, and you never know where your most fierce competitor will emerge from. Ever hear of Bentonville, Arkansas? That's where Walmart started (and is still headquartered).

Source: Hiroko Tabuchi and Rachel Abrams, "4 Different Turnaround Tales at Retailers Sears, Kohl's, Gap and J.C. Penney," *New York Times*, Feb. 26, 2015.

ADVERTISING AS A MONOPOLIST The monopolist sells a unique product without close substitutes. The fact that consumers have few, if any, good alternatives when deciding to buy the good makes the monopolist less likely to advertise than a monopolistic competitor. When consumer choice is limited, the firm does not have to advertise to get business. In addition, the competitive aspect is missing, so there is no need to advertise to prevent consumers from switching to rival products. However, that does not mean that the monopolist never advertises.

The monopolist may wish to advertise to inform the consumer about its product and stimulate demand. This strategy can be beneficial as long as the gains from advertising are enough to cover the cost of advertising. For example, De Beers, the giant diamond cartel, controls most of the world's supply of rough-cut diamonds. The company does not need to advertise to fend off competitors, but it advertises nevertheless because it is interested in creating more demand for diamonds. De Beers created the famous "A diamond is forever" campaign.

The Negative Effects of Advertising

We have seen the benefits of advertising, but there are also drawbacks. Two of the most significant drawbacks are that advertising raises costs and can be deceitful.

ADVERTISING AND COSTS Advertising costs are reflected in the firm's average total cost curve. Figure 12.6 shows the paradox of advertising for most firms. When a firm advertises, it hopes to increase demand for the product and sell more units—say, from point 1 at Q_1 to point 2 at the higher quantity Q_2. If the firm can sell enough additional units, it will enjoy economies of scale, and the average total cost will fall from ATC_1 to ATC_2. This return on the advertising investment looks like a good business decision.

However, the reality of advertising is much more complex. Under monopolistic competition, each firm is competing with many other firms selling somewhat different products. Rival firms will respond with advertising of their own. This dynamic makes advertising the norm in monopolistic competition. Each firm engages in competitive advertising to win new customers and keep the old ones. As a result, the impact on each individual firm's demand largely cancels out. This result is evident in the movement from point 1 to point 3 in Figure 12.6. Costs rise from ATC_1 to ATC_3 on the higher LRATC curve, but the quantity demanded may remain at Q_1. The net result is that advertising creates higher costs but no change in quantity produced and a decrease in profit. In this case, we can think of advertising as causing a negative *business-stealing externality* whereby no individual firm can easily gain market share but feels compelled to advertise to protect its customer base.

We have seen that advertising raises costs for the producer. It also raises prices for consumers. In fact, consumers who consistently favor a particular brand of a product have more inelastic demand than those who are willing to switch from one product to another. Therefore, brand loyalty often means higher prices. Let's look at an example.

FIGURE 12.6

Advertising Increases Cost

By advertising, the firm hopes to increase demand (or quantity) from point 1 to point 2. In this scenario, the increase in demand from Q_1 to Q_2 is large enough to create economies of scale even though advertising causes the long-run average total cost curve (LRATC) to rise. Because monopolistically competitive firms each advertise, the advertising efforts often cancel one another out. As a result, long-run average total costs rise without demand increasing much, so the firm may move from point 1 to point 3 instead.

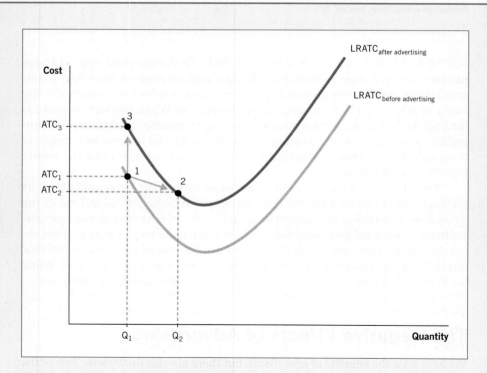

Pearl ear studs are a nice gift, but they are even better when they come in a . . .

. . . blue box.

Suppose you buy all your jewelry at Tiffany's. One day, you enter the store to pick up pearl ear studs. You can get a small pair of pearl studs at Tiffany's for $300. But it turns out you can get studs of the same size, quality, and origin (freshwater) at Pearl World for $43, and you can find them online at Amazon for $19. There are no identifying marks on the jewelry that would enable you, or a seasoned jeweler, to tell the ear studs apart! Why would you buy them at Tiffany's when you can purchase them for far less elsewhere? The answer, it turns out, is that buying ear studs is a lot like consuming many other goods: name recognition matters. So do perception and brand loyalty. Many jewelry buyers also take cues from the storefront, how the staff dress, and how the jewelry is packaged. Spending $300 total is a lot of money for the privilege of getting Tiffany's blue box. Consumers believe that Tiffany's jewelry is better, when all the store is doing is charging more markup.

TRUTH IN ADVERTISING Finally, many advertising campaigns are not just informative—they are designed to produce a psychological response. When an ad moves you to buy or act in a particular way, it becomes manipulative. Because advertising can be such a powerful way to reach customers, there is a temptation to lie about a product. To prevent firms from spreading misinformation about their products, the Federal Trade Commission (FTC) regulates

PRACTICE WHAT YOU KNOW

Advertising: Brands versus Generics

Why do some frozen pizzas cost more than others when brands that offer similar quality are only a few feet away in the frozen foods aisle? To answer that question, consider the following questions:

QUESTION: What would graphs showing price and output look like for DiGiorno and for a generic pizza? What is the markup for DiGiorno?

DiGiorno or generic?

ANSWER: Here is the graph for DiGiorno.

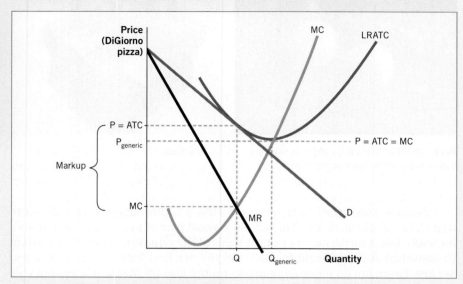

And here is the graph for the generic pizza.

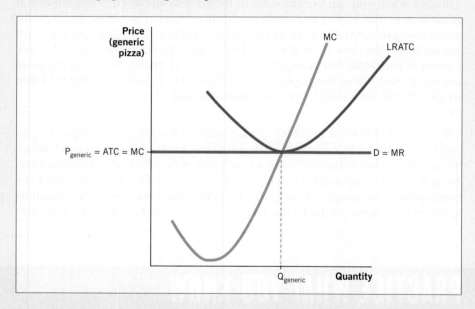

QUESTION: Which company has a stronger incentive to maintain strict quality control in the production process, DiGiorno or a generic brand? Why?

ANSWER: DiGiorno has a catchy slogan: "It's not delivery. It's DiGiorno!" This statement tries to position the product as being just as good as a freshly delivered pizza. Some customers who buy frozen pizzas will opt for DiGiorno over comparable generics because they are familiar with the company's advertising claim about its quality. Therefore, DiGiorno has a stronger incentive to make sure the product delivers as advertised. Because generic, or store-name, brands are purchased mostly on the basis of price, the customer generally does not have high expectations about the quality.

2xSnickers should really be called 1.5xSnickers. Shame on Mars for the deception.

advertising and promotes economic efficiency. At the FTC, the Division of Advertising Practices protects consumers by enforcing truth-in-advertising laws. While the commission does not have enough resources to track down every violation, it does pay particular attention to claims involving food, non-prescription drugs, dietary supplements, alcohol, and tobacco. Unsubstantiated claims are particularly prevalent on the Internet, and they tend to target vulnerable populations seeking quick fixes to a variety of medical conditions.

Of course, even with regulatory oversight, consumers must still be vigilant. At best, the FTC can remove products from the market and levy fines against companies that make unsubstantiated claims. However, the damage is often already done. The Latin phrase *caveat emptor*, or "buyer beware," sums up the dangers of false information.

Sometimes the way a product is advertised is not illegal but is still border-line unethical. Firms often engage in price deception, or tricks to make you think a price is lower than it really is. Gas stations deploy this technique by quoting prices ending in a 9/10 of a cent fraction, to slightly understate how much you are paying. But a more egregious example of price deception comes from Mars, which sells Snickers, far and away the most popular snack-sized candy bar sold in the United States. For a time, Mars sold Snickers and 2xSnickers. One would think that "two times" Snickers would be two Snickers in one longer package, right? That's the deception: the bars in 2xSnickers are smaller!

ECONOMICS IN THE REAL WORLD

THE FEDERAL TRADE COMMISSION VERSUS 1-800 CONTACTS

The FTC found 1-800 Contacts guilty of manipulative advertising.

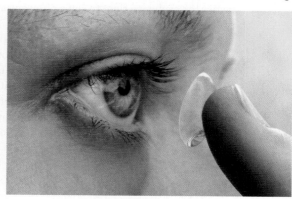

When we search online, we trust that the most pertinent results are shown first. How would you feel—and how would it change your buying behavior—if you knew that the search results were being manipulated? That's what happened with 1-800 Contacts, America's largest online retailer of contact lenses. The firm was found guilty of unlawfully orchestrating a web of anticompet-itive agreements with rival online contact lens sellers, to sup-press competition in certain online search forums that advertise to consumers. So instead of buying contacts in a monopolisti-cally competitive online space, consumers were shown search results with much higher prices.

Product Differentiation: Would You Buy a Franchise?

- Restaurant failures are very high and running a franchise can lower your risk.
- Franchises provide brand familiarity.
- However, rights to franchise can come with very high fees. The five restaurants with the highest combined franchise and start-up costs are:

  Golden Corral, $6.8M

  Buffalo Wild Wings, $3.2M

  Culver's, $2.8M

  KFC, $2.5M

  Denny's, $2.4M

Franchises are valuable in markets where product differentiation matters. McDonald's, Panera Bread, and KFC all have a different take on serving fast food. But what does it mean to own a franchise?

Franchises are sold to individual owners, who operate subject to the terms of their agreement with the parent company. For instance, purchasing a McDonald's franchise and opening a new store can cost over $2 million. McDonald's also requires the individual restaurant owner to charge certain prices and offer menu items selected by the parent corporation. As a result, customers who prefer a certain type and quality of food know that the dining experience at each McDonald's will be similar. Most franchises also come with noncompete clauses that guarantee that another franchise will not open nearby. This guarantee gives the franchise owner the exclusive right to sell a differentiated product in a given area.

Suppose you want to start a restaurant. Why would you, or anyone else, be willing to pay over $2 million just for the right to sell food? For that amount, you could open your own restaurant with a custom menu and interior, create your own marketing plan, and locate anywhere you like. For example, Golden Corral and Buffalo Wild Wings

are two restaurants with high start-up costs exceeding $3 million. Golden Corral is the largest buffet-style restaurant in the country, and Buffalo Wild Wings is one of the top locations to watch sporting events. You might think it would make more sense to avoid the franchising costs by opening your own buffet or setting up a bank of big-screen TVs. However, failures in the restaurant industry are high. With a franchise, the customer knows what to expect. Translation: high franchise fees enable firms to charge a higher markup because consumer demand is more inelastic.

Franchise owners are assured of visibility and a ready supply of customers. Purchasing a franchise means more potential customers will notice your restaurant, and that drives up revenues. Is that worth $2 million or more? Yes, in some cases. Suppose you'll do $1 million in annual sales as part of a franchise, but only $0.5 million on your own. That half-million difference over 20 years means $10 million more in revenue, a healthy chunk of which will turn into profits. This is the magic of franchising.

How much would you pay for a KFC franchise?

Conclusion

Firms willingly spend on advertising because it can increase demand, build brand loyalty, and provide consumers with useful information about differences in products. Monopolistic competitors advertise and mark up their products like monopolists, but, like firms in a competitive market, they cannot earn long-run profits. While an economic profit is possible in the short run in all three types of market structure (perfect competition, monopolistic competition, and monopoly), only the monopolist, whose business has significant barriers to entry, can earn an economic profit in the long run. Entry and exit cause long-run profits to equal zero in competitive and monopolistically competitive firms.

Monopolistic competitors are price makers who fail to achieve the most efficient welfare-maximizing output for society. But this observation does not tell the entire story. Monopolistic competitors do not have as much market power or create as much excess capacity or markup as monopolists. Consequently, the monopolistic competitor lacks the ability to exploit consumers. The result is not perfect, but widespread monopolistic competition generally serves consumers and society well.

In the next chapter, we continue our exploration of market structure with *oligopoly*, which produces results that are much closer to monopoly than monopolistic competition. ✳

▪ ANSWERING *the* BIG QUESTIONS ▪

What is monopolistic competition?

- Monopolistic competition is a market structure characterized by low barriers to entry and many firms selling differentiated products.
- Differentiation of products takes three forms: differentiation by style or type, location, and quality.

What are the differences among monopolistic competition, competitive markets, and monopoly?

- Monopolistic competitors, like monopolists, are price makers with downward-sloping demand curves. Whenever the demand curve is downward sloping, the firm is able to mark up the price above marginal cost. The results are excess capacity and an inefficient level of output.
- In the long run, barriers to entry enable a monopoly to earn an economic profit. This is not the case for monopolistic competition or competitive markets.

Why is advertising prevalent in monopolistic competition?

- Advertising performs useful functions under monopolistic competition: it conveys information about the price of the goods offered for sale, the location of products, and new products. It also signals differences in quality. However, advertising also encourages brand loyalty, which makes it harder for other businesses to successfully enter the market. Advertising can be manipulative and misleading.

·CHAPTER PROBLEMS·

Concepts You Should Know

excess capacity (p. 375)
markup (p. 375)

monopolistic competition (p. 368)
product differentiation (p. 368)

Questions for Review

1. Why is product differentiation necessary for monopolistic competition? What are three types of product differentiation?

2. How is monopolistic competition like competitive markets? How is monopolistic competition like monopoly?

3. Why do monopolistically competitive firms produce less than those operating at the most efficient scale of production?

4. Draw a graph that shows a monopolistic competitor making an economic profit in the short run and a graph that shows a monopolistic competitor making no economic profit in the long run.

5. Monopolistic competition produces a result that is inefficient. Does this outcome mean that monopolistically competitive markets should be regulated? Discuss.

6. Draw a typical demand curve for competitive markets, monopolistic competition, and monopoly. Which of these demand curves is the most inelastic? Why?

7. How does advertising benefit society? In what ways can advertising be harmful?

8. When you buy a generic product instead of its name-brand counterpart, is the good you purchase really inferior, or is it the same good, simply repackaged by the name-band manufacturer under another label?

Study Problems (*solved at the end of the section)

✳ 1. At your high school reunion, a friend describes his plan to take a break from his florist shop and sail around the world. He says that if he continues to make the same economic profit for the next five years, he will be able to afford the trip. Do you think your friend will be able to achieve his dream in five years? What do you expect to happen to his firm's profits in the long run?

2. Which of the following could be considered a monopolistic competitor?

   a. a local corn farmer
   b. the Tennessee Valley Authority, a large electricity producer
   c. a pizza delivery business
   d. a grocery store
   e. Stella McCartney, fashion designer

3. Which of the following are the same under monopolistic competition and in a competitive market in the long run?

   a. the markup the firm charges
   b. the price the firm charges to consumers

   c. the firm's excess capacity
   d. the average total cost of production
   e. the amount of advertising
   f. the firm's profit
   g. the efficiency of the market structure

4. In competitive markets, price is equal to marginal cost in the long run. Explain why this statement is not true for monopolistic competition.

5. Econoburgers, a fast-food restaurant in a crowded local market, has reached a long-run equilibrium.

   a. Draw a diagram showing demand, marginal revenue, average total cost, and marginal cost curves for Econoburgers.
   b. How much profit is Econoburgers making?
   c. Suppose that the government decides to regulate burger production to make it more efficient. Explain what would happen to the price of Econoburgers and the firm's output.

6. Consider two different companies. The first manufactures cardboard, and the second sells books. Which firm is more likely to advertise?

7. In the diagram that follows, identify the demand curve that is consistent with a monopolistic competitor making zero long-run economic profit. Explain why you have chosen that demand curve and why the other two demand curves are not consistent with monopolistic competition.

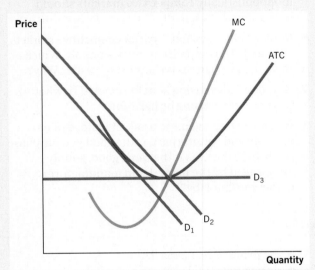

8. Titleist has an advertising slogan: "#1 ball in golf." Consumers can also buy generic golf balls. The manufacturers of generic golf balls do not engage in any advertising. Assume that the average total

cost of producing Titleist and generic golf balls is the same.

   a. Create a graph showing the price and the markup for Titleist.

   b. In a separate graph, show the price and the output for the generic firms.

   c. Who has a stronger incentive to maintain strict quality control in the production process—Titleist or the generic firms? Why?

9. Taste of India is a small restaurant in a small town. The owner of Taste of India marks up his dishes by 300%. Indian Cuisine is a small restaurant in a large city. The owner of Indian Cuisine marks up her dishes by 200%. Explain why the markup is higher in the small town.

* 10. Read the following online article: http://20 somethingfinance.com/why-eyeglasses-are-so -expensive-how-you-can-pay-less. Using your understanding of monopolistic competition and markup, explain why retail customers pay so much more for eyeglasses than online customers do. You can also watch this video from *Adam Ruins Everything* for an interesting explanation: www.youtube.com/watch?v=CAeHuDcy_bY.

* 11. Consider a monopolistically competitive firm. From the point of view of the remaining firms, as firms leave the industry we can think of this as a shift to the

   a. left for each individual firm's supply curve.

   b. left in each individual firm's MC curve.

   c. right in each individual firm's ATC curve.

   d. right in each individual firm's demand curve.

Solved Problems

1. The florist business is monopolistically competitive. This means firms are free to enter and exit at any time. Firms will enter because your friend's shop is making an economic profit. As new florist shops open, the added competition will drive prices down, causing your friend's profits to fall. In the long run, this means he will not be able to make an economic profit. He will earn only enough to cover his opportunity costs, or what is known as a *fair return* on his investment. That is not to say he won't be able to save enough to sail around the

world, but it won't happen as fast as he would like because other firms will enter the market and limit his profits going forward.

6. The cardboard firm manufactures a product that is a component used mostly by other firms that need to package final products for sale. As a result, any efforts at advertising will only raise costs without increasing the demand for cardboard. This situation contrasts with that of the bookseller, who advertises to attract consumers to the store. More traffic means more purchases of books and other items sold in the store. The bookstore has some market power and markup. In this case, it pays to advertise. A cardboard manufacturing firm sells exactly the same product as other cardboard producers, so it has no market power, and any advertising expenses will only make its cost higher than its rivals'.

10. There are many retailers (LensCrafters, Pearle, Sears, Target), but the brands they sell all come from Italian eyeglass manufacturer Luxottica. Luxottica prevents these major retailers from discounting the frames and will pull their brands if they do. However, if you don't care about the brand of eyeglasses you wear, you can find a pair online for well under $100. Online retailers aren't selling a brand, so they attract customers with much more elastic demand compared with customers who want their frames to be fashionable. This scenario fits perfectly with the idea of markup. Firms with brand-loyal customers have much higher markup than firms with customers who do not care about the brand they purchase.

11. The correct answer is d: each individual firm's demand curve shifts to the right. The reason is that as firms exit, each remaining firm picks up additional customers.

Oligopoly and Strategic Behavior

Cell Phone Companies are Competitive.

If you have a cell phone, chances are that you receive service from one of three major cell phone carriers in the United States: AT&T, Verizon, or T-Mobile. Together, these firms control 95% of all cellular service. In some respects, this market is very competitive. For example, cell phone companies advertise intensely, and they offer a variety of phones with voice and data plans. Also, there are differences in network coverage and in the number of applications users can access. But despite outward appearances, the cell phone companies do not do business in a competitive or even a monopolistically competitive market. One important reason for this is the expense of building and maintaining a cellular network. The largest cell phone companies have invested billions of dollars in infrastructure in order to attract customers based on cell phone network quality and speed and the plans and services the companies provide. Therefore, the cost of entry is very high. As we learned in Chapter 10, barriers to entry are a key feature of monopolies.

The cell phone industry has features of both competition and monopoly: competition is fierce, but smaller firms and potential entrants into the market find it difficult to enter and compete. This mixture of characteristics represents another form of market structure—*oligopoly*. In this chapter, we examine oligopoly by comparing it with other market

Gamers delight, 5G networks will make your cell phones even more powerful! Whatever this customer is seeing in her 3D display has apparently made quite an impression.

structures already familiar to you. We then look at some of the strategic behaviors firms in an oligopoly employ, an examination that leads us into the fascinating topic of game theory.

- BIG QUESTIONS -

- What is oligopoly?
- How does game theory explain strategic behavior?
- How do government policies affect oligopoly behavior?
- What are network externalities?

What Is Oligopoly?

Oligopoly
is a form of market structure that exists when a small number of firms sell a differentiated product in a market with high barriers to entry.

Oligopoly is a form of market structure that exists when a small number of firms sell a product in a market with significant barriers to entry. An oligopolist is like a monopolistic competitor in that it often sells a differentiated product. But like pure monopolists, oligopolists enjoy significant barriers to entry. Table 13.1 compares the differences and similarities between the four market structures.

We have seen that firms in monopolistically competitive markets usually have a limited amount of market power. As a result, buyers often find low prices (but not as low as competitive markets) and wide availability. In contrast, an oligopolist sells in a market with significant barriers to entry and fewer rivals. Thus, the oligopolist has more market power than a firm operating under monopolistic competition. However, because an oligopolistic market has more than one seller, no single oligopolist has as much market power as a monopolist.

Our study of oligopoly begins with a look at how economists measure market power in an industry. We then work through a simplified model of oligopoly to explore the choices that oligopolists make.

TABLE 13.1

Comparing Oligopoly to Other Market Structures

Competitive market	Monopolistic competition	Oligopoly	Monopoly
Many sellers	Many sellers	A few sellers	One seller
Similar products	Differentiated product	Differentiated product (most of the time)	Unique product without close substitutes
Free entry and exit	Easy entry and exit	Barriers to entry	Significant barriers to entry

TABLE 13.2

Highly Concentrated Industries in the United States

Industry	Concentration ratio of the four largest firms (%)	Top firms
Search engines	98.5	Google, Yahoo, Microsoft
Wireless telecommunications	94.7	Verizon, AT&T, T-Mobile, Sprint
Satellite TV providers	94.5	DIRECTV, DISH Network
Soda production	93.7	Coca-Cola, PepsiCo, Dr Pepper Snapple
Sanitary paper products	92.7	Kimberly-Clark, Procter & Gamble, Georgia-Pacific
Lighting and bulb manufacturing	91.9	General Electric, Philips, Siemens
Tire manufacturing (domestic)	91.3	Goodyear, Michelin, Cooper, Bridgestone
Major household appliances	90.0	Whirlpool, Electrolux, General Electric, LG
Automobile manufacturing (domestic)	87.0	General Motors, Toyota, Ford, Fiat-Chrysler

Source: *Highly Concentrated: Companies That Dominate Their Industries*, www.ibisworld.com. Special Report, February 2012.

Measuring the Concentration of Industries

In markets with only a few sellers, industry output is highly concentrated among a few large firms. Economists use *concentration ratios* as a measure of the oligopoly power present in an industry. The most common measure, known as the four-firm concentration ratio, expresses the sales of the four largest firms in an industry as a percentage of that industry's total sales. Table 13.2 lists the four-firm concentration ratios for highly concentrated industries in the United States. This ratio is determined by taking the output of the four largest firms in an industry and dividing that output by the total production in the entire industry.

In highly concentrated industries like search engines, wireless telecommunications, and satellite TV providers, the market share held by the four largest firms approaches 100%. At the bottom of our list of most concentrated industries is domestic automobile manufacturing. General Motors, Fiat Chrysler, Ford, and Toyota (which has seven manufacturing plants in the United States) dominate the domestic automobile industry. These large firms have significant market power.

However, when evaluating market power in an industry, it is important to be aware of international activity. In several industries, including automobile and tire manufacturing, intense global competition keeps the market power of U.S. companies in check. For instance, domestic manufacturers that produce automobiles also must compete globally against cars produced elsewhere. This means that vehicles produced by Honda, Nissan, Volkswagen, Kia, and Volvo, to name just a few companies, limit the market power of domestic producers. As a result, the concentration ratio is a rough gauge of oligopoly power—not an absolute measure.

Competition from foreign car companies keeps the market power of the U.S.-based automobile companies in check.

Collusion and Cartels in a Simple Duopoly Example

In this section, we explore the two conflicting tendencies found in oligopoly: oligopolists would like to act like monopolists, but they often end up competing like monopolistic competitors. To help us understand oligopoly behavior, we start with a simplified example: an industry consisting of only two firms, known as a *duopoly*. Duopolies (such as Boeing and Airbus in the wide-body jet market) are rare in national and international markets, but not that uncommon in small, local markets. For example, in many small communities, the number of cell phone carriers is limited. Imagine a small town where only two providers have cell phone towers. In this case, the cell towers are a sunk cost (see Chapter 9); both towers were built to service all of the customers in the town, so each carrier has substantial excess capacity when the customers are divided between the two carriers. Also, because there is extra capacity on each network, the marginal cost of adding additional customers is zero.

Table 13.3 shows the community's demand for cell phones. Because the prices and quantities listed in the first two columns are negatively related, the data are consistent with a downward-sloping demand curve.

Column 3 calculates the total revenue from columns 1 and 2. With Table 13.3 as our guide, we will examine the output in this market under three scenarios: competition, monopoly, and duopoly.

Duopoly sits between the two extremes. Competition still exists, but it is not as extensive as you would see in competitive markets, which ruthlessly drive the price down to cost. Nor does the result always mirror that of monopoly, where competitive pressures are completely absent. In an oligopoly, a small number of firms feel competitive pressures and also enjoy some of the advantages of monopoly.

TABLE 13.3

The Demand Schedule for Cell Phones

Here we assume that 1 customer = 1 cell phone = 1 purchase of cell phone service.

(1) Price/month (P)	(2) Number of customers (Q)	(3) Total revenue (TR) (P) × (Q)
$180	0	$0
165	100	16,500
150	200	30,000
135	300	40,500
120	400	48,000
105	500	52,500
90	600	54,000
75	700	52,500
60	800	48,000
45	900	40,500
30	1,000	30,000
15	1,100	16,500
0	1,200	0

COMPETITIVE OUTCOME Recall that competitive markets drive prices down to the point at which marginal revenue is equal to the marginal cost. So if the market is highly competitive and the marginal cost is zero, we would expect the final price of cell phone service to be zero and the quantity supplied to be 1,200 customers—the number of people who live in the small town. At this point, anyone who desires cell phone service would be able to receive it without cost. Because efficiency exists when the output is maximized, and because everyone who lives in the community would have cell phone service, the result would be socially efficient. However, it is unrealistic to expect this outcome. Cell phone companies provide a good that is nonrival and also excludable; in other words, they sell a club good (see Chapter 7). Because these firms are in business to make money, they will not provide something for nothing.

Marginal thinking

MONOPOLY OUTCOME At the other extreme of the market structure continuum, a monopolist faces no competition, and price decisions do not depend on the activity of other firms. A monopolist can search for the price that brings it the most profit. Looking at Table 13.3, we see that total revenue peaks at $54,000. At this point, the price is $90 per month, and 600 customers sign up for cell phone service. Compared with a competitive market, the monopoly price is higher and the quantity sold is lower. The result is a loss of efficiency.

DUOPOLY OUTCOME In a duopoly, the two firms can decide to cooperate—even though this practice is illegal in the United States, as we will discuss shortly. If the duopolists cooperate, we say that they collude. **Collusion** is an agreement between rival firms that specifies the price each firm charges and the quantity it produces. The firms that collude can act like a single monopolist to maximize their profits. In this case, the monopolist would maximize its profit by charging $90 and serving 600 customers. If the duopolists divide the market equally, they will each have 300 customers who pay $90, for a total of $27,000 in revenue each.

When two or more firms act in unison, economists refer to them as a **cartel**. Many countries prohibit cartels. In the United States, **antitrust laws** prohibit collusion. However, even if collusion were legal, it would probably fail more often than not. Imagine that two theoretical cell phone companies, AT-Phone and Horizon, have formed a cartel and agreed that each will serve 300 customers at a price of $90 per month per customer. But AT-Phone and Horizon each have an incentive to earn more revenue by lowering their price while the rival company keeps the agreement. Suppose AT-Phone lowers its price to $75. Looking at Table 13.3, we see that at this price the total market demand rises to 700 customers—and AT-phone will capture the entire market, by selling at the lowest price. So AT-Phone will serve 700 customers, and its revenue will be 700 × $75, or $52,500. This is an improvement of $25,500 over what AT-Phone made when the market price was $90 and the customers were equally divided.

How would Horizon react? At the very least, unless it wants to earn $0, it had better match AT-Phone's lower price. Horizon would then attract 350 customers, half the market at a price of $75, and now AT-Phone and Horizon would each bring in revenue of 350 × $75, or $26,250, leaving each firm making $750 less than when they served only 600 customers total. From what we know about competitive markets, we might expect the competition

Collusion
is an agreement among rival firms that specifies the price each firm charges and the quantity it produces.

A **cartel** is a group of two or more firms that act in unison.

Antitrust laws
attempt to prevent oligopolies from behaving like monopolies.

Incentives

TABLE 13.4

Outcomes under Competition, Duopoly, and Monopoly

	Competitive markets	Duopoly	Monopoly
Price	$0	$0–90	$90
Output	1,200	600–1200	600
Socially efficient?	Yes	Only when the price is $0 and output is 1200	No
Explanation	Because the marginal cost of providing cell phone service is zero, the price is eventually driven to zero. Since firms are in business to make a profit, it is unrealistic to expect this result.	Because firms are mutually interdependent, each adopts a strategy based on the actions of its rival. The two firms may decide to collude and charge $90, or competitive pressures may lead them to charge a much lower price.	The monopolist is free to choose the profit-maximizing output. In the cell phone example, it maximizes its total revenue. As a result, the monopolist charges $90 and serves 600 customers.

between the two firms to cause a price war in which price eventually falls to zero. Duopolists are unlikely to participate in an all-out price war because both firms would no longer be making any profit, but we cannot know to what extent competitive pressures will determine each firm's decision.

Table 13.4 summarizes the different results under competition, duopoly, and monopoly using our cell phone example. From this example, we see that a market with a small number of sellers is characterized by **mutual interdependence**, which is a market situation in which the actions of one firm have an impact on the price and output of its competitors. As a result, a firm's market share is determined by the products it offers, the prices it charges, and the actions of its rivals.

Oligopolists want to emulate the monopoly outcome, but the push to compete with their rivals often makes it difficult to maintain a cartel. Yet the idea that cartels are unstable is not guaranteed. When a stable cartel is not achieved, firms in oligopoly fall short of fully maximizing profits. But they also do not compete to the same degree as firms in competitive markets. Therefore, when a market is an oligopoly, output is likely to be higher than under a monopoly and lower than within a competitive market. As you would expect, the amount of output affects the prices. The higher output (compared with monopoly) makes oligopoly prices generally lower than monopoly prices, and the lower output (compared with a competitive market) makes oligopoly prices higher than those found in competitive markets.

In many industries, smaller firms may take a cue from the decisions made by the price leader. **Price leadership** occurs when a single firm, known as the price leader, produces a large share of the total output in the industry. The price leader sets the price and output level that maximizes its own profits. Smaller firms then set their prices to match the price leader. Because the impact on price is small to begin with, it makes sense that smaller rivals tend to follow the price leader.

Price leadership is not illegal because it does not involve collusion. Rather, it relies on an understanding that an effort to resist changes implemented by the price leader will lead to both increased price competition and lower

Mutual interdependence is a market situation where the actions of one firm have an impact on the price and output of its competitors.

Price leadership occurs when a dominant firm in an industry sets the price that maximizes its profits and the smaller firms in the industry follow by setting their prices to match the price leader.

profits for every firm in the industry. Because the firms act in accordance with one another, this practice is commonly known as *tacit collusion*.

One well-known example of price leadership is pricing patterns in the airline industry. On almost any route with multiple carrier options, a price search for flights will reveal almost identical prices on basic economy-class flights. This similarity of prices happens even though the firms do not collude to set a profit-maximizing price. Rather, when one firm sets a fare, the other carriers feel compelled to match it. Price leadership works best when the largest firm in an industry raises or lowers its price and smaller rivals follow suit.

ECONOMICS IN THE REAL WORLD

OPEC: AN INTERNATIONAL CARTEL

The best-known cartel is the Organization of the Petroleum Exporting Countries, or OPEC, a group of oil-exporting countries that have a significant influence on the world price of crude oil and the output of petroleum. To maintain relatively high oil prices, the member nations collude to limit the overall supply of oil. While OPEC's activities are legal under international law, collusion is illegal under U.S. antitrust law.

OPEC controls almost 80% of the world's known oil reserves and accounts for almost one-third of the world's crude production, giving the cartel's 14 member nations significant control over the world price of oil. As is the case within any organization, conflict inevitably arises. In the 50 years OPEC has existed, there have been embargoes (government prohibitions on the trade of oil), oil gluts, production disputes, and periods of falling prices. As a result, OPEC has been far from perfect in consistently maintaining high prices. In addition, OPEC has been careful to keep the price of oil below the cost of alternative energy options. Despite the limitations on OPEC's pricing power, OPEC has effectively acted as a cartel during the periods when it adopted output rationing to maintain price. However, the oil shale boom in the United States and Canada has significantly reduced OPEC's control over worldwide oil production, and as a result, the price is lower today than it was just a few years ago.

What would oil prices be like if OPEC didn't exist?

Oligopoly with More Than Two Firms

We have seen how firms behave in a duopoly. What happens when more firms enter the market? The addition of a third firm complicates efforts to maintain a cartel and increases the possibility of a more competitive result.

We can see this interaction in the cell phone market. The three major companies are not all equal. If AT&T and Verizon were the only two providers, the market might have very little competition. However, T-Mobile plays a crucial role in changing the market dynamic. Even though T-Mobile has significantly less market share than either of its bigger rivals, it still has developed an extensive cellular network in order to compete. Because T-Mobile has a smaller subscriber base and significant excess capacity, it aggressively competes on price. As a result, in many (but not all) respects, the entire cell phone industry functions competitively.

To see why, consider what the addition of a third firm will do to the market. When the third firm enters the market, there are two effects to consider—price and output. For example, if the third firm builds a cell tower, it will increase the overall capacity to provide cell phone service. As we observed in the duopoly example, if the total number of cell phone contracts (the supply) increases, all the firms must charge a lower price. This is the **price effect**, and it reflects how a change in price affects the firm's revenue. But because the marginal cost of providing cell phone service is essentially zero, the price each firm charges is substantially higher than the marginal cost of adding a new customer to the network. When the firm sells an additional unit, it generates additional revenues for the firm. This **output effect** occurs when a change in price affects the number of customers in a market.

The price effect and output effect make it difficult to maintain a cartel when there are more than two firms. Generally, as the number of firms grows, each individual firm becomes less concerned about its impact on the overall price, because any price above marginal cost creates a profit. Therefore, individual firms are more willing to lower prices because doing so creates a large output effect for the individual firm and only a small price effect in the market.

Of course, not all firms are the same size. Therefore, smaller and larger firms in an oligopolistic market react differently to the price and output effects. Increased output at smaller firms will have a negligible impact on overall prices because small firms represent only a tiny fraction of the market supply. But the same is not true for firms with a large market share. Decisions at these firms will have a substantial impact on price and output because the overall amount supplied in the market will change appreciably. In other words, in an oligopoly, the decisions of one firm directly affect other firms.

The **price effect** reflects how a change in price affects the firm's revenue.

The **output effect** occurs when a change in price affects the number of customers in a market.

PRACTICE WHAT YOU KNOW

Oligopoly: Can You Recognize the Oligopolist?

QUESTION: Which firm is the oligopolist?

a. Firm A is in retail. It is one of the largest and most popular clothing stores in the country. It also competes with many rivals and faces intense price competition.

b. Firm B is in the auto rental business. It is not the nation's largest rental company, but significant barriers to entry enable it to serve customers across the United States more conveniently and at a lower price than local rivals.

c. Firm C is a restaurant in a small, isolated community. It is the only local eatery. People drive from miles away to eat there.

ANSWER: Firm A sells clothing, a product with many competing brands and outlets. The competition is intense, which means that the firm has little market power. As a result, firm A is a player in a competitive market. It is not an oligopolist. Firm B faces competition from other large national car rental companies, but barriers to entry at many airports prevent smaller firms from securing space inside the terminal. This means that car rental companies are oligopolists. Firm C is a monopolist. It is the only place to eat out in the isolated community, and no other restaurant is nearby. It is not an oligopolist.

CHALLENGE QUESTION: Is the airline industry (a number of major airlines but many smaller rivals) a good example of oligopoly, or of monopolistic competition?

ANSWER: If you simply look at the number of airlines operating in the United States, you find dozens—more than enough, on a ground-level view—to make cartels and other monopoly-like behaviors seem unlikely. But if you look again, this time from 30,000 feet, you see that four major carriers (American, Delta, Southwest, and United) account for 80% of all domestic departures. In addition, many small airports are only served by one or two carriers, making price collusion relatively easy on many routes. Finally, significant start-up costs make the cost of entry into the market relatively high. That's not to say that airlines face no competition—one of the four largest U.S. carriers, Southwest, used to be a small regional airline but was so successful at building its brand and keeping cost low that it was able to expand across the country. Still, with the high barriers to entry (it is hard to secure gates at airports), consolidation among the largest carriers, and differentiated routes, each carrier enjoys pricing power. This makes the airline industry a better example of oligopoly than of monopolistic competition.

How Does Game Theory Explain Strategic Behavior?

Decision-making under oligopoly can be complex. **Game theory** is a branch of mathematics that economists use to analyze the strategic behavior of decision-makers who have to consider the behavior of others around them. In particular, game theory can help us determine what level of cooperation is most likely to occur. A game consists of a set of players, a set of strategies available to those players, and a specification of the payoffs for each combination of strategies. The game is usually represented by a payoff matrix that shows the players, strategies, and payoffs. It is presumed that each player acts simultaneously or without knowing the actions of the other.

In this section, we will learn about the prisoner's dilemma, an example from game theory that helps us understand how dominant strategies often frame short-run decisions. (In its simplest form, the prisoner's dilemma is a game played just once, not repeatedly over time.) We will use the idea of the dominant strategy to explain why oligopolists often choose to advertise. Finally, we will come full circle and argue that the dominant strategy in a game may be overcome in the long run, through repeated interactions.

Game theory is a branch of mathematics that economists use to analyze the strategic behavior of decision-makers.

Strategic Behavior and the Dominant Strategy

We have seen that in oligopoly there is mutual interdependence: a rival's business choices affect the earnings the other rivals can expect to make. To learn more about the decisions firms make, we will explore a fundamental problem in game theory known as the *prisoner's dilemma*. The dilemma takes its name from a famous scenario devised by pioneer game theorist Al Tucker soon after World War II.

The scenario goes like this: Two prisoners are being interrogated separately about a crime they both participated in, and each is offered a plea bargain to cooperate with the authorities by testifying against the other. If both suspects refuse to cooperate with the authorities, neither can be convicted of a more serious crime, though they will both have to spend some time in jail. But the police have offered full immunity if one cooperates and the other does not. This means that each suspect has an incentive to betray the other. The rub is that if they both confess, they will spend more time in jail than if they had both stayed quiet. When decision-makers face incentives that make it difficult to achieve mutually beneficial outcomes, we say they are in a **prisoner's dilemma**. This situation makes the payoff for cooperating with the authorities more attractive than the result of keeping quiet.

We can understand the outcomes of the prisoner's dilemma by looking at the payoff matrix in Figure 13.1. Starting with the white box in the upper left corner, we see that if both suspects testify against each other, they each get 10 years in jail. If one suspect testifies while his partner remains quiet—the

The **prisoner's dilemma** occurs when decision-makers face incentives that make it difficult to achieve mutually beneficial outcomes.

FIGURE 13.1

The Prisoner's Dilemma

The two suspects know that if they both keep quiet, they will spend only 1 year in jail. The prisoner's dilemma occurs because the decision to testify results in no jail time for the one who testifies if the other does not testify. However, this outcome means that both are likely to testify and get 10 years.

		Tony Montana	
		Testify	**Keep quiet**
Manny Ribera	**Testify**	10 years in jail / 10 years in jail	25 years in jail / goes free
	Keep quiet	goes free / 25 years in jail	1 year in jail / 1 year in jail

upper right and lower left boxes—he goes free and his partner gets 25 years in jail. If both keep quiet—the result in the lower right corner—they each get off with 1 year in jail. This result is better than the outcome in which both prisoners testify.

Because each suspect is interrogated separately, the decision about what to tell the police cannot be made cooperatively; thus, each prisoner faces a dilemma. The interrogation process makes the situation a noncooperative "game" and changes the incentives each party faces.

Under these circumstances, what will our suspects choose? Let's begin with the outcomes for Tony Montana. Suppose he testifies. If Manny Ribera also testifies, Tony will get 10 years in jail (the upper left box). If Manny keeps quiet, Tony will go free (the lower left box). Now suppose that Tony decides to keep quiet. If Manny testifies, Tony can expect 25 years in jail (the upper right box). If Manny keeps quiet, Tony will get 1 year in jail (the lower right box). No matter what choice Manny makes, Tony is always better off choosing to testify. If his partner testifies and he testifies, he gets 10 years in jail as opposed to 25 if he keeps quiet. If his partner keeps quiet and he testifies, Tony goes free as opposed to spending a year in jail if he also keeps quiet. The same analysis applies to the outcomes for Manny.

When a player always prefers one strategy, regardless of what his opponent chooses, we say it is a **dominant strategy**. We can see a dominant strategy at work in the case of our two suspects. They know that if they both keep quiet, they will spend one year in jail. The dilemma occurs because both suspects are more likely to testify and get 10 years in jail. The choice to testify is obvious for two reasons. First, neither suspect can monitor the actions of the other after they are separated. Second, once each suspect understands that his partner will save jail time if he testifies, he realizes that the incentives are not in favor of keeping quiet.

The dominant strategy in our example is also a Nash equilibrium, named for mathematician John Nash. A **Nash equilibrium** occurs when all economic decision-makers have no incentive to change their current decision. If each suspect reasons that the other will testify, the best response is also to testify. Each suspect may wish that he and his partner could coordinate their actions and agree to keep quiet. However, without the possibility of coordination, neither has an incentive to withhold testimony. So they both think strategically and decide to testify.

Duopoly and the Prisoner's Dilemma

The prisoner's dilemma example suggests that cooperation can be difficult to achieve. What this means for oligopoly is that it is not natural or easy for firms to collude. To get a better sense of the incentives that oligopolists face, let's revisit the situation of AT-Phone and Horizon, each trying to decide whether to charge $90 or $75 for cell phone plans. Figure 13.2 puts some of the information from Table 13.3 into a payoff matrix and highlights the revenue AT-Phone and Horizon could earn, depending on the price each firm chooses.

We see that when AT-Phone sets a high price ($90), Horizon can earn either $27,000, by setting a high price, or $52,500, by setting a low price. When AT-Phone sets a low price ($75), Horizon can earn either $0 with a high price or $26,250 with a low price. Either way, Horizon is better off setting the low price. The same reasoning holds for AT-Phone: choosing the low price instead of the high one means getting either $52,500 instead of $27,000 or else $26,250 instead of $0, depending on what Horizon does. So the low price is the

Incentives

A **dominant strategy** exists when a player will always prefer one strategy, regardless of what his opponent chooses.

A **Nash equilibrium** occurs when all economic decision-makers opt to keep the status quo.

Incentives

Nash Equilibrium

A BRILLIANT MADNESS AND A BEAUTIFUL MIND

A Brilliant Madness (2002) is the story of a mathematical genius, John Nash, whose career was cut short by a descent into madness. At the age of 30, Nash began claiming that aliens were communicating with him. He spent the next three decades fighting paranoid schizophrenia. Before this time, while he was a graduate student at Princeton, Nash wrote a proof about noncooperative equilibrium. The proof established the Nash equilibrium and became a foundation of modern economic theory. In 1994, Nash was awarded a Nobel Prize in Economics. The documentary features interviews with John Nash, his wife, his friends and colleagues, and experts in both economics and mental illness. Nash died in 2015.

The 2001 film *A Beautiful Mind*, directed by Ron Howard, is based on the life of Nash but does not adhere strictly to the facts. If you watch *A Brilliant Madness* and then watch the famous bar scene in *A Beautiful Mind*, you'll see that Ron Howard attempts to depict a Nash equilibrium when we see the men and women dancing together. *A Beautiful Mind* won the Academy Award for Best Picture, but the film's most famous scene is infamous among economists because it does not depict a Nash equilibrium. If you are curious about why this is the case, read the spoiler in the conclusion of this chapter.

Russell Crowe plays John Nash, who revolutionized modern microeconomics.

Incentives

dominant strategy for both firms. This produces a Nash equilibrium, where both firms make $26,250. This is the prisoner's dilemma: each firm has an incentive to lower its price to generate more revenue than if they had colluded and kept prices high, but acting on this incentive causes them both to earn less revenue than if they had kept prices high.

Unfortunately for the two firms, it's not just a matter of settling for $26,250 instead of $27,000, because the Nash equilibrium is only for the given payoff matrix. Once the possibility of dropping the price to $60 floats into view, there's a new payoff matrix in which $75 is the high price and $60 is the low price. Lather, rinse, repeat with the price war "shampoo," and pretty soon both firms are practically giving cell phone service away for free. At that point they're

FIGURE 13.2

		AT-Phone	
		High price: $90	Low price: $75
Horizon	High price: $90	$27,000 revenue $27,000 revenue	$52,500 revenue $0 revenue
	Low price: $75	$0 revenue $52,500 revenue	$26,250 revenue $26,250 revenue

The Prisoner's Dilemma in Duopoly

Each company has a dominant strategy to serve more customers by lowering its price. But when both firms pursue that strategy, they end up in a Nash equilibrium where both firms are worse off than if they'd both chosen differently. They earn just $26,250, when $27,000 was seemingly within reach.

really, really wishing they'd figured out how to operate as a cartel and both earn $27,000, instead.

Advertising and Game Theory

We have seen that oligopolists function like monopolistic competitors in that they sell differentiated products. We know that advertising is commonplace in markets with a differentiated product. In the case of an oligopoly, mutual interdependence means that advertising can create a contest between firms trying to gain customers. The result may be skyrocketing advertising budgets and little, or no, net gain of customers. Therefore, oligopolists have an incentive to scale back their advertising, but only if their rivals also agree to scale back. Like all cooperative action among competitors, this is easier said than done.

Incentives

Figure 13.3 highlights the advertising choices of Coca-Cola and PepsiCo, two fierce rivals in the soft-drink industry. Together, Coca-Cola and PepsiCo account for 72% of the soft-drink market, with Coca-Cola being the slightly larger of the two firms. Both companies are known for their advertising campaigns, which cost hundreds of millions of dollars. To determine if they gain anything by spending so much on advertising, let's look at the dominant strategy. In the absence of cooperation, each firm will choose to advertise, because the payoffs under advertising ($100 million or $150 million) exceed those of not advertising ($75 million or $125 million). When each firm chooses to advertise, it generates a profit of $100 million. This is a second-best outcome

Prisoner's Dilemma

WHY DO SUPERHEROES FIGHT?

The movie *Captain America: Civil War* (2016) features a common comic trope: two groups of heroes end up fighting each other. After a superhero mishap results in the deaths of hundreds of people, the public demands that the government regulate the conduct of those with superpowers. Iron Man agrees with having the Avengers put under government control, while Captain America does not. The two heroes reach a stalemate, and they start to recruit members of the hero fraternity to their respective sides. Eventually Iron Man tries to bring Captain America in, and an epic battle ensues.

It's all very dramatic—but what is going on here? These are heroes, after all. Why would they fight each other, when there are so many villains to worry about? Many of the heroes are indeed concerned that fighting each other sends a bad message. And of course any battle where the fighters have superpowers is liable to result in a lot of civilian casualties. Nevertheless, the two sides lurch pell-mell into a messy (but of course highly watchable) confrontation.

While this seems like an outrageous outcome, fit only for the comics, there is a perfectly good economic explanation for this faceoff between two of Marvel's great protagonists: it's a prisoner's dilemma. In the payoff matrix, the dominant strategy is to fight. While we might like to see the two sides sit down and hash out their differences, each of them gets a bigger payoff for digging in their heels. The largest joint payoff (the combined benefit to both sides) occurs when both sides talk things out, but if one side decides to fight while the other side opts for peaceful talk, the "fight" side can get everything it wants, without compromising. These are the payoffs in the upper right and lower left boxes. Because

If you were a superhero, would you rather fight or talk it out?

the dominant strategy is to fight, the parties end up in the lower right box, even though the joint payoff is lowest there. Now it's time for civilians to head indoors and stay there, because things are about to get ugly.

		Captain America	
		Talk it out	Fight for what you believe
Iron Man	Talk it out	4 4	6 1
	Fight for what you believe	1 6	2 2

Why is there an Avengers Civil War? Or for that matter, why is it Batman versus Superman? The answer isn't that the comic characters are irrational, or are being blackmailed, or even that someone is controlling their minds. The answer is that they are in a prisoner's dilemma.

FIGURE 13.3

	Coca-Cola	
	Advertises	**Does not advertise**
PepsiCo — Advertises	$100 million profit $100 million profit	$75 million profit $150 million profit
PepsiCo — Does not advertise	$150 million profit $75 million profit	$125 million profit $125 million profit

The Prisoner's Dilemma and Advertising

The two companies each have a dominant strategy to advertise. We can see this strategy by observing that Coca-Cola and PepsiCo each make $25 million more profit by choosing to advertise. As a result, they both end up in the upper left box earning $100 million profit when they could have each made $125 million profit in the lower right box if they had agreed not to advertise.

compared with the $125 million profit each could earn if neither firm advertises. The dilemma is that each firm needs to advertise to market its product and retain its customer base, but most advertising expenditures end up canceling each other out and costing the companies millions of dollars.

ECONOMICS IN THE REAL WORLD

THE COLD WAR

The idea that companies benefit from spending less on advertising has an analogue in warfare. Countries benefit from a "peace dividend" whenever war ends. There is no better example than the Cold War between the Soviet Union and the United States that began in the 1950s. By the time the Cold War ended in the late 1980s, both countries had amassed thousands of nuclear warheads in an effort to deter aggression.

This buildup put enormous economic pressure on each country to keep up with the other. During the height of the Cold War, each country found itself in a prisoner's dilemma in which spending more in an arms race was the dominant strategy. When the Soviet Union ultimately dissolved, the United States was able to spend less money on deterrence. In the post–Cold War world of the 1990s, the U.S. military budget fell from 6.5% to 3.5% of gross domestic product (GDP) as the nation reaped a peace dividend. However, with China now aggressively upgrading its navy and the associated ability to project air power, and with Russia sinking money into advanced submarine technology, we may be sliding back into the same dynamic, this time with three players.

The Cold War created a prisoner's dilemma for the United States and the Soviet Union.

Airlines in the Prisoner's Dilemma

American Airlines and Delta Airlines once found themselves in a classic prisoner's dilemma. It all started when Delta wanted to expand its share of the lucrative Dallas-to-Chicago route, where American was the dominant carrier. Delta offered a substantial fare cut on that route to attract new travelers. American threatened a price war by offering its own fare cut on the Delta-dominated Dallas-to-Atlanta route.

> Both airlines had a dominant strategy to cut their fare on the targeted route. Why? If one airline cut its fares and the other did not, the airline that did would earn a large profit ($100,000) while the other suffered a large loss (-$200,000). This was each airline's best possible outcome.

> Even if the rival cut its fare too, lowering the price was still the right move—the dominant strategy—for each airline. Why? Because if an airline failed to match the fare of its rival, it would make less profit than before.

The hallmark of a prisoner's dilemma is when two rivals follow their dominant strategy and the result is not the best result for both. It would have been better if no fare discounts were ever considered.

What happened? Fortunately for both airlines, they posted their planned fare cuts on a computer system that allowed them to see what their rival was doing. They each saw the price war starting, backed down, and escaped the prisoner's dilemma!

REVIEW QUESTIONS

- Which expected outcome in the matrix reflects the outcome of this American/Delta pricing war?

- Explain how the ability to communicate can allow two parties to escape a prisoner's dilemma.

Escaping the Prisoner's Dilemma in the Long Run

We have seen how game theory can be a useful tool for understanding strategic decision-making in noncooperative environments. However, the dominant strategy does not consider the possible long-run benefits of cooperation.

Game theorist Robert Axelrod decided to examine the choices participants make in a long-run setting. He ran a sophisticated computer simulation in which he invited scholars to submit strategies for securing points in a prisoner's dilemma tournament over many rounds. All the submissions were collected and paired, and the results were scored. After each simulation, Axelrod eliminated the weakest strategy and reran the tournament with the remaining strategies. This evolutionary approach continued until the best strategy remained. Among all strategies, including those that were solely cooperative or noncooperative, tit-for-tat dominated. **Tit-for-tat** is a long-run strategy that promotes cooperation among participants by mimicking the opponent's most recent decision with repayment in kind. As the name implies, a tit-for-tat strategy is one in which you do whatever your opponent does. If your opponent breaks the agreement, you break the agreement, too. If the opponent behaves properly, then you behave properly, too.

Because the joint payoffs for cooperation are high in a prisoner's dilemma, tit-for-tat begins with the players cooperating. In subsequent rounds, the tit-for-tat strategy mimics whatever the other player did in the previous round. The genius behind tit-for-tat is that it changes the incentives and encourages cooperation. Turning back to our example in Figure 13.3, suppose that Coca-Cola and PepsiCo want to save on advertising expenses. The companies expect to have repeated interactions, so they both know from past experience that any effort to start a new advertising campaign will be immediately countered by the other firm. Because the companies react to each other's moves in kind, any effort to exploit the dominant strategy of advertising will ultimately fail. This dynamic can alter the incentives the firms face in the long run and lead to mutually beneficial behavior.

Tit-for-tat
is a long-run strategy that promotes cooperation among participants by mimicking the opponent's most recent decision with repayment in kind.

Incentives

The Long-Run Benefits of Cooperation

THE EVOLUTION OF TRUST

Designer Nicky Case (a member of Forbes' "30 under 30" list for Games development) created an interactive simulation (https://ncase.me/trust/) based on Robert Axelrod's groundbreaking 1984 book, *The Evolution of Cooperation*. When you play the simulation, you encounter a variety of strategies that you might deploy in the repeated prisoner's dilemma.

In the repeated version of the game, it's important that neither player knows when the last round is. Why? If the players knew, then in the last round they would both definitely cheat, since there'd be no later rounds to worry about. But then by backward induction, each player should cheat in the second-last round, as well, since there will be no effect on the other player's choice in the last round. This logic continues until both players simply decide to cheat in the first round. That's a pretty depressing outcome, but it's not what Axelrod found in the long run with an unknown stopping point. Instead, he found that tit-for-tat did better than all other approaches. To observe Axelrod's result, Case has you play against five different strategies to show which are the most effective at creating cooperative outcomes. The entire simulation takes about thirty minutes to play—give it a try!

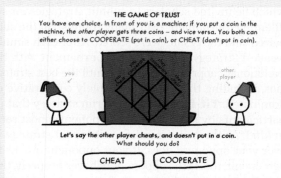

Should your strategy be "copycat," "all cheat," "all cooperate," "grudger," or "detective"? Find out by trying the simulation!

Opportunity cost

Tit-for-tat makes it less desirable to advertise by eliminating the long-run benefits. Advertising is still a dominant strategy in the short run because the payoffs with advertising ($100 million or $150 million) exceed those of not advertising ($75 million or $125 million). In the short run, the firm that advertises could earn $25 million extra, but in every subsequent round—if the rival responds in kind—the firm should expect profits of $100 million because its rival will also be advertising. As a result, there is a large long-run opportunity cost for not cooperating. If one firm stops advertising and the other follows suit, they will each find themselves making $125 million in the long run. Why hasn't this outcome happened in the real world? Because Coke and Pepsi don't trust each other enough to earn the dividend that comes from an advertising truce.

The prisoner's dilemma nicely captures why cooperation is so difficult in the short run. But most interactions in life occur over the long run. For example, scam artists and sketchy companies take advantage of short-run opportunities that cannot last because relationships in the long run—with businesses and with people—involve mutual trust. Cooperation is the default because you know that the other side is invested in the relationship. Under these circumstances, the tit-for-tat strategy works well.

Sequential Games

Not all games involve simultaneous decisions. Sometimes one player must move first and then the other player responds to the first move. In this case it is possible for the first player to utilize **backward induction** to get the best possible result. Backward induction in game theory is the process of deducing backward from the end of a scenario to infer a sequence of optimal actions.

Backward induction in game theory is the process of deducing backward from the end of a scenario to infer a sequence of optimal actions.

To help visualize this situation, look at Figure 13.4. The payoff matrix summarizes the payoffs that Iggy and Azalea face in a noncooperative game. Neither Iggy nor Azalea has a dominant strategy, so it is impossible to predict what the final outcome will be.

However, if we let one player go first, the game has a predictable conclusion. To see this process at work, look at Figure 13.5. This type of diagram is known as a **decision tree**; it illustrates all of the possible outcomes in a sequential game. Let's imagine that Azalea goes first and Iggy chooses second.

A **decision tree** illustrates all of the possible outcomes in a sequential game.

In a sequential game, the first player can restrict the set of outcomes to one of the branches at the top of the decision tree. When Azalea chooses Agree, Iggy works off the lower left set of branches and must choose between making $20,000 if she agrees or $75,000 if she disagrees. Of course, Iggy chooses to disagree. In this case, the final outcome is $50,000 for Azalea and $75,000 for Iggy. If Azalea instead chose Disagree to start, Iggy would be faced with the payoffs on the lower right side of the decision tree. Here, Iggy would get $50,000 if she agrees and $25,000 if she disagrees,

FIGURE 13.4

To Cooperate or Not

Iggy and Azalea do not have dominant strategies, so the outcome of this game cannot be determined.

		Iggy: Agree	Iggy: Disagree
Azalea	Agree	$20,000 $60,000	$75,000 $50,000
	Disagree	$50,000 $35,000	$25,000 $75,000

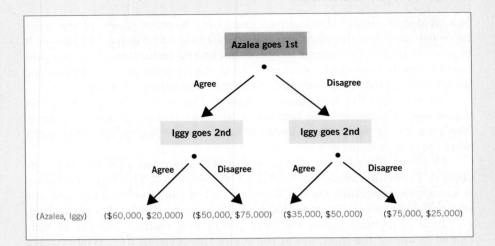

FIGURE 13.5

Decision Tree for a Sequential Game

Azalea will agree, knowing that Iggy will disagree. This game guarantees Azalea $50,000 and Iggy $75,000.

so this time she agrees. Now the final outcome is $35,000 for Azalea and $50,000 for Iggy.

Because Azalea has full information about all of the payoffs in the matrix, she knows what Iggy will choose at the end of each set of branches. This knowledge allows her to use backward induction to earn $50,000 for herself by selecting Agree with the full knowledge that Iggy will choose Disagree.

There are many examples of sequential games in life. Chess and checkers are two popular board games that utilize backward induction. Likewise, many business decisions are also sequential in nature, and once a particular path is taken, it becomes easier to predict how future decisions will unfold. For instance, when a firm decides to launch a new advertising campaign, it is easier for the firm to predict how a rival will react by examining the remaining choices along a decision tree.

A Caution about Game Theory

Game theory is a decision-making tool, but not all games have dominant strategies that make player decisions easy to predict. Perhaps the best example is the game known as rock-paper-scissors. This simple game has no dominant strategy: paper beats rock (because the paper will cover the rock) and rock beats scissors (because the rock will break the scissors), but scissors beats paper (because the scissors will cut the paper). The preferred choice is strictly a function of what the other player selects. Many situations in life and business are more like rock-paper-scissors than the prisoner's dilemma. Winning at business in the long run often occurs because you are one step ahead of the competition, not because you deploy a strategy that attempts to take advantage of a short-run opportunity.

Consider two sisters who enjoy playing racquetball together. They are of equal ability, so each point comes down to whether a player guesses correctly about where the other player will hit the ball. Take a look at Figure 13.6. The

Rock-paper-scissors is a game without a dominant strategy.

· ECONOMICS *in the* MEDIA ·

Sequential Games

WHY DID RACHEL LET ELEANOR WIN A GAME OF MAHJONG?

In *Crazy Rich Asians* (2018), the lead character, Rachel, is an economics professor who teaches game theory at NYU, where her boyfriend, Nick, teaches history. After they've dated seriously for a year, Nick invites Rachel to Singapore to meet his crazy-rich family. Things do not go well. Nick's mother, Eleanor, wants to protect Nick from ending up with someone who, Eleanor thinks, is not right for Nick. The upshot is that Rachel and Eleanor end up in a prisoner's dilemma, making suboptimal decisions.

Rachel wants to keep Nick for herself because she earns either 2 or 5 "happiness points" playing that strategy, whereas giving Nick up brings her only 1 or 4 points. Eleanor's reasons for wanting to keep Nick for herself are exactly the same. As a result, there is a Nash equilibrium at (2, 2) in the upper left box.

The plot takes a remarkable turn when Rachel recognizes that she and Eleanor are stuck, and that if they remain at odds, neither of them will ever win. Ever the economist, Rachel decides to break the prisoner's dilemma by initiating a sequential game where she moves first, deliberately leaving herself vulnerable if Eleanor continues to play the dominant strategy.

An inspired scene where the two play mahjong sets the stage. As the game unfolds, Rachel lets Eleanor know that Nick has proposed to her earlier but Rachel did not accept. She goes on to explain that she knows Nick would never really be happy if he had to leave his family to be with her. Rachel then lays down a tile that Eleanor picks up in order to win the mahjong game. After Rachel finishes explaining her decision, she stands up and reveals all her tiles. The tile she gave Eleanor would have won Rachel the game. Rachel has communicated to Eleanor that she could have accepted Nick's proposal, but she respects Eleanor in her role as family matriarch enough to sacrifice for Nick's good. Rachel's strategic gesture, proving that she was willing to bend for the sake of family, breaks the cycle of mistrust and prompts Eleanor to bless the marriage.

We see the result of Rachel's actions in the following decision tree and payoff matrix.

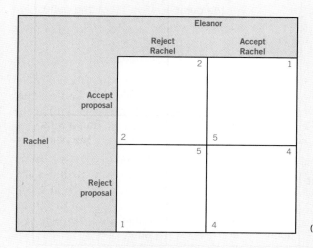

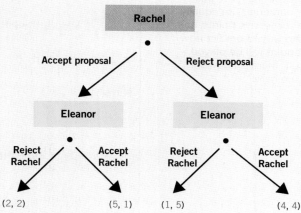

By saying no to Nick's proposal, Rachel has made Eleanor's choice simpler: she will gain either 5 or 4. She can still choose the 5 outcome, but Rachel has given her a very powerful reason to accept the (4, 4) outcome. Rachel makes one last statement before leaving: "So, I just wanted you to know that one day, when he marries another lucky girl who is enough for you . . . that it was because of me . . . a poor, raised-by-a-single-mother, low-class, immigrant nobody." Soon after, Eleanor understands that Rachel guaranteed her at least a 4, when Rachel could have chosen to say yes, and Eleanor would have earned no more than 2. This prompts Eleanor to reject the short-run dominant strategy and choose Rachel as her daughter-in-law. From that point forward, they are entering a long-run cooperative equilibrium, and (4, 4) maximizes their joint welfare by maximizing the sum of all payouts!

Good luck beating a game theorist at Mahjong!

FIGURE 13.6

No Dominant Strategy Exists

Neither Raina nor Nimah has a dominant strategy that guarantees winning the point. The four outcomes are equally likely on successive points, and there is no way to predict how the next point will be played. As a result, there is no Nash equilibrium here.

		Raina	
		Guesses to the left	Guesses to the right
Nimah	**Hits to the left**	Raina wins the point Nimah loses the point	Raina loses the point Nimah wins the point
	Hits to the right	Raina loses the point Nimah wins the point	Raina wins the point Nimah loses the point

success of Nimah and Raina depends on how well each one guesses where the other one will hit the ball.

In this competition, neither Raina nor Nimah has a dominant strategy that guarantees success. Sometimes Nimah wins when hitting to the right; at other times she loses the point. Sometimes Raina wins when she guesses to the left; at other times she loses. Each player guesses correctly only half the time. Because we cannot say what each player will do from one point to another, there is no Nash equilibrium. Any of the four outcomes are equally likely on successive points, and there is no way to predict how the next point will be played. In other words, we cannot expect every game to include a prisoner's dilemma and produce a Nash equilibrium. Game theory, like real life, has many different possible outcomes.

How Do Government Policies Affect Oligopoly Behavior?

When oligopolists in an industry form a cooperative alliance, they function like a monopoly. Competition disappears, which is not good for society. One way to improve the social welfare of society is to restore competition and limit monopoly practices through policy legislation.

Antitrust Policy

Efforts to curtail the adverse consequences of oligopolistic cooperation began with the **Sherman Antitrust Act** of 1890, the first federal law to place limits on cartels and monopolies. The Sherman Act was created in response to the increase in concentration ratios in many leading U.S. industries, including steel, railroads, mining, textiles, and oil. Prior to passage of the Sherman Act, firms were free to pursue contracts that created mutually beneficial outcomes. Once the act took effect, however, certain cooperative actions became criminal. Section 2 of the Sherman Act reads, "Every person who shall monopolize, or attempt to monopolize, or combine or conspire with any other person or persons, to monopolize any part of the trade or commerce among the several States, or with foreign nations, shall be deemed guilty of a felony."

The **Clayton Act** of 1914 targets corporate behaviors that reduce competition. Large corporations had been vilified during the presidential election of 1912, and the Sherman Act was seen as largely ineffective in curbing monopoly power. To strengthen antitrust policy, the Clayton Act added to the list of activities deemed socially detrimental, including:

1. *price discrimination* if it lessens competition or creates monopoly
2. *exclusive dealings* that restrict a buyer's ability to deal with competitors
3. *tying arrangements* that require the buyer to purchase an additional product in order to purchase the first
4. *mergers and acquisitions* that lessen competition, or situations in which a person serves as a director on more than one board in the same industry

As the Clayton Act makes clear, there are many ways to reduce competition.

The **Sherman Antitrust Act** (1890) was the first federal law limiting cartels and monopolies.

The **Clayton Act** (1914) targets corporate behaviors that reduce competition.

Dominant Strategy: To Advertise or Not—That Is the Question!

How much should a sandwich shop in a small college town charge for this sandwich?

QUESTION: University Subs and Savory Sandwiches are the only two sandwich shops in a small college town. If neither runs a special 2-for-1 promotion, both are able to keep their prices high and earn $10,000 a month. However, when both run promotions, their profits fall to $1,000. Finally, if one runs a promotion and the other does not, the shop that runs the promotion earns a profit of $15,000 and the other loses $5,000. What is the dominant strategy for University Subs? Is there a Nash equilibrium in this example?

ANSWER:

If University Subs runs the 2-for-1 promotion, it will make either $1,000 or $15,000, depending on its rival's actions. If University Subs keeps the price high, it will either lose $5,000 or make $10,000, depending on what Savory Sandwiches does. Suppose that Savory Sandwiches decides to run a 2-for-1 promotion. In this case, University Subs's best response is also to run a 2-for-1 promotion because $1,000 > −$5,000. Now imagine that Savory Subs uses the strategy of keeping the price high. University Subs's best response remains running the 2-for-1 promotion because $15,000 > $10,000. So regardless of what Savory Subs does, University Subs's best response—and therefore its dominant strategy—is to run a 2-for-1 promotion. Savory Sandwiches has the same dominant strategy and the same payoffs. Therefore, both companies will run the promotion and each will make $1,000. Neither firm has a reason to switch to the high-price strategy because one would lose $5,000 if the other company runs the 2-for-1 promotion. A Nash equilibrium occurs when both companies run the promotion.

| | | University Subs | |
		Runs a 2-for-1 promotion	Keeps price high
Savory Sandwiches	**Runs a 2-for-1 promotion**	Makes $1,000 Makes $1,000	Loses $5,000 Makes $15,000
	Keeps price high	Makes $15,000 Loses $5,000	Makes $10,000 Makes $10,000

Over the past hundred years, lawmakers have continued to refine antitrust policy. Additional legislation along with court interpretations of existing antitrust law have made it difficult to determine whether a company has violated the law. The U.S. Justice Department is charged with oversight, but it often lacks the resources to fully investigate every case. Antitrust law is complex, and cases are hard to prosecute, but these laws are essential to maintaining a competitive business environment. Without effective restraints on excessive market power, firms would organize into cartels more often or would find other ways to restrict competition. Table 13.5 briefly describes the most influential antitrust cases in history.

TABLE 13.5

Influential Antitrust Cases in History

Defendant	Year	Description
Standard Oil	1911	Standard Oil was founded in 1870. By 1897, the company had driven the price of oil down to 6 cents a gallon, which put many of its competitors out of business. Subsequently, Standard Oil became the largest company in the world. In 1906, the U.S. government filed suit against Standard Oil for violating the Sherman Antitrust Act. Three years later, the company was found guilty and forced to break up into 34 independent companies.
ALCOA	1944	The Aluminum Company of America (ALCOA), founded in 1907, maintained its position as the only producer of aluminum in the United States for many years. To keep that position, the company acquired exclusive rights to all U.S. sources of bauxite, the base material from which aluminum is refined. It then acquired land rights to build and own hydroelectric facilities in both the United States and Canada. By owning both the base materials and the only sites where refinement could take place, ALCOA effectively barred other firms from entering the U.S. aluminum market. In 1937, the Department of Justice filed suit against ALCOA. Seven years later, the Supreme Court ruled that ALCOA had taken measures to restrict trade and functioned as a monopoly. ALCOA was not broken apart because two rivals, Kaiser and Reynolds, emerged soon after.
AT&T	1982	In 1974, the U.S. Attorney General filed suit against AT&T for violating antitrust laws. It took seven years before a settlement was reached to split the company into seven new companies, each serving a different region of the United States. However, five of the seven have since merged to become AT&T Incorporated, which is now one of the largest companies in the world.
Microsoft	2001	When Internet Explorer was introduced in 1995, Microsoft insisted that it was a feature rather than a new Windows product. The U.S. Department of Justice did not agree and filed suit against Microsoft for illegally discouraging competition to protect its software monopoly. The government argued that Microsoft leveraged its monopoly power from the operating systems market into the browser market by strong-arming personal computer manufacturers like Dell into favoring Internet Explorer over Netscape. After a series of court decisions and appeals, a settlement ordered Microsoft to share application programming interfaces with third-party companies. Today, Internet Explorer has largely been replaced by Chrome and Firefox.
Google	2015	The European Union began investigating whether Google used its dominant market share as a search engine to gain an unfair advantage over competitors. After a lengthy investigation, the EU fined Google $2.8 billion in 2017 for diverting traffic away from search results that favored its rivals and toward results that favored Google's own products. As of 2019, Google remains the search engine of choice in 92% of all searches in Europe, and competitors continue to press for additional sanctions.

Predatory Pricing

While firms have a strong incentive to cooperate in order to keep prices high, they also want to keep potential rivals out of the market. **Predatory pricing** is the practice of setting prices deliberately below average variable costs with the intent of driving rivals out of the market. The firm suffers a short-run loss in order to prevent rivals from entering the market or to drive rival firms out of business in the long run. Once the rivals are gone, the firm should be able to act like a monopolist.

Predatory pricing is illegal, but it is difficult to prosecute. Neither the court system nor economists have a simple rule that helps to determine when a firm steps over the line. Predatory pricing can look and feel like spirited competition. Moreover, the concern is not the competitive aspect or lower prices, but the effect on the market when all rivals fail. To prove that predatory pricing has occurred, the courts need evidence that the firm's prices increased significantly after its rivals failed.

Walmart is often cited as a firm that engages in predatory pricing because its low prices effectively drive many smaller companies out of business. However, there is no evidence that Walmart has ever systematically raised prices after a rival failed. Therefore, its price strategy does not meet the legal standard for predatory pricing. Similarly, Microsoft came under intense scrutiny in the 1990s for giving away its browser, Internet Explorer, in order to undercut Netscape, which also ended up giving away its browser. Microsoft understood that the key to its long-term success was the dominance of the Windows platform. Bundling Internet Explorer with Microsoft Office enabled the company not only to gain over 80% of the browser market but also to keep its leadership with the Windows operating system. Eventually, Microsoft was prosecuted by the government—but not for predatory pricing, which could not be proved because Microsoft never significantly raised the price of Internet Explorer. Instead, the government prosecuted Microsoft for tying the purchase of

Because Walmart keeps its prices low, there is no evidence that it engages in predatory pricing.

PRACTICE WHAT YOU KNOW

Predatory Pricing: Price Wars

You've undoubtedly encountered a price war at some point. It could be two gas stations, clothing outlets, or restaurants charging prices that seem unbelievably low.

QUESTION: Is a price war between two adjacent pizza restaurants evidence of predatory pricing?

ANSWER: One essential element for proving predatory pricing is evidence of the intent to raise prices after others are driven out of business. That is a problem in this example. Suppose one of the pizza places closes. The remaining firm could then raise its price substantially. But barriers to entry in the restaurant industry are low in most metropolitan areas, so any efforts to maintain high prices for long will fail. Customers will vote with their feet and wallets by choosing another pizza place a little farther away that offers a better value. Or a new competitor will sense that the victor is vulnerable

Predatory pricing? Check out the competing signs in the photo!

because of the high prices and will open a new pizza parlor nearby. Either way, the market is monopolistically competitive, so any market power created by driving out one rival will be fleeting.

The aggressive price war is not evidence of predatory pricing. Instead, it is probably just promotional pricing to protect market share. Firms often price some items below their variable costs to attract customers. These firms hope to make up the difference and then some with high profit margins on other items, such as beverages and side dishes.

Internet Explorer to the Windows operating system in order to restrict competition. The Microsoft case lasted over four years, and it ended in a settlement that placed restrictions on the firm's business practices.

What Are Network Externalities?

We end this chapter by considering a special kind of externality that often occurs in oligopoly. A **network externality** occurs when the number of customers who purchase or use a good influences the demand. When a network externality exists, firms with many customers often find it easier to attract new customers and to keep their regular customers from switching to other rivals. In the early days of social networking, for example, MySpace had many more users than Facebook. How did Facebook gain over 2.2 billion users when it had to play catch-up? Facebook built a better social network, and MySpace was slow to respond to the threat. By the time MySpace did respond, it was too late: Facebook was on its way. Now the tables are turned, as Facebook is the dominant social networking platform. Moreover, among most demographics, the sheer size of Facebook makes it a better place to do social networking than Google+, Twitter, or LinkedIn. However, even though Facebook now enjoys significant network externalities, it must be mindful to keep innovating or else it might end up forgotten like MySpace.

Most network externalities involve the introduction of new technologies. For instance, some technologies need to reach a critical mass before consumers can effectively use them. Consider that today everyone seems to have a cell phone. However, when cell phones were introduced in the United States in 1983, coverage was quite limited. The first users could not surf the Internet, roam, text, or use many of the applications we enjoy today. Moreover, the phones were large and bulky. How did we get from that situation in 1983 to today? As additional people bought cell phones, networks expanded and manufacturers and telephone companies responded by building more cell towers and offering better phones. The expansion of networks brought more users, and the new adopters benefited from the steadily expanding customer base.

Other technologies have gone through similar transformations. The Internet, fax machines, and apps all depend on the number of users. If you were the only person on the Internet or the only person with the ability to send and receive a fax, your technical capacity would have little value. In a world with ever-changing technology, first adopters pave the way for the next generation of users.

In addition to the advantages of forming a larger network, customers may face significant switching costs if they leave. **Switching costs** are the

A **network externality** occurs when the number of customers who purchase or use a product influences the quantity demanded.

Switching costs are the costs incurred when a consumer changes from one supplier to another.

Users of the first-generation cell phone, the Motorola DynaTAC 8000X, created a positive network externality for future users.

costs incurred when a consumer changes from one supplier to another. For instance, the transition from listening to music on CDs to using digital music files involved a substantial switching cost for many users. Today, there are switching costs among the many digital music options. Once a consumer has established a library of MP3s or uses iTunes, the switching costs of transferring the music from one format to another create a significant barrier to change. When consumers face switching costs, the demand for the existing product becomes more inelastic. As a result, oligopolists not only leverage the number of customers they maintain in their network, but also try to make switching to another network more difficult. For instance, firms promote customer loyalty through frequent flier benefits, hotel reward points, and credit card reward programs to create higher switching costs.

An excellent example of the costs of switching are the costs associated with cell phone services. Contract termination fees apply to many cell phone agreements if the contract is broken. This tactic creates high switching costs for many cell phone customers. To reduce switching costs, the Federal Communications Commission in 2003 began requiring that phone companies allow customers to take their cell phone numbers with them when they change to a different provider. This change in the law has reduced the costs of switching from one provider to another and has made the cell phone market more competitive.

PRACTICE WHAT YOU KNOW

Examples of Network Externalities

Does Netflix benefit from network externalities?

QUESTION: In which two of these examples are network externalities important?

a. college alumni

b. Netflix

c. a local bakery that sells fresh bread

ANSWERS:

a. Colleges and universities with more alumni are able to raise funds more easily than smaller schools, so the size of the alumni network matters. The number of alumni also matters when graduates look for jobs, because alumni are often inclined to hire individuals who went to the same school. For example, Penn State University has the nation's largest alumni base. This means that each PSU graduate benefits from network externalities.

b. Netflix's size enables it to offer a vast array of DVDs, downloads, and streaming video. If it were smaller, Netflix would be unable to make as many obscure titles available. This means that Netflix customers benefit from network externalities by having more DVDs to choose from.

c. The local bakery is a small company. If it attracts more customers, each one will have to compete harder to get fresh bread. Because the bakery's supply of bread is limited, additional customers create congestion, and network externalities do not exist.

Oligopolists are keenly aware of the power of network externalities. As new markets develop, the first firm into an industry often gains a large customer base. When there are positive network externalities, the customer base enables the firm to grow quickly. In addition, consumers are often more comfortable purchasing from an established firm. These two factors favor the formation of large firms and make it difficult for smaller competitors to gain customers. As a result, the presence of significant positive network externalities causes small firms to be driven out of business or forces them to merge with larger competitors.

ECONOMICS IN THE REAL WORLD

NEW YORK CITY TAXIS

In 1932, during the depths of the Great Depression, New York City decided to license taxicabs. The goal was to standardize fares, operating procedures, and safety requirements. At that time, a taxicab license, or medallion, was available at no cost. Today, if you find one on the resale market, it costs around $200,000. That's a lot of money, but medallion prices peaked in 2013 at over $1,000,000! How did prices get so high, and why have they fallen so much? Let's find out.

The city did not intend to create an artificial oligopoly but that's what happened. From 1932 until the 1990s, the number of medallions, which represents the supply of taxis, was fixed at approximately 12,000. During the same 60-year period, population growth and an increase in tourism caused the demand for taxi services to rise steeply. The number of medallions would have had to quadruple to keep up with demand.

Medallion holders made huge profits and successfully lobbied the city to keep the supply of medallions low. Imagine what would happen if the city lifted restrictions on the number of available medallions and gave them out to any qualified applicant. Applications for licenses would increase, and profits for cab drivers and cab companies would fall until quantity supplied equalled quantity demanded. Conversely, if taxicab drivers experienced economic losses, the number of taxis operating would decline until the losses disappeared.

The medallion oligopoly worked effectively, until ridesharing came along. In 2012 it became possible to grab a ride without using a taxi. As ridesharing has caught on, the prices of the medallions have plummeted. Therefore, it is not surprising that medallion holders seek to keep the number of medallions as low as possible and to keep out Uber, Lyft, and other rivals. Because oligopolists make profits by charging higher prices than firms in competitive markets do, no one who already has a medallion wants the supply to expand.

Despite medallion owners' efforts to restrict the supply, ridesharing companies are having a big impact in the medallion market. The added competition has driven down medallion prices to $200,000 today.

Conclusion

Firms in oligopoly markets can compete or collude to create monopoly conditions. The result is often hard to predict. In many cases, the presence of a dominant short-run strategy causes firms to compete on price and advertising even though doing so yields a lower economic profit. In contrast, the potential success of a tit-for-tat strategy suggests that oligopolistic firms are capable of cooperating to jointly maximize their long-run profits. Whether oligopoly mirrors the result found in monopolistic competition or monopoly matters a

How Oligopolies Shape Our Lives as Consumers

- The rate at which new businesses are created has been steadily falling since the 1970s.
- Vertical integration allows a firm to exert enormous control over the prices consumers pay.
- Heavily consolidated industries can lose the incentive to innovate.

Who do you trust to tell you the truth? Jim Cramer or John Oliver?

Oligopolies are big business, and they shape our lives in many ways. HBO's John Oliver has a really informative and funny take on corporate consolidation on his show *Last Week Tonight* (stream this on YouTube). Oliver points out many of the features of oligopoly that are potentially problematic for consumers, but he also gives some screen time to Jim Cramer, a well-known pro-business personality. Watching this video will make you think about how consolidation plays a key role in a wide range of industries—everything from air travel to eyewear to beer.

Here are some ways corporate consolidation is shaping our lives:

- The rate at which new businesses are created has been steadily falling since the 1970s, and one reason for that is that big businesses are becoming more consolidated.
- Some brands you might think are indie, like Burt's Bees, Tom's deodorant, and Goose Island beer, are actually run by large corporations.

- Airline industry consolidation has allowed firms to raise $4.2 billion in ancillary fees for additional baggage, seat assignments, and priority check-in.
- In the eyewear industry, most of the name-brand frames (e.g., Prada, Dolce & Gabbana, Burberry, and Ralph Lauren) are manufactured by the same firm, Luxottica, which also owns most of the eyewear retailers (Pearle, Lens Crafters, Sunglass Hut, and Target Optical). This level of vertical integration allows Luxottica to exert enormous control over the prices consumers pay.
- Heavily consolidated industries can lose the incentive to innovate. (Think about your cable TV box and how antiquated the technology is!)

great deal because society's welfare is higher when more competition is present. Because oligopoly is not a market structure with a predictable outcome, each oligopolistic industry must be assessed on a case-by-case basis by examining data and utilizing game theory. For these reasons, the study of oligopoly is one of the most fascinating parts of the theory of the firm.

Revisiting *A Beautiful Mind*: Recall that a Nash equilibrium exists when all economic decision-makers opt to keep the status quo. In *A Beautiful Mind*, the famous bar scene is not a Nash equilibrium. If the most beautiful woman in the bar was without a dance partner, each of the gentlemen would have had an incentive to change his behavior and switch to her. ✳

Incentives

· ANSWERING *the* BIG QUESTIONS ·

What is oligopoly?

- Oligopoly is a type of market structure that exists when a small number of firms sell a differentiated product in a market with significant barriers to entry. An oligopolist is like a monopolistic competitor in that it sells differentiated products. It is like a monopolist in that it enjoys significant barriers to entry. The small number of sellers in oligopoly leads to mutual interdependence.

- Oligopolists have a tendency to collude and to form cartels in the hope of achieving monopoly-like profits.

- Oligopolistic markets are socially inefficient because price and marginal cost are not equal. The result under oligopoly falls somewhere between the competitive market and monopoly outcomes.

How does game theory explain strategic behavior?

- Game theory helps to determine when cooperation among oligopolists is most likely to occur. In many cases, cooperation fails to occur because decision-makers have dominant strategies that lead them to be uncooperative. As a result, firms compete with price or advertising when they could potentially earn more profit by curtailing these activities.

- Games become more complicated when they are played multiple times, so short-run dominant strategies often disappear. Whenever repeated interaction occurs, decision-makers fare better under tit-for-tat, an approach that maximizes the long-run profit.

How do government policies affect oligopoly behavior?

- Antitrust law is complex, and cases are hard to prosecute. Nevertheless, these laws are essential in providing oligopolistic firms an incentive to compete rather than collude.

- Antitrust policy limits price discrimination, exclusive dealings, tying arrangements, mergers and acquisitions that limit competition, and predatory pricing.

What are network externalities?

- A network externality occurs when the number of customers who purchase or use a good influences the quantity demanded. The presence of significant positive network externalities can cause small firms to go out of business.

· CHAPTER PROBLEMS ·

Concepts You Should Know

antitrust laws (p. 401)
backward induction (p. 415)
cartel (p. 401)
Clayton Act (p. 419)
collusion (p. 401)
decision tree (p. 415)
dominant strategy (p. 407)

game theory (p. 405)
mutual interdependence (p. 402)
Nash equilibrium (p. 407)
network externality (p. 423)
oligopoly (p. 398)
output effect (p. 404)
predatory pricing (p. 422)

price effect (p. 404)
price leadership (p. 402)
prisoner's dilemma (p. 406)
Sherman Antitrust Act (p. 419)
switching costs (p. 423)
tit-for-tat (p. 413)

Questions for Review

1. Compare the price and output under oligopoly with that of monopoly and monopolistic competition.

2. How does the addition of another firm affect the ability of the firms in an oligopolistic industry to form an effective cartel?

3. What is predatory pricing?

4. How is game theory relevant to oligopoly? Does it help to explain monopoly? Give reasons for your response.

5. What does the prisoner's dilemma indicate about the longevity of collusive agreements?

6. What is a Nash equilibrium? How does it differ from a dominant strategy?

7. What practices do antitrust laws prohibit?

8. What are network externalities? Explain why network externalities matter to an oligopolist.

Study Problems (*solved at the end of this section)

1. Some places limit the number of hours that alcohol can be sold on Sunday. Is it possible that this sales restriction could help liquor stores? Use game theory to construct your answer. (*Hint:* Even without restrictions on the hours of operation, individual stores could still limit Sunday sales if they wanted to.)

2. Which of the following markets are oligopolistic?
   a. passenger airlines
   b. cereal
   c. fast food
   d. wheat
   e. golf equipment
   f. the college bookstore on your campus

✳ 3. Imagine that your roommate's alarm goes off at 4:30 every morning, and she hits snooze every 10 minutes until 6:00, when you both need to get up. She insists that this maddening procedure is the only way she is able to wake up. How would you respond? Is there a nonviolent way you

can convince her to change her morning wake-up routine? (*Hint:* Think about a tit-for-tat strategy.)

4. After teaching a class on game theory, your instructor announces that if every student skips the last question on the next exam, everyone will receive full credit for that question. However, if one or more students answer the last question, all responses will be graded and those who skip the question will get a zero on that question. Will the entire class skip the last question? Explain your response.

5. For which of the following are network externalities important?
   a. gas stations
   b. American Association of Retired Persons (AARP)
   c. eHarmony, an Internet dating site

6. Your economics instructor is at it again (see question 4). This time, you have to do a two-student project. Assume that you and your partner

are both interested in maximizing your grade, but you are both very busy and would be happier if you could get a good grade with less work.

| | Your partner | |
	Work hard	Work less hard
Work hard (You)	Grade = A, but your partner had to work 10 hours. Happiness = 7/10. / Grade = A, but you had to work 10 hours. Happiness = 7/10.	Grade = A, and your partner only worked 5 hours. Happiness = 9/10. / Grade = A, but you had to work 15 hours. Happiness = 4/10.
Work less hard	Grade = A, but your partner had to work 15 hours. Happiness = 4/10. / Grade = A, and you only worked 5 hours. Happiness = 9/10.	Grade = B, but your partner only worked 5 hours. Happiness = 6/10. / Grade = B, but you only worked 5 hours. Happiness = 6/10.

a. What is your dominant strategy? Explain.
b. What is your partner's dominant strategy? Explain.
c. What is the Nash equilibrium in this situation? Explain.
d. If you and your partner are required to work together on a number of projects throughout the semester, how might this requirement change the outcome you predicted in parts (a), (b), and (c)?

7. Suppose that the marginal cost of mining gold is constant at $300 per ounce and the demand schedule is as follows:

Price (per oz.)	Quantity (oz.)
$1,000	1,000
900	2,000
800	3,000
700	4,000
600	5,000
500	6,000
400	7,000
300	8,000

a. If the number of suppliers is large, what would be the price and quantity?
b. If there is only one supplier, what would be the price and quantity?
c. If there are only two suppliers and they form a cartel, what would be the price and quantity?
d. Suppose that one of the two cartel members in part (c) decides to increase its production by 1,000 ounces while the other member keeps its production constant. What will happen to the revenues of both firms?

✳ **8.** Trade agreements encourage countries to curtail tariffs (taxes on imports) so that goods may flow across international boundaries without restrictions. Using the following payoff matrix, determine the best policies for China and the United States.

| | | China | |
		Low tariffs	High tariffs
United States	Low tariffs	China gains $50 billion / U.S. gains $50 billion	China gains $100 billion / U.S. gains $10 billion
	High tariffs	China gains $10 billion / U.S. gains $100 billion	China gains $25 billion / U.S. gains $25 billion

a. What is the dominant strategy for the United States?
b. What is the dominant strategy for China?
c. What is the Nash equilibrium for these two countries?
d. Suppose that the United States and China enter into a trade agreement that simultaneously lowers trade barriers in both countries. Is this agreement a good idea? Explain your response.

9. A small town has only one pizza place, The Pizza Factory. A small competitor, Perfect Pies, is thinking about entering the market. The profits of these two firms depend on whether Perfect Pies enters the market and whether The Pizza Factory—as a price leader—decides to set a high price or a low price. Use the payoff matrix below to answer the questions that follow.

		Perfect Pies	
		Enter	Stay out
The Pizza Factory	**High price**	Perfect Pies makes $10,000 The Pizza Factory makes $20,000	Perfect Pies makes $0 The Pizza Factory makes $50,000
	Low price	Perfect Pies loses $10,000 The Pizza Factory makes $10,000	Perfect Pies makes $0 The Pizza Factory makes $25,000

a. What is the dominant strategy of The Pizza Factory?

b. Does Perfect Pies have a dominant strategy?

c. What is the Nash equilibrium in this situation?

d. The combined profit for both firms is highest when The Pizza Factory sets a high price and Perfect Pies stays out of the market. If Perfect Pies enters the market, how will this entry affect the profits of The Pizza Factory? Would The Pizza Factory be willing to pay Perfect Pies not to enter the market? Explain.

10. Two brands of coffee makers, Keurig and Tassimo, are vying for the convenience market. Keurig is the market-share leader and has the largest variety of cups used to make coffees and teas. Tassimo makes a smaller machine that brews faster, but it lacks the variety of coffees and teas sold by Keurig. To complicate matters, Keurig and Tassimo users cannot easily switch from one manufacturer to the other, because the cups that each manufacturer uses are a different size. Which manufacturer is likely to dominate the market in the long run?

✳ **11.** On the TV show *The Big Bang Theory*, the characters have an interesting way of resolving disputes. Watch the video at this link: www.youtube.com/watch?v=cSLeBKT7-sM. Is there a dominant strategy in rock-paper-scissors-lizard-Spock? Why do the guys always answer with Spock?

12. Most large banks charge the same or nearly the same interest rate. When market conditions require an adjustment, one of the major banks announces a change in its rate and other banks quickly follow suit. What model of oligopoly behavior explains why this happens?

✳ **13.** Suppose that Muber is currently the only firm providing rideshares, but a second firm, Wyft, is considering entering the market. Prior to learning what Wyft will do, Muber must decide whether to make a costly investment to improve its own product. The decision tree for this game is diagrammed below, with the payoffs assumed to be the ones shown.

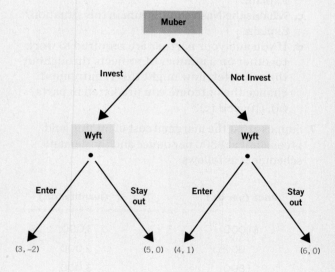

What is the equilibrium outcome of this game?

✳ **14.** The owner of a small restaurant has one person who is responsible for keeping things clean throughout the day. Should the owner be more concerned that the restrooms are always clean, or the kitchen? Is there a dominant strategy?

Solved Problems

3. If your roommate does not wake up immediately, a tit-for-tat response would be for you to get up. Once up, you should turn on the lights, get dressed, and make enough noise that your roommate cannot easily sleep. If you use this approach, it won't take long for your roommate to realize that she should set the alarm for a more reasonable time and *not* hit the snooze button. When your roommate no longer relies on the snooze button to wake up, you can return to your normal sleeping pattern and stay in bed for as long as you wish.

8. a. The dominant strategy for the United States is to impose high tariffs, because it always earns more from that strategy than if it imposes low tariffs, no matter what policy China pursues.
   b. The dominant strategy for China is to impose high tariffs, because it always earns more from that strategy than if it imposes low tariffs, no matter what policy the United States pursues.
   c. The Nash equilibrium for both countries is to levy high tariffs. Each country will earn $25 billion.
   d. China and the United States would each benefit from cooperatively lowering trade barriers. In that case, each country would earn $50 billion.

11. There is not a dominant strategy in this variation of rock-paper-scissors, but the guys can't bring themselves to answer with paper, even though it disproves Spock, because they respect him so much.

13. Muber will invest, and Wyft will stay out. How do we know this? Muber will use backward induction to solve this sequential problem. If Muber decides to invest, it restricts Wyft's outcomes to either −2 (if it enters) or 0 (if it stays out). Wyft prefers 0 to −2, so it stays out. Now consider what happens if Muber does not invest. In this case, Wyft makes 1 (if it enters) or 0 (if it stays out). Wyft prefers 1 to 0, so it enters. Since Muber knows what Wyft will choose in both cases, Muber must examine how well it does based on Wyft's choices. When Muber invests, Wyft stays out and Muber earns 5. If Muber decides to not invest, Wyft enters and Muber earns 4. Muber prefers 5 to 4, so Muber will choose to invest.

14. Dirty restrooms cost businesses lost sales, customer referrals, and repeat business. This is especially important for restaurants. So the owner will direct the employee to clean the restrooms more often than the kitchen. Cleaning the restrooms is the dominant strategy, because customers routinely use the restrooms but rarely see the kitchen.

PART IV

Labor Markets and EARNINGS

14

The Demand and Supply of Resources

Is Outsourcing Bad for the Economy?

When U.S. jobs are outsourced (sent to other countries), workers in the United States lose their jobs. People commonly think that outsourcing is bad for the U.S. economy, but the situation is not that simple. Outsourced jobs are relocated from high-labor-cost areas to low-labor-cost areas. Often, a U.S. job lost to outsourcing creates more than one job in another country. In addition, outsourcing lowers the cost of manufacturing goods and providing services. Those lower costs translate into lower prices for U.S. consumers and streamlined production processes for U.S. businesses. The improved efficiency helps U.S. firms compete in the global economy. In this chapter, we examine the demand and supply of resources throughout the economy. The outsourcing of jobs is a very visible result of these resource flows and an essential part of the market economy.

Consider Allen Edmonds, an American shoe company that has selectively shifted some of their production to the Dominican Republic. Quality footwear is stylish and hip, but consumers don't have unlimited budgets. To keep prices in the right range for the target market, Allen Edmonds decided to trim production costs by offshoring some of the early production stages. That enabled them to keep final assembly stateside. This move has made

These wingtips are assembled in the USA, but the uppers are probably stitched together overseas. If you want to buy American, how "American" must your shoes be?

their shoes a little more affordable for Americans who appreciate fine footwear, and it has helped keep the doors open at the main plant in Wisconsin. The point is that outsourcing is not a binary outcome. Products aren't made 100% in the United States or 100% elsewhere. The components are generally sourced from around the globe, and designed, manufactured, and assembled wherever these are most cost-effective.

In earlier chapters, we saw that profit-maximizing firms must decide how much to produce. For production to be successful, firms must combine the right amounts of labor and capital to maximize output while simultaneously holding down costs. Because labor often constitutes the largest share of the costs of production, we begin by looking at the labor market. We use supply and demand to illustrate the role of the labor market in the U.S. economy. We then extend the lessons learned about labor into the markets for land and capital. In Chapter 15, we expand our understanding of the labor market by examining income inequality, unemployment, discrimination, and poverty.

· BIG QUESTIONS ·

- What are the factors of production?
- Where does the demand for labor come from?
- Where does the supply of labor come from?
- What are the determinants of demand and supply in the labor market?
- What role do land and capital play in production?

What Are the Factors of Production?

Wages and salaries account for two-thirds of all the income generated by the U.S. economy. The remaining one-third of income goes to the owners of land and capital. Together, labor, land, and capital make up the *factors of production*, or the *inputs* used in producing goods and services. (For a review of these terms, see Chapter 8.)

For instance, let's imagine that Sophia wants to open a Mexican restaurant named Agaves. Sophia will need a dining room staff, cooks, dishwashers, and managers to coordinate everyone else; these are the labor inputs. She also will need a physical location; this is the land input. Finally, she will need a building in which to operate, along with ovens and other kitchen equipment, seating and tableware, and a cash register; these are the capital inputs.

Of course, Sophia's restaurant won't need any inputs if there is no demand for the food she plans to sell. The demand for each of the factors of production that go into her restaurant (land, labor, and capital) is said to be a *derived demand* because the factors are inputs the firm uses to supply a good in another market—in this case, the market for Mexican cuisine. Let's say Sophia secures the land, builds a building, and hires employees to produce the food she will serve. She is willing to spend a lot of money up front to build and staff the restaurant because she expects there to be demand for the food her restaurant will prepare and serve.

Derived demand—the demand for an input used in the production process—is not limited to the demand for a certain type of cuisine. For example,

A lack of customers is an ominous sign for restaurant workers.

Derived demand is the demand for an input used in the production process.

PRACTICE WHAT YOU KNOW

Derived Demand: Tip Income

Your friend waits tables 60 hours a week at a small restaurant. He is discouraged because he works hard but can't seem to make enough money to cover his bills. He complains that the restaurant does not have enough business and that is why he has to work so many hours just to make ends meet.

QUESTION: As an economist, what advice would you give him?

ANSWER: Because labor is a derived demand, he should apply for a job at a more popular restaurant. Working at a place with more customers will help him earn more tip income.

Want more tip income? Follow the crowd.

Why do economists generally earn more than elementary school teachers?

consumer demand for iPads causes Apple to demand the resources needed to make them. The switches, glass, memory, battery, and other parts have little value alone, but when assembled into an iPad, they become a device that many people find very useful. Therefore, when economists speak of derived demand, they are differentiating between the demand for a product or service and the demand for the resources used to make or produce that product or service.

Where Does the Demand for Labor Come From?

As a student, you are probably hoping that one day your education will translate into tangible skills that employers will seek. As you choose a major, you might be thinking about potential earnings in different occupations. Have you ever wondered why there is so much variability in levels of salary and wages? For instance, economists generally earn more than elementary school teachers but less than engineers. Workers on night shifts earn more than those who do the same job during the day. And professional athletes and successful actors make much more for jobs that are not as essential as the work performed by janitors, construction workers, and nurses. In one respect, the explanation is surprisingly obvious: demand helps to regulate the labor market in much the same way that it helps to determine the prices of goods and services sold in the marketplace.

To understand why some people get paid more than others, we need to explore each worker's output at the margin, or the *marginal product of labor*. In fact, the value that each worker creates for a firm is highly correlated with the demand for labor. Then, to develop a more complete understanding of how the labor market works, we will examine the factors that influence labor demand.

The Marginal Product of Labor

To gain a concrete appreciation for how labor demand is determined, let's look at the restaurant business—a highly competitive market. In Chapter 8, we saw that a firm determines how many workers to hire by comparing the output of labor with the wages the firm must pay. We will apply this analysis of production to the labor market in the restaurant business. Table 14.1 should look familiar to you; it highlights the key determinants of the labor hiring process.

Let's work our way through the table. Column 1 lists the number of laborers, and column 2 reports the daily numbers of meals that can be produced with differing numbers of workers. Column 3 shows the **marginal product of labor**, or the change Δ (Greek delta) in output associated with adding one additional worker. For instance, when the firm moves from three employees to four, output expands from 120 meals to 140 meals. The increase of 20 meals is the marginal product of labor for the fourth worker. Note that the values in column 3 decline as additional workers are added. Recall from Chapter 8 that each successive worker adds less value, a phenomenon known as *diminishing marginal product*.

The **marginal product of labor** is the change in output associated with adding one additional worker.

TABLE 14.1

Deciding How Many Laborers to Hire

(1) Labor (number of workers)	(2) Output (daily meals produced)	(3) Marginal product of labor	(4) Value of the marginal product of labor	(5) Wage (daily)	(6) Marginal profit
		Δ Output	Price ($10) × marginal product of labor		Value of the marginal product of labor − wage
0	0				
		50	$500	$100	$400
1	50				
		40	400	100	300
2	90				
		30	300	100	200
3	120				
		20	200	100	100
4	140				
		10	100	100	0
5	150				
		0	0	100	−100
6	150				

It is useful to know the marginal product of labor, which tells us how much each additional worker adds to the firm's output. Combining the marginal product of labor with the price the firm charges gives us a tool we can use to explain how many workers the firm will hire. Suppose that Agaves charges $10 for each meal. When the firm multiplies the marginal product of labor in column 3 by the price it charges, $10 per meal, we see the value of the marginal product in column 4. The **value of the marginal product (VMP)** is the marginal product of an input multiplied by the price of the output it produces. The firm compares the gain in column 4 with the cost of achieving that gain—the wage that must be paid—in column 5. This process reduces the hiring decision to a simple cost-benefit analysis in which the wage (column 5) is subtracted from the value of the marginal product (column 4) to determine each worker's marginal profit (column 6).

You can see from the green numbers that the marginal profit is positive for the first four workers. You might be tempted to argue that the firm should quit hiring once it has four workers because the marginal profit is zero for the fifth worker, shown in black. However, this argument is not valid because the firm can hire part-time workers. If the firm hires four full-time workers plus a fifth part-time worker, the fifth worker's VMP is greater than the wage the firm pays. Because the marginal profit is negative for the sixth worker, shown in red, the firm would not hire the sixth worker.

Figure 14.1 plots the value of the marginal product (VMP) from Table 14.1. Look at the curve: What do you see? Does it remind you of a demand curve? The VMP is the firm's willingness to pay for each laborer. In other words, it is the firm's labor demand curve.

The VMP curve slopes downward due to diminishing marginal product— which we see in column 3 of Table 14.1. As long as the value of the marginal product is higher than the market wage, shown in column 5 as $100 a day, the firm will hire more workers. For example, when the firm hires the first worker, the VMP is $500. This amount easily exceeds the market wage of hiring an

The **value of the marginal product (VMP)** is the marginal product of an input multiplied by the price of the output it produces.

Marginal thinking

FIGURE 14.1

The Value of the Marginal Product

The value of the marginal product (VMP) is the firm's labor demand curve. When the value of the marginal product is higher than the market wage, the firm will hire more workers. However, because labor is subject to diminishing marginal product, eventually the value created by hiring additional labor falls below the market wage.

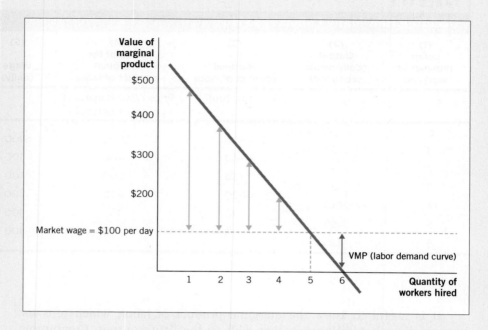

extra worker and creates a marginal profit of $400. Figure 14.1 illustrates the additional profit from the first worker with the longest green arrow under the labor demand curve and above the market wage. The second, third, and fourth workers generate additional profit of $300, $200, and $100, respectively, represented by the progressively shorter green arrows. As the value of the marginal product declines, there will be a point at which hiring additional workers will cause profits to fall. Because labor is subject to diminishing marginal product, the value created by hiring additional labor eventually falls below the market wage.

Changes in the Demand for Labor

We know that customers desire good food and that restaurants like Agaves hire workers to satisfy their customers. Figure 14.2 illustrates the relationship between the demand for restaurant meals and the demand for restaurant workers. Notice that the demand for labor is downward sloping; at high wages Agaves will use fewer workers; at lower wages it will hire more workers. We illustrate the law of demand with the blue arrow that moves along the original demand curve (D_1). Recall from Chapter 3 that a change in price results in a change in the quantity demanded. In addition, the demand for workers depends on, or is derived from, the number of customers who place orders. So changes in the restaurant business as a whole can shift the original demand curve and influence the number of workers the restaurant hires. For example, if the number of customers increases, the demand for workers will increase, or shift to the right to D_2. Likewise, if the number of customers decreases, the demand for workers will decrease, or shift to the left to D_3.

FIGURE 14.2

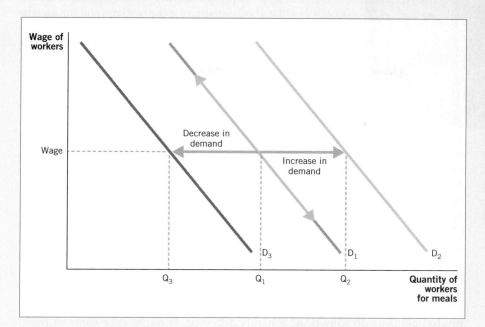

When the wages of workers change, the quantity of workers demanded, shown by the blue arrow moving along the demand curve D_1, also changes. Changes that shift the entire labor demand curve, shown by the gray horizontal arrows, include changes in demand for the product that the firm produces and changes in cost.

Two primary factors shift labor demand: (1) a change in demand for the product the firm produces and (2) a change in the cost of producing that product.

CHANGES IN DEMAND FOR THE PRODUCT THE FIRM PRODUCES

Because a firm is primarily interested in making a profit, it hires workers only when the value of the marginal product of labor is higher than the cost of hiring labor. Consider Agaves. If a rival Mexican restaurant closes down, many of its customers will likely switch to Agaves. Then Agaves will need to prepare more meals, which will cause the entire demand curve for cooks, table clearers, and waitstaff to shift outward to D_2 in Figure 14.2.

CHANGES IN COST

A change in the cost of production can sometimes be positive, such as when a new technology makes production less expensive. It can also be negative, such as when an increase in the cost of a needed raw material makes production more expensive.

In terms of a positive change for the firm, technology can act as a substitute for workers or can make existing workers more efficient. For example, microwave ovens enable restaurants to prepare the same number of meals with fewer workers compared to earlier technology. The same is true with the growing trend of using conveyor belts and automated systems to help prepare meals or even serve them. Therefore, changes in technology can lower a firm's demand for workers.

Marginal thinking

Touch screens at McDonald's automate order taking.

One John Deere 1270G harvester can replace 10 lumberjacks.

In the short run, substituting technology for workers may seem like a bad outcome for the workers and for society in general. However, in the long run that is not typically the case. Consider how technological advances affect the demand for lumberjacks in the forestry business. As timber companies invest in new harvesting technology, they can replace traditional logging jobs, which are dangerous and inefficient, with equipment that is safer and more efficient. By deploying the new technology, the lumber companies can cut down trees faster and more safely, and the workers are freed up to work in other parts of the economy. In the short run, the result is fewer timber jobs; those workers must find employment elsewhere. Admittedly, this adjustment is painful for the workers involved, and they often have difficulty finding jobs that pay as well as the job they lost. However, the new equipment requires trained, highly skilled operators who can fell more trees in a shorter period than traditional lumberjacks can. As a result, harvester operators have a higher marginal product of labor and can command higher wages.

For every harvester operator employed at a higher wage, there are perhaps 10 traditional lumberjacks displaced and in need of a job. But consider what happens after the short-run job losses. Overall production rises because while 1 worker harvests trees, the 9 other workers are forced to move into related fields or do something entirely different. It might take some of these displaced workers many years to find new work, but when they eventually do, society benefits in the long run. What once required 10 workers to produce now takes only 1, and the 9 other workers are able to work in other jobs and grow the economy in different ways.

PRACTICE WHAT YOU KNOW

Value of the Marginal Product of Labor: Flower Barrettes

How many flower barrettes could you make in an hour?

In *The Big Bang Theory*, Penny starts a business making flower barrettes. Sheldon wonders if she can make a profit.

QUESTION: Penny can make five flower barrettes each hour. She works 8 hours each day. Penny is paid $75.00 a day. The firm can sell the barrettes for $1.99 each. What is Penny's value of the marginal product of labor? What is the barrette firm's marginal profit from hiring her?

ANSWER: In 8 hours, Penny can make 40 barrettes. Because each barrette sells for $1.99, her value of the marginal product of labor, or VMP_{labor}, is $40 \times \$1.99$, or $79.60. Her VMP_{labor} is greater than the daily wage she receives, so the marginal profit from hiring her is $79.60 − $75.00, or $4.60.

CHALLENGE QUESTION: Suppose that the market price of barrettes begins to drop. At what price would Penny's job be in jeopardy?

ANSWER: Penny's VMP_{labor} is her output times the price the firm charges. Penny's wage is $75 a day, so with her making 40 barrettes per day, the VMP_{labor} pencils out to $75/40 = $1.875 per barrette. That's a scant 11.5 cents less than the current selling price. A small price drop will cause Penny to lose her job.

Changes in the Demand for Labor

WALL·E

In this classic animated sci-fi film from 2008, a future megacorporation called Buy N Large has caused so much overconsumption that Earth's resources are entirely used up. Humans escape their ruined home planet on spaceships where automation has rendered human labor superfluous. The humans become obese and ride around in hovering chairs while staring at computer screens all day long. The people in *Wall-E* drink "cupcakes-in-a-cup," they never exercise, and if they happen to fall off their hovering chairs, they can no longer walk and must wait for a robot to help them up.

This dystopian future occurs because automation and robots have left people with nothing to do, economically speaking. Yikes! But what will happen if, instead, automation and robotics *augment* our productivity? In that alternative future, we will have less work to do, but we will be able to devote our leisure time to travel and other hobbies and passions. There is

Getting replaced by automation and robots would be a drag, but the future doesn't have to look like *Wall-E*.

no doubt that the age of robots is nearing. You can be replaced, or you can find a way to work with, or alongside, robots to increase the value of the marginal product of your labor. The time to think about this is now, before you enter a field where automation is likely to replace you entirely.

To summarize, if labor becomes more productive, the VMP curve (demand for labor) shifts to the right, driving up both wages and employment, which is exactly what occurs with the demand for harvester operators. There is the potential for substitution as well, causing the demand for traditional labor to fall. This is what has happened to traditional lumberjack jobs, leading to a decrease in those workers' wages.

Where Does the Supply of Labor Come From?

In this section, we examine the connection between the wage rate and the number of workers who are willing to supply their services to employers. Because workers also value leisure, the supply curve is not always directly related to the wage rate. Indeed, at high wage levels, some workers may desire to cut back the number of hours they work. Other factors that influence the labor supply include other employment opportunities, the changing composition of the workforce, migration, and immigration; we explore these factors as well.

The Labor-Leisure Trade-Off

Trade-offs

People work because they need to earn a living. While it is certainly true that many workers enjoy their jobs, this does not mean they would work for nothing. In other words, while many people experience satisfaction in their work, most of us have other interests, obligations, and goals. As a result, the supply of labor depends both on the wage that is offered and on how individuals want to use their time. We call this relationship the *labor-leisure trade-off*.

In our society today, most individuals must work to meet their basic needs. However, once those needs are met, a worker might be more inclined to use his or her time in leisure. Would higher wages induce an employee to give up leisure and work more hours? The answer is both yes and no!

The **substitution effect** occurs when laborers work more hours at higher wages, substituting labor for leisure.

At higher wage rates, workers may be willing to work more hours, or substitute labor for leisure. This effect is known as the **substitution effect**. One way to think about the substitution effect is to note that higher wages make leisure time more expensive, because the opportunity cost of enjoying more leisure means giving up more income. For instance, suppose Emeril is a short-order cook at Agaves. He works 40 hours at $10 per hour and can also work 4 hours overtime at the same wage. If Emeril decides to work the overtime, he ends up working 44 hours and earns $440. In that case, he substitutes more labor for less leisure.

Opportunity cost

But at higher wage rates, some workers may work fewer hours, or substitute leisure for labor. This effect is known as the **income effect**. Leisure is a normal good (see Chapter 3), so as income rises, some workers may use their additional income to demand more leisure. As a consequence, at high income levels the income effect may outweigh the substitution effect and cause the supply curve to bend backward. For example, suppose Rachael chooses to work overtime for $10 per hour. Her total pay (like Emeril's) will be $10 × 44, or $440. If her wage rises to $11, she may continue to work the overtime at a higher wage. However, if she does not work overtime, she will earn as much as she earned before the wage increase ($11 × 40 = $440), and she might choose to discontinue the overtime altogether or work fewer overtime hours. The income effect is at work when Rachael's wage goes up and she chooses to work fewer hours.

The **income effect** occurs when laborers work fewer hours at higher wages, using their additional income to demand more leisure.

Figure 14.3 shows what can happen to the labor supply curve when the supply of labor responds directly to wage increases. When the wage rises progressively from W_1 to W_2 to W_3, the number of hours worked increases from Q_1 to Q_2 to Q_3, along the curve labeled S_{normal}. However, at high wage rates the number of hours worked is large. As a result, workers might experience diminishing marginal utility from the additional income and thus might value increased leisure time more than increased income. In this situation, workers might choose to work less, and the normal supply curve bends backward between W_2 and W_3 because as the wage goes up, the hours worked go down.

A **backward-bending labor supply curve** occurs when workers value additional leisure more than additional income.

The **backward-bending labor supply curve** occurs when workers value additional leisure more than additional income. The labor supply curve bends backward when the income effect is large enough to offset the substitution effect that typically causes individuals to work more when the wage rate is higher. Because most workers in the real world do not reach wage level W_2 (that is, a wage at which they might begin to value leisure more than labor), we will draw the supply curve as upward sloping throughout the chapter. Nevertheless, it is important to recognize that the direct relationship we normally observe does not always hold.

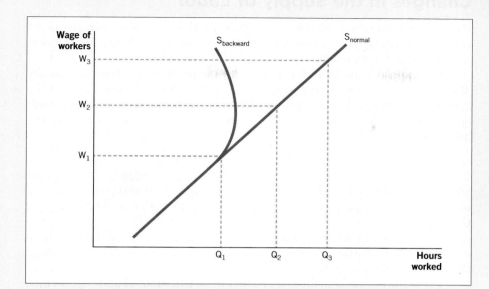

FIGURE 14.3

The Labor Supply Curve

At high wage levels (in this figure, above W_2), the income effect may become larger than the substitution effect and cause the labor supply curve to bend backward. The backward-bending supply curve occurs when additional leisure time becomes more valuable than additional income.

ECONOMICS IN THE REAL WORLD

THE LABOR-LEISURE TRADE-OFF

The statistician Nathan Yau created a simulation called "A Day in the Life of Americans," available at his site flowingdata.com, using data from the American Time Use Survey. As the clock on the upper left ticks along, you see 1,000 dots representing the ways Americans' days typically unfold. Watching the entire simulation will deepen your appreciation for what Americans typically do with their time, and all the trade-offs that take place during a work day.

Trade-offs

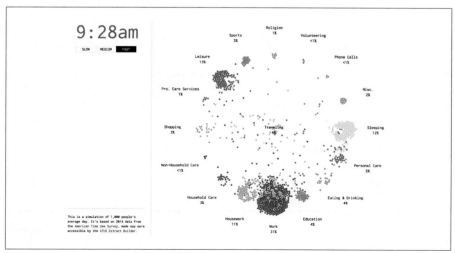

What do you do with your time when you are not working?

Changes in the Supply of Labor

If we hold the wage rate constant, a number of additional factors determine the supply of labor. In this section, we look beyond the wage rate to other forces governing the supply of labor.

Turning to Figure 14.4, the orange arrow along S_1 shows that the quantity of workers increases when the wage rate rises. But what will cause a shift in the supply curve? Three primary factors affect the supply curve: other employment opportunities, the changing composition of the workforce, and migration and immigration.

OTHER EMPLOYMENT OPPORTUNITIES The supply of workers for any given job depends on the employment opportunities and prevailing wage in related labor markets. Let's consider the supply of labor at Agaves. Notice that the supply curve for labor in Figure 14.4 is upward sloping; if Agaves offers higher wages, more workers, such as table clearers, will be willing to work there. We illustrate this situation with the orange arrow that moves along the original supply curve (S_1).

The supply of table clearers also depends on a number of nonwage factors. Because table clearers are generally young and largely unskilled, the number of laborers willing to work is influenced by the prevailing wages in similar jobs. For instance, if the wages of baggers at local grocery stores increase, some of the table clearers at Agaves will decide to bag at local grocery stores instead. The supply of table clearers will decrease and cause a leftward shift to S_3. If the wages of baggers were to fall below the wages of table clearers, the supply of

---

FIGURE 14.4

The Labor Supply Curve

A change in the quantity supplied of labor occurs when wages change, causing a movement along the supply curve S_1, shown by the orange arrow. Changes in the supply of labor (the quantity of workers), shown by the gray horizontal arrows, can occur due to other employment opportunities, the changing composition of the workforce, immigration, and migration.

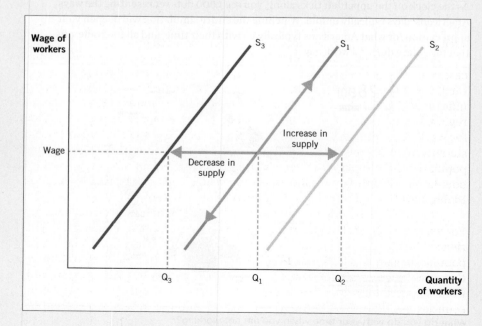

---

table clearers would increase, or shift to the right to S_2. These shifts reflect the fact that when jobs requiring comparable skills have different wage rates, the number of workers willing to supply labor for the lower-wage job will shrink and the number willing to supply labor for the better-paid job will grow.

THE CHANGING COMPOSITION OF THE WORKFORCE Over the last 30 years, the labor force participation rate (as measured by the female/male ratio) has increased significantly in most developed countries. A ratio of 100% indicates that females and males participated equally. According to the United Nations Development Programme, the United States saw its female/male ratio rise from 66% to 82%, Switzerland from 67% to 81%, and New Zealand from 65% to 84%. Overall, there are many more women employed in the workforce today than there were a generation ago, and the supply of workers in many occupations has expanded significantly as a result.

IMMIGRATION AND MIGRATION Demographic factors, including immigration and migration, also play a crucial role in the supply of labor. For example, immigration—both legal and illegal—increases the available supply of workers by a significant amount each year.

In 2015, over half a million people from foreign countries entered the United States through legal channels and gained permission to seek employment. There are over 40 million legal immigrants in the United States. In addition, illegal immigrants account for close to 10 million workers in the United States, many of whom enter the country to work as hotel maids, janitors, and fruit pickers. Often when states suggest or pass a tough immigration law, businesses in food and beverage, agriculture, and construction protest because they need inexpensive labor to remain competitive, and U.S. citizens are reluctant to work these jobs. Many states have wrestled with the issue, but policies that address illegal immigration remain controversial, and the solutions are difficult. The states need the cheap labor but don't want to pay additional costs, such as medical care and the cost of schooling the illegal immigrants' children.

For the purposes of this discussion, we consider migration to be the process of moving from one place to another within the United States. Although the U.S. population grows at an annual rate of approximately 1%, there are significant regional differences. Indeed, large population influxes lead to marked regional changes in the demand for labor and the supply of people looking for work. According to the U.S. Census Bureau, in 2010 the 10 fastest-growing states were in the South or West, with some states adding as much as 4% to their population in a single year. States in these areas provided 84% of the nation's population growth from 2000 to 2010, with Nevada, Utah, North Carolina, Idaho, and Texas all adding at least 20% to their populations.

It is worth noting that statewide data can hide significant localized changes. For example, census data from 2010 indicate that a number of counties experienced 50% or more population growth between 2000 and 2010. The biggest population gain was in Kendall County, Illinois, a far-flung suburb of Chicago that grew by nearly 100% between censuses. The county has been transitioning from an agricultural area to a bedroom community. Most of the fastest-growing counties are, like Kendall, relatively distant suburbs of major metropolitan areas. These are areas where new homes are available at comparatively reasonable prices.

SUPPLY OF LABOR

Where Have All the Teenagers Gone (and Who Is Going to Replace Them)?

In the mid-1990s there were 56 teenagers in the labor force for every fast-food restaurant. Today, there are half that many. Two factors are at work: teenagers are far less likely to participate in the workforce, and there has been explosive growth in the fast-food sector. Historically, fast-food restaurants relied on cheap labor to produce inexpensive food. Today, automation is being used to make up for the lack of workers. In 2018, Caliburger introduced Flippy, the first hamburger-flipping robot. Flippy costs $60,000, and there is also a $12,000 recurring annual fee for cleaning and maintenance, but Caliburger is confident that the investment is worth the high fixed cost. Caliburger is banking on decreased wait times, better consistency in food preparation, and less food waste. Plus, Flippy doesn't need health insurance. Also, he shows up for work on time and doesn't complain about the heat from the griddle.

Can't find reliable workers? No problem. Get a robot to do the job.

What Are the Determinants of Demand and Supply in the Labor Market?

In earlier chapters, we saw how markets reconcile the forces of demand and supply through pricing. Now that we have considered the forces governing demand and supply in the labor market, we are ready to see how the equilibrium

PRACTICE WHAT YOU KNOW

If you got a big raise, would you travel the world?

The Labor Supply Curve: What Would You Do with a Big Raise?

QUESTION: Your friend is concerned about his uncle, who just received a big raise. Your friend doesn't understand why his uncle wants to take time off from his job to travel. Can you help him understand why his uncle might want to cut back on his hours?

ANSWER: Ordinarily, we think of the labor supply curve as upward sloping, in which case higher wages translate into more hours worked and less leisure time. However, when the wage rate becomes high enough, some workers choose to substitute leisure for labor because they feel that enjoying free time is more valuable than earning more money. In this case, the labor supply curve bends backward, and the worker spends fewer hours working as his wage rises. Your friend's uncle is reflecting this tendency.

wage is established. We can then examine the labor market in greater detail and identify what causes shortages and surpluses of labor, why outsourcing occurs, and what happens when there is a single buyer of labor. The goal of this section is to provide a rich set of examples that help you become comfortable using demand and supply curves to understand how the labor market operates.

How Does the Market for Labor Reach Equilibrium?

We can think about wages as the price at which workers are willing to "rent" their time to employers. Turning to Figure 14.5, we see that at wages above equilibrium (W_E), the supply of workers willing to rent their time exceeds the demand for that time. The result is a surplus of available workers. The surplus, in turn, places downward pressure on wages. As wages drop, fewer workers are willing to rent their time to employers. When wages drop to the equilibrium wage, the surplus of workers is eliminated. At that point, the number of workers willing to work in that profession at that wage is exactly equal to the number of job openings that exist at that wage.

A similar process guides the labor market toward equilibrium from low wages. At wages below the equilibrium, the demand for labor exceeds

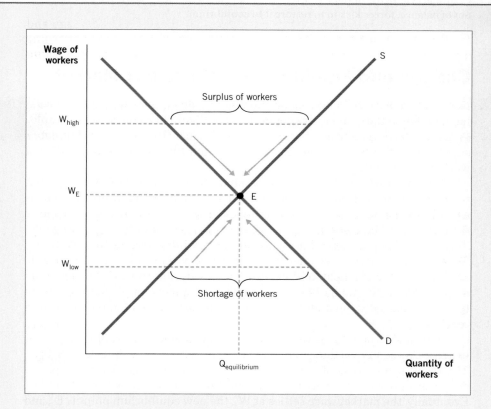

FIGURE 14.5

Equilibrium in the Labor Market

At high wages (W_{high}), a surplus of workers exists. The wage rate is driven down until the supply of workers and the demand for workers reach equilibrium. At low wages (W_{low}), a shortage occurs. The shortage forces the wage rate up until the equilibrium wage is reached and the shortage disappears.

the available supply. The shortage forces firms to offer higher wages to attract workers. As a result, wages rise until the shortage is eliminated at the equilibrium wage.

ECONOMICS IN THE REAL WORLD

WHERE ARE THE NURSES?

The United States is experiencing a shortage of nurses. A stressful job with long hours, nursing requires years of training. As baby boomers age, demand for nursing care is expected to rise. At the same time, the existing pool of nurses is rapidly aging and nearing retirement. According to the Bureau of Labor Statistics, the shortage of nurses in America will approach 1 million by 2025, making nursing the number one job in the country in terms of growth prospects.

Because the training process takes two or more years to complete, the labor market for nurses won't return to equilibrium immediately. The nursing shortage will persist for a number of years, until the quantity of nurses supplied to the market increases. The median pay of nurses was $70,000 in 2017. Given the ongoing shortage, not only will you find immediate employment once trained, you'll also experience rising wages while the shortage lasts.

Economics tells us that the combination of more newly trained nurses entering the market and the transfer of certain nursing services to assistants and technicians will eventually cause the nursing shortage to disappear. Remember that when a market is out of balance, forces kick in to restore it to equilibrium.

Entering an occupation with a shortage of workers will result in higher pay.

Change and Equilibrium in the Labor Market

Now that we have seen how labor markets find an equilibrium, let's see what happens when the demand or supply changes. Figure 14.6 contains two graphs. Panel (a) shows a shift in labor demand, and panel (b) shows a shift in labor supply. In both cases, the equilibrium wage and the equilibrium quantity of workers employed adjust accordingly.

Let's start with a shift in labor demand, shown in panel (a). Imagine that the demand for medical care increases due to an aging population and that, as a result, the demand for nurses increases, causing a shift in the demand curve from D_1 to D_2. The result is a shortage of workers equal to $Q_3 - Q_1$ at wage W_1. The shortage places upward pressure on wages, which increase from W_1 to W_2. As wages rise, nursing becomes more attractive as a profession. More people choose to enter the field, and existing nurses decide to work longer hours or postpone retirement. Thus, the number of nurses employed rises from Q_1 to Q_2. Eventually, the wage settles at W_2, and the number of nurses employed reaches Q_2.

Turning to panel (b), we see what happens when the supply of nurses increases. As additional nurses are certified, the overall supply shifts from S_1 to S_2. The result is a surplus of workers equal to $Q_3 - Q_1$ at wage W_1, which places downward pressure on wages. As a result, the wage rate falls from W_1 to W_2. Eventually, the market wage settles at W_2, the new equilibrium point is E_2, and the number of nurses employed reaches Q_2.

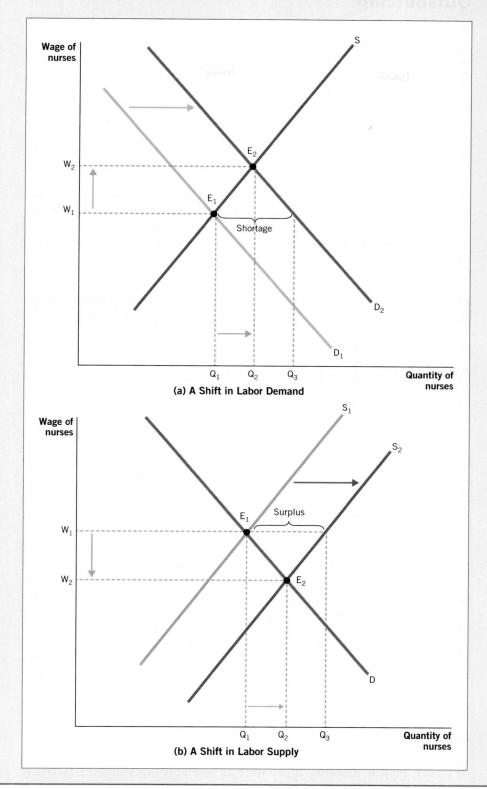

FIGURE 14.6

Shifting the Labor Market Equilibrium

In panel (a), the demand for nurses increases, creating a shortage of workers equal to $Q_3 - Q_1$, which leads to a higher equilibrium wage (W_2) and a higher quantity of nurses employed (Q_2) than before. In panel (b), the supply of nurses increases. The result is a surplus of workers equal to $Q_3 - Q_1$, causing the equilibrium wage to fall (to W_2) and the number of nurses employed to rise (to Q_2).

(a) A Shift in Labor Demand

(b) A Shift in Labor Supply

Outsourcing

Why would a firm hire someone from outside if it has a qualified employee nearby? This practice, known as *outsourcing*, has gotten a lot of attention in recent years. In this section, we explain how outsourcing works, why companies do it, and how it affects the labor market for workers.

The **outsourcing of labor** occurs when a firm shifts jobs to an outside company, usually overseas, where the cost of labor is lower. In the publishing industry, for example, page make-up (also known as composition) is often done overseas to take advantage of lower labor costs. This outsourcing has been facilitated by the Internet, which eliminates the shipping delays and costs that used to constitute a large part of the business. Today, a qualified worker can lay out book pages anywhere in the world.

When countries outsource, their pool of potential workers expands. But whether a labor expansion is driven by outsourcing or by an increase in the domestic supply of workers, those who are already employed in that particular industry find that they earn less. Moreover, a rise in unemployment occurs in the occupation that can be outsourced.

ECONOMICS IN THE REAL WORLD

INTERNATIONAL SURROGACY

Kaival Hospital in Anand, India, matches infertile couples with local women, such as these surrogate mothers.

When we think of outsourced jobs, we don't generally think of childbirth. But a growing number of infertile couples have outsourced pregnancy to surrogate mothers in India. The process involves surrogate mothers being impregnated with eggs previously fertilized in vitro. While often controversial, surrogacy is a growing practice in India, and has been legal in India since 2002, as it is in many other countries including the United States. While no reliable numbers track such pregnancies nationwide, doctors work with surrogates in virtually every major city in India. Surrogate mothers earn roughly $5,000 for a nine-month commitment. This amount is the equivalent of what low-skilled workers in India earn in 10 or more years. Couples typically pay approximately $10,000 for all of the costs associated with the pregnancy. Critics question the ethics of the entire business, especially inequality issues.

THE GLOBAL IMPLICATIONS OF OUTSOURCING IN THE SHORT RUN Recall our chapter-opening question, "Is outsourcing bad for the economy?" Many people hold that opinion because when they think of outsourcing, they immediately imagine the jobs lost in the short run. However, the reality is more complex. Outsourced jobs are not lost; they are relocated from high-labor-cost areas to low-labor-cost areas. Outsourcing also creates benefits for firms in the form of lower production costs. The lower costs translate into lower prices for consumers and also help the firms that outsource to compete in the global economy.

Outsourcing need not cost the United States jobs. Consider what happens when foreign countries outsource their production to the United States. For example, the German auto manufacturer Mercedes-Benz currently has many of its cars built in Alabama. If you were an assembly-line worker in Germany

who had spent a lifetime making cars for Mercedes, you would likely be upset if your job was outsourced to North America. You would feel just like the American technician who loses a job to someone in India or the software writer who is replaced by a worker in China. Outsourcing always produces a job winner and a job loser. In the case of foreign outsourcing to the United States, employment in this country rises. In fact, the Mercedes-Benz plant in Alabama employs more than 3,000 workers. Those jobs were transferred to the United States because the company felt that it would be more profitable to hire American workers and make the vehicles in the United States rather than construct them in Germany and ship them across the Atlantic.

The Mercedes-Benz plant near Tuscaloosa, Alabama, illustrates that outsourcing is more than just a one-way street.

Figure 14.7 shows how outsourcing by foreign firms helps to increase U.S. labor demand. In panel (a), we see the job loss and lower wages that occur in Germany when jobs are outsourced to the United States. As the demand for labor in Germany falls from D_1 to D_2, wages drop to W_2 and employment declines to Q_2. Panel (b) illustrates the corresponding increase in demand for U.S. labor in Alabama. As demand shifts from D_1 to D_2, wages rise to W_2 and employment rises to Q_2.

Because each nation will experience outsourcing flows out of and into the country, it is impossible to say anything definitive about the overall impact of outsourcing on labor in the short run. However, it is highly unlikely that workers who lose high-paying jobs toward the end of their working lives will be able to find other jobs that pay equally well.

THE GLOBAL IMPLICATIONS OF OUTSOURCING IN THE LONG RUN

Although we see mixed results for outsourcing in the short run, we can say that in the long run outsourcing benefits domestic consumers and producers. In fact, outsourcing is a key component in international trade. Throughout this book, we have seen that trade creates value. When companies and even countries specialize, they become more efficient. The efficiency gains, or cost savings, help producers to expand production. In the absence of trade barriers, lower costs benefit consumers in domestic and international markets through lower prices, and the outsourcing of jobs provides the income for foreign workers to purchase domestic imports. Therefore, the mutually interdependent nature of international trade enhances overall social welfare.

Trade creates value

FIGURE 14.7

Shifting the Labor Market Equilibrium

Outsourcing creates more demand in one market at the expense of the other. In panel (a), the demand for German labor declines from D_1 to D_2, leading to lower wages and less employment. Panel (b) shows the increase in the demand for labor from D_1 to D_2 in Alabama. The results are higher wages and more employment.

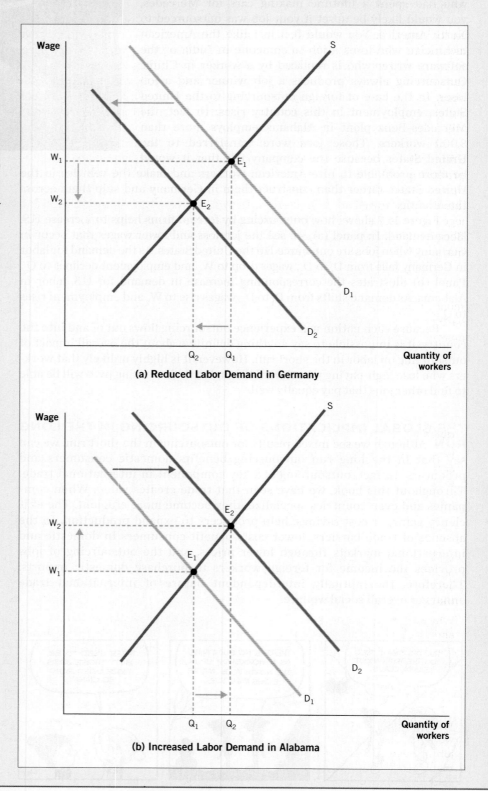

(a) Reduced Labor Demand in Germany

(b) Increased Labor Demand in Alabama

Monopsony

In looking at supply, demand, and equilibrium in the labor market, we have assumed that the market for labor is competitive. But that is not always the case. Sometimes the labor market has only a few buyers or sellers who are able to capture market power. One extreme form of market power is **monopsony**, which occurs when only a single buyer exists. Like a monopolist, a monopsonist has a great deal of market power. As a consequence, the output in the labor market will favor a monopsonist whenever one is present.

In Chapter 10, we examined how a monopolist behaves. Compared with a firm in a competitive market, the monopolist charges a higher price for the product it sells. Likewise, a monopsonist in the labor market can leverage its market power. Because it is the only firm hiring, it can pay its workers less. Isolated college towns are a good example. Workers who wish to live in such college towns often find that almost all the available jobs are through the college. Because it is the chief provider of jobs, the college has a monopsony in the labor market. It can use its market power to hire many local workers at low wages.

Monopsony
is a situation in which there is only one buyer.

WHY DO SOME WORKERS MAKE MORE THAN OTHERS? While most workers generally spend 35 to 40 hours a week at work, the amount they earn varies dramatically. Table 14.2 presents a number of simple questions that answer the larger question, "Why do some workers make more than others?"

TABLE 14.2

Why Some Workers Make More than Others

Question	Answer
Why do economists generally earn more than elementary school teachers?	Supply is the key. There are fewer qualified economists than certified elementary school teachers. Therefore, the equilibrium wage in economics is higher than it is in elementary education. It's also important to note that demand factors may be part of the explanation. The value of the marginal product of labor of economists is generally higher than that of most elementary school teachers because many economists work in industry, which pays higher wages than the public sector.
Why do people who work the night shift earn more than those who do the same job during the day?	Again, supply is the key. Fewer people are willing to work at night, so the wage necessary to attract labor to perform the job must be higher. (That is, night shift workers earn what is called a *compensating differential*, which we discuss in Chapter 15.)
Why do professional athletes and successful actors make so much when what they do is not essential?	Demand and supply both play important roles here. The paying public is willing, even eager, to spend a large amount of income on entertainment. Thus, demand for entertainment is high. On the supply end of the equation, the number of individuals who capture the imagination of the paying public is small, and they are therefore paid handsomely. Since the value of the marginal product that they create is incredibly high, and the supply of workers with these skills is quite small, accomplished athletes and actors earn huge incomes.
Why do janitors, construction workers, and nurses—whose jobs are essential—have salaries that are a tiny fraction of celebrities' salaries?	Demand again. The value of the marginal product of labor created in these essential jobs is low, so their employers are unable to pay high wages.

Changes in Labor Demand

Labor is always subject to changes in demand.

QUESTION: A company builds a new facility that doubles its workspace and equipment. How is labor affected?

ANSWER: The company has probably experienced additional demand for the product it sells. Therefore, it needs additional employees to staff the facility, causing a positive shift in the demand curve. When the demand for labor rises, wages increase and so does the number of people employed.

QUESTION: A company decides to outsource 100 jobs from a facility in Indiana to Indonesia. How is labor affected in the short run?

ANSWER: This situation leads to two changes. First, a decrease in demand for labor in Indiana results in lower wages there and fewer workers hired. Second, an increase in demand for labor in Indonesia results in higher wages there and more workers hired.

The table shows how demand and supply determine wages in a variety of settings. Workers with a high-value marginal product of labor invariably earn more than those with a lower-value marginal product of labor. It is important to note that working an "essential" job does not guarantee a high income. Instead, the highest incomes are reserved for jobs with a high demand for workers and a low supply of them. In other words, our preconceived notions of fairness take a backseat to the underlying market forces that govern pay. In the next chapter, we consider many additional factors that determine wages, including wage discrimination.

What Role Do Land and Capital Play in Production?

In addition to labor, firms need land and capital to produce goods and services. In this section, we complete our analysis of the resource market by considering how land and capital enter into the production process. Returning to the restaurant Agaves, we know that the business hires labor to make meals. But to do their jobs, the workers need equipment, tables, chairs, cash registers, and a kitchen. Without a physical location and a host of capital resources, labor would be irrelevant.

The Market for Land

Like the demand for labor, the demand for land is determined by the value of the marginal product it generates. However, unlike the supply of labor, the supply of land is ordinarily fixed. We can think of it as nonresponsive to prices, or perfectly inelastic.

In Figure 14.8, the vertical supply curve reflects the inelastic supply. The price of land is determined by the intersection of supply and demand. Notice the label on the vertical axis, which reflects the price of land as the rental price necessary to use it, not the price necessary to purchase it. When evaluating a firm's economic situation, we do not count the entire purchase price of the land it needs. To do so would dramatically overstate the cost of land in the production process because the land is not used up, but only occupied for a certain period. For example, consider a car that you buy. You drive it for a year and put 15,000 miles on it. Counting the entire purchase price of the car would overstate the true operating cost for one year of service. The true cost of operating the vehicle includes wear and tear along with operating expenses, such as gasoline, maintenance, and service visits. A similar process is at work with land. Firms that own land consider the rent they could have earned if they had rented the land out for the year. This method nicely captures the opportunity cost of using the land.

Opportunity cost

Because the supply of land is usually fixed, changes in demand determine the rental price. When demand is low—say, at D_1—the rental price received, P_1, is also low. When demand is high—say, at D_2—the rental price of land is high, at P_2. Apartment rentals near college campuses provide a good example of the conditions under which the demand for land is high. Because students and faculty want to live near campus, the demand for land is often much higher there than even a few blocks away. Like labor, the demand for land is derived from

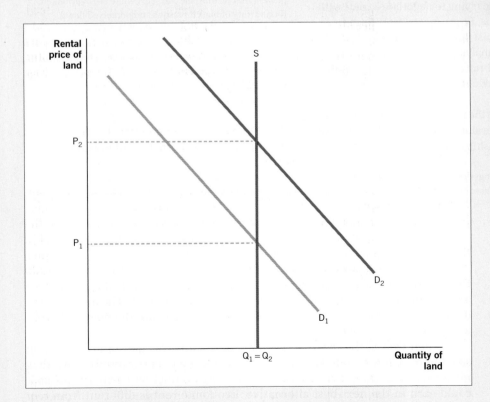

FIGURE 14.8

Supply and Demand in the Market for Land

Because the supply of land is fixed, the price it commands depends on demand. If demand increases from D_1 to D_2, the price will rise from P_1 to P_2. Note that "price" here reflects the rental price of the land, not the purchase price.

· ECONOMICS *in the* MEDIA ·

Value of the Marginal Product of Labor

MONEYBALL

Moneyball (2011), a film based on Michael Lewis's 2003 book of the same name, details the struggles of the Oakland Athletics, a major-league baseball team. The franchise attempts to overcome some seemingly impossible obstacles with the help of its general manager, Billy Beane, by applying innovative statistical analysis, known as sabermetrics, pioneered by Bill James.

Traditional baseball scouts use experience, intuition, and subjective criteria to evaluate potential players. However, Beane, formerly a heavily recruited high school player who failed to have a successful professional career, knows firsthand that this method of scouting does not guarantee success. The Oakland A's lack the financial ability to pay as much as other teams. While trying to negotiate a trade with the Cleveland Indians, Beane meets Peter Brand, a young Yale economist who has new ideas about applying statistical analysis to baseball in order to build a better team. Brand explains that evaluating a player's marginal product would be a better tool for recruitment.

In the key scene in the movie, Brand briefly explains his methodology for evaluating players and how the A's can build a championship team:

> It's about getting things down to one number. Using the stats the way we read them, we'll find value in

Can a young economist's algorithm save the Oakland A's?

players that no one else can see. People are overlooked for a variety of biased reasons and perceived flaws: age, appearance, and personality. Bill James and mathematics cut straight through that. Billy, of the 20,000 notable players for us to consider, I believe that there is a championship team of 25 people that we can afford, because everyone else in baseball undervalues them.

The A's go on to have a remarkable season by picking up "outcasts" that no other team wanted.

Thanks to Kim Holder (the University of West Georgia).

Marginal thinking

Economic rent
is the difference between what a factor of production earns and what it could earn in the next-best alternative.

the demand for the products it is used to produce. In this case, the demand for apartments, homes, and retail space near campus is very high. The high demand drives up the rental price of land closer to campus because the marginal product of land there is higher.

When we see the term "rent," most of us think of the rental price of an apartment or house. But when economists talk about an **economic rent**, they mean the difference between what a factor of production earns and what it could earn in the next-best alternative. Economic rent is different from *rent seeking*. Recall from Chapter 10 that rent seeking occurs when firms compete to

A satellite photo shows manufactured islands in Dubai, United Arab Emirates—an exception to our assumption that the amount of land is fixed.

seek a monopoly position. In contrast, economic rent refers to investors' ability to beat their opportunity cost. For instance, in the case of housing near college campuses, a small studio apartment generally commands a much higher rent than a similar apartment located 10 miles away. Why? The rent near campus must be high enough to compensate the property owners for using their land for an apartment instead of in other ways that might also be profitable in the area—for example, for a single residence, a business, or a parking lot. Once you move 10 miles farther out, the number of people interested in using the land for these purposes declines.

More generally, in areas where many people would like to live or work, rental prices are often very high. Take San Francisco, where the average rental unit costs a staggering $3,500 a month. That eye-popping amount makes most apartment rental prices in the United States seem downright inexpensive. Similarly, owners of property in Manhattan, Boston, and Washington, D.C., all receive more economic rent on properties than those who own similar rentals in Peoria, Idaho Falls, Scranton, or Chattanooga. The ability to earn a substantial economic rent comes back to opportunity costs: because there are so many other potential uses of property in densely populated areas, rents are correspondingly higher.

Opportunity cost

The Market for Capital

Capital, or the equipment and materials needed to produce goods, is a necessary factor of production. The demand for capital is determined by the value of the marginal product it creates. Like the demand for land and labor, the demand for capital is a derived demand: a firm requires capital only if the product it produces is in demand. The demand for capital is also downward sloping, reflecting the fact that the value of the marginal product associated with its use declines as the amount used rises.

When to Use More Labor, Land, or Capital

Firms must evaluate whether hiring additional labor, utilizing more land, or deploying more capital will constitute the best use of their resources. To do this, they compare the value of the marginal product per dollar spent across the three factors of production.

Let's consider an example. Suppose that a company pays its employees $15 per hour, the rental rate of land is $5,000 per acre per year, and the rental rate of capital is $1,000 per year. The company's manager determines that the value of the marginal product of labor is $450, the value of the marginal product of an acre of land is $125,000, and the value of the marginal product of capital is $40,000. Is the firm using the right mix of resources? Table 14.3 compares the ratios of the value of the marginal product (VMP) of each factor of production with the cost of attaining that value (this calculation gives us the "bang per buck" for each resource, or the relative benefit of using each resource).

Looking at these results, we see that the highest bang per buck (column 4) is the value $40 created by dividing the VMP of capital by the rental price of capital. When we compare this value with the bang per buck for labor and land, we see that the firm is getting more benefit per dollar spent on capital than from labor ($30) or land ($25). Therefore, the firm would benefit from using capital more intensively. As it does so, the VMP of capital in column 2 will fall due to diminishing returns, and the bang per buck for capital will drop from $40 in column 4 to a number that is more in line with bang per buck for labor and land. Conversely, the firm is using land ($25) too intensively, and it would benefit from using less. Doing so will raise the VMP it produces and increase its bang per buck for land. By using less land and more capital and by tweaking the use of labor as well, the firm will eventually bring the value created by all three factors to a point at which the bang per buck spent is equal for each of the factors. At that point, the firm will be utilizing its resources efficiently.

Why does all this matter? Because the world is always changing: wages rise and fall, as do property values and the cost of acquiring capital. A firm must constantly adjust the mix of land, labor, and capital it uses to get the largest return. Moreover, the markets for land, labor, and capital are connected. The amount of labor that a firm uses depends not only on the marginal product of labor, but also on the marginal product of land and capital. Therefore, a change in the supply of one factor will alter the returns of all factors. For instance, if wages fall, firms will be inclined to hire more labor. But if they hire more labor, they will use less capital. Capital itself is not any more, or less, productive. Rather, lower wages reduce the demand for capital. In this situation, the demand curve for capital would shift to the left, lowering the rental price of capital as well as the quantity of capital deployed.

Marginal thinking

TABLE 14.3

Determining the Bang per Buck for Each Resource

(1) Factor of production	(2) Value of the marginal product	(3) Wage or rental price	(4) Bang per buck
Labor	$450	$15	$450 ÷ 15 = $30
Land	125,000	5,000	125,000 ÷ 5,000 = 25
Capital	40,000	1,000	40,000 ÷ 1,000 = 40

Outsourcing

Outsourcing, though painful for those whose jobs are outsourced, is simply the application of a fundamental economic principle—keep costs as low as possible. Labor is usually the most expensive input for a business, so all managers must seek to pay the lowest wage that still ensures an effective workforce. Firms seek the right balance of costs and relevant skills when outsourcing jobs. Here is a look at three representative jobs in the United States, Mexico, China, and India, with salaries measured as a percentage of the typical U.S. salary.

U.S. Salary   China   India   Mexico

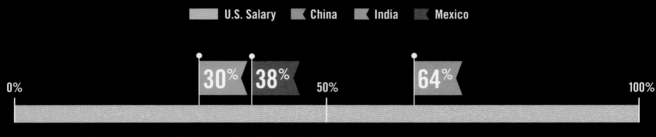

INFORMATION TECHNOLOGY PROJECT MANAGER

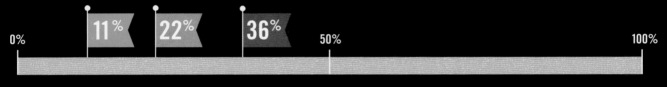

SOFTWARE ENGINEER

CUSTOMER SERVICE REPRESENTATIVE

The communications and transportation revolutions, along with the increasing skill level of foreign labor, have created conditions for the outsourcing of millions of U.S. jobs to China, India, and Latin America.

Outsourcing is about comparative advantage. Firms hire foreign workers who hold a comparative advantage and can produce a good or service more cheaply and at a lower opportunity cost than domestic workers.

REVIEW QUESTIONS

- Software engineering jobs are outsourced from the United States to India. Use supply and demand curves to sketch the effects on the U.S. and Indian labor forces.

- Outsourcing is controversial. Explain why by citing effects to the economy both in the short run and long run.

SKILLED WORK WITHOUT THE WORKER

Tesla factory in California. Where are the workers?

While the many robots in auto factories typically perform only one function, at the Tesla electric automobile factory in Fremont, California, a robot might perform up to four tasks. And it does it all without a coffee break—three shifts a day, 365 days a year. This is the future. A new wave of robots, far more adept than those now commonly used by automakers and other heavy manufacturers, are replacing workers around the world in both manufacturing and distribution. Factories like Tesla's are a striking counterpoint to those used by Apple and other consumer electronics giants, which employ hundreds of thousands of low-skilled workers.

The falling costs and growing sophistication of robots have touched off a renewed debate among economists and technologists over how quickly jobs will be lost. MIT economists Erik Brynjolfsson and Andrew McAfee argue that the transformation will be rapid: "The pace and scale of this encroachment into human skills is relatively recent and has profound economic implications." In their minds, the advent of low-cost automation foretells changes similar to those of the revolution in agricultural technology over the last century, which decreased farming employment in the United States from 40% of the workforce to about 2% today.

Robot manufacturers in the United States say that in many applications, robots are already more cost-effective than humans. In one example, a robotic manufacturing system initially cost $250,000 and replaced two machine operators, each earning $50,000 a year. Over the 15-year life of the system, the machines yielded $3.5 million in labor savings.

Some jobs are still outside the range of automation: construction jobs that require workers to move in unpredictable settings and perform different tasks that are not repetitive; assembly work that requires tactile feedback like placing fiberglass panels inside airplanes, boats, or cars; and assembly jobs where only a limited quantity of the product is made or where there are many versions of each product, which would require expensive reprogramming of robots. Moreover, Tesla may rely on automation in its Fremont plant, but it is still the area's biggest employer, with 10,000 workers compared to 3,200 for the local school district in the #2 spot—so there are still plenty of jobs that automation can't reach—yet.

But that list is growing shorter. Older robots cannot do such work because computer vision systems were costly and limited to carefully controlled environments where the lighting was just right. But thanks to an inexpensive stereo camera and software that lets the system see shapes with the same ease as humans, new types of robot can quickly discern the irregular dimensions of randomly placed objects.

"We're on the cusp of completely changing manufacturing and distribution," says Gary Bradski, a machine-vision scientist. "I think it's not as singular an event, but it will ultimately have as big an impact as the Internet."

Adapted from "Skilled Work, Without the Worker" by John Markoff, *New York Times*, August 18, 2012.

Conclusion

Throughout this chapter, we learned that the compensation for factor inputs depends on the interaction between demand and supply. Resource demand is derived from the demand for the final product a firm produces, and resource

Bang for the Buck: When to Use More Capital or More Labor

Suppose Agaves is considering the purchase of a new industrial dishwasher. The unit cleans faster and uses less labor and less water, but it costs $10,000. Should the restaurant make the capital expenditure, or would it be better off saving the money and incurring higher operating costs? To help decide what Agaves should do, consider this information: the dishwasher has a usable life of five years before it will need to be replaced. It will save the restaurant $300 a year in water and 10 hours of labor each week. Human dishwashers are currently paid $8 per hour.

How are all those dishes going to get clean?

QUESTION: Should Agaves purchase the new dishwasher?

ANSWER: This is the kind of question every business wrestles with on a regular basis. And the way to answer it is very straightforward. A firm should invest in new capital when the value of the marginal product it creates per dollar spent is greater than the value of the marginal product per dollar spent on the next-best alternative. In other words, a firm should invest in new capital when the bang per buck exceeds that of labor and other investments.

Let's compare the total cost of purchasing the dishwasher with the total savings. The total cost of the dishwasher is $10,000, but the savings are larger.

Item	Amount saved	Total for five years
Water	$300/year	$1,500
Labor	10 hours per week × $8/hour = $80/week × 52 weeks = $4,160/year	20,800
Total		22,300

The total savings over five years is $22,300. This makes the investment in the dishwasher the best choice!

supply depends on the other opportunities and compensation levels that exist in the market. As a result, the equilibrium prices and outputs in the markets for land, labor, and capital reflect, in large part, the forces of demand and supply.

In the next chapter, we examine income and poverty. As you will discover, there are many factors beyond the demand for and supply of workers that explain why some workers make more than others. For instance, wages also depend on the amount of human capital required for a job, as well as location, lifestyle choices, union membership, and the riskiness of the profession. Understanding these elements will deepen your understanding of why workers earn what they do.

It is true that outsourcing destroys some jobs in high-labor-cost areas, but it also creates jobs in low-labor-cost areas. As a result, it lowers the cost of manufacturing goods and providing services. This improved efficiency helps firms that outsource by enabling them to better compete in the global economy.

Will Your Future Job Be Automated?

- The best way to ensure that your future job is not automated is to be valuable to your organization.

- Developing new skills and knowledge is integral to maintaining and increasing the value of the marginal product of your labor.

- When you are highly valued, it will be difficult to replace you.

- Low-skill occupations tend to be the most at risk.

When you select an academic major and learn a set of skills, you hope they will enable you to find stable employment. Finding stable employment becomes more challenging in an environment where labor is easily automated. So as you seek employment, you need to consider the long-term likelihood that your job could be replaced. To help you think about your future career, let's consider jobs that are likely to be automated and jobs that are more likely to still be done by humans.

Researchers estimate that nearly half of all U.S. jobs may be at risk in the coming decades, with lower-paid occupations among the most vulnerable. In 2017 Bloomberg.com created a tool in an article to "Find Out If Your Job Will Be Automated." It projected which jobs are at increased risk of being replaced, which included nearly 50% of all U.S. jobs. Type your occupation into the search bar (as shown in the figure) to see where the researchers peg the probability of your job being automated.

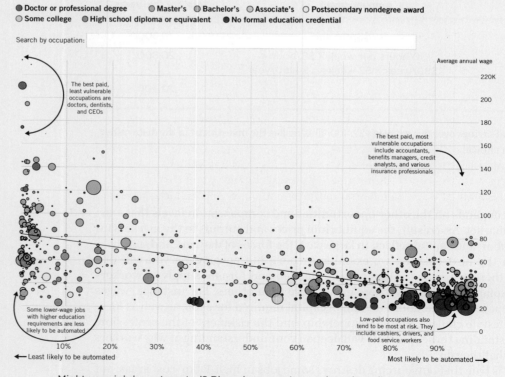

Might your job be automated? Bloomberg.com's search tool predicts it may be.

Outsourcing is one of the many ways firms adapt when labor costs rise. Firms also utilize more capital and deploy more technology when labor costs increase. And, workers must create a high value of the marginal product of labor to keep automation and robotics from making them superfluous as workers. ✳

· ANSWERING *the* BIG QUESTIONS ·

What are the factors of production?

- Labor, land, and capital are the factors of production, or the inputs used in producing goods and services.

Where does the demand for labor come from?

- The demand for each factor of production is a derived demand that stems from a firm's desire to supply a good in another market. Labor demand is contingent on the value of the marginal product that is produced, and the value of the marginal product is equivalent to the firm's labor demand curve.

Where does the supply of labor come from?

- The supply of labor comes from the wage rate that is offered. Each worker faces the labor-leisure trade-off. At high wage levels, the income effect may become larger than the substitution effect and cause the labor supply curve to bend backward. Changes in the supply of labor can result from other employment opportunities, the changing composition of the workforce, immigration, and migration.

What are the determinants of demand and supply in the labor market?

- Labor markets bring the forces of demand and supply together in a wage signal that conveys information to both sides of the market. At wages above the equilibrium, the supply of workers exceeds the demand for labor. The result is a surplus of available workers that places downward pressure on wages until they reach the equilibrium wage, at which point the surplus is eliminated. At wages below the equilibrium, the demand for labor exceeds the available supply of workers, and a shortage develops. The shortage forces firms to offer higher wages to attract workers. Wages rise until they reach the equilibrium wage, at which point the shortage is eliminated.
- There is no definitive result for outsourcing of labor in the short run. In the long run, outsourcing moves jobs to workers who are more productive and enhances overall social welfare.

What role do land and capital play in production?

- Land and capital (as well as labor) are the factors of production across which firms compare the value of the marginal product per dollar spent. Firms seek to equalize the revenue per dollar spent on each input, thereby maximizing their efficiency.

Concepts You Should Know

backward-bending labor supply
   curve (p. 444)
derived demand (p. 437)
economic rent (p. 458)

income effect (p. 444)
marginal product of
   labor (p. 438)
monopsony (p. 455)

outsourcing of labor (p. 452)
substitution effect (p. 444)
value of the marginal product
   (VMP) (p. 439)

Questions for Review

1. Why is the demand for factor inputs a derived demand?

2. What rule does a firm use when deciding to hire an additional worker?

3. What are the two shifters of labor demand? What are the four shifters of labor supply?

4. What can cause the labor supply curve to bend backward?

5. If wages are below the equilibrium level, what would cause them to rise?

6. What would happen to movie stars' wages if all major film studios merged into a single firm, creating a monopsony for film actors?

7. If workers became more productive (that is, produced more output in the same amount of time), what would happen to the demand for labor, the wages of labor, and the number of workers employed?

8. How is economic rent different from rent seeking?

9. How does outsourcing affect wages and employment in the short run and in the long run?

Study Problems (* solved at the end of this section)

1. Maria is a hostess at a local restaurant. When she earned $8 per hour, she worked 35 hours per week. When her wage increased to $10 per hour, she decided to work 40 hours per week. However, when her wage increased again to $12 per hour, she decided to cut back to 37 hours per week. Draw Maria's supply curve. How would you explain her actions to someone who is unfamiliar with economics?

2. Would a burrito restaurant hire an additional worker for $10.00 an hour if that worker could produce an extra 30 burritos and each burrito made added $0.60 in revenues?

* 3. Pam's Pretzels has a production function shown in the following table. It costs Pam's Pretzels $80 per day per worker. Each pretzel sells for $3.

Quantity of labor	Quantity of pretzels
0	0
1	100
2	180
3	240
4	280
5	310
6	330
7	340
8	320

a. Compute the marginal product and the value of the marginal product that each worker creates.

b. How many workers should Pam's Pretzels hire?

4. Jimi owns a music school that specializes in teaching guitar. Jimi has a limited supply of rooms for his instructors to use for lessons. As a result, each successive instructor adds less to Jimi's output of lessons. The following table lists Jimi's production function. Guitar lessons cost $25 per hour.

Quantity of labor	Quantity of lessons (hours)
0	0
1	10
2	17
3	23
4	28
5	32
6	35
7	37
8	38

a. Construct Jimi's labor demand schedule at each of the following daily wage rates for instructors: $75, $100, $125, $150, $175, $200.
b. Suppose that the market price of guitar lessons increases to $35 per hour. What does Jimi's new labor demand schedule look like at the daily wage rates listed in part (a)?

5. In an effort to create a healthcare safety net, the government requires employers to provide healthcare coverage to all employees. What impact will this increased coverage have in the following labor markets in the short run?

a. the demand for doctors
b. the demand for medical equipment
c. the supply of hospital beds

6. A million-dollar lottery winner decides to quit working. How can you explain this behavior using economics?

7. Illustrate each of the following changes with a labor supply and demand diagram. (Use a separate diagram for each part.) Diagram the new equilibrium point, and note how the wage and quantity of workers employed changes.

a. There is a sudden migration out of an area.
b. Laborers are willing to work more hours.
c. Fewer workers are willing to work the night shift.
d. The demand for California wines suddenly increases.

✳ **8.** A football team is trying to decide which of two running backs (A or B) to sign to a one-year contract.

Predicted statistics	Player A	Player B
Touchdowns	7	10
Yards gained	1,200	1,000
Fumbles	4	5

The team has done a statistical analysis to determine the value of each touchdown, yard gained, and fumble to the team's revenue. Each touchdown is worth an extra $250,000, each yard gained is worth $1,500, and each fumble costs $75,000. Player A costs $3.0 million and player B costs $2.5 million. Based on their predicted statistics in the table above, which player should the team sign?

9. Farmers in Utopia experience perfect weather throughout the entire growing season, and as a result their crop is double its normal size. Draw a labor supply and demand diagram and use the diagram to explain how this bumper crop will affect each of the following.

a. the price of the crop
b. the marginal product of workers who harvest the crop
c. the demand for the workers who harvest the crop

10. What will happen to the equilibrium wage of crop harvesters in Dystopia if the price of the crop falls by 50% and the marginal product of the workers increases by 25%?

11. Suppose that the current wage rate is $20 per hour, the rental rate of land is $10,000 per acre, and the rental rate of capital is $2,500. The manager of a firm determines that the value of the marginal product of labor is $400, the value of the marginal product of an acre of land is $200,000, and the value of the marginal product of capital is $4,000. Is the firm maximizing profit? Explain your response.

✳ 12. What country made the shirt you are wearing? Go ahead and check the tag and write down your answer. Even though we can't predict the exact country your shirt is from, there is a surprising answer in the Solved Problems section, which you should check out.

13. Why are most iPhones manufactured and assembled in China and then shipped to the United States, even though Apple was founded in California and most of Apple's workforce still reside in this country?

✳ 14. We saw that a backward-bending supply curve of labor can cause individual workers to work less at high wage levels. But one doesn't generally see market supply curves bend backward. Can you explain why we don't generally see that but see it here?

15. Use labor supply and demand curves to illustrate what will happen to the wages of each of the following as the United States ages.

a. teachers
b. dog walkers

Solved Problems

3. a.

Quantity of labor	Quantity of pretzels	Marginal product	Value of the marginal product
0	0	0	$0
1	100	100	300
2	180	80	240
3	240	60	180
4	280	40	120
5	310	30	90
6	330	20	60
7	340	10	30
8	320	−20	−60

b. The VMP of the fifth worker is $90 and each worker costs $80, so Pam should hire five workers. Hiring the sixth worker would cause her to lose $20.

8.

Predicted statistics	Player A	VMP of Player A	Player B	VMP of Player B
Touchdowns	7	$1,750,000	10	$2,500,000
Yards gained	1,200	1,800,000	1,000	1,500,000
Fumbles	4	−300,000	5	−375,000
Total value		3,250,000		3,625,000

Player A has a predicted VMP of $3.25 million and a cost of $3.0 million. Player B has a predicted VMP of $3.625 million and a cost of $2.5 million. Since player B's predicted VMP exceeds his salary by $1.125 million and player A's predicted VMP exceeds his salary by only $0.25 million, the team should sign player B.

12. Forget the country of origin on your tag—that is just where the final product was assembled. Your shirt is actually a product of a global supply

chain that includes cotton seeds engineered in the United States, cotton grown in India, sewing machines manufactured in Germany, a collar lining from Brazil, and inexpensive labor from the place on your tag (where all the pieces were sewn together). The tag chronicles the end of your shirt's journey, so it gets the credit; but behind the scenes it takes a planet to make every shirt, and that is the surprising answer to the question.

14. In general, rising prices draw more suppliers. This is also true for wages in a particular market: as wages rise, more workers will choose that occupation, thereby ensuring that the market supply of labor increases. For the labor market as a whole, however, the supply of workers is more or less fixed (barring unrestricted immigration), and so there is a cap on the number of worker-hours per month that the market can supply. If wages continue to rise, the supply of labor becomes completely inelastic and the supply curve becomes vertical. This makes it possible for the income effect to begin to overtake the substitution effect if wages rise still further, as workers enjoy the same pay while working fewer hours.

Income, Inequality, and Poverty

Do You Think the Structure of Compensation in the Working World is Unfair?

If you wish to earn a sizable income, it is not enough to be good at something; that "something" needs to be an occupation that society values highly. What matters are your skills, what you produce, and the supply of workers in your chosen profession. How hard you work often has little to do with how much you get paid.

Just think about schoolteachers. They put in long hours, including evenings spent grading and prepping for the next day's classes. But the pay that teachers earn is low relative to the hours they put in and often teachers need to look for other income streams. One modern idea is to monetize their lesson plans. Second-grade teacher Nicki Dingraudo has an Instagram account, *The Sprinkle Topped Teacher*, with over thirty thousand followers. She lives in Arizona, where teachers are paid, on average, about $50,000 per year. That may sound like decent money, but it is not enough if you're a single parent who hopes to own a home and raise a family. Teachers like Nicki who have followers on Instagram or Pinterest in the tens or hundreds of thousands can earn more from social influence than they do from their salaries. How? On Instagram the same teacher helps thousands of other teachers by creating unique tools that make course preparation easier. Since

Social media puts one in touch with many thousands of adult followers. Teachers and many other "influencers" are using it to turn their work efforts into additional income.

time is the scarce resource many teachers wish they had more of, teachers often pay for lesson plans from trusted social influencers.

In this chapter, we continue our exploration of labor by examining income and inequality in labor markets, including the characteristics of successful wage earners and the impediments the poor face when they try to escape poverty. Examining those at the top and the bottom of the income ladder helps us explain the many forces that determine income. In addition, we explore the incidence of poverty, poverty trends, and measurement issues. Examining the poverty statistics, and understanding the causes of poverty, allows society to craft economic policies that more effectively help those in need.

· BIG QUESTIONS ·

- What are the determinants of wages?
- What causes income inequality?
- How do economists analyze poverty?

What Are the Determinants of Wages?

The reasons why some workers get paid more than others are complex. We learned in Chapter 14 that the forces of supply and demand explain a large part of wage inequality. However, numerous additional factors contribute to differences in earnings. Various nonmonetary factors cause some occupations to pay higher or lower wages than supply and demand would seem to dictate. In other contexts, discrimination on the basis of gender, race, or other characteristics is an unfortunate but very real factor in wages. And in some markets, a "winner-take-all" structure can lead to a small number of workers capturing a large majority of the total earnings.

The Nonmonetary Determinants of Wages

Some jobs have characteristics that make them more desirable or less desirable. Also, no two workers are exactly alike. Differences in jobs and worker ability affect the supply and demand of labor. In this section, we examine the nonmonetary determinants of wages, including compensating differentials, education and human capital, location and lifestyle, unions, and efficiency wages.

Are you being paid enough to risk a fall?

COMPENSATING DIFFERENTIALS Some jobs are more unpleasant, risky, stressful, inconvenient, or monotonous than others. If the characteristics of a job make it unattractive, firms must offer more to attract workers. For instance, roofing, logging, and deep-sea fishing are some of the most dangerous occupations in the world. Workers who do these jobs must be compensated with higher wages to offset the higher risk of injury. A **compensating differential** is the difference in wages offered to offset the desirability or undesirability of a job. If a job's characteristics make it unattractive, the compensating wage differential must be positive.

A **compensating differential** is the difference in wages offered to offset the desirability or undesirability of a job.

In contrast, some jobs are highly desirable. For example, restaurant critics sample a lot of great food, radio DJs spend the day playing their favorite music, and video game testers try beta versions before they are released. Some jobs are simply more fun, exciting, prestigious, or stimulating than others. In these cases, the compensating differential is negative and the firm offers lower wages. For example, newspaper reporters and radio DJs earn low pay. Video game testing is so desirable that most people who do it are not paid at all.

Incentives

EDUCATION AND HUMAN CAPITAL Many complex jobs require substantial education, training, and industry experience. Qualifying to receive the specialized education required for certain occupations—for example, getting into medical school—is often very difficult. Relatively few students are able to pursue these degrees. In addition, such specialized education is expensive, in terms of both tuition and forgone income.

Opportunity cost

The set of skills that workers acquire on the job and through education are collectively known as **human capital**. Unlike other forms of capital, investments in human capital accrue to the employee. As a result, workers who have high human capital can market their skills among competing firms. Engineers, doctors, and members of other professions that require extensive education and training can command high wages in part because the human capital needed to do those jobs is high. In contrast, low-skilled workers such as ushers, baggers, and sales associates earn less because the human capital required to do those jobs is quite low; it is easy to find replacements.

Human capital is the set of skills workers acquire on the job and through education.

Table 15.1 shows the relationship between education and pay. Increased human capital (education) qualifies a worker for jobs paying higher wages. Workers who earn advanced degrees have a higher marginal product of labor because their extra schooling has presumably given them additional skills for the job. But they also have invested heavily in education. Higher wages are a compensating differential that rewards additional education.

TABLE 15.1

The Relationship between Education and Pay

Education level	Median usual weekly earnings ($)
Doctoral degree	$1,825
Professional degree	$1,884
Master's degree	$1,434
Bachelor's degree	$1,198
Associate's degree	$862
Some college, no degree	$802
High school diploma	$730
Less than a high school diploma	$553
All workers	$932

Note: Data are for persons age 25 and over. Earnings are for full-time wage and salary workers.
Source: U.S. Bureau of Labor Statistics, Current Population Survey.

ECONOMICS IN THE REAL WORLD

DOES EDUCATION *REALLY* PAY?

An alternative perspective on the value of education argues that the returns to increased education are not the product of what a student learns, but rather a signal to prospective employers. In other words, the degree itself (specifically, the classes taken to earn that degree) is not evidence of a set of skills that makes a worker more productive. Rather, earning a degree and attending prominent institutions is a signal of a potential employee's quality. Prospective employers assume that a student who gets into college must be intelligent and willing to work hard. Students who have done well in college send another signal: they are able to learn quickly and perform well under stress.

It is possible to test the importance of signaling by looking at the returns to earning a college degree, controlling for institutional quality. At many elite institutions, the four-year price tag has reached extraordinary levels. For example, to attend Columbia University in New York City, the most expensive institution in the country, it cost $74,173 in 2018–2019. Over four years, that adds up to more than a quarter of a million dollars! What type of return do graduates of such highly selective (and expensive) institutions make on their sizable investments? And are those returns the result of a rigorous education or a result of the institution's reputation? It is difficult to answer this question because the students who attend more selective institutions are more likely to have higher earnings potential regardless of where they attend college. These students enter college as high achievers, a trait that carries forward into the workplace no matter where they attend school.

Is it the amount of education you obtain or other traits that determine your financial success?

Economists Stacy Dale and Alan Krueger examined the financial outcomes for over 6,000 students who were accepted or rejected by a comparable set of colleges. They found that 20 years after graduation, students who had been accepted at more selective colleges but decided to attend a less selective college earned the same amount as their counterparts from more selective colleges. This finding indicates that actually attending a prestigious school is less important for future career success than the qualities that enable students to get *accepted* at a prestigious school.

Although Table 15.1 shows that additional education pays, the reason is not simply an increase in human capital. There is also a signal that employers can interpret about other, less observable qualities. For instance, Harvard graduates presumably learn a great deal in their time at school, but they were also highly motivated and likely to be successful even before they went to college. Part of the increase in income attributable to completing college depends on a set of other traits that the student already possessed, independent of the school or the degree.

LOCATION AND LIFESTYLE For most people, sipping margaritas in Key West, Florida, sounds more appealing than living in Eureka, Nevada, along the most isolated stretch of road in the continental United States. Likewise, being able to see a show, visit a museum, or go to a Yankees game in New York City constitutes a different lifestyle from what you'd experience in Dodge City, Kansas. People find some places more desirable than others. So how does location affect wages? Where the climate is more pleasant, all other things being equal, people are willing to accept lower wages because the nonmonetary benefits of enjoying the weather act as a compensating differential. Similarly, jobs in metropolitan areas—where the cost of living is significantly higher than in most other places—pay higher wages as a cost-of-living adjustment. The higher wage helps employees afford a quality of life similar to what they would enjoy if they worked in less expensive areas.

How much more would you pay to live near here?

Choice of lifestyle is also a major factor in determining wage differences. Some workers are not particularly concerned with maximizing their income; instead, they care more about working for a cause. This is true for many employees of nonprofits or religious organizations or even for people who take care of loved ones. Others follow a dream of being a musician, writer, or actor. And still others are guided by a passion such as skiing or surfing. Indeed, many workers view their pay as less important than doing something they are passionate about. For these workers, lower pay functions as a compensating differential.

UNIONS A **union** is a group of workers who bargain collectively for better wages and benefits. Unions are able to secure increased wages by creating significant market power over the supply of labor available to a firm. A union's ability to achieve higher wages depends on a credible threat of a work stoppage, known as a **strike**. In effect, unions can raise wages because they represent labor, and labor is a key input in the production process. Because firms cannot do without labor, an effective union can use the threat of a strike to negotiate higher wages for its workers.

U.S. law prohibits some unions from going on strike, including those representing many transit workers, some public school teachers, law enforcement officers, and workers in other essential services. If workers in one of these industries reach an impasse in wage and benefit negotiations, the employee union is required to submit to the decision of an impartial third party, a process known as *binding arbitration*. The television show *Judge Judy* is an example of binding arbitration

A **union** is a group of workers who bargain collectively for better wages and benefits.

A **strike** is a work stoppage designed to aid a union's bargaining position.

Does going on strike result in higher wages?

in action: two parties with a small claims grievance agree in advance to accept the verdict of Judith Sheindlin, a noted family court judge.

The effect of unions in the United States has changed since the early days of unionization in the late 1800s. Early studies of the union wage premium found wages to be as much as 30% higher for unionized workers. At the height of unionization approximately 60 years ago, one in three jobs was a unionized position. Today, only about one in eight workers belongs to a union. Today, most empirical studies find the wage premium to be between 10% and 20%. The demise of many unions has coincided with the transition of the U.S. economy from a manufacturing base to one with a greater emphasis on the service sector, which is less centralized.

Efficiency wages
are wages higher than equilibrium wages, offered to increase worker productivity.

EFFICIENCY WAGES In terms of paying wages, one approach stands out as unique. Ordinarily, we think of wages being determined in the labor market at the intersection of supply and demand. When the labor market is in equilibrium, the wage guarantees that every qualified worker can find employment. However, some firms willingly pay more than the equilibrium wage. **Efficiency wages** exist when an employer pays its workers more than the equilibrium wage. Why would a business do that? Surprisingly, the answer is to make *more* profit. That outcome hardly seems possible when a firm using efficiency wages pays its workers more than its competitors do. But think again. Above-equilibrium wages (1) decrease turnover; (2) increase productivity by attracting a larger applicant pool, from which the most productive ones can be chosen; and (3) increase the cost of being fired, because other jobs in the same industry don't pay as well—giving every worker a greater incentive to work hard and not shirk. **Productivity** is the effectiveness of effort as measured in terms of the rate of output per unit of input. If the gains in overall labor productivity are higher than the increased cost, the result is greater profit for the firm.

Productivity
is the effectiveness of effort as measured in terms of the rate of output per unit of input.

Incentives

Henry Ford developed a visionary assembly process and also implemented efficiency wages at his plants.

Automaker Henry Ford used efficiency wages to generate more productivity on the Model T assembly line. In 1914, Ford decided to more than double the pay of assembly-line workers to $5 a day—an increase that his competitors did not match. He also decreased the workday from 9 hours to 8 hours. Ford's primary goal was to reduce worker turnover, which was frequent because of the monotonous nature of assembly-line work. By making the job so lucrative, he hoped that most workers would not quit so quickly. He was right. The turnover rate plummeted from over 10% per day to less

than 1%. As word of Ford's high wages spread, workers flocked to Detroit. The day after the wage increase was announced, over 10,000 eager job seekers lined up outside Ford's Highland Park, Michigan, plant. From this crowd, Ford hired many temporary workers and gave each a 30-day trial. At the end of the trial period, he permanently hired the most productive workers and let the others go. The resulting productivity increase per worker was more than enough to offset the wage increase. In addition, reducing the length of each shift enabled Ford to add an extra shift, which increased productivity even more.

We have seen that wages are influenced by factors that include compensating differentials, human capital, location and

TABLE 15.2

The Key Nonmonetary Determinants of Wage Differences

Determinant	Impact on wages	In pictures
Compensating differentials	Some workers are eager to have jobs that are more fun, exciting, prestigious, or stimulating than others. As a result, they are willing to accept lower wages. Conversely, jobs that are unpleasant or risky require higher wages.	
Human capital	Many jobs require substantial education, training, and experience. As a result, workers who acquire additional amounts of human capital can command higher wages.	
Location and lifestyle	When the location is desirable, the compensating wage will be lower. Similarly, when employment is for a highly valued cause, wage is less important. In both situations, the compensating wage will be lower.	
Unions	Because firms cannot do without labor, unions can threaten a strike to negotiate higher wages.	
Efficiency wages	The firm pays above-equilibrium wages to help reduce slacking, decrease turnover, and increase productivity.	

lifestyle, union membership, and the presence of efficiency wages. Table 15.2 summarizes these nonmonetary determinants of income differences.

Wage Discrimination

When workers with the same ability as others are not paid the same because of their race, ethnic origin, sex, age, religion, or some other group characteristic, we say they are experiencing **wage discrimination**. Because of its importance for individuals and for policymakers, economists study the topic of wage discrimination by trying to understand its effects in the past and to help address wage discrimination today. In this section, we explore some of their observations. While most economists acknowledge that bias plays a role in wage discrimination, they believe that broader factors related to human capital play the major roles.

Wage discrimination occurs when workers with the same ability as others are not paid the same because of their race, ethnic origin, sex, age, religion, or some other group characteristic.

LOOKING AT THE DATA Table 15.3 presents median weekly earnings in the United States by sex, race or ethnic group, and age. Looking at the data, we see large earnings differences across many groups in U.S. society. In particular, female workers earn 19% less than their male counterparts. While most of us would like to believe that employers no longer pay men more than women for doing the same job, wage discrimination does still exist. In 2009, President Obama signed the Lilly Ledbetter Fair Pay Act, which

TABLE 15.3

Median Weekly Earnings by Group

Group	Median earnings in 2018	Percentage difference within each group
Males	$959	–
Females	780	–19%
White	907	–
Black	683	–25
Asian	1083	19
Hispanic	674	–26
Early-career workers (25–34)	794	–20
Mid-career workers (35–54)	978	–2
Late-career workers (55–64)	993	–

Source: U.S. Bureau of Labor Statistics, 2018. https://www.bls.gov/news.release/pdf/wkyeng.pdf.

gives victims of wage discrimination more time to file a complaint with the government. The act is named after a former Goodyear employee who sued the company in 2007. The courts determined that she was paid 15% to 40% less than her male counterparts. The fact that a major U.S. corporation was violating the Equal Pay Act of 1963 almost 50 years after its passage was a poignant reminder that wage discrimination still occurs in our society.

PRACTICE WHAT YOU KNOW

Efficiency Wages: Which Company Pays an Efficiency Wage?

You are considering two job offers. Company A is well known and respected and offers a year-end bonus based on your productivity relative to other workers. This could substantially boost your income but the company's base wage is relatively low. Company B is not as well known, but its wages are higher than the norm in your field. This company does not offer a year-end bonus.

QUESTION: Which company, A or B, is the efficiency wage employer?

ANSWER: Efficiency wages are a mechanism that some companies use to reduce turnover, encourage teamwork, and create loyalty. Company A's bonus plan will reward the best producers, but the average and less-than-average workers will become frustrated and leave. Company A is not paying efficiency wages; it is simply using incentives tied to productivity. Company B is the efficiency wage employer because it pays every worker somewhat higher wages to reduce turnover.

CHALLENGE QUESTION: If firms in a given industry can become more profitable by paying efficiency wages rather than equilibrium wages, why don't all firms pay efficiency wages?

Forbes magazine calls Facebook the best company to work for—and not just because you eat for free at work.

(CONTINUED)

ANSWER: Efficiency wages work as an incentive to reduce turnover and boost productivity because they are higher than the equilibrium wage in the industry. If every firm paid higher wages, none of the firms would be at a competitive advantage in retaining workers or finding more productive workers from a larger-than-normal applicant pool. Therefore, if efficiency wages became the norm, they would lose their effectiveness.

Incentives

But economists try to study the topic of wage discrimination further by examining the data. For example, women and men often hold different types of jobs, and certain jobs pay more than others. Higher wages in jobs such as road work and construction reflect in part a compensating differential for exposure to extreme temperatures, bad weather, and other dangers, and men are more likely to work in these jobs. Additionally, more women than men take time off from work to raise a family, meaning that women ultimately have fewer years of work experience, put in fewer paid work hours per year, are less likely to work a full-time schedule, and leave the labor force for longer periods. In contrast, men normally take less, if any, time off to raise children. In the long term, these differences tend to lead to lower levels of human capital and overall lower wages for women.

Claudia Goldin's careful examination of the gender wage gap data suggests that the gap stems not from gender discrimination, but from work design. She found that people who work the longest and least flexible hours make the highest salaries per unit of time—and those people tend to be men, because women are more likely to be juggling caregiving responsibilities. Framed differently, one way to help close the gap is for employers to be more flexible about work hours and pay part-time workers a pro-rated share of what full-time workers earn. This is also more of a work-life balance issue. Added flexibility helps all workers juggle careers, family, and other interests. The work of Francine Blau and Lawrence Kahn explains some of the important causes of the gender pay gap. Their research finds that 62% of the pay gap is attributable to the first six causes listed in Figure 15.1. Unmeasured factors—including discrimination—account for the other 38% of the gap.

Similarly, differences in human capital can help explain wide gaps in earnings data by race or ethnic group. Asian Americans (56% of whom have a bachelor's degree or higher) have higher education levels than whites (44%), who in turn generally have much higher levels than blacks (24%) and Hispanics (20%). Economists expect the wage disparities between groups to decrease as these educational differences (and the resulting differences in human capital) become less pronounced. Socioeconomic factors also play a significant role in these disparities. For instance, the low quality of some inner-city schools can limit the educational attainment of students, many of whom are minorities.

For every $1 men make, women make, on average, 81 cents.

HUMAN CAPITAL AND THE LIFE-CYCLE WAGE PATTERN The earnings gap between mid-career workers and others also reflects differences in human capital. After all, workers who are just starting out have limited experience. As these workers age, they accumulate on-the-job training and experience that make them more productive

FIGURE 15.1

What Do We Know about What Causes the Gender Pay Gap?

Studies show that a large portion of the gender pay gap comes from factors that cannot be measured.

Source: Journal of Economic Literature, 2017.

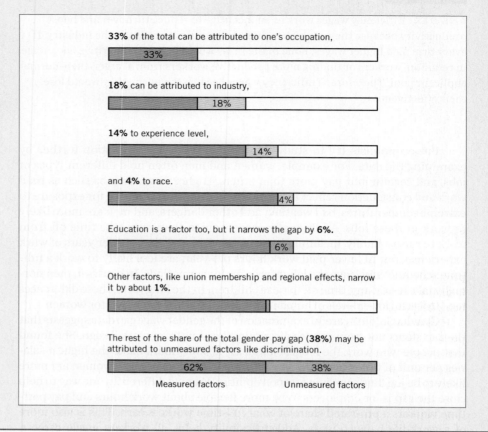

33% of the total can be attributed to one's occupation,

33%

18% can be attributed to industry,

18%

14% to experience level,

14%

and **4%** to race.

4%

Education is a factor too, but it narrows the gap by **6%**.

6%

Other factors, like union membership and regional effects, narrow it by about **1%**.

The rest of the share of the total gender pay gap (**38%**) may be attributed to unmeasured factors like discrimination.

62%	38%
Measured factors	Unmeasured factors

The **life-cycle wage pattern** refers to the predictable effect age has on earnings over the course of a person's working life. Wages peak for people in their early 60s and then slowly fall thereafter.

and enable them to obtain higher wages. However, for older workers the gains from increased experience are eventually offset by diminishing returns. Consequently, wages peak when these workers are in their early 60s and then slowly fall thereafter. This pattern, known as the **life-cycle wage pattern**, refers to the predictable effect age has on earnings over a person's working life.

ECONOMICS IN THE REAL WORLD

THE EFFECTS OF BEAUTY ON EARNINGS

According to research that spans the labor market from the law profession to college teaching and in countries as different as the United States and China, beauty matters. How much? You might be surprised. As related by economist Daniel S. Hamermesh in his book *Beauty Pays*, beautiful people make as much as 10% more than people with average looks, while those whose looks are considered significantly below average may make as much as 25% below normal.

The influence of beauty on wages can be viewed in two ways. First, beauty can be seen as a marketable trait that has value in many professions. Actors, fashion models, restaurant servers, and litigators all rely on their appearance to make a living, so it is not surprising that beauty is correlated with wages in those professions. If beautiful

Sandra Bullock, Lupita Nyong'o, Chris Hemsworth—three of the decade's most beautiful people.

people are more productive in certain jobs because of their beauty, then attractiveness is simply a measure of the value of the marginal product they generate. In other words, being beautiful is a form of human capital the worker possesses.

However, a second interpretation finds evidence of discrimination. If employers prefer "beautiful" people as employees, then part of the earnings increase associated with beauty might reflect that preference. In addition, the success of workers who are more beautiful could also reflect the preferences of customers who prefer to buy products and services from attractive people.

Because it is impossible to determine whether the beauty premium is a compensating differential or the result of overt discrimination, we have to acknowledge the possibility that the truth, in many situations, could be a little bit of both.

Also, height and earnings are correlated. A study found that for every inch taller you are, you make on average $800 more per year (the study controlled for gender, weight, and age).

OCCUPATIONAL CROWDING: HOW DISCRIMINATION AFFECTS WAGES   Another factor deserving particular attention is **occupational crowding**—the phenomenon of relegating a group of workers to a narrow range of jobs in the economy. To understand how occupational crowding works, imagine a community named Utopia with only two types of jobs: a small number in engineering and a large number in secretarial services. Furthermore, men and women are equally proficient at both occupations, and everyone in the community is happy to work either job. Under these assumptions, we would expect the wages for engineers and secretaries to be the same.

Now imagine that not everyone in Utopia has the same opportunities. Suppose we roll back the clock to a time when women in Utopia are not allowed to work as engineers. Women who want to work can only find employment as secretaries. As a result of this occupational crowding, workers who have limited opportunities (women, in this example) find themselves competing with one another, as well as with the men who cannot get engineering jobs, for secretarial positions. As a result, wages fall in secretarial jobs and rise in engineering. Because only men can work in engineering, they are paid more than their similarly qualified female counterparts, who are crowded into secretarial positions and

Occupational crowding is the phenomenon of relegating a group of workers to a narrow range of jobs in the economy.

earn less. Furthermore, because women who want to work can only receive a low wage as a secretary, many effectively decide to stay at home and produce nonmarket services, such as child-rearing. These services have a higher value to the women who make this choice than the wages they could earn as secretaries.

Of course, women today are not restricted to secretarial jobs, but they still hold more of the lower-paying jobs in our society. The first column of Figure 15.2

FIGURE 15.2

Percentages of Male and Female Workers in the Most Common Occupations

In the United States, the most common jobs categories tend to be occupied by either women or men. Very few occupations have a roughly equal split of women and men. Women are also paid less than men across the board, though this is improving.

Source: US Census Bureau, 2017.

Common Occupations in USA, Gender and Pay Level

Occupation	Share of female workers in the occupation (percent)	Women's median weekly earnings	Men's median weekly earnings	Women's earnings as a percent of men's
Secretaries and admin assistants	94.5	735	852	86.3
Receptionists and information clerks	92.6	599	652	91.9
Registered nurses	88.8	1143	1260	90.7
Nursing, psychiatric, and home health aides	88.2	493	583	84.6
Bookkeeping, accounting, and auditing clerks	87.0	716	743	96.4
Office clerks, general	84.8	670	780	85.9
Maids and housekeeping	84.3	439	508	86.4
Elementary and middle school teachers	78.4	987	1139	86.7
Cashiers	72.2	422	493	85.6
Supervisors of office and admin support	67.7	819	987	83.0
Customer service representatives	65.6	637	712	89.5
Accountants and auditors	58.9	1065	1389	76.7
Retail supervisors	42.4	639	891	71.7
Retail salespersons	38.8	523	704	74.3
Managers, all other	38.7	1251	1629	76.8
Cooks	37.1	436	481	90.6
Stock clerks and order fillers	34.5	538	571	94.2
Janitors and building cleaners	28.8	481	574	83.8
Sales representatives, wholesale and manufacturing	27.9	956	1222	78.2
Software developers, applications and systems software	18.4	1543	1863	82.8
Laborers and freight, stock, and material movers, hand	17.5	500	595	84.0
Driver/sales workers and truck drivers	4.9	589	807	73.0
All full-time workers	**44.4**	**770**	**941**	**81.8**

shows the percentages of female workers in many of the most common jobs in the United States. Not surprisingly, given the low wages, neither men nor women rush into many of the lowest-paying jobs.

Why do occupational crowding and wage differentials continue? Rigidity in changing occupations, social customs (including discrimination), and personal preferences are all part of the explanation. However, many economists see a change coming. Because more women than men attend colleges and universities, women are now primarily responsible for expanding the supply of workers in most fields. As the supply of workers expands, the net effect will likely be lower wages in traditionally male-dominated jobs. At the same time, traditionally female-dominated jobs will see rising wages as women leave those jobs for better opportunities. The net result is that the wage gap will narrow over time.

Was your kindergarten teacher male or female?

A CAUTIOUSLY OPTIMISTIC OUTLOOK Because no employer will admit to discriminating, researchers can only infer the amount of bias driven discrimination after first correcting for observable differences from compensating differentials and differences in human capital. The unobservable differences that remain are presumed to reflect discrimination. While the number is hotly debated, most economists estimate that discrimination accounts for less than 5% of observed wage differences. They also see many signs of improvement.

Though it is still real, the gender gap is shrinking. In 1960 women in the workforce earned, on average, 60 cents for every dollar men earned. Today women earn 81 cents for every dollar men earn (see the second, third, and fourth columns of Figure 15.2), and the gap continues to close by about half a cent each year. In addition, women are no longer clustered in less rigorous academic programs than men, so women are more prepared to get jobs that pay better. In 2018, for example, more women than men in the United States received doctoral degrees. The number of women at every level of academia has been rising for decades. There are now three women for every two men enrolled in postsecondary education. Over time, this education advantage may offset some of the other compensating differentials that have kept men's wages higher than women's.

ECONOMICS IN THE REAL WORLD

WAGE INEQUALITY: WHAT UBER CAN TEACH US ABOUT THE GENDER PAY GAP

Uber pays drivers based on an algorithm that is gender-blind. Driver pay is determined by a pay structure tied to output (rides completed) and a surge multiplier (for peak demand times). Researchers studied data from over one million Uber drivers and found that men earned 6% more per hour than women. Perplexed, they dug deeper into the data to find the causes of the gender pay gap. What they found was that the entire gender gap could be explained by three factors: experience (men, on average, have worked for Uber longer), preferences over when and where to work (men tend to work later at night and more often in less-safe areas), and preferences for driving speed

Do male Uber drivers earn more than females? Read more to find out.

	All	Men	Women
Weekly earnings	$376.38	$397.68	$268.18
Hourly earnings	$21.07	$21.28	$20.04
Hours per week	17.06	17.98	12.82
Trips per week	29.83	31.52	21.83
Six-month attrition rate	68.1%	65.0%	76.5%
Number of drivers	1,873,474	1,361,289	512,185
Number driver/weeks	24,832,168	20,210,399	4,621,760
Number of Uber trips	740,627,707	646,965,269	93,662,438

(men drive faster, on average, than women). One of the researchers, Rebecca Diamond, sums up the findings nicely:

> Uber shows that even when you strip away all of this stuff, you definitely don't go to a gender gap of zero, and you still have this important experience component, where you work more and you learn about how to do the job better, and you get better at doing the job. So you can't say it's all going to be perfect in this new gig economy. [But it's] not because of discrimination, or problems in how we compensate workers. It really is about working more hours and gaining knowledge on the job, and differences in gender preferences.

Since Uber's algorithm does not discriminate, gender-based preferences are the cause of the pay gap.

Source: Cody Cook et al., "The Gender Earnings Gap in the Gig Economy: Evidence from over a Million Rideshare Drivers," (Stanford: Stanford Institute for Economic Policy Research [SIEPR], 2018).

Winner-Take-All

In 1930, baseball legend Babe Ruth demanded and received a salary of $80,000 from the New York Yankees. This would be approximately $1 million in today's dollars. Babe Ruth earned a lot more than the other baseball players of his era. When told that President Herbert Hoover earned less than he was asking for, Ruth famously said, "I had a better year than he did." In fact, the annual salary of the president of the United States is far less than that of top professional athletes, movie stars, college presidents, and many corporate CEOs.

Why does the most important job in the world pay less than jobs with far less value to society? Part of the answer involves compensating differentials. Being president of the United States means being the most powerful person in the world, so paid compensation is only a small part of the benefit of holding that office. The other part of the answer has to do with the way labor markets function. Pay at the top of most professions is subject to a form of competition known as **winner-take-all**, which occurs when extremely small differences in ability lead to sizable differences in compensation. This compensation structure has been common in professional sports and in the entertainment industry for many years, but it also exists in the legal profession, medicine, journalism, investment banking, fashion design, and corporate management.

Winner-take-all occurs when extremely small differences in ability lead to sizable differences in compensation.

In a winner-take-all market, being a little bit better than one's rivals can be worth a tremendous amount. For example, in 2019, baseball star Manny Machado earned $30 million with the San Diego Padres. As good as Machado is, he is not 7.5 times better than an average major-league baseball player, who makes $4 million. Nor is he a thousand times better than a typical minor-league player, who earns a few thousand dollars a month. In fact, it is hard to tell the difference between a baseball game played by major- and minor-leaguers. Minor-leaguers run almost as fast, and the fielding is almost as good. Yet major-league players make hundreds of times more.

Paying so much to a relatively small set of workers may seem unfair, but the prospect of much higher pay or bonuses motivates many ambitious employees to exert maximum effort. If we look beyond the amount of money that some people earn, we can see that winner-take-all creates incentives that encourage supremely talented workers to maximize their abilities.

Manny Machado has 30 million reasons a year to practice, but not all professional baseball players are as fortunate.

Incentives

What Causes Income Inequality?

Income inequality occurs when some workers earn more than others. Compensating differentials, discrimination, corruption, and differences in the marginal product of labor all lead to inequality of income. In this section, we first examine why income inequality exists. Once we understand the factors leading to income inequality, we examine how it is measured. Because income inequality is difficult to measure and easy to misinterpret, we explain how observed income inequality statistics are constructed and what they mean. We end by discussing income mobility, a characteristic in many developed nations that can lessen the impact of income inequality on the life-cycle wage pattern.

Factors That Lead to Income Inequality

To illustrate the nature of income inequality, we begin with a simple question: what would it take to equalize wages? For all workers to get the same wages, three conditions would have to be met. First, every worker would have to have the same skills, ability, and productivity. Second, every job would have to be equally attractive to potential employees. Third, all workers would have to be perfectly mobile. In other words, perfect equality of income would require that workers be clones who perform the same job. Needless to say, we do not live in such a world. In the real world, some people work harder than others and are more productive. Some people, such as humanitarian aid workers, missionaries, teachers, and even ski bums, choose occupations where they know they will earn less. In fact, our traits, our desires, and our differences all help to explain income inequality, which is the natural result of a market economy.

Next we look at five factors that can contribute to income inequality: ability, training and education, discrimination, wealth, and corruption.

ABILITY Workers who have more ability (for example, mental acuity, physical strength, fortitude) than less-able workers generally earn higher wages. Differences in ability can lead to large differences in wages because more-able workers have the potential to create much larger marginal products than their less-able counterparts.

TRAINING AND EDUCATION More ability is a necessary but not sufficient condition for high wages. Workers of all ability levels benefit from receiving additional training and education. The acquisition of specific skills through training and additional education enhances each worker's human capital. More human capital often makes workers more valuable in the marketplace, helping them earn higher wages.

DISCRIMINATION Discrimination harms the workers who are discriminated against, and it makes the overall distribution of income in a country more unequal. Workers who are passed over for promotions or job openings because of their gender, race, age, religion, or other traits earn lower wages that do not reflect their ability, training, or education. Discrimination in this context acts as a price ceiling that limits some workers' ability to earn more. Since discriminated workers are concentrated among women and minorities, the net effect is that discriminated groups end up concentrated among the lowest-paid groups—leading to more income inequality.

THE ROLE OF WEALTH How much does a privileged background matter? According to controlled studies, children born into wealthy households earn about 10% more than children born into low-income households. Wealth gives a child from an affluent home access to better education, private tutoring, a healthier diet, and many other intangible benefits that provide a head start in life. These early advantages often lead to higher levels of human capital that translate into higher wages.

THE ROLE OF CORRUPTION IN INCOME INEQUALITY All economic systems require trust in order to achieve gains from trade. However, some societies value the rule of law more than others. Many less developed countries suffer from widespread corruption. Consider Somalia, a country without a functional central government. This situation has led to lawlessness in which clans, warlords, and militia groups fight for control. The situation is so dire that international aid efforts often require the bribing of government officials to ensure that the aid reaches those in need.

Corruption can play a large role in income inequality. In societies where corruption is common, working hard or being innovative is not enough; getting ahead often requires bribing officials to obtain business permits or to ward off competitors. Moreover, when investors cannot be sure their assets are safe from government seizure or criminal activity, they are less likely to develop a business. Under political systems that are subject to bribery and other forms of corruption, dishonest people benefit at the expense of the poor. Corruption drives out legitimate business opportunities and magnifies income inequality.

Measuring Income Inequality

How do we measure income inequality in a country? To answer this question, we begin by looking at income inequality in the United States. Economists study the distribution of household income in the United States by quintiles, or five groups of equal size, ranging from the poorest fifth (20%) of households to the top fifth. Figure 15.3 shows the data from 2017.

According to the U.S. Bureau of the Census, the poorest 20% of households makes just 3.1% of all income earned in the United States. The next quintile, the second fifth, earns 8.2% of income. In other words, fully 40% of U.S. households (the bottom two quintiles) account for only 11.3% of earned income. The middle quintile earns 14.3%, the second-highest quintile 23.0%, and the top quintile 51.4%. Being a pie chart, Figure 15.3 vividly shows the wide disparity between the percentage of total U.S. income earned by the poorest households (3.1%) and by the richest households (51.4%). If we divide the percentage of income earned by households in the top fifth (51.4%) by the percentage of income earned by households in the bottom fifth (3.1%), we get an **income inequality ratio** of about 16.5. Looking at the numbers this way, we can say that households in the top fifth have approximately 16 to 17 times the income of those in the bottom fifth. Viewing that number in isolation makes the amount of income inequality in the United States seem large. However, we have not yet adjusted the data to reflect disposable income. When taxes and subsidies are included the U.S. income inequality ratio drops to 9.9.

The **income inequality ratio** is calculated by dividing the top quintile's income percentage by the bottom quintile's income percentage.

To provide some perspective, Table 15.4 compares the income inequality in various other countries using disposable income. The countries above the line are more developed, and those below are less developed.

As you can see, the U.S. income inequality ratio of 9.9 after controlling for taxes and subsides is high compared with that of other highly developed nations but relatively low compared with that of less developed nations. In general, highly developed nations have lower degrees of income inequality.

FIGURE 15.3

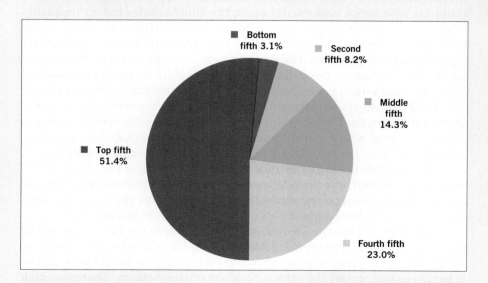

The Distribution of Income in the United States by Quintile

The top fifth of income earners makes 51.4% of all income, an amount greater than the combined incomes of the four remaining quintiles. Income declines across the quintiles, falling to 3.1% in the lowest fifth.

Source: U.S. Census Bureau, 2017.

TABLE 15.4

Income Inequality Ratios (after controlling for taxes and subsidies) in Selected Countries

Country	Inequality ratio (richest 20% ÷ poorest 20%)
Germany	4.7
Japan	5.4
Canada	5.8
United Kingdom	7.6
United States	9.9
Mexico	11.1
Brazil	16.9
Bolivia	15.2
Namibia	19.6

Source: Adapted from United Nations Development Programme, *Human Development Report*.

Why? More-developed countries have less poverty, so those individuals who are at the bottom of the income ladder in the developed countries earn more than those at the bottom in less developed countries.

UNDERSTANDING OBSERVED INEQUALITY Translating income inequality into a number, as we've done with the income quintiles, can mask the true nature of income inequality. In this section, we step back and consider what the income inequality ratio can tell us and what it cannot tell us.

Because the income inequality ratio measures the success of top earners against that of bottom earners, if the bottom group is doing relatively well, then the inequality ratio will be smaller, which explains why many highly developed countries have ratios under 6. However, the United States has an inequality ratio close to 10. What is driving the difference? The United States has many highly successful workers and a poverty rate similar to those found in other highly developed countries. The **poverty rate** is the percentage of the population whose income is below the poverty threshold. The **poverty threshold** is the income level below which a person or family is considered impoverished.

According to the Organization for Economic Cooperation and Development (OECD), the United States has a poverty rate quite similar to that of Japan, a country with a markedly lower inequality ratio (5.4). Given that the poverty rate in the United States is not unusually large compared with Japan's, we cannot explain the higher inequality ratio by pointing to the percentage of poor people. Rather, it is the relative success of the top income earners in the United States that causes the markedly higher inequality ratio. In other words, there are more high-income earners in the United States than in Japan.

High levels of income inequality also occur when the poorest are *really* poor. For example, there are many successful people in Mexico, Brazil, Bolivia, and Namibia. The problem in these countries is that the success of some people is benchmarked against the extreme poverty of many others. Therefore, high inequality ratios can be a telltale sign of a serious poverty problem. Suppose that the poorest quintile of the population in Bolivia has an average disposable

The **poverty rate** is the percentage of the population whose income is below the poverty threshold.

The **poverty threshold** is the income level below which a person or family is considered impoverished.

income of $4,000, while those in the top quintile have a disposable income of $60,800. The income inequality ratio is $60,800/$4,000 = 15.2. By comparison, consider Canada. If the poorest quintile of the population in Canada has an average disposable income of $10,500, while those in the top quintile have an average of $60,800, the income inequality ratio there is $60,800/$10,500 = 5.8. In both countries, the top quintile is doing equally well, but the widespread poverty in Bolivia produces an alarming income inequality ratio. In this example, the inequality ratio signals a significant poverty problem.

In sum: A high income inequality ratio can occur if people at the bottom earn very little or if the income of high-income earners is much greater than the income of others. The key point to remember is that even though income inequality ratios give us some idea about the degree of inequality in a society, a single number cannot fully reflect the sources of the underlying differences in income.

THE GINI INDEX An alternative way of representing income inequality across countries is to use the **Gini index**, which represents the income distribution of a nation's residents. Its value fluctuates between 0 (no income inequality) and 100 (extreme income inequality). If every individual's income is equal in a society, the Gini index (or Gini coefficient) is 0. A nation where one individual gets all the income, while everyone else gets nothing, would have a Gini index of 100. The average Gini index is approximately 40 (Figure 15.4).

The **Gini index** is a measurement of the income distribution of a country's residents.

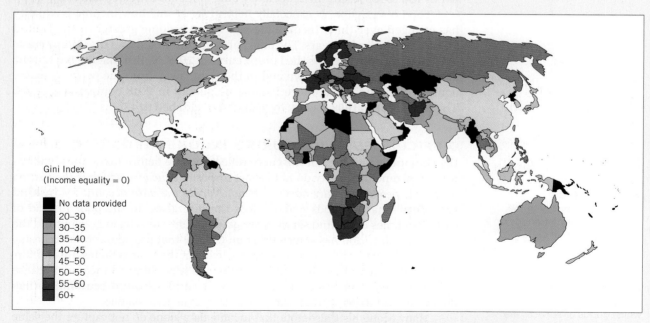

FIGURE 15.4

The Gini Index Across the World, 2014

Countries color-coded in green have the lowest Gini index, while those in shades of red have the highest Gini index.

SOURCE: CIA World Factbook.

Gini Index
(Income equality = 0)

- No data provided
- 20–30
- 30–35
- 35–40
- 40–45
- 45–50
- 50–55
- 55–60
- 60+

FIGURE 15.5

The Gini Index and the Lorenz Curve

The green curve indicates complete income equality. As income inequality increases, the orange curve shifts down and to the right.

Source: M. Tracy Hunter, https://commons.wikimedia.org/wiki/File:2014_Gini_Index_World_Map,_income_inequality_distribution_by_country_per_World_Bank.svg.

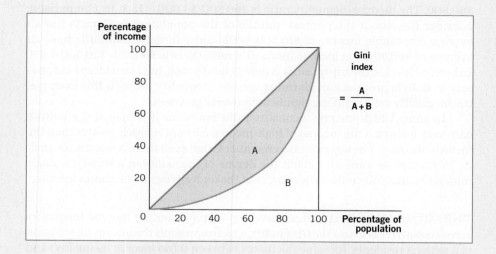

The **Lorenz curve** is a visual representation of the Gini index.

The **Lorenz curve** is a visual way of representing the Gini index. A perfectly equal distribution of income is represented by the green 45-degree line in Figure 15.5. As the income distribution becomes more unequal, the Lorenz curve, represented by the orange line in Figure 15.5, shifts downward and to the right. The Gini index is calculated by taking the area between the two curves, shaded and labeled A, and dividing that amount by the total of area A plus area B. Area A represents the amount of income *inequality* in society, while area B represents the amount of income *equality* in society. Calculating the Gini index gives us a number between 0 and 1. Economists multiply this number by 100 to represent the score as a whole number between 0 and 100.

The Lorenz curve is especially helpful for seeing how income inequality has changed over time. Income inequality has become greater in the United States over the last 50 years. The blue line in Figure 15.6 shows the Lorenz curve in 1968. The red line shows the Lorenz curve in 2018. Notice that the red Lorenz curve from 2018 shifted down and to the right, away from the perfect income equality line, indicating more income inequality in 2018 compared to 1968. The Gini index in 1968 was 34; by 2018, it had climbed to 42.

DIFFICULTIES IN MEASURING INCOME INEQUALITY Because the Gini index and the Lorenz curve reflect income before taxes, these indicators of income inequality do not reflect *disposable income, which is the portion of income people actually have to spend. Nor do the data account for* **in-kind transfers**—that is, goods and services that are given to the poor instead of cash. Examples of in-kind services are government-subsidized housing and the Subsidized Nutrition Assistance Program (SNAP) that provides food-purchasing assistance for low- and no-income people living in the United States. In addition, the data do not account for unreported or illegally obtained income. Because less developed countries generally have larger **underground economies** than developed countries do, their income data are even less reliable.

Many economists also note that income data alone do not capture the value created from goods and services produced in the household. For example, if you

In-kind transfers
are transfers (mostly to the poor) in the form of goods or services instead of cash.

Underground economies
are composed of markets in which goods or services are traded illegally.

FIGURE 15.6

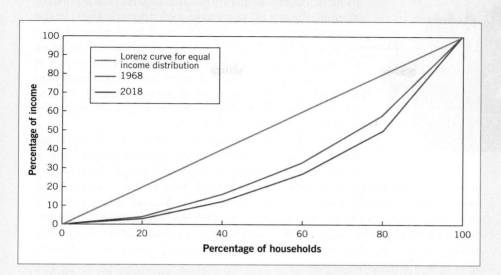

The Gini index in the United
States was 34 in 1968. By 2018,
it had climbed to 42, indicating
an increase in income inequality.

mow your own lawn or grow your own vegetables, those activities have a positive
value not expressed in your income data. In less developed countries, many households engage in very few market transactions and produce a large portion of their
own goods and services. If we do not count these, our comparison of data with
other countries will overstate the amount of inequality present in the less developed countries. Finally, the number of workers per household and the median age
of each worker differ from country to country. When households contain more
workers or those workers are, on average, older and therefore more experienced,
comparing inequality across countries is more likely to be misleading.

Individually, none of these shortcomings poses a serious measurement issue
from year to year. However, if we try to measure differences in income across
generations, the changes can be significant enough to invalidate the *ceteris paribus*
("all other things being equal") condition that allows us to assume that outside
factors are held constant. In short, comparing inequality data from this year with
data from last year is generally fine, but comparing inequality data from this year
with data from 50 years ago is more difficult. For instance, we might note that
income inequality in the United States increased very slightly from 2017 to 2018.
However, because we are looking at just two data points, we must be cautious
about assuming a trend. To eliminate that problem, we can extend the time frame
back to 1968. Comparing the data over that range shows an unmistakable upward

Growing your own vegetables is an activity not counted in official income data.

trend in income inequality but also violates *ceteris paribus*; after all, the last 50 years have seen dramatic shifts in the composition of the U.S. labor force, changes in tax rates, a surge in in-kind transfers, a lower birthrate, and an aging population. It is a complex task to determine the impact of these changes on income inequality. A good economist tries to make relevant comparisons by examining similar countries over a relatively short period during which there were no significant socioeconomic changes.

Finally, the standard calculations and models we have discussed assume that the income distribution is a direct reflection of a society's well-being. However, we must be very careful not to infer too much about how well people are living based on their income alone. Indeed, income analysis does not offer a complete picture of human welfare. In Chapter 16, we will see that income is only one factor determining human happiness and well-being. People also value leisure time, nonwage benefits, a sense of community, safety from crime, and social networks, among other things.

Income Mobility

Income mobility
is the ability of workers to move up or down the economic ladder over time.

When workers have a realistic chance of moving up the economic ladder, each person has an incentive to work harder and invest in human capital. **Income mobility** is the ability of workers to move up or down the economic ladder over time. Think of it this way: if today's poor must remain poor 10 years from now, income inequality remains high. However, if someone in the lowest income category can expect to experience enough economic success to move to a higher income quintile, being poor is a temporary condition. In other words, economic mobility reduces inequality over long periods of time.

The dynamic nature of the U.S. economy is captured by income mobility data. Table 15.5 reports the income mobility in the United States over a series of

TABLE 15.5

Income Mobility in the United States, 1970–2010

(1) Ten-year period	(2) % Poorest quintile that move up at least one quintile	(3) % Highest quintile that move down at least one quintile	(4) % Poorest quintile that move up at least two quintiles	(5) % Highest quintile that move down at least two quintiles
1970–1980	43.2%	48.8%	19.1%	22.8%
1975–1985	45.3	50.9	20.6	24.8
1980–1990	45.2	47.6	21.3	25.7
1985–1995	41.8	45.8	17.8	21.5
1990–2000	41.7	46.7	15.2	20.7
1995–2005	41.9	45.0	15.4	20.2
2000–2010	41.8	44.8	14.9	19.9

Source: Katharine Bradbury, *Trends in U.S. Family Income Mobility, 1969–2006*, Working Paper, Federal Reserve Bank of Boston, No. 11-10. Data for 1990–2005 was interpolated. Author's adjustments.

Income Inequality around the World

"The rich get richer, and the poor get poorer" is a simple yet profound way to think about income inequality. As top earners make more and bottom earners make less, the inequality rate increases. It's a combination of these factors, not just extreme wealth or extreme poverty, that leads to huge gaps between those at the very top and those at the very bottom.

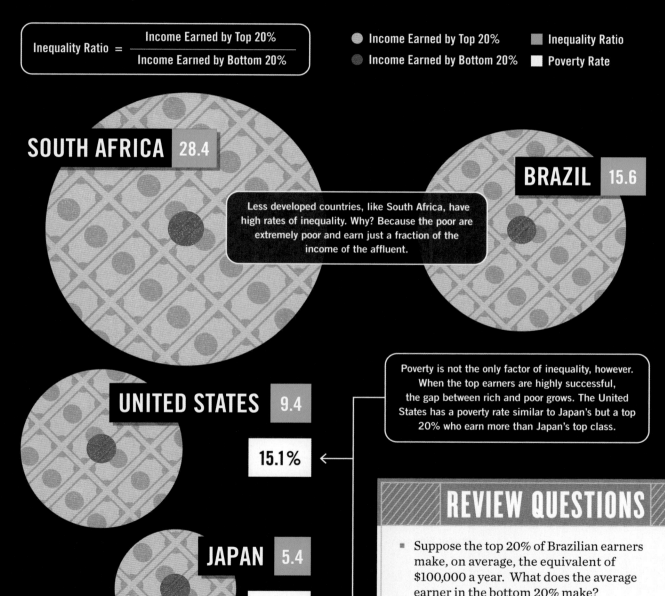

$$\text{Inequality Ratio} = \frac{\text{Income Earned by Top 20\%}}{\text{Income Earned by Bottom 20\%}}$$

- Income Earned by Top 20%
- Income Earned by Bottom 20%
- Inequality Ratio
- Poverty Rate

SOUTH AFRICA 28.4

BRAZIL 15.6

Less developed countries, like South Africa, have high rates of inequality. Why? Because the poor are extremely poor and earn just a fraction of the income of the affluent.

UNITED STATES 9.4

15.1%

Poverty is not the only factor of inequality, however. When the top earners are highly successful, the gap between rich and poor grows. The United States has a poverty rate similar to Japan's but a top 20% who earn more than Japan's top class.

JAPAN 5.4

16.1%

REVIEW QUESTIONS

- Suppose the top 20% of Brazilian earners make, on average, the equivalent of $100,000 a year. What does the average earner in the bottom 20% make?

- A friend tells you he wants to live in a world without income inequality. Discuss the pros and cons using at least one of the five foundations of economics from Chapter 1.

Sources: United Nations Development Programme, Human Development Reports 2018; CIA World Factbook

· ECONOMICS *in the* MEDIA ·

Income Mobility

THE SIMPSONS: EXAMINING ALL OF HOMER'S JOBS

The long-running cartoon series *The Simpsons* features Homer Simpson as a lazy doofus who has somehow managed to work an amazing variety of jobs over the years. In 2017, the website *Vox* did an economic analysis of all the jobs Homer ever held over the course of 600 episodes, from 1989 to 2016. The 100-plus jobs ranged from convenience store clerk, bodyguard, and ordained minister to more exotic gigs such as a moonshine taste tester and a cannonball performance artist (for both of which Homer's practically bomb-proof stomach was an asset). Sometimes Homer caught a break and temporarily ended up in a high-paying position. Other times, his pay was even lower than what he earned in his regular job as a safety inspector ($37,500 in today's money per Homer's paycheck in Season 7) at the local nuclear power plant.

Having identified a hundred or so of Homer's jobs and assigned each a salary, *Vox*'s team then tracked the fluctuations in Homer's average earnings over time. They found that he stays stuck in the lower-middle-class income quintile; he has stagnated like much of the middle class during the time of the show's run. In many ways that is not surprising, since Homer lacks a college education and is not a very motivated worker. After three decades, he remains right where he started: a reminder of why income mobility (or in this case the lack of it) matters so much. When people are able to move across the income quintiles easily, long-term poverty is less likely.

Source: Zachary Crockett, "What Homer Simpson's 100+ jobs tell us about America's middle class," Vox.com, https://www.vox.com/2016/9/6/12752476/the-simpsons-homer-middle-class. Updated Sept 16, 2016.

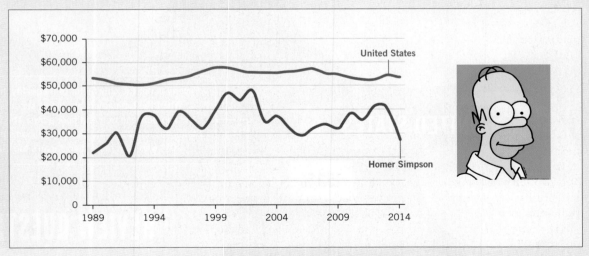

Homer Simpson's fictional pay places him in the lower-middle class.

PRACTICE WHAT YOU KNOW

Income Inequality: The Beginning and End of Inequality

Consider two communities, Alpha and Omega. Alpha has 10 residents, 5 who earn $90,000 and 5 who earn $30,000. Omega also has 10 residents, 5 who earn $250,000 and 5 who earn $50,000.

QUESTION: What is the income inequality ratio in each community?

ANSWER: To answer this question, we must use quintile analysis. Because there are 10 residents in Alpha, the top 2 earners represent the top quintile and the lowest 2 earners represent the bottom quintile. Therefore, the degree of income inequality in Alpha using quintiles analysis is $90,000 ÷ $30,000, or 3. In Omega, the top 2 earners represent the top quintile and the lowest 2 earners represent the bottom quintile. Therefore, the degree of income inequality in Omega is $250,000 ÷ $50,000, or 5.

QUESTION: Which community has the more unequal distribution of income, and why?

ANSWER: Omega has the more unequal distribution of income because the quintile analysis yields an income inequality ratio of 5, versus 3 for Alpha.

QUESTION: Can you think of a reason why someone might prefer to live in Omega?

ANSWER: Each rich citizen of Omega earns more than each rich citizen of Alpha, and each poor citizen of Omega earns more than each poor citizen of Alpha. Admittedly, there is more income inequality in Omega, but there is also more income across the entire income distribution. Thus, one might prefer Omega if the absolute amount of income is what matters more, or one might prefer Alpha if relative equality is what matters more.

The good life: so near, yet so far.

10-year periods from 1970 to 2010. We can see that mobility increased through the late 1980s, but thereafter declined for both the poorest and the highest quintiles. Columns 4 and 5 show the percentage of households that moved up or down at least two quintiles.

Mobility data enable us to separate those at the bottom of the economic ladder into two groups: (1) the *marginal poor*, or people who are poor at a particular point in time but have the skills necessary to advance up the ladder, and (2) the *long-term poor*, or people who lack the skills to advance to the next quintile. The differences in income mobility between these two groups provide a helpful way of understanding how income mobility affects poverty.

For the marginal poor, low earnings are the exception. Because most young workers expect to enjoy higher incomes as they get older, many are willing to borrow in order to make a big purchase—for example, a car or a home. Conversely, middle-aged workers know that a comfortable retirement will be possible only if they save now for the future. As a result, workers in their 50s have much higher savings rates than young workers and retirees. On reaching retirement, earnings fall; but if the worker has saved enough, retirement need

Income Inequality

CAPITAL IN THE TWENTY-FIRST CENTURY

Capital in the Twenty-First Century, by Thomas Piketty, focuses on wealth and income inequality in Europe and the United States since the eighteenth century. The book quickly became a best seller, selling over a million copies in 2014.

Piketty used historical data to examine income inequality beginning with the Industrial Revolution. He found that high levels of income inequality were the norm during the eighteenth and nineteenth centuries. Wealth and income were highly concentrated among rich households. During the twentieth century this pattern changed. Higher tax rates, increased government provision of services, and turbulent economic times caused the concentration of wealth to decline dramatically by the late 1960s. However, Piketty's data show a marked increase in income inequality beginning in the late twentieth century.

Piketty developed a theory that in normal times wealth grows faster than economic output. This means that the world's natural state is a highly unequal distribution of wealth unless economic calamities (such as war or depressions) or government intervention reduce the impact of inherited wealth on the rest of society. For this reason, Piketty recommends that governments increase tax rates on accumulated wealth with the goal of reducing income inequality.

Not all economists are convinced by Piketty's argument. Will the future really look like the past? The answer is not clear. Over time, technological progress

could lead to a more equal income distribution, not a less equal one.

More generally, standard economic theory holds that any asset (wealth included) is subject to diminishing returns. Therefore, the more wealth there is, the harder it is for the wealthy to earn an above-normal return on their investments. In other words, wealth cannot grow faster than economic output indefinitely. Also, inherited wealth accounts for only about 10% of income inequality.

Despite these criticisms, many skeptics have kind words for Piketty because he succeeded in bringing rising income inequality to the forefront of public discussion and debate.

Marginal thinking

not be a period of low consumption. The life-cycle wage pattern argues that changes in borrowing and saving patterns over one's life smooth out the consumption pattern. In other words, for many people, a low income at a point in time does not necessarily reflect a low standard of living.

When we examine how people live in societies with substantial income mobility, we see that the annual income inequality data can create a false impression about the spending patterns of young and old. The young are generally upwardly mobile, so they spend more than one might expect by borrowing. The middle-aged, who have relatively high incomes, spend less than one might expect because they are saving for retirement. And the elderly, who have lower incomes, spend more than one might expect because they are drawing down their retirement savings.

In the next section, we turn our attention to the long-term poor, who do not escape the lowest quintile. Members of this group spend their entire lives near or below the poverty threshold.

How Do Economists Analyze Poverty?

Poverty remains an ongoing challenge in the United States. According to the Census Bureau, close to 15% of all households are below the poverty threshold. To help us understand the issues, we begin with poverty statistics. Then, once we understand the scope of the problem, we examine possible policy solutions.

The Poverty Rate

For the last 50 years, the U.S. Bureau of the Census has been tracking the poverty rate, or the percentage of the population whose income is below the poverty threshold. To keep up with inflation, the poverty threshold is adjusted each year for changes in the overall level of prices in the economy. However, an individual family's threshold is calculated to include only the money that represents income earned by family members in the household. It does not include in-kind transfers, nor are the data adjusted for cost-of-living differences in the family's specific geographical area. For these reasons, poverty thresholds are a crude yardstick. Figure 15.7 shows the poverty rate for households in the United States from 1960 to 2017.

In 1964, Congress passed the Equal Opportunity Act and a number of other measures designed to fight poverty. Despite those initiatives, the rate of poverty today is slightly higher than it was 50 years ago. This result is surprising, because the U.S. economy's output has roughly doubled in that time. One would

Those below the poverty threshold are unable to make ends meet.

have hoped that the economy's progress could be enjoyed at the bottom of the economic ladder as well as at the top. Unfortunately, the stagnant poverty rate suggests that the gains from economic growth over that period have accrued to households in the middle and upper quintiles, rather than to the poor. Poverty has remained persistent, in part, because many low-income workers lack the necessary skills to earn a living wage and, at the same time, investments by firms in automation and technology have reduced the demand for these workers.

Table 15.6 illustrates that children, female heads of household, and certain minorities disproportionately feel the incidence of poverty. When we combine at-risk groups—for example, black or Hispanic women who are heads of household—the poverty rate can exceed 50%.

FIGURE 15.7

Poverty Rate for U.S. Households, 1960–2017

Poverty rates for households fluctuated from 1960 through 2017.

Source: U.S. Bureau of the Census.

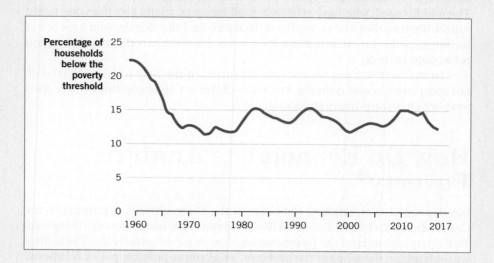

TABLE 15.6

The Poverty Rate for Various Groups, 2017

Group	Poverty rate (percentage)
Age	
Children (under 18)	19
Adults (18–64)	11
Elderly (65 or older)	9
Race/Ethnicity	
White	9
Asian	13
Hispanic	22
Black	20
Type of household	
Married couple	6
Male head only	16
Female head only	31

Source: U.S. Bureau of the Census, 2017.

Trade-offs

Poverty Policy

In this section, we outline a number of policies related to the problem of poverty. These policies are hotly debated because each policy carries both associated costs and assumed benefits, and assumptions about the benefits differ widely.

WELFARE "Welfare" is not the name of a specific government program, but rather an umbrella term for a series of initiatives designed to help the poor by supplementing their income. The term "welfare" in this section should not be confused with our earlier discussions of "social welfare." Here we focus on how government assistance programs ("welfare") operate and the incentives that these programs create.

Welfare can take a variety of forms, such as monetary payments, subsidies and vouchers, health services, or subsidized housing. Welfare is provided by the government and by other public and private organizations. It is intended to help the unemployed, those with illnesses or disabilities that prevent them from working, the elderly, veterans, and households with dependent children. An individual's eligibility for welfare is often limited to a set amount of time and is valid only as long as the recipient's income remains below the eligibility cutoff. Examples of welfare programs include Temporary Assistance for Needy Families (TANF), which provides financial support to families with dependent children; the Supplemental Security Income (SSI) program, which provides financial support to those who are unable to work; and the Subsidized Nutrition Assistance Program (SNAP), which gives financial assistance to those who need help to purchase basic foods.

IN-KIND TRANSFERS In addition to financial assistance, the poor can receive direct assistance in the form of goods and services. The government provides health care to the poor through Medicaid. **Medicaid** is a joint federal and state program that helps low-income individuals and households pay for the costs associated with long-term medical care. Communities or cities often provide organized assistance like shelters, and local community food banks, religious organizations, and private charities like Habitat for Humanity and Toys for Tots all provide in-kind benefits to the poor.

The idea behind in-kind transfers is that they protect recipients from the possibility of making poor decisions if they receive cash instead. For example, some recipients may use cash transfers to support drug or alcohol addictions, to gamble, or to buy unnecessary goods and services. To limit the likelihood of such poor decisions, in-kind transfers can be targeted at essential services. However, not everyone agrees that in-kind transfers are a good idea. Skeptics view them as paternalistic, inefficient, and disrespectful, and they argue that cash payments allow recipients to make the choices that best fit their needs.

THE EARNED INCOME TAX CREDIT (EITC) The Earned Income Tax Credit (EITC) is a tax credit designed to encourage low-income workers to work more. At very low income levels, EITC offers an incentive to work by supplementing earned income with a tax credit of approximately $6,000 a year. The amount is determined, in part, by the number of dependent children in the household and the location. Once a family reaches an income level above its earnings threshold, EITC is phased out, and workers gradually lose the tax credit. Under many welfare and in-kind transfer programs, the qualifying income is a specific cutoff point; an individual or household is either eligible or not. In contrast, EITC is gradually reduced, which means that workers do not face a sizable disincentive to work as the program is phased out.

Medicaid
is a joint federal and state program that helps low-income individuals and households pay for the costs associated with long-term medical care.

Poverty

THE HUNGER GAMES

The *Hunger Games* series of dystopian-themed books written by Suzanne Collins (and later made into feature films) chronicles the life of Katniss Everdeen, a teenager living in the post-apocalyptic country of Panem, which has been divided into twelve districts. Life in each district is unique, with vast differences in wealth, resources, and production. The wealthy Capitol district governs the economy by heavily regulating all aspects of life in the other poverty-stricken districts. One of the methods of control is the annual Hunger Games, where a boy and a girl are chosen from each district to battle to the death. The survivor earns extra food and a life of luxury.

Katniss Everdeen lives in District 12, an area with striking similarities to the coal mining Appalachian region of the United States. In District 12, inhabitants work in the mines. They struggle to make ends meet, often go hungry, and have a permeating sense of desolation because there is no escape.

The rising income inequality we see in the United States is not as extreme as we find in *The Hunger Games*, but it does remind us that we need to pay attention to income inequality in our society. When an income distribution becomes too unequal, the result

Where would you rather live, the Capitol district or District 12?

is often political and social instability. *The Hunger Games* challenges us to think about economic freedom, the role of institutions in creating growth, the extent to which governments should regulate economic activity, and how policy decisions made today will shape the future world.

Incentives

EITC, which was established in 1975, helps over 25 million families, making it the largest poverty-fighting tool in the United States. The government estimates that EITC payments are sufficient to lift more than 5 million households out of poverty each year. In addition, EITC creates stronger work incentives than those found under traditional antipoverty programs that critics argue discourage recipients from working.

Trade-offs

THE MINIMUM WAGE The minimum wage is often viewed as an antipoverty measure. However, we learned in Chapter 6 that the minimum wage creates trade-offs. Predictably, firms respond to higher minimum wages by hiring fewer workers and utilizing more capital-intensive production processes, such as self-checkout lanes and robotic production. Because the minimum wage does not guarantee employment, the most it offers to a low-skill worker is a slightly larger paycheck. At the same time, a higher minimum wage makes those jobs more difficult to find.

Problems with Traditional Aid

While trying to be well meaning, many welfare programs can create unintended work disincentives, especially when we examine the combined effects of welfare and in-kind transfer programs.

Incentives

As an example, consider a family of five with a combined income of $30,000 a year. Suppose that the family qualifies for public assistance that amounts to another $10,000 in benefits. The family's combined income from employment and benefits thus rises to $40,000. What happens if another family member gets a part-time job and income from wages rises from $30,000 to $40,000? Under the current law, an income of $40,000 disqualifies the family from receiving most of the financial assistance it had been getting. As a result, the family's benefits fall from $10,000 to $2,000 per year. Now the family nets $42,000 total. The person who secured part-time employment may feel that working isn't worth it, because even though the family earned an additional $10,000, they lost $8,000 in welfare benefits. Because the family is able to raise its net income by only $2,000, it has effectively returned $8,000. The loss of those benefits as they are phased out feels like an 80% tax, which creates a large disincentive to work.

This is a basic dilemma that poverty-reducing programs face: those that provide substantial benefits can discourage participation in the workforce because a recipient who starts to work, in many cases, no longer qualifies for the benefits and loses them.

While few people dispute that welfare programs are well intentioned, many economists are concerned about the programs' unintended consequences. A society that establishes a generous welfare package for the poor will find that it faces a Samaritan's dilemma. A **Samaritan's dilemma** occurs when an act of charity creates disincentives for recipients to take care of themselves. President Bill Clinton's 1996 vow "to end welfare as we know it" and for welfare to be "a second chance, not a way of life" attempted to address this dilemma by providing benefits for only a limited period of time. Clinton changed the payout structure for federal assistance and encouraged states to require employment searches as a condition for receiving aid. In addition, the TANF program imposed a five-year maximum for the time during which a recipient can receive benefits. This strategy changed welfare from an entitlement under the law into a temporary safety net, thereby reducing the Samaritan's dilemma.

A **Samaritan's dilemma** occurs when an act of charity creates disincentives for recipients to take care of themselves.

Incentives

ECONOMICS IN THE REAL WORLD

MUHAMMAD YUNUS AND THE GRAMEEN BANK

In 2006, economist Muhammad Yunus received the Nobel Peace Prize for his work helping poor families in Bangladesh. What did Yunus do to win that honor? He founded the Grameen Bank, which was instrumental in creating a new type of loan that has

In 2006, Yunus received the Nobel Peace Prize.

loaned more than $10 billion to poor people in Bangladesh in an effort to eliminate extreme poverty.

The Grameen Bank gives out very small loans, known as *microcredit*, to poor Bangladeshis who are unable to qualify for conventional loans from traditional lenders. The loans are provided without collateral, and repayment is based on an honor system. By conventional standards that sounds preposterous, but it works! The Grameen Bank reports a 97% repayment rate, and according to one survey, over 50% of the families of Grameen borrowers have moved above the poverty line.

It all started with just a few thousand dollars. In 1974, Yunus, who was trained as an economist in the United States, returned to Bangladesh and lent $27 to each of 42 villagers who made bamboo furniture. The loans, which were all paid back, enabled the villagers to cut out middlemen and purchase their own raw materials. A few years later, Yunus won government approval to open the Grameen Bank, named for the Bengali word for "rural."

Yunus had a truly innovative idea. To receive a loan, applicants must belong to a five-member group. Once the first two members begin to pay back their loans, the others can get theirs. While there is no group responsibility for returning the loans, the Grameen Bank believes that it creates a sense of social responsibility, ensuring that all members will pay back their loans. More important, Yunus trusted that people would honor their commitments, and he was proved right.

PRACTICE WHAT YOU KNOW

Welfare is an economic means of lending a helping hand.

Incentives

Samaritan's Dilemma: Does Welfare Cause Unemployment?

The state you live in is considering two different welfare programs. The first plan guarantees $8,000 for each person. The second plan does not guarantee any payments, but it doubles any income earned up to $12,000.

QUESTION: Which program creates the lesser amount of unemployment?

ANSWER: Think about incentives. Under the first plan, recipients' benefits are not tied to work. The $8,000 is guaranteed. However, the second plan will pay more if recipients do work. This policy acts as a positive incentive to get a job. For instance, someone who works 20 hours a week and earns $10 per hour would make $200 per week, or about $10,000 a year. Under the second plan, that person would receive an additional $10,000 from the government. Therefore, we can say that the second program reduces the amount of unemployment.

It's Expensive to Be Poor

- The poor pay more for staples than the rich do, since they can't afford to buy in bulk.
- The poor pay more for auto insurance.
- The poor pay more to maintain checking accounts and credit cards.
- The poor are more likely to rent than own their housing, and this is more costly in the long run.

Imagine what it's like to earn $25,000 a year versus $250,000. A person earning $25,000 annually makes about $12.50 an hour—an amount near the minimum wage. A person making $250,000, on the other hand, is in the top five percent of all earners. Suppose these two people with different income levels are trying to do the same things: buy toilet paper and other staples, purchase car insurance, use a checking account and credit cards, and find a place to live.

The person making $25,000 annually is likely to be living paycheck to paycheck. When they buy staples, they rarely have enough extra cash to buy things like toilet paper in bulk, so they end up paying a lot more for those items in smaller units and also spending a lot more time in the process. A study by the Consumer Federation of America (CFA) found that the five major car insurers charge low-income drivers almost $700 a year more for minimum coverage than they do drivers with higher incomes. People living paycheck to paycheck don't have a lot in their checking accounts, so they often pay monthly fees imposed by financial institutions for insufficient deposits. Likewise, people who can't pay off their credit card each month end up paying hefty fees in interest. In addition, most poor people rent a place to live rather than own one. This is costly in two ways: they don't receive the mortgage

"Anyone who has ever struggled with poverty knows how extremely expensive it is to be poor."—James Baldwin

interest deduction on their taxes, and they're not building up equity.

Conversely, our quarter-million per year rich person is able to buy many household items in bulk, receiving a significant discount in the process. Because of the socioeconomic group they are in, they get much lower quotes on auto insurance. They have enough in the bank to avoid monthly minimums, and they pay off their credit card bills every month—not only avoiding high interest charges but also profiting from promotions that provide air travel points, cash back, and other goodies. The wealthy also are far more likely to own the home they live in. (For Americans who can afford it, home ownership is often their single biggest financial investment.)

Conclusion

Income and work have long been a subject of discussion and contention. We find that some jobs pay much more than others, and working hard and performing well at one's job do not guarantee good pay. People and jobs differ in many dimensions, and wages usually respond accordingly, though wages are affected by compensating differentials, location, education and human capital, union membership, and efficiency wages, all of which create significant income inequality.

This chapter is ultimately about trade-offs and incentives—two of our five foundations of economics. The debate about how society should handle income, poverty, and inequality is complex, and passions run deep. Depending on your perspective, you can point to data showing that society is improving (the narrowing wage gap between females and males) or worsening (increased levels of income inequality). In economics there are always trade-offs. Policies designed to reduce income inequality may cause highly productive workers to work less. Poverty initiatives may have unintended consequences as well. Unfortunately, good intentions alone won't close the wage gap or decrease income inequality, but the judicious use of incentives just might. ✳

· ANSWERING *the* BIG QUESTIONS ·

What are the determinants of wages?

- Supply and demand play a key role in determining wages, along with a number of nonmonetary determinants of earnings, such as compensating differentials, education and human capital, location, lifestyle, union membership, and efficiency wages.

- Economic studies estimate that wage discrimination accounts for less than 5% of wage differences.

- Despite recent gains, women still earn significantly less than men. Occupational crowding partially explains the wage gap. As long as supply imbalances remain in traditional male and female jobs, significant wage differences will persist.

What causes income inequality?

- Five factors can contribute to income inequality: ability, training and education, discrimination, wealth, and corruption. The income inequality ratio is sometimes used to measure a nation's level of inequality. Another measure of income inequality is the Gini index.

- Economic mobility reduces income inequality over long periods. Due to the life-cycle wage pattern, distinct borrowing and saving patterns over an individual's life smooth out his or her spending pattern. Therefore, in societies with substantial income mobility, the annual income inequality data overstate the amount of inequality.

How do economists analyze poverty?

- Economists determine the poverty rate by establishing a poverty threshold.

- The poverty rate in the United States is now slightly higher than it was 50 years ago, despite many efforts (welfare, in-kind transfers, and EITC) to reduce it.

- Efforts to reduce poverty are subject to the Samaritan's dilemma because they can create disincentives for recipients to support themselves.

·CHAPTER PROBLEMS·

Concepts You Should Know

compensating differential (p. 473)
efficiency wages (p. 476)
Gini index (p. 489)
human capital (p. 473)
income mobility (p. 492)
income inequality ratio (p. 487)
in-kind transfers (p. 490)

life-cycle wage pattern (p. 480)
Lorenz curve (p. 490)
Medicaid (p. 499)
occupational crowding (p. 481)
poverty rate (p. 488)
poverty threshold (p. 488)
productivity (p. 476)

Samaritan's dilemma (p. 501)
strike (p. 475)
underground economies (p. 490)
union (p. 475)
wage discrimination (p. 477)
winner-take-all (p. 484)

Questions for Review

1. Why do garbage collectors sometimes make more than furniture movers?

2. What are efficiency wages? Why are some employers willing to pay them?

3. Why is it difficult to determine the amount of wage discrimination in the workplace?

4. Discuss some of the reasons why full-time working women make, on average, 81% as much as full-time working men.

5. How does the degree of income inequality in the United States compare with that in similarly developed countries? How does U.S. income inequality compare with that in less developed nations?

6. Why do high rates of income mobility mitigate income inequality?

7. Which antipoverty program (welfare, in-kind transfers, or EITC) creates the strongest incentive for recipients to work? Why?

Study Problems (✶ solved at the end of this section)

1. Suppose that society restricted the economic opportunities of right-handed persons to jobs in construction, while left-handed persons can work any job.

   a. Would wages in construction be higher or lower than wages for other jobs?
   b. Would left-handed workers make more or less than right-handed workers?
   c. Now suppose that right-handers are allowed to work any job they like. What effect would this change have on the wages of right-handers and left-handers over time?

2. Internships are considered a vital stepping-stone to full-time employment after college, but not all internship positions are paid. Why do some students take unpaid internships when they could be working summer jobs and earning an income? Include a discussion of human capital in your answer.

3. Consider two communities. In Middletown, two families earn $40,000 each, six families earn $50,000 each, and two earn $60,000 each. In Polarity, four families earn $10,000 each, two earn $50,000 each, and four earn $90,000 each. Which

community has the more unequal distribution of income as measured by the income inequality ratio? Explain your response.

4. The United States has attracted many highly productive immigrants who work in fields such as education, health, and technology. How do these immigrants affect income inequality in the United States? Is this type of immigration good or bad for the United States, and why? What impact is this type of immigration having on the countries that are losing some of their best workers?

✶ 5. Suppose that a wealthy friend asks for your advice on how to reduce income inequality. Your friend wants to know if it would be better to give $100 million to poor people who will never attend college or to offer $100 million in financial aid to students who could not otherwise afford to attend college. What advice would you give, and why?

6. What effect would doubling the minimum wage have on income inequality? Explain your answer.

✶ 7. Suppose that a company has 10 employees. It agrees to pay each worker on the basis of productivity. The individual workers' outputs are 10, 14, 15, 16, 18, 19, 21, 23, 25, and 30 units. However, some of the workers complain that they are earning less than the other workers, so they appeal to management to help reduce the income inequality. As a result, the company decides to pay each worker the same salary. But the next time the company measures each worker's output, they find that 6, 7, 7, 8, 10, 10, 11, 11, 12, and 12 units are produced. Why did this happen? Would you recommend that the company continue the new compensation system? Explain your response.

8. The government is considering three possible welfare programs:

    a. Give each low-income household $10,000.
    b. Give each low-income household $20,000 minus the recipient's income.
    c. Match the income of each low-income household, where the maximum it can receive in benefits is capped at $10,000.

    Which program will do the most to help the poor? Describe the work incentives under each program.

9. A number of very famous people (Ellen DeGeneres, Brad Pitt, Mark Zuckerberg, Bill Gates) all dropped out of college. Why would anyone drop out of college when college graduates typically make significantly more than college dropouts?

✳ 10. Tracy Chapman's song "Fast Car" reminds us how difficult it is to escape poverty. Identify the reasons in the song that keep Tracy trapped in poverty. (To listen to the song, visit www.youtube.com/watch?v=uTIB10eQnA0.)

11. Suppose that next summer you get two job offers, one as a lifeguard and the other as a garbage collector. Each job pays $15 an hour, and you are required to work 30 hours a week.

    a. Which job are you more likely to take?
    b. If no one wants to work as a garbage collector and everyone wants to be a lifeguard, what will happen to the wages in both jobs?

✳ 12. Which of the following explanations (compensating differentials, discrimination, human capital, occupational crowding, winner-take-all) describes each of the following situations?

    a. A person who is perceived as unattractive earns less than a person seen as attractive.
    b. Alexa is more educated and better trained than Felix.
    c. A Nobel-prize winning economist earns significantly more than other economists.
    d. More women work as elementary school teachers than men.

13. In a society where 25% of the people earn $30,000 per year, 50% earn $60,000, and 25% earn $90,000, draw the Lorenz curve and calculate the Gini index.

Solved Problems

5. The return on your wealthy friend's investment will be higher if the money is given to students with the aptitude, but not the income, to go to college. After all, college students earn substantially more than high school graduates do. Therefore, an investment in additional education will raise the marginal revenue product of the poor students' labor. With the higher earning power a college degree provides, more people will be lifted out of poverty, thereby reducing the amount of income inequality in the future.

7. Begin by calculating the average output when each worker's wage is based on the amount he or she produces: $10 + 14 + 15 + 16 + 18 + 19 + 21 + 23 + 25 + 30 = 191$, and $191 (\div 10 = 19.1$. Then compute the average output when the company decides to pay each worker the same wage: $6 + 7 + 7 + 8 + 10 + 10 + 11 + 11 + 12 + 12 + 94$, and $94 (\div 10 = 9.4$. The output has dropped by approximately one-half! Why? The

company forgot about incentives. In this case, an attempt to create equal pay caused a disincentive problem (because hard work is not rewarded), and the workers all reduced their work effort. The new compensation system should be scrapped.

10. Tracy's condition is difficult because she lives in the country and the jobs are in the city—which is why she wants a "fast car" to drive away in. She also comes from a broken family; her mother left her father because he had a drinking problem. The lack of nearby job opportunities and the necessity of caring for her father prevents Tracy from taking advantage of economic opportunities elsewhere.

12. a. discrimination
    b. human capital
    c. winner-take-all
    d. occupational crowding

PART
V

Special Topics in
MICROECONOMICS

Consumer Choice

The More Money You Have, the Happier You'll Be? Not So Fast.

As a college student, you would probably be delighted if someone surprised you with a gift of $100. But to a successful stockbroker, $100 is mere pocket change. The more dollars you have, the less you value each additional one. And there can come a point where more money is actually undesirable. Consider Jack Whittaker, who won a $315 million Powerball jackpot in 2002, which at the time was the biggest single-winner jackpot in American lottery history. He later divorced and went completely broke, was arrested for DUI, and was robbed on two separate occasions while carrying over $100,000. (Who carries *that much* money?) Worst of all, he lost his granddaughter to a drug overdose, which he blamed on the lottery win, as well. Whittaker told an interviewer in 2007: "My wife said she wished that she had torn the ticket up. Well, I wish that we tore the ticket up too." Too much money can make you very unhappy!

Some lottery winners do just fine, of course. But it's so common for winners to deal badly with the sudden wealth, and all the attention from "friends" who suddenly emerge from the woodwork, that there's a name for this phenomenon: the lottery curse. The root problem is that winners suddenly face a whole ton of choices they hadn't faced

"Are we ready to ruin another life? The (un)lucky number is...!" Let's hope winners of these payoffs escape the lottery curse.

before and aren't well-equipped to make. In this chapter, we use our understanding of income constraints, price, and personal satisfaction to determine which economic choices yield the greatest benefits.

· BIG QUESTIONS ·

- How do economists model consumer satisfaction?
- How do consumers optimize their purchasing decisions?
- What is the diamond-water paradox?

How Do Economists Model Consumer Satisfaction?

Trade-offs

Imagine that it is a hot afternoon and you decide to stop at a convenience store for a cold drink. While you're there, you decide to get a snack as well. Brownies are your favorite, but apple pie is on sale and you choose that instead. You may not think about these purchases very carefully, but they involve several trade-offs, including the time you could use to do something else and the money you could be spending on something else. If brownies are your favorite snack, why do you sometimes choose to eat apple pie? Why do many people pay thousands of dollars for diamond jewelry, which is not essential for life, and yet pay only pennies for water, which is essential for life? These are the kinds of questions we must answer if we are to understand how people make personal buying decisions.

To better understand the decisions that consumers make, economists attempt to measure the satisfaction that consumers get when they make purchases. **Utility** is a measure of the level of satisfaction that a consumer enjoys from the consumption of goods and services. Utility theory seeks to measure contentment, or satisfaction. To understand why people buy the goods and services they do, we need to recognize that some products produce more utility than others and that everyone receives different levels of satisfaction from the same good or service. In other words, utility varies from individual to individual. To quantify this idea of relative satisfaction, economists measure utility with a unit they refer to as a **util**.

There is tremendous value in modeling decisions this way. When we understand utility, we can predict what people are likely to purchase. We model consumer behavior in a manner similar to the way we model how a firm makes

Utility
is a measure of the level of satisfaction that a consumer enjoys from the consumption of goods and services.

A **util** is a personal unit of satisfaction used to measure the enjoyment from consumption of a good or service.

decisions or how the labor market works. We expect the firm to maximize profits, the laborer to accept the best offer, and the consumer to find the combination of goods that gives the most utility. For example, a brownie lover may get 25 utils from her favorite snack, but someone who is less susceptible to the pleasures of chewy, gooey chocolate may rate the same brownie at 10 utils. However, these are not completely accurate measurements of relative utility. Who can say whether one person's 25 utils represents more actual satisfaction than another person's 10? Even if you and a friend agree that you each receive 10 utils from eating brownies, you cannot say that you both experience the same amount of satisfaction; each of you has a unique personal scale. However, the level of enjoyment one receives can be internally consistent. For example, if you rate a brownie at 25 utils and a slice of apple pie at 15 utils, we know that you like brownies more than apple pie.

Utility, or what most of us think of as satisfaction, is a balance between economic and personal factors. Even though there is an inherent problem with equating money and satisfaction, this has not stopped researchers from exploring the connection.

In the next section, we explore the connection between total utility and marginal utility. This connection will help us understand why more money does not necessarily bring more satisfaction.

Do you prefer a slice of apple pie . . .

. . . or a fudge brownie?

ECONOMICS IN THE REAL WORLD

HAPPINESS INDEX

Since 2006, the Organisation for Economic Co-operation and Development (OECD) has published the Better Life Index—popularly called the "happiness index"—which compiles social and economic data for 34 highly developed countries. The OECD measures well-being across these countries, based on 11 topics it has identified as essential in the areas of material living conditions and quality of life.

Which countries are happiest? The OECD doesn't rank them, and the results depend on the relative importance assigned to the different measurements. Australia rates highly in most categories. What makes Australians so happy? It's not their income, which averages only $35,000 per year in U.S. dollars. However, Australians live to an average age of 82 (two years longer than typical in developed countries), experience low amounts of pollution, display a high degree of civic engagement, and enjoy a very high life satisfaction rating.

"Down under" is a satisfying place to live!

In contrast, the OECD identifies the United States as having the highest income, but it scores substantially lower in work-life balance than many of the other top countries do. Just as with individuals, with nations it's hard to make comparisons. Are Australians happier than Americans, or vice versa? Without knowing how much importance people attach to longevity compared to income, it's hard to say. Still, when one country outscores another in virtually every category, we can be pretty sure there's a corresponding difference in happiness levels. Thus it seems clear that Americans and Australians are better off overall than the citizens of Mexico, where safety concerns, poor education, and low levels of income combine to produce a very low rating.

The OECD Better Life Index

The OECD Better Life Index attempts to measure 11 key factors of material well-being in each of its 34 member countries. The goal of the index is to provide member governments with a snapshot of how their citizens are living, thus providing a road map for future policy priorities. Some factors are objectively measured, such as average household income. Others are more subjective, such as "life satisfaction," and are measured from survey responses. Below is a look at the results in three countries.

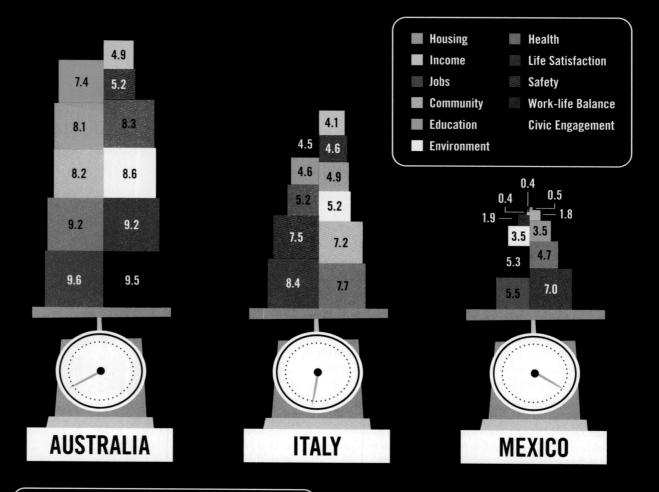

Legend:
- Housing
- Income
- Jobs
- Community
- Education
- Environment
- Health
- Life Satisfaction
- Safety
- Work-life Balance
- Civic Engagement

AUSTRALIA

| 4.9 |
7.4	5.2
8.1	8.3
8.2	8.6
9.2	9.2
9.6	9.5

ITALY

| 4.1 |
4.5	4.6
4.6	4.9
5.2	5.2
7.5	7.2
8.4	7.7

MEXICO

| 0.4 |
0.4	0.5
1.9	1.8
3.5	3.5
5.3	4.7
5.5	7.0

0.0

Each factor is ranked on a scale of zero to 10, with 10 being the highest. One to three indicators go into each measurement. For instance, "Jobs" is measured through the unemployment rate, job security, and personal earnings.

What do these numbers say about a nation's quality of life? It depends on which factors you think are most important. At www.oecdbetterlifeindex.org you can weight the different categories, create an index, and see how nations compare.

REVIEW QUESTIONS

- Mexico has five glaring challenges to the well-being of its citizens. What are they?

- Visit the OECD website and create your own index. Are any of the 11 factors trade-offs?

Total Utility and Marginal Utility

Thinking about the choices that consumers make can help us understand how to increase total utility. Consider a person who really likes brownies. In this case, the **marginal utility** is the additional satisfaction enjoyed from consuming one more brownie. In the table on the left-hand side of Figure 16.1, we see that the first brownie eaten brings 25 total utils. Eating additional brownies increases total utility until it reaches 75 utils after eating five brownies.

The graph in panel (a) of Figure 16.1 reveals that while the total utility (the green curve) rises until it reaches 75, the rate of increase (that is, the increase

Marginal thinking

Marginal utility
is the additional satisfaction derived from consuming one more unit of a good or service.

FIGURE 16.1

Total Utility and Marginal Utility

The relationship between total utility and marginal utility can be seen by observing the dashed line that connects panels (a) and (b). Because the marginal utility becomes negative after five brownies are consumed, the total utility eventually falls after a certain number of brownies are eaten. To the left of the dashed line, the marginal utility is positive in panel (b) and the total utility is rising in panel (a). Conversely, to the right of the dashed line, the marginal utility is negative and the total utility is falling.

Number of brownies eaten	Total utility (utils)	Marginal utility (utils per brownie)
0	0	
		25
1	25	
		20
2	45	
		15
3	60	
		10
4	70	
		5
5	75	
		0
6	75	
		−5
7	70	
		−10
8	60	
		−15
9	45	
		−20
10	25	

(a) Total Utility

(b) Marginal Utility

Running is fun for only so long.

Diminishing marginal utility occurs when marginal utility declines as consumption increases.

in marginal utility) falls from 25 utils for the first brownie down to 5 additional utils for the fifth. The marginal utility values from the table are plotted in panel (b), which shows that marginal utility declines steadily as consumption rises.

The relationship between total utility and marginal utility is evident when we observe the dashed line that connects panels (a) and (b). Because the marginal utility becomes negative after five brownies are consumed, the total utility eventually falls. To the left of the dashed line, the marginal utility is positive in panel (b) and the total utility is rising in panel (a). Conversely, to the right of the dashed line, the marginal utility is negative and the total utility is falling.

When marginal utility becomes negative, the consumer is tired of eating brownies. At that point, the brownies are no longer adding to the consumer's utility, and he or she will stop eating them.

Diminishing Marginal Utility

As you can see in panel (b) of Figure 16.1, the satisfaction that a consumer derives from consuming a good or service declines with each additional unit consumed. Consider what happens when you participate in a favorite activity for an hour and then decide to do something else. **Diminishing marginal utility** occurs when marginal utility declines as consumption increases. The concept of diminishing marginal utility is so universal that it is one of the most widely held ideas in all of economics.

In rare cases, marginal utility can rise—but only temporarily. Consider running. Many people choose to run for recreation because it is both healthy and pleasurable. Often, the first mile is difficult as the runner's body gets warmed up. Thereafter, running is easier—for a while. No matter how good you are at distance running, eventually the extra miles become more exhausting and less satisfying, and you stop. This does not mean that running is not healthy or pleasurable. Far from it! But it does mean that forcing yourself to do more running after you have already pushed your limit yields less utility. Your own intuition should confirm this theory. If increasing marginal utility were possible, you would find that with every passing second you would enjoy what you were doing more and never want to stop. Because economists do not observe this behavior among rational consumers, we can be highly confident that diminishing marginal utility has tremendous explanatory power.

PRACTICE WHAT YOU KNOW

Diminishing Marginal Utility

QUESTION: A friend confides to you that a third friend has gradually lost interest in watching *Empire* with her and has begun saying she's too busy. How would you advise your friend to handle the situation?

ANSWER: Tell your friend about diminishing marginal utility! Even the best television show runs its course. After a while, the same humor or drama that once made the show interesting no longer seems as interesting. Then suggest to your friend that they mix it up and do something different together. If that doesn't work, it may not be *Empire* that is the problem—it may be that your friend's friend has grown tired of her.

CHALLENGE QUESTION: How could you tell whether the marginal utility someone derived from a TV show had not just gone down to zero but gone negative?

ANSWER: A person whose marginal utility had gone negative would not just show a lack of interest in the show but would be willing to pay a price to avoid watching it. "If you agree to watch something else, I'll do the dishes!"

Cookie Lyon wants you to keep watching.

Table 16.1 highlights how diminishing marginal utility can serve to explain a number of interesting real-world situations. Do not skip this table! It is very useful in helping you understand the concept of diminishing marginal utility.

TABLE 16.1

Examples of Diminishing Marginal Utility

	Example	Explanation using diminishing marginal utility
	Discounts on two-day passes to amusement parks	The excitement on the first day is palpable. You run to rides, don't mind waiting in line, and experience the thrill for the first time. By the second day, the enthusiasm has worn off and the lower price entices you to return.
	Discounts on season tickets	Over the course of any season, people anticipate some games and concerts more highly than other games and concerts. To encourage patrons to buy the entire season package, venues must discount the total price.
	All-you-can-eat buffet	All-you-can-eat buffets offer the promise of unlimited food, but the average diner has a limited capacity. Eating more eventually leads to negative marginal utility. Restaurants assume that diminishing utility will limit how much their customers eat.
	Unlimited minutes with cell phone plans	Cell phone companies rely on the diminishing marginal utility of conversation. Cell phone companies offer "unlimited" plans because they know that consumers will not stay on their phones indefinitely.
	Pokémon GO	Remember the summer of 2016 when Pokémon GO first appeared? Everyone was playing, and capturing digital monsters was so much fun. But you soon tired of the grind . . . and most people quit—that's diminishing marginal utility.
	Nathan's Famous Hot Dog Eating Contest	Many people enjoy eating a hot dog or two or three, but Nathan's Eating Contest is very difficult to watch. The idea of eating so many hot dogs makes a lot of people queasy.

How Do Consumers Optimize Their Purchasing Decisions?

Maximizing utility requires that consumers get the most satisfaction out of every dollar they spend, or what is commonly called "getting the biggest bang for the buck." When a consumer gets the most bang for the buck, we say that the consumer has *optimized* his or her purchasing decisions. However, optimization is easier said than done. Over the course of the year, each of us will make thousands of purchases of different amounts. Our budgets are generally not unlimited, and we try to spend in a way that enables us to meet both our short-run and our long-run needs. The combination of goods and services that maximizes the satisfaction, or utility, we get from our income or budget is the **consumer optimum**. In this section, we examine the decision process that leads to the consumer optimum. We start with two goods and then generalize those findings across a consumer's entire income or budget.

The **consumer optimum** is the combination of goods and services that maximizes the consumer's utility for a given income or budget.

Consumer Purchasing Decisions

Opportunity cost

Let's begin by imagining a world with only two goods: Pepsi and pizza. This example will help us focus on the opportunity cost of purchasing Pepsi instead of pizza, or pizza instead of Pepsi.

Pepsi is available for $1 per can, and each pizza slice costs $2. Suppose you have $10 to spend. How much of each good should you buy in order to maximize your satisfaction? Before we can answer that question, we need a rule for making decisions. To reach your consumer optimum, you must allocate your available money by choosing goods that give you the most utility per dollar spent. By getting the biggest bang for your buck, you will end up optimizing your choices. This relationship, shown below in terms of marginal utility (MU), helps quantify the decision. So if you get more for your money by purchasing Pepsi rather than pizza, then you should buy Pepsi—and vice versa.

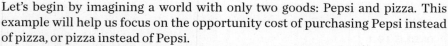

$$\frac{MU_{Pepsi}}{Price_{Pepsi}} \quad \textbf{Which is larger?} \quad \frac{MU_{pizza}}{Price_{pizza}}$$

If we divide the marginal utility of a good by its price, we get the utility per dollar spent. Because you wish to optimize your utility, a direct comparison of the marginal utility per dollar spent on Pepsi versus pizza gives you a road map to your consumer satisfaction. Table 16.2 shows the marginal utility for each can of Pepsi (column 2) and the marginal utility for each slice of pizza (column 5).

To decide what to consume first, look at column 3, which lists the marginal utility per dollar spent for Pepsi, and column 6, which lists the marginal utility per dollar spent for pizza. Now it's time to make your first spending decision—whether to drink a Pepsi or eat a slice of pizza. Because the marginal utility per dollar spent for the first slice of pizza (10) is higher than the marginal utility for the first can of Pepsi (9), you order a slice of pizza, which costs $2. You have $8 left.

After eating the first slice of pizza, you can choose between having a second slice of pizza, which brings 8 utils per dollar spent, and having the first can of Pepsi, which brings 9 utils per dollar spent. This time you order a Pepsi, which costs $1. You have $7 left.

TABLE 16.2

The Consumer Optimum with Pepsi and Pizza

(1) Pepsi consumed (cans)	(2) Marginal utility (MU Pepsi)	(3) MU Pepsi / Price Pepsi (Pepsi $1/can)	(4) Pizza consumed (slices)	(5) Marginal utility (MU pizza)	(6) MU pizza / Price pizza (pizza $2/slice)
1	9	9/1 = 9	1	20	20/2 = 10
2	8	8/1 = 8	2	16	16/2 = 8
3	7	7/1 = 7	3	12	12/2 = 6
4	6	6/1 = 6	4	8	8/2 = 4
5	5	5/1 = 5	5	4	4/2 = 2
6	4	4/1 = 4	6	0	0/2 = 0
7	3	3/1 = 3	7	−4	−4/2 = −2
8	2	2/1 = 2	8	−8	−8/2 = −4
9	1	1/1 = 1	9	−12	−12/2 = −6
10	0	0/1 = 0	10	−16	−16/2 = −8

Now you can choose between having a second slice of pizza, representing 8 utils per dollar spent, and having a second can of Pepsi, also 8 utils per dollar spent. Because both choices yield the same amount of utility per dollar spent and you have enough money to afford both, we'll assume you would probably purchase both at the same time. Your purchase costs another $3, which leaves you with $4.

Your next choice is between the third slice of pizza at 6 utils per dollar spent and the third can of Pepsi at 7 utils per dollar spent. Pepsi is the better value, so you buy that. You are left with $3 for your final choice: between the third slice of pizza at 6 utils per dollar spent and the fourth can of Pepsi at 6 utils per dollar spent. Since you have exactly $3 left and the items are of equal utility, you buy both, and you have no money left.

Let's see how well you have done. Looking at column 2 in Table 16.2, we calculate that the four Pepsis you consumed yielded a total utility of 9 + 8 + 7 + 6 = 30 utils. Looking at column 5, we see that three slices of pizza yielded a total utility of 20 + 16 + 12 = 48. Adding the two together (30 + 48) gives 78 total utils of satisfaction. This is the most utility you can afford with $10. To see why, look at Table 16.3, which reports the maximum utility for every affordable combination of Pepsi and pizza.

The optimum combination of Pepsi and pizza is highlighted in red. This is the result we found by comparing the marginal utilities per dollar spent in Table 16.2. Notice that Table 16.3 confirms that this process results in the highest total utility. All other affordable combinations of Pepsi and pizza produce less utility. Table 16.3 also illustrates diminishing marginal utility. If you select either pizza or Pepsi exclusively, you will have a much lower total utility: 60 utils with pizza and 45 utils with Pepsi. In addition, the preferred outcome of four Pepsis and three pizza slices corresponds to a modest amount of each good; this outcome avoids the utility reduction associated with excessive consumption of either good.

By thinking at the margin about which good provides the highest marginal utility, you also maximize your total utility. Of course, most people

TABLE 16.3

The Maximum Utility from Different Combinations of Pepsi and Pizza

Affordable combination of pizza and Pepsi	Total utility
5 pizza slices (20 + 16 + 12 + 8 + 4)	60 utils
2 Pepsis (9 + 8) and 4 pizza slices (20 + 16 + 12 + 8)	73 utils
4 Pepsis (9 + 8 + 7 + 6) and 3 pizza slices (20 + 16 + 12)	78 utils
6 Pepsi (9 + 8 + 7 + 6 + 5 + 4) and 2 pizza slices (20 + 16)	75 utils
8 Pepsi (9 + 8 + 7 + 6 + 5 + 4 + 3 + 2) and 1 pizza slice (20)	64 utils
10 Pepsi (9 + 8 + 7 + 6 + 5 + 4 + 3 + 2 + 1 + 0)	45 utils

rarely think this way. But as consumers we make marginal choices all the time. Instead of adding up utils, we think "that isn't worth it" or "that's a steal." Consumer choice is not so much a conscious calculation as an instinct to seek the most satisfaction. Next we extend our analysis by generalizing the two-good example.

Marginal Thinking with More Than Two Goods

The idea of measuring utility makes our instinctive sense more explicit and enables us to solve simple optimization problems. For instance, when you travel without the aid of GPS, you instinctively make choices about which route to take to save time. The decision to turn left or right when you come to a stop sign is a decision at the margin: one route will be better than the other. If you consistently make the best choices about which way to turn, you will arrive at your destination sooner. This is why economists focus on marginal thinking.

Marginal thinking

In reality, life is more complex than the simple two-good model implies. When you have $10 to spend, you may choose among many goods. Because you buy many items at all kinds of prices over the course of a year, you must juggle hundreds (or thousands) of purchases so that you enjoy roughly the same utility per dollar spent. Consumer optimum captures this idea by comparing the utility gained with the price paid for every item a consumer buys. In other words, a consumer's income or budget is balanced so that the ratio of the marginal utility (MU) per dollar spent on every item, from good A to good Z, is equal. In mathematical terms:

$$\frac{MU_A}{Price_A} = \frac{MU_B}{Price_B} = \ldots = \frac{MU_Z}{Price_Z}$$

Left or right? One way will get you to your destination sooner.

It should be noted that, because goods aren't infinitely divisible (we can't buy a fraction of a soda can), we can't always make the fractions come out exactly equal. Still, we maximize utility by buying the goods with the higher fractions, and in the end the marginal utilities per dollar spent for each good end up approximately equal.

In the next section, we explore the relationship between changes in price and changes in the consumer optimum.

Price Changes and the Consumer Optimum

Recall our example of pizza and Pepsi: you reached an optimum when you purchased four Pepsis and three slices of pizza. At that point, the marginal utility per dollar spent for Pepsi and pizza was equal:

$$\frac{MU_{pizza}\ (12\ utils)}{\$2} = \frac{MU_{Pepsi}\ (6\ utils)}{\$1}$$

In the earlier example, the prices of a slice of pizza ($2) and a can of Pepsi ($1) were held constant. But suppose that the price of a slice of pizza drops to $1.50. This new price causes the ratio of $MU_{pizza} \div Price_{pizza}$ to change from $12 \div 2$, or 6 utils per dollar, to $12 \div 1.5$, or 8 utils per dollar. The lower price for pizza increases the quantity of slices the consumer will buy:

$$\frac{MU_{pizza}\ (12\ utils)}{\$1.50} > \frac{MU_{Pepsi}\ (6\ utils)}{\$1}$$

As a result, we can say that lower prices increase the marginal utility per dollar spent and cause consumers to buy more of a good. Higher prices have the opposite effect by lowering the marginal utility per dollar spent. If that conclusion sounds an awful lot like the law of demand, it is! We have just restated the law of demand in terms of marginal utility.

We know that according to the law of demand (see Chapter 3), the quantity demanded falls when the price rises, and the quantity demanded rises when the price falls—all other things being equal. If we think of consumer desire for a particular product as demand, it makes sense to find a connection between the prices consumers pay, the quantity they buy, and the marginal utility they receive.

A lower price has two effects. First, because the marginal utility per dollar spent is now higher, consumers substitute the product that has become relatively less expensive—this is the **substitution effect**. Second, at the same time, a lower price can also change the purchasing power of income—this is the **real-income effect**. (For a basic discussion of the trends behind these effects, see Chapter 3.)

Let's go back to our Pepsi and pizza example to separate these two effects. A lower price for a slice of pizza makes it more affordable. If slices are $2 each, a consumer with a budget of $10 can afford five slices. If the price drops to $1.50 per slice, the consumer can afford six slices and still have $1 left over.

When the price of a slice of pizza is $2, your optimum is three slices of pizza and four Pepsis. If we drop the price of a slice of pizza to $1.50, you save 50 cents per slice. Because you are purchasing three slices, you save $1.50— which is enough to buy another slice. Looking back at column 5 in Table 16.2, we see that the fourth slice of pizza yields an additional 8 utils. Alternatively, you could use the $1.50 you saved on pizza to buy a fifth can of Pepsi—which has a marginal utility of 5—and still have 50 cents left over.

The lower price of pizza may cause you to substitute pizza for Pepsi because pizza has become relatively less expensive. This is the substitution effect at work. In addition, you have more purchasing power through the money you save from the lower-priced pizza. This is the real-income effect.

The real-income effect matters only when prices change enough to cause a measurable effect on the purchasing power of the consumer's income or

Marginal thinking

The **substitution effect** occurs when consumers substitute a product that has become relatively less expensive as the result of a price change.

The **real-income effect** occurs when there is a change in purchasing power as a result of a change in the price of a good.

budget. For example, suppose that a 10% price reduction in peanut butter cups occurs. Will there be a substitution effect, a real-income effect, or both? The key to answering this question is to consider how much money is saved. Most candy bars cost less than a dollar, so a 10% reduction in price would be less than 10 cents. The lower price will motivate some consumers to switch to peanut butter cups—a substitution effect that can be observed through increased purchases of peanut butter cups. However, the real-income effect is negligible. The consumer has saved less than 10 cents. The money saved could be used to purchase other goods; but very few goods cost so little, and the enhanced purchasing power is effectively zero. Thus, the answer to the question is that there will be a modest substitution effect and essentially no real-income effect.

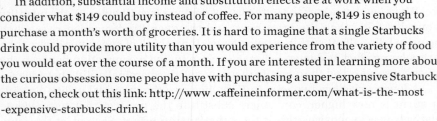

ECONOMICS IN THE REAL WORLD

WOULD YOU PAY $149 FOR A DRINK AT STARBUCKS?

Your favorite Starbucks creation typically costs about $5. Now suppose you do what the guy on the left did, and spend over $100 on extra shots, add-ins, and flavors, all in a punchbowl-sized "cup." Would you enjoy the drink more? Maybe. But 20 times more? Not a chance. How do we know this? The law of diminishing marginal utility tells us that additional units of the same good will eventually bring less marginal utility.

In addition, substantial income and substitution effects are at work when you consider what $149 could buy instead of coffee. For many people, $149 is enough to purchase a month's worth of groceries. It is hard to imagine that a single Starbucks drink could provide more utility than you would experience from the variety of food you would eat over the course of a month. If you are interested in learning more about the curious obsession some people have with purchasing a super-expensive Starbucks creation, check out this link: http://www.caffeineinformer.com/what-is-the-most-expensive-starbucks-drink.

A $149 cup of Starbucks coffee, and yes, that's the actual size. What's the most *you* would pay for your favorite drink?

The **diamond-water paradox** explains why water, which is essential to life, is inexpensive, while diamonds, which do not sustain life, are expensive.

What Is the Diamond-Water Paradox?

Now that you understand the connection between prices and utility, we can tackle one of the most interesting puzzles in economics—the **diamond-water paradox**. First described by Adam Smith in 1776, the diamond-water paradox explains why water, which is essential to life, is inexpensive, while diamonds, which do not sustain life, are expensive. Many people of Smith's era found the paradox perplexing. Today, we can use consumer choice theory to answer the question.

Essentially, the diamond-water paradox unfairly compares the amount of marginal utility a person receives from a small quantity of something rare (the diamond) with the marginal utility received from consuming a small amount of additional water after already consuming a large amount.

We know that marginal utility is captured in the law of demand and therefore by the price of a good. For example, when the price of diamonds increases, the quantity demanded declines. We learned in Chapter 5 that in graphical

PRACTICE WHAT YOU KNOW

Consumer Optimum

QUESTION: Suppose your favorite magazine, *The Economist*, costs $6 per issue and *People* magazine costs $4 per issue. If you receive 20 utils when you read *People*, how many additional utils would you need to get from reading *The Economist* to prompt you to pony up the extra $2 to purchase it instead of *People* magazine?

ANSWER: To answer the question, you first need to equate the marginal utility (MU) per dollar spent for both magazines and solve for the missing variable, the utility from *The Economist*:

$$\frac{MU_{The\ Economist}\ (X\ utils)}{\$6} = \frac{MU_{People}\ (20\ utils)}{\$4}$$

$$\frac{X}{\$6} = \frac{20}{\$4}$$

$$X = \frac{\$120}{\$4}$$

$$X = 30$$

When the $MU_{The\ Economist}$ is equal to 30 utils, you are indifferent between purchasing either of the two magazines (that is, each magazine would bring you equal satisfaction). Because the question asks how many *additional* utils are needed to justify purchasing *The Economist*, you should subtract the utils from *People*, or 20, to get the difference, which is $30 - 20$, or 10 utils.

terms, the consumer surplus is the area under the demand curve and above the price, or the gains from trade that a consumer enjoys. Therefore, if the price of diamonds rises, consumers will enjoy less surplus when buying them.

Figure 16.2 contrasts the demand and supply equilibrium in both the market for water and the market for diamonds. Notice that the consumer surplus is the area highlighted in blue for water and the triangular area highlighted with dots for diamonds. The blue area of total utility for water (TU_w) is much larger than the dotted area of total utility for diamonds (TU_d) because water is essential for life. Therefore, water creates significantly more total utility than diamonds do. However, in most places in the United States, water is very plentiful, so people take additional units of it for granted. In fact, it is so plentiful that if someone were to offer you a gallon of water right now, you would probably hesitate to take it. But what if someone offered you a gallon-size bucket of diamonds? You bet you would take that! Therefore, it should not surprise you that something quite plentiful, water, would yield less marginal utility than something rare, diamonds ($MU_w < MU_d$). However, if water were as rare as diamonds, there is no doubt that the price of water would exceed the price of diamonds.

Let's consider how we use water. We bathe in it, cook with it, and drink it. Each of those uses has high value, so the marginal utility of water is high. But we also use it to water our lawns and fill our fish tanks. Those uses are not nearly as essential, so the marginal utility of water for these uses is much lower. The

FIGURE 16.2

The Diamond-Water Paradox

The diamond-water paradox exists because people fail to recognize that demand and supply are equally important in determining the value a good creates in society. The demand for water is large, while the demand for diamonds is small. If we look at the amount of consumer surplus, we observe that the blue area (TU_w, which represents the consumer surplus for water) is much larger than the dotted area (TU_d, which represents the consumer surplus for diamonds) because water is essential for life. As a result, water creates significantly more total utility (TU) than diamonds. However, because water is abundant in most places, the price, P_{water}, is low. In contrast, diamonds are rare and the price, $P_{diamond}$, is high.

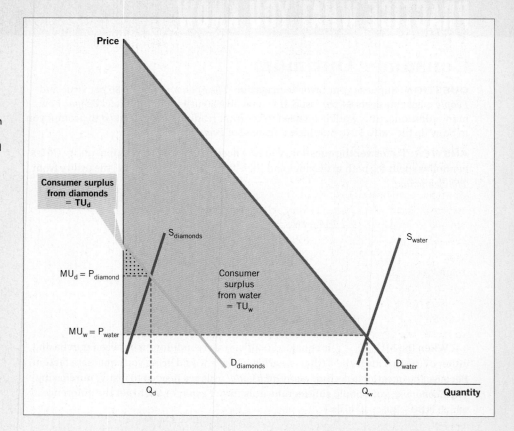

reason we use water in both essential and nonessential ways is that its price is relatively low, so low-value uses, like filling fish tanks, yield enough utility to justify the cost. Because water is abundant in most places, the price (P_{water}) is low. In contrast, diamonds are rare, and their price ($P_{diamond}$) is high. The cost of obtaining a diamond means that a consumer must get a great deal of marginal utility from the purchase of a diamond to justify the expense, which explains why diamonds are given as gifts for extremely special occasions.

Conclusion

Does having more money make people more satisfied? The answer is no. More money enables people to buy more goods, but because of diminishing marginal utility, the increases in satisfaction from being able to buy more goods or higher-quality goods become progressively smaller with rising income. So we could say that having more money makes people somewhat more satisfied. But it seems appropriate to add that the relationship between quality of life and money is not direct. More money sometimes leads to more utility, and at other times more money means more problems.

The Diamond-Water Paradox

SUPER SIZE ME

What would happen if you ate all your meals at McDonald's for an entire month—without ever exercising? *Super Size Me*, a 2004 documentary by Morgan Spurlock, endeavored to find out. It is the absurd nature of Spurlock's adventure that pulls viewers in. No one would *actually* eat every meal at the same restaurant for a month, because diminishing marginal utility would cause the utility from the meals to plunge. (This is especially true with McDonald's, which is not known for high-quality cuisine.)

Why did Spurlock take aim at McDonald's and more generally the fast-food industry? His aim was to reveal how unhealthy fast food really is, but the documentary also happens to unintentionally offer a modern parallel to the diamond-water paradox.

The key is the business model that many fast-food restaurants follow. These restaurants provide filling food at low prices, a combination that encourages consumers to eat more than they would if the price were higher. Eating a lot of food causes diminishing marginal utility; often, the last bite of a sandwich or fries or the last gulp of a 32-ounce drink brings very little additional utility, so it is not uncommon for consumers to discard the excess.

In contrast, consider fine dining. Fancy establishments serve smaller portions by design. A five-course meal is meant to be savored, and the experience trumps price. What makes someone willing to pay

A Big Mac a day for 30 days! What could possibly go wrong?

significantly more when dining out at such places? Upscale restaurants are creating high marginal utility by making every bite mouthwatering. They do not want to diminish the marginal value through overeating.

To summarize, McDonald's is a lot like water in the diamond-water paradox. It is easy to find a McDonald's restaurant almost anywhere, and the chain serves close to 70 million customers a day. Therefore, the total utility the chain creates is high, despite the fact that the marginal utility of the last bite is low. Upscale restaurants are a lot like diamonds: they are uncommon, and the number of customers they serve is small. The total utility that upscale restaurants create is low compared with McDonald's, but the marginal utility of the last individual bite at an upscale restaurant is quite high.

As we have seen in this chapter, price plays a key role in determining utility. Because consumers face a budget and wish to maximize their utility, the prices they pay determine their marginal utility per dollar spent. Comparing the marginal utility per dollar spent across many goods helps us understand individuals' consumption patterns. Diminishing marginal utility also helps to describe consumer choice. Because marginal utility declines with additional consumption, consumers do not exclusively purchase their favorite products. Instead, they diversify their choices in order to gain more utility. In addition,

Worth It

- You really need or want it (inelastic demand).
- No acceptable substitute good is available at a lower price.
- It is a good bang for the buck (MU/P is high).
- You can afford it without spending beyond your means.

Would you buy a $47 taco and eat it in one bite?

Buzzfeed's *Worth It* is the #1 show on YouTube. The show features Steven Lim and Andrew Ilnyckyj. The premise is simple: the hosts try an inexpensive, a moderately-priced, and a very expensive version of the same good. They then debate the merits of each version and explain why it is either "worth it" or not.

Life works the same way! We make thousands of decisions over the course of each year to either make a purchase, not purchase, or find a substitute product instead. *Worth It* is really about the hunt for the consumer optimum, where the extra value we get from buying one more unit of a good is the same across all the items we purchase. Whether something is "worth it" also applies to how we spend our time and energy. In a world of scarcity we must use our limited resources wisely, or else we end up with fewer utils (less enjoyment).

changes in prices have two different effects: one on real income and a separate substitution effect that together determine the composition of the bundle of goods purchased.

In the next chapter, we question how much individuals use consumer choice theory to make their decisions. The approach known as behavioral economics argues that decision-makers are not entirely rational about the choices they make.

Finally, in the appendix that follows, we refine consumer theory by discussing indifference curves. Please read the appendix to get a glimpse into how economists model consumer choice in greater detail. ✳

· ANSWERING *the* BIG QUESTIONS ·

How do economists model consumer satisfaction?

- Economists model consumer satisfaction by examining utility, which is a measure of the level of satisfaction that a consumer enjoys from the consumption of goods and services.

- Utility diminishes with additional consumption. This property limits the amount of any particular good or service that a person will consume.

How do consumers optimize their purchasing decisions?

- Consumers optimize their purchasing decisions by finding the combination of goods and services that maximizes the level of satisfaction from a given income or budget. The consumer optimum occurs when a consumer maximizes the utility from his or her income or budget, so that the marginal utility per dollar spent on every item purchased is equal to that of every other item purchased.

- Changes in price have two distinct effects on consumer behavior. If the price falls, the marginal utility per dollar spent will be higher. As a result, consumers will substitute the product that has become relatively less expensive. This is the substitution effect. If the lower price also results in substantial savings, it causes an increase in purchasing power, known as the real-income effect.

What is the diamond-water paradox?

- The diamond-water paradox explains why water, which is essential to life, is inexpensive, while diamonds, which do not sustain life, are expensive. Many people of Adam Smith's era, in the eighteenth century, found the paradox perplexing. We can solve the diamond-water paradox by recognizing that the price of water is low because its supply is abundant, and the price of diamonds is high because their supply is small. If water were as rare as diamonds, there is no doubt that the price of water would exceed the price of diamonds.

·CHAPTER PROBLEMS·

Concepts You Should Know

consumer optimum (p. 518)
diamond-water paradox (p. 522)
diminishing marginal utility (p. 516)

marginal utility (p. 515)
real-income effect (p. 521)
substitution effect (p. 521)

util (p. 512)
utility (p. 512)

Questions for Review

1. After watching a movie, you and your friend both indicate that you liked it. Does this mean that each of you received the same amount of utility? Explain your response.

2. What is the relationship between total utility and marginal utility?

3. How is diminishing marginal utility reflected in the law of demand?

4. What does it mean when we say that the marginal utility per dollar spent is equal for two goods?

Study Problems (✳ solved at the end of the section)

1. A local pizza restaurant charges full price for the first pizza but offers 50% off on a second pizza. Using marginal utility, explain the restaurant's pricing strategy.

2. Suppose that the price of trail mix is $4 per pound and the price of cashews is $6 per pound. If you get 30 utils from the last pound of cashews you consume, how many utils would you have to get from the last pound of trail mix to be in consumer equilibrium?

3. Fill in the missing information in the table below:

Number of cookies	Total utility of cookies	Marginal utility of cookies	Number of pretzels	Total utility of pretzels	Marginal utility of pretzels
0	0	—	0	0	—
1	—	25	1	10	—
2	—	15	2	18	—
3	—	10	3	24	6
4	—	5	4	—	4
5	55	—	5	—	2
6	50	—	6	—	0

4. Use the table in problem 3. Suppose that you have a budget of $8 and that cookies and pretzels cost $1 each. What is the consumer optimum?

5. Use the table in problem 3. What is the consumer optimum if the price of cookies rises from $1 to $1.50 and the price of pretzels remains at $1?

6. You are considering either dining at Cici's, an all-you-can-eat pizza chain, or buying pizza by the slice at a local pizzeria for $2 per slice. At which restaurant are you likely to obtain the most marginal utility from the last slice you eat? Explain your response.

7. In consumer equilibrium, a person buys four cups of coffee at $2 per cup and two muffins at $2 per muffin each day. If the price of a cup of coffee rises to $3, what would you expect to happen to the amount of coffee and muffins this person consumes?

8. How do dollar stores survive when *none* of the items sold brings a high amount of total utility to consumers?

✳ 9. Imagine that the total utility from consuming five tacos is 10, 16, 19, 20, and 17 utils, respectively. When does marginal utility begin to diminish?

10. You and your friends are considering vacationing in either Cabo San Lucas or Cancun for spring break. When you first researched the cost of your hotel and flights, the total price was $1,000 to each destination. However, a sale has lowered the total cost of going to Cancun to $800. Does this change create a substitution effect, a real-income effect, or both? Explain.

★ **11.** Everyone wears underwear, but comparatively few people wear ties. Why are ties so much more expensive than underwear if the demand for underwear is so much greater than the demand for ties?

12. Do you agree with Henry David Thoreau's quote, "Happiness is like a butterfly; the more you chase it, the more it will elude you, but if you turn your attention to other things, it will come and sit softly on your shoulder"? Explain your answer using diminishing marginal utility.

★ **13.** A health study found that patients who experience severe pain may feel better if they curse as a coping mechanism. Based on what you have learned about economics, would you expect to see a difference in pain relief between people who normally use profanity and those who do not normally use profanity?

14. Suppose that Gina's marginal utility from drinking milk is 5 utils per ounce, and her marginal

utility from eating cereal is 10 utils per ounce. If the price of milk is 50 cents per ounce and the price of cereal is 80 cents per ounce, is Gina maximizing her utility? If so, explain how you know. If not, explain how she should change her spending to increase her utility.

15. Refer to the following Marginal Utility (MU) table:

$Q_{mangoes}$	$MU_{mangoes}$	$Q_{pineapples}$	$MU_{pineapples}$
1	20	1	24
2	15	2	18
3	10	3	12
4	5	4	6

You have a budget of $10. Pineapples cost $2, and mangoes cost $1. How many of each should you buy to maximize total utility?

Solved Problems

9. The key to answering this question is to realize that the data are expressed in total utils. The first taco brings the consumer 10 utils. Consuming the second taco yields $16 - 10$, or 6 additional utils. Since there are fewer extra utils from the second taco (6) than the utils from the first taco (10), diminishing marginal utility begins after the first taco.

11. Recall that demand is only half of the market. The other half is supply. Far fewer ties are produced than items of underwear. The supply of ties also plays a role in determining the price. In addition, ties are a fashion statement, which makes ties a luxury good. Underwear is a necessity. As a result, ties are a lot like diamonds: there is a small overall market, and prices are high. Underwear is a lot

like water: there is a very large overall market, and prices are low. The fact that ties generally cost more does not mean that ties are more valuable to society. Rather, people get more marginal utility from purchasing the "perfect" tie as opposed to finding the "perfect" underwear.

13. The researchers found that patients who infrequently cursed in their daily lives experienced more pain relief when they were in severe pain. Those who regularly cursed in their daily lives experienced almost no pain relief from cursing. This result is not surprising when you recall the law of diminishing marginal utility. For additional information, see http://www .ncbi .nlm.nih.gov/m/pubmed/22078790/.

Indifference Curve Analysis

There is much more to economic analysis than the simple supply and demand model can capture. Chapter 16 considered how consumers can get the biggest bang for their buck, or the greatest utility out of their purchases. Here we explore the question in more detail, using the tool of indifference curve analysis. The purpose of this appendix is to get you thinking at a deeper level about the connections between price changes and consumption decisions.

Indifference Curves

Indifference curves are a tool that economists use to describe the trade-offs that exist when consumers make decisions.

An **indifference curve** represents the various combinations of two goods that yield the same level of satisfaction, or utility. The simplest way to think about indifference curves is to envision a topographical

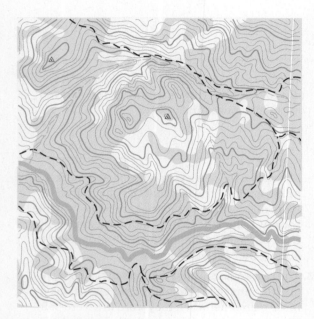

A topographical map and indifference curve analysis share many of the same properties.

An **indifference curve** represents the various combinations of two goods that yield the same level of personal satisfaction, or utility.

A **maximization point** is the point at which a certain combination of two goods yields the greatest possible utility.

map on which each line represents a specific elevation. When you look at a topographical map, you see ridges, mountains, valleys, and the subtle flow of the land. An indifference curve conveys the same complex information about personal satisfaction. Indifference curves visually rise to a peak called the **maximization point**, or the point at which utility is maximized. The only limitation of this analysis is that this book is a two-dimensional space used to illustrate a three-dimensional concept. Let's set this concern aside and focus on achieving the maximization point, where total utility is highest.

Returning to our example of pizza and Pepsi, recall that you had $10 to spend and only two items to purchase: Pepsi at $1 per can and pizza at $2 per slice. Like all consumers, you will optimize your utility by maximizing the marginal utility per dollar spent, so you select four Pepsis and three slices of pizza. But what happens if your budget is unlimited? If you're free to spend as much you like, how much pizza and Pepsi would you want?

Economic "Goods" and "Bads"

To answer the question we just posed, we'll start with another question. Are Pepsi and pizza always economic "goods"? This may seem like a strange question, but think about your own consumption habits. Do you keep eating something after you feel full? Do you continue to eat even if your stomach aches? At some point, we all stop eating and drinking. In this sense, economic goods, like Pepsi and pizza, are "good" only up to a point. Once we are full, however, the utility from attaining another unit of the good becomes negative—a "bad."

Each indifference curve represents lines of equal satisfaction. For simplicity, Figure 16A.1 shows the indifference curve as circles around the point of maximum satisfaction. The closer the indifference curve is to the maximization point, the higher the consumer's level of satisfaction.

FIGURE 16A.1

Indifference Curves

The maximization point indicates where a consumer attains the most utility. In quadrant I, both Pepsi and pizza are "goods" (because their consumption involves the reactions of either tasting great or getting full), so attaining more of each will cause utility to rise toward the maximization point. In quadrants II, III, and IV, either pizza or Pepsi is a "bad" or both are (because at those levels of consumption they make the consumer feel either too full or sick). Because the consumer must pay to acquire pizza and Pepsi, and because at least one of the items is reducing the consumer's utility in quadrants II, III, and IV, the most affordable path to the highest utility—that is, the maximization point—is quadrant I. (Notice that the labels are qualitative and reflect decreasing utility with additional consumption.)

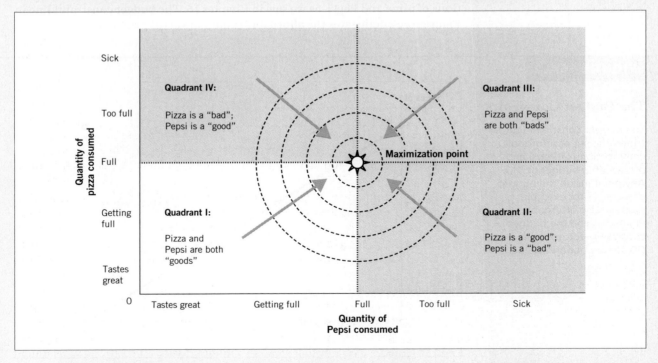

Indifference curves are best seen as approaching the maximization point from all directions (like climbing up a mountain on four different sides). In any hike, some paths are better than others. Figure 16A.1 illustrates four separate ways to reach the maximization point. However, only one of the paths makes any sense. In quadrants II, III, and IV, either pizza or Pepsi is a "bad" or both are "bads" (because at those levels of consumption one or both of them make the consumer feel too full or sick). Because the consumer must pay to acquire pizza and Pepsi, and because at least one of them is reducing the consumer's utility, the consumer's satisfaction will increase by purchasing less of the "bad." In other words, why would anyone willingly pay to feel worse? Quadrants II, III, and IV are highlighted in orange because people are unlikely to choose an option that makes them feel too full or sick. That leaves quadrant I as the preferred path to the highest utility. In quadrant I, increasing amounts of pizza and Pepsi produce more utility. (Notice that the labels in Figure 16A.1 are qualitative and reflect decreasing utility with additional consumption.)

The Budget Constraint

Figure 16A.1 illustrates the choices facing a consumer with an unlimited budget and no opportunity costs. However, in real life we need to account for a person's budget and the cost of acquiring each good. The amount a person has to spend is the **budget constraint**, or the set of consumption bundles that represent the maximum amount the consumer can afford. If you have $10 to spend on pizza ($2 per slice) and Pepsi ($1 per can), you could choose to purchase 10 cans of Pepsi and forgo the pizza. Alternatively, you could purchase 5 slices of pizza and do without the Pepsi. Or you could choose a number of different combinations of pizza and Pepsi, as we saw in Chapter 16. The budget constraint line in Figure 16A.2 delineates the affordable combinations of pizza and Pepsi.

The **budget constraint** is the set of consumption bundles that represent the maximum amount the consumer can afford.

The Budget Constraint

The budget constraint line shows the set of affordable combinations of Pepsi and pizza with a budget of $10. Any point inside the budget constraint—for example (2,2)—is also affordable. Points beyond the budget constraint—for example (10,5)—are not affordable.

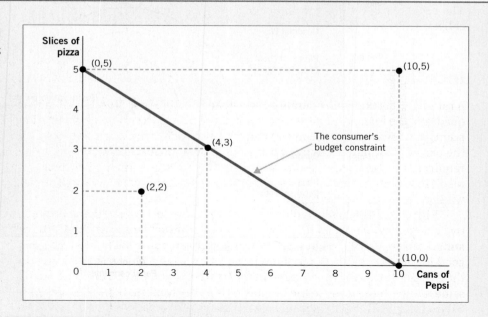

There are many different affordable combinations of the two goods. Let's take the pairs along the budget constraint line first. If you spend your entire $10 on Pepsi, the combination of coordinates would be the point (10,0), which represents 10 cans of Pepsi and 0 slices of pizza. If you spend your entire budget on pizza, the coordinates would be (0,5). These two points are the extreme outcomes. By connecting these two points with a line—the budget constraint—we can see the many combinations that would fully exhaust $10. As a consumer, your goal is to pick the combination that maximizes your satisfaction, subject to your budget constraint. One possibility would be to spend the $10 on four cans of Pepsi and three slices of pizza (4,3), which happens to be the point of utility maximization we discovered in the chapter (see Table 16.3).

What about the points located below and above the budget constraint? For example, looking again at Figure 16A.2, at the point (2,2) you would be spending $6—that is, $2 on Pepsi and $4 on pizza. You would still have $4 to spend on more of either good. Because both goods are desirable, spending the leftover money in your budget will increase your level of satisfaction. So the combination (2,2) represents a failure to maximize utility. On the other side of the budget constraint line, we find the point (10,5). This combination, which would cost you $20 to attain, represents a combination of items you cannot afford. From this example, you can see that the budget constraint is a limiting set of choices, or a constraint imposed by scarcity.

In the next section, we examine indifference curves in greater detail. Once we fully understand the properties that characterize indifference curves, we can join them with the budget constraint to better describe how consumers make choices.

Properties of Indifference Curves

It is useful to keep in mind several assumptions about indifference curves. The properties described in this section help ensure that our model is logically consistent.

Indifference Curves Are Typically Bowed Inward

A rational consumer will operate only in quadrant I in Figure 16A.1. Within that quadrant, the higher indifference curves (those nearer the utility maximization point) are bowed inward (convex) and are preferred to the lower ones (nearer the origin). Our model eliminates any outcome in quadrants II through IV by requiring that goods be "good," not "bad." Because quadrants II through IV result in less utility and greater expenditures, no rational consumer would ever willingly operate in these regions.

Figure 16A.3 shows an indifference curve that reflects the trade-off between two goods. Because the indifference curve bows inward, the **marginal rate of substitution (MRS)**, or the rate at which a consumer is willing to trade one good for another along the indifference curve, varies. The MRS is reflected in the slope of the indifference curve in the figure. Points A and B are both on the same indifference curve, so the consumer finds the combinations (1,5) and (2,3) to be equally attractive. Between points A and B, the consumer must receive two slices of pizza to compensate for the loss of a can of Pepsi. We can see this in the

The **marginal rate of substitution (MRS)** is the rate at which a consumer is willing to trade one good for another along an indifference curve.

Trade-offs

FIGURE 16A.3

The Marginal Rate of Substitution

The marginal rate of substitution (MRS) along an indifference curve varies, as reflected in the slope of the indifference curve. Because Pepsi and pizza are both subject to diminishing marginal utility, it takes more of the plentiful good to keep the consumer indifferent when giving up another good that is in short supply.

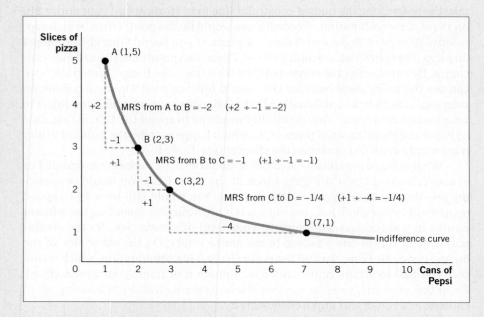

figure by observing that the consumer chooses only two cans of Pepsi and three slices of pizza at (2,3). Because the marginal utility from consuming Pepsi is high when the amount consumed is low, giving up an additional Pepsi requires that the consumer receive back two slices of pizza to reach the point (1,5). Therefore, the marginal rate of substitution (MRS) is −2 (because +2 ÷ −1 = −2).

However, if we examine the same indifference curve between points C and D, we see that the consumer is also indifferent between the combinations (3,2) and (7,1). However, this time the consumer is willing to give up four cans of Pepsi to get one more slice of pizza, so the MRS is −4 (because +1 ÷ −4 = −1/4). Why is there such a big difference between (3,2) and (7,1) compared with (2,3) and (1,5)? At (7,1), the consumer has a lot of Pepsi and very little pizza to enjoy it with. As a result, the marginal utility of the second slice of pizza is so high that it is worth four Pepsis! We can see the change in the marginal rate of substitution visually, because the slope between points A and B is steeper than it is between points C and D.

Marginal thinking

What explains why Pepsi is more valuable between points A and B? The consumer starts with only two cans. Pizza is more valuable between points C and D because the consumer starts with only two slices of pizza. Because Pepsi and pizza are both subject to diminishing marginal utility, it takes more of the plentiful good to keep the consumer indifferent when giving up another good that is in short supply.

Indifference Curves Cannot Be Thick

Another property of indifference curves is that they cannot be thick. If they could be thick, then it would be possible to draw two points inside an indifference curve where one of the two points was preferred to the other. Therefore, a

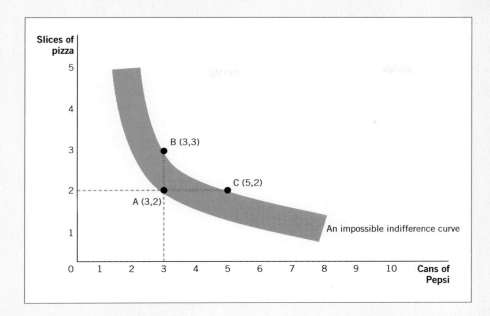

Indifference Curves Cannot Be Thick

If indifference curves could be thick, it would be possible to draw two points inside the curve in a way that indicates that one of the two points is preferred to the other. Point B has one extra slice of pizza and point C has two extra cans of Pepsi compared with point A. Therefore, the consumer cannot be indifferent between these three points, and the indifference curve cannot be thick.

consumer could be indifferent between those points. In Figure 16A.4, points A, B, and C are all located on the same (impossible) indifference curve. However, points B and C are both strictly preferred to point A. Why? Because point B has one extra slice of pizza compared with point A, and point C has two extra cans of Pepsi compared with point A. Because more pizza and Pepsi adds to the consumer's utility, the consumer cannot be indifferent between these three points.

Indifference Curves Cannot Intersect

Indifference curves, by their very nature, cannot intersect. To understand why, let's look at a hypothetical case. Figure 16A.5 shows two indifference curves crossing at point A. Points A and B are both located along the light orange curve (IC_1), so we know that those two points bring the consumer the same utility. Points A and C are both located along the darker orange curve (IC_2), so those two points also yield the same utility for the consumer. Therefore, the utility at point A equals the utility at point B, and the utility at point A also equals the utility at point C. This means that the utility at point B should also equal the utility at point C, but that cannot be true. Point B is located at (1,3), and point C is located at (2,4). Because (2,4) strictly dominates (1,3), point C is preferred to point B. Therefore, we can say that indifference curves cannot intersect without violating the assumption that consumers are rational utility maximizers.

We have seen that indifference curves have three properties: they are bowed inward toward the origin (convex); they cannot be thick; and they cannot intersect. These properties guarantee that they take the general levels shown in quadrant I of Figure 16A.1.

Indifference Curves Cannot Intersect

The utility at point B should equal the utility at point C, but that cannot be true even though the utility at point B is equal to the utility at point A (along IC$_1$) and the utility at point C is equal to the utility at point A (along IC$_2$). Point B is located at (1,3) and point C is located at (2,4). Because (2,4) strictly dominates (1,3), point C is preferred to point B. Indifference curves cannot intersect.

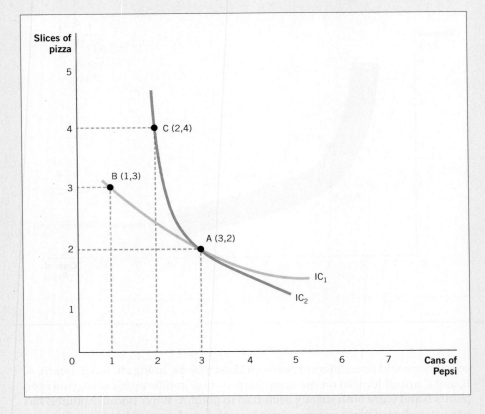

Extreme Preferences: Perfect Substitutes and Perfect Complements

As we have just seen, indifference curves typically are convex and bow inward toward the origin. However, there are two exceptions: *perfect substitutes* and *perfect complements*. These are found on either side of the standard-shaped, convex indifference curve.

Perfect substitutes exist when a consumer is completely indifferent between two goods. Suppose that you cannot taste any difference between Aquafina and Evian bottled water. You would be indifferent between drinking one additional bottle of Aquafina or one additional bottle of Evian. Turning to panel (a) of Figure 16A.6, you can see that the indifference curves (IC$_1$, IC$_2$, IC$_3$, IC$_4$) for these two goods are straight, parallel lines with a marginal rate of substitution, or slope, of –1 everywhere along the curve. However, it's important to note that the slope of an indifference curve of perfect substitutes need not always be –1; it can be any constant rate. Because perfect substitutes have a marginal rate of substitution with a constant rate, they are drawn as straight lines.

Perfect complements exist when a consumer is interested in consuming two goods in fixed proportions. Shoes are an excellent example. We buy shoes in pairs because the left or right shoe is not valuable by itself; we need both shoes

Perfect substitutes
exist when the consumer is completely indifferent between two goods, resulting in a straight-line indifference curve with a constant marginal rate of substitution.

Perfect complements
exist when the consumer is interested in consuming two goods in fixed proportions, resulting in a right-angle indifference curve.

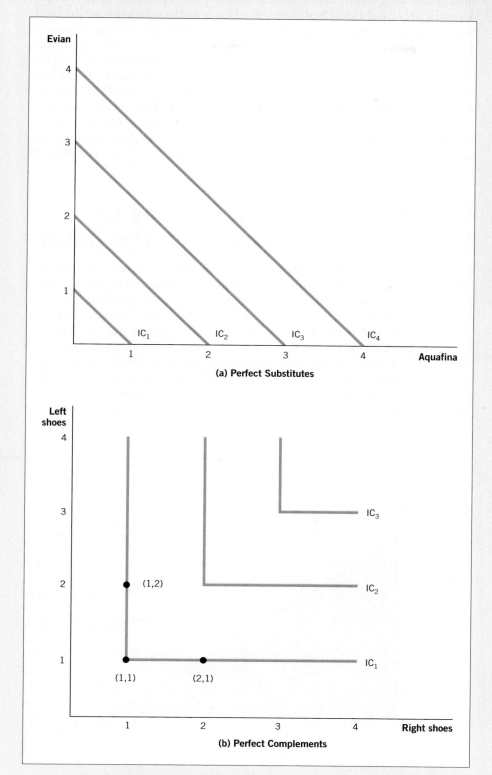

Perfect Substitutes and Perfect Complements

(a) Because perfect substitutes have a marginal rate of substitution that is constant, they are drawn as straight lines. In this case, the MRS, or slope, is −1 everywhere along the lines, or curves. (b) Perfect complements are drawn as right angles. A typical indifference curve that reflects the trade-off between two goods that are not perfect substitutes or perfect complements has a marginal rate of substitution that falls between these two extremes.

(a) Perfect Substitutes

(b) Perfect Complements

to be able to walk comfortably. This explains why shoes are not sold individually. An extra left or right shoe has no marginal value to the consumer, so the indifference curves are right angles. For instance, left and right shoes are needed in a 1:1 ratio. Let's look at indifference curve IC_1 in panel (b) of Figure 16A.6. This curve forms a right angle at the point (1,1) where the person has one left and one right shoe. Now notice that the points (1,2) and (2,1) are also on IC_1. Because an extra left or right shoe by itself does not add utility, the points (1,2), (1,1), and (2,1) are all connected, since the individual has only one pair of usable shoes.

Perfect complements can also occur in combinations other than 1:1. For instance, an ordinary chair needs four legs for each seat. In that case, the indifference curve is still a right angle, but additional chair legs do not enhance the consumer's utility unless they come in groups of four.

Using Indifference Curves to Illustrate the Consumer Optimum

Figure 16A.7 shows the relationship between indifference curves and the budget constraint. The area bounded by the budget constraint (shaded in purple) represents the set of possible choices—what the consumer can afford. The highest indifference curve that can be attained within the set of possible choices is IC_3, where the budget constraint is just tangent to (that is, just touches) IC_3. Even though all the points on IC_4 are more desirable than those on IC_3, the consumer lacks the purchasing power to reach the level of satisfaction represented by IC_4. Moreover, the point (4,3) is now clearly the preferred choice among the set of possible decisions. Other choices that are also affordable—for example, the combination (2,4)—fall on a lower (and hence less preferable) indifference curve. Point (4,3) is the consumer optimum.

FIGURE 16A.7

Consumer Optimum

Progressively higher indifference curves bring the consumer closer to the maximization point. Because the budget constraint limits what the consumer can afford, the tangency of the budget constraint with the highest indifference curve represents the highest level of affordable satisfaction—that is, the consumer optimum. In this case, the point (4,3) represents the consumer's preferred combination of Pepsi and pizza.

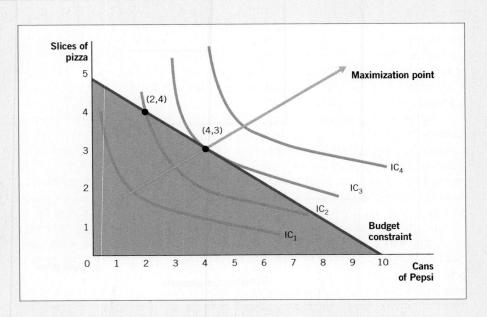

Progressively higher indifference curves bring the consumer closer to the maximization point. Because the budget constraint limits what the consumer can afford, the tangency of the budget constraint with the highest indifference curve represents the highest affordable level of satisfaction—that is, the consumer optimum.

Using Indifference Curves to Illustrate the Real-Income and Substitution Effects

The power of indifference curve analysis is its ability to display how price changes affect consumption choices. Part of the intuition behind the analysis involves understanding when the substitution effect is likely to dominate the real-income effect, and vice versa.

In our example, you have only $10, so a price increase on Pepsi from $1 to $2 per can would represent a financial burden, significantly lowering your real purchasing power. However, we can easily think of cases in which a change in the price of Pepsi wouldn't matter. Suppose yours is a typical American household with a median annual income of $60,000. While out shopping, you observe that a local Toyota car dealer is offering 10% off new cars and a nearby grocery store is selling Pepsi at a 10% discount. Because of the substitution effect, more people will buy Toyotas instead of Hondas, and more people will buy Pepsi instead of Coca-Cola. However, the real-income effects will be quite different. Saving 10% on the price of a new car could easily amount to a savings of $3,000 or more. In contrast, saving 10% on a 2-liter bottle of Pepsi will save only a couple of dimes. In the case of the new car, there is a substantial real-income effect, while the amount you save on the Pepsi is almost immaterial.

As we have just seen, changes in prices can have two distinct effects. The first is a substitution effect, under which changes in price will cause the consumer to substitute toward a good that becomes relatively less expensive. In our Pepsi/pizza example, suppose that the price of Pepsi rises to $2 per can. This price increase reduces your marginal utility per dollar of consuming Pepsi. As a result, you would probably buy fewer Pepsis and use the remaining money to purchase more pizza. In effect, you would substitute the relatively less expensive good (pizza) for the relatively more expensive good (Pepsi).

However, this is not the only effect at work. The change in the product price will also alter the purchasing power of your money, or income. And a change in purchasing power generates a real-income effect. In this case, your $10 will not go as far as it used to. In Figure 16A.8, we can see that the inward rotation of the budget constraint along the x axis from BC_1 to BC_2 is a result of the rise in the price of Pepsi. At $2 per can, you can no longer afford to buy 10 cans; the most you can purchase is 5. Therefore, the budget constraint moves inward along the x axis to 5 units while remaining constant along the y axis (because the price of pizza did not change). As a result, the combination (4,3) is no longer affordable. The higher price of Pepsi produces a new consumer optimum at (2,3) along IC_2. The end result is predictable: a rise in the price of Pepsi causes you to purchase less Pepsi and yields a lower level of satisfaction at IC_2 than your former point on IC_3 did, which is no longer possible.

How a Change in Price Rotates the Budget Constraint

The inward rotation of the budget constraint along the x axis from BC_1 to BC_2 is a result of the rise in the price of Pepsi. At the price of $2 a can, you can no longer afford to buy 10 cans; the most you can purchase is 5. Therefore, the budget constraint moves inward along the x axis to 5 units (causing utility to fall from IC_3 to IC_2) while remaining constant along the y axis (because the price of pizza slices did not change).

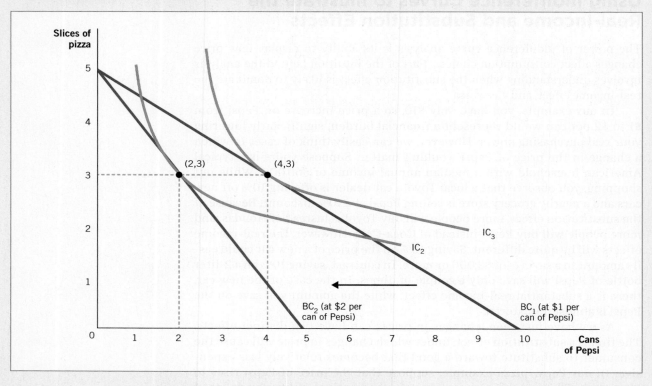

Separating the Substitution Effect from the Real-Income Effect

In this section, we separate the substitution effect from the real-income effect, and we see how the two effects can either reinforce each other or tend to cancel each other out (see Figure 16A.9).

With Pepsi at its new $2-per-can price, you're ready to buy your revised optimum quantities, 2 cans of Pepsi and 3 slices of pizza. Then you learn that Pepsi has briefly gone on sale, at its old price of $1 per can. How will you respond? Since at the old Pepsi price, your optimum was at (4, 3), we know you'll end up back there again. But let's break your move from (2, 3) to (4, 3) into two steps.

Step 1. You were about to content yourself with 2 Pepsis and 3 pizza slices. Since that purchase now comes to $8 instead of $10, you just caught a break. But notice: theoretically you could be equally happy *for even less* than $8. Simply slide along curve IC_2 to the consumption point that is cheapest, given the sale on Pepsi. That would be point A, where you're buying about 2 1/2 cans of Pepsi and 2 1/2 slices of pizza, for a total price of right around $7.50. We can even draw a new budget constraint through this point—call it BC "two point five"—based on the new prices, where we pretend that you have only $7.50 to spend. With that budget, Point A is your consumer optimum. You're just as happy as you would have been at (2, 3), but you've saved money by substituting Pepsi for pizza, because Pepsi is cheaper compared to pizza than it was before. This is the substitution effect. (You would also, by the way, be substituting Pepsi for pizza if instead the price of pizza had gone up. What matters for the substitution effect is how *relative* prices change.)

Step 2. Okay, so you can't actually buy fractional Pepsis and pizza slices. It doesn't matter, though, because you're not actually on a $7.50 budget. You're on a $10 budget, and therefore able to buy both more pizza and more Pepsi. So, we shift the $7.50 line out to make it a $10 constraint, keeping the slope the same to reflect the current pizza-to-Pepsi price ratio. This is the real-income effect,

FIGURE 16A.9

Separating the Substitution Effect from the Real-Income Effect

Breaking down the movement from IC_2 to IC_3 into the substitution effect and the real-income effect allows us to see how each impacts the consumer's choice. The substitution effect increases the amount of Pepsi consumed and decreases the consumption of pizza, as indicated by the blue arrows and the leveling out of the budget constraint, from BC_2 to $BC_{2.5}$. The real-income effect increases the amounts of both Pepsi and pizza, as indicated by the green arrows and the shift of the budget constraint, from $BC_{2.5}$ to BC_3.

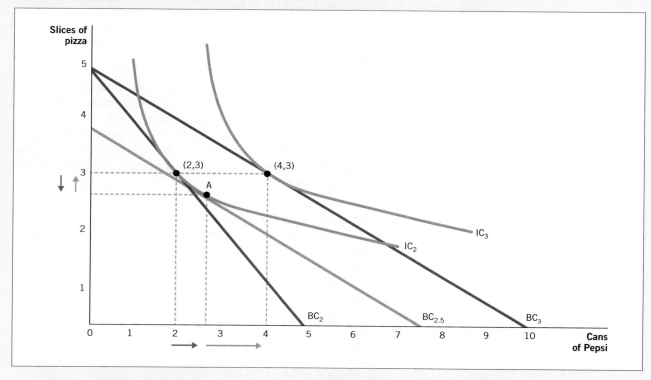

which is based on purchasing power. Again you seek your consumer optimum, where the $10 budget constraint, BC_3 (formerly known as BC_1), grazes curve IC_3, and that's point (4, 3). Enjoy your meal!

The substitution and real-income effects influenced the consumption quantities of pizza and Pepsi in different ways. With pizza the effects canceled out: you bought less pizza because of the substitution effect (the blue arrow pointing down) but more pizza because of the real-income effect (the green arrow pointing up). That's how you started and ended at 3 slices. With Pepsi, on the other hand, the two effects reinforced each other: you bought more Pepsi because of the substitution effect, going from 2 cans to 2 1/2 (the blue arrow pointing right), and yet more because of the real-income effect, going from 2 1/2 cans to 4 (the green arrow pointing right). More generally, whenever the price of a good decreases, the result will be an increase in the amount consumed, because the real-income and substitution effects point in the same direction. By contrast, because the real-income effect and substitution effect move in opposite directions with respect to the good whose price has not changed, the result is ambiguous for that good (pizza), and any change in consumption depends on which effect—the substitution effect or the real-income effect—is greater. Here, they happened to be equal.

In our example, when the price of Pepsi drops back to $1 per can, it produces a large real-income effect. Prior to the price drop, you were spending $4 out of your $10 budget on Pepsi, so Pepsi expenditures represented 40% of your budget. Because Pepsi is a big component of your budget, a halving of its price causes a sizable real-income effect. This is not always the case, however. For example, if the price of a candy bar were to halve, the typical household would barely notice this change. In cases like that, the real-income effect is negligible and the substitution effect tends to dominate.

Conclusion

Economists use indifference curve analysis to gain additional insights into consumer behavior. This analysis extends the basic understanding found in supply and demand analysis by incorporating utility theory. Because indifference curves are lines of equal utility, we can impose a budget constraint to describe the bundle of goods that maximizes utility. This framework enables us to illustrate the effect of price changes and budget constraints on the decisions that consumers make. ✳

· APPENDIX PROBLEMS ·

Concepts You Should Know

budget constraint (p. 532)
indifference curve (p. 530)
marginal rate of substitution (MRS) (p. 533)

maximization point (p. 530)
perfect complements (p. 536)
perfect substitutes (p. 536)

Questions for Review

1. If your budget increases, what generally happens to the amount of utility you experience?

2. If your budget increases, is it possible for your utility to fall? Explain your response.

3. What is the difference between an economic "good" and an economic "bad"?

4. Describe what happens to your budget constraint if the price of one item in your budget decreases. Show the result on a graph.

5. A friend mentions to you that the campus coffee shop offers a 10% discount each Thursday morning before 10 a.m. Is this discount more likely to cause a significant substitution effect or a significant real-income effect? Explain.

Study Problems *(* solved at the end of the section)*

1. Kate has $20. Fish sandwiches cost $5, and a cup of espresso costs $4. Draw Kate's budget constraint. If espresso goes on sale for $2 a cup, what does her new budget constraint look like?

2. When you head home for dinner, your mother always sets the table with one spoon, two forks, and one knife. Draw her indifference curves for forks and knives.

✳ 3. Frank's indifference curves for movies and bowling look like the figure to the right.

Each game of bowling costs $4, and each movie costs $8. If Frank has $24 to spend, how many times will he go bowling? How many times will he go to the movies?

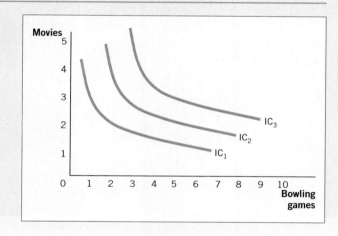

Solved Problem

3. Because Frank has $24 to spend, he can afford $24 ÷ $4, or six games of bowling. If he spends his money instead on movies, he can afford $24 ÷ $8, or three movies. Because Frank's budget constraint (BC) is just tangent to IC_1 at the point (2,2), Frank will go to two movies and bowl two games.

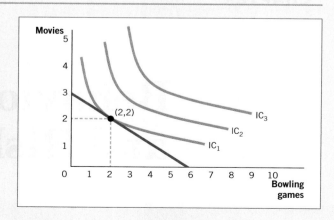

Behavioral Economics and Risk Taking

People Don't Always Make Rational Decisions.

In this textbook, we have proceeded as if every person were *Homo economicus*, a rationally self-interested decision-maker. This idealized individual is acutely aware of opportunities in the environment and strives to maximize the benefits received from each course of action while minimizing the costs. What does *Homo economicus* look like? If you are a fan of *Star Trek*, you'll recall Spock, the Vulcan with perfect logic. He eschewed human emotion and didn't face many of the complications it creates for making decisions. Spock is *Star Trek*'s *Homo economicus*.

Kirk, by contrast, famously goes with his gut when the chips are down. In *Star Trek Into Darkness*, he saves a planet's inhabitants by making a snap decision to ignore the Prime Directive (not for the first time) and letting them see the *Enterprise*. Kirk's seat-of-his-pants style of decision-making often serves him and his shipmates, and various and sundry aliens, well. Remember, though: this is fiction! In the real world, the story is more complicated. Sometimes our instincts do steer us in the right direction. More commonly, however, they lead us astray in various subtle ways. In this chapter, we'll see how that happens. To fold the broadest possible set of human behavior into economic analysis, we must turn to the field of *behavioral*

Yet again, Spock has his mind blown by Kirk trusting his gut and getting away with it. "Why does he *do* that?" he's thinking. Answer: It's a movie, folks. Don't try this at home.

economics, which enables us to capture a wider range of human motivations than the rational-agent model alone affords.

- How do economists explain irrational behavior?
- What is the role of risk in decision-making?

How Do Economists Explain Irrational Behavior?

Like economics, psychology endeavors to understand the choices people make. One key difference is that psychologists do not assume that people always behave in a fully rational way. As a result, psychologists have a much broader toolbox at their disposal to describe human behavior. **Behavioral economics** is the field of economics that draws on insights from experimental psychology to explore how people make economic decisions.

Until relatively recently, economists have ignored many human behaviors that do not fit their models. For example, because traditional economic theory assumed that people make optimal decisions, economic theorists did not try to explain why people might make an impulse purchase. Behavioral economists, however, understand that many behaviors contradict standard assumptions about rationality. They employ the idea of **bounded rationality**, which proposes that although decision-makers want a good outcome, either they are not capable of performing the problem-solving that traditional economic theory assumes or they are not inclined to do so.

Bounded rationality, or limited reasoning, can be explained in three ways. First, the information the individual uses to make the decision may be limited or incomplete. Second, the human brain has a limited capacity to process information. Third, there is often a limited amount of time in which to make a decision. These limitations prevent the decision-maker from reaching the results predicted under perfect rationality.

For example, suppose you're about to get married and find yourself at Kleinfeld Bridal with your bridesmaids. You enter the store to begin your search for the perfect wedding dress. You find a dress you like, but its price is higher than you were planning to spend. Do you make the purchase or not? The decision to buy depends on whether you believe that the value is high enough to justify the price. But there is a problem: you have a limited amount of information. In a fully rational world, you would check out alternatives in other stores and on the Internet and then make the decision to purchase the dress only

Behavioral economics is the field of economics that draws on insights from experimental psychology to explore how people make economic decisions.

Bounded rationality (also called limited reasoning) proposes that although decision-makers want a good outcome, either they are not capable of performing the problem solving that traditional economic theory assumes or they are not inclined to do so.

after you were satisfied it was the best possible choice. Full rationality also assumes that your brain is able to recall the features of every dress. However, a dress you tried on at one location often blurs into another dress you tried on elsewhere. Wedding dresses are selected under a binding deadline. This deadline means that you, the bride, must reach a decision quickly. Collectively, these three reasons often prevent a bride from achieving the result that economists' rational models predict. In reality, you walk into a store, see something you love, and make the purchase using partial information. Whenever people end up making decisions without perfect information, the decisions reflect bounded rationality.

We will continue our discussion of behavioral economics by examining various behaviors that do not fit assumptions about fully rational behavior. These include misperceptions of probabilities, inconsistencies in decision-making, and judgments about fairness when making decisions. The goal in this section is to help you recognize and understand many of the behaviors that lead to contradictions between what economic models predict and what people actually do.

Will you say yes to the dress?

Misperceptions of Probabilities

Economic models that assume rationality in decision-making do not account for the way people perceive the probability of events. Low-probability events are often overanticipated, and high-probability events are often underanticipated. To understand why, we consider several familiar examples, including games of chance, difficulties in assessing probabilities, and seeing patterns where none exist.

GAMES OF CHANCE Playing games of chance—for example, a lottery or a slot machine—is generally a losing proposition. Yet even with great odds against winning, millions of people spend money to play games of chance. How can we explain this behavior?

For some people, the remote chance of winning a lottery offers hope that they will be able to purchase something they need but cannot afford or even to escape from poverty. In many cases, people have incomplete information about the probabilities and prize structures. Most lottery players do not calculate the exact odds of winning. Lottery agencies typically highlight winners, as if the game has a positive expected value, which gets people excited about playing. Imagine how sobering it would be if every headline trumpeting the newest lottery millionaire was followed by all the names of people who lost. In fact, almost all games of chance have *negative expected values* for the participants, meaning that players are not likely to succeed at the game.

Players often operate under the irrational belief that they have control over the outcome. They are sure that playing certain numbers or patterns (for example, birthdays, anniversaries, or other lucky numbers) will bring success. Many players also feel they must stick with their favorite numbers to

Many games of chance return only about 50 cents for every dollar played.

Incentives

avoid regret; everyone has heard stories about players who changed from their lucky pattern only to watch it win.

In contrast, some gaming behaviors are rational. For example, the film *21* depicts how skilled blackjack players, working in tandem, can beat the casinos by betting strategically and paying close attention to the cards on the table. In fact, some individuals are able to win at blackjack by counting the cards that have been dealt. Anytime the expected value of a gamble is positive, there is an incentive to play. For instance, if a friend wants to wager $10.00 on the flip of a coin and promises you $25.00 if you guess right, the expected value is half of $25.00, or $12.50. (There are only 2 possible outcomes, heads or tails, so your chances of winning are 1 in 2, or 1/2. So $1/2 \times \$25.00 = \$12.50$.) Because $12.50 is greater than the $10.00 you are wagering, we say that the gamble has a *positive expected value*. When the expected value of a gamble is positive, we actually expect that the more you play, the more likely it is that your earnings will be larger than your losses.

Gambles can also make sense when you have very little to lose or no other options. And some people find the thrill of gambling enjoyable as entertainment, whether they win or lose. However, most gambling behaviors do not have rational motivations. Gambling often creates addictions that lead players to make poor financial decisions.

THE DIFFICULTIES IN ASSESSING PROBABILITIES In our discussion of games of chance, we saw that people who gamble do not usually evaluate probabilities in a rational way. But this irrational decision-making also happens with many other behaviors besides gambling. For example, on a per-mile basis, traveling by airplane is approximately 10 times safer than traveling by automobile. However, millions of people who refuse to fly because they are afraid of a crash do not hesitate to get into a car. Driving seems to create a false sense of control over one's surroundings.

The long-running television game show *Let's Make a Deal* provides a well-known example of the difficulties in assessing probabilities accurately. At the end of the show, the host would ask a contestant to choose one of three curtains. Behind each curtain was one of three possible prizes: a car, a nice but less expensive item, or a worthless joke item. Contestants could have maximized their chances of winning the car if they had used probability theory to make a selection. However, contestants rarely chose in a rational way.

Suppose you are a contestant on a game show like *Let's Make a Deal*. You pick curtain number 3. The host, who knows what is behind the curtains, opens a different one—say, curtain number 1, which has a pen filled with chickens (the joke prize). He then offers you the opportunity to switch your choice to curtain number 2. According to probability theory, what is the right thing to do? Most contestants would stay with their original choice because they figure that now they have a 50/50 chance of winning the car. But the probability of winning with your original

If you were a contestant, would you make a rational choice?

Misperceptions of Probabilities

THE BIG BANG THEORY: THE SEPTUM DEVIATION

At the start of the episode, Leonard returns from a visit with his doctor, who explained to Leonard why he snores and gets sinus infections.

SHELDON: Hey, how did it go?

LEONARD: Oh, not fun. The doctor shoved a camera up into my sinuses.

AMY: Did they figure out what's wrong?

LEONARD: Yeah. It's a deviated septum. The surgery to correct it is simple. He's gonna do it next week.

Alarmed, Sheldon tries to convince Leonard that the risk of death from elective surgery is higher than most people realize. However, Sheldon seems fixated on a series of extremely unlikely possibilities.

SHELDON: I've been crunching the numbers, and so far, I've gotten your probability of death all the way to a sphincter-tightening one in 300 . . . What about epilepsy?

LEONARD: I don't have epilepsy.

SHELDON: You don't, but the surgeon might, hmm? And your carotid artery is just one shaky scalpel away from becoming the dancing fountain at Disneyland.

LEONARD: Sheldon, do you realize that driving is riskier than surgery?

Is Sheldon overthinking the risks of Leonard's minor surgery?

SHELDON: I do. I have the drive to the hospital right here. That is if you make it to the car without falling down the stairs.

LEONARD: Buddy, I, I get that you're worried about me and I, I appreciate that, but I'm not going to die.

SHELDON: You don't know that.

LEONARD: Well, I do know that it won't be from an asteroid strike.

SHELDON: You know who else said that? Every cocky *T. Rex* currently swimming around in the gas tank of your car.

choice remains 1/3, because the chance that you guessed correctly the first time is unchanged. Equally, the chance that one of the other curtains contains the car is still 2/3. But with curtain number 1 revealed as the joke prize, that 2/3 probability now belongs entirely to curtain number 2. Therefore, the contestant should take the switch, because it upgrades the chance of winning the car from 1/3 to 2/3. Few contestants make the switch, though. Almost all contestants think that each of the two remaining unopened curtains has an equal probability of holding the car, so they decide not to switch for fear of regretting their decision. Not switching indicates a failure to understand the opportunity costs involved in the decision.

Opportunity cost

The difficulty in recognizing the true underlying probabilities, combined with an irrational fear of regret, leads to many poor decisions. Understanding these tendencies helps economists to evaluate why some decisions are difficult to get right.

SEEING PATTERNS WHERE NONE EXIST Two fallacies, or false ways of thinking, help explain how some people make decisions: the *gambler's fallacy* and the *hot hand fallacy*.

The gambler's fallacy is the belief that recent outcomes are unlikely to be repeated and that outcomes that have not occurred recently are due to happen soon.

The **gambler's fallacy** is the belief that recent outcomes are unlikely to be repeated and that outcomes that have not occurred recently are due to happen soon. For example, studies examining state lotteries find that bets on recent winning numbers decline. Because the selection of winning numbers is made randomly, just like flipping coins, the probability that a certain number will be a winner in one week is not related to whether the number came up in the previous week. In other words, someone who uses the gambler's fallacy believes that if many "heads" have occurred in a row, then "tails" is more likely to occur next.

The hot hand fallacy is the belief that random sequences exhibit a positive correlation (relationship).

The **hot hand fallacy** is the belief that random sequences exhibit a positive correlation (relationship). The classic study in this area examined perceptions about the game of basketball. Most sports enthusiasts believe that a player who has scored several baskets in a row—one with a "hot hand"—is more likely to score a basket with his or her next shot than at another time. However, the study found no positive correlation between success in one shot and success in the next shot.

ECONOMICS IN THE REAL WORLD

HOW BEHAVIORAL ECONOMICS HELPS TO EXPLAIN STOCK PRICE VOLATILITY

Let's examine some of the traps that people fall into when they invest in the stock market. In a fully rational world, the gambler's fallacy and the hot hand fallacy would not exist. In the real world, however, people are prone to seeing patterns in data even when there are none. Investors, for example, often believe that the rise and fall of the stock market is driven by specific events and by underlying metrics such as profitability, market share, and return on investment. But, in fact, investors often react with a herd mentality by rushing into stocks that appear to be doing well—reflecting the hot hand fallacy—and selling off stocks when a downward trend seems to be occurring. Similarly, there are times when investors believe that the stock market has run up or down too rapidly and they expect its direction to change soon—reflecting the gambler's fallacy.

Ulrike Malmendier studies behavioral economics and is a leading expert on how biases affect corporate decisions, stock prices, and markets in general. "Biases don't only affect decision-making by small investors and consumers; they also affect top business leaders," Malmendier says. She likes to quote Warren Buffett, who once remarked, "I'd be a bum on the

Ulrike Malmendier, *Homo economicus* mythbuster.

street with a tin cup if the markets were efficient." In her work on hubris, she found that executives who won prestigious awards, such as "CEO of the Year," tended to underperform their noncelebrity peers in the years just after the prestigious award was bestowed, proving that overconfidence could be detrimental to profits. One likely way this plays out is that award-winning CEOs think they have a hot hand and therefore take risks they shouldn't.[*]

In addition, some segments of the market are driven by investor psychology instead of metrics that measure valuation. Research has also shown that mood matters: believe it or not, there is a small correlation between the weather and how the stock market trades on a particular day. The market is more likely to move higher when it is sunny on Wall Street than when it is cloudy! The very fact that the weather in Lower Manhattan could have anything to do with how the overall stock market performs is strong evidence that some market participants are not rational.

*Source: http://www.haas.berkeley.edu/groups/pubs/berkeleyhaas/summer2014/faculty-rock-stars-toby-stuart-ulrike-malmendier.html.

PRACTICE WHAT YOU KNOW

Gambler's Fallacy or Hot Hand Fallacy? Patterns on Exams

Your instructor is normally conscientious and makes sure that exam answers are randomly distributed. However, you notice that the first five answers on the multiple-choice section are all C. Unsure what this pattern means, you consider the next question. You do not know the answer and are forced to guess. You decide to avoid C because you figure that C cannot happen six times in a row.

Do you ever wonder what it means when the same answer comes up many times in a row?

QUESTION: Which is at work: the gambler's fallacy or the hot hand fallacy?

ANSWER: According to the gambler's fallacy, recent events are less likely to be repeated again in the near future. So it is the gambler's fallacy at work here in your decision to avoid marking another C. If you had acted on the hot hand fallacy, you would have believed that random sequences exhibit a positive correlation and therefore would have marked the next answer as C.

CHALLENGE QUESTION: Suppose that instead of all C's, the first five answers are B, A, C, D, B. Again you are forced to guess. You avoid B because it's the one answer that was already used twice. Is this reasonable?

ANSWER: It's the same gambler's fallacy again, just in subtler form. If the answers are random, it doesn't matter what the first five answers were. They have *nothing to do* with the sixth answer.

Inconsistencies in Decision-Making

Trade-offs

If people were entirely rational, they would always be consistent. So the way a question is asked should not alter our responses, but research has shown that it does. Likewise, rational decision-making requires the ability to take the long-run trade-offs into account: if the returns are large enough, people should be willing to sacrifice current enjoyment for future benefits. Yet many of us make shortsighted decisions. In this section, we examine a variety of decision-making mistakes, including framing effects, priming effects, status quo bias, and inter-temporal decision-making.

FRAMING EFFECTS AND PRIMING EFFECTS We have seen a number of ways in which economic models do not entirely account for the behavior of real people. One common mistake that people make involves the **framing effect,** which occurs when an answer is influenced by the way a question is asked or a decision is influenced by the way alternatives are presented. Consider an employer-sponsored retirement plan. Companies can either (1) ask employees if they want to join or (2) use an automatic enrollment system and ask employees to let them know if they do not wish to participate. Studies have shown that workers who are asked if they want to join tend to participate at a much lower rate than those who are automatically enrolled and must say they want to opt out. Surely, a rational economic decision-maker would determine whether to participate by evaluating the plan itself, not by responding to the way the employer presents the option to participate. However, people are rarely that rational!

> The **framing effect** occurs when people change their answer depending on how the question is asked (or change their decision depending on how alternatives are presented).

Another decision-making pitfall, known as the **priming effect**, occurs when the order of the questions influences the answers. For example, consider two groups of college students. The first group is asked "How happy are you?" followed by "How many dates have you had in the last year?" The second group is asked "How many dates have you had in the last year?" followed by "How happy are you?" The questions are the same, but they are presented in reverse order. In the second group, students who had gone out on more dates reported being much happier than similar students in the first group! In other words, because they were reminded of the number of dates first, those who had more dates believed they were happier.

> The **priming effect** occurs when the order of the questions influences the answers.

STATUS QUO BIAS When people want to keep things the way they are, they may exhibit what is known as the **status quo bias**. This bias leads decision-makers to try to protect what they have, even when an objective evaluation of their circumstances suggests that a change would be beneficial.

> **Status quo bias** exists when decision-makers want to keep things the way they are.

The status quo bias causes people to behave conservatively. The cost of this behavior is missed opportunities that could potentially enhance welfare. For example, an individual with status quo bias would maintain a savings account with a low interest rate instead of actively shopping for better rates elsewhere. This person would lose the potential benefits from higher returns on savings.

Status quo bias also explains why new products and ideas have trouble gaining traction: many potential customers prefer to leave things the way they are, even if something new might make more sense. Consider the $1 coin. It is far more durable than the $1 bill. It is also easier to tell the $1 coin apart from

Framing

INSIDE OUT

Pixar's *Inside Out* (2015) is a hilarious romp that illustrates how five human emotions impact everyday decisions. The film shows that humans do not behave rationally but instead are guided by mental shortcuts and influenced by emotional biases. Moreover, our different emotions provide different ways of framing the same situation. If there's an opportunity to go out in the rain, Joy will ask if we want to go jump around in puddles, while Sadness will ask if we want to stand outside while our boots fill with water. Fear will wonder if it is safe and suggest we stay inside—that's the status quo bias.

Joy, the default emotion in the movie, influences us in ways that are usually good, but not always. Joy helps us face challenges and makes life worth living. Joy also derives utility from small acts of kindness and gives us the pluck to smile when life gets tough. But too much optimism is itself a kind of bias. When we are happy, we don't believe that bad things will happen to us, like traffic accidents—so we may drive too fast. (Joy rides, anyone?) Riley, the teenage girl who is the film's main character,

Our lives are a whirlwind of emotions that make fully rational decisions impossible most of the time.

needed more than simply Joy in her life. Riley also needed Sadness to help her cope with her cross-country move. Our emotions are complex, and each plays a crucial role in helping us navigate life. So it shouldn't be surprising to anyone trying to explain human behavior that our emotional states will influence our choices and how rationally or irrationally we make them.

---

the other coins and bills in your wallet, and if people used the coin, the government would save about $5 billion in production costs over the next 30 years. That sounds like a slam-dunk policy change, but it is not. Americans like their dollar bills and rarely use the $1 coins in circulation even though they repeatedly use nickels, dimes, and quarters to make change, to feed parking meters, and to buy from vending machines. Introducing more of the $1 coin and eliminating the $1 bill would be rational, but the status quo bias has prevented the change from happening.

Are you on Team Dollar Bill or Team Dollar Coin?

ECONOMICS IN THE REAL WORLD

ARE YOU AN ORGAN DONOR?

More than 25,000 organ transplants take place every year in the United States, with the vast majority coming from deceased donors. Demand greatly exceeds supply. Over 100,000 people are currently on organ donation waiting lists. Most Americans are

In the United States, you must opt in to become an organ donor.

aware of the need, and 90% of all Americans say they support donation. But only 30% know the essential steps to take to become a donor.

There are two main donor systems: the "opt-in" system and the "opt-out" system. In an opt-in system, individuals must give explicit consent to be a donor. In an opt-out system, anyone who has not explicitly refused is considered a donor.

In the United States, donors are required to opt in. Because opting in generally produces fewer donors than opting out, many states have sought to raise donation awareness by allowing consent to be noted on individual driver's licenses.

In Europe, many countries have opt-out systems, where consent is presumed. The difference is crucial. After all, in places with opt-in systems, many people who would be willing to donate organs never actually take the time to complete the necessary steps to opt in. In countries like France and Poland, where people must opt out, over 90% of citizens do not explicitly opt out, which means they give consent. This strategy yields organ donation rates that are significantly higher than those of opt-in programs.

According to traditional economic analysis, opting in or opting out should not matter—the results should be the same. The fact that we find strong evidence to the contrary is a compelling illustration of the framing effect.

Intertemporal decision-making involves planning to do something over a period of time, which requires valuing the present and the future consistently.

INTERTEMPORAL DECISION-MAKING Intertemporal decisions occur across time. **Intertemporal decision-making**—that is, planning to do something over a period of time—requires the ability to value the present and the future consistently. For instance, many people, despite their best intentions, do not end up saving enough for retirement. The temptation to spend money today ends up overwhelming the willpower to save for tomorrow. In a perfectly rational world, a person would not need outside assistance to save enough for retirement. In the real world, however, workers depend on 401(k) plans and other work-sponsored retirement programs to deduct funds from their paycheck so that they don't spend that portion of their income on other things. It may seem odd that people would need an outside agency to help them do something that is in their own long-term interest, but as long as their intertemporal decisions are likely to be inconsistent, the additional commitment helps them to achieve their long-run objectives.

Can you resist eating one marshmallow now in order to get a second one later?

The ability to resist temptation is illustrated by a classic research experiment conducted at a preschool at Stanford University in 1972. One at a time, individual children were led into a room devoid of distractions and were offered a marshmallow. The researchers explained to each child that he or she could eat the marshmallow right away or wait for 15 minutes and be rewarded with a second marshmallow. Very few of the 600 children in the study ate the marshmallow immediately. Most tried to fight the temptation. Of those who tried to wait, approximately one-third held out long enough to earn the second marshmallow. That finding is interesting by itself, but what happened next is truly amazing. Many of the parents of the children in the original study noticed that the children who had delayed gratification seemed to perform better as they progressed through school. Researchers have tracked the participants over the course of 40 years and found that the delayed-gratification group had higher SAT scores, more savings, and larger retirement accounts.

Opt-Out Is Optimal

Some of the most successful applications of behavioral economics are "opt-out" programs, which automatically enroll eligible people unless they explicitly choose not to participate. The incentives and freedom of choice are exactly the same as in "opt-in" programs, where members must choose to participate, but enrollments are significantly higher under opt-out. Here's a look at three remarkable results.

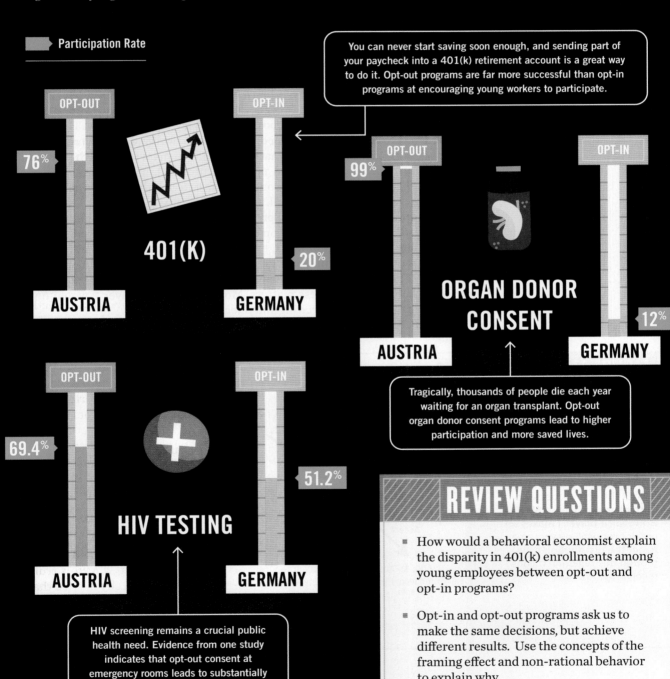

▰ Participation Rate

You can never start saving soon enough, and sending part of your paycheck into a 401(k) retirement account is a great way to do it. Opt-out programs are far more successful than opt-in programs at encouraging young workers to participate.

401(K)

OPT-OUT — 76% — AUSTRIA

OPT-IN — 20% — GERMANY

ORGAN DONOR CONSENT

OPT-OUT — 99% — AUSTRIA

OPT-IN — 12% — GERMANY

Tragically, thousands of people die each year waiting for an organ transplant. Opt-out organ donor consent programs lead to higher participation and more saved lives.

HIV TESTING

OPT-OUT — 69.4% — AUSTRIA

OPT-IN — 51.2% — GERMANY

HIV screening remains a crucial public health need. Evidence from one study indicates that opt-out consent at emergency rooms leads to substantially more individuals agreeing to be tested.

REVIEW QUESTIONS

- How would a behavioral economist explain the disparity in 401(k) enrollments among young employees between opt-out and opt-in programs?

- Opt-in and opt-out programs ask us to make the same decisions, but achieve different results. Use the concepts of the framing effect and non-rational behavior to explain why.

Judgments about Fairness

The pursuit of fairness is another common behavior that is important in economic decisions but that standard economic theory cannot explain. For example, fairness is one of the key drivers in determining tax rate structure for income taxes. Proponents of fairness believe in progressive taxation, whereby the rich pay a higher tax rate on their income than those in lower income brackets do. Likewise, some people object to the high pay of chief executive officers or the high profits of some corporations because they believe there should be an upper limit to what constitutes fair compensation.

The **ultimatum game** is an economic experiment in which two players decide how to divide a sum of money.

While fairness is not normally modeled in economics, behavioral economists have developed experiments to determine the role of fairness in personal decisions. The **ultimatum game** is an economic experiment in which two players decide how to divide a sum of money. The game shows how fairness enters into the rational decision-making process. In the game, player 1 is given a sum of money and is asked to propose a way of splitting it with player 2. Player 2 can either accept or reject the proposal. If player 2 accepts, the sum is split according to the proposal. However, if player 2 rejects the proposal, neither player gets anything. The game is played only once, so the first player does not have to worry about reciprocity.

Consider an ultimatum game that asks player 1 to share $1,000 with player 2. Player 1 must decide how fair to make the proposal. The decision tree in Figure 17.1 highlights four possible outcomes to two very different proposals—a fair proposal and an unfair proposal.

Traditional economic theory presumes that both players are fully rational and wish to maximize their income. Player 1 should therefore maximize his gains by offering the minimum, $1, to player 2. The reasoning is that player 2 values $1 more than nothing and so will accept the proposal, leaving player 1 with $999. But real people are not always economic maximizers because they generally believe that fairness matters. Most of the time, player 2 would find such an unfair division infuriating and reject it.

FIGURE 17.1

The Decision Tree for the Ultimatum Game

The decision tree for the ultimatum game has four branches. If player 1 makes a fair proposal, player 2 will accept the distribution and both players will earn $500. However, if player 1 makes an unfair proposal, player 2 may reject the distribution even though this rejection means receiving nothing.

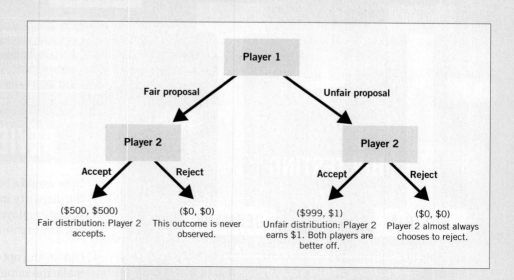

Player 1 knows that player 2 will definitely accept an offer of $500; this division of the money is exactly equal and therefore fair. Thus, the probability of a 50/50 agreement is 100%. In contrast, the probability of player 2 accepting an offer of $1 is close to 0%. Offering increasing amounts from $1 to $500 will continue to raise the probability of an acceptance until it reaches 100% at $500.

Player 2's role is simpler: her only decision is whether to accept or reject the proposal. Player 2 desires a fair distribution but has no direct control over the division. To punish player 1 for being unfair, player 2 must reject the proposal altogether. The trade-off of penalizing player 1 for unfairness is a complete loss of any prize. So while player 2 may not like any given proposal, rejecting it would cause a personal loss. Player 2 might therefore accept a number of unfair proposals because she would rather get something than nothing.

Trade-offs

Each of the ideas that we have presented in this section, including misperceptions of probability, inconsistency in decision-making, and judgments about fairness, represent a departure from the traditional economic model of rational maximization. In the next section, we focus on risk-taking. As you will soon learn, not everyone evaluates risk in the same way. This fact has led economists to reconsider their models of human behavior.

ECONOMICS IN THE REAL WORLD

UNFAIR PAY MATTERS TO CAPUCHIN MONKEYS

Traditional economic theory suggests that when two traders each expect gains from a trade, no matter how unequal those gains may be, the traders will reach an agreement. Researchers on fairness disagree with that conclusion. Frans de Waal, a primatologist, uses capuchin monkeys to argue that fairness matters throughout the animal kingdom. His short TED talk, which is equal parts *America's Funniest Home Videos* and Econ 101, is available on YouTube. It shows how a capuchin monkey given cucumbers as a reward is beside itself when it realizes its companion is receiving grapes. If you're thinking, "Okay, but they're just monkeys," consider how you'd react if you were invited to a party and were served cantaloupe while everyone else got lobster salad. Would you say, "Hey, free cantaloupe"? Or would you find a way to express your displeasure?

Sour grapes? A capuchin monkey throws away cucumber to protest unfairness.

What Is the Role of Risk in Decision-Making?

In this section, we examine the role that risk plays in decision-making. The standard economic model of consumer choice assumes that people are consistent in their risk-taking preferences. However, people's risk tolerances actually vary widely and are subject to change. Thus, risk-taking behavior is not nearly as simple or predictable as economists once believed. We begin with a phenomenon known as *preference reversal*. We then consider how negative surprises can cause people to take more risk, which is explained by *prospect theory*.

Preference Reversals

As you know, trying to predict human behavior is not easy. Maurice Allais, the recipient of the 1988 Nobel Prize in Economics, noticed that people's tolerance for risk appeared to change in different situations. This observation did not agree with the standard economic model, which assumes that an individual's risk tolerance is constant and places the individual into one of three distinct groups: **risk-averse people**, who prefer a sure thing over a gamble with a higher expected value; **risk-neutral people**, who choose the highest expected value regardless of the risk; and **risk-takers**, who prefer gambles with lower expected values, and potentially higher winnings, over a sure thing.

Allais developed a means of assessing risk behavior by presenting the set of choices (known as the Allais paradox) depicted in Table 17.1. Individuals were asked to choose their preferred options between gambles A and B and then again between gambles C and D.

Economic science predicts that people will choose consistently according to their risk preference. As a result, economists understood that risk-averse individuals would choose the pair A and D. Likewise, the pair B and C makes sense if the participants are risk-neutral and wish to maximize the expected value of the gambles. Let's see why.

1. *Risk-Averse People:* People who select gamble A over gamble B take the sure thing. If they are asked to choose between C and D, we would expect them to try to maximize their chances of winning something by selecting D, because it has the higher probability of winning.

2. *Risk-Neutral People:* Gamble B has a higher expected value than gamble A. We know that gamble A always pays $1 million because it occurs 100% of the time. Calculating gamble B's expected value is more complicated. The expected value is computed by multiplying each outcome by its respective probability. For gamble B, this means that the expected value is ($5 million × 0.10) + ($1 million × 0.89), which equals $1.39 million. So a risk-neutral player will select gamble B. Likewise, gamble C has a higher expected value than gamble D. Gamble C has an expected value of ($5 million × 0.10), or $0.5 million. Gamble D's expected value is ($1 million × 0.11), or $0.11 million. Therefore, a risk-neutral player who thinks at the margin will choose gambles B and C in order to maximize potential winnings from the game.

Risk-averse people
prefer a sure thing over a gamble with a higher expected value.

Risk-neutral people
choose the highest expected value regardless of the risk.

Risk-takers
prefer gambles with lower expected values, and potentially higher winnings, over a sure thing.

Marginal thinking

TABLE 17.1	
The Allais Paradox	
Choose gamble A or B	
Gamble A	**Gamble B**
No gamble—receive $1 million in cash 100% of the time	A lottery ticket that pays $5 million 10% of the time, $1 million 89% of the time, and nothing 1% of the time
Choose gamble C or D	
Gamble C	**Gamble D**
A lottery ticket that pays $5 million 10% of the time and nothing 90% of the time	A lottery ticket that pays $1 million 11% of the time and nothing 89% of the time

Preference Reversals

"MINE"

The music video for Taylor Swift's 2010 hit begins with Swift walking into a coffee shop. When she sits down, she notices a couple arguing at a nearby table. This reminds Swift about her parents arguing when she was very young. Just then, the waiter drops by to take Swift's order. She looks up and dreams of what life would be like with him. We see them running together in the waves at the beach, then unpacking boxes as they move in together. Later, the two argue, resulting in Swift running away from their house and crying, just like she did when she was young and saw her parents arguing. Her boyfriend follows her, and they reconcile. They get married and have two sons. The video ends with Swift reemerging from her dream and ordering her food at the coffee shop.

In the song's refrain, Swift sings, "You made a rebel of a careless man's careful daughter." Think about that line, keeping in mind that a "rebel" is a risk-taker. Does that remind you of a concept from this chapter? It should—this is a preference reversal. The entire song is about someone (Swift) who is normally risk-averse but falls for this guy so hard that she lets her guard down and acts differently. Instead of running

Taylor's dream illustrates one version of a preference reversal.

away when it comes time to fall in love, she stays in the relationship. In other words, the song is about finding someone who makes you believe in love so much that you are willing to take a chance for the first time in your life.

---

3. *Risk-Takers:* Because risk-takers prefer risk, they would choose gambles B and C even if they were not already the gambles with the highest expected values.

While we would expect people to be consistent in their choices, Allais found that approximately 30% of his research population selected gambles A and C, which are contrasting pairs. Gamble A is the sure thing; however, Gamble C, even though it has the higher expected value, carries more risk. This scenario illustrates a *preference reversal*. A **preference reversal** occurs when risk tolerance is not consistent. Allais argued that a person's risk tolerance depends on his or her financial circumstances. Someone who chooses gamble A over gamble B prefers the certainty of a large financial prize—the guarantee of $1 million over the uncertainty of the larger prize. Choosing gamble A could be seen as similar to purchasing insurance: you pay a fee, known as a *premium*, to protect your winnings. In this case, you forfeit the chance to win $5 million. In contrast,

A **preference reversal** occurs when risk tolerance is not consistent.

Withholding too much in the previous year and then paying your accountant to file for a rapid refund is a good example of a preference reversal.

gambles C and D offer small chances of success, and therefore the choice is more like playing the lottery.

People who play games of chance are more likely to participate in games with large prizes—for example, Powerball—because the winnings will measurably improve their financial status. Allais showed that people care about how much they might win and also how much they stand to lose. This distinction causes people to choose gambles A and C. By establishing that many people behave this way, Allais reshaped the traditional economic view of risk-taking behavior.

It turns out that preference reversals are more common than economists once believed. For example, almost 80% of all income tax filers expect to get a refund because they overpaid in the previous year. This behavior is odd, since there is an opportunity cost of waiting to get money back from the government when it didn't need to be paid in the first place. Employees could have asked their employers to withhold less and enjoyed their money sooner. Individuals who choose to wait to receive their money later are said to have a time preference that is weakly positive. In most circumstances, people have strongly positive time preferences: they prefer to have what they want sooner rather than later. So what do these taxpayers do when they learn the amount of their refund? In many cases, they pay their tax preparers an additional fee to have their refunds sent to their bank accounts electronically so they can receive the money sooner! Traditional economic analysis is unable to explain this behavior; but armed with Allais's insights, we now see this behavior as a preference reversal.

Prospect Theory

Opportunity cost

The television game show *Deal or No Deal* (2005–2010, 2018–) provides an opportunity for economists to examine the risk choices that contestants make in a high-stakes setting. *Deal or No Deal* creates particular excitement among researchers who study game shows, because it involves no skill whatsoever. Taking skill out of the equation made it easier to analyze the contestants' strategy choices. Other TV game shows, such as *Jeopardy!,* require skill to win prizes. Highly skilled players may have different risk tolerances than their less skilled counterparts. As a result, part of the beauty of studying *Deal or No Deal* is that the outcome is a pure exercise in probability theory.

For those who are unfamiliar with *Deal or No Deal,* here is how the show works. Each of 26 models holds a briefcase containing a sum of money, varying from 1 cent to $1 million. The contestant picks one briefcase as her own and then begins to open the other 25 briefcases one at a time, slowly revealing a little more about what her own case might contain. Suspense builds, and the contestant's chance of a big payoff grows as small sums are eliminated and the $1 million case and other valuable cases remain unopened. As cases are eliminated, a "banker" periodically calls the host to offer the contestant a "deal" in exchange for quitting the game.

At the start of the game, the expected value (EV) of the chosen briefcase is determined as follows:

$$EV_{briefcase} = \$0.01 \times (1/26) + \$1 \times (1/26) + \$5 \times (1/26) + \ldots + \$1M \times (1/26)$$

This value computes to about $131,000. As the game progresses and more and more cases are opened, the "banker's" settlement offers are based on whether the expected value of the briefcase has increased or decreased since the last offer.

Some contestants behave as the traditional model of risk behavior predicts: they maximize the expected value of the briefcase while remaining risk-neutral. Because contestants who are risk neutral don't make for exciting television, the "banker" typically offers a "deal" that is far less than the expected value of the remaining cases throughout the early part of the game. This move encourages contestants to play longer, so that the excitement and tension have a chance to build.

But not all contestants did what the traditional model expected them to do. For example, some contestants took more risks if they suffered setbacks early in the game, such as opening the $1 million briefcase. This behavior is consistent with *prospect theory* from psychology. **Prospect theory**, developed by Daniel Kahneman and Amos Tversky, suggests that people weigh decisions according to subjective utilities of gains and losses. The theory implies that people evaluate the risks that lead to gains separately from the risks that lead to losses. This concept is useful because it explains why some investors try to make up for losses by taking more chances rather than by maximizing the utility they receive from money under a rigid calculation of expected value.

Deciding when to take the "deal" makes the show compelling.

Prospect theory
suggests that individuals weigh the utilities and risks of gains and losses differently.

PRACTICE WHAT YOU KNOW

Risk Aversion: Risk-Taking Behavior

QUESTION: You have a choice between selecting heads or tails. If your guess is correct, you earn $2,000. But you earn nothing if you are incorrect. Alternatively, you can simply take $750 without the gamble. You decide to take the $750. Is your choice evidence of risk aversion or risk-taking?

ANSWER: The expected value of a 50/50 outcome worth $2,000 is $1,000. Therefore, the decision to take the sure thing, which is $250 less, is evidence of risk aversion.

QUESTION: You have a choice between (a) predicting the roll of a six-sided die, with a $3,000 prize for a correct answer, or (b) taking a sure $750. You decide to roll the die. Is your choice evidence of risk aversion or risk-taking?

ANSWER: The expected value of the roll of the die is $1/6 \times \$3,000$, or $500. Therefore, the $750 sure thing has an expected value that is $250 more. By rolling the die, you are taking the option with the lower expected value and also more risk. Therefore, you are a risk-taker.

How do you handle risky decisions?

WHY ARE THERE COLD OPENINGS AT THE BOX OFFICE?

The line for tickets is long. Do you suppose this movie was cold-opened?

Movie studios generally make a film available for review if the screenings are expected to generate a positive buzz. Also, access to movie reviews provides moviegoers with a measure of a film's quality. So a rational moviegoer should infer that if a movie studio releases a film without reviews, it is signaling that the movie is not very good: the studio didn't want to risk negative reviews, so it didn't show the movie to reviewers.

Economists Alexander L. Brown, Colin F. Camerer, and Dan Lovallo studied 856 widely released movies and found that cold openings—movies withheld from critics (that is, not screened) before their release—produced a significant increase (15%) in domestic box office revenue compared with poor films that were reviewed and received predictably negative reviews. Most movie openings are accompanied by a marketing campaign to increase consumer demand. As a consequence, cold openings provide a natural field setting to test how rational moviegoers are. Their results are consistent with the hypothesis that some moviegoers do not infer low quality from a cold opening as they should.

The researchers showed that cold-opened movies earned more than prescreened movies after a number of characteristics were controlled for in the study. An important point is that the researchers also found that cold-opened films did not fare better than expected once they reached foreign film or video rental markets. In both of those cases, movie reviews were widely available, which negated any advantage from cold-opening the films. This finding is consistent with the hypothesis that some moviegoers fail to realize that no advance review is a signal of poor quality. The fact that moviegoer ratings from the Internet Movie Database are lower for movies that were cold-opened also suggests that in the absence of information, moviegoers overestimate the expected quality.

It's not that moviegoers are idiots. But over time, distributors have learned that there's a certain amount of moviegoer naiveté, especially among teenagers. Somebody says "Let's go see *Floundernado*," and nobody in the group thinks about the fact that they haven't seen any reviews. Or they do think about it, but they don't realize that it's because there *aren't* any reviews out. If they did figure that out, they'd probably know that it's a bad sign. But moviegoers often don't recognize a cold open when they see one, and so distributors have overcome their earlier reluctance and have cold-opened more movies in recent years.

These findings provide evidence that the best movie distribution strategy does not depend entirely on generating positive movie reviews. Cold openings work because some people are unable to process the negative signal implied by incomplete information, despite what traditional economic analysis would lead us to expect.

Bounded Rationality: How to Guard Yourself against Crime

- Raise the probability the criminal will be seen (trim bushes around your property, install motion-sensing lights).
- Raise the costs of entering (deadbolts, security doors, and security bars on windows).
- Raise the probability the criminal will be caught (alarm systems, barking dog).

A rational thief would look for an easier target.

Suppose that a recent crime wave has hit your community and you are concerned about your family's security. Determined to make your house safe, you consider many options: an alarm system, bars on your windows, deadbolts for your doors, better lighting around your house, and a guard dog. Which of these solutions will protect you from a criminal at the lowest cost? All of them provide a measure of protection—but there's another solution that provides deterrence at an extremely low cost.

The level of security you need depends, in part, on how rational you expect the burglar to be. A fully rational burglar would stake out a place, test for an alarm system before breaking in, and choose a home that is an easy target. In other words, the burglar would gather full information. But what if the burglar is not fully rational?

Because criminals look for the easiest target to rob, they will find a house that is easy to break into without detection. If you trim away the shrubs and install floodlights, criminals will realize they can be seen approaching your home. A few hundred dollars spent on better lighting will dramatically lower your chances of being robbed. However, if you believe in bounded rationality, there is an even better answer: a criminal may not know what is inside your house, so a couple of prominently displayed "Beware of

dog!" signs would discourage the burglar for less than $10! In other words, the would-be thief has incomplete information and only a limited amount of time to select a target. A quick scan of your house would identify the "Beware of dog!" signs and cause him to move on.

This is an example of bounded rationality because only limited, and in this case unreliable, information is all that is easily available regarding possible alternatives and their consequences. Knowing that burglars face this constraint can be a key to keeping them away. Of course, you could also buy a "Beware of owner!" sign like the one shown. On the one hand, yes, you'll deter some burglars. On the other hand, you may end up attracting *armed* burglars who are after your (nonexistent) gun collection. Now who's the person with the bounded rationality?

Conclusion

Behavioral economics challenges the traditional economic model and invites a deeper understanding of human behavior. Armed with the insights from behavioral economics, we can answer questions that span a wider range of behaviors. We have seen behavioral economics at work in the examples in this chapter, which include the "opt-in" or "opt-out" debate, the economics of risk-taking, the effects of question design, and the status quo bias. These ideas do not fit squarely into traditional economic analysis. You have learned enough at this point to question the assumptions we have made throughout this book. In the next chapter, we apply all of the tools we have acquired to examine one of the most important sectors of the economy—health care and health insurance. ✳

· ANSWERING *the* BIG QUESTIONS ·

How do economists explain irrational behavior?

* Economists use a number of concepts from behavioral economics to explain how people make choices that display irrational behavior. These concepts include bounded rationality, misperceptions of probabilities, framing effects and priming effects, the status quo bias, intertemporal decision-making, judgments about fairness, preference reversals, and prospect theory.

* Folding the behavioral approach into the standard model makes economists' predictions about human behavior much more robust.

What is the role of risk in decision-making?

* Risk influences decision-making because people can be risk-averse, risk-neutral, or risk-takers.

* In the traditional economic model, risk tolerances are assumed to be constant. If an individual is a risk-taker by nature, he or she will take risks in any circumstance. Likewise, if an individual does not like to take chances, he or she will avoid risk.

* Maurice Allais proved that many people have inconsistent risk preferences, or what are known as preference reversals. Moreover, he showed that simply because some people's preferences are not constant does not necessarily mean that their decisions are irrational.

* Prospect theory suggests that individuals weigh the utilities and risks of gains and losses differently and are therefore willing to take on additional risk to try to recover losses caused by negative shocks.

· CHAPTER PROBLEMS ·

Concepts You Should Know

behavioral economics (p. 546)
bounded rationality (p. 546)
framing effect (p. 552)
gambler's fallacy (p. 550)
hot hand fallacy (p. 550)

intertemporal decision-making (p. 554)
preference reversal (p. 559)
priming effect (p. 552)
prospect theory (p. 561)

risk-averse people (p. 558)
risk-neutral people (p. 558)
risk-takers (p. 558)
status quo bias (p. 552)
ultimatum game (p. 556)

Questions for Review

1. What is bounded rationality? How is this concept relevant to economic modeling?

2. What are the hot hand fallacy and the gambler's fallacy? Give an example of each.

3. How does the status quo bias reduce the potential utility that consumers enjoy?

4. Economists use the ultimatum game to test judgments of fairness. What result does economic theory predict?

5. What is prospect theory? Have you ever suffered a setback early in a process (for example, seeking a job or applying for college) that caused you to alter your behavior later on?

Study Problems (∗ *solved at the end of the section*)

∗ 1. You have a choice between two jobs. The first job pays $50,000 annually. The second job has a base pay of $40,000 with a 30% chance that you will receive an annual bonus of $25,000. You decide to take the $50,000 job. On the basis of this decision, can we tell if you are risk-averse or a risk-taker? Explain your response.

2. Suppose that Danny Ocean decides to play roulette, one of the most popular casino games. Roulette is attractive to gamblers because the house's advantage is small (less than 5%). If Danny Ocean plays roulette and wins big, is this evidence that Danny is risk-averse or a risk-taker? Explain.

3. Many voters go to the polls every four years to cast their ballot for president. The common refrain from those who vote is that their vote "counts" and that voting is important. A skeptical economist points out that with over 100 million ballots cast, the probability that any individual's vote will be decisive is close to 0%. What idea, discussed in this chapter, explains why so many people actually vote?

4. Your instructor is very conscientious and always makes sure that exam answers are randomly distributed. However, you notice that the first five answers on the true/false section are all "true." Unsure what this pattern means, you consider the sixth question. However, you do not know the answer. What answer would you give if you believed in the gambler's fallacy? What answer would you give if you believed in the hot hand fallacy?

∗ 5. Suppose that a university wishes to maximize the response rate for teaching evaluations. The administration develops an easy-to-use online evaluation system that each student can complete at the end of the semester. However, very few students bother to complete the survey. The registrar's office suggests that the online teaching evaluations be linked to course scheduling. When students access the course scheduling system, they are redirected to the teaching evaluations. Under this plan, each student can opt out and go directly to the course scheduling system. Do you think this plan will work to raise the response rate on teaching evaluations? What would traditional economic theory predict? What would a behavioral economist predict?

6. Ray likes his hamburgers with American cheese, lettuce, and ketchup. Whenever he places an order

for a burger, he automatically orders these three toppings. What type of behavior is Ray exhibiting? What does traditional economic theory say about Ray's preferences? What would a behavioral economist say?

7. Many people give to charity and leave tips. What prediction does traditional economic theory make about each of these activities? (**Hint:** Think of the person's narrow self-interest.) What concept from behavioral economics explains this behavior?

8. Given a choice of an extra $1,000 or a gamble with the same expected value, a person prefers the $1,000. But given a choice of a loss of $1,000 or a gamble with the same expected value, the same person prefers the gamble. How would a behavioral economist describe this decision?

✳ 9. A researcher asks you the following question: "Would you rather have a 10% chance of mortality or a 90% chance of survival?" What concept

from behavioral economics is illustrated here? What is the difference between the two choices, if any? Which choice do you think most people make?

✳ 10. How might the concept of diminishing marginal utility, from Chapter 16, be used to compare and contrast the preferences of the risk-averse and the risk-neutral person?

✳ 11. Under what circumstances would it make economic sense to be a risk-taker?

12. Two people are playing an ultimatum game with $100. Player 1 can make an offer to player 2, who can either accept or reject it. If player 2 accepts, then they split the money according to player 1's offer. If player 2 rejects, neither of them get any money. Player 1 offers $2 to player 2. What does *traditional economic theory* say player 2 will do?

Solved Problems

1. The first job pays $50,000 annually, so it has an expected value of $50,000. The second job has a base pay of $40,000 with a 30% chance that you will receive an annual bonus of $25,000. To determine the expected value of the second job, the calculation looks like this: $40,000 + (0.3 × $25,000) = $40,000 + $7,500 = $47,500. Since you decided to take the job with higher expected value, we cannot tell if you are a risk-taker or risk-averse.

5. Because students who access the course scheduling system are redirected to the teaching evaluations, they are forced to opt out if they do not wish to evaluate the instructors. As a result, a behavioral economist would predict that the new system will raise the teaching evaluation response rate. Traditional economic theory would predict that the response rate will not change simply based on whether or not students opt in or opt out.

9. According to traditional economics, how the question is framed should not matter. But behavioral economics correctly predicts that it does: when asked to choose which of the two outcomes they prefer, a significant majority chooses "a 90% chance of survival," even though this statement is equivalent to "a 10% chance of mortality."

10. Let's use Table 17.1 to think about the answer. A person whose marginal utility of money is constant, or decreases only modestly as the amount of money increases, will choose gambles B and C, the gambles with the highest expected monetary value and therefore the highest expected utility. This is the risk-neutral person. The risk-averse person, who chooses gamble A over gamble B, is giving up a 10% chance of getting lots more than $1M in order eliminate a 1% chance of getting nothing. Apparently this person's marginal utility of money diminishes very sharply after $1M.

11. Again let's use Table 17.1 to formulate an answer, and this time imagine a choice between gamble A and gamble C. Someone who prefers a 10% chance of $5M (and otherwise nothing) over a guarantee of $1M would qualify as a risk-taker, because their expected payoff is only $500,000. This kind of preference would make sense for someone in the middle of a very expensive life crisis, where $1M would not be enough to make a difference but $5M would make a big difference.

18

Health Insurance and Health Care

There's No Such Thing as a Free Lunch.

We have come a long way in our exploration of microeconomics. In this chapter, we apply our economic toolkit to one particular industry: health care. The debate over healthcare spending is at the core of the healthcare crisis in the United States. The goal of this chapter is not to sway your opinion but to provide a simple set of tools to focus your thinking about how medical care can best serve individuals and society as a whole.

When you are young, health care is often the last thing on your mind—until you need it. Imagine you just turned 26. Out biking the next day, and thinking happy thoughts about the party your friends threw you, you fail to notice a nasty pothole. An instant later, you're sprawled on the pavement, seriously injured. You are no longer covered under your parents' plan. Now what?

Many people believe that the best way to handle all such scenarios would be universal health care: just cover everyone with government-funded national health insurance. As a step in that direction, the Affordable Care Act passed under President Obama (the federal healthcare law often called "Obamacare") mandated expanded coverage. It's the reason you could stay on your parents' plan until your 26th birthday.

But what about the costs? Proponents of universal health care argue that it would make health care less expensive on

A biking accident hurts more when you turn 26 and are no longer able to stay on your parents' insurance plan. Now the damage to your wallet is going to be much greater.

a per-person basis. Conservative policymakers, however, push back and argue that mandatory coverage is inefficient and intrusive, and that universal coverage would be a budget-buster for the government. Even Obamacare is controversial, and neither side of the aisle is satisfied with the political compromises that led to the legislation. So for now, the United States is stuck with a patchwork system of health care and coverage that is neither market based nor government run, and certainly not anywhere near efficient.

Trade-offs

That means we can all benefit from taking a closer look at ways to improve health insurance and health care, and what trade-offs would make sense. In this chapter, we describe how the health-care industry works and how the government and the market can each make the delivery of health care more efficient. We consider how health care is delivered, who pays, and what makes the provision of medical care unlike the delivery of services in any other sector of the economy. Then we use supply and demand analysis to look at how the medical market functions. One important aspect of medical care is the role that information plays in the incentive structure for patients and providers. Finally, we examine a number of case studies to pull all this information together, so you can decide for yourself where you stand on one of the most important issues of the twenty-first century.

· BIG QUESTIONS ·

- What are the important issues in the healthcare industry?
- How does asymmetric information affect healthcare delivery?
- How do demand and supply contribute to high medical costs?
- How do incentives influence the quality of health care?

What Are the Important Issues in the Healthcare Industry?

Health care is big business. If you add the education and automobile sectors together, they represent about 10% of national economic output. But health care alone accounts for more than 17% of the nation's economic output. That's 1 out of every 6 dollars spent annually in the United States—roughly $3.5 trillion, or over $10,000 for every citizen. No matter how you slice it, that is a lot of money.

In this section, we examine the key issues in health care: how much is spent on it, where the money goes, and who the key players in the industry are. The goal is to give you a sense of how the sector functions. Then we turn our attention to supply and demand. First, though, we take a brief look at how health care has changed over the past hundred or so years.

The History of U.S. Health Care

At the start of the twentieth century, life expectancy in the United States was slightly less than 50 years. Now life expectancy is close to 80 years—a longevity gain that would have been unthinkable a few generations ago. Let's go back in time to examine the way medical care was delivered and see some of the advances that have improved the human condition.

Early in the twentieth century, infectious diseases were the most common cause of death in the United States. Typhoid, diphtheria, gangrene, gastritis, smallpox, and tuberculosis were major killers. Today, because of antibiotics, they have either been completely eradicated or are extremely rare. Moreover, the state of medical knowledge was so dismal that a cure was often far worse than the condition it was supposed to treat. For instance, tobacco was recommended for the treatment of bronchitis and asthma, and leeches were used to fight laryngitis. Throughout the first half of the twentieth century, a trip to the doctor was painful, and it rarely produced positive results.

Cutting-edge medical equipment: then . . .

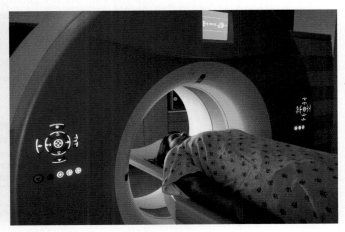

. . . and now.

Since 1950, advances in cellular biology and discoveries in biochemistry have led to a better understanding of diseases and more precise diagnostic tests. In addition, discoveries in biomedical engineering have led to the widespread use of imaging techniques such as ultrasound, computerized axial tomography (CAT scans), and nuclear magnetic resonance imaging (MRI). These and other technological innovations have replaced the medical practices of the past and made medical care safer, gentler, and more effective. In addition, pharmaceutical companies have developed a number of "miracle" drugs for fighting many conditions, including high blood pressure, leukemia, and bad cholesterol, thereby limiting the need for more invasive treatments. Each of these amazing medical advances costs money—sometimes, lots of money. As a society, we have made a trade-off: in exchange for a dramatically longer life expectancy, we now devote much more of our personal and government budgets to health care.

Trade-offs

Healthcare Expenditures

We have noted that healthcare expenditures in the United States are more than 17% of economic output. As you can see in Table 18.1, this total is quite a bit higher than similar expenditures in Canada and Mexico. Canada spends about 10% of its economic output on health care, and Mexico spends slightly more than 5%.

The United States spends significantly more on health care than our neighbors to the north and south, but life expectancy in the United States is lower than in Canada. How does Canada achieve a higher life expectancy while spending less money? And why doesn't Mexico, which spends only about one-tenth of what we do on health care per capita (see Table 18.1), trail farther behind the United States than it does? To answer those questions, consider the usual assumption of *ceteris paribus,* or other things being constant. We all agree that increased healthcare expenditures are making people healthier, probably happier (because they feel better), and more productive—this is true for most countries. However, longevity is also a function of environmental factors, genetics, and lifestyle choices—variables that are not constant across countries. The question we should be asking is not how much money we are spending, but whether we are getting our money's worth. In other words, in this context economists are most concerned with the impediments to the efficient delivery of medical care.

Why does health care take up so much of our budget? There are a number of reasons. Health insurance plays a contributing role. When private insurance covers most treatment costs, many patients agree to tests or medical visits

TABLE 18.1
Selected Healthcare Facts

Country	Total expenditure on health (percentage of economic output)	Per capita expenditure on health (in U.S. dollars)	Life expectancy at birth, total population (in years)
Mexico	5.4	989	75.4
Canada	10.4	4,826	81.9
U.S.	17.2	10,209	78.6

Source: OECD Health Division, *Health Data 2018: Frequently Requested Data.*

they wouldn't be willing to pay for out of pocket. Also, doctors are more willing to order tests that might not be necessary if they know the patient isn't paying directly. Medicare and Medicaid, the two government-sponsored forms of health insurance, add to the overall demand for medical services by providing medical coverage to the elderly and poor. And we know that anytime there is more demand for services, the market price rises in response, as long as supply remains constant.

Another reason for high healthcare costs is the number of uninsured people in the United States—approximately 28 million in 2017. When uninsured people need immediate medical treatment, they often seek care from emergency rooms and clinics, which raises costs in two ways. First, emergency care is extraordinarily expensive—much more so than routine care. Second, waiting until one has an acute condition that requires immediate attention often requires more treatment than would occur with preventive care or an early diagnosis. For example, an insured person who develops a cough with fever is likely to see a physician. If the patient has bronchitis, a few days of medicine and rest will be all it takes to feel better. However, an uninsured person who develops bronchitis is less likely to seek medical help and risks the possibility of a worsening condition, such as pneumonia, which can be difficult and costly to treat.

Medical demand is quite inelastic, so when competition is absent (which is usually the case), hospitals and other providers can charge what they want, and patients will have to pay. In addition, many people are not proactive about their health. Many health problems could be dramatically reduced and costs contained if people curbed habits such as cigarette use, excessive alcohol consumption, and overeating and if they exercised more. Finally, heroic end-of-life efforts are extraordinarily expensive. These efforts may extend life for a few months, days, or hours, and they come at a steep price.

Diminishing Returns

In the United States, it has become the norm to spare no expense in the effort to extend life for even a few days. However, providing more medical care is subject to diminishing returns, as we can see in Figure 18.1. The orange curve shows a society's aggregate health production function, a measure of health reflecting the population's longevity, general health, and quality of life. This function initially rises rapidly when small amounts of health care are provided, but the benefits of additional care are progressively smaller. To understand why, compare points A and B. At point A, only a small amount of medical care is provided (Q_A), but this care has a large impact on health. The slope at point A represents the marginal product of medical care. However, by the time we reach point B at a higher amount of care provided (Q_B), the marginal product of medical care (the slope) is much flatter, indicating that diminishing returns have set in.

Marginal thinking

Higher medical care expenditures, beyond some point, are unlikely to measurably improve longevity and quality of life because many other factors—for example, disease, genetics, and lifestyle—also play a key role in determining health, quality of life, and longevity. As we move out along the medical production function, extending life becomes progressively more difficult, so it is not surprising that medical costs rise appreciably. Given this pattern, society must answer two questions. First, what is the optimal mix of expenditures on medical care? Second, could society get more from each dollar spent by reallocating

FIGURE 18.1

Health Production Function

The marginal product of medical care, indicated by the slope of the health production function, is higher at point A than at point B.

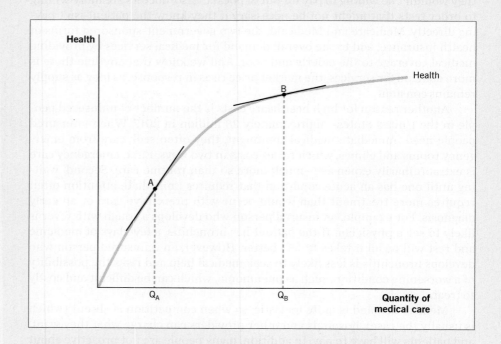

dollars away from heroic efforts to extend life and toward prevention and medical research instead?

Figure 18.2 shows where the typical health dollar goes. Hospital care, physicians, and clinics account for a little more than half of all medical expenses. After that, prescription drugs, dental care, home health care, and nursing homes each represent smaller parts of healthcare expenditures. Here we note a paradox. On the one hand, medical care has become much more efficient as medical records are increasingly computerized and many procedures that required days of hospitalization a generation ago can now take place on an outpatient basis. Thus, reducing medical costs through efficiency gains is ongoing. Yet, on the other hand, costs continue to rise. What is going on? In the next section, we examine the incentives that patients, providers, and insurance companies face when making medical decisions and how the incentive structure contributes to escalating costs.

Who's Who in Health Care, and How Does Insurance Work?

Incentives

Healthcare consumption is different from that of most other goods and services. Like the others, healthcare services have consumers and producers; but because of intermediaries, such as insurance companies, the two rarely interact directly. This situation generates a unique set of incentives and leads to distortions in the standard supply and demand analysis. It is important to understand how medical care is delivered and paid for, as well as the incentives that patients, medical providers, and insurers face when making decisions.

FIGURE 18.2

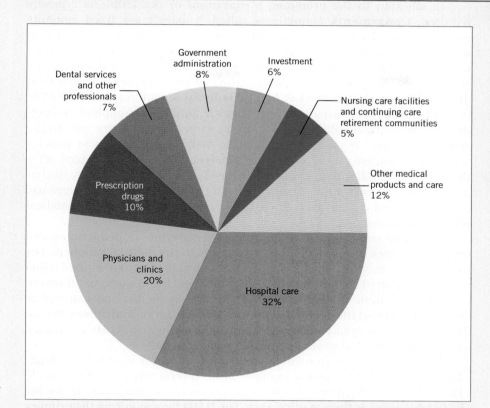

Hospital care, physicians, and clinics make up over half of all healthcare expenditures, which totaled $3.5 trillion in 2018.

Source: Centers for Medicare and Medicaid Services, Office of the Actuary, National Health Statistics Group. See "National Health Expenditure Data," cms.gov.

CONSUMERS The two biggest consumers of medical care are patients and the government. Patients demand medical care to prevent and treat illness. The federal government runs Medicare, a program that provides medical assistance to the elderly, and Medicaid, a program that provides medical assistance to the poor. Medicare and Medicaid are social insurance programs that each serve over 40 million enrollees. The two programs account for approximately one-third of all medical spending in the United States and represent about one-fourth of all U.S. government expenditures.

PRODUCERS The medical care industry employs millions of workers, including doctors, nurses, psychologists, technicians, and many more. There are also over 500,000 medical facilities in this country, including small medical offices, large regional hospitals, nursing homes, pharmacies, and stores that supply medical equipment. In addition, pharmaceutical companies generate over $300 billion in annual sales in the United States.

INTERMEDIARIES Intermediaries—for example, insurance companies—cover certain medical expenses in exchange for a set monthly fee, known as a *premium*. Medical insurance enables consumers to budget their expenses and limit what they will have to pay out of pocket in the event of a serious condition.

In addition to the premium, a *copayment* or deductible is typically required. **Copayments** (sometimes called "copays") are fixed amounts that the insured pays when receiving a medical service or filling a prescription. Insurance companies use copayments in part to share expenses with the insured. In addition to covering a small portion of the costs, the copay serves to prevent most people from seeking care for common conditions that are easy to treat at home. **Deductibles** are fixed amounts the insured must pay before most of the policy's benefits can be applied. Deductibles are sometimes subject to exceptions, such as a necessary visit to the emergency room or preventive physician visits and tests. Some policies also require **coinsurance payments**, a percentage the insured pays after the insurance policy's deductible is exceeded up to the policy's contribution limit. These services vary with each type of plan. Like coinsurance, copayments and deductibles work to encourage consumers to use medical services judiciously.

Insurance companies use the premiums, copayments, deductibles, and coinsurance they receive from their customers to pay medical suppliers. For example, you may not need an appendectomy this year, but a predictable number of insured customers will. Using statistical techniques, an insurance company with millions of customers can accurately predict how many of its customers will visit the doctor and require hospitalization and other services. This statistical analysis enables the company to estimate its costs in advance and set premiums that generate a profit for the company.

Many people receive medical care through *health maintenance organizations,* or HMOs—another example of an intermediary. HMOs provide managed care for their patients by assigning them a primary care physician (PCP) who oversees their medical care. The HMO then monitors the primary care provider to ensure that unnecessary care is not prescribed. HMOs earn revenue from premiums, copayments, deductibles, and coinsurance. Many insurance plans allow the insured to make choices. *Preferred provider organizations,* or PPOs, are a type of health insurance arrangement that gives plan participants relative freedom to choose the doctors and hospitals they want to visit.

Another kind of insurance company sells insurance against medical malpractice, or negligent treatment on the part of doctors. The doctor pays a set fee to the insurer, which in turn pays for the legal damages that arise if the doctor faces a malpractice claim. By analyzing statistics about the number of malpractice cases for each type of medical procedure performed each year, insurers can estimate the probability that a particular physician will face a malpractice claim; the insurers then incorporate that risk into the premium they charge to doctors.

PHARMACEUTICAL COMPANIES Constituting another major player in the healthcare industry are the many pharmaceutical companies that develop the drugs used to treat a wide variety of conditions. Global pharmaceutical sales are almost $1 trillion. The United States accounts for about 30% of this $1 trillion—that's a lot of prescriptions! Pharmaceutical companies spend billions of dollars developing and testing potential drugs. One drug can take years or decades to develop. Once a drug is developed, it must receive approval by the U. S. Food and Drug Administration (FDA) before it can be sold. The development cost, time required, and risk that a drug may turn out to be problematic or ineffective combine to make the development of new drugs an expensive proposition.

Medical Costs

To understand why medical costs are so high, we must look at the incentives that drive the decisions of the major players. Consumers want every treatment to be covered, providers want a steady stream of business and don't want to be sued for malpractice, and the insurance companies and pharmaceutical companies want to make profits. These market dynamics showcase the inherent conflict that exists between consumers, producers, and intermediaries, and it helps explain the difficulty of providing medical care at a reasonable cost.

Because patient copayments are only a tiny fraction of the total cost of care, the effective marginal cost of seeking medical treatment is quite low. As a result, consumers increase the quantity of medical care they demand. Some physicians prescribe more care than is medically necessary in order to earn more income and to avoid malpractice lawsuits. Meanwhile, insurance companies, which are caught in the middle between patients and medical providers, do their best to contain costs, but they find that controlling the behavior of patients and providers is difficult. Consequently, escalating costs result from a system with poorly designed incentive mechanisms. In the case of Medicare and Medicaid, the government attempts to control costs by setting caps on the reimbursements paid to providers for medical treatments. An unintended consequence of government price setting is that it forces physicians and medical centers to raise prices for other procedures not covered by Medicare and Medicaid.

Incentives

Physical Fitness

QUESTION: You go in for a physical, and your doctor suggests that you get more exercise. So you decide to start working out. The increased physical activity has a big payoff and soon you feel much better, so you decide to double your efforts and get in even better shape. However, you notice that the gains from doubling your workout effort do not make you feel much better. What economic concept explains this effect?

ANSWER: More of a good thing isn't always better. Physical activity extends longevity and increases quality of life up to a point. However, working out is subject to *diminishing returns*. In other words, a small amount of physical activity has a big payoff, but lifting more weights or running more miles, after a certain point, does not increase your overall health—it simply maintains your health.

"I work out . . ."

How Does Asymmetric Information Affect Healthcare Delivery?

We have seen that incentives play an important role in the delivery of medical care. Another important element is the information and lack of information available to participants. Imbalances in information, known as **asymmetric information**, occur whenever one party knows more than the other. Asymmetric information has two forms: *adverse selection* and the *principal-agent problem*.

Adverse Selection

Most of us know very little about medicine. We know when we don't feel well and that we want to feel better, so we seek medical attention. Because we know very little about the service we are buying, we are poor judges of quality. For example, how can you know if your doctor is qualified or better than another doctor? **Adverse selection** exists when one party has information about some aspect of product quality that the other party does not have. As a result, the party with the limited information should be concerned that the other party will misrepresent information to gain an advantage.

When one side knows more than the other, the only way to avoid an adverse outcome is to gather better information. Suppose that you are new in town and need medical care. You haven't had a chance to meet anyone and find out whom to see or where to go for care. Fortunately, there is a way to avoid the worst doctors: websites like ratemds.com provide patient feedback on the quality of care they have received. Armed with knowledge from sources like these, you can request to be treated by doctors whom you know to be competent and have strong reputations. Conducting this research helps new residents avoid below-average care. More generally, it is important for patients to take charge of their own health care and learn all they can about a condition and its treatment so they are prepared to ask questions and make better decisions about treatment options. When patients are better informed, adverse selection is minimized.

Adverse selection also applies when buyers are more likely to seek insurance if they are more likely to need it. Consider a life insurance company. The company wants to avoid selling an inexpensive policy to someone who is likely to die prematurely, so before selling a policy to that applicant, the insurance company has to gather additional information about the person. It can require a medical exam and delay eligibility for full benefits until it can determine that the applicant has no preexisting health conditions. The process of gathering information about the applicant is crucial to minimizing the risk associated with adverse selection. In fact, the process is similar for automobile insurance, in which drivers with poor records pay substantially higher premiums and safe drivers pay substantially lower ones.

The Principal-Agent Problem

Patients generally trust doctors to make good treatment decisions. A **principal-agent problem** arises when a principal entrusts an agent to complete a task and the agent does not do so in a satisfactory way. Some nonmedical examples will be familiar to you. Parents (the principal) hire a babysitter (the agent) to

Moral Hazard

"KING-SIZE HOMER"

In this episode of *The Simpsons*, a new corporate fitness policy is intended to help the power plant workers become healthier. Morning exercises are instituted, and the employees are whipped into shape. But Homer hates working out, so he decides to gain a lot of weight in order to claim disability and work at home. To qualify, he must weigh at least 300 pounds. To get to that weight, he must go on an eating binge. Of course, his behavior is not what the designers of the fitness policy had in mind.

This amusing episode is a good example of moral hazard, and it showcases how well-intentioned policies can often be abused.

Moral hazard makes Homer decide to gain weight.

watch their children, but the babysitter might talk on the phone instead. A company manager (the agent) might try to maximize his own salary instead of working to increase value for the shareholders (the principal). Finally, a politician (the agent) might be more likely to grant favors to interest groups than to focus on the needs of his or her constituents (the principal).

In a medical setting, the principal-agent problem occurs whenever patients cannot directly observe how medical providers and insurers are managing their patients' interests. The lack of oversight on the part of patients gives their agents, the physicians and insurance companies, some freedom to pursue other objectives that do not directly benefit patients. In the case of medicine, doctors and hospitals may order more tests, procedures, or visits to specialists than are medically necessary. The physician or the hospital may be more concerned about making profits or avoiding medical malpractice lawsuits than ensuring the patient's health and well-being. At the same time, insurance companies may want to save on treatment costs in order to maximize profit. In both cases, the patient's desire for the best medical care conflicts with the objectives of the agents who deliver their care.

Behavioral Dynamics in Healthcare Delivery

Healthcare is also subject to the problem of **moral hazard**, which is the lack of incentive to guard against risk where one is protected from its consequences. Moral hazard does not necessarily refer to behavior that is "immoral"

Moral hazard is the lack of incentive to guard against risk where one is protected from its consequences.

or "unethical." But it does imply that some people will change their behavior when their risk exposure is reduced and an "it's insured" mentality sets in. This mentality can lead to inefficient outcomes, such as visiting the doctor more often than necessary.

In the example mentioned, there is a moral hazard problem that can be lessened by restructuring the incentives. For the patient, a higher copayment will discourage unnecessary visits to the doctor.

To solve a moral hazard problem in medical care, it is necessary to fix the incentive structure. Many health insurance companies address moral hazard by encouraging preventive care, which lowers medical costs. They also impose payment limits on treatments for preventable conditions, such as gum disease and tooth decay.

Incentives

PRACTICE WHAT YOU KNOW

Asymmetric Information

QUESTION: You decide to use an online dating site, but you are not entirely sure if the posted picture of someone is accurate. Is adverse selection, the principal-agent problem, moral hazard, or some combination of these at work?

ANSWER: Adverse selection is at work. The person you are interested in knows more about herself than you do. She can, and probably would, post a flattering picture of herself. When you finally meet her, you are likely to be disappointed.

QUESTION: You hire a friend to feed your cat and change the litter twice a day while you are on spring break. However, your friend only visits your apartment every other day, and your cat shows its disapproval by using your bedspread as a litter box. Why is this an example of the principal-agent problem?

ANSWER: Because you have arranged for your friend to act on your behalf, but he cares less about your cat than you do and therefore wasn't conscientious about looking after it.

CHALLENGE QUESTION: How are adverse selection and moral hazard also involved in the cat-sitting fiasco?

ANSWER: Adverse selection is involved because you relied on a friend in a one-time arrangement. If you used a professional pet-sitter, you would have more information about his or her performance—first through references and after that through your own experiences. Moral hazard is involved because your friend won't have to sleep in that bed the cat peed on. Because your friend was protected from the consequences of his negligence, he wasn't as worried as you would have been about making sure the cat stuck to the litter box.

How Do Demand and Supply Contribute to High Medical Costs?

Now that we have a basic understanding of how the healthcare industry functions and who the key players are, we can examine the way demand and supply operate in the market for health care. On the demand side, we consider what makes healthcare demand stubbornly inelastic. Health care, when you need it, is not about the price—it is about getting the care you need. When you consider this fact and the presence of third-party payments, or payments made by insurance companies, you can begin to understand why medical expenses have risen so rapidly. On the supply side, medical licensing requirements help explain why the supply of medical services is limited. The combination of strongly inelastic demand and limited supply pushes up prices for medical services.

Healthcare Demand

Health care is usually a necessity, and it doesn't have many good alternatives. These two facts explain why the demand for health care is typically inelastic. For example, going without a heart transplant when you need one isn't an option. In fact, a 2002 RAND Corporation study found that health care has an average price elasticity coefficient of -0.17. This means that a 1% increase in the price of health care will lead to a 0.17% reduction in healthcare expenditures. Recall that as an elasticity coefficient approaches zero, demand becomes more inelastic. So we can say that the demand for medical care is quite inelastic. (For a refresher on elasticity, see Chapter 4.)

But there are some situations in which healthcare expenditures can be reduced. For example, otherwise healthy people with minor colds and other viruses can use home remedies, such as drinking fluids and resting, rather than make an expensive visit to the doctor. So the price elasticity of demand depends on the severity of the medical need and the sense of urgency involved in treatment. Urgent needs have the most inelastic demand. As the time horizon expands from the short run to the long run, the demand for health care becomes progressively more elastic. Nonemergency long-term treatments have the greatest price elasticity. For instance, a significant portion of the adult population postpones routine dental visits, despite the obvious benefits. Later, when a tooth goes bad, some people choose extractions, which are less expensive (though less attractive) than root canals and crowns.

In recent years, demand for health care has grown. As people live longer, demand rises for expensive medical goods and services, including hearing aids, replacement joints, and assisted living and nursing home facilities. In an aging population, the incidence of certain illnesses and conditions—for example, cancer and Alzheimer's disease—rises. In addition, new technologies have made it possible to treat medical conditions for which there previously was no treatment. While these medical advances have improved the quality of life for many consumers, they drive up demand for more advanced medical procedures, equipment, and specialty drugs.

People who are risk averse (see Chapter 17) generally choose to purchase health insurance because it protects them against the possibility of extreme financial hardship in the case of severe illness or other medical problems. But

Health Insurance

SUPERSTORE

The sitcom *Superstore* features Amy Dubanowski (America Ferrera) and her fellow employees at Cloud 9, a big-box establishment where you can buy everything from toothpaste to a sofa. In the episode "Health Fund," the employees try to create a fund to pay for medical expenses within their group. While they only mention the word *insurance* with respect to the poor coverage they get through their employer, what they are trying to create is really a group insurance plan. They are attempting to pool their risk by all chipping in up front and then covering actual expenses as they arise.

Within a few hours, however, the plan is overextended by tens of thousands of dollars, due to an immediate flood of participant claims. At this point the simple plan becomes increasingly complex, as Amy and Jonah (Ben Feldman) try to separate people into high- and low-risk groups with differentiated premiums. They also confront traditional insurance problems, like adverse selection, where the high-risk people are the ones most eager to get coverage. There is also evidence of moral hazard, where people change their behavior—or at least their interest in seeing a doctor—due to insurance coverage. Further complex

Do you think America Ferrera and Ben Feldman have better health insurance than the characters they play on Superstore?

adjustments to the plan lead an exasperated employee to declare, "Guys, we're making it too difficult. We just gotta simplify. Cover everything, exclude no one, and make it affordable."

Credit: Thanks to Clair Smith, of St. John Fisher College, for this idea.

insurance may distort their idea of costs and cause them to change their behavior, which creates a moral hazard problem. For example, if an insurance policy does not require the patient to pay anything, or requires very little, to see the doctor, the patient may wind up seeing the doctor more often than necessary.

Consider how this situation affects two patients. Abigail does not have insurance and therefore must pay the full cost of medical care out of pocket. Brett has an insurance policy that requires a small copayment for medical care. Figure 18.3 illustrates the difference between how Abigail (point A) and Brett (point B) might react. Let's suppose they both get sick five times during the year. Because Abigail pays the full cost of seeking treatment ($100 per physician office visit), she will go to the doctor's office only three times. She ends up paying $300. Brett pays $10 per visit, so he will go to the doctor's office five times for a total cost to him of $50. The insurance company picks up the rest of the cost for Brett, or $90 per visit.

FIGURE 18.3

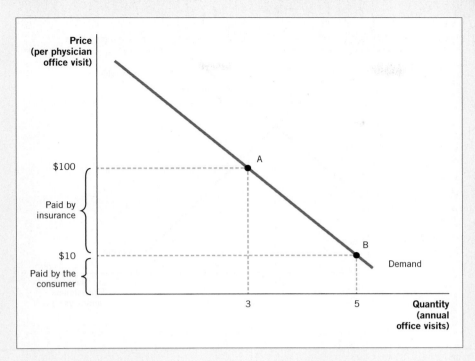

Without insurance, the consumer bears the entire cost of an office visit, or $100. At this amount, the consumer (Abigail) might think twice about whether the medical care is truly necessary. As a result of these costs, Abigail makes three office visits per year, represented by point A. However, when a consumer has insurance and pays only a $10 copayment per visit, the marginal price drops and the quantity demanded increases. This insured consumer, Brett, makes five office visits per year, represented by point B.

The overall impact of a $10 copayment on healthcare costs is large. In the Abigail/Brett scenario, since each visit costs $100, total healthcare costs for the office visits are only $300 when a patient is uninsured, but $500 with healthcare coverage—a $200 increase in total healthcare costs. Because in our example the insurance companies are paying 90% of the cost, the consumer has little reason not to seek medical attention, even for minor problems that will respond to home treatment. The two extra visits per year illustrate a change in consumer behavior as a result of the lower copayment, helping to explain why insurance costs are so high.

Healthcare Supply

While consumers worry about the price, or premium, they pay for health insurance, producers are concerned about profits. As much as we might like to think that medical providers care only about our health, we must acknowledge that they are providing a service for which they expect to be paid. Therefore, it is more accurate to think of healthcare providers in the same way we think of any other producers: when the price rises, they are willing to supply additional health care. Producers of medical care such as physicians and hospitals also enjoy significant market power. In this section, we consider how licensing requirements limit the supply of certain healthcare providers and thereby impact the market.

Becoming a skilled medical provider is a lengthy process that requires extensive training, education, and certification. Physicians must secure licenses

FIGURE 18.4

Barriers to Entry Limit the Supply of Certain Medical Workers

Restrictions associated with entering the medical profession limit the supply of certain workers. These restrictions cause a decrease in the quantity supplied of physicians and nurses from Q_1 to Q_2 and an increase in wages from W_1 to W_2.

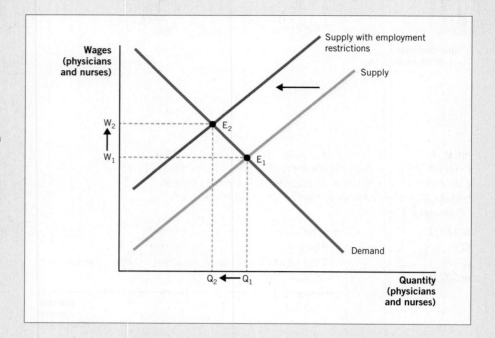

from a medical board before they can practice, and nurses must become registered. Thus, restrictions associated with entering the medical profession limit the supply of workers. This point is captured in Figure 18.4, which illustrates how barriers to entry limit the number of physicians and nurses and the associated effect on their wages.

Barriers to entry in the medical profession restrict the supply of physicians and nurses. The subsequent decrease in the quantity supplied of these medical workers (from Q_1 to Q_2) causes their wages to increase (from W_1 to W_2). In addition, many medical facilities do not face direct competition. For example, many small communities have only one hospital. In these cases, familiarity, the need for immediate care, and convenience make the nearest hospital the default option for most patients. Because economies of scale are important in the provision of medical care, even large metropolitan areas tend to have only a few large hospitals rather than many smaller competitors. As the population base expands, larger hospitals can afford to offer a wider set of services than smaller hospitals do. For instance, the need for pediatric care units, oncology centers, organ transplant centers, and a host of other services require that the hospital develop a particular expertise. The availability of specialized care is, of course, a good thing. However, as hospitals become larger and more highly specialized, competitive pressures subside and they are able to charge higher fees.

The market power of suppliers is held in check to some extent by insurance companies and by the Medicare and Medicaid programs. Also, some services are not reimbursed by insurance. And the insurance companies push back against certain other medical charges by limiting the amount they reimburse, as do Medicare and Medicaid for certain treatments. In addition, elective medical services, such as Lasik eye surgery, are typically not reimbursed by

Demand for Health Care: How Would Universal Health Care Alter the Demand for Medical Care?

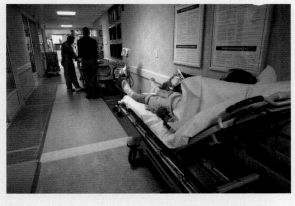

QUESTION: Suppose that the United States scraps its current healthcare system, and citizens are 100% covered for all medical care with no copayments or deductibles. How would the new system affect the demand for medical care? Illustrate your answer on a graph.

ANSWER: Without any copayment or deductibles, each patient's out-of-pocket expense would be zero. Society would pick up the tab through taxes. As a result, the quantity of medical care demanded by each patient would increase from point A to point B.

At point B, demand is no longer contingent on price, so this represents the largest potential quantity of care demanded.

An increase in the quantity of medical care demanded for services might mean that "hurry up and wait" becomes a common experience for most patients.

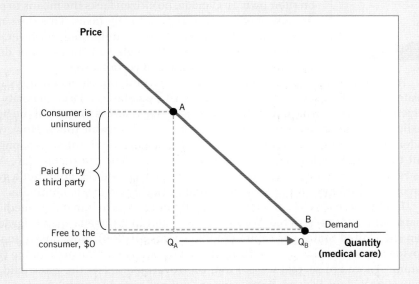

insurance plans. As a result, consumer demand is quite elastic for some services. While high medical care costs continue to be a significant policy concern, one researcher, Melinda Buntin, a professor in the Vanderbilt University School of Health Policy, has found that Medicare spending did not rise as fast as the overall economy and inflation from 2010 to 2016. If this trend holds, healthcare spending as a percentage of GDP will slowly decline over time.[*]

---

[*] Source: https://www.help.senate.gov/imo/media/doc/Buntin.pdf.

How Do Incentives Influence the Quality of Health Care?

Incentives

In this section, we apply what we've learned about health care. First, we look at the universal healthcare debate by comparing the healthcare systems in the United States and Canada. Then we examine the shortage of human organs available for transplant. By considering these two issues, we can see how incentives influence the quality of health care patients receive.

Single-Payer versus Private Health Care

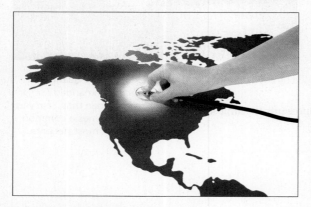

Which country has better health care, the United States or Canada?

Rationing is a fact of life because we live in a world of scarcity. The simplest way of thinking about the healthcare issue is to understand how different rationing mechanisms are used in medical care. In the United States, the primary rationing mechanism is the consumer's ability to pay. One consequence of using prices to ration medical care is that close to 35 million U.S. citizens forgo some medical care because they lack insurance or the means to pay for care on their own. In Canada, no citizen lacks the means to pay because medical care is paid for by taxes. This does not mean that medical care there is unlimited, however. In Canada, rationing occurs through wait times, fewer doctors, and limited availability of certain drugs.

As in almost all things economic, there is a trade-off. No medical system creates the perfect set of incentives. In the United States, a large majority of citizens have the means to pay for medical care, have access to some of the best medical facilities in the world, and face relatively short wait times. However, under the current U.S. system, access to the best facilities is limited, and longer wait times exist for the poorest members of society. The Affordable Care Act has reduced some of the disparities between the rich and the poor, but a system of private health care makes those differences impossible to eliminate.

Trade-offs

In Canada, each citizen is treated equally, but access to immediate medical treatment is more restricted. We saw in Table 18.1 that Canada spends far less than the United States per capita ($4,826 versus $10,209). How does Canada provide medical care to every citizen at approximately half the price of the U.S. system? There are several ways. First, the government sets the rates paid to medical providers. Second, physicians are not permitted to have private practices. Third, hospitals receive grants from the government to cover the costs of providing care. This system, in which there is only a *single payer*, makes the government the single buyer, or monopsonist, of most medical care. (See Chapter 14 for a discussion of monopsony.) In other words, in a **single-payer system**, the government covers the cost of providing most health care, and citizens pay their share through taxes.

In a **single-payer system**, the government covers the cost of providing most health care, and citizens pay their share through taxes.

The Canadian government uses its leverage as a monopsonist to set compensation levels for physicians below the competitive market wage rate. Under Canada's Health Act, government funding is required for medically necessary care, but only if that care is delivered in hospitals or by certified physicians. This means that the Canadian government funds about 70% of all medical expenses,

Health: United States vs. Canada

The healthcare dollar being spent as efficiently as possible to maintain the health of Americans? To answer this question, it's helpful to compare our situation to other countries, such as Canada. The United States and Canada have very different healthcare systems. Canada's is primarily a publicly funded, single-payer system with the government paying 70% of all health-related expenses. The United States' is primarily a privately funded, multi-payer system with the government paying approximately 48% of all health-related expenses.

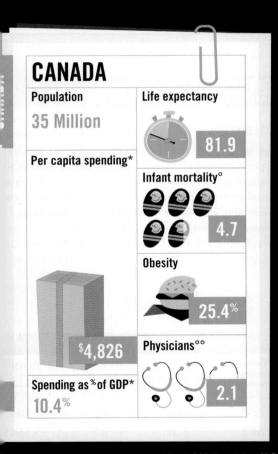

CANADA

Population
35 Million

Per capita spending*
$4,826

Spending as % of GDP*
10.4%

Life expectancy
81.9

Infant mortality°
4.7

Obesity
25.4%

Physicians°°
2.1

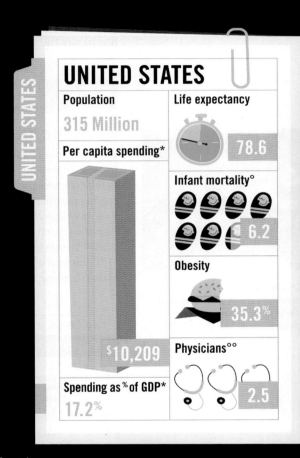

UNITED STATES

Population
315 Million

Per capita spending*
$10,209

Spending as % of GDP*
17.2%

Life expectancy
78.6

Infant mortality°
6.2

Obesity
35.3%

Physicians°°
2.5

*Total expenditure, public and private   ° Per 1,000 live births   °° Per 1,000 people
Sources: OECD, World Health Organization, CIA World Factbook.

Both countries achieve similar health outcomes, but health care is a clear example of trade-offs. The Canadian system cuts costs, while patients in the United States benefit from shorter wait times for care and the best medical facilities in the world.

REVIEW QUESTIONS

- How do you think the obesity level in the United States contributes to healthcare costs?

- What are the benefits and costs of a private versus a public healthcare system?

with the remaining 30% of costs being generated by prescription medications, long-term care, physical therapy, and dental care. In these areas, private insurance operates in much the same way it does in the United States.

Patients seeking medical care in Canada are far more likely to seek additional care in the United States than U.S. patients are to seek care in Canada. This fact might strike you as odd. After all, Canada has national health care, and health services there are covered under the Canadian Health Act. However, there is a difference between access and availability. Because Canada keeps tight control over medical costs, people with conditions that are not life-threatening often face extended waits. Services that are not regulated—for example, veterinarian visits—provide access to medical care without waiting. Dogs in Canada have no trouble getting MRIs and chemotherapy quickly—unlike their human counterparts, who have to wait—but of course the pet owner has to pay the full expense.

ECONOMICS IN THE REAL WORLD

HEALTHCARE EFFICIENCY

The Bloomberg Health Efficiency Index tracks medical costs and value-for-the-dollar for over 50 economically developed nations. The Efficiency Index was created in 2015 to rank countries whose citizens have average lifespans of at least 70 years, GDP per capita exceeding $5,000, and a minimum population of 5 million. The findings show that Americans aren't getting their money's worth. Only Switzerland spent more than the United States—but Switzerland's investment in medical care delivered an extra 4.2 years of extra life. A sampling of nations is shown in Table 18.2.

When your efficiency score places you between Russia and Bulgaria, something is seriously amiss.

Creating a more efficient health-care delivery system is one of the United States' greatest challenges of the 21st century.

TABLE 18.2

Health Care Efficiency in Selected Countries, 2015

Rank	Economy	Efficiency score	Life expectancy	Relative cost %	Absolute cost in USD
1	Hong King	87.3	84.3	5.7	2,222
2	Singapore	85.6	82.7	4.3	2,280
3	Spain	69.3	82.8	9.2	2,354
7	Japan	64.3	83.8	10.9	3,733
12	Switzerland	58.4	82.9	12.1	9,818
16	Canada	55.5	82.1	10.4	4,508
20	China	54.6	76.1	5.3	426
53	Russia	31.3	71.2	5.6	524
54	United States	29.6	78.7	16.8	9,536
56	Bulgaria	29.4	74.6	8.2	572

Source: https://www.bloomberg.com/news/articles/2018-09-19/u-s-near-bottom-of-health-index-hong-kong-and -singapore-at-top.

The Human Organ Shortage

Many altruistic people donate blood each year to help save the lives of tens of thousands of other people. Their generosity makes transplants and other surgeries possible. Unfortunately, the same level of generosity does not apply to organ donations. The quantity of replacement organs demanded exceeds the quantity of replacement organs supplied each year, resulting in thousands of deaths. Many of these deaths would be preventable if people were allowed to sell organs. However, the National Organ Transplant Act of 1984 makes it illegal to do so in the United States. Restrictions do not cover the entire body: people can sell platelets, sperm, and ova (the female reproductive cell). In those markets, prices determine who donates. With blood, kidneys, livers, and lungs, the donors are not paid. This discrepancy has created two unintended consequences. First, many people die unnecessarily: in the United States, more than 7,000 patients on transplant waiting lists die each year. Second, the demand for human organs has created a billion-dollar-a-year black market.

Let's consider the market for kidneys. Figure 18.5 illustrates how the supply of and demand for human kidneys works. Almost everyone has two kidneys, and a person's life can continue almost normally with only one healthy kidney. Of course, there are risks associated with donation, including complications from the surgery and during recovery, as well as no longer having a backup kidney. However, since there are roughly 300 million "spare" kidneys in the United States (because the population is 300 million), there is

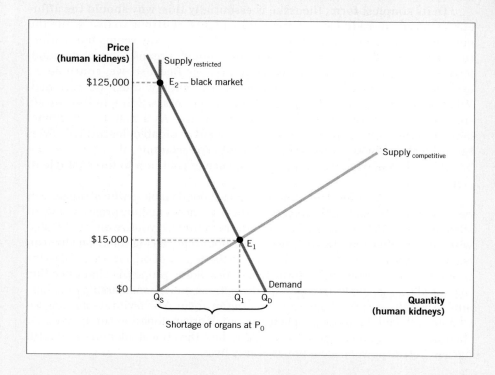

FIGURE 18.5

The Supply and Demand for Human Kidneys

Restrictions on selling kidneys limit the supply of organs as shown by Supply$_{restricted}$ and cause the shortage noted between Q_D and Q_S. A black market develops with an illegal price of $125,000.

a large pool of potential donors who are good matches for recipients awaiting a transplant.

Because kidneys cannot be legally bought and sold, the supply curve shown in Figure 18.5 does not respond to price. As a result, the curve becomes a vertical line at point Q_S (quantity supplied). Notice that the quantity supplied is not zero because many people donate kidneys to friends and family members in need. Others participate in exchange programs under which they donate a kidney to someone they don't know in exchange for someone else agreeing to donate a kidney to their friend or family member. (Exchange programs help to provide better matches so that the recipient is less likely to reject the kidney transplant.) Moreover, a few altruistic persons donate their kidneys to complete strangers. Nevertheless, the quantity supplied still falls short of the quantity demanded, because $Q_D > Q_S$ at a price of \$0.

Trade creates value

Markets would normally reconcile a shortage by increasing prices. In Figure 18.5, an equilibrium market price of \$15,000 is shown (E_1). Economists have estimated that this would be the market price if the sale of kidneys were legal in the United States. Because such sales are illegal, the nation faces the shortage illustrated in Figure 18.5. Over 4,000 people die each year in this country waiting for a kidney transplant. Many others have a low quality of life while waiting to receive a kidney. Because patients waiting for human organs eventually die without a transplant, a black market for kidney transplants has developed outside the United States. However, the price—typically \$125,000 or greater—requires doctors, hospitals, staff, and patients to circumvent the law. As a consequence, the black-market price (at E_2) is much higher than it would be if a competitive market for human kidneys existed.

In its simplest form, the issue is essentially this: why should the affluent, who can afford to pay for organ transplants, continue to live, while the poor, who also need organ transplants, die? That hardly seems fair. Unfortunately, altruism alone has not provided enough organs to meet demand, leading to a shortage of many vital organs. Because we continue to experience shortages of human organs, the supply must be rationed. Whether the rationing takes place through markets, waiting in line, or via some other mechanism is a matter of efficiency. As a result, using markets, in some form, may be one way to prevent avoidable deaths. However, the ethical considerations are significant. For example, if organs can be bought and sold, what would prevent the use of coercion to force people to sell their organs?

Of course, the ethical dilemma becomes moot if viable artificial organs can be created. And in fact, in this regard medical science is making progress toward someday solving the organ shortage. In the meantime, if you are uncomfortable with markets determining the price, remember that relying solely on altruism is not enough. If we really want to increase the supply of organs, we need to try incentives and harness behavioral economics. Some proposals along this line include allowing people to receive tax deductions, college scholarships, or guaranteed health care in exchange for donating an organ. A behavioral solution (see Chapter 17) would require people to opt out of organ donations in the event of their death. All these suggestions would reduce the ethical dilemma while still harnessing the power of economics to save lives.

Incentives

SELLING OVA TO PAY FOR COLLEGE

Did you know that young, bright, American women with college loans can help pay off their debts by donating their ova? In 2012, *The Atlantic* reported on this phenomenon, exploring the donation process and experience. The donor is paid to travel to a fertility clinic, and several weeks of hormone treatments begin. Afterward, pairs of the donor's ova are removed surgically, then fertilized in a laboratory and implanted inside the womb of a woman who is infertile. With careful lab work and a little luck, the procedure works. The donor receives between $5,000 and $15,000, depending on her track record as a donor. Those whose ova have been successfully implanted and led to the birth of a healthy child are in high demand.

"Baby, baby, baby, oh."

The procedure is not without risks, including rare but potentially serious complications for donors and a high incidence of multiple births among recipients; additionally, long-term risks are not well understood. And, clearly, volunteering for elective surgery isn't a choice everyone would feel comfortable making. But that said, the existence of a market allows a trade that can greatly benefit both the donor and the recipient.

Human Organ Shortage: Liver Transplants

Most liver transplants make use of organs from cadavers. However, liver transplants are also possible with live donors, who give a portion of their liver to a needy recipient. Donating a live liver involves major surgery that lasts between 4 and 12 hours. The complication rate for the donor is low, but the recovery time is typically two to three months. Not surprisingly, there is still a shortage of live livers for transplant.

QUESTION: What solutions can you think of that would motivate more people to donate part of their liver to help save the life of someone else?

ANSWER: One answer would be to repeal the National Organ Transplant Act. This move would create a market for livers and establish a price that would eliminate the shortage. Other ways to increase donations would be to allow donors to claim a tax deduction equal to the value of the portion of the liver donated or to receive scholarships for themselves or members of their family.

The Human Organ Black Market

LAW & ORDER: SPECIAL VICTIMS UNIT

In one episode of *Law & Order: Special Victims Unit*, the officers try to track down a sleazy kidney dealer. What makes the episode compelling is the tension between doing what the law requires—stopping an illegal kidney transplant mid-surgery—and subsequently wrestling with watching the patient suffer as a result. In addition, the officers interview the dealer, the physician, patients on kidney waiting lists, and an administrator of the national kidney wait list. Their opinions, which run a wide gamut, allow the viewer to experience all of the emotions and arguments for and against the purchase of kidneys.

Each character tugs on viewers' emotions in a different way. The sleazy dealer proudly proclaims that he is making his customers happy and that the officers wouldn't be so judgmental if one of their own family members needed a kidney. The physician who does the transplant explains he is not driven by making money but by saving lives. The patients all know where they can get an illegal kidney, but most accept their fate within the current system. The administrator of the wait list argues that "they have enough trouble getting people to volunteer as it is. What would happen if

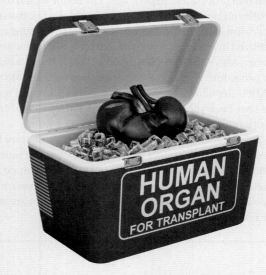

On the track of a black-market kidney dealer.

donors learned that we had made an exception and approved the transplant of an illegally purchased kidney?" By the end of the episode, we see that the economic and ethical dimensions of the issue are not clear-cut.

Conclusion

When people speak about health care, they often debate the merits of universal health care versus private medical care, as if the issue involves just those two factors. This obscures the important economic considerations at work on the micro level. The reality is that the healthcare debate exists on many margins and requires complex trade-offs. The way the various participants deal with different healthcare issues affects how well our nation's overall healthcare system functions. Supply and demand works just fine in explaining the incentives that participants face when considering healthcare options; what complicates the analysis is the impact of third parties on the incentives patients face.

Obamacare: A Primer

Formally called the Affordable Care Act (ACA), Obamacare is a federal law, signed by President Barack Obama in 2010, that provided fundamental reform of the U.S. healthcare and health insurance system, signed by President Barack Obama in 2010. To help you understand the Affordable Care Act, we have created this primer.

Learn about the Affordable Care Act.

1. The ACA does not create health insurance. The legislation regulates the health insurance industry and is designed to increase the quality, affordability, and availability of private insurance.

2. Young adults can stay on their parents' plan until age 26. Before the ACA was passed, it was common for young adults to fall off their parents' plans and, due to low income, forgo health care. Under the ACA, most young adults qualify for federal subsidies or Medicaid through the Health Insurance Marketplace.

3. The ACA created new health insurance exchanges to promote increased enrollment, deliver subsidies, and help spread risk to ensure that the costs associated with expensive medical treatments are shared more broadly across large groups of people, rather than spread across just a few beneficiaries. If you don't have coverage, you can use the Health Insurance Marketplace (healthcare .gov) to buy a private insurance plan. The cost of your marketplace health insurance works on a sliding scale. Those who make less pay less. Poorer Americans are eligible for premium tax credits through the marketplace. These tax credits subsidize the cost of insurance premiums.

4. All new plans sold on or off the marketplace must include a wide range of new benefits. These include wellness visits and preventive tests and treatments at no additional out-of-pocket cost. Preventive care is much cheaper than addressing serious medical issues too late, so this provision of the ACA is intended to lower overall costs.

5. The ACA does away with discrimination based on preexisting conditions and gender, so these factors no longer affect the cost of insurance on or off the marketplace. You can't be denied health coverage based on health status. You can't be dropped from coverage when you are sick. These changes spread risk more evenly and encourage people to get medical care sooner.

Health care straddles the boundary between microeconomic analysis, which focuses on individual behavior, and macroeconomics, in which society's overarching concern is how to best spend so large an amount of money. Moreover, health decisions are an unavoidable part of our individual lives. Medical expenditures account for one out of every six dollars spent in the United States. Therefore, micro forces that lead to fundamental changes to the healthcare system will have a large impact—a macro effect—on our economy. ✳

What are the important issues in the healthcare industry?

- The healthcare debate is about efficiency and cost containment. Increases in longevity and quality of life are subject to diminishing returns and require choices with difficult trade-offs.

- The widespread use of insurance alters the incentives consumers and producers face when making healthcare decisions. Consumers pay premiums up front and much smaller deductibles and copayments when seeking medical care. Producers receive the bulk of their revenue from intermediaries such as insurance companies. The result is a system in which consumers demand more medical care because they are insured and many providers have an incentive to order additional tests or procedures that may not be absolutely necessary.

How does asymmetric information affect healthcare delivery?

- Asymmetric information (adverse selection, the principal-agent problem, and moral hazard) affects incentives in healthcare delivery. Insurance companies try to structure their plans to encourage patients to seek care only when it is needed and also to seek preventive care. The companies can achieve these goals by making many preventive care visits free and establishing deductibles and copayments that are high enough to discourage unnecessary trips to the doctor or a demand for additional procedures.

- Inelastic demand for many medical services, combined with third-party payments that significantly lower out-of-pocket expenses to consumers, gives rise to a serious moral hazard problem in which patients demand more medical care than is medically advisable. To solve a moral hazard problem, it is necessary to fix the incentive structure. Moral hazard explains why many insurance companies encourage preventive care: it lowers medical costs. It also explains why insurance companies impose payment limits on preventable conditions.

How do demand and supply contribute to high medical costs?

- Inelastic demand and third-party payments help explain why medical expenses have risen so rapidly. The combination of third-party payments and inelastic demand for medical care increases the quantity of medical care demanded; both factors also result in increased expenditures. As we learned previously, more demand means higher prices, all else equal.

- In addition, licensing requirements limit the supply of key healthcare providers. Licensing requirements provide a supply-side explanation for increased medical expenditures. In addition, hospital charges are rarely subject to competitive pressures. In many small communities, there is only one local hospital, clinic, or specialist nearby. Providers therefore have market power, which they can use in setting prices.

How do incentives influence the quality of health care?

- A single-payer system makes the government the single buyer, or monopsonist, of most medical care. The government uses its leverage as a monopsonist to set compensation levels for providers below the competitive market wage rate.

- Single-payer systems ration medical services through increased wait times, whereas private healthcare systems ration medical care through prices.

- The demand for many replacement organs exceeds the supply made available each year. However, because of the National Organ Transplant Act of 1984, it is illegal to sell most organs in the United States. This restriction results in thousands of deaths annually, many of which would be preventable if people were allowed to sell organs in legal markets.

Concepts You Should Know

adverse selection (p. 578)
asymmetric information (p. 578)
coinsurance payments (p. 576)

copayments (p. 576)
deductibles (p. 576)
moral hazard (p. 579)

principal-agent problem (p. 578)
single-payer system (p. 586)

Questions for Review

1. What is asymmetric information? How is it relevant to medical care?

2. Give one example each of adverse selection, moral hazard, and the principal-agent problem.

3. For each of the examples you gave in question 2, discuss a solution that lessens the asymmetric information problem.

4. Describe why the marginal product of medical care declines as medical expenditures rise.

5. What are two primary reasons healthcare demand has increased dramatically over the last 20 years?

6. What is a supply-related reason for high medical care costs?

7. What are the two primary ways in which health care is rationed?

Study Problems (✻ solved at the end of the section)

1. Suppose that a medical specialist charges $300 per consultation. If your insurance charges you a $25 copay, what is the marginal cost of your consultation? Suppose that a second patient has a different policy that requires a 25% coinsurance payment, but no copay. What is the second patient's marginal cost of the consultation? Which patient is more likely to see the specialist?

✻ **2.** Newer automobiles have many safety features, including antilock brakes, side air bags, traction control, and rear backup sensors, to help prevent accidents. Do these safety features lead the drivers of newer vehicles to drive more safely? In your answer, consider how an increased number of safety features affects the problem of moral hazard.

3. A customer wants a new life insurance policy. Even though the customer's medical records indicate a good health history, the insurance company requires a physical exam before coverage can be extended. Why would the insurance company insist on a physical exam?

4. Indicate whether the following medical services have elastic or inelastic demand.

    a. an annual physical for someone between the ages of 20 and 35

    b. an MRI used to detect cancer

    c. the removal of a noncancerous mole on your back

    d. seeing a physician when your child has a temperature of 104°F

5. Most people have two working kidneys, but humans need only one working kidney to survive. If the sale of kidneys were legalized, what would happen to the price and the number of kidneys sold in the market? Would a shortage of kidneys continue to exist? Explain your response.

✻ **6.** An isolated community has one hospital. The next closest hospital is 2 hours away. Given what you have learned about monopoly, what prices would you expect the hospital to charge? How much care would you expect it to provide? Compare the prices and amount of care provided to those of a comparably sized hospital in a major metropolitan area where competition is prevalent.

7. One insurance plan costs $100 a month and has a $50 copayment for all services. Another insurance plan costs $50 a month and requires patients to pay a 15% coinsurance. A consumer is trying to decide which plan to purchase. Which plan would the consumer select with an anticipated $200 per month in medical bills? What about $600 per month in medical bills? Set up an equation to determine the monthly amount of medical expenses at which the consumer would be indifferent between the two plans.

8. For each of the following situations, determine whether adverse selection, moral hazard, or the principal-agent problem is at work.

   a. You decide to buy a scalped ticket before a concert, but you are not entirely sure the ticket is legitimate.

   b. A contractor takes a long time to finish the construction work he promised after you gave him his final payment.

   c. You hire a neighborhood teenager to mow your grass once a week over the summer while you are traveling. The teenager mows your grass every three weeks instead.

✳ **9.** "To economists, human life is not of infinite value." Explain this statement and its economic implications for end-of-life care.

10. What characteristics make the market for health care different from other markets?

11. Suppose you recently broke your arm, and as part of your recovery process, you are considering how many times to go to physical therapy. The marginal cost (MC) of a visit to the physical therapist is constant and equal to $300. That is what you have to pay per visit, assuming you don't have insurance.

   a. How many times should you visit the physical therapist?

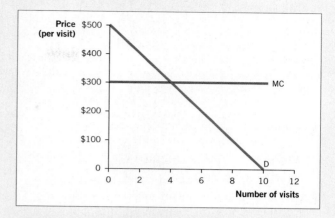

   b. If you have full health coverage (with no copay or deductible) how many times will you visit the physical therapist?

   c. What is the deadweight loss that arises due to full health coverage? (***Hint:*** Deadweight loss is the difference between the willingness to pay and the additional cost of production that arises when the consumer has no copay or deductible.)

✳ **12.** We learned that when caps are placed on how much a physician can be paid for a service under Medicare, doctors charge more for other services. Can you think of anything else a physician might decide to do if they feel that what Medicare pays is insufficient to cover their costs?

Solved Problems

2. When drivers feel safer, they drive faster—not more safely. The higher speed offsets the safety gain from safety features that help prevent accidents or make them survivable. Drivers of vehicles who feel especially safe are more likely to take on hazardous conditions and become involved in accidents. In other words, they alter their behavior when driving a safer car. The change in behavior is evidence of a moral hazard problem.

6. Because the demand for medical care is quite inelastic, an isolated hospital with significant monopoly power will charge more and offer fewer services. In contrast, a comparably sized hospital in a major metropolitan area where competition is prevalent is forced to charge the market price and offer more services to attract consumers.

9. Human life is not of infinite value because we live in a world of trade-offs. An "infinite value" implies

that the value is so high that all medical paths are worth pursuing. However, one must be mindful of the marginal cost of care versus the amount of additional life that end-of-life care buys. This consideration is especially important at the end of life when extraordinary medical efforts might mean only a few extra days of low-quality life. The law of diminishing returns applies, and the application of this economic principle suggests that resources should be redirected from end-of-life care to preventive care with larger returns.

12. Medicare is a government program, but physicians are not required to participate. Therefore, another option is not to participate, which is exactly what some doctors decide to do. These doctors have decided that as long as they're able to keep their appointment books reasonably full with non-Medicare patients, the opportunity cost of taking Medicare patients is too high.

19

International Trade

Nations Gain Through International Trade, Even if they can Produce their Goods and Services Domestically.

It's often assumed that nations should try to produce their own goods and services. In particular, it seems intuitive that if the United States *can* produce a particular good more efficiently than any other nation can, then the United States *should* produce that good. But way back in Chapter 2, we learned how individuals gain by specializing in the production of certain goods and obtaining other goods through trade, even when the individuals could produce those other goods more efficiently themselves. Here we will see how the same principles apply to trade between nations. This second look at trade will give us a chance to go deeper into the theory.

International trade is greatly facilitated by an invention that gets little fanfare: the stackable shipping container, conceived and developed in the mid-1950s by trucking magnate Malcolm McLean and engineer Keith Tantlinger. Prior to that time, ships had cargo holds. Wooden crates of cargo were loaded individually and meticulously fitted together like a jigsaw puzzle, to maximize the use of interior space. All of this took time, and more time on the unloading end. McLean and Tantlinger's inspired insight was that on- and off-loading time could be reduced dramatically by using metal containers of uniform shape and size, and using large

Without the invention of the container ship, getting imports from overseas would be a lot more expensive. Imports come into the United States from all over the globe. But does importing goods from other countries harm our economy?

cranes to stack the containers, securely locked together, on the decks of specially configured ships, instead of down in the holds.

Today every container is geo-tagged, so manufacturing plants know exactly when the components they need are offloaded. This arrangement makes just-in-time manufacturing possible. Overall, the "containerization" of shipping has reduced costs by approximately 35% compared to the use of cargo holds. With transoceanic transport dramatically more cost effective, the past few decades have seen the volume of trade among the world's nations rise dramatically.

To help illustrate the extent of international trade, we begin this chapter with a look at global trade data. We then consider how international trade affects an economy. Finally, we have to reckon with the fact that, despite the theoretical arguments for free trade and the practical advances that make it easy and cheap, not everyone is convinced that free trade is a good idea. So we conclude the chapter by examining trade barriers and the reasons for their existence.

· BIG QUESTIONS ·

- Is globalization for real?
- How does international trade help the economy?
- What are the effects of tariffs and quotas?

Is Globalization for Real?

Over the past 75 years, trade among nations all over the world is way up. What this means for you and me is that we can buy fresh Peruvian strawberries (in February!), roses from Kenya, cars from Mexico, and electronics from South Korea. But the United States also exports more now than in any earlier era. Imports and exports are both up for other countries, as well, and that means

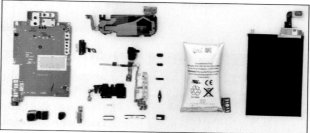

How many borders does an iPhone cross before it is sold?

economies around the globe are more and more interdependent. This interdependence is the essence of *globalization*, and it is changing not only what you purchase but also your future job prospects.

Consider a single popular item: the iPhone. Inside the iPhone are parts made in Germany, Japan, Korea, and the United States. The phone is famously "designed by Apple in California," but it is assembled in China. This single item requires thousands of miles of global shipping before anyone ever touches its screen.

The modern trade explosion has occurred for many reasons. Among these are lower shipping and communication costs, reduced trade barriers, and increased specialization in world economies. Total world exports of goods and services are now about one-fourth the size of world GDP. In this section, we look first at the growth in total world trade and then at trends in U.S. trade.

Trade creates value

Growth in World Trade

World trade has grown, but not just in market value. It has also grown as a percentage of total world output. That is, not only are nations trading more, but they are also trading a greater portion of their GDP. Figure 19.1 shows merchandise trade as a percentage of world GDP. This has expanded dramatically, doubling over 50 years, from 11% in 1970 to 22% in 2017.

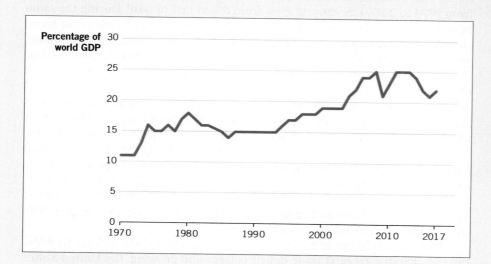

FIGURE 19.1

World Trade as a Percentage of World GDP, 1970–2017

Even as a percentage of world GDP, trade has grown significantly. It doubled from 11% in 1970 to 22% in 2017.

Sources: World Trade Organization; World Bank.

NICARAGUA IS FOCUSED ON TRADE

Nicaragua, the second-poorest nation in the Western Hemisphere, is trying to escape poverty through international trade. Between 2007 and 2017, its real exports grew from $1.8 billion to $5.3 billion.

Trade with Nicaragua is growing in part because the country has established "free zones," where companies can produce goods for export and avoid standard corporate tax rates. Typical Nicaraguan companies pay a myriad of sales taxes, value-added taxes, corporate profit taxes, and dividend taxes. But these do not apply to output that a company exports to other nations. U.S. companies that have taken advantage of production in these free zones include Levi's, Under Armour, and Nike.

All else equal, market-driven international trade certainly helps nations to prosper. Yet while the free zones are increasing exports, the effect on domestic consumers in Nicaragua may not be entirely positive. Because the goods have to be exported for the manufacturers to take advantage of the tax breaks, there is very little incentive to produce goods for domestic purchase and consumption.

The Levi-Strauss company produces many of its blue jeans in Nicaragua.

Trends in U.S. Trade

Trends in U.S. international trade are similar to overall global trends. The United States is the world's biggest economy. A huge amount of trade takes place between the individual states *inside* the country. For example, residents of Michigan buy oranges from Florida, and Floridians buy cars from Michigan. Still, even with the ability to produce and trade so much within U.S. borders, the nation's participation in international trade has risen dramatically in recent years. Figure 19.2 shows U.S. exports and imports as a percentage of GDP from 1970 to 2017.

As you look at the data in Figure 19.2, note three features. First, in panel (a), notice that both imports and exports increased significantly over the 50 years from 1970 to 2017. U.S. exports grew from 5% to 12% of GDP. During the same period, imports rose from less than 5% to 15% of GDP. Note also that these changes occurred even as real GDP grew by 3% each year. These numbers provide another clear glimpse at the modern trend toward globalization: the world's largest economy is becoming ever more intertwined with those of other nations.

Second, since 1975, U.S. imports have exceeded U.S. exports. **Net exports** is the total exports of final goods and services minus total imports of final goods and services. The difference between a nation's total exports and total imports is its **trade balance**. If a nation exports more than it imports, it has a positive trade balance, or a **trade surplus**. However, if a nation imports more than it exports, it has a negative trade balance, or a **trade deficit**. The United States has had a trade deficit since 1975. In 2017 alone, the United States exported $2.35 trillion in goods and services and imported $2.9 trillion, leading to a trade deficit of $550 billion—no small sum.

Panel (c) of Figure 19.2 reveals a little-known fact about U.S. trade: while the merchandise (goods) trade deficit is large and growing, the United States actually has a service trade surplus. Popular U.S. service exports include financial,

Net exports is the total exports of final goods and services minus total imports of final goods and services.

A nation's **trade balance** is the difference between its total exports and total imports.

A **trade surplus** occurs when exports exceed imports, indicating a positive trade balance.

A **trade deficit** occurs when imports exceed exports, indicating a negative trade balance.

FIGURE 19.2

U.S. Exports and Imports, 1970–2017 (as a percentage of GDP)

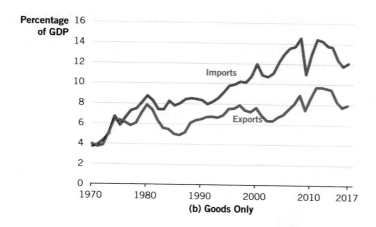

Percentage of GDP

Imports

Exports

(a) Total Goods and Services

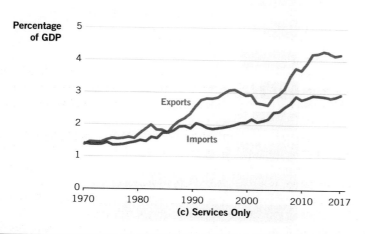

Percentage of GDP

Imports

Exports

(b) Goods Only

Percentage of GDP

Exports

Imports

(c) Services Only

(a) Both imports and exports are rising in the United States. In addition, the trade balance is becoming more negative over time, as imports are exceeding exports by an increasingly wider margin. This trade deficit grows during economic expansions and shrinks during recessions (shaded regions). (b) The trade deficit is driven by a merchandise (goods) deficit, and yet, (c) the United States enjoys a trade surplus in services.

Source: U.S. Bureau of Economic Analysis: *U.S. International Transactions.*

Foreign students who purchase their education in the United States are one type of U.S. service export.

travel, and education services. To put a face on service exports, think about students in your classes who are from outside the United States (perhaps this category even includes you). In 2017, the United States exported over $43 billion worth of education services.

Finally, notice how the business cycle affects international trade. During recessionary periods (indicated by the light blue bars in Figure 19.2a), imports generally drop. As the economy recovers, imports begin to rise again. In addition, while exports often drop during recessions, the trade deficit tends to shrink during downturns. Part of this fluctuation reflects the way imports and exports are calculated. In short, note the strong relationship between trade and economic activity: trade expands during economic expansions and contracts during recessions.

Major Trading Partners of the United States

In 2017, the United States imported goods and services from 238 nations. However, over 60% of goods imports came from just nine nations. Figure 19.3 shows the value of imports from and exports to these top nine trading partners of the United States.

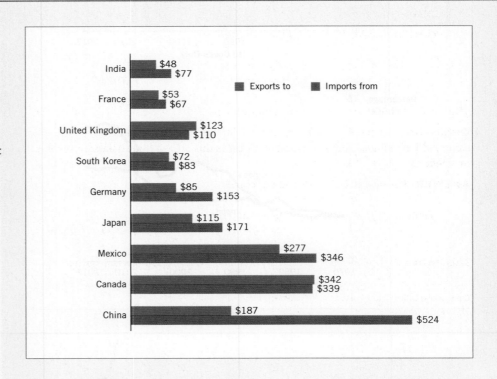

Country	Exports to	Imports from
India	$48	$77
France	$53	$67
United Kingdom	$123	$110
South Korea	$72	$83
Germany	$85	$153
Japan	$115	$171
Mexico	$277	$346
Canada	$342	$339
China	$187	$524

Trade in Goods and Services: Deficit or Surplus?

The United States imports many goods from Japan, including automobiles, electronics, and medical instruments. But we also export many services to Japan, such as financial and travel services. The table below reflects trade between the United States and Japan in 2014. (All figures are in billions of U.S. dollars.)

Sony PlayStations are a popular U.S. import from Japan.

	Exports to Japan	Imports from Japan
Goods	$20	$103
Services	47	31

QUESTION: Using the data shown above, how would you compute the U.S. goods trade balance with Japan? Is the balance a surplus or a deficit?

ANSWER: The U.S. goods trade balance equals

goods exports − goods imports
= $20 billion − $103 billion = −$83 billion

This is a trade deficit. Imports exceed exports, and the trade balance is negative.

QUESTION: Now how would you compute the U.S. services trade balance with Japan? Is the balance a surplus or a deficit?

ANSWER: The U.S. services trade balance equals

service exports − service imports
= $47 billion − $31 billion = $16 billion

This is a trade surplus. Exports exceed imports, and the trade balance is positive.

QUESTION: Finally, how would you compute the overall U.S. trade balance with Japan, which includes both goods and services? Is this overall trade balance a surplus or a deficit?

ANSWER: The overall U.S. trade balance equals

Goods and service exports − goods and service imports
= $67 billion − $134 billion = −$67 billion

This is a trade deficit. Imports exceed exports, and the trade balance is negative.

Data source: Office of the United States Trade Representative.

In this picture from a dollar store, is there anything that is *not* produced in China?

In the past, our closest neighbors—Canada and Mexico—were our chief trading partners. From Canada we get motor vehicles, oil, natural gas, and many other goods and services. From Mexico we get motor vehicles, coffee, computers, household appliances, and gold. More recently, falling transportation costs have led to increased trade with other countries, as well. For example, total imports from China alone are now roughly $524 billion, up from $350 billion (adjusted for inflation) a little more than a decade ago. Popular Chinese imports include electronics, toys, and clothing.

Canada and Mexico buy the most U.S. exports. To Canada we export cars, car parts, computers, and agricultural products. To Mexico we export cars, car parts, computers, and meat, among many other items. Financial and travel services are major U.S. exports to all our major trading partners.

How Does International Trade Help the Economy?

Trade creates value

In this section, we explain how comparative advantage and specialization make it possible to achieve gains from trade between nations. To keep the analysis simple, we assume that two trading partners—the United States and Mexico—produce only two items, clothes and food. This example will enable us to demonstrate that trade creates value in the absence of any restrictions.

Comparative Advantage

Comparative advantage refers to the situation where an individual, business, or country can produce at a lower opportunity cost than a competitor can.

In Chapter 2, we saw that trade creates value and that **comparative advantage** makes the creation of value possible. Gains arise when a nation specializes in production and exchanges its output with a trading partner. In other words, each nation should produce the good it is best at making and trade with other nations for the goods they are best at making. Trade leads to lower costs of production and maximizes the combined output of all nations involved. (Comparative advantage is very important to the discussion that follows. If you don't remember the details of comparative advantage, be sure to review Chapter 2 before proceeding.)

Suppose the United States and Mexico both produce clothing and food. Also assume that the production of one unit of food requires a greater quantity of capital per unit of labor than the production of one unit of clothing (in economics, we say that food is *capital intensive* and clothing is *labor intensive*). Because the United States is generally viewed as abundant in skilled labor but not so much in unskilled labor, while at the same time abundant in capital, it makes sense that it will specialize and produce food. Mexico, which is generally viewed as abundant in unskilled labor, will specialize in clothing.

In Figure 19.4, we see the production possibilities frontier (PPF) for each country when it does *not* specialize and trade. In panel (a), Mexico can produce at any point along its PPF. It can produce 900 million units, or articles, of clothing if it does not make any food, and it can produce 300 million tons of food if it

FIGURE 19.4

The Production Possibilities Frontier for Mexico and the United States without Specialization and Trade

(a) Mexico chooses to operate along its production possibilities curve at 450 million articles of clothing and 150 million tons of food. Each ton of food incurs an opportunity cost of three articles of clothing—a food–clothing ratio of 1:3.
(b) The United States chooses to operate along its production possibilities curve at 300 million articles of clothing and 200 million tons of food. Each ton of food incurs an opportunity cost of one-half an article of clothing—a food–clothing ratio of 2:1.

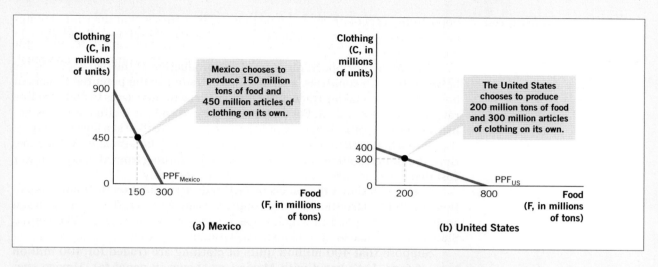

(a) Mexico

(b) United States

does not make any clothing. Neither extreme is especially desirable because it would mean that Mexico would have to do without either clothing or food. As a result, Mexico will prefer to operate somewhere in between the two extremes. We show Mexico operating along its production possibilities frontier at 450 million articles of clothing and 150 million tons of food. Panel (b) shows that the United States can produce 400 million articles of clothing if it does not make any food, and it can produce 800 million tons of food if it does not make any clothing. Like Mexico, the United States will prefer to operate somewhere in between—for example, at 300 million articles of clothing and 200 million tons of food.

To see whether gains from trade are able to make both countries better off, we must first examine the opportunity cost that each country faces when making these two goods. In Mexico, producing 150 million tons of food means giving up the production of 450 million articles of clothing (900 − 450 = 450). Thus, each ton of food incurs an opportunity cost of three articles of clothing, yielding a ratio of 150:450, or 1:3, or one ton of food per three articles of clothing. In the United States, producing 200 million tons of food means giving up production of 100 million articles of clothing (400 − 300 = 100). The ratio here is therefore 200:100, or 2:1. (Notice that both ratios are in the format food:clothing.) In the United States, then, a ton of food incurs an opportunity cost of one-half an article of clothing. Table 19.1 shows the initial production choices and the opportunity costs for both nations. Because the United States has a lower

Opportunity cost

TABLE 19.1

Output and Opportunity Costs for Mexico and the United States

	Chosen output level		Opportunity cost	
	Food (millions of tons)	Clothing (millions of units)	Food (F)	Clothing (C)
Mexico	150	450	3 C	⅓ F
United States	200	300	½ C	2 F

Opportunity cost

opportunity cost of producing food than Mexico, we say that the United States has a comparative advantage in producing food and therefore will specialize in food production.

As long as the opportunity cost of the production of the two goods differs between the two countries, as it does here, trade has the potential to benefit both. The key to making trade mutually beneficial in this case is to find a trading ratio between 1:3 and 2:1. For instance, if Mexico and the United States establish a 1:1 trading ratio, Mexico would be able to acquire food at a lower cost from the United States than it would cost to produce food domestically. At the same time, the United States would be able to acquire clothing from Mexico at a lower cost than it would cost to produce clothing domestically.

Figure 19.5 shows the effects of a 1:1 trade agreement on the joint production possibilities frontier for each country. If the two countries trade, each can specialize in the good in which it has a comparative advantage. The United States will produce food and Mexico will produce clothing.

Suppose that 400 million units of clothing are traded for 400 million tons of food. Let's begin with Mexico, as shown in panel (a). Mexico specializes in the production of clothing, producing 900 million units. It then exports 400 million units of clothing to the United States and imports 400 million tons of food from the United States in return—this is the 1:1 trade ratio we identified previously. Therefore, Mexico ends up at point M_2 with 500 million units of clothing and 400 million tons of food. Notice that Mexico's production without trade (at point M_1) was 450 million units of clothing and 150 tons of food. Therefore, specialization and trade have made Mexico better off by enabling it to consume 50 million more units of clothing and 250 more million tons of food.

Now let's look at the United States in panel (b). The United States specializes in the production of food, producing 800 million tons. It exports 400 million tons of food to Mexico and imports 400 million units of clothing from Mexico in return. Therefore, the United States ends up at point US_2 with 400 million units of clothing and 400 million tons of food. Notice that U.S. production without trade (at point US_1) was 300 million units of clothing and 200 tons of food. Therefore, specialization and trade have made the United States better off by allowing it to consume 100 million more units of clothing and 200 million more tons of food.

The combined benefits that Mexico and the United States enjoy are even more significant. As we saw in Figure 19.4, when Mexico did not specialize and trade, it chose to make 450 million units of clothing and 150 million tons of food. Without specialization and trade, the United States chose to produce 300 million units of clothing and 200 million tons of food. The combined output without specialization was 750 million units of clothing and 350 million tons

FIGURE 19.5

The Production Possibilities Frontier for Mexico and the United States with Specialization and Trade

(a) After Mexico specializes in clothing and trades with the United States, it is better off by 50 million units of clothing and 250 million tons of food (compare points M_1 and M_2). (b) After the United States specializes in food and trades with Mexico, it is better off by 100 million units of clothing and 200 million tons of food (compare points US_1 and US_2).

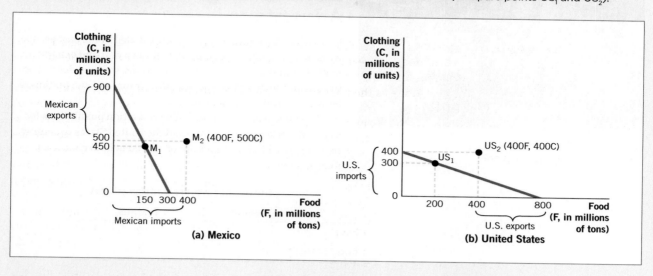

(a) Mexico   (b) United States

of food. However, as we see in Figure 19.5, the joint output with specialization is 900 million units of clothing and 800 million tons of food. In economics, we call this a *positive-sum game* because both players, in this case both countries, win by trading with each other.

Other Advantages of Trade

Although comparative advantage is the biggest reason that many nations trade with other nations, there are other good reasons for nations to engage in trade. In this section, we consider how international trade encourages both economies of scale and increased competition and how these factors can help an economy to grow.

ECONOMIES OF SCALE When a nation specializes its production, it can take advantage of the lower production costs that can accompany large-scale production processes. Economies of scale are especially important for smaller nations that do not have a population big enough to support the domestic production of large-scale items such as automobiles, television sets, steel, and aluminum. However, once a smaller nation has free access to larger markets, it can effectively specialize in what it does best and generate low per-unit costs through exports.

Does China enjoy a comparative advantage in textile production?

Opportunity Cost and Comparative Advantage: Determining Comparative Advantage

U.S. trade with mainland China has exploded in the past decade, with goods imports reaching $467 billion a year and exports up to $124 billion. For the following questions, we consider a hypothetical production possibilities frontier for food and textiles in both China and the United States.

The table below presents daily production possibilities for a typical worker in both China and the United States, assuming that only two kinds of goods are produced in both countries: food and textiles.

	Output per worker per day (units)	
	Food	**Textiles**
China	1	2
United States	9	3

QUESTION: What are the opportunity costs of food production for both China and the United States?

ANSWER: The opportunity cost of food production in China is the amount of textile production forgone for a single unit of food output. Because a Chinese worker can produce 2 textile units in a day or 1 unit of food, the opportunity cost of 1 unit of food is 2 textile units.

In the United States, a worker can produce 3 textile units in one day or 9 units of food. Thus, the opportunity cost of 1 unit of food is just $\frac{1}{3}$ textile unit.

QUESTION: What are the opportunity costs of textile production for both China and the United States?

ANSWER: The opportunity cost of textile production in China is the amount of food production forgone for a single textile produced. Because a Chinese worker can produce 1 unit of food in a day or 2 textile units, the opportunity cost of 1 textile unit is $\frac{1}{2}$ unit of food.

In the United States, a worker can produce 9 units of food in one day or 3 textile units. Thus, the opportunity cost of 1 textile unit is 3 units of food.

QUESTION: Which nation has a comparative advantage in food production? Which nation has a comparative advantage in textile production?

ANSWER: The United States has a lower opportunity cost of food production ($\frac{1}{3}$ versus 2 textile units), so it has a comparative advantage in food production. China has a lower opportunity cost of textile production ($\frac{1}{2}$ versus 3 units of food), so it has a comparative advantage in textile production.

In Figures 19.4 and 19.5, the production possibilities frontier is shown as a straight line, which makes the computation of the ratios fairly simple and holds the opportunity cost constant. However, in the real world, access to new markets allows countries to take advantage of economies of scale and therefore lower per-unit costs as production expands. Increased production gives companies the opportunity to economize on distribution costs and marketing and to utilize assembly lines and other forms of automation.

Consider how a small textile company based in Mexico fares under this arrangement. With international trade, the company can expand its sales into the United States—a much larger market. This move creates additional demand, which translates into added sales. A larger volume of sales enables the textile firm's production, marketing, and sales to become more efficient. The firm can purchase fabrics in bulk, expand its distribution network, and use volume advertising.

INCREASED COMPETITION Another largely unseen benefit from trade is increased competition. In fact, increased competition from foreign suppliers forces domestic firms to become more innovative and to compete in terms of both price and quality. Competition also gives consumers more options to choose from, which enables consumers to purchase a broader array of products that better match their needs. For example, many cars are produced in the United States, but foreign automobiles offer U.S. consumers greater variety and help to keep the prices of domestically made cars lower than they would be otherwise.

TRADE AGREEMENTS Gains from trade often spur nations to sign trade agreements, to reduce tariffs and clear the way for mutually beneficial exchange. One prominent example is the North American Free Trade Agreement (NAFTA), which was signed in 1992 by the United States, Canada and Mexico. NAFTA eliminated many of the barriers to trade that had been erected between the three nations.

When Donald Trump campaigned for president in 2016, he pledged to make trade more fair for the United States. After he became president, his administration renegotiated the terms of NAFTA and signed a new agreement in 2018. The new agreement, called the United States-Mexico-Canada Agreement (USMCA) altered the provisions of NAFTA slightly but also insured a continuation of trade among the three nations.

Even though trade agreements often stipulate protections for particular industries (most notably, agriculture), they still increase trade between nations. For example, as a result of NAFTA, real U.S. imports and exports of goods with Canada and Mexico have doubled. Between 1993 and 2017, inflation-adjusted exports to Canada rose from $120 billion to $282 billion. Over the same period, inflation-adjusted exports to Mexico grew from $50 billion to $240 billion. The reduction in trade barriers has enabled all three nations to move toward the production of goods and services in which they enjoy a comparative advantage.

The World Trade Organization (WTO) is an international organization that facilitates trade agreements between nations. Created in 1995 by the 123 countries that were then signatories of the General Agreement on Tariffs and Trade, the WTO regulates the trade of various goods and services, including textiles, investment, intellectual property, even agriculture. Moreover, the WTO works to resolve trade disputes. For example, in 2012 the WTO helped to end a 20-year disagreement between Latin American banana exporters and the European Union over a tax on imported bananas.

What Are the Effects of Tariffs and Quotas?

Despite the benefits of free trade, significant trade barriers, such as import taxes, often exist. For example, almost every shoe purchased in the United States is made overseas; but with few exceptions, the U.S. government taxes each pair of shoes that comes across its borders to be sold. For example, a new pair of Nike tennis shoes imported from Vietnam is subject to a 20% import tax. If these shoes are valued at $100, the foreign producer has to pay a $20 tax on them.

Import taxes like those on footwear are not unusual. In this section, we explore two of the most common types of trade barriers: *tariffs* and *quotas*. We then look more closely at common economic and political justifications for **protectionism**, which is a blanket term for governmental actions and policies that restrict or restrain international trade, often with the intent of protecting local businesses and jobs from foreign competition. We close by examining whether or not protectionism is effective.

Protectionism
is a blanket term for governmental actions and policies that restrict or restrain international trade, often with the intent of protecting local businesses and jobs from foreign competition.

Tariffs

Tariffs
are taxes levied on imported goods and services.

Tariffs are taxes levied on imported goods and services. A tariff is paid by the producer of the good when the good arrives in a foreign country. A tariff can be a percentage of the value of the good (called an *ad valorem tax*), a per-unit tax (called a *specific tax*), or a mix of the two. Figure 19.6 illustrates the impact of a per-unit tariff on foreign shoes. To assess how a tariff affects the market price of shoes in the United States, we observe the relationship between domestic demand and domestic supply.

We begin by noting that domestic supply ($S_{domestic\ only}$) and domestic demand ($D_{domestic}$) would be in equilibrium at $140 per pair of shoes. However, this is not the market price if free trade prevails. If trade is unrestricted, imports are free to enter the domestic market, so that supply increases to $S_{free\ trade}$. Now, because trade is unrestricted, domestic producers who might wish to charge a price higher than that charged by foreign producers would find that they could not sell their shoes at that price. As a result, the domestic price (P_D) decreases to the world price (P_W), which is $100. At $100, the total quantity demanded is Q_W. Part of this quantity is produced domestically (Q_{D1}), and part is imported from foreign sources ($Q_W - Q_{D1}$).

Now let's see what happens when a tariff of $20 per pair of shoes is levied. When the country imposes the tariff per pair of shoes, the cost that foreign producers must bear when they export shoes rises by $20 per pair, the amount of the tariff. Supply decreases to $S_{with\ tariff}$. The tariff pushes the domestic price up from $100 to $120 (represented as P_T, reflecting the price with tariff). Foreign producers must pay the tariff, but domestic producers do not have to pay it. One

FIGURE 19.6

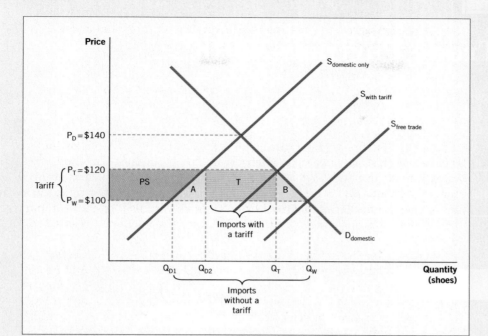

The Impact of a Tariff

Without a tariff, the domestic market is dominated by imports. However, when a tariff is imposed, the price rises and domestic production expands from Q_{D1} to Q_{D2}. At the same time, imports fall to $Q_T - Q_{D2}$. Tariffs also create deadweight loss (shaded areas A and B), revenue for the government (area T), and increased producer surplus for domestic firms (area PS).

consequence of this situation is that the amount imported drops to $Q_T - Q_{D2}$. At the same time, the amount supplied by domestic producers rises along the domestic-only supply curve from Q_{D1} to Q_{D2}. Because domestic suppliers are now able to charge $120 and also sell more, they are better off.

We can see this outcome visually by noting that domestic suppliers gain producer surplus equal to the shaded area marked PS. The government also benefits from the tariff revenue, shown as shaded area T. The tariff is a pure transfer from foreign suppliers to the government. In this case, the tariff is $20 per pair of shoes, so total tax revenue is $20 times the number of imported pairs of shoes. In addition, there are two areas of deadweight loss, A and B. Consumers are harmed because the price is higher and some people are forced to switch from foreign brands to domestic shoes. In addition, inefficient domestic producers now get to enter the market. Areas A and B represent the efficiency loss associated with the tariff—or the unrealized gains from trade. The economy as a whole loses from the tariff because the loss in consumer surplus is greater than the gains obtained by producers and the government.

Consider for a moment just how damaging a tariff is. Foreign producers are the lowest-cost producer of shoes, but they are limited in how much they can sell. This situation makes little sense from an import/export standpoint. If foreign shoe manufacturers cannot sell as many shoes in the United States, they will acquire fewer dollars to use in purchasing U.S. exports. So not only does the tariff mean higher shoe prices for U.S. consumers, but it also means fewer sales for U.S. exporters.

Major U.S. Trade Partners, 2018

Though the United States imports goods from over 230 nations in the world, just 7 of those countries account for over 60% of these imports. These same 7 countries also buy more U.S. goods exports than any other country. Clearly, our major trade partners produce numerous items that Americans demand, and the United States produces numerous items that these countries desire.

— U.S. goods imports from trade partner (2018)   — U.S. goods exports to trade partner (2018)

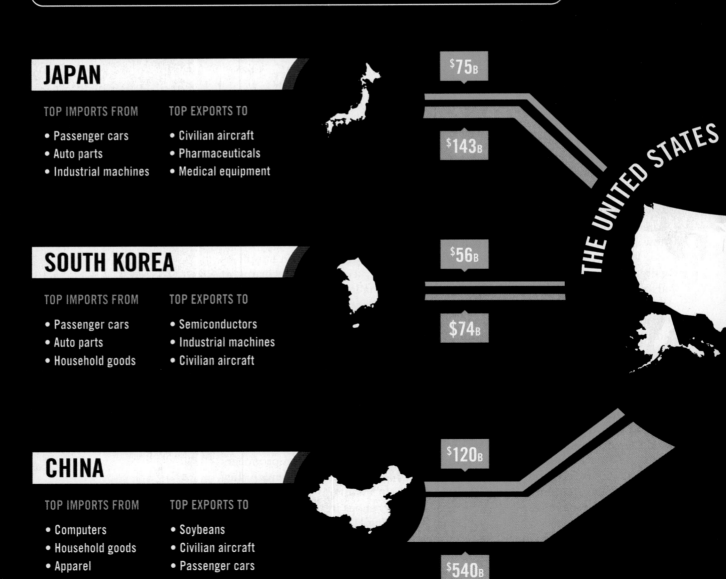

JAPAN

TOP IMPORTS FROM
- Passenger cars
- Auto parts
- Industrial machines

TOP EXPORTS TO
- Civilian aircraft
- Pharmaceuticals
- Medical equipment

$75B

$143B

SOUTH KOREA

TOP IMPORTS FROM
- Passenger cars
- Auto parts
- Household goods

TOP EXPORTS TO
- Semiconductors
- Industrial machines
- Civilian aircraft

$56B

$74B

CHINA

TOP IMPORTS FROM
- Computers
- Household goods
- Apparel

TOP EXPORTS TO
- Soybeans
- Civilian aircraft
- Passenger cars

$120B

$540B

THE UNITED STATES

Source: U.S. Bureau of Economic Analysis

REVIEW QUESTIONS

- What U.S. industry generates the most universal demand from our trading partners?

- Based on the list of U.S. imports, how would you finish this sentence? "Americans sure love their _____!"

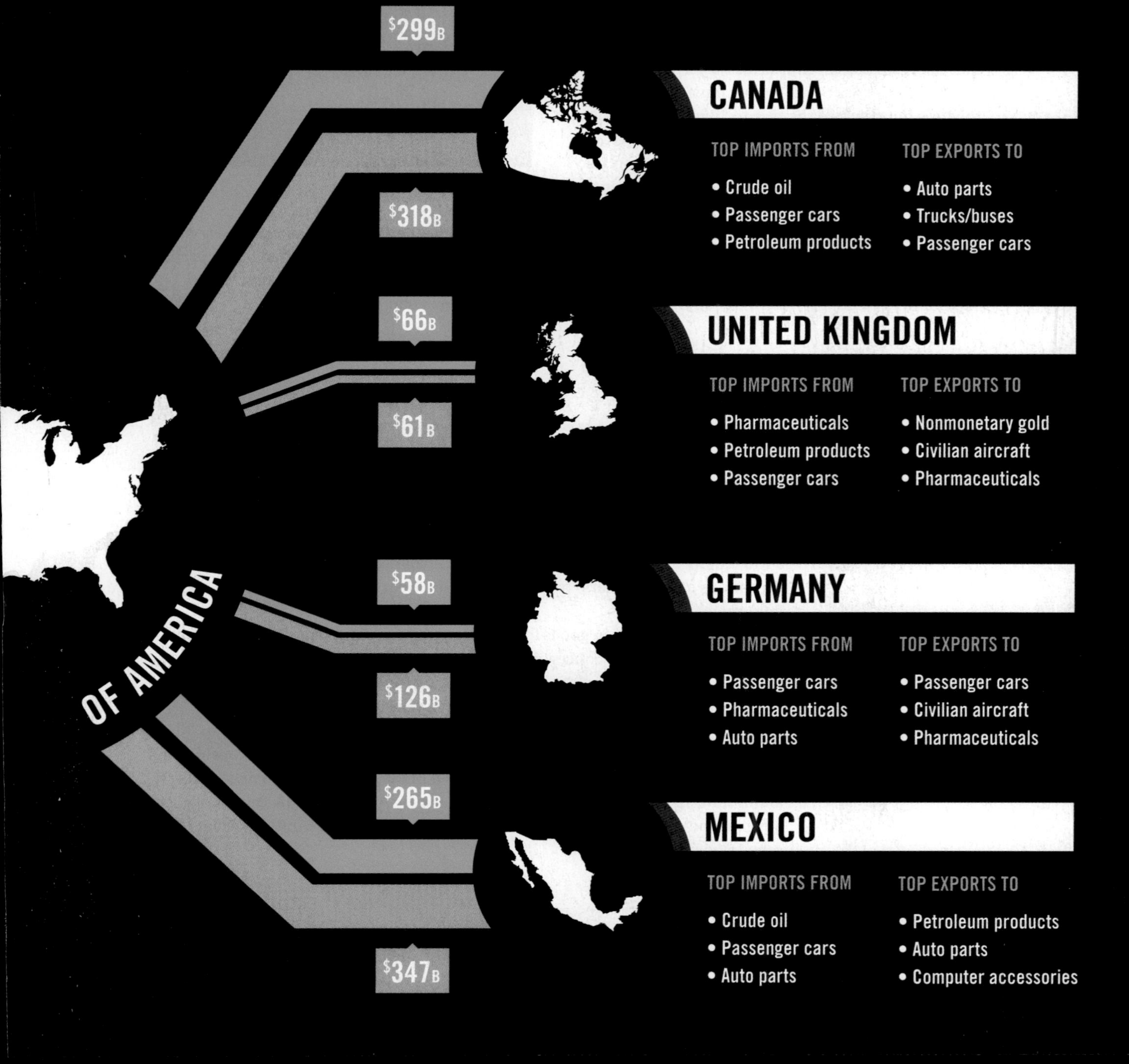

$299B

$318B

$66B

$61B

$58B

$126B

$265B

$347B

OF AMERICA

CANADA

TOP IMPORTS FROM
- Crude oil
- Passenger cars
- Petroleum products

TOP EXPORTS TO
- Auto parts
- Trucks/buses
- Passenger cars

UNITED KINGDOM

TOP IMPORTS FROM
- Pharmaceuticals
- Petroleum products
- Passenger cars

TOP EXPORTS TO
- Nonmonetary gold
- Civilian aircraft
- Pharmaceuticals

GERMANY

TOP IMPORTS FROM
- Passenger cars
- Pharmaceuticals
- Auto parts

TOP EXPORTS TO
- Passenger cars
- Civilian aircraft
- Pharmaceuticals

MEXICO

TOP IMPORTS FROM
- Crude oil
- Passenger cars
- Auto parts

TOP EXPORTS TO
- Petroleum products
- Auto parts
- Computer accessories

Tariffs: A Parody

REMY: "BANANA" (FREE-TRADE "HAVANA" PARODY)

"Havana," recorded by Camila Cabello (with guest vocals by Young Thug) is a very catchy tune that reflects Cabello's Latin roots. In 2018, the song won the American Music Awards for Best Video and Favorite Pop/Rock Song. Parody musician Remy kept the tune but changed the title to "Banana," with lyrics that explain how tariffs would bring back jobs from Havana to East Atlanta. Quite hilariously, Remy plays the president and also all his advisors at a trade policy planning meeting. Each of the advisors weighs in as the song progresses: "Take jobs back from Havana," "Why can't we grow bananas ourselves? They'd taste worse and cost more," and "You'd have to pump in water and heat, dude." If all of this sounds like a bad

THEY SHOULD BE GROWN IN EAST ATLANTA

idea, it is. Placing a tariff on bananas and trying to grow them in the southeast United States is evidence that "We've gone absolutely bananas." Check out the video on YouTube!

ECONOMICS IN THE REAL WORLD

U.S.–CHINA TRADE WAR

Since the 1980s, the U.S. trade deficit with China has increased from $4 billion to almost $400 billion. Figure 19.7 shows the U.S. trade balance with China adjusted for inflation (in billions of 2018 dollars) from 2000 to 2018. Nearly every year brings more and more imports from China.

While this increase in goods for U.S. consumers is viewed positively by economists, the trade deficit is very concerning to some in the United States. President Trump, for example, views the trade deficit as China taking funds from the United States. In March 2018, Trump said the U.S. "lost $500 billion" a year to China.*

To try to reduce this deficit, President Trump began imposing tariffs on Chinese imports in January of 2018. The first items affected were solar panels, washing machines, steel, and aluminum. China retaliated immediately by imposing tariffs on U.S. aluminum, airplanes, cars, pork, and soy beans. By August of 2018, the list of goods affected had grown into the hundreds. Many tariff levels were initially set at 10%, with scheduled increases to 25%.

---

*Source: Jim Tankersley, "Trump Hates the Trade Deficit. Most Economists Don't," *New York Times*, March 5, 2018, https://www.nytimes.com/2018/03/05/us/politics/trade-deficit-tariffs-economists-trump.html.

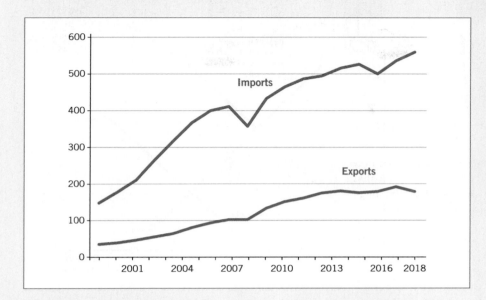

FIGURE 19.7

U.S. Goods and Services Trade with China (billions of 2018 dollars)

Nearly every year, the United States imports more goods and services from China. Exports typically grow too, but the gap between them (the trade deficit) widens almost every year.

Source: Bureau of Economic Analysis.

If the trade war continues to escalate, trade between the two nations will fall drastically over the next few years, and this is not good news for U.S. consumers. Economists are generally against tariffs, because they limit the value-creating benefits of trade. Put simply: consumers benefit from additional options.

Trade creates value

Quotas

Sometimes, instead of taxing imports, governments use *import quotas* to restrict trade. **Import quotas** are limits on the quantity of products that can be imported into a country. Quotas function like tariffs with one crucial exception: the government does not receive any tax revenue. In the United States today, there are quotas on many products, including milk, tuna, olives, peanuts, cotton, and sugar.

One famous example of quotas comes from the automobile industry in the 1980s and 1990s. During that period, Japan agreed to a "voluntary" quota on the number of vehicles it would export to the United States. Why would any group of firms agree to supply less than it could? The answer involves politics and economics. By voluntarily limiting the quantity they supply, foreign producers avoid having a tariff applied to their goods. Also, because the quantity supplied is somewhat smaller than it would otherwise be, foreign suppliers can charge higher prices. The net result is that a "voluntary" quota makes financial sense if it helps a producing nation to avoid a tariff.

Figure 19.8 shows how a quota placed on foreign-made shoes would work. The figure looks quite similar to Figure 19.6, which is not an accident. If we set the quota amount on foreign shoes equal to the imports after the tariff illustrated in Figure 19.6, the result is exactly the same with one notable exception: the green tariff rectangle, T, in Figure 19.6 has been replaced with a green rectangle, F, which is called the tariff-equivalent quota.

Import quotas
are limits on the quantity of products that can be imported into a country.

FIGURE 19.8

The Impact of a Quota

Without a quota, the domestic market is dominated by imports. However, when a quota is imposed, the price rises and domestic production expands from Q_{D1} to Q_{D2}. At the same time, imports fall to $Q_Q - Q_{D2}$. Quotas create deadweight loss (shaded areas A and B), a gain for foreign suppliers (area F), and increased producer surplus for domestic firms (area PS).

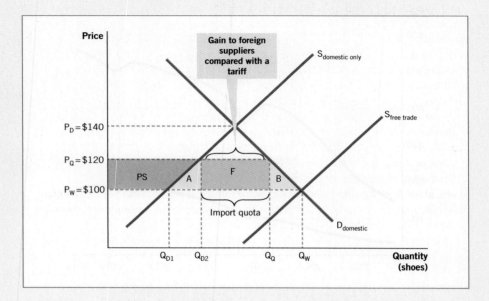

The quota is a strict limit on the number of shoes that may be imported into the United States. This limit pushes up the domestic price of shoes from $100 to $120 (represented as P_Q, reflecting the price under a quota). Because foreign producers must abide by the quota, one consequence is that the amount imported drops to $Q_Q - Q_{D2}$ (where Q_Q represents the total quantity supplied after the imposition of the quota). The smaller amount of imports causes the quantity supplied by domestic producers to rise along the domestic-only supply curve from Q_{D1} to Q_{D2}. Because domestic suppliers are now able to charge $20 more and also sell more, they are better off. We can see this result visually by noting that domestic suppliers gain producer surplus equal to shaded area PS (as we observed in Figure 19.6). As a result, domestic suppliers are indifferent between a tariff and a quota that has the same results. So, like before, there are two areas of deadweight loss, A and B, in which consumers lose because the price is higher and some people are forced to switch from foreign brands to domestic ones.

As you can see by the deadweight loss in shaded areas A and B, a quota results in the same efficiency loss as a tariff. Even though domestic suppliers are indifferent between a tariff and a quota system, foreign producers are not. Under a quota, they are able to keep the revenue generated in the green rectangle, F. Under a tariff, the equivalent rectangle, T, shown in Figure 19.6, is the tax revenue generated by the tariff.

ECONOMICS IN THE REAL WORLD

INEXPENSIVE SHOES FACE THE HIGHEST TARIFFS

Overall, U.S. tariffs average less than 2%, but inexpensive shoes face tariffs that are often at least 10 times more than that amount. What makes inexpensive imported shoes so "dangerous"? To help answer this question, a history lesson is in order.

Just 40 years ago, shoe manufacturers in the United States employed 250,000 workers. Today, the number of shoe workers is less than 3,000—and none of those workers assemble cheap shoes. Most of the shoe jobs have moved to low-labor-cost countries. But the shoe tariff, which was enacted to save domestic jobs, remains the same. Not a single sneaker costing less than $3 a pair is made in the United States, so the protection isn't saving any jobs. In contrast, goods such as cashmere sweaters, snake-skin purses, and silk shirts face low or no import tariffs. Other examples range from the 2.5% tariff on cars, tariffs of 4% and 5% for TV sets, and duty (tax)-free treatment for cell phones.

Shoppers who buy their shoes at Walmart and Zappos face the impact of shoe tariffs approaching 50% for the cheapest shoes, about 20% for a pair of name-brand running shoes, and about 9% for designer shoes from Gucci or Prada. This situation has the unintended consequence of passing along the tax burden to those who are least able to afford it.

Why do cheap imported shoes face such a high tariff?

One could reasonably argue that the shoe tariff is one of the United States' worst taxes. First, it failed to protect the U.S. shoe industry—the shoe jobs disappeared a long time ago. Second, consumers who are poor pay a disproportionate amount of the tax. And third, families with children pay even more because the more feet in a family, the more shoes are needed.

Incentives

Reasons Given for Trade Barriers

Considering all that we have discussed about the gains from trade and the inefficiencies associated with tariffs and quotas, you might be surprised to learn that trade restrictions are quite common. In this section, we consider some of the reasons for the persistence of trade barriers. These include national security, protection of infant industries, retaliation for *dumping*, and favors to special interests.

NATIONAL SECURITY Many people believe that certain industries, such as weapons, energy, and transportation, are vital to our nation's defense. They argue that without the ability to produce its own missiles, firearms, aircraft, and other strategically significant assets, a nation could find itself relying on its enemies. Thus, people often argue that certain industries should be protected in the interest of national security.

Although it is certainly important for any trade arrangement to consider national security, this argument has been used to justify trade restrictions on goods and services from friendly nations with whom we have active, open trade relations. For example, in 2002, the United States imposed tariffs on steel imports. Some policymakers argued that the steel tariffs were necessary because steel is an essential resource for national security. But, in fact, most imported steel comes from Canada and Brazil, which are traditional allies of the United States.

INFANT INDUSTRIES Another argument in support of steel tariffs in the United States was that the U.S. steel industry needed some time to implement new technologies that would enable it to compete with steel producers in other

Free Trade

STAR WARS EPISODE I: THE PHANTOM MENACE

The Phantom Menace (1999) is an allegory about peace, prosperity, taxation, and protectionism. As the movie opens, we see the Republic slowly falling apart. Planetary trade has been at the heart of the galactic economy. The central conflict in the movie is the Trade Federation's attempt to enforce its franchise by trying to intimidate a small planet, Naboo, which believes in free trade and peace.

The leader of the Naboo, Queen Amidala, refuses to pursue any path that might start a war. Her country is subjected to an excessive tariff and blockade, so she decides to appeal to the central government for help in ending the trade restrictions. However, she discovers that the Republic's Galactic Senate is ineffectual, so she returns home and prepares to defend her country.

Meanwhile, two Jedi who work for the Republic are sent to broker a deal between Naboo and the Trade Federation, but they get stranded on Tatooine, a desert planet located in the Outer Rim. In the Outer Rim, three necessary ingredients for widespread trade—the rule of law, sound money, and honesty—are missing. As a consequence, when the Jedi try to purchase some new parts for their ship, they find out that no one accepts the credit-based money of

Disruptive, barriers to trade are!

the Republic. The Jedi are forced to barter, a process that requires each trader to have exactly what the other wants. This situation results in a complicated negotiation between one of the Jedi and a local parts dealer. The scenes on Tatooine show why institutions, economies of scale, and competition matter so much for trade to succeed.

We encourage you to watch *The Phantom Menace* again with a fresh pair of eyes trained on the economics behind the special effects!

The **infant industry argument** states that domestic industries need trade protection until they are established and able to compete internationally.

nations. This **infant industry argument** states that domestic industries need trade protection until they are established and able to compete internationally. According to this point of view, once the fledgling industry gains traction and can support itself, the trade restrictions can be removed.

However, reality doesn't work this way. Firms that lobby for protection are often operating in an established industry. For example, the steel industry in the United States is over 100 years old. Establishing trade barriers is often politically popular, but finding ways to remove them is politically difficult. There was a time when helping to establish the steel, sugar, cotton, or peanut industries might have made sense based on the argument for helping new industries. But the tariffs that protect those industries have remained, in one form or another, for over 100 years.

Tariffs and Quotas: The Winners and Losers from Trade Barriers

We have seen that tariffs definitely affect trade balances. One clear example is the U.S. tariff on Chinese tires that was imposed in 2009. The result of this tariff was a drop in imports of these tires from 13 million tires to just 5.6 million tires in one quarter. In addition, within a year, average radial car tire prices rose by about $8 per tire in the United States: the average price of Chinese tires rose from $30.79 to $37.98, while the average price of tires from all other nations rose from $53.94 to $62.05.

QUESTION: Who were the winners and losers domestically from this tire tariff?

ANSWER: The primary winners are domestic tire makers and the government since it collects the tariffs. The primary losers were U.S. tire consumers, who saw prices rise by about $8 per tire, or $32 for a set of four tires.

CHALLENGE QUESTION: Who would be the winners and losers overseas?

ANSWER: The primary winners were the producers of tires from everywhere except China. Because this tariff was targeted at a single nation, it did not affect tire producers in other nations. Non-Chinese tire producers realized an average of $8 more per tire. The losers were Chinese tire manufacturers.

Why would we penalize Chinese tire imports?

Data Source: Gary Clyde Hufbauer and Sean Lowry, "U.S. Tire Tariffs: Saving Few Jobs at High Cost," Policy Brief (Washington, D.C.: Peterson Institute for International Economics, April 9, 2012).

RETALIATION FOR DUMPING In 2009, the U.S. government imposed tariffs on radial car tires imported from China. These tariffs began at 35% and then gradually decreased to 25% before being phased out after three years. The argument in support of this tariff was that Chinese tire makers were *dumping* their tires in U.S. markets. **Dumping** occurs when a foreign supplier sells a good below the price it charges in its home country. As the name implies, dumping is often a deliberate effort to gain a foothold in a foreign market. It can also be the result of subsidies within foreign countries.

In cases of dumping, the WTO allows for special *countervailing duties* to offset the subsidies. Thus, the United States placed a tariff on the imported tires to restore a level playing field. In essence, anytime a foreign entity decides to charge a lower price to penetrate a market, the country that is dumped on is likely to respond by imposing a tariff or quota to protect its domestic industries from foreign takeover. However, retaliation is also problematic. British economist Joan Robinson understood the risks well. She argued that the threat of trade barriers might conceivably work as a negotiation ploy, but when it came to actually enacting a retaliatory tariff, it "would be just as sensible to drop rocks into our harbours because other nations have rocky coasts."[*]

Dumping
occurs when a foreign supplier sells a good below the price it charges in its home country.

[*]Source: Joan Robinson, *Essays in the Theory of Employment* (New York: MacMillan, 1937).

The Impact of Tariffs on Domestic Prices

To help you out, we've identified a few of the products with the highest tariffs, to give you a sense of how much the prices of those imports are affected:

- French chocolates—100% tariff
- European truffles—100%
- Sneakers—48%
- Chinese tires—35%

New Balance gets a "kick" out of tariffs on Nike.

The U.S. International Trade Commission (Office of Tariff Affairs and Trade Agreements) is responsible for publishing the applicable tariff rates for all merchandise imported into the United States. If you are interested in digging deeper, the full schedule can be found here: https://hts.usitc.gov/current. But be warned, the entire tariff schedule runs to almost four thousand pages!

From that list, sneakers are the item that most of us own. U.S. tariffs on sneakers benefit New Balance, the last large shoemaker to keep its entire production process stateside. If you have ever wondered why popular brands of shoes such as Nike and Adidas have higher prices, this is part of the reason. Since Nike and most other retailers produce many of their final products outside the United States, they must pay the tariff that protects domestic suppliers such as New Balance, and they pass those costs through to the customer.

FAVORS TO SPECIAL INTERESTS The imposition of trade barriers is often referred to as "protection." This term raises the questions *Who is being protected?* and *What are they being protected from?* We have seen that trade barriers drive up domestic prices and lead to a lower quantity of goods or services in the market where the barriers are imposed. This situation does not protect consumers. In fact, tariffs and quotas protect domestic producers from international competition. Steel tariffs were put in place to help domestic steel producers, and tire tariffs were put in place to help domestic tire producers.

When we see trade barriers, the publicly stated reason is generally one of the three reasons we have already discussed: national security, infant industry protection, or retaliation for dumping. But we must also recognize that these barriers may be put in place as a favor to special interest groups that have much to gain at the expense of domestic consumers. For example, as a result of sugar import regulations, U.S. consumers pay twice as much for sugar as the rest of the world does. Thus, while sugar tariffs and quotas protect U.S. sugar producers from international competition, they cost U.S. consumers more than $3 billion in 2014 alone. This outcome represents a special interest gain at the expense of U.S. consumers. If it were a tax transferred from consumers to producers, it would likely not persist. However, this kind of favor doesn't appear in the federal budget.

Conclusion

We began this chapter by rejecting the misconception that nations should not trade for goods and services they can produce for themselves. An analysis of the concept of comparative advantage shows that nations can gain by (1) specializing in the production of goods and services for which they have the lowest opportunity cost and then (2) trading for the other goods and services they wish to consume.

International trade is expanding all over the world. The United States now imports and exports more than at any time in its history. Increased trade is generally positive for all nations involved. However, trade barriers still exist around the globe for various reasons, including national security, the protection of infant industries, retaliation for dumping and subsidies, and favors to special interests. ✳

▪ ANSWERING *the* BIG QUESTIONS ▪

Is globalization for real?

- Since 1970, world exports have grown from 11% to about 25% of world GDP. In the United States, imports and exports have both grown rapidly over the past five decades. Between 1965 and 2014, U.S. exports grew from less than 5% of GDP to 13% of GDP. Over the same period, U.S. imports grew from 4% of GDP to over 16% of GDP. There's no doubt that the world economy is becoming more integrated.

How does international trade help the economy?

- Gains from trade occur when a nation specializes in production and exchanges its output with a trading partner. For this arrangement to work, each nation must produce goods for which it is a low-opportunity-cost producer and then trade them for goods for which it is a high-opportunity-cost producer.

- In addition, trade benefits nations' economies through economies of scale and increased international competition.

What are the effects of tariffs and quotas?

- Protectionism in the form of trade restrictions, such as tariffs and quotas, is common. A tariff is a tax on imports; a quota is a quantity restriction on imports.

- Proponents of trade restrictions often cite the need to protect defense-related industries and fledgling firms and to fend off dumping. But protectionist policies can also serve as political favors to special interest groups.

·CHAPTER PROBLEMS·

Concepts You Should Know

comparative advantage (p. 606)
dumping (p. 621)
import quotas (p. 617)
infant industry argument (p. 620)

net exports (p. 602)
protectionism (p. 612)
tariffs (p. 612)

trade balance (p. 602)
trade deficit (p. 602)
trade surplus (p. 602)

Questions for Review

1. What are three problems with trade restrictions? What are three reasons often given in support of trade restrictions?

2. What would happen to the standard of living in the United States if all foreign trade were eliminated?

3. How might a nation's endowment of natural resources, labor, and climate shape the nature of its comparative advantage?

4. Why might foreign producers voluntarily agree to a quota rather than face an imposed tariff?

5. Tariffs reduce the volume of imports. Do tariffs also reduce the volume of exports? Explain your response.

Study Problems (* solved at the end of the section)

1. Consider the following table for the neighboring nations of Quahog and Pawnee. Assume that the opportunity cost of producing each good is constant.

Product	Quahog	Pawnee
Meatballs (per hour)	4,000	2,000
Clams (per hour)	8,000	1,000

a. What is the opportunity cost of producing meatballs in Quahog? What is the opportunity cost of harvesting clams in Quahog?

b. What is the opportunity cost of producing meatballs in Pawnee? What is the opportunity cost of producing clams in Pawnee?

c. Based on your answers in parts (a) and (b), which nation has a comparative advantage in producing meatballs? Which nation has a comparative advantage in producing clams?

2. Suppose that the comparative-cost ratios of two products—mangoes and sardines—are as follows in the hypothetical nations of Mangolia and Sardinia:

Mangolia: 1 mango = 2 cans of sardines
Sardinia: 1 mango = 4 cans of sardines

In what product should each nation specialize? Explain why the terms of trade of 1 mango = 3 cans of sardines would be acceptable to both nations.

3. What are the two trade restriction policies we discussed in this chapter? Who benefits and who loses from each of these policies? What is the new outcome for society?

* 4. Germany and Japan both produce cars and beer. The table below shows production possibilities per worker in each country. For example, one worker in Germany produces 8 cars or 10 cases of beer per week. (For a review of absolute versus comparative advantage, see Chapter 2.)

	Labor force	Cars (C)	Beer (B)
Germany	200	8	10
Japan	100	20	14

a. Which nation has an absolute advantage in car production? Which one has an absolute advantage in beer production? Explain your answers.

b. Which nation has a comparative advantage in car production? Which one has a comparative advantage in beer production? Explain your answers.

✳ 5. Continuing with the example given in the previous problem, assume that Germany and Japan produce their own cars and beer and allocate half their labor force to the production of each.

    a. What quantities of cars and beer does Germany produce? What quantities does Japan produce?

Now suppose that Germany and Japan produce only the good for which they enjoy a comparative advantage in production. They also agree to trade half of their output for half of what the other country produces.

    b. What quantities of cars and beer does Germany produce now? What quantities does Japan produce?

    c. What quantities of cars and beer does Germany consume now? What quantities does Japan consume?

    d. People often act as if international trade is a zero-sum game, meaning that when one party wins, the other party must lose an equal amount. State this book's foundational principle that contradicts this idea.

✳ 6. Determine whether each statement is true or false.

Developing countries stand to gain from international trade because

    a. trade enables them to specialize in producing where they have a comparative advantage.

    b. trade gives them access to the greater variety of goods produced abroad.

    c. trade subjects their local producers to greater competition.

    d. trade allows them to produce larger amounts than they could consume themselves, allowing them to take advantage of increasing returns to scale.

7. Is it possible for a producer to have both an absolute advantage and a comparative advantage?

Solved Problems

4.a. Japan has an absolute advantage in both because $20 > 8$ and $14 > 10$.

    b. Japan has a comparative advantage in car production because its opportunity cost is less than Germany's ($0.7 < 1.25$). Germany has a comparative advantage in beer production because its opportunity cost is less than Japan's ($0.8 < 1.43$).

5.a. Germany: $(C, B) = (800, 1,000)$;
    Japan: $(C, B) = (1,000, 700)$

    b. Germany: $(C, B) = (0, 2,000)$;
    Japan: $(C, B) = (2,000, 0)$

    c. Germany: $(C, B) = (1,000, 1,000)$;
    Japan: $(C, B) = (1,000, 1,000)$

    d. Trade creates value for all involved because each party must benefit from the terms of trade or they would not agree to trade.

6. All four statements are true: (a) Trade is built on the concept of specialization and the application of comparative advantage in that process. (b) Trade allows countries to obtain a greater variety of goods and services from abroad than they could produce on their own. (c) Because trade effectively increases the number of potential competitors in the market, local producers are subject to more competition than would exist without trade. (d) When countries export goods, they benefit from being able to access a larger marketplace, which gives them the opportunity to produce at a larger scale than they would without trade.

GLOSSARY

absolute advantage one producer's ability to make more than another producer with the same quantity of resources

accounting profit profit calculated by subtracting a firm's explicit costs from total revenue

adverse selection phenomenon existing when one party has information about some aspect of product quality that the other party does not have

antitrust laws laws that attempt to prevent collusion (that is, prevent oligopolies from behaving like monopolies)

asymmetric information an imbalance in information that occurs when one party knows more than the other

average fixed cost (AFC) an amount determined by dividing a firm's total fixed costs by the output

average total cost (ATC) the sum of average variable cost and average fixed cost

average variable cost (AVC) an amount determined by dividing a firm's total variable costs by the output

backward-bending labor supply curve supply curve occurring when workers value additional leisure more than additional income

backward induction in game theory, the process of deducing backward from the end of a scenario to infer a sequence of optimal actions

barriers to entry restrictions that make it difficult for new firms to enter a market

behavioral economics the field of economics that draws on insights from experimental psychology to explore how people make economic decisions

black markets illegal markets that arise when price controls are in place

bounded rationality the concept that although decision-makers want a good outcome, either they are not capable of performing the problem solving that traditional economic theory assumes or they are not inclined to do so; also called *limited reasoning*

budget constraint the set of consumption bundles that represent the maximum amount the consumer can afford

cap and trade an approach used to curb pollution by creating a system of emissions permits that are traded in an open market

capital goods goods that help produce other valuable goods and services in the future

cartel a group of two or more firms that act in unison

causality condition existing when one variable influences another

ceteris paribus meaning "other things being equal," the concept under which economists examine a change in one variable while holding everything else constant

circular flow diagram a diagram that shows how goods, services, and resources flow through the economy

Clayton Act law of 1914 targeting corporate behaviors that reduce competition

club good a good with two characteristics: it is nonrival in consumption and excludable

Coase theorem theorem stating that if there are no barriers to negotiations, and if property rights are fully specified, interested parties will bargain to correct externalities

coinsurance payments a percentage of costs the insured must pay after exceeding the insurance policy's deductible up to the policy's contribution limit

collusion an agreement among rival firms that specifies the price each firm charges and the quantity it produces

common cause a single cause responsible for two phenomena observed to correlate with each other

common-resource good a good with two characteristics: it is rival in consumption and nonexcludable

comparative advantage the situation where an individual, business, or country can produce at a lower opportunity cost than a competitor can

compensating differential the difference in wages offered to offset the desirability or undesirability of a job

competitive market a market in which there are so many buyers and sellers that each has only a small (negligible) impact on the market price and output

complements two goods that are used together; when the price of a complementary good rises, the quantity demanded of that good falls and the demand for the related good goes down

constant returns to scale condition occurring when long-run average total costs remain constant as output expands

consumer goods goods produced for present consumption

consumer optimum the combination of goods and services that maximizes the consumer's utility for a given income or budget

consumer surplus the difference between the willingness to pay for a good (or service) and the price paid to get it

copayments fixed amounts the insured must pay when receiving a medical service or filling a prescription

cost-benefit analysis a process that economists use to determine whether the benefits of providing a public good outweigh the costs

cross-price elasticity of demand measurement of the percentage change of the quantity demanded of one good to the percentage change in the price of a related good

deadweight loss the decrease in economic activity caused by market distortions

decision tree diagram that illustrates all of the possible outcomes in a sequential game

deductibles fixed amounts the insured must pay before most of the policy's benefits can be applied

demand curve a graph of the relationship between the prices in the demand schedule and the quantity demanded at those prices

demand schedule a table that shows the relationship between the price of a good and the quantity demanded

derived demand the demand for an input used in the production process

diamond-water paradox concept explaining why water, which is essential to life, is inexpensive, while diamonds, which do not sustain life, are expensive

diminishing marginal product condition occurring when successive increases in inputs are associated with a slower rise in output

diminishing marginal utility condition occurring when marginal utility declines as consumption increases

diseconomies of scale condition occurring when long-run average total costs rise as output expands

dominant strategy in game theory, a strategy that a player will always prefer, regardless of what his opponent chooses

dumping behavior occurring when a foreign supplier sells a good below the price it charges in its home country

economic profit profit calculated by subtracting both the explicit costs and the implicit costs from a firm's total revenue

economic rent the difference between what a factor of production earns and what it could earn in the next-best alternative

economics the study of how individuals and societies allocate their limited resources to satisfy their unlimited wants

economic thinking a purposeful evaluation of the available opportunities to make the best decision possible

economies of scale condition occurring when long-run average total costs decline as output expands

efficiency wages wages higher than equilibrium wages, offered to increase worker productivity

efficient describing an outcome when allocation of resources maximizes total surplus

efficient scale the output level that minimizes average total cost in the long run

elasticity a measure of the responsiveness of buyers and sellers to changes in price or income

endogenous factors the variables that are inside a model

equilibrium condition occurring at the point where the demand curve and the supply curve intersect

equilibrium price the price at which the quantity supplied is equal to the quantity demanded; also known as the *market-clearing price*

equilibrium quantity the amount at which the quantity supplied is equal to the quantity demanded

equity the fairness of the distribution of benefits among the members of a society

excess capacity phenomenon occurring when a firm produces at an output level smaller than the output level needed to minimize average total costs

excise taxes taxes levied on a particular good or service

excludable good a good for which access can be limited to paying customers

exogenous factors the variables that are outside a model

explicit costs tangible out-of-pocket expenses

external costs the costs of a market activity imposed on people who are not participants in that market

externalities the costs or benefits of a market activity that affect a third party

factors of production the inputs (labor, land, and capital) used in producing goods and services

fixed costs costs that do not vary with a firm's output in the short run; also known as *overhead*

framing effect a phenomenon seen when people change their answer depending on how the question is asked (or change their decision depending on how alternatives are presented)

free-rider problem phenomenon occurring when someone receives a benefit without having to pay for it

gambler's fallacy the belief that recent outcomes are unlikely to be repeated and that outcomes that have not occurred recently are due to happen soon

game theory a branch of mathematics that economists use to analyze the strategic behavior of decision-makers

Gini index a measurement of the income distribution of a country's residents

hot hand fallacy the belief that random sequences exhibit a positive correlation

human capital the set of skills workers acquire on the job and through education

immediate run a period of time when there is no time for consumers to adjust their behavior

imperfect market a market in which either the buyer or the seller can influence the market price

implicit costs the costs of resources already owned, for which no out-of-pocket payment is made

import quotas limits on the quantity of products that can be imported into a country

incentives factors that motivate a person to act or exert effort

incidence the burden of taxation on the party who pays the tax through higher prices, regardless of whom the tax is actually levied on

income effect phenomenon occurring when laborers work fewer hours at higher wages, using their additional income to demand more leisure

income elasticity of demand measurement of how a change in income affects spending

income inequality ratio ratio calculated by dividing the top quintile's income percentage by the bottom quintile's income percentage

income mobility the ability of workers to move up or down the economic ladder over time

indifference curve a graph representing the various combinations of two goods that yield the same level of personal satisfaction, or utility

infant industry argument the idea that domestic industries need trade protection until they are established and able to compete internationally

inferior good a good for which demand declines as income rises

in-kind transfers transfers (mostly to the poor) in the form of goods or services instead of cash

inputs the resources (labor, land, and capital) used in the production process

internal costs the costs of a market activity paid only by an individual participant

internalize relating to a firm's handling of externalities, to take into account the external costs (or benefits) to society that occur as a result of the firm's actions

intertemporal decision-making planning to do something over a period of time, which requires valuing the present and the future consistently

investment the process of using resources to create or buy new capital

invisible hand a phrase coined by Adam Smith to refer to the unobservable market forces that guide resources to their highest-valued use

law of demand the law that, all other things being equal, quantity demanded falls when the price rises, and rises when the price falls

law of increasing opportunity cost law stating that the opportunity cost of producing a good rises as a society produces more of it

law of supply the law that, all other things being equal, the quantity supplied of a good rises when the price of the good rises, and falls when the price of the good falls

law of supply and demand law stating that the market price of any good will adjust to bring the quantity supplied and the quantity demanded into balance

life-cycle wage pattern the predictable effect age has on earnings over the course of a person's working life

long run in microeconomics, the period of time when consumers make decisions that reflect their long-term wants, needs, or limitations and have time to fully adjust to market conditions

Lorenz curve a visual representation of the Gini index

loss the result when total revenue is less than total cost

macroeconomics the study of the overall aspects and workings of an economy

marginal cost (MC) the increase in cost that occurs from producing one additional unit of output

marginal product the change in output associated with one additional unit of an input

marginal product of labor the change in output associated with adding one additional worker

marginal rate of substitution (MRS) the rate at which a consumer is willing to trade one good for another along an indifference curve

marginal revenue the change in total revenue a firm receives when it produces one additional unit of output

marginal thinking the evaluation of whether the benefit of one more unit of something is greater than its cost

marginal utility the additional satisfaction derived from consuming one more unit of a good or service

market demand the sum of all the individual quantities demanded by each buyer in the market at each price

market economy an economy in which resources are allocated among households and firms with little or no government interference

market failure condition occurring when there is an inefficient allocation of resources in a market

market power a firm's ability to influence the price of a good or service by exercising control over its demand, supply, or both

markets systems that bring buyers and sellers together to exchange goods and services

market supply the sum of the quantities supplied by each seller in the market at each price

markup the difference between the price the firm charges and the marginal cost of production

maximization point the point at which a certain combination of two goods yields the greatest possible utility

Medicaid a joint federal and state program that helps low-income individuals and households pay for the costs associated with long-term medical care

microeconomics the study of the individual units that make up the economy

minimum wage the lowest hourly wage rate that firms may legally pay their workers

monopolistic competition a type of market structure characterized by low barriers to entry, many different firms, and product differentiation

monopoly condition existing when a single company supplies the entire market for a particular good or service

monopoly power measure of a monopolist's ability to set the price of a good or service

monopsony a situation in which there is only one buyer

moral hazard the lack of incentive to guard against risk where one is protected from its consequences

mutual interdependence a market situation where the actions of one firm have an impact on the price and output of its competitors

Nash equilibrium a phenomenon occurring when all economic decision-makers opt to keep the status quo

natural monopoly the situation that occurs when a single large firm has lower costs than any potential smaller competitor

negative correlation condition occurring when two variables move in opposite directions

net exports total exports of final goods and services minus total imports of final goods and services

network externality condition occurring when the number of customers who purchase or use a product influences the quantity demanded

normal good a good consumers buy more of as income rises, holding all other factors constant

normative statement an opinion that cannot be tested or validated; it describes "what ought to be"

occupational crowding the phenomenon of relegating a group of workers to a narrow range of jobs in the economy

oligopoly a form of market structure that exists when a small number of firms sell a differentiated product in a market with high barriers to entry

opportunity cost the highest-valued alternative that must be sacrificed to get something else

output the product the firm creates

output effect how a change in price affects the number of customers in a market

outsourcing of labor a firm's shifting of jobs to an outside company, usually overseas, where the cost of labor is lower

perfect complements two goods the consumer is interested in consuming in fixed proportions, resulting in a right-angle indifference curve

perfect price discrimination the practice of selling the same good or service at a unique price to every customer

perfect substitutes two goods the consumer is completely indifferent between, resulting in a straight-line indifference curve with a constant marginal rate of substitution

positive correlation condition occurring when two variables move in the same direction

positive statement an assertion that can be tested and validated; it describes "what is"

poverty rate the percentage of the population whose income is below the poverty threshold

poverty threshold the income level below which a person or family is considered impoverished

predatory pricing the practice of a firm deliberately setting its prices below average variable costs with the intent of driving rivals out of the market

preference reversal phenomenon arising when risk tolerance is not consistent

price ceiling a legally established maximum price for a good or service

price controls an attempt to set prices through government regulations in the market

price discrimination the practice of selling the same good or service at different prices to different groups of customers

price effect how a change in price affects the firm's revenue

price elasticity of demand a measure of the responsiveness of quantity demanded to a change in price

price elasticity of supply a measure of the responsiveness of the quantity supplied to a change in price; sometimes called *elasticity of supply* or *supply elasticity*

price floor a legally established minimum price for a good or service

price gouging laws temporary ceilings on the prices that sellers can charge during times of emergency

price leadership phenomenon occurring when a dominant firm in an industry sets the price that maximizes its profits and the smaller firms in the industry follow by setting their prices to match the price leader

price maker a firm with some control over the price it charges

price taker a firm with no control over the price set by the market

priming effect phenomenon seen when the order of the questions influences the answers

principal-agent problem a situation in which a principal entrusts an agent to complete a task and the agent does not do so in a satisfactory way

prisoner's dilemma a situation in which decision-makers face incentives that make it difficult to achieve mutually beneficial outcomes

private good a good with two characteristics: it is excludable and rival in consumption

private property provision of an exclusive right of ownership that allows for the use, and especially the exchange, of property

producer surplus the difference between willingness to sell a good (or service) and the price the seller receives

product differentiation the process firms use to make a product more attractive to potential customers

production function the relationship between the inputs a firm uses and the output it creates

production possibilities frontier (PPF) a model that illustrates the combinations of outputs a society can produce if all of its resources are being used efficiently

productivity the effectiveness of effort as measured in terms of the rate of output per unit of input

profit the result when total revenue is higher than total cost

profit-maximizing rule the rule stating that profit maximization occurs when a firm chooses the quantity of output that equates marginal revenue and marginal cost, or MR = MC

property rights an owner's ability to exercise control over a resource

prospect theory a theory suggesting that individuals weigh the utilities and risks of gains and losses differently

protectionism a blanket term for governmental actions and policies that restrict or restrain international trade, often with the intent of protecting local businesses and jobs from foreign competition

public good a good that can be consumed by more than one person, and from which nonpayers are difficult to exclude

purchasing power the value of your income expressed in terms of how much you can afford

quantity demanded the amount of a good or service that buyers are willing and able to purchase at the current price

quantity supplied the amount of a good or service producers are willing and able to sell at the current price

real-income effect a change in purchasing power as a result of a change in the price of a good

rent control a price ceiling that applies to the market for apartment rentals

rent seeking occurs when resources are used to secure monopoly rights through the political process

reverse causation condition occurring when causation is incorrectly assigned among associated events

risk-averse people those who prefer a sure thing over a gamble with a higher expected value

risk-neutral people those who choose the highest expected value regardless of the risk

risk-takers those who prefer gambles with lower expected values, and potentially higher winnings, over a sure thing

rival good a good that cannot be enjoyed by more than one person at a time

Samaritan's dilemma a situation in which an act of charity creates disincentives for recipients to take care of themselves

scale the size of the production process

scarcity refers to the inherently limited nature of society's resources, given society's unlimited wants and needs

scatterplot a graph that shows individual (x, y) points

Sherman Antitrust Act the first federal law (1890) limiting cartels and monopolies

shortage market condition when the quantity supplied of a good is less than the *quantity* demanded; also called *excess demand*

short run in microeconomics, the period of time when consumers make decisions that reflect their short-term wants, needs, or limitations and can partially adjust their behavior

signals information conveyed by profits and losses about the profitability of various markets

single-payer system government coverage of most healthcare costs, with citizens paying their share through taxes

slope the change in the rise along the y axis (vertical) divided by the change in the run along the x axis (horizontal)

social costs the sum of the internal costs and external costs of a market activity

social optimum the price and quantity combination that would exist if there were no externalities

social welfare see *total surplus*

specialization the limiting of one's work to a particular area

status quo bias condition existing when decision-makers want to keep things the way they are

strike a work stoppage designed to aid a union's bargaining position

subsidy a payment made by the government to encourage the consumption or production of a good or service

substitutes goods that are used in place of each other; when the price of a substitute good rises, the quantity demanded of that good falls and the demand for the related good goes up

substitution effect (1) the decision by laborers to work more hours at higher wages, substituting labor for leisure; (2) a consumer's substitution of a product that has become relatively less expensive as the result of a price change

sunk costs unrecoverable costs that have been incurred as a result of past decisions

supply curve a graph of the relationship between the prices in the supply schedule and the quantity supplied at those prices

supply schedule a table that shows the relationship between the price of a good and the quantity supplied

surplus market condition when the quantity supplied of a good is greater than the quantity demanded; also called *excess supply*

switching costs the costs incurred when a consumer changes from one supplier to another

tariffs taxes levied on imported goods and services

third-party problem a situation in which those not directly involved in a market activity experience negative or positive externalities

tit-for-tat a long-run strategy that promotes cooperation among participants by mimicking the opponent's most recent decision with repayment in kind

total cost the amount a firm spends to produce and/or sell goods and services

total revenue the amount a firm receives from the sale of goods and services

total surplus the sum of consumer surplus and producer surplus; a measure of the well-being of all participants in a market, absent any government intervention; also known as *social welfare*

trade the voluntary exchange of goods and services between two or more parties

trade balance the difference between a nation's total exports and total imports

trade deficit condition occurring when imports exceed exports, indicating a negative trade balance

trade surplus condition occurring when exports exceed imports, indicating a positive trade balance

tragedy of the commons the depletion of a common-resource good

ultimatum game an economic experiment in which two players decide how to divide a sum of money

underground economies markets in which goods or services are traded illegally

union a group of workers who bargain collectively for better wages and benefits

util a personal unit of satisfaction used to measure the enjoyment from consumption of a good or service

utility a measure of the level of satisfaction that a consumer enjoys from the consumption of goods and services

value of the marginal product (VMP) the marginal product of an input multiplied by the price of the output it produces

variable a quantity that can take on more than one value

variable costs costs that change with the rate of output

wage discrimination unequal payment of workers because of their race, ethnic origin, sex, age, religion, or some other group characteristic

welfare economics the branch of economics that studies how the allocation of resources affects economic well-being

willingness to pay the maximum price a consumer will pay for a good or service; also called the *reservation price*

willingness to sell the minimum price a seller will accept to sell a good or service

winner-take-all phenomenon occurring when extremely small differences in ability lead to sizable differences in compensation

CREDITS

Commons, Alex Belomlinsky/iStockphoto; **p. 128** (top to bottom): BraunS/iStockphoto, Rick Rhay/iStockphoto, Alex Belomlinsky/iStockphoto, Wikimedia Commons; **p. 133**: Ty Lim/Shutterstock; **p. 134** (top): Barbara Helgason/Dreamstime.com, (bottom): Wilf Doyle/Alamy Stock Photo; **p. 137**: Xpogo LLC; **p. 138**: Eliza Snow/iStockphoto; **p. 139** (top): Aleksandar Mijatovic/Dreamstime.com; **p. 139** (Table 4.4 top to bottom): Svetlana Foote/Dreamstime.com, Steven von Niederhausern/iStockphoto, Ragoarts/Dreamstime.com; **p. 140** (Table 4.5 clockwise): Steve Shepard/iStockphoto, Steve Shepard/iStockphoto, Chaoss/Dreamstime.com, Daniel R. Burch/iStockphoto, Olga Lyubkina/iStockphoto, Ljupco Smokovski/Dreamstime.com; **p. 140** Pibb Xtra: W. W. Norton & Co., Inc., Red Vines: Keith Homan/Shutterstock; **p. 141**: dotshock/Shutterstock; **p. 142**: Daniel Bendjy/iStockphoto; **p. 143** (top to bottom): Yuri Arcurs/Dreamstime.com, Yuri Arcurs/Dreamstime.com, jakelv7500/Shutterstock, Julie Feinstein/Dreamstime.com; **p. 145**: George Peters/iStockphoto; **p. 146**: PSL Images/Alamy; **p. 148**: Jeffry W. Myers/Getty Images; **p. 149**: Rich Legg/iStockphoto.

CHAPTER 5

P. 154: Giuseppe Masci/Alamy Stock Photo; **p. 157** (left): dpa picture alliance/Alamy Stock Photo, (center): Allstar Picture Library/Alamy Stock Photo, (right): Kristin Callahan/Everett Collection/Alamy Stock Photo; **p. 162** (top): Matt Baron/Shutterstock, (bottom): Hero Images Inc./Alamy Stock Photo; **p. 164**: Chuck Place/iStockphoto; **p. 165**: AP Photo/Ann Hermes/The Christian Science Monitor; **p. 166**: Jen Grantham/iStockphoto; **p. 167** (left): Versluis Photography/iStockphoto, (right): Dan Van Den Broeke/Dreamstime.com; **p. 171** (top): Perry van Munster/Alamy Stock Photo, (bottom): AP Photo/Kiichiro Sato; **p. 175**: Uros Petrovic/Dreamstime.com; **p. 177**: Rui Matos/Dreamstime.com; **p. 178**: apcuk/iStockphoto; **p. 182**: Cultura Creative (RF)/Alamy Stock Photo.

CHAPTER 6

P. 188: Federico Parra/AFP/Getty Images; **p. 191** (top): Carlos Garcia Rawlins/Reuters/Newscom; **p. 191** (Table 6.1 top to bottom): Chhob/Dreamstime.com, Michael Neelon(misc)/Alamy Stock Photo, ermess/Shutterstock, Justin Sullivan/Getty Images, BluIz60/Alamy Stock Photo; **p. 192**: ESB Professional/Shutterstock; **p. 195**: Str/EPA/Shutterstock; **p. 196**: Benoit Daoust/Alamy Stock Photo; **p. 197**: Alex Craig/Getty Images; **p. 198**: Lisa F. Young/Dreamstime.com; **p. 201** (top): Yuri Arcurs/Dreamstime.com, (bottom): Steven von Niederhausern/iStockphoto; **p. 202** (top): Julie Feinstein/Dreamstime.com, (center): Courtesy of Andrew Le, (bottom): Chris Graythen/Getty Images; **p. 203**: Anthony Aneese Totah Jr/Dreamstime.com; **p. 205**: Peter Booth/iStockphoto; **p. 206**: Goran Bogicevic/Shutterstock; **p. 211** (left): calimedia/Shutterstock, (right): Kyoungil Jeon/iStockphoto, (bottom): Robert Churchill/iStockphoto; **p. 213**: Howard Greenblatt via Planetpix/Alamy Stock Photo.

CHAPTER 7

P. 218: Greg Taylor/Alamy Stock Photo; **p. 221**: Christophe Testi/Dreamstime.com; **p. 222**: Charlieb34/Dreamstime.com; **p. 224**: wwing/iStock/Getty Images Plus; **p. 225**: Sean Locke/iStockphoto; **p. 226** (clockwise): Charlieb34/Dreamstime.com, Yarinca/iStockphoto, Jonathan Cohen/iStockphoto, River NorthPhotography/iStockphoto, Stef Bennett/Dreamstime.com, Steve Lovegrove/Dreamstime.com; **p. 227**: Roy Morsch/Getty Images; **p. 229** (top): Charlene Key/Dreamstime.com, (left): Stephen Ausmus/ARS/USDA, (right): Michael Thompson/ARS/USDA; **p. 230**: Vplut/Dreamstime.com; **p. 231**: Annie Su Yee Yek/Dreamstime.com; **p. 232**: U.S. Navy photo by Mass Communication Specialist 3rd Class John Grandin; **p. 233** (top): The Family Circus ©2006 Bil Keane, Inc. Dist. by King Features Syndicate, Inc., (left): Crystal Kirk/Dreamstime.com; (right): lightasafeather/e+/Getty Images; **p. 234** (Table 7.3 clockwise): Annie Su Yee Yek/Dreamstime.com, Crystal Kirk/Dreamstime.com, U.S. Navy photo by Mass Communication Specialist 3rd Class John Grandin, light-asafeather/Getty Images; **p. 234** (bottom): Oscity/Shutterstock; **p. 235**: Kenneth Sponsler/iStockphoto; **p. 236**: stuar/Shutterstock; **p. 238**: Stockbyte/Getty Images; **p. 239** (top): Karl Dolenc/iStockphoto, (bottom): The Ocean Cleanup (Handout)/EPA-EFE/Shutterstock; **p. 240**: Stephanie Keith/Polaris/Newscom; **p. 241**: kali9/iStockphoto; **p. 242**: Daniel DeSlover/ZUMA Wire/Alamy Live News.

PART III

P. 248: Gpointstudio/Cultura Creative/Alamy Stock Photo.

CHAPTER 8

P. 250: Westend61 GmbH/Alamy Stock Photo; **p. 252**: Photoshot/Newscom; **p. 253**: Zits ©2002 Zits Partnership, Dist. by King Features Syndicate,

me/trust; **p. 416**: Nickilford/iStockphoto; **p. 418**: Sanja Bucko/Warner Bros/Kobal/Shutterstock; **p. 420**: TheCrimsonMonkey/iStockphoto; **p. 422** (top): YvanDube/iStockphoto, (bottom): Richard Levine/Alamy; **p. 424** (top): Tim Boyle/Bloomberg/Getty Images; (bottom): Alex Ruhl/Shutterstock; **p. 426** (left): Bobby Bank/WireImage/Getty Images (right): Sixteen String Jack Prods/Avalon Tv/Kobal/Shutterstock.

PART IV

P. 432: Monkey Business Images/Shutterstock.

CHAPTER 14

P. 434: Dean Drobot/Shutterstock; **p. 437** (top): Ernesto Diaz/iStockphoto, (bottom): Candybox Images/Dreamstime.com; **p. 438**: Daniel Laflor/iStockphoto; **p. 442** (top): South West Images Scotland/Alamy Stock Photo, (bottom): Robert Kneschke/Alamy Stock Photo; **p. 443**: ©Walt Disney Studios Motion Pictures/courtesy Everett Collection; **p. 448 (**top): Ringo Chiu/ZUMA Wire/Alamy Live News, (bottom): Kt/Dreamstime.com; **p. 450**: Eric Hood/iStockphoto; **p. 452**: AP Photo/Ajit Solanki; **p. 453** (top): The Protected Art Archive/Alamy, (bottom): GRAND AVENUE ©2003 Steve Breen and Mike Thompson. Reprinted by permission of Andrews McMeel for UFS. All rights reserved.; **p. 456**: EPA/Newscom; **p. 458**: ©Columbia Pictures/courtesy Everett Collection; **p. 459**: MCT/Newscom; **p. 462**: Jasper Juinen/Bloomberg via Getty Images; **p. 463**: jez gunnell/iStockphoto.

CHAPTER 15

P. 470: Nicki Dingraudo; **p. 473**: pete collins/iStockphoto; **p. 474**: Ljupco/iStockphoto; **p. 475**: pete collins/iStockphoto; **p. 476** (top): Matthew Simmons/Stringer/WireImage/Getty Images, (bottom): Getty Images; **p. 477** (top to bottom): pete collins/iStockphoto, Stockbyte/Getty Images, pete collins/iStockphoto, Matthew Simmons/Stringer/WireImage/Getty Images, Getty Images; **p. 478**: Phillipe Wojazer/Reuters/Newscom; **p. 479**: Nyul/Dreamstime.com; **p. 481** (left): DFree/Shutterstock, (center): Elizabeth Goodenough/Everett Collection/Newscom, (right): Featureflash/Shutterstock; **p. 483** (top): Stockbroker/MBI/Alamy Stock Photo, (bottom): Tero Vesalainen/Shutterstock; **p. 484:** Table 1 reprinted from The Gender Earnings Gap in the Gig Economy: Evidence from over a Million Rideshare Drivers by Cody Cook, Rebecca Diamond, Jonathan Hall, John A. List, Paul Oyer, June 7, 2018, Stanford Graduate School of Business. Working Paper No. 3637. Reprinted by permission of the authors; **p. 485**: Chris Brown/CSM/Alamy Live News; **p. 491**: THE BORN LOSER ©2005 Art and Chip Sansom. Reprinted by permission of Universal Uclick for UFS. All rights reserved.; **p. 492**: nilgun bostanci/iStockphoto; **p. 494** (left): from Vox.com video, "Homer Simpson: An economic analysis", September 9th, 2016. Zachary Crockett/Vox Media, Inc. Data source: The Simpsons (seasons 1-27), BLS, Glassdoor; US Census Bureau. https://www.vox.com/2016/9/6/12752476/the-simpsons-homer-middle-class, right: ©20th Century Fox Film Corp. All rights reserved/ Everett Collection; **p. 495**: Design Pics/Carson Ganci/Getty Images; **p. 496**: Magali Delporte/eyevine/Redux; **p. 497**: Ken Backer/Dreamstime.com; **p. 500**: Murray Close/©Lionsgate/Courtesy Everett Collection; **p. 502** (top): Roberto Serra/Iguana Press/Getty Images, (bottom): zhang bo/iStockphoto; **p. 503**: Album/Alamy Stock Photo.

PART V

P. 508: Stockbroker/MBI/Alamy Stock Photo.

CHAPTER 16

P. 510: Erik Pendzich/Shutterstock; **p. 513** (top): Stephen Walls/iStockphoto, (center): john shepherd/iStockphoto; (bottom): Rawpixel.com/Shutterstock; **p. 516**: Mathias Wilson/iStockphoto; **p. 517** (top): Chuck Hodes/©Fox/courtesy Everett Collection; **p. 517** (Table 16.1 top to bottom): Christian Degroote/Dreamstime.com, Robert Billstone/iStockphoto, Juanmonino/iStockphoto, iStockphoto, Stoyan Yotov/Shutterstock, Cal Vornberger/Alamy; **p. 520**: Vividpixels/Dreamstime.com; **p. 522**: South Florida Reporter; **p. 525**: SUPER SIZE ME, Morgan Spurlock, 2004, ©Samuel Goldwyn/courtesy Everett Collection; **p. 526**: Rimma Bondarenko/Alamy Stock Photo; **p. 530**: AiVectors/Shutterstock.

CHAPTER 17

P. 544: Photo by CBS via Getty Images; **p. 547**: iofoto/iStockphoto; **p. 548** (top): Jennifer Pitiquen/Dreamstime.com, (bottom): Monty Brinton/CBS Photo Archive/Getty Images; **p. 549**: Monty Brinton/CBS via Getty Images; **p. 550**: Photo courtesy of Ulrike Malmendier. ©Edward Caldwell; **p. 551**: Ryan Balderas/iStockphoto; **p. 553** (top): ©Walt Disney

Studios Motion Pictures/Courtesy Everett Collection, (bottom): Filmfoto/Dreamstime.com; **p. 554** (top): Marc De Simone/Alamy Stock Photo, (bottom): Courtesy of University of Rochester; **p. 557**: National Science Foundation; **p. 559**: Everett Collection Inc/Alamy; **p. 560**: Mark Stahl/iStockphoto; **p. 561** (top): Jason Merritt/FilmMagic/Getty Images, (bottom): Alex Slobodkin/iStockphoto.com; **p. 562**: Kyodo News via Getty Images; **p. 563**: iunewind/Alamy Stock Vector.

CHAPTER 18

P. 568: B-D-S Piotr Marcinski/Shutterstock; **p. 571** (left): Brown-Brooks/Photo Researchers/Getty Images, (right): Mark Kostich/iStockphoto; **p. 577**: D Dipasupil/FilmMagic/Getty Images: **p. 579**: Matt Groening/20th Century Fox/Kobal/Shutterstock; **p. 580**: Hero Images Inc./Alamy Stock Photo; **p. 582**: Kathy Hutchins/Shutterstock; **p. 585**: ZUMA Wire Service/Alamy; **p. 586**: Jovan Jaric/iStockphoto; **p. 588**: Michael Burrell/Alamy Stock Photo; **p. 591**: Vesna Andjic/iStockphoto; **p. 592**: Olekcii Mach/Alamy Stock Photo; **p. 593**: sjscreens/Alamy Stock Photo.

CHAPTER 19

P. 598: Kiln Enterprises Limited/www.shipmap.org; **p. 601** (left and right): Phil Crean A/Alamy Stock Photo; **p. 602**: Aleksandra Yakovleva/iStockphoto; **p. 604**: Craig Hastings/Getty Images; **p. 605**: Chris Ratcliffe/Bloomberg via Getty Images; **p. 606**: UrbanZone/Alamy Stock Photo; **p. 610**: Andrew Rowat/Getty Images; **p. 616**: Reason.com; **p. 619**: AP Photo/Damian Dovarganes; **p. 620**: Mary Evans/LUCASFILMS/Ronald Grant/Everett Collection; **p. 621**: Larry Leung/FeatureChina/Newscom; **p. 622** (left): 2p2play/Shutterstock, (right): Sergio Azenha/Alamy Stock Photo.

INDEX

Page numbers where key terms are defined are in **boldface**.